# *The* Patterns *of* World Politics

**KIM RICHARD NOSSAL**
**McMaster University**

**Prentice Hall Allyn and Bacon Canada**
**Scarborough, Ontario**

**Canadian Cataloguing in Publication Data**

Nossal, Kim Richard
   The patterns of world politics

Includes index.
ISBN 0-13-907478-3

1. International relations.  I. Title.

JX1395.N677 1998          326.1'01         C98-930247-4

 © 1998 Prentice-Hall Canada Inc., Scarborough, Ontario
A Division of Simon & Schuster/A Viacom Company

Prentice-Hall, Inc., Upper Saddle River,
   New Jersey

Prentice-Hall International (UK) Limited, London

Prentice-Hall of Australia, Pty. Limited, Sydney

Prentice-Hall Hispanoamericana, S.A.,
   Mexico City

Prentice-Hall of India Private Limited, New Delhi

Prentice-Hall of Japan, Inc., Tokyo

Simon & Schuster Southeast Asia Private Limited,
   Singapore

Editora Prentice-Hall do Brasil, Ltda.,
   Rio de Janeiro

ISBN 0-13-907478-3

Vice President, Editorial Director: Laura Pearson
Acquisitions Editor: Dawn Lee
Developmental Editor: Carol Steven
Marketing Manager: Christine Cozens
Production Editor: Andrew Winton
Copy Editor: Rosemary Tanner

Production Coordinator: Kathrine Pummell
Permissions/Photo Research: Susan Wallace-Cox
Cover and Interior Design: Julia Hall
Cover Image: Photonica/Chris Ferebee
Page Layout: Debbie Fleming/Joan Wilson

1 2 3 4 5    RRD    02 01 00 99 98

Printed and bound in United States of America.

Visit the Prentice Hall Canada web site! Send us your comments, browse our catalogues, and more at
**www.phcanada.com**. Or reach us through e-mail at **phabinfo_pubcanada@prenhall.com**

**Photo Credits**: p.2 Hong Kong Tourist Association; p.4 AP/Wide World Photos; p.13 First Light; p.23
UPI/Corbis-Bettman; p.38 AP/Wide World Photos; p.49 Corbis-Bettman; p.57 Canadian National; p.89
Reuters/Corbis-Bettman; p.101 AP/Wide World Photos; p.118 AP/Wide World Photos; p.182 Corbis-
Bettman; p.199 The Granger Collection; p.227 The Toronto Sun/H.Rosettani; p.228 AP/World Wide
Photos; p.258 Corbis-Bettman; p.263 UPI/Corbis-Bettman; p.277 AP/Wide World Photos; p.284
AP/Wide World Photos; p.304 Canapress/Jockel Finck; p.317 UPI/Corbis-Bettman; p.344 UPI/Corbis-
Bettman; p.382 UPI/Corbis-Bettman; p.418 AP/Wide World Photos; p.451 AP/Wide World Photos;
p.482 NASA; p.491 AP/Wide World Photos

# BRIEF CONTENTS

# CONTENTS

# *Preface*

One of the most difficult challenges facing those who have the important task of introducing students to the study of world politics is striking the right balance among the often contending objectives of an introduction. Normally, an introduction must try to offer students a sense of the subject and an exposure to what they should try to understand. It should provide a theoretical map to guide inquiry. And indeed, in the case of international relations, an introduction should also try to give students some sense of the rich and often contentious theoretical quarrels that divide the discipline of international relations (IR). An introduction should provide students with some factual knowledge about events—not only contemporary events, but also some historical background that normally is not covered in secondary school curricula. It should give students the technical vocabulary so necessary for understanding a specialized discipline. And, above all, an introduction to international relations should fire students' fascination and puzzlement over this sphere of human activity.

This book tries to strike a balance among these objectives. It is written for first or second year students at the post-secondary level, taking IR for the first time. It assumes that most will not have been exposed to IR as an academic subject. Some will have broad familiarity with the contours of world history, but not necessarily a detailed knowledge. This book is thus designed to provide a framework for thinking about—and working toward an understanding of—the puzzles of world politics in a way that is both theoretically oriented and historically grounded. It seeks to provide both factual information and the beginnings of the vocabulary of world politics. It tries to highlight the enduring patterns of politics at a global level, while at the same time providing an appropriate historical context within which to interpret those patterns.

## ORGANIZATION

**Part One** explores the nature of world politics, and in particular the problems that come from the absence of an agreed-upon set of theoretical principles to guide exploration. A chapter is devoted to surveying the major schools of thought in the field of IR and discussing the difficulties of theorizing in a field that is marked by theoretical diversity.

**Part Two** defines some key terms and explores some central assumptions that can be used to analyze world politics. It looks at what politics at a world level might entail, providing a discussion of the anarchic environment in which world politics occurs, examining the goals and interests of actors in world politics. A separate chapter focuses on how the actors seek to attain their goals through the use of influence, power, and authority. We also examine some of the implications of drawing a distinction between "insides" and "outsides" in world politics.

**Part Three** consists of a single chapter on actors and agents in world politics. Rather than dividing a consideration of actors into the usual state/nonstate dichotomy, this single chapter looks systematically at the full range of actors on the world stage, arguing for a more inclusive approach to thinking about agency at a global level.

**Part Four** begins an examination of the many boundaries that human beings create between each other that are so much the mark of world politics. Tracing division back to the Paleolithic era, it surveys some key ways in which political divisions have been created. Three chapters focus on the emergence of the modern state, the evolution of the idea of sovereignty, and how the sovereign idea works in practice—framed within a discussion of entrenching political divisions between human beings.

**Part Five** carries this discussion of division further by looking at the nation as a type of political community and the ideology of nationalism that binds members of nations. Different chapters look at nationalism and imperialism, and nationalism and war.

**Part Six** looks at other forms of division that go beyond the state divide. Two chapters examine divisions that were layered over the divisions created by the sovereign nation-state: one chapter examines the ideological cleavage between East and West, and another explores the economic divide between North and South. A third chapter looks at challenges to the dominant ways of dividing the world, looking at the impact of globalization and other conceptions of political identity, such as race and civilization. This chapter also examines political forms that rival the sovereign nation-state, both actual and notional.

The concluding chapter explores the consequences of division and examines the patterns of conflict and cooperation that are the essence of politics at any level, including the global.

## KEY FEATURES

*Pedagogical Features*    To assist in building students' vocabulary in IR, important terms are bold-faced and listed in a **Keyword File** at the end of each chapter. These terms, and biographical sketches of key actors and thinkers who appear in the book, are featured in a **Glossary of Names, Events**, and Terms that appears at the end of the book. A bibliographic guide, **For Further Exploration**, appears at the end of each chapter. **Hardcopy** provides suggestions for further reading in the huge literature on international politics; the works suggested have been selected for their interest and relevance for the beginning student of world politics. **Weblinks** give students an illustrative list of useful Web sites relating to the topics discussed in the chapter. In addition, a discussion of sources and references in IR is including in Chapter 1. Throughout the text, **Focus** boxes provide an opportunity to explore issues in more detail. **Maps, graphics**, and **tables** are used to illustrate important points without disrupting the flow of text.

*Supplements*    An **Instructor's Resource Manual with Test Item File** is available. The manual provides chapter summaries, lecture outlines for each chapter, and suggestions for multimedia presentations. It also has a test item file, containing essay and multiple choice question formats. The lecture outlines in the Instructor's Resource Manual are also available as Microsoft Powerpoint templates that can be modified and personalized by instructors.

*Focus on Analysis*    To encourage students to search for connections between phenomena, this text tries to explain the different elements of world politics, and  links these elements together in a holistic fashion. The analysis seeks to cover all the major phenomena that one would want an introductory student to get to know without trying to provide a mini-encyclopedia of factoids about world politics.

*Discrete Sections*    Although this book provides an exposition of world politics that follows a particular sequence, it is arranged so that its parts can be used in different sequences by instructors who want to organize their course differently. Many of the discussions that I use to illustrate some factors are written in such a way that they can readily be used to illustrate different phenomena.

*Historical Perspective*    Many students come to the study of world politics from secondary school systems that tend not to emphasize the teaching of history. Some IR texts address this problem by providing an introductory section that summarizes the history of the world in a few pages. But presented without context or purpose, a "Plato-to-NATO" survey becomes just a set of dates strung out in a linear, and often unconnected, fashion, difficult to absorb and impossible to place in context. By contrast, this text seeks to weave an account of key historical themes into the discussion of the patterns of world politics throughout the book. Moreover, an effort is made to provide students with an understanding of why an historical event occurred. By the end of the book, students will have been exposed to a discussion of key historical themes that range from ancient times to the present.

*Theoretical Approach*    Among the more notable features of IR as a discipline is the huge diversity of theoretical approaches that may be used to introduce students to world politics. This text provides an introductory discussion of the different theoretical approaches dominant in the field, though the analysis presented in the subsequent chapters does not follow any one theoretical line or any particular and identifiable "school" of thought; it is written from neither a "realist" nor a "liberal internationalist" perspective. Rather, this book stresses the essential pluralism that marks the IR field and the need to explore the rich theoretical contentions that make the study of world politics so challenging. What theoretical smudges can be observed tend to be an admittedly idiosyncratic amalgam, the result of having visited a number of different pigeon-holes in the IR roost.

The approach taken in this book stresses the importance of classical factors that have been considered important by some students of world politics: the impact of political identity, the interaction of politics and economics, the importance of individual actors and agents, the search for community at a global level, the interplay between politics at a local level and politics at a global level, and the importance of the past on constructions of the present. The central problematique of this text is likewise classical: how and why humans can and do go to war with one another, exhibiting the deepest cruelty, while at the same time engaging in the kind of cooperation at a global level that makes a complex global community possible. In other words, this text suggests that the central issues facing the student of international politics continue to be the causes of war and the conditions of peace.

# *Acknowledgments*

Many thanks to the team at Prentice Hall Allyn & Bacon Canada who were so important in making this book a reality. I am grateful to the two acquisitions editors, Cliff Newman and Dawn Lee, who oversaw this project. Cliff, who signed this book before his retirement in 1997, deserves special mention, for under his leadership, Prentice Hall Canada became Canada's leading publisher of international relations textbooks. A special thanks to Carol Steven, the development editor, who shepherded the book (and its author) with grace, good humour—and the patience of Job. My gratitude to Andrew Winton, the production editor, who deftly pulled the different elements of the project together; and to the other members of the production team—Susan Wallace-Cox, the photo editor; the designer, Julia Hall; and the formatters, Debbie Fleming and Joan Wilson. Finally, I was most fortunate that Prentice Hall Canada engaged Rosemary Tanner as the copy editor for this book. All authors depend on copy editors to make them appear more fluent and logical than they actually are, and I am no exception. Rosemary is wonderfully skilled at the demanding art of editing: she has an unerring eye for errors, inelegancies, and non sequiturs, but her blue pencil treads lightly on an author's stylistic idiosyncrasies. I am deeply indebted to her for improving this book immeasurably.

To the reviewers engaged by Prentice Hall Allyn and Bacon Canada and other colleagues who commented on the ms. at various stages—Ronald Deibert of the University of Toronto, Michael Hawes of Queen's University, Tom Keating of the University of Alberta, George MacLean of the University of Manitoba, Tony Porter of McMaster University, and Sandra Whitworth of York University—my thanks for useful comments and criticisms, many of which I have incorporated.

It was not until I began to write this book that I came to realize how much my understanding of world politics has been shaped by the colleagues and students I have known over the last 25 years. Some are scholars whom I have never met, but whose writings and thoughts on world politics I have found compelling. Others are the many teachers, colleagues, teaching assistants, and friends who over the years and in countless ways—in lectures, conversations, e-mail messages, and letters—have left a mark. And there is nothing like a second-year class of 150 often sceptical but always engaged students to prompt a more careful thinking through of a problem—or how to phrase it. To all go my thanks for your (often unwitting) contributions to my own thinking about world politics.

KRN
Hamilton, Ontario

# About the Author

Kim Richard Nossal was born in London, England, and was schooled in Melbourne, Beijing, Toronto, and Hong Kong. He received his B.A. from St. Michael's College, University of Toronto, and his M.A. and Ph.D. in the Department of Political Economy, University of Toronto. In 1976 he joined the Department of Political Science at McMaster University, Hamilton, Ontario, Canada, and served as chair of the department from 1992 to 1996. He is a former editor of the *International Journal*, the quarterly of the Canadian Institute of International Affairs, and is a member of editorial boards of scholarly journals in Australia, Britain, and Canada. His articles are published in a number of journals, including *Review of International Studies, International Organization, Foreign Affairs, Political Science Quarterly, Études internationales*, and *Australian Journal of International Affairs*. Among his books are *The Politics of Canadian Foreign Policy* (Scarborough, ON: Prentice Hall Canada, 1997, 3d edition), *Rain Dancing: Sanctions in Canadian and Australian Foreign Policy* (Toronto: University of Toronto Press, 1994), and (with Andrew Cooper and Richard Higgott) *Relocating Middle Powers: Australia and Canada in a Changing World Order* (Vancouver: University of British Columbia Press, 1993).

# Acronyms and Other Abbreviations

| | |
|---|---|
| ABC | American Broadcasting Company; Australian Broadcasting Corporation |
| ACTU | Australian Confederation of Trade Unions |
| ADB | Asian Development Bank |
| AfDB | African Development Bank |
| AFL–CIO | American Federation of Labor-Congress of Industrial Organizations (United States) |
| AI | Amnesty International |
| AIDAB | Australian International Development Assistance Bureau |
| AIDS | Acquired immune deficiency syndrome |
| ALP | Australian Labor Party |
| AMU | Arab Maghreb Union |
| ANZAC | Australia–New Zealand Army Corps |
| ANZCERTA | Australia New Zealand Closer Economic Relationship Trade Agreement (CER for short) |
| ANZUS | Australia–New Zealand–United States Defence Agreement |
| APEC | Asia Pacific Economic Cooperation |
| ARF | ASEAN Regional Forum |
| ARVN | Army of the Republic of Vietnam |
| ASEAN | Association of Southeast Asian Nations |
| ASIO | Australian Security Intelligence Organisation |
| ASIS | Australian Secret Intelligence Service |
| BBC | British Broadcasting Corporation |
| BCIE | *Banco Centroamericano de Integración Económico*—Central American Bank for Economic Integration |
| BIG | Bougainville Interim Government (Papua New Guinea) |
| BIS | Bank for International Settlements |
| BOAD | *Banque Ouest-Africaine de Développement*—West African Development Bank |
| BOSS | Bureau of State Security (apartheid South Africa) |
| CAP | Common Agricultural Policy (European Communities) |
| CARICOM | Caribbean Community and Common Market |
| CBM | Confidence-building measure |
| CBS | Columbia Broadcasting Service (United States) |
| CCP | Chinese Communist Party |
| CDB | Caribbean Development Bank |
| CDI | Christian Democrat International |
| CEDAW | Convention on Elimination of All Forms of Discrimination Against Women |
| CENTO | Central Treaty Organization |
| CER | see ANZCERTA |
| CGDK | Coalition Government of Democratic Kampuchea (Cambodia) |
| CHOGM | Commonwealth Heads of Government Meeting |
| CIA | Central Intelligence Agency (United States) |
| CIDA | Canadian International Development Agency |
| CIEC | Conference on International Economic Cooperation |
| CIS | Commonwealth of Independent States |
| CITES | Convention on International Trade in Endangered Species |
| CNN | Cable News Network |

| | |
|---|---|
| CNNE | *CNN en Español* |
| COMECON | Council for Mutual Economic Assistance |
| CPSU | Communist Party of the Soviet Union |
| CSCE | see OSCE |
| CSIS | Canadian Security Intelligence Service |
| DAC | Development Assistance Committee (OECD) |
| DAEs | Dynamic Asian economies |
| DEA | Department of External Affairs (India); Drug Enforcement Agency (United States) |
| DF | *Distrito Federal* (Mexico) |
| DFAIT | Department of Foreign Affairs and International Trade (Canada) |
| DFAT | Department of Foreign Affairs and Trade (Australia) |
| DGSE | *Direction générale de la Sécurité extérieure* (France) |
| DIA | Defense Intelligence Agency (United States) |
| DoD | Department of Defense (United States) |
| EBRD | European Bank for Reconstruction and Development |
| EC | European Community (see Note #2 on names below) |
| ECB | European Central Bank |
| ECOMOG | ECOWAS Monitoring Group (Liberia) |
| ECOSOC | Economic and Social Council (United Nations) |
| ECOWAS | Economic Community of West African States |
| ECSC | European Coal and Steel Community (see Note #2 on names below) |
| ECU | European Currency Unit |
| EEC | European Economic Community (see Note #2 on names below) |
| EEZ | Exclusive economic zone |
| EMI | European Monetary Institute |
| EMS | European monetary system |
| EMU | Economic and Monetary Union (EU) |
| EO | Executive Outcomes (South Africa) |
| EPOS | Electronic point of sale |
| ERM | Exchange rate mechanism |
| ERP | European Recovery Program (Marshall Plan) |
| ETA | *Euzkadi ta Azkatasuna*—Basque Homeland and Liberty (Spain) |
| EU | European Union (see Note #2 on names below) |
| EZLN | *Ejército Zapatista de Liberación Nacional*—Zapatista National Liberation Army (Mexico) |
| FAQs | Frequently-asked questions |
| FCO | Foreign and Commonwealth Office (Britain) |
| FDI | Foreign direct investment |
| FEMA | Foreign Extraterritorial Measures Act (Canada) |
| FIS | Foreign Intelligence Service (Russia); *Front islamique de salvation*—Islamic Salvation Front (Algeria) |
| FLN | *Front de Libération nationale* (Algeria) |
| FLQ | *Front de Libération du Québec* (Canada) |
| FMLN | *Frente Farabundo Martí para la Liberación Nacional*—Farabundo Martí National Liberation Front (El Salvador) |
| FNLA | *Frente nacional de libertação de Angola*—National Liberation Front of Angola |
| FRELIMO | *Frente de Libertação de Moçambique*—Liberation Front of Mozambique |
| FRETILIN | *Frente Revolucionário do Timor Leste Independente*—Revolutionary Front for an Independent East Timor |

| | |
|---|---|
| FRG | Federal Republic of Germany; West Germany |
| FSB | *Federalnaja sluzhba besopasnosti*—Federal Security Service (Russia) |
| FSLN | *Frente Sandinista de Liberación Nacional*—Sandinista National Liberation Front (Nicaragua) |
| FYROM | Former Yugoslav Republic of Macedonia (see Note #1 on names below) |
| G-7 | Group of Seven |
| G-10 | Group of Ten |
| G-77 | Group of 77 |
| GAB | General Arrangements to Borrow |
| GATS | General Agreement on Trade in Services |
| GATT | General Agreement on Tariffs and Trade |
| GDP | Gross Domestic Product |
| GDR | German Democratic Republic; East Germany |
| GI | Government Issue (slang for U.S. soldier) |
| GIA | *Groupe islamique armée*—Armed Islamic Group (Algeria) |
| GNP | Gross National Product |
| GSP | Generalized system of preferences |
| HDI | Human Development Index |
| HIV | Human immunodeficiency virus |
| HKSAR | Hong Kong Special Administrative Region |
| IADB | Inter-American Development Bank |
| IAEA | International Atomic Energy Agency |
| IBRD | International Bank for Reconstruction and Development (the World Bank) |
| ICA | International commodity agreement |
| ICBM | Inter-continental ballistic missile |
| ICC | International Criminal Court |
| ICJ | International Court of Justice |
| ICRC | International Committee of the Red Cross |
| IDA | International Development Association |
| IDB | Islamic Development Bank |
| IFC | International Finance Corporation |
| IFI | International financial institution |
| IFOR | Implementation Force (former Yugoslavia) |
| IGO | Intergovernmental organization |
| IISS | International Institute for Strategic Studies (Britain) |
| IJC | International Joint Commission (Canada-United States) |
| ILO | International Labour Organization |
| IMB | International Maritime Bureau |
| IMF | International Monetary Fund |
| INS | Immigration and Naturalization Service (United States) |
| IOC | International Olympic Committee |
| INC | Iraqi National Congress |
| IPE | International political economy |
| IPRs | Intellectual property rights |
| IRA | Irish Republican Army |
| IRBM | Intermediate-range ballistic missile |
| ISIS | Institute of Strategic and International Studies (Malaysia) |
| ISO | International Standards Organization |
| ITO | International Trade Organization |
| JIT | Just-in-time |

| | |
|---|---|
| KGB | *Komitet gosudarstvennoi bezopasnosti*—Committee on State Security (Soviet Union) |
| KKK | Ku Klux Klan (United States) |
| KMT | Kuomintang: National People's Party (China); (see Note #5 on names below) |
| LDC | "Less developed country" |
| LLDC | "Least developed country" |
| LTTE | Liberation Tigers of Tamil Eelam (Sri Lanka) |
| MAD | Mutual assured destruction/deterrence |
| MADD | Mothers Against Drunk Driving |
| MAI | Multilateral Agreement on Investment |
| MEP | Member of the European Parliament |
| MERCOSUR | *Mercado común del Cono sur*—Common Market of the Southern Cone. In Portuguese, MERCOSUL: *Mercado comun de Cone sul* |
| METO | Middle East Treaty Organization (after 1959, CENTO) |
| MFA | Multifibres Arrangement |
| MFN | Most favoured nation |
| MI5/MI6 | Military Intelligence, Section 5/Section 6 (Britain) |
| MIA | Missing in action |
| MIRV | Multiple independently-targetable re-entry vehicle |
| MNC | Multinational corporation |
| MPLA | *Movimento popular de libertação de Angola*—Popular Movement for the Liberation of Angola |
| MPRI | Military Professional Resources Inc. |
| MSA | Most Seriously Affected |
| MSF | *Médecins sans Frontières*—Doctors without Borders |
| MTN | Multilateral trade negotiation |
| MTV | Music Television |
| NAFO | North Atlantic Fisheries Organization |
| NAFTA | North American Free Trade Agreement |
| NAM | Non-Aligned Movement |
| NASA | National Aeronautics and Space Administration (United States) |
| NATO | North Atlantic Treaty Organization |
| NBC | National Broadcasting Corporation (United States); nuclear-biological-chemical |
| NDA | National Democratic Alliance (Sudan) |
| NGO | Non-governmental organization |
| NIC | Newly industrializing country |
| NIEO | New International Economic Order |
| NIF | National Islamic Front (Sudan) |
| NJM | New Jewel Movement (Grenada) |
| NORAD | North American Air Defence (after 1981, North American Aerospace Defence) |
| NSC | National Security Council (United States) |
| NSDAP | *Nationalsocialistische Deutsche Arbeiterpartei*—National Socialist German Workers Party—i.e., Nazi (Nazi Germany) |
| NTB | Non-tariff barrier |
| OAPEC | Organization of Arab Petroleum Exporting Countries |
| OAS | Organization of American States |
| OAU | Organization of African Unity |
| ODA | Official Development Assistance; Overseas Development Administration (Britain) |
| OECD | Organisation for Economic Cooperation and Development |
| OIC | Organization of the Islamic Conference |
| OPEC | Organization of Petroleum Exporting Countries |

| | |
|---|---|
| OSCE | Organization on Security and Cooperation in Europe (before 1994, Conference on Security and Cooperation in Europe) |
| P-5 | Permanent five members of the UN Security Council |
| PBS | Public Broadcasting System (United States) |
| PEMEX | *Petróleos Mexicanos* |
| PLA | People's Liberation Army (China) |
| PLO | Palestine Liberation Organization |
| PNG | Papua New Guinea |
| PNGDF | Papua New Guinea Defence Force |
| POW | Prisoner of war |
| PPP | Purchasing power parity |
| PQ | *Parti québécois* (Canada) |
| PRC | People's Republic of China (see Note #1 on names below) |
| PRI | *Partido Revolucionario Institucional*—Institutional Revolutionary Party (Mexico) |
| R&D | Research and development |
| R&R | Rest and recreation |
| RIIA | Royal Institute of International Affairs (Britain) |
| RENAMO | *Resistência Nacional Moçambicana*—Mozambiquean National Resistance |
| ROC | Republic of China on Taiwan (see Note #1 on names below) |
| RSS | *Rashtriya Swayamsevak Sangh*—National Volunteer Corps (India) |
| RUF | Revolutionary United Front (Sierra Leone) |
| SA | *Sturmabteilungen*—storm troops (Nazi Germany) |
| SAARC | South Asian Association for Regional Cooperation |
| SACEUR | Supreme Allied Commander in Europe (NATO) |
| SADC | Southern African Development Community |
| SADR | Saharan Arab Democratic Republic |
| SAM | Surface-to-air missile |
| SAP | Structural adjustment program |
| SDI | Strategic Defense Initiative (United States) |
| SDR | Special Drawing Rights |
| SEA | Single European Act |
| SEATO | Southeast Asia Treaty Organization |
| SFOR | Stabilization Force (former Yugoslavia) |
| SII | Strategic Impediments Initiative (US-Japan) |
| SLORC | State Law and Order Restoration Council (Myanmar) |
| SOM | Senior Officials Meeting |
| SPLA | Sudanese People's Liberation Army |
| SS | *Schutzstaffel*—defence squad (Nazi Germany) |
| STDs | Sexually-transmitted diseases |
| TEUs | Twenty-foot equivalent units (measurement of capacity of intermodal containers) |
| TNC | Transnational corporation |
| TRIMs | Trade-related investment measures |
| TRIPs | Trade-related aspects of intellectual property rights |
| UAE | United Arab Emirates |
| UAR | United Arab Republic |
| UDI | Unilateral declaration of independence |
| UK | United Kingdom of Great Britain and Northern Ireland (see Note #3 on names below) |
| UN | United Nations |
| UNAMIR | UN Assistance Mission to Rwanda |

| UNCED | UN Conference on Environment and Development |
| UNCLOS | UN Conference on the Law of the Sea |
| UNCTAD | UN Conference on Trade and Development |
| UNDP | UN Development Fund |
| UNEF | UN Emergency Force |
| UNESCO | UN Economic and Social Council |
| UNICEF | UN Children's Fund |
| UNITA | *União nacional para a indepêndencia total de Angola*—National Union for the Total Independence of Angola |
| UNITAF | United Task Force (Somalia) |
| UNOSOM | United Nations Operation in Somalia |
| UNPROFOR | UN Protection Force (former Yugoslavia) |
| UNSCOM | UN Special Commission (Iraq) |
| UNTAC | UN Transitional Authority in Cambodia |
| US | United States (of America) |
| USAF | United States Air Force |
| USAID | United States Agency for International Development |
| USSR | Union of Soviet Socialist Republics (see Notes #3 and #4 on names below) |
| USTR | United States Trade Representative |
| UTI | *Union télégraphique internationale* (after 1934, UIT—*Union internationale des télé-communications*) |
| VAT | Value-added tax |
| VERs | Voluntary export restraints |
| VRA | Voluntary restraints agreement |
| WEU | Western European Union |
| WFP | World Food Program |
| WHO | World Health Organization |
| WTO | Warsaw Treaty Organization (before 1991); World Trade Organization (after 1995) |
| WWW | World Wide Web |

# Notes on Names

## 1. Place Names

With the exception of countries divided during the Cold War (East/West Germany, North/South Korea, North/South Vietnam), this book refers to countries (and cities in those countries) by the English version of names preferred by the governments in power, regardless of the preferences of others. Thus Macedonia is called Macedonia, despite its official UN designation as the Former Yugoslav Republic of Macedonia (FYROM), and despite the claim of the government of Greece that it has exclusive rights to the name Macedonia. Myanmar is used for the country formerly known as Burma, even though some argue that using the name selected by the military dictatorship which seized power in 1989 confers inappropriate legitimacy on that regime. There are two Congos; context is provided by attaching the names of the capital cities—hence Congo-Kinshasa refers to the country formerly known as Zaire; Congo-Brazzaville is the country to the north of the Congo and Ubangi rivers. Where sovereignty is contested, the names used by those political authorities actually controlling the territory in question are used: hence the People's Republic of China (PRC) and the Republic of China on Taiwan (ROC on Taiwan) are both used. Current city designations are used for contemporary references: Beijing for Peking, Guangzhou for Canton; Ho Chi Minh City for Saigon; Mumbai for Bombay; Saint Petersburg for Leningrad; Yangon for Rangoon.

## 2. European Union

Names for the supranational organizations of Europe can be confusing. In the 1950s, three European "communities" were created. In 1952, the European Coal and Steel Community (ECSC) came into force, and the Treaty of Rome, signed on 25 March 1957, created the European Economic Community (EEC) and the European Atomic Energy Community (Euratom). In 1967, these three communities began to be served by what is legally known as the Common Institutions of the European Communities—usually contracted to EC. While legal documents must refer to the EC in the plural (European Communities, or EC), in day-to-day parlance, the EC referred to itself informally in the singular, the European Community (also EC). On 1 November 1993, the EC became the European Union (EU), with the three original Communities remaining in existence. However, just to ensure that some confusion would remain, it was also decided that as of 1 November 1993, the EEC's name would be changed to the European Community (EC).

## 3. Short Forms

For convenience, the official names of some countries have been shortened in accordance with common usage. Britain is used instead of United Kingdom of Great Britain and Northern Ireland. Soviet Union and USSR are used interchangeably.

## 4. Historical Usage

For historical discussions, I have generally used the names of political communities, countries, nations, colonies, imperial possessions, cities, or organizations in use at the time.

## 5. Chinese Names

Chinese names are rendered in the system for transliterating Chinese to English dominant in that place. The PRC uses the Pinyin system, while in the ROC on Taiwan and the Hong Kong Special Administrative Region (HKSAR), the Yale system tends to be dominant. Historically, another system, called Wade-Giles, was also used. Thus, Chinese on both sides of the Strait of Formosa would pronounce the name of the National People's Party as *gwo min daang*, but it would be transliterated differently: in Wade-Giles it would be written Kuomintang; in Pinyin it would be Guomindang; in Yale, it would be Gwomindang.

I have followed the PRC/ROC/HKSAR divide in names of individuals and places. For the PRC, they are rendered in Pinyin: Mao Zedong rather than Mao Tse-tung and Guangzhou rather than Canton. For the ROC, the Yale system is used: Taipei rather than Daibei (though because it is so deeply entrenched in common usage, Chiang Kai-shek continues to be rendered in the historical Wade-Giles system rather than Jiang Kaishek). For Hong Kong, names are given in Yale (e.g., Tung Chee-hwa, the chief executive of the HKSAR). Note that in Chinese, the family name precedes the given names; in Hong Kong, English Christian names are often added to the Chinese name, e.g., Martin Lee Chu-ming. A guide to pronunciation of Chinese names referred to is provided in the Glossary.

## 6. Arabic Names

Arabic must also be transliterated into English. For consistency, usage follows Arthur Banks et al., *Political Handbook of the World* (1996). Some exceptions are made where historical usage is deeply entrenched: for example, Gamal Abdel Nasser is used rather than the more correct Jamal 'Abd al-Nasir.

# PART ① 

# Thinking *about* World Politics

# *An* Introduction
# *to* World Politics

**I N T R O D U C T I O N** We begin by asking a simple question: what is world politics "about"? What puzzles does the student of world politics try to work through? And when one studies world politics, what does one study?

At first blush, such questions may seem obvious, but in fact there is little agreement about what world politics is "about": about the boundaries of the discipline known as "International Relations" (or IR, as it is commonly called), about what should be studied, and about how to study it. Indeed, the very language we use to describe the area of study itself is problematic, as we will see. For this reason, it is not good enough to simply gloss over the issue of what a student of world politics studies as though it were self-evident.

## EXPERIENCING WORLD POLITICS

At one level, getting to know what world politics is about is easy. The events that comprise the raw material of international politics can be experienced with relative ease—by opening a newspaper or a newsmagazine, or turning on the television. There, in pictures and words, one can experience world politics. Mostly the stories are about governments and leaders. Many concern international organizations, treaties, conventions, or operations, and one will need a program to understand the alphabet soup of acronyms that dot the contemporary international scene: ANZUS, APEC, CITES, ILO, IMF, NAFO, NAFTA, OAU, OSCE, SAADC, UNDP, UNESCO, UNPROFOR, WHO, and WTO to name just a few of them (see list of abbreviations and acronyms on pp. xxii–xxvii). For contemporary international politics is highly institutionalized: there are global organizations, regional organizations, regional development banks, functional organizations, economic cooperation forums, military organizations, and treaties and conventions covering a variety of issues. And most of the nongovernmental and intergovernmental organizations in existence today use acronyms for convenience. Moreover, less formal and institutional groups are everywhere, adding to the mix: the G-7, P-5, G-77, the Group of Ten, the Quadrilateral, the Cairns Group, the Commonwealth, Caricom.

## The Images of World Politics

Some of the images we see are from the pleasant side of international affairs: people in the midst of conducting interstate relations, posing for the photo opportunity that may

*Pictures of summit meetings are mostly of men, and mostly wearing suits.*

serve as the lead-off on the nightly news back home, getting in or out of the long black Cadillacs or Mercedes that seem to be the only cars suitable for international diplomacy. The leaders are snapped posing in front of foreign ministries, presidential palaces, or state guesthouses, usually attended by a retinue of advisers, spin-doctors, and gofers. They sign treaties; shake hands; cut ribbons on new facilities paid for by development assistance grants; tour model factories, farms, or labs, often decked out in incongruous headgear or clothing intended to add to the photo-op; make toasts at lavish state dinners; sit around tables behind little nameplates embossed with their countries' names; or give press conferences on any number of topics, from the design of a new European currency to the latest developments in boundary negotiations. Pictures of summit meetings are mostly of men, and mostly wearing suits.* Indeed, Madeleine Albright, the first woman to be appointed secretary of state in the United States, liked to draw attention to this androcentric feature of international politics by insisting on describing herself, when she was the U.S. representative on the 15-member United Nations Security Council, as "a skirt among fourteen suits."[1]

But we also see images from the darker side of world politics: disputes between peoples; angry protests against foreigners; assassinations; acts of terrorism, torture and other human rights abuses; famine; abject and grinding poverty, sometimes jarringly juxtaposed next to wealth and luxury. We are shown wars that come in numerous variations: large, small, civil, global, declared, undeclared, low-intensity, and guerrilla.

---

* Except at annual summit meetings of the Asia Pacific Economic Cooperation (APEC) forum. There, leaders have taken to wearing common leisure-wear supplied by the host leader, a tradition started by the United States president, Bill Clinton, who provided sporty windbreakers to all the leaders at the first heads-of-state meeting in Seattle in November, 1993. In Bogor, Indonesia, it was Batik shirts; in the Philippines, the straight-bottomed tagalog business shirts; in Vancouver, denim shirts and leather jackets.

We see images of the brutality, savagery, and death that is also so very much an integral part of world politics: a mud-covered corpse in the middle of no-man's land during the First World War; a Japanese officer executing a prisoner on a city street in China; an American soldier taking part in the Normandy invasion on D-Day, slowly slumping into the water after being hit by a round from a German machine-gun; piles of bodies dumped unceremoniously in giant stacks around Nazi death camps; partisans sprawled dead on a Budapest street, killed by Soviet machine-gunners; the famous image, shown here, of an unidentified Viet Cong guerrilla being paraded before the TV cameras by Col. Nguyen Ngoc Loan, South Vietnam's chief of police—and then without warning Loan raising his revolver and shooting the guerrilla in the head; the charred corpse of an Iraqi soldier, frozen in his tank during the Gulf War of 1991; the dusty and bleeding naked body of a United States peacekeeper dragged by an angry crowd through the streets of the Somali capital of Mogadishu; red-stained bodies sprawled in unnatural and misshapen angles—over a fence in a Sarajevo marketplace, in pews in a Rwandan church, a Tel Aviv street, an Algerian village.

This is, of course, an armchair exposure. It is very much removed from the realities being portrayed, and therefore does not provide the full sense of the experiences of world politics. After all, how can you experience from afar the gripping pains of dehydration and malnourishment? Or the elation felt when a colonial flag comes down the pole for the last time, and the colours of a new nation are run up? Or the putrid atmosphere of a crowded shantytown slum? Or the adrenalin rush of making it unscathed through a firefight? Or the fear of being forced out of one's home in an ethnic cleansing? Or the sense

A Viet Cong guerrilla being summarily executed in Saigon on 1 February 1968.

of violation after being raped by an invading soldier? Or the humiliation of having to pay tribute to a conqueror?

Moreover, the view from the armchair may encourage the idea that world politics is something that only happens "out there"—and to "other people." The reality, however, is rather different: world politics affects virtually everyone in some way; there is no escaping its reach. Indeed, many readers of this book will already have been introduced to world politics in a more direct and personal way, even if, like Molière's Monsieur Jourdain (who was surprised to discover that he had been talking in prose for years without realizing it), they might not have thought about these experiences as *world politics*. Consider, for example, how many of us live where we do now because our parents, our grandparents, or perhaps more distant forebears chose (or were forced) to move countries. Throughout history, people have always moved and migrated, pushed by war, oppression, poverty, or famine, or pulled by the prospect of fortune or simply a better life. This has been particularly true during the 19th and 20th centuries. The result is that large numbers of people, particularly in the world's primary "settler" societies or "immigrant" countries—Australia, Canada, Israel, New Zealand, South Africa, and the United States*—are where they are now because of the forces of global politics. Perhaps they were fleeing the upheavals caused by quarrels among nations; perhaps they were trying to find a safer or more liberal political environment; perhaps they were prompted to flee religious persecution; perhaps they were seeking a better life for their families by escaping the general poverty of their homelands or a more specific catastrophe, such as a plague or a blight; perhaps they were hired to fill a labour shortage in another country and ended up staying; perhaps they were seeking to avoid military service in an unpopular war; perhaps they were sent overseas to a penal colony as a punishment for a crime; or perhaps they were simply expelled en masse by oppressive regimes.

Many readers may have family members who were involved in the wars that have occurred over the course of the 20th century. How many have family members who spent time in prisoner-of-war camps or who were interned as "enemy aliens" by their own governments, their property seized and confiscated? How many have family members who experienced the massive killing operation we know as the Holocaust? How many can go to the war memorials in our communities and see the public commemoration of family members who died in those wars as soldiers? How many have family members who died in those wars as ordinary civilians, for whom there is no public remembrance?

---

* Of course the phenomenon is not limited to these countries: political upheaval and the search for economic gain have affected numerous countries in this way. For example, after the Algerian war of independence, hundreds of thousands of refugees moved to France. Germany has been host to hundreds of thousands of *gastarbeiter* ("guestworkers") who came from poorer parts of Europe seeking work in the 1970s and 1980s. Large numbers of refugees settled in Germany after the breakup of Yugoslavia in the early 1990s. We have seen similar patterns in Asia: consider the Koreans who settled in Japan after their country was annexed by the Japanese in 1910; or the large number of Chinese who fled to what was then the British colony of Hong Kong following the Communist revolution in 1949; or, more recently, the numerous Filipino women working as domestic servants in Hong Kong.

## The Effects of the Global Economy

It is not only international strife that provides us with direct experience of world politics; the way in which the global economy operates also affects us. How many readers are from families that have experienced the wrenching effects of sudden unemployment caused by downsizing? or gains or losses in family wealth as a result of changes in international money markets that affect personal investment portfolios and employee pension plans? How many readers are from farm families which have seen increases or declines in the price of produce? How many are from fishing families, and experienced the effects of overfishing or the mismanagement of fishery stocks?

Finally, the ordinary patterns and routines of our daily lives are very much the consequences of world politics. These routines, which we take so much for granted, involve the movement of goods, services, labour, technology, and ideas across borders on an immense scale, possible only because of the global political environment. For example, much of what we eat and drink comes from abroad, transported thousands of kilometres at minimal cost to the eventual consumer: Australian wine, Canadian wheat, Filipino mangoes, French champagne, Kenyan coffee, New Zealand lamb, and South African oranges are all moved around the world at great speed and low cost. Much of the junk food we eat is produced locally under licence from foreigners.

Most of the durable consumer products we buy are developed, manufactured, or assembled in other countries, sometimes with components from around the world. Some people point to "world jet fighters" or "world cars" as examples of this multinational production. Those readers who are not able to have a close look at an F-16 or who do not want to get greasy exploring the innards of their car can simply take a look at their bicycle for just as good an example of this, as the Focus suggests.

Computer software for the American market may be programmed in India or Malaysia. Clothing and footwear manufacturing long ago migrated from Europe and North America to Asia and Central America. Even some service industries are located multinationally: for example, animation for *The Simpsons*, the animated comedy produced by the Fox Network of Los Angeles, is done by a Korean company; some North American insurance companies have started to process their claims across the Atlantic Ocean in Ireland.

Much of our entertainment has crossed a border or two before we enjoy it. What we see on television is a mixture of local and foreign programming, though that mix varies greatly depending on where one is and what language one speaks. In the United States, the only major network to run foreign-produced news is CNN (Cable News Network) through its international network, CNN International. Beyond that, virtually all TV programming seen by Americans on the four main networks (ABC, CBS, Fox, and NBC) is locally produced. If Americans want to watch non-American television entertainment, they have to watch smaller networks or specialty cable channels: the foreign (and mostly British) productions aired by the Public Broadcasting System (PBS); co-productions sponsored by the Disney channel, such as the Canadian Broadcasting Corporation's *Road to Avonlea*; foreign-produced music videos on MTV (Music Television); or Hispanic productions aired on specialty cable channels.

# FOCUS

## A "World Bike"

Raleigh Industries, a firm located in Nottingham, England, began making bicycles in 1887; today Raleigh bikes are made around the world. In Canada, for example, Raleighs are manufactured by a wholly owned subsidiary, Raleigh Industries Canada, of Oakville, Ontario. Bikes are assembled at a plant in Waterloo, Québec, but the finished product is a "world bike." Tubular parts—the frame, handlebars, and seat post—are cut and welded at the Waterloo plant from Canadian-manufactured metals; the paint is also purchased from Canadian suppliers. Everything else is sourced overseas: the calliper brakes, the rear carrier, and the hand grips are made by firms in Taiwan, while the handlebar steering lug and pedal footrests come from two companies in China. The rims are made in Belgium, the tires in Korea, the seat in Italy, the kick-stand in Germany. Many components come from Japan: the chain assembly, the cranks, the derailleur variable transmission, the wheel hubs, the steering column, and the rear reflector are made by five different Japanese companies. But not a single component comes from England; indeed, the only thing English about this bike is the name.

In other English-speaking countries, the mix is less parochial. A great deal of the non-local programming is imported from the United States as is, or franchised for particular national audiences (as in *Australia's Funniest Home Videos* or the Australian version of CBS's *60 Minutes*). But local production also follows the American lead: in most countries, for example, one can find a *Good Morning, Ruritania* news-and-interview show, modelled on *Good Morning, America*. Indeed, most of the TV genres—game shows, sitcoms, soaps, and even "reality-TV" crime shows—are reproduced locally in miniature replica. Sometimes the American idea is taken to new highs (or lows, depending on one's taste): in Russia, for example, Moscow TV-6's *Road Patrol*, modelled after *Rescue 911*, shows in exceedingly graphic detail the gory results of accidents and crimes of violence, images that would never get past a network censor in the United States.

*"Morning drive" shows can be found on stations that bill themselves as their city's "best rock" from Melbourne to Manchester and many points between.*

The films and videos we see tend to be dominated by the American film industry, which sells its cultural products worldwide. In the process, it dominates not only big screens, particularly in English-speaking countries, but even the little screens of the world's major airlines. The music we listen to, from alternative to classical, is written, recorded, performed, and marketed on a multinational basis. The progressive globalization of television music is indicative of this trend: MTV, MuchMusic, Channel V, and Viva all broadcast multinationally, reaching millions of young adults throughout the world.[*] Even the format of FM radio programming has been imported from the United States. "Morning drive" shows can be found on stations that bill themselves

---

[*] MTV provides a good example of this trend: it began in the United States in 1981 and expanded to Europe in 1987, Brazil in 1990, Japan in 1992, Latin America in 1993, Asia and China in 1995, India in 1996, and Australia in 1997; at last count, the network reached 282 million households in 79 countries. *Christian Science Monitor*, 6–12 June 1997.

as their city's "best rock" from Melbourne to Manchester and many points between; only the names of the always-clogged highways in the traffic reports change.

Our spectator sports also have an international dimension. Cricket, rugby, and soccer are played locally, and also organized for international competition. There is some interest in sports played in the United States and Canada—baseball, basketball, football, and hockey—in other parts of the world, but they pose no threat to the dominant place of soccer. In Canada and the United States, there is some interest in sports played in other parts of the world (mainly on the part of those who have immigrated from overseas), but the main spectator sports in these countries remain baseball, basketball, football, and hockey. But these sports are "international" only to the extent that some of the players are non-Americans, and in some cases have teams across one border—in Canada. (The major leagues in baseball, basketball, hockey, and Canadian football are more properly *bi-national*, including teams from Canada and the United States; the American Football League contains only American teams.) Even this essential difference between two of the three North American countries and the rest of the world is transcended every four years when athletes are brought together for what has become the ultimate global spectator sport: the Olympic Games.

As well, we tend to take for granted how cheap, easy, and dependable global communication and transportation is. We can reach virtually anywhere in the world by regular postal service, telephone, cell phone, fax, or e-mail—even if the reach of these services and technologies in some countries is partial or inconsistent. We can put our bank card into any one of thousands of ATM machines dotted around the world, and make withdrawals on our account in local currency. Investment funds can be moved between countries instantaneously and on a 24-hour basis. Over 900 airlines operating some 14 000 aircraft link thousands of cities and towns, and transport millions of passengers daily all over the globe. We can move across the globe in less than a day—London to Sydney, one of the world's longest air routes, takes only 22 hours—and incredibly cheaply—the 13-hour flight from Hong Kong to the west coast of North America costs a mere eight cents a kilometre.

We tend to take for granted the hundreds of millions of daily transborder transactions and movements, occurring relatively smoothly and predictably. But the fact is that the ease of these transactions can be attributed to the nature of contemporary world politics—an environment that allows such transactions to occur in safety and with considerable predictability.

Of course, the same environment that makes the intercontinental movement of oranges so easy also makes possible the transborder movement of goods, services, and peoples that are rather less seemly. For example, psychotropic drugs flow in mass quantities from source country to final user, moving effortlessly through countries and across borders, greased by the vast profits their very illegality commands. Child pornography flows instantaneously over the World Wide Web, making it difficult (but not impossible) for authorities to track and prosecute. Arms large and small, laundered money, prohibited goods such as nonregulated ivory, illegal live animals, illegal migrants, pirated software and videos, illicit brand-name knock-offs—all move relatively freely across borders.

## STUDYING WORLD POLITICS: FOR FURTHER EXPLORATION

Noting the existence of all of these complex webs of linkages across borders is, however, merely to catalogue the features of contemporary global life. The catalogue itself does not tell us much about what world politics is, or how politics on a global scale manifests itself, or what is sufficiently puzzling about world politics that should prod our interest. To make some sense of this otherwise unconnected jumble of observations and images, we have to study world politics.

Studying world politics means trying to sort out the disorderly mass of information, knowledge, events, personalities, concepts, and terminology that comprise the discourse of world politics, rendering it intelligible. Part of that process involves taking courses, which are organized efforts to make sense of disciplinary topics. But part of that process involves reading, not only to write the papers that are inevitably required for courses, but also to expand understanding and knowledge. This section provides a brief map to the resources available for further reading.

The literature on world politics in English is, to put it simply, overwhelming. No one individual is able to keep abreast of the output of books, journals, working papers, conference proceedings, and occasional papers that are produced in prodigious quantities by academics, researchers, think tanks, journalists, politicians, and nongovernmental organizations. No one is able to read the vast number of words posted each day to hundreds of thousands of home page sites on the World Wide Web. No one is able to read all of the English-language newspapers in the world, even though most of them are available—in electronic edition—at one's home or office.

There are, however, methods of making one's way through the blizzard of words and making further exploration easier, whether the purpose is to prepare an essay or simply to expand one's knowledge. The following sources might prove useful.

### Basic Reference Material

Basic information on world politics can be found in an annual series edited by Arthur Banks and his colleagues, *Political Handbook of the World* (CSA Publications). This series annually surveys every country and every international organization in the world and includes highly detailed information.

For those who would like to flesh out their historical knowledge, the most engaging history of the world is J.M. Roberts, *The Penguin History of the World* (Harmondsworth, U.K.: Penguin, 1992). A magisterial overview of the relations among the world's great powers for the last 500 years is to be found in Paul Kennedy's *The Rise and Fall of the Great Powers* (London: Unwin Hyman, 1988).

### Memoirs and Biographies

Another way to access the world of world politics is through biographies and memoirs of individuals who have played roles—major or minor—in global politics. The vast majority of those individuals listed in the Glossary have either a biography written about them, or have turned their hand to writing about themselves. Biographies offer an often fascinating window into politics from an individual's point of view. And provided that memoirs are read with an appropriate dose of salt—for their authors inevitably tailor their remembrances to make themselves look good—they too can provide important "insider" perspectives that can enhance understanding.

## Journals

There are two kinds of international relations (IR) journals. One kind, often published by national institutes of international affairs, provides detailed and informative discussions of world politics for the informed but not necessarily specialist reader. Anyone who has been admitted to university will readily make sense of articles and book reviews in such journals as *Foreign Affairs, Foreign Policy, International Affairs, The World Today, International Journal,* and *Australian Journal of International Affairs.* The other kind is specialist journals, which publish articles aimed at other scholars. Frequently, the terminology or methodology (or both) will be impenetrable to the outsider or nonspecialist. More often than not, articles in these journals take the form of scholarly debates, their articles assuming a deep knowledge of the squabbles in contention. Few contributions to these specialist journals are likely to be useful to the undergraduate student just embarking on the study of world politics.

The most "penetrable" of the leading IR journals are the *Review of International Studies,* published by the British International Studies Association; *International Organization,* published by the World Peace Foundation; and *Millennium,* the student journal of the London School of Economics. Articles in *Review of International Studies* tend to be topical, thought-provoking, and theoretical, and are written in an accessible style; a good resource for beginning student and advanced scholar alike. *International Organization* tends to be somewhat more ponderous as a journal, but the contributions are informative. Although *Millennium* is a student journal, the theoretical quality of its articles is very high.

Browsing the world's English-language journals has been made enormously easier with services like CARL, a firm at the University of Colorado. Accessible on the Internet by telnetting to pac.carl.org, or directly available through many university libraries, this service allows users to browse the tables of contents of journals or find articles. (And, if CARL is supplied with credit card and fax numbers, articles can be faxed, sometimes within an hour, for a modest fee—a convenient, if somewhat expensive, way to conduct research.)

## World Wide Web

*"'Surfing' the Internet can at times feel like groping through a dark labyrinth of seemingly endless loops of links, dead-links, and false leads."*

One of the consequences of the spread and expansion of the Internet and the World Wide Web in the last decade has been to make even more information available to people around the world. With the Web one can read what the president of the United States said yesterday in a speech; indeed, because of the international date line, North Americans can know what is on the front page of tomorrow's *Sydney Morning*

*Herald* before most Sydneysiders see their morning paper. One can research South African attitudes toward a civil war in Sierra Leone, or analyze what the Hong Kong press is saying about American mid-term Congressional elections, or read the latest communiqué from the National Democratic Alliance seeking to overthrow the government of Sudan.

Because of its capacity to provide global access to these resources, the Internet is often seen as a "revolutionary" development in human communication. But for the researcher, the revolutionary change in the material available must be seen in the context of two major down-sides. First, even with a solid search engine and well-honed Boolean search skills, the researcher is confronted with a mass of data that must be sorted, read, assessed, and digested. The Web may bring the libraries, information ministries, and newspapers of the world to the top of one's desk, but that does not make the process of working with that data any easier. As Ronald Deibert notes, "'surfing' the Internet can at times feel like groping through a dark labyrinth of seemingly endless loops of links, dead-links, and false leads."[2] Indeed, for students working under deadline, hunting for useful information on the Internet can be a hugely time-consuming process. That is why Deibert's guide to WWW resources on international relations is so valuable. Indeed, many of the suggested URLs that appear at the end of each chapter of this book have been drawn from this excellent guide, which can be accessed at Deibert's home page: *www.chass.utoronto.ca/~rdeibert/irweb.html*

The second problem is that there is a vast amount of junk on the World Wide Web. "Gutenberg technology"—the printed page stored in libraries—features a series of gatekeepers, from the editors who make choices about what to publish to librarians who make choices about what to acquire. This gatekeeping function allows library users to make some relatively easy judgments about quality. By contrast, anything can be posted to the WWW by anyone, with the result that wholly bogus statistics from a racist militia can surface in a search next to wholly reliable statistics from a United States federal agency. And while this essentially anarchic feature is what makes the Web attractive for some, it does not help the student looking for reliable sources for learning.

## An Invitation

If you have comments, suggestions, or questions about this book, please do not hesitate to e-mail me at nossalk@mcmaster.ca

## CONCLUSION

This chapter has focused on images of world politics as a way to provide an introduction to what lies ahead. Much of the discussion has shown the *multiplicity* of images that one can draw on to convey what world politics is "about." But, since each of the chapters opens with an image that tries to convey graphically the different elements of world politics being explored, for this chapter I needed one *single* image to capture the essence not only of this chapter but of the book itself.

I decided that a picture of Hong Kong should open this chapter and this book. That city is emblematic of so many of the different strands of world politics that we will meet later on: imperialism, colonialism, nationalism, communism, economic dynamism, diplomacy, politics, trade, refugees, finance, drugs, sovereignty, shipping, spies, war, crime, the conflicts of the great powers past and present—all have crossed in this city, making it an appropriate image to convey the essence of world politics.

Exploring the different images of world politics in this chapter has involved laying out a number of different strands of argument, many of which may seem rather tangled by now. To sort through those tangles, we have to think theoretically; we now turn to a discussion of theory in world politics.

## Notes to Chapter 1

1. Quoted in *Globe and Mail* (Toronto), 6 December 1996.
2. Ronald Deibert, *Virtual Resources: International Relations on the Internet*, Working Paper 13 (Vancouver: Institute of International Relations, University of British Columbia, 1997), 1.

# C H A P T E R ( 2 )

# Theorizing *About*
# World Politics

It would be difficult to make sense of world politics—or any other set of social phenomena—without a way to take a vast array of seemingly disconnected facts, events, and assumptions and render them intelligible. That is the role of theory. Theory is the way that we organize what we see and what we know, shape our assumptions, make complex phenomena understandable, identify puzzles, and provide explanations for those puzzles. In the context of a discipline in the arts or sciences, theory suggests the set of rules or principles for the study or practice of that discipline. All "disciplined" human endeavours are guided by theory: imagine setting out to build a tunnel under the English Channel, perform arthroscopic surgery on an injured knee, fly a jumbo jet from Nairobi to London, play the viola part of a Bach concerto, or land astronauts on the moon without the various theories that inform civil engineering, medicine, navigation, music, or physics. In these disciplines, it is not difficult to arrange the principles that underlie a theory into a coherent account that finds general agreement among practitioners and professors alike. Thus, the average university library has on its shelves well over a

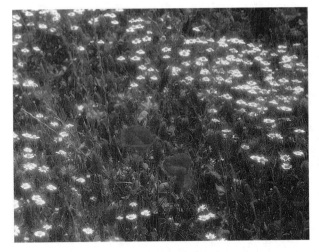

thousand books outlining the principles of different disciplines, with titles ranging from *The Principles of Aquatic Chemistry* to *The Principles of Zoological Micropaleontology*.

One would, however, be hard-pressed to find a book with a title like *The Principles of World Politics*.[1] This is not because there are no principles to articulate; rather, it is because in the field of International Relations (commonly called IR) there is no widely accepted theory of international politics, and thus no principles that command wide agreement among those who teach about world politics—or those who practise it. There is no agreement on the elements needed to guide inquiry or on the boundaries of their field. Indeed, some even deny that disciplinary boundaries do—or should—exist. There is no agreement on the most important questions to be asked or the essential assumptions to be used in analysis. There is no agreement on what is sufficiently puzzling about world politics as to command our attention. In short, scholars who study international relations are deeply divided on the most appropriate theoretical approach to the discipline. As a consequence, **international relations theory**, as Kal J. Holsti put it succinctly, is in "a state of disarray."[2]

Thus, instead of a relatively unified approach to first principles—the kind one finds in economics, astrophysics, or immunology, for example—there has been a huge diversity in theoretical approaches to international politics. Viewing the contending perspectives in the field of IR, one is reminded of the exhortation of Mao Zedong, the Chinese leader, in May 1957: "Let a hundred flowers bloom," Mao said. "Let a hundred schools of thought contend."* For in the fields and meadows of international relations, a hundred flowers—and more—have bloomed; and unlike China, where the blossoms were quickly nipped in the bud, numerous schools of thought continue to compete in happy heterodoxy.

*"Let a hundred flowers bloom. Let a hundred schools of thought contend."*

## "LET A HUNDRED SCHOOLS OF THOUGHT CONTEND"

There are numerous alternative theoretical approaches to world politics. Each one purports to offer the most accurate, logical, and comprehensible theoretical insights into the nature of global politics, its dominant puzzles, and explanations for those puzzles. Each of the contending perspectives works on differing sets of philosophical assumptions, seeks different answers, and comes to rather different conclusions. Some schools of thought have even evolved a highly specialized terminology, or methodology, often accessible only to the cognoscenti. Each perspective tends to have its enthusiasts. Quarrels are frequent, and occasionally vicious.[3]

---

* The Hundred Flowers campaign was designed to encourage a struggle against orthodoxy by openly criticizing the Chinese Communist Party (CCP). However, so many intellectuals took the call to heart that Mao quickly changed his mind about the wisdom of the movement, and instead launched a vicious campaign to clamp down on his critics. By the end of 1957, some 300 000 intellectuals had been stripped of their positions; many of them were jailed or "sent down to the countryside" in exile, forbidden to teach. Others were driven to suicide by public criticism. One measure of the brutality of the clampdown was the fate of three middle school students in Hanyang who had criticized the administration of their school: they were put on trial and then executed by firing squad in front of 10 000 people. Jonathan D. Spence, *The Search for Modern China* (London: Hutchinson, 1990), 568–73.

However, this profusion of blossoms poses a serious problem for the beginning student of international politics. In other disciplines, where basic theoretical assumptions enjoy widespread agreement, the student can be introduced to the essential theoretical principles of the discipline at the outset. In IR, this is just not possible. Rather, the student must contend with a profusion of approaches, theories, and methodologies.

## Approaches to IR

Those who teach international politics tend to adopt one of a number of theoretical approaches to the study of their subject. Each school of thought is tagged with the suffix "-ism" to denote its status as a doctrine or theory. Three theoretical approaches are usually presented as the dominant schools in the field: **realism**, **liberalism**, and **Marxism** (sometimes called **radicalism**). Two other theoretical perspectives, **feminism** and **postmodernism**, constitute major—and much more radical—challenges to the dominant theoretical approaches.

### Realist Theories

As its name suggests, realism seeks to portray world politics as *realistically* as possible. It is usually contrasted with **idealism**, the view common in the period between the two world wars, that war could be brought to an end by establishing international institutions. If idealists held out the possibility of optimism, the realist (or power politics) approach is marked by a certain pessimism. The classical realist approach embraces an interrelated set of assumptions about the world:

- international politics is about states and their interactions

- states seek power, particularly military power, because there is nothing to guarantee their security

- the relations between states are guided by an amoral calculation of whatever best serves the interests of the state

- the political realm is distinct from the economic realm

- in such an amoral, power-driven world, one must always be on guard

The philosophers usually associated with the realist approach to international politics are Thucydides (circa 460–400 BC), Niccolò Machiavelli (1469–1527), and Thomas Hobbes (1588–1679). Modern exponents of realist thought in world politics include E.H. Carr and Hans J. Morgenthau.[4]

*"Because some states may at any time use force, all states must be prepared to do so—or live at the mercy of their militarily more vigorous neighbors."*

A variant of classical realism is **structural realism** (sometimes called neorealism), commonly associated with an American academic, Kenneth N. Waltz, and his 1979 book, *Theory of International Politics*. As its name suggests, structural realism focuses on how the structures of the international system shapes the behaviour of the various units in the system, the states. Waltz compares the international system to a market, with states (like firms) engaging in activities that keep them alive and operating. Just as firms that do not pursue profit-maximizing strategies will go bankrupt, so too will states disappear that do not pursue self-protective and power-seeking strategies. Thus, conflict rather than cooperation marks world politics: "Because some states may at any time use force, all states must be prepared to do so—or live at the mercy of their militarily more vigorous neighbors."[5]

### Liberal Theories

Taking their cue from the liberal individualism of political philosophers such as John Locke (1632–1704) and Immanuel Kant (1724–1804), classical liberal theories of international politics focus on the individual and the possibilities for the improvement in the condition of individual existence. For liberals, international politics is not the grim struggle for power among competing states. Rather, the actors in world politics are an amalgam of states, governments, groups, and individuals. Liberals do not see international relations as an endless and vicious struggle for power among states, but as relations between individuals and societies engaged in highly cooperative activities. Moreover, liberals tend to see that cooperation between some societies is more likely than with others. In particular, liberal perspectives suggest that liberal democracies are more inclined to remain at peace and engage in cooperative behaviour with other liberal democracies than with states with other kinds of political systems. Thus much liberal theorizing is concerned with an explicitly normative concern to expand the realm of liberal democracy.

**Neoliberalism**, sometimes known as **liberal institutionalism**, emerged in the 1980s as a variant on classical liberal ideas. Usually associated with the work of such scholars as Robert O. Keohane,[6] neoliberalism tends to focus on one aspect of international cooperation—the degree to which institutions play an important part in tempering the anarchical nature of international relations. It rejects the realist separation of the economic and political realms, and instead focuses on the consequences of economic exchange between individuals organized into states. Here the assumptions of classical liberal economists such as Adam Smith (1723–1790) and David Ricardo (1772–1823) are used to examine how economic exchange between states produces harmony and natural patterns of cooperation as each individual pursues his or her own economic self-interest.

### Marxist Theories

A third approach is inspired by the thought of Karl Marx (1818–1883). Marxist approaches are often called "radical" theories because of their focus on nontraditional factors of analysis, such as the impact of modes of production on politics and particularly on the formation of class. This theoretical perspective thus highlights the importance of socioeconomic factors in relations between states and peoples. It also suggests that the real political struggle in world politics is not between states or peoples, but between classes, organized into different nation-states. This approach fixes on the fundamental inequalities between peoples, not only within states but also between states.[7]

This theoretical perspective includes a number of diverse strands. **Dependency** and **world economy theories** seek to explain why some parts of the international capitalist economy remain underdeveloped and dependent on other parts.[8] Likewise, world economy perspectives like those of Immanuel Wallerstein or Christopher Chase-Dunn suggest that the capitalist world system that developed after the middle of the 15th century divided the world's labour into three basic areas: **core**, **periphery**, and **semi-periphery**. Core states developed high-skill modes of production and dominated both the states of the periphery, which supply the core, and the states of a semi-periphery which fall into neither category.[9] Some scholars, such as Robert W. Cox, have been influenced by the work of Antonio Gramsci (1891–1937) and focus on the centrality of production for the shaping of politics and society and systems of power.[10]

## Radical Challenges: Feminism and Postmodernism

After a century of orthodox existence, Marxist theories are no longer really *radical*, in the sense of being marked by a departure from the usual or traditional. By contrast, feminist and postmodernist theories of international politics are quite radical, for they reject the dominant and orthodox approaches to the discipline of IR.

**Feminist Theories**    There are numerous approaches within feminist theorizing about international politics, but one central and abiding concern has been to demonstrate the degree to which orthodox theories about world politics tend to ignore gender. Realist theory and its focus on states, liberal theory and its focus on individuals, and Marxist theory with its focus on class all assume that gender relations are fundamentally unimportant to political outcomes. Feminist scholarship, by contrast, has been concerned with uncovering how gender matters in international politics. It asks: in what ways is international politics "gendered"—in other words, how is it thought about so as to hide important differences between men and women? For example, does the overwhelming **androcentrism** (or male-centred nature) of political structures around the world have an impact on how politics at a world level is practised? What hidden or unconscious assumptions do we make about gender? Consider our assumptions of what is "private" and what is "public"—ideas that are central to the very idea of the modern state. This basic dichotomy has a huge impact on the way we look at the domestic work done by women, for example. The labour devoted to childcare, husbandcare, and homecare simply disappears in an aggregate statistic like the Gross National Product (GNP), which generally does not count the huge unpaid domestic labour of the world's women. And given the invisibility of women's work, what should the role of women be in the development process? In short, feminist theorizing about world politics demands that we think about the world in ways that are indeed radically different from the realist, liberal, and Marxist approaches.[11]

**Postmodern Theories**    The revolution in thinking about the world that we call the **Age of Enlightenment** occurred during the 18th century, but cast a long shadow over the next two hundred years. Enlightenment thinkers themselves conceived of their contributions in terms of emerging from the "darkness" of beliefs about the world informed by superstition and religion to the "enlightenment" provided by reason and science. The physical laws uncovered by observation and logic suggested that laws could also be found to understand society and human behaviour. The Enlightenment project, in short, held that an objective and discernible Truth could be discovered. And the logical corollary of that was that humankind itself could be made better through the application of reason and education. This was—and is—the essence of **modernity**.

**Postmodernism**, by contrast, casts doubt on modernity's belief in the existence of an "objective reality" that can be readily discerned. Rather, postmodernist theory is concerned with showing the degree to which the social world does not *exist* in reality, but rather is created—or *constructed*—by social scientists, among others. To be sure, the events and the actors are real enough, but how we understand them and their interactions is largely a matter of how we choose to interpret those interactions; all writing (and lecturing and teaching) are "stories" or "discourses" that get passed on. Postmodernists seek to "deconstruct" how those stories are told and to reveal what assumptions underlie them. Some, inspired by the work of Michel Foucault (1926–1984), try to show how the way we are led to interpret the world around us tends to reflect and promote the interests of the powerful: *discourse*, then, is an exercise in power. Some postmodernists seek to tell a new "story" (or, as they might say, "re-inscribe" that story, creating a new discourse). But most post-modernists, precisely because they are postmodernists, are not necessarily concerned with providing *explanations* for phenomena; that, after all, is part of the modernist project. As Ole Wæver points out, this can lead to frustrations when a modernist reads a postmodern critique of IR theorizing: "'But what is *your* explanation?' the establishment asks... 'It is not!' the new critics reply to the bewilderment of the establishment."[12] In IR, there is no one school of postmodernism, but rather a group of scholars concerned with critiquing how the orthodox modernists, or the establishment, think about world politics.[13] It is perhaps not surprising that many feminist students of IR are also postmodernists (and vice versa), for the two approaches share many of the same analytical and critical concerns.[14]

### Other Approaches, Schools, and Methodologies

To this list of "isms" could be added a variety of approaches and schools. The **rational choice** approach to IR, dominant in the United States but not in other English-speaking countries, suggests that political outcomes are the consequences of groups of individuals each seeking to maximize their objectives.[15] The **peace research** approach focuses on the problem of war and the conditions of peace, primarily using insights gleaned from many disciplines, including psychology, sociology, economics, philosophy, and medicine.[16] The **international political economy** approach sees world politics as not simply the competition among states, but rather the intersection of states and markets.[17] The **English School** is the name given to an approach outlined by scholars mainly but not exclusively in England, that focuses on the evolution of society and community at a world level.[18] The **Frankfurt School**, influenced by the thought of the German sociologist Jurgen Habermas, seeks to examine world politics from a sociological, critical, and explicitly normative perspective.[19]

Students will also encounter what is called "mid-level" theory—perspectives that help us understand particular elements of IR but do not provide a full and comprehensive theory of all the phenomena of world politics. Mid-level theoretical approaches include decision-making theory, integration theory, regime theory, long-cycle theory, hegemonic stability theory, or prospect theory.[20]

Among the blooms, students will find these various approaches bundled and organized into dichotomies (realism/idealism or neorealism/neoliberalism) or even trichotomies (realism/liberalism/socialism; Hobbesian/Grotian/Kantian). Sometimes they are organized into numbered Great Debates™ that ran their course over the latter half of the 20th century: the "first" debate between realism and idealism in the 1940s and 1950s; a "second" debate in the 1960s between **behaviouralism** (or the scientific approach) and traditionalism; the so-called Third Debate[21] of the 1970s between globalism and realism; and a fourth, more philosophical, debate in the 1980s and 1990s over **epistemology** (how one knows what one knows about something) and **ontology** (how one categorizes what one knows).

Finally, along with the huge range of theoretical perspectives that guide students of international politics, there are also contending methodologies. These include historical analysis, which seeks to reveal the essence of international politics by exploring the past; behavioural analysis, which seeks to construct if/then hypotheses on the basis of statistical techniques and tries to bring scientific methodology to the study of IR; formal modelling and game theory, used by rational choice theorists to reveal the nature of international interactions; and **semiotics** (the study of signs and symbols) and **hermeneutics** (the study of interpretation), the methodology of choice for postmodern scholars seeking to deconstruct a text.[22]

## THINKING THEORETICALLY

What is the beginning student of international politics to make of such a profusion of theory and methodology? How can these competing perspectives guide inquiry? Which is the right one? Which one does one choose—and on what criteria does one make that choice? Unfortunately, there can be no definitive answers to such questions.

### Exploring the Meadow: A Cautionary Note

One can, however, caution against choosing a particular "ism" to make one's own at the outset of one's studies. There are three reasons for such caution. First, any single theoretical approach noted above is rarely able to capture the complexity of international politics. On the contrary: simplification encourages caricature and pigeon-holing. Take Thucydides, Machiavelli, and Hobbes, who are usually considered as realist writers. These three men lived at different times in history, in different societies; they had different worldviews, which were expressed in long and theoretically rich books that some people have spent lifetimes trying to understand. It is difficult to sum up these thinkers and their work by tagging them with the single word "realist."[23] (More importantly, the caricatures offered of their work are sometimes simply erroneous, as we will see in the case of Hobbes in Chapter 3.)

A second reason for caution is that these theoretical perspectives are often difficult to compare. One can lay out the different schools of thought and try to assess which school most appropriately reflects world politics. But one should never forget that some of these contending theoretical perspectives are simply incompatible. For example, one cannot just pick up feminist theory to look at one issue, then discard it and pick up realist theory for other issues. The feminist critique of international relations, if it is to be taken seriously, means reshaping the very way in which one understands world politics and sees the world. By the same token, realism as an approach speaks right past feminist theory; it is utterly blind to gender differences. The two approaches, in short, cannot simply be substituted for one another. The same is true of most theoretical approaches.

*The feminist critique of international relations, if it is to be taken seriously, means reshaping the very way in which one understands world politics and sees the world.*

A third problem with choosing an "ism" at the outset is that it encourages one to overlook the work of the theorists themselves; it suggests that one does not need to go and actually *read* the works of those who have presented us with some markedly different ways of looking at world politics, such as the authors listed in the Focus below. But these are books that deserve to be read in the original as part of one's IR education.

For these three reasons, there is much to be said for avoiding trying to cram oneself into a tight pigeon-hole, as some committed "-ist" or other, at the outset of one's studies about world politics. Instead, know that there is no one theory of world politics; be alert to the fact that international relations has a rich intellectual history that should be explored; set aside—for the moment, at least—the intense theoretical quarrels of the various schools of

# FOCUS

## *Blooming Flowers: Some Contemporary English-Language Contributions to International Theory*

Hans J. Morgenthau, *Politics Among Nations: The Struggle for Power and Peace*, 5th ed. (New York: Alfred A. Knopf, [1948] 1973)

John W. Burton, *World Society* (Cambridge: Cambridge University Press, 1972)

Hedley Bull, *The Anarchical Society: A Study of Order in World Politics* (London: Macmillan, 1977)

Kenneth N. Waltz, *Theory of International Politics* (Reading, MA: Addison-Wesley, 1979)

Robert O. Keohane, *After Hegemony: Cooperation and Discord in the World Political Economy* (Princeton: Princeton University Press, 1984)

Robert W. Cox, *Production, Power and World Order: Social Forces in the Making of History* (New York: Columbia University Press, 1987)

Cynthia Enloe, *Bananas, Beaches, and Bases: Making Feminist Sense of International Politics* (Berkeley: University of California Press, 1990)

R.B.J. Walker, *Inside/Outside: International Relations as Political Theory* (Cambridge: Cambridge University Press, 1993)

Fred Halliday, *Rethinking International Relations* (Vancouver: University of British Columbia Press, 1994)

thought; and acquire an exposure to some of the elements of world politics before delving into the contentions of international theory.

## Inquiry and Understanding

This is not to suggest that one should abandon thinking theoretically about world politics. On the contrary: if we are to make some sense of the world around us, we cannot avoid theory. We have to give shape to our inquiry and develop ways of increasing our understanding of the patterns of politics.

Thinking theoretically about world politics means, in the first instance, trying to identify the boundaries of inquiry and explanation—selecting phenomena that are critical for understanding of world politics, and, just as importantly, setting aside phenomena that are irrelevant. Drawing boundaries in this fashion is not easy, however, because the exclusionary nature of the exercise makes it highly contested.

Second, thinking theoretically means organizing phenomena to make them intelligible. Part of this process involves taxonomy—in other words, identifying, naming, and defining phenomena. This definitional exercise is crucial for building the vocabulary of international politics necessary for analyzing events, facts, and phenomena. This too can involve pitfalls, for definitions can vary, sometimes widely.

Third, as Ralph Pettman has argued, thinking theoretically also means acquiring a knowledge of context and meaning.[24] This is an often inchoate process that we often take for granted, but it is crucial for theorizing about the world around us. Pettman cites Mervyn Frost's example of how much we need to know in order to understand a simple and commonplace event like a summit meeting between two political leaders. If an external observer knew nothing about human society, Frost suggests, consider what the observer would see:

> a large aircraft, which was met by crowds assembled beside a strip of red carpet. [W]hen a man emerged from the aircraft, lights popped and bands played and...then the man walked up and down rows of men all uniformly dressed in unusual clothes.[25]

As Frost says, to make sense of all of this, one needs a considerable amount of contextual knowledge. One would need to understand what a summit, a state, a leader, a national flag, a national anthem, an honour guard, a red carpet, and a press photographer are. One would also need to know what these people were *doing* there; what they were trying to accomplish; how they all fit together in these particular circumstances; and why their interaction might be important. In fact, most of us already have developed this level of understanding, but consider how much time it required. Spending time accumulating and refining context will provide, as Charles McClelland put it a generation ago, "an 'understanding' that is not quite intuitive; it is more a synthesis constructed privately from particular facts and general meanings."[26]

## THE SEARCH FOR PATTERNS IN WORLD POLITICS

Thinking theoretically also means trying to develop a general understanding of the phenomena of world politics. The purpose here is not to identify quantifiable independent and dependent variables or to construct testable hypotheses intended to yield predictions about how world politics will unfold in the future. It can be argued that prediction in international politics is difficult, if not impossible.

## Prediction and the Unpredictable

There is little that is smooth and regular about the way in which world politics happens. On the contrary: global politics tends to be marked by unpredictable and unexpected events that can alter the course of human affairs. An assassination, an invention, a plague, the downing of a plane, a market collapse, an electoral defeat (or victory), a leader's sudden illness or death, a riot spiralling out of control, even a sudden storm—all can "trigger" outcomes, and affect the course of world politics, as the Focus suggests.

# FOCUS

## *Sudden and Unpredictable "Triggers" in World Politics*

**ASSASSINATIONS:** On 28 June 1914, Archduke Francis Ferdinand, heir to the throne of Austria-Hungary, was assassinated by a Serbian nationalist, Gavrilo Princip. Usually cited as the spark that ignited the First World War, it set in train a series of events that led to war.

**MARKET COLLAPSES:** The collapse of the New York stock market in the fall of 1929 triggered a deep economic depression, not only in the United States, but eventually spreading throughout the international capitalist system as protectionism increased and trade declined. By contrast, the stock market crash of October 1987 was immediately global: in one night stocks around the world lost billions in value. This crash prompted a series of crises and conflicts over the relative value of international currencies.

**DEFENESTRATIONS:** On 23 May 1618, Protestants in Prague, angered by the Catholic king of Bohemia, stormed the royal palace and threw two of his ministers from a window. The Defenestration of Prague was the immediate cause of the Thirty Years' War, a series of bitter and destructive wars that altered the political landscape of Europe. A much later defenestration in Prague was that of Jan Masaryk, foreign minister in the Czech government following the Second World War. Masaryk opposed the efforts of Communists, backed by the Soviet Union, to take over the government; on 10 March 1948, he either jumped to his death, or, more likely, was thrown from a window and murdered. His death galvanized support in the United States for a defensive alliance with Western Europe that eventually resulted in the formation of NATO.

**DOWNING OF AIRCRAFT:** On 1 September 1983, a fighter from the Soviet Union shot down a Korean Air Lines 747 jumbo jet which had accidentally strayed into Soviet airspace, killing 269 people. This crisis triggered the beginning of a reversal in the tensions of the Cold War. On 6 April 1994, unknown assailants fired rockets at a plane carrying the presidents of Rwanda and Burundi, Juvénal Habyarimana and Cyprien Ntaryamira, as it landed at Kigali. It crashed into Habyarimana's own garden, killing all on board and triggering a wave of ethnic violence in which hundreds of thousands of Rwandans died.

**IMPETUOUS DECISIONS:** Following the outbreak of war in Europe in September 1939, many Americans believed that the struggle between the European powers was none of their concern. As a result, the government of Franklin Delano Roosevelt remained neutral, even if openly sympathetic to Britain. On 7 December 1941, Japanese aircraft attacked the United States naval base at Pearl Harbor; the next day, Congress approved a declaration of war against

Japan. While the United States was now involved in the war in the Pacific, it would have been difficult to justify an American declaration of war against Germany. On 11 December, Adolf Hitler impetuously declared war on the United States, thus ensuring that American resources would also be devoted to the war in Europe.

**ILLNESS:** On 18 January 1989, Pieter W. Botha, the president of South Africa, suffered a stroke. Although he refused to resign for over seven months, he was replaced as head of his party by the education minister, Frederik W. De Klerk. The incapacitation that brought De Klerk to power accelerated the dismantling of apartheid and the creation of a multiracial state in South Africa.

**STORMS:** In 1281, the Mongols attacked Japan with a naval force of 140 000 soldiers. However, a violent typhoon destroyed over half of the Mongol fleet, stranding soldiers on Japanese territory and forcing the retreat of the remaining ships; only about 70 000 men returned. Because it had preserved their independence, the Japanese called the typhoon "kamikaze"—

divine wind. Winds also had a dramatic effect on the fortunes of the 130 ships and 30 000 soldiers assembled by Philip II of Spain to invade England. In August 1588, following the defeat of the Spanish Armada by the English navy, strong winds forced the remaining Spanish ships to sail home around the top of the British Isles. However, storms wrecked numerous ships off the Irish coast. Thousands drowned, and many of the survivors who made it to shore were killed by the English. Only sixty ships and 15 000 men made it back to Spain, marking the beginning of Spain's decline as a great European power.

**VOLCANIC ERUPTION:** On 9 June 1991, Mount Pinatubo in the Philippines erupted, blanketing nearby Clark Air Base, a facility operated by the United States Air Force, in ash and forcing its closure. When the United States decided it would not reopen Clark, the Philippine Senate decided that the United States Navy would no longer be able to use Subic Bay Naval Station. Thus, the eruption proved to be the trigger for ending the American military presence in the Philippines.

Following the Japanese attack on Pearl Harbor, Nazi Germany impetuously declared war on the United States. (See "Impetuous Decision" in the Focus.)

## Path Dependency and Chaos Theory

The sudden and often random intrusion of events makes prediction virtually impossible, for the evolution of world politics is highly dependent on a particular sequence of events. Thus how we got to where we are now is highly **path dependent** (in other words, the evolution of any particular event is highly dependent on the sequence of events, or path, that came before it). In path-dependent analysis, if you change one element in the sequence, the outcome is likely to be different. It is true that some path-dependent analyses are grossly reductionist, in the sense that they attribute major consequences to minor and often trivial events. Such analysis is reflected in the nursery rhyme notion that the fall of the House of York in 15th-century English politics can be explained by the loss of a horseshoe nail. While fighting the Battle of Bosworth Field against the Lancastrians on 22 August 1485, King Richard III was unhorsed in a bog and killed. The nursery rhyme is a classic of reductionist path-dependent analysis:

> For want of a nail, the shoe was lost;
> For want of a shoe, the horse was lost;
> For want of a horse, the rider was lost;
> For want of a rider, the battle was lost;
> For want of a battle, the kingdom was lost.

The problem with such reductionism is that it ignores the huge variety of other factors that "cause" major events like the dynastic Wars of the Roses. "A horse! a horse! my kingdom for a horse!" makes a good closing line for a Shakespearean Richard, who the audience knows is doomed, but it is by no means certain that had the horseshoe nail remained intact, the House of York would have remained equally intact.

But path-dependent analysis alerts us to the essentially *contingent* nature of world politics, where nothing is predetermined, preordained, natural, inevitable, or unavoidable. Rather, if some key conditions had been changed, the sequence of events that shaped world politics would have been different.

*"Wind the tape of life back to Burgess times, and let it play again. If* Pikaia *does not survive in the replay, we are wiped out of future history."*

Stephen Jay Gould has demonstrated the usefulness of this kind of thinking when theorizing about the evolution of species. Using as his inspiration the 1946 Frank Capra film *It's a Wonderful Life* (in which George Bailey, played by Jimmy Stewart, is shown what his town would have been like without him), Gould reflects on the vast number of species found in the 570-million-year-old Burgess Shale in British Columbia that simply went extinct. Among the diverse life forms found in the Burgess Shale was a relatively rare little chordate, *Pikaia gracilens*, one of the earliest life forms to have a very primitive spinal column. That *Pikaia* survived, while the more numerous other species found in the shale did not, suggested to Gould just how hugely contingent the evolution of the species *Homo sapiens sapiens* was: had but one adaptation gone one way rather than another hundreds of millions of years ago, life forms would have evolved in an entirely different way. As Gould puts it evocatively: "Wind the tape of life back to Burgess times, and let it play again. If *Pikaia* does not survive in the replay, we are wiped out of future history—all of us, from shark to robin to orangutan."[27] This kind of thinking is equally useful for reflecting on patterns in international politics.

World politics can thus be seen as highly "chaotic" in the sense that that term is used in chaos theory in physics. **Chaos theory** denies the possibility of "infinite predictability," since even systems that appear to behave according to very precise laws are in fact sensitive to differences in initial conditions that alter subsequent behaviour. Thus systems like a pendulum or a dripping faucet, which on the surface appear quite simple, are in fact quite unpredictable. Chaos theory has been applied to complex systems such as the solar system and even human systems like national economies.

Niall Ferguson has applied chaos theory to history, which he calls "chaostory." He argues that it is useful to reflect on the **counterfactual**—the hypothesizing of what might have happened. Counterfactual history has long been used for entertainment. In its halcyon days, NBC's *Saturday Night Live* ran a regular segment called "What If?" that featured "talking-head" experts earnestly discussing such silly historical counterfactual questions as "What if Napoleon Bonaparte had had F-15 jet fighters at the Battle of Waterloo?" Less frivolous is Robert Harris's 1992 novel *Fatherland*, a detective story set in the early 1960s in a Germany that won the Second World War. But counterfactual history can also be done seriously to demonstrate the chaotic and contingent nature of world politics. For example, Ferguson gathered eminent historians to analyze some of the key conflicts that have shaped contemporary world politics.[28] The studies ask such plausible counterfactual questions as "What if Nazi Germany had defeated the Soviet Union?" and "What if Communism had not collapsed?"* Ferguson's book provides not only an excellent introduction to historical theorizing, but a nice illustration of the contingent nature of world politics.

## Thinking Historically...

Thus, to think theoretically is not necessarily to search for a basis for predictability; rather, thinking theoretically means trying to discern particular patterns in world politics. In this context, thinking theoretically means thinking historically—always mindful that human beings have been recording their engagement in world politics for some five thousand years.

Thinking historically also means avoiding the trap of becoming mesmerized by current events, headline news, the personalities of the day, and the fads of the present. Indeed, trying to develop an appreciation of world politics by getting to know the international affairs that were dominant in those few years spent in post-secondary education is actually of quite limited benefit analytically. First, these years represent about 1/1000 of the historical experience that humankind has had with world politics; one is unlikely to acquire an appreciation of a subject by overlooking history. This is not simply a matter of citing George

---

* On the basis of the various studies, Ferguson himself contributes a "virtual history" of the world from 1646 to 1996. Unfortunately, Ferguson's concluding history ends up contradicting the broader point of the book—that if one changes "initial conditions," subsequent events simply do not fall into place. Thus, for example, if there had been a German victory in 1915, as Ferguson counterfactually hypothesizes, would there have been a Treaty of Versailles with punitive reparations, hyperinflation, and political dislocation in Germany that created the fertile soil in which Adolf Hitler and the National Socialist German Workers (Nazi) party thrived? Change the conditions in 1915 to those painted by Ferguson, and a more plausible counterfactual future is that Corporal Hitler was demobilized in 1916, returned to Vienna where he set up a moderately successful portrait studio, and lived an unremarkable bourgeois existence, dying of prostate cancer in 1963 at the age of 74.

Santayana's well-worn saying that "Those who cannot remember the past are condemned to repeat it." In fact, history's "lessons" are by no means automatic and self-revealing; indeed, there is another, and quite opposite, conclusion: "Those who remember the past are condemned to repeat it."

Rather, thinking historically stresses the importance of the past in understanding the present—and the future. In particular, as I will argue throughout this book, in order to understand world politics today, one has to appreciate that the politics of the contemporary era emerged out of an historical context, one that is constantly unfolding.

Indeed, it is this feature that suggests a second, and perhaps even more important, reason for thinking historically about world politics. As dramatic as the events of today's headlines may be, as pressing as today's issues may appear, as fascinating as today's personalities may seem, one should never forget that in a blink of an eye they will be gone, the stuff of history, remembered only mistily, if at all. Ten or 20 years into the 21st century, what lessons will today's events hold? How useful will it be to know them, unless they are placed in the context of broad patterns of human experience, observed over a considerable period of time?

## ...But Not Universally

However, to search for *patterns* is not to search for *universals*. It is often argued that over the five thousand years that the species *Homo sapiens sapiens* has been recording its history, humankind has manifested a good deal of sameness over time and space. It is said that some aspects of human existence have changed over time—political, social, and religious ideas; modes of production; systems of economic exchange; socioeconomic and political institutions; culture; and technological innovation—but many other aspects of human behaviour have remained relatively unchanged. Some argue that the point of theory is **universalism**—the discovery of patterns that apply to human behaviour universally, everywhere and at all times.

It is true that much of our genetically-coded and instinctual behaviour really is universal: fear, for example, increases the flow of adrenalin in all humans. Likewise, there are similarities of behaviour across time and space—even if the actual manifestations of that behaviour may differ. Human courtship rituals are not at all universal in the *way* they are conducted: contemporary teenagers in the city of Teheran behave very differently from their American counterparts in San Diego; the courtship rituals of 19th-century Victorian England, 18th-century Masai, and 17th-century Tokugawa Japan differ considerably. But there can be no denying that all who engage in such rituals have a final *end* in mind that *is* universal.

Similarly, humans everywhere and at all times will laugh at a joke, find some things beautiful, or feel anger at a slight. But since humans are an intensely social species, their behaviour is deeply culturally determined, always dependent on time and place. Thus a joke in one culture may be distinctly unfunny in another (which is why humour is one form of entertainment that does not travel well internationally); likewise, a joke in the same culture can become distinctly unfunny over time. What may be considered beautiful in one culture at one time may not arouse similar feelings in another culture or at another time. What provokes anger in one place or at one time may not evoke such a sentiment everywhere.

So too is international politics largely dependent on time and place; thus one should view with considerable skepticism universalistic assertions that human beings will behave politically the same way at all times in all places.

## The Pitfall of the Universal: A (Qian)long Digression

To get some sense of how differences in time and space can affect political behaviour and our understanding of it, consider once again the summit meeting mentioned by Mervyn Frost on p. 21. We could conceive of this in universalist terms: i.e., a summit is a summit is a summit. But is it? Consider two summits—one in the 1760s in China, and another in the 1990s in the Asia Pacific.

### Imperial China, 1760s

Imagine what 20th-century observers would have seen if they had attended the imperial court of Hongli, the Qianlong emperor in the Qing dynasty,* who ruled from 1736 to 1795. They would have seen non-Chinese leaders from all around what is now China—Korea, Liuqiu (the Ryukyu islands, now part of Japan), Annam (Vietnam), Siam (Thailand), Laos, Burma, and Tibet—travel regularly to the imperial Qing courts in Beijing and other cities. As these leaders and their retinues approached the Chinese heartland, they were met by escorts and led to the capital. They lodged at official guest houses by the bureaucracies responsible for foreign visits, the Board of Rites and the Office of Guest Ceremony. A special day was chosen for the emperor to receive the visiting delegation. In the presence of the full Chinese court, the visitors approached the emperor, who always sat facing south for ritualistic reasons. They then performed the "three kneelings and nine knockings" of the *koutou*: three times they knelt, and each time bowed their foreheads against the floor three times. They then presented petitions, offered greetings and special gifts, and thanked the emperor for granting them imperial grace and showering them with gifts. The visitors were then allowed to open a market for a short period to sell local products before being escorted out of China.

This is what we would have *seen*, but we really would not understand very much about what we saw if we tried to use universalizing notions to describe and understand it. For example, we would probably make the mistake of calling it a "tribute system"—because we remembered that the Roman Empire forced conquered peoples to present tribute (*tributum*), supposedly "just like" what we saw in China (i.e., tribute is tribute is tribute). Using 20th century European and American (or Euro-American) and Christian assumptions about the significance of kneeling and prostration, we would be both appalled at the humiliation that the emperor was inflicting on the visitor and wonder what would lead for-

---

* In English, the Chinese *q* is pronounced *ch*: Qing is "ching" and Qianlong is "chee-an-lung." In Chinese history, periods of rule are called dynasties and each dynasty was marked by a number of reigns, with each emperor choosing a "reign name" (e.g., Hongli was the Qianlong emperor). The Ming dynasty, for example, began in 1368 and ran until a rebellion in April 1644, when the last Ming, the Chongzen emperor, committed suicide. Manchus, a people from the north, seized the throne, and established the Qing dynasty, which lasted through ten reigns until 1911, when imperial rule was abolished. A republic was established in 1912.

eign leaders to accept such humiliation. Using more Euro-American assumptions about economic value, we might also be puzzled at the emperor's showers of gifts to the visitors. Trying to solve these puzzles, we might look for explanations grounded in economic rationality, or rooted in the raw military power of the emperor's troops.

And if we did this, we would simply misinterpret what we saw, for these rituals cannot be fully understood from a 20th century, Euro-American, economic-rationalist perspective.

*In the Chinese conception the world was filled with lords, but ruling over all of them was the Son of Heaven.*

First, we would misname the very process: the Chinese themselves did not call this a "tribute system"—that is a term imposed by Europeans and Americans. Rather, for those who participated in this system, it was part of *Binli*, or the **Guest Ritual**—a highly stylized means of giving non-Chinese an audience with the emperor. Likewise, the offerings brought to Beijing were nothing like *tributum*; rather, they were *gong*, offerings of precious things and local products (*fangwu*) that had great symbolic but little material value.

Second, we would misname the players if we characterized the central player as "China" and its leader as "emperor." As we will see in more detail in Chapter 8, the Chinese and their Manchu leaders did not conceive of "China" as a single territorial state the way a 20th-century person would. Instead, they lived in *Jungguo: jung* is the Chinese character for central or middle, *guo* is usually translated as kingdom or country—hence "Middle Kingdom." But a better translation for *guo* is "domain," in other words, a geographic/geopolitical space with highly fluid boundaries that could incorporate both Chinese and the *yi*, the foreign peoples who were considered part of the Chinese empire. In the Chinese conception the world was filled with lords, but ruling over all of them was the Son of Heaven, the *huangdi* (often translated as "emperor," but better rendered as "lord of all lords"). In this view—shaped by the teachings of the philosopher Kongfuzi (Confucius) that humans would be in harmony with the universe if they adhered to specific social roles—there could be no equality between lords: all lesser lords (*fanwang*) owed obedience and subservience to the *huangdi*, whose authority extended over the whole world. Those at the furthest corners of the world would want to visit the *huangdi* and receive his *en*, or imperial grace. Thus, lesser lords were never *commanded* to perform these rituals; on the contrary, they eagerly *asked* for the privilege of an audience with the "south-facing emperor." They were proud to offer *fangwu* on behalf of their *guo*, and regarded the performance of the *koutou* as a natural and proper expression of the *necessary* inequality between them and the *huangdi*.[29]

In short, these practices only make sense when Chinese words, embedded in a particular Chinese and Confucian worldview dominant in the 18th century, are used to analyze them. If we read "backward" and "transculturally"—by discussing 18th-century Chinese practices using the English language and 20th-century Euro-American assumptions—we misunderstand and miss context.

## Asia Pacific, 1990s

But the same is also true in reverse: reading "forward" and across cultures would lead to just as much confusion. Consider, for example, if we dropped the Qianlong *huangdi* into a contemporary meeting of the Asia Pacific Economic Cooperation (APEC) forum. What sense could he make of what he saw if he used 18th-century classical Confucian assumptions about contemporary summit diplomacy?

He would of course see much that was familiar. Of the 21 "lords" present, he would recognize Chinese, Japanese, Koreans, Vietnamese, and others from Southeast Asian countries. He would also recognize the Russians, but he would probably think that all the other "round eyes" present also came from the West Ocean Kingdoms (i.e., Europe) rather than from Australia, Canada, New Zealand, and the United States. But the people from Papua New Guinea, Mexico, and Chile would be unfamiliar; and he would probably be puzzled that the lord of Peru was a Japanese.

The diplomacy he saw would look somewhat familiar, but he would lack some important contextual understanding. What would he make of the fact that of all the *guo* there, only China got to send three representatives to this meeting? Would he conclude (incorrectly) that this privilege was a reflection of China's natural superiority over other kingdoms? Would he understand why *Jungguo* was divided into three—the People's Republic of China (PRC), the Republic of China on Taiwan (ROC), and the Hong Kong Special Administrative Region (HKSAR)? Would he understand why of all the *guos*, only the ROC was not allowed to send a lord, and why no one was allowed to call it the Republic of China, but only "Chinese Taipei"? What would he make of another compatriot, the chief executive of the HKSAR, who attended using the name "Hong Kong, China"? And why Hong Kong—which in his time was an obscure fishing village—but not other great Chinese cities like Shanghai or Guangzhou? What would he make of the fact that the chief executive of this apparently important place was a merchant who owned a number of boats—which the *huangdi* would consider a very lowly station in life—and the secretary of the Hong Kong government was a woman—unthinkable in his day? And how could it be that the leader of Singapore was Chinese, but Singapore was not part of China?

And what would he think of the other *fanwang* present? He surely would be surprised at the fact that the "lesser lords" of Japan, Korea, and Vietnam, vassals during his day, were there as equal members. Would he understand why the lords from Australia, Canada, New Zealand, and Papua New Guinea had the same queen, but she lived in another country on the other side of the world, and amazingly was never consulted by them on matters of state? And why was this same queen regarded by some leaders as the head of another association of *guo*, the Commonwealth?

The *huangdi* would no doubt be surprised at what the APEC leaders actually did during their summit meeting. The eating, the drinking, the speeches, and the toasting would be familiar—though he would be surprised that much of the conversation was in a barbarian language, *Yingwen*, or English, which most of them seemed to know. But why was so much of their time spent talking not about the affairs of state, as proper lords would do, but about financial and commercial affairs, like a group of grubby merchants?

He would surely be horrified at the lack of dignity in some of the proceedings, such as all the leaders dressing up in the same clothes to have their portraits taken, or going one day to a park, where they tried to hit small white balls into holes in the ground hundreds of *ma* away with thin sticks. But above all, he would surely be shocked that all of the lords treated one another with familiarity and as *equals*, a practice that simply could not be reconciled with a Confucian worldview. In short, the Qianlong emperor would be just as much at a disadvantage if he tried to use universalizing notions to analyze contemporary summit diplomacy as we would be trying to examine diplomatic practices in 18th-century China.

This digression suggests that we should take some care when thinking about practices, ideas, and behaviour in universal terms. However, we would not want to go to the other extreme and declare that each act in history is unique. We can find similarities, parallels, and recurring patterns, both across time and between different cultures. While it is important to guard against the problems inherent in thinking universally, we should also recognize that some of the political behaviour of human beings today would be quite recognizable to those who lived at other times and in other cultures, and vice versa.

For that reason, we should be just as careful about claims that come from the other end of the spectrum about the uniqueness of humankind's capacity for fundamental change, its ability to progress ever more assuredly toward a better world. This, for example, has been a common interpretation of the end of the Cold War. Humankind is now in a "new era," it is often said, and has somehow changed its essence. But statements about the "newness" of humankind's essence should be met with no less skepticism than universalistic claims of the essential sameness of human affairs.

In short, some of the patterns we will find in world politics reflect some recurrences from the past, long-forgotten in contemporary memory. At the same time—because there is actually something new under the sun from time to time—we will see new patterns never before observed.

## CONCLUSION

This chapter has established the beginnings of a path for an understanding of world politics. In Chapter 1, we observed that virtually everybody has experienced world politics in some form; part of the task ahead is to put those experiences in some kind of context. This means thinking historically about world politics, seeing that some of the phenomena of international relations fit patterns that have been repeated many times in human experience, and that others, by contrast, are indeed new and innovative ways of dealing with politics at a global level. It means always keeping in mind that the phenomena of world politics observable in any era—including our own—will always reflect a particular historical correlation of political, social, economic, and philosophic forces.

It also means thinking theoretically about world politics, something difficult to do in a discipline where theory is so deeply contested, where theoretical agreement is so lacking, and where disciplinary maps are rudimentary at best. The chapters ahead, it must be admitted, do not pretend to offer a freshly-drawn chart of those theoretical waters. Rather, my intention is to "cross the river by feeling the stones," as the Chinese expression has it—in other words, to look systematically at the nature of world politics step by step, and in the process providing, I hope, an introductory answer to the essential puzzles of world politics.

Moreover, I hope that the chapters ahead will provide an introductory sense of what world politics is "about" and the beginnings of an understanding of why politics at a global level is as it is. I also hope that by the end of this book, you will come away with a sense that there is a great deal more to learn about the intriguing and at times horrific puzzles of world politics. But to get a sense of what those puzzles might be, we must turn to a more explicit consideration of what world politics is and how we might analyze it; this is the focus of the next part of this book.

## Keyword File

| | |
|---|---|
| International relations theory | Androcentrism |
| Realism | Modernity |
| Liberalism | Age of Enlightenment |
| Marxism | Rational choice |
| Radicalism | Peace research |
| Feminism | International political economy |
| Postmodernism | English School |
| Idealism | Frankfurt School |
| Structural realism | Behaviouralism |
| Neorealism | Epistemology |
| Neoliberalism | Ontology |
| Liberal institutionalism | Semiotics |
| Dependency theory | Hermeneutics |
| World economy theory | Path dependency |
| Core | Chaos theory |
| Periphery | Counterfactual |
| Semi-periphery | Universalism |

## For Further Exploration

HARD COPY: *This section in each chapter suggests interesting readings on topics raised in the chapter.*

Cohn, Carol. "Sex and death in the rational world of defense intellectuals," *Signs* 12 (1987), 687–718.

Doyle, Michael W. *Ways of War and Peace: Realism, Liberalism, and Socialism.* New York/London: W.W. Norton, 1997.

Enloe, Cynthia. *The Morning After: Sexual Politics at the End of the Cold War.* Berkeley: University of California Press, 1993.

Ferguson, Niall, ed. *Virtual History: Alternatives and Counterfactuals.* London: Picador, 1997.

Gould, Stephen Jay. *Wonderful Life: The Burgess Shale and the Nature of History.* New York: W.W. Norton, 1989.

Halliday, Fred. *Rethinking International Relations.* London/Vancouver: Macmillan/University of British Columbia Press, 1994.

Holsti, K.J. "International relations at the end of the millennium," *Review of International Studies* 19:4 (1993), 401–408.

Light, Margot and A.J.R. Groom, eds. *International Relations: A Handbook of Current Theory,* 2d ed. London: Frances Pinter, 1994.

Neumann, Iver B. and Ole Wæver, eds. *The Future of International Relations.* London and New York: Routledge, 1997.

Strange, Susan. "Cave! Hic dragones: a critique of regime analysis," *International Organization* 36 (Spring 1982), 479–96.

Wight, Martin. "Why is there no international theory?" in H. Butterfield and Martin Wight, eds., *Diplomatic Investigations: Essays in the Theory of International Politics.* London: Allen and Unwin, 1966, 17–34.

**WEBLINKS:** *This section in each chapter includes useful URLs for World Wide Web sites related to topics covered in the chapter.*

**http://www.aber.ac.uk/~inpwww/resour.html**

Department of International Politics, University of Wales, Aberystwyth; jumping-off point for international relations links

**http://www.wesleyan.edu/gov/gallagher/resources.html**

Women and World Politics, Wesleyan University; annotated bibliography on feminist theories and critiques of IR and other subjects

**http://www.vuw.ac.nz/atp/**

*AntePodium,* a fully electronic journal on world affairs run from the Victoria University of Wellington, New Zealand

## Notes to Chapter 2

1. In fact, there is at least one book with such a title: back in 1972, George Modelski penned *The Principles of World Politics* (New York: Free Press). However, unlike his well-known work on long cycles in international relations, this book is little known and rarely cited.

2. K.J. Holsti, *The Dividing Discipline: Hegemony and Diversity in International Theory* (Boston: Allen and Unwin, 1985), 1.

3. See, for example, the exchange between R.E. Jones and R.B.J. Walker in *Review of International Studies* 20 (1994), 299–311.

4. E.H. Carr, *The Twenty Years' Crisis, 1919–1939*, 2d ed. (London: Macmillan, 1946); Hans J. Morgenthau, *Politics Among Nations: The Struggle for Power and Peace*, 5th ed. (New York: Alfred A. Knopf, [1948] 1973).

5. Kenneth N. Waltz, *Theory of International Politics* (Reading, MA: Addison-Wesley, 1979), 102; see the survey of Waltz's work in Hans Mouritzen, "Kenneth Waltz: a critical rationalist between international politics and foreign policy," in Iver B. Neumann and Ole Wæver, eds., *The Future of International Relations* (London and New York: Routledge, 1997), 66–89.

6. Robert O. Keohane, *After Hegemony: Cooperation and Discord in the World Political Economy* (Princeton, NJ: Princeton University Press, 1984); a useful survey of Keohane's work is to be found in Michael Suhr, "Robert O. Keohane: a contemporary classic," in Neumann and Wæver, eds., *Future of International Relations*, 90–120.

7. Andrew Linklater, "Marxism and international relations: antithesis, reconciliation, and transcendence," in Richard Higgott and J.L. Richardson, eds., *International Relations: Global and Australian Perspectives on an Evolving Discipline* (Canberra: Australian National University, 1991), 70–91.

8. For example, André Gunder Frank, *Capitalism and Underdevelopment in Latin America* (New York: Monthly Review Press, 1967).

9. Immanuel Wallerstein, *The Modern World System* (New York: Academic Press, 1979); also Christopher Chase-Dunn, *Global Formation: Structures of the World Economy* (Cambridge: Basil Blackwell, 1989).

10. Robert W. Cox, *Production, Power, and World Order: Social Forces in the Making of History* (New York: Columbia University Press, 1987).

11. For example, see J. Ann Tickner, *Gender in International Relations: Feminist Perspectives on Achieving Global Security* (New York: Columbia University Press, 1992); Nancy McGlen and Meredith Reid Sarkees, *Women in Foreign Policy: The Insiders* (New York: Routledge, 1993); Sandra Whitworth, *Feminism and International Relations* (New York: St Martin's, 1994). Craig N. Murphy, "Seeing women, recognizing gender, recasting international relations," *International Organization* 50 (1996), 513–38, provides a survey of the recent literature.

12. Ole Wæver, "Figures of international thought: introducing persons instead of paradigms," in Neumann and Wæver, *Future of International Relations*, 15.

13. For example, R.B.J. Walker, *Inside/Outside: International Relations as Political Theory* (Cambridge: Cambridge University Press, 1993); James Der Derian, *On Diplomacy: A Genealogy of Western Estrangement* (London: Basil Blackwell, 1987); and the contributions in Claire Turenne Sjolander and Wayne S. Cox, *Beyond Positivism: Critical Reflections on International Relations* (Boulder, CO: Lynne Rienner, 1994).

14. For example, Cynthia Enloe, *Bananas, Beaches, and Bases: Making Feminist Sense of International Politics* (Berkeley: University of California Press, 1990); Rebecca Grant and Kathleen Newland, eds. *Gender and International Relations* (Indianapolis: Indiana University Press, 1991); V. Spike Peterson, "Introduction," in Peterson, ed., *Gendered States: Feminist (Re)visions of International Relations Theory* (Boulder, CO: Lynne Rienner, 1992); Christine Sylvester, *Feminist Theory and International Relations in a Postmodern Era* (New York: Cambridge University Press, 1994).

15. For example, Elizabeth Nunn, "The rational choice approach to IPE," in David N. Balaam and Michael Veseth, *Introduction to International Political Economy* (Upper Saddle River, NJ: Prentice Hall, 1996), 77–98.

16. For example, F.M. Cancian and J.W. Gibson, *Making War/Making Peace: The Social Foundations of Violent Conflict* (Belmont, CA: Wadsworth Publishing, 1990).

17. For example, Richard Stubbs and Geoffrey R.D. Underhill, *Political Economy and the Changing Global Order* (London/New York/Toronto: Macmillan/St Martin's/McClelland and Stewart, 1994).

18. A useful survey of the English School is found in Barry Buzan, "From international system to international society: structural realism and regime theory meet the English school," *International Organization* 47 (Summer 1993), 327–52.

19. See, for example, Andrew Linklater, "The question of the next stage in international relations theory: a critical-theoretical point of view," *Millennium: Journal of International Studies* 21:1 (1992), 77–98.

20. On decision-making, see Graham T. Allison, *Essence of Decision: Explaining the Cuban Missile Crisis* (Boston: Little, Brown, 1971); on integration, see Ernest B. Haas, *Beyond the Nation-State: Functionalism and International Organization* (Stanford, CA: Stanford University Press, 1964); on regimes, see Stephen D. Krasner, ed., *International Regimes* (Ithaca, NY: Cornell University Press, 1983); on long cycles, see George Modelski, *Long Cycles in World Politics* (Seattle, WA: University of Washington Press, 1987); on hegemonic stability theory, see Robert Gilpin, *The Political Economy of International Relations* (Princeton, NJ: Princeton University Press, 1987); and on prospect theory, see Janice Gross Stein and Louis W. Pauly, *Choosing to Cooperate: How States Avoid Loss* (Baltimore: Johns Hopkins University Press, 1993).

21. Ray Maghoori and Bennet Ramberg, eds., *Globalism versus Realism: International Relations' Third Debate?* (Boulder, CO: Westview Press, 1982).

22. Exemplars of these approaches would be: historical analysis, Kalevi J. Holsti, *Peace and War: Armed Conflicts and International Order, 1648–1989* (Cambridge: Cambridge University Press, 1991); behaviouralism, James N. Rosenau, *The Scientific Study of Foreign Policy* (New York: Free Press, 1971); game theory, Frank P. Harvey, *The Future's Back: Nuclear Rivalry, Deterrence Theory, and Crisis Stability after the Cold War* (Montreal/Kingston: McGill-Queen's University Press, 1997); semiotics, James Der Derian, *On Diplomacy* (London: Basil Blackwell, 1987).

23. By contrast, it took Michael J. Doyle 160 pages to explore the realism of these thinkers (and others besides) as revealed by a careful textual analysis of their works: see his *Ways of War and Peace: Realism, Liberalism, and Socialism* (New York: W.W. Norton, 1997), part 1, 41–201.

24. Ralph Pettman, *International Politics: Balance of Power, Balance of Productivity, Balance of Ideologies* (Melbourne: Longman Cheshire/Boulder: Lynne Rienner, 1991), 21.

25. Mervyn Frost, *Towards a Normative Theory of International Relations* (Cambridge: Cambridge University Press, 1986), 17.

26. Charles McClelland, "International relations: wisdom or science?" in James N. Rosenau, ed., *International Politics and Foreign Policy: A Reader in Research and Theory* (New York: Free Press, 1969), 4.

27. Stephen Jay Gould, *Wonderful Life: The Burgess Shale and the Nature of History* (New York: W.W. Norton, 1989), 323.

28. Niall Ferguson, "Introduction: virtual history: towards a 'chaotic' theory of the past," in Ferguson, ed., *Virtual History: Alternatives and Counterfactuals* (London: Picador, 1997), 1–90.

29. For discussions, see James L. Hevia, *Cherishing Men from Afar: Qing Guest Ritual and the Macartney Embassy of 1793* (Durham, NC: Duke University Press, 1995); Mark Mancall, *China at the Center: 300 Years of Foreign Policy* (New York: Free Press, 1984), chap. 2; Immanuel C.Y. Hsü, *China's Entrance into the Family of Nations* (Cambridge, MA: Harvard University Press, 1960).

# PART 2

# Definitions *and* Assumptions

# CHAPTER 3

*Defining* World

Politics

**INTRODUCTION**
When we think theoretically, we draw boundaries that identify what we seek to examine. To begin this process, we focus on defining world politics in a more systematic way—always keeping in mind that in international politics any definition will be highly contested. We begin by examining the phrase "world politics," and then outline a broad definition to guide our inquiry.

## A DEFINITIONAL EXPLORATION: WHAT IS WORLD POLITICS?

It is one thing to say what world politics is "about"; it is harder to provide an agreed-upon definition of the term, partly because of the lack of theoretical agreement (explored in Chapter 2). But we cannot avoid trying to define our area of study. One way to engage in this exercise is to explore each of the words separately—the adjective "world" and the noun "politics"—as a way of thinking about them together.

## The Adjective: What Kind of Politics Are These?

Not only do scholars disagree on the theoretical approach, but they also disagree on what to call the kind of politics we are exploring. They use at least four common designations: international relations, international politics, world politics, and global politics. The terminology one uses, however, is important to how one conceives of what one is interested in studying and understanding.

### "International" and its Problems

The commonest modifier in use is *international*. While the word "nation" first appears in English around 1300, the word "international" was not used until 1780. In that year, the English philosopher Jeremy Bentham used it to describe the "law of nations," which up to that point had been generally referred to using a Latin root: *jus gentium* (literally, the law of peoples, from the Latin *gens*, tribe), or in French, *le droit des gens*. Bentham expressed the hope that his new word would catch on, and it did. Indeed, international is so often used in ordinary discourse that there is something to be said for simply adopting it without further ado.

The difficulty, however, is that *international* is a deeply problematic term. When taken literally, its etymology—inter+nation—suggests that we are only interested in the politics (or relations) between nations. That is problematic for two reasons: first, we are not just interested in the politics between *nations*; second, we are not just interested in the politics *between* nations.

**Politics Between *Nations*?**    First, we do not want to restrict our attention merely to the nation, which, as we will see below, is a unique political form of relatively recent invention. Rather, we are interested in looking at politics involving a much wider range of actors and agents than just nations.

Moreover, using inter+national could refer as reasonably to "domestic" politics as to "international" politics. After all, the politics between the English and Scottish and Welsh *nations*, between the Québécois and Canadian *nations*, between the Cree *nation* on the one hand and the Québécois and Canadian *nations* on the other, between the Catalan and Spanish *nations*, could be considered inter+national—even though these politics are not normally considered international since they occur within the boundaries of the United Kingdom, Canada, and Spain.

Using *interstate* to describe these politics is not much better. First, there is the possibility of confusion, since this adjective is commonly used in Australia, India, Mexico, and the United States to describe politics between the constituent units of these federations. Moreover, the "state" is also what we call the modern governing apparatus (or government).

More importantly, the limitations of using "state" are similar to those of using "nation." The state is a relatively young political formation: one could not call a *polis* in ancient Greece, a Ostrogoth tribe, a Mongol khanate, a Japanese shōgunate, a Maori *waka*, or a village of the Yanomamö in the tropical forests of Venezuela a "state" for the same reason that it would be inappropriate to call an 18th-century Chinese *guo* a "state," as I argued in Chapter 2.

However, trying to find a more apt generic description leads one to unorthodox adjectives that are jargonistic, experimental, or simply bizarre. "Polity" (a political community) is one possibility, though "inter-polity politics" does not exactly roll smoothly off the tongue. Nor do generic synonyms work any better: inter-group, inter-country, or inter-unit. "Independent political community" is a reasonably accurate generic descriptor for all the units mentioned above—and more besides. However, while it might be somewhat more accurate, "inter-independent-political-community politics" is unlikely to find a place in common usage.

**Politics *Between* Nations?**    Not only the name of the unit, "nation," but also the "inter" makes "international" problematic. We are interested in more than simply looking at how independent political entities—whether they be states, nations, fiefdoms, kingdoms, tribes, or countries—interact politically *between* each other. The relationships between different countries today—Zimbabwe and Zambia, Australia and Papua New Guinea, Canada and Belgium, Britain and Germany, Russia and Ukraine, China and the United States—are all *international* and often highly *political*, but international politics is more than simply the sum of the 18 000 possible bilateral relationships between the 190 states in the world today. While we are interested in the bilateral relationships of different countries, we are also interested in looking at much broader political processes.

**Politics at a World Level**
That is why reflecting on modifying politics by specifying its domain is useful. We all have a sense of "politics by domain" that can begin with units as small as the family, the clan, or the tribe. As the aperture widens, the domain expands: for example, "urban politics" is about the politics of the city, both "inside" the city and "outside" in its relations with a broader socio-political environment. "State" or "provincial" politics is about the politics of the constituent parts of a federation, again both "inside" the state/province and "outside" with other constituent units and the federal government, and indeed, outside the federation itself with other countries. More broadly still, the same is true for "national" politics, which includes all the lower layers as well as the relations between the nation-state and the "outside"—or what is usually called **foreign policy** (discussed in more detail in Chapter 7).

Beyond the nation are two further levels of politics. The next step is **supranational politics**, where a separate and independent political community exists "above" the nation-state. At the end of the 20th century, there is only one active site of supranational politics: the European Union (EU), which we examine in Chapter 17. This a supranational community of 15 European nation-states which have joined together to create a higher level of government in Brussels. Consequently, the politics of the EU are a mixture of national and international politics, similar to the politics one finds in a federal state, where different levels of government share political authority over the same territory and the same people.

The domain beyond that is "world" politics. The next step up from supranational politics, world politics deals with politics at the level of the whole world. We could call these politics "global politics" or "planetary politics," or "Earth politics," but "world" is both a common and a common-sense way of naming this level. By its very nature, then, world politics seeks to provide an account of politics at a global level, which is the broadest domain of politics. (Unless, of course, the truth really *is* out there, and in that case we will get to open the aperture wider still. In the meantime, we will have to leave imaginings on "galactic politics" to the dim bulbs of Hollywood, and content ourselves with such offerings as *Independence Day*, a 1996 film in which American forces, led by the president himself no less, save the world from would-be alien invaders.*)

*World politics seeks to provide an account of politics at a global level, which is the broadest domain of politics.*

While the term "world politics" is intended to convey the broad domain of the subject, this is not to suggest that the term "international" should be rigorously avoided. There is no point in being so rigid, particularly when the term is in such common use. Moreover, as noted above, International Relations (capitalized) is a common term to describe the field, even by those who are highly critical of the term itself. It is more a matter of being conscious about what baggage "international" carries with it.

## The Noun: What Are the Politics of the World?

We might begin to answer the question about the nature of the politics of the world by asking what politics is "about" more generically. Numerous political scientists have tried to come up with a pithy definition of politics. For many political philosophers, politics is the pursuit of the good. For others, politics is the struggle for power; for others still, politics is the art and science of governing. Two contemporary definitions are routinely given in standard English-language introductions to political science: Harold Lasswell's definition that politics is who gets what, when, and how (and why); and David Easton's "politics is the authoritative allocation of values for a society."[1]

## Politics and Political Economy: A Generic Definition

Although it might be tantalizing to be able to capture the essence of a huge sphere of human activity in a single phrase, simple definitions cannot capture the multifaceted nature of the political realm. One can count at least six different but related facets: community, rules, economic structure, conflict, governance, and power.

---

* Like most of its genre, this film was amusingly Americo-centric (why do aliens never seem to make Earthfall in places likes Mumbai, Mombasa, Melbourne, or Manchester?) and unimaginatively anthropocentric (i.e., constructed using human-centred assumptions): why do non-earthly species imagined by Hollywood always *look* different enough, but invariably *behave* precisely like humans, and usually American humans?

**Community**   Politics is about the **communities** into which human beings organize themselves. Asserting the universality of political community is easy; providing a precise definition is rather more difficult. Some insist that political communities must have three necessary elements: a *people* living in a particular *territory* under a common *government*. The problem is that this definition excludes the possibility that a political community can (and does) exist without these three interlinked attributes. We will examine a particular kind of political community—the primitive community—in more detail below, and we will see that one can indeed have communities without government. Likewise, consider medieval European communities, where strict territorial divisions were difficult to identify and where "government" represented a number of overlapping layers of authority. Or the large number of nomadic communities that regularly travelled across different parts of the world for much of human history. Or consider the contemporary Sikh community, which exists in a number of different places. Note that political communities may not even comprise all the people living in a particular space: consider the ancient Greek *polis* (plural: *poleis*), in which only a small number of those who lived in the city-state were actually considered members of the political community. Likewise, communities may "nest" within a variety of other communities. Thus a university student who lives in Montréal is a member of at least four political communities: Canada, Québec, Montréal and that of the university.

Political communities come in markedly different shapes, sizes, and types: tiny clan-based hunter-gatherer bands, small agricultural villages, the small *poleis* of ancient Greece, the vast empires of antiquity, nomadic tribes like the Vandals or the Mongols, the feudal fiefdoms of medieval Europe, the kingdoms of West Africa, the continental-sized contemporary states with hundreds of millions of members, or the supranational community of the European Union. Politics focuses on the community and its nature, and the relationship of individuals and groups to the community.

**Rules**   Politics is about the rules for the community. **Rules** in this context means not just the formal written laws developed to guide human action, but rather "ways of doing things" in a broad context—the "rules of the game," as it were. All political communities have such rules: written laws, informal customs, ideas, and philosophies that guide action and belief; and norms and mores that govern how individuals relate to one another and how the individual relates to the community as a whole. These rules determine what is "good" and what is "bad," and how people should behave. The rules also govern relations between children and adults and between men and women, often entrenching in law informal customary patterns of **androcentrism**—in other words, with men at the centre—and patriarchal dominance. Rules determine how "good things" are allocated to different members of the community. Rules also shape the nature of community projects, how they will be built, and how they will be paid for. Rules determine who in the community is rich and who is poor, who is powerful and who is marginalized, who is valued and who is discriminated against, who is revered and who is despised. There are rules about what is divine and who (or what) is to be worshipped.

Moreover, all communities have rules about making rules: who gets to make the rules and how they are to be made. The rules determine what kind of governing structure there will be, how complex it will be, and how the structures of governance will be paid for by the community. The rules decree what kind of leaders the community will have, how they will be chosen, and who they will be. Some communities have rules that govern what is **public**, and thus appropriate for the community to involve itself in, and what is **private**, in which the community has no business; other communities make no such distinction. In short, the rules are about the huge complex of human interactions in a community setting.

**Economic Structure: A Special Subset of the Rules** Each community has its own economic structure that could be considered part of the rules, but which is important enough that we should consider it separately. Economic structures do not miraculously or spontaneously occur, the preachings of some colleagues in the "dismal science" of economics to the contrary notwithstanding. Rather, the **economy** of a community is heavily dependent on extensive rule-making. Economic rules determine the very way we think about economic intercourse: what is of value, what is treated as a commodity, what money is, how property is to be regarded. Rules determine the nature of economic relationships within the community as well as the nature and complexity of economic exchange; for example, whether the economy is barter-based or monetarized or whether land and labour are commodified. Rules govern how markets within communities operate, if they operate at all. Rules determine how wealth is generated and distributed and how much of the production or labour of individuals and groups is appropriated by the community as taxation. In short, rules about the economy are deeply intertwined with the rules that govern other spheres of human existence.

**Interests, Goals, and Conflict** Politics is about conflict over the rules that govern the community. Conflict is pervasive among the species *Homo sapiens sapiens*, a logical consequence of the consciousness of our species that is reflected in the very name we give ourselves: *Homo sapiens sapiens*, from the Latin *sapere*, to be wise; the second *sapiens* added to indicate that not only do we know, but we *know* that we know.

This self-consciousness is crucial, for it enables us to know what we like, to know what we want, to know what we think is good and righteous and just, to know what we think is bad and unjust; in other words, to know what we have come to call our **interests**. This capacity means that there is no way that the scores, or hundreds, or thousands, or millions of such knowing individuals who make up a community will all think alike on every issue. On the contrary: humans able to understand what they want and like will inexorably come to different conclusions on many matters; **conflict** with one another is inevitable.

Note that conflict in this context does not mean that everyone fights one another; rather, conflict means a disharmony or an incompatibility. That disharmony is worked out in numerous ways—fighting is only one way. In the context of the community, conflicts are likely to emerge over the nature of the political community and the rules that govern the community.

**Governance**    Politics is also about the **governance** of the community. Governance in-

*Governance also involves the exercise of authority, that fascinating human practice of submitting obediently to the orders of others without having to be forced, coerced, induced, or persuaded to do so.*

volves establishing rules for the community, making alloca-
tive decisions for the community as a whole, settling conflicts
over the rules, and mediating disputes between individuals
and groups. Governance also involves the exercise of authority, that fascinating human practice of submitting obediently to the orders of others without having to be forced,
coerced, induced, or persuaded to do so. Note that for governance to occur, one does not need a formal set of structures
such as a government; this issue is addressed at length below.

**Power**    Finally, politics is about power within the community. Power has been described
as the central concept of politics, and for good reason, since power and its exercise shape
so many of the outcomes of politics. Briefly put, **power** is the ability to prevail over others in a conflict of interests—or, to put it more crudely, the ability to get your way. Not
everyone can "get their own way," but some people are always able to exercise power over
others: the rules, the allocations, and the very nature of the community reflect *their* interests,
wants, desires, and definitions of the "good."

**A Multifaceted Definition**    The above multifaceted definition helps us to focus
on some of the puzzles of politics: how are hundreds, thousands, millions, and in some cases,
hundreds of millions of human beings, each capable of calculating what they want, able to live
in communities in sufficient peace and harmony that, at the very least, they sustain and reproduce themselves? Thus political science is about understanding why and how communities live in peace—and why occasionally they disintegrate into war. In short, while politics is
"about" community, rules, economic structure, conflict, governance, and power, political science is basically concerned with elucidating the causes of war and the conditions of peace.

## POLITICS AND POLITICAL ECONOMY AT A GLOBAL LEVEL

A multifaceted definition also helps focus our thinking about world politics by directing our
attention to similar elements of politics at the global level. To do this, we must examine the
broad setting in which community, rules, economic structures, conflict, governance, and
power intersect. And that means looking at the anarchical nature of world politics.

### "No Common Power": Anarchy and World Politics

The governance of political communities takes many different forms: tribal systems of
governance by elders, the singular rule of absolute monarchies, or the highly institutionalized
structures of the 20th-century bureaucratic state. But in most political communities,
institutional systems of governance that we call the government, or the state, have evolved.
While the degree of institutionalization varies widely, this form always involves a basic
hierarchy, a division between the governors and the governed, between those *entitled to*

*command*, and those *obligated to obey*.[*] Generally, the governors seek to establish laws, rules, policies, and day-to-day practices for the community. As noted above, these rules not only cover the behaviour of individuals toward each other, but also govern the nature and operation of economic relationships within the community. Importantly, governors generally seek to impose these rules on the community as a whole, securing the obedience of the governed by legitimate authority if possible, but by brute force if necessary. Moreover, in many (but not all) communities, the governors seek to monopolize the legitimate use of force, not only to make the task of ruling easier, but in many cases also to provide a safe and secure environment for the operation of economic activity.

**Anarchy**, by contrast, is the absence of government. Coming to English from the Greek *anarchos*, without a chief or governor (*an + archos*), anarchy describes a system of social, political, and economic relations without formal institutions of governance to define enforceable rules or exact obedience from the governed. In an anarchical condition, no hierarchy exists between governors and governed, nor any comparable entitlement to command or obligation to obey. In an anarchy, there is no institution with coercive powers—the state or the government—telling people what to do, defining what is right and wrong, or proscribing a whole range of forbidden acts.

At one level, anarchy is an apt description for the setting of world politics. There is indeed no "government of the world"—no institution with coercive powers to regulate the political relations among all six billion human beings, to make laws for all people that can be enforced over all the globe, or to arbitrate and settle disputes. In short, in world politics there is neither entitlement to command nor obligation to obey. In this way, politics at the world level differs substantially from politics *within* communities. But what implications can be drawn from this observation? How does this affect world politics?

## Misconstructing Anarchy

One has to be careful with the observation that at a world level no one is entitled to command and no one obligated to obey. All too often, instead of being analyzed as *politics without government*, anarchy is frequently misconstructed as *life without politics*. Such a misconstruction has huge implications for how we interpret politics at a world level.

### The "Law of the Jungle"?

For some, the anarchical condition of world politics suggests chaos and disorder, existence without politics. These scholars tend to use phrases that evoke fearsome images of politics at the global level. Joshua S. Goldstein, for example, likens international politics to the "law of the jungle"; Jonathan Mercer writes of the "nightmare of state-eat-state competition."[2]

---

[*] Note that this says nothing about how governors come to their positions. Some come to govern as a result of brute force, some claim their entitlement to govern from divine right, some from nothing more than an accident of birth, some because of their age relative to the rest of the community, and some as a result of legalistic systems of elections and the consent of the governed.

Perhaps such phrases are meant to summon images of survival-of-the-fittest behaviour among animals that are the staple of television nature shows: a lion bringing down a wide-eyed wildebeest in a cloud of dust and flailing legs; a leopard seal skinning a hapless penguin with a practised flick of its head; a wriggling field mouse being carried aloft in the claws of a hawk. The implicit message of the jungle analogy is unambiguous: Life at the level of world politics is raw, instinctual, unleavened by any civilizing influences, and always pregnant with danger; other communities, higher up on the food chain as it were, are always looking for a chance to gobble up unsuspecting peoples—and will always do so if given the chance.

It is true that the annals of world politics includes a great deal of predatory behaviour. For political communities *do* "eat" other communities. History abounds with invasions, conquests, or absorptions of some peoples by others. Israel, for example, emerged as a unified community after 993 BC under King David only by vanquishing the Philistines, Moabites, Arameans, Edomites, Ammonites, and Jebusites. Contemporary Britain emerged from a thousand years of invasions and occupations—from 55 BC to AD 1066—by a succession of peoples from the European mainland: Romans, Saxons, Angles, Jutes, Franks, Danes, and Normans. Likewise, the modern era in Chinese history has its beginnings in the conquest of the country in 1644 by the Jürchen, a foreign people occupying what is now Manchuria.

Indulging the appetites in this fashion has not been limited to antiquity. Many countries founded in the last three centuries were in fact only "founded" in the sense that they were

*"One of the chief myths of early colonial history [of Australia] was the idea...that the First Fleet sailed into an 'empty' continent, speckled with primitive animals and hardly less primitive men."*

created by overrunning, destroying, supplanting, or absorbing existing communities. It is true that many communities weave into their histories comforting assurances that the original settlers were occupying either *terra nullius*—in legal terms, no one's rightfully claimed land—or land occupied by what were inevitably described as merely a few "uncivilized savages."* Such histories rarely describe the actual process by which the contemporary community came into being—usually through a conquest of some kind. This is true of all the states in the western hemisphere, as well as the "settler" societies in the antipodes, Australia, New Zealand, and South Africa.

At some times in human history, the feasting, if it can be called that, was nothing short of gluttonous. In Chapter 13, we will look at the scramble of Europeans, Americans, and Japanese for colonial possessions. Only a few countries managed to avoid being swallowed: Abyssinia (now called Ethiopia), Liberia, and Siam (Thailand). Likewise, "state-eat-state" behaviour is most readily seen in the great wars of the contemporary era. Consider the huge

---

* "One of the chief myths of early colonial history," Robert Hughes has noted of Australia, "was the idea...that the First Fleet sailed into an 'empty' continent, speckled with primitive animals and hardly less primitive men." Robert Hughes, *Fatal Shore: The Epic of Australia's Founding* (Toronto: Random House, 1987), 7.

territorial expansion of France during the Napoleonic Wars from 1799 to 1815 or the number of countries invaded by Japan, Italy, Germany, and the Soviet Union during the 1930s and 1940s.

At other times, the predatory behaviour is less widespread. There have been relatively few such acts since 1945. However, even in this period we can still see examples of such carnivorous behaviour: the Chinese takeover of Tibet in 1950–51, the Indian annexation of Goa in 1961, the Indonesian invasion of East Timor in 1975, or the Iraqi attempt to annex Kuwait in 1990.

It is also true that these kinds of human predations tend to be far more ferocious and bloody than anything seen in the animal world. As the Focus on p. 48 suggests, when political communities are seized by others, the process tends to be marked by brutality.

In short, it is not hard to point to many examples of predatory "state-eat-state" behaviour, some quite nightmarish. However, the jungle analogy is misleading in a number of ways. First, it suggests that states, like lions, engage in predatory behaviour for survival reasons: eat or die. This is an erroneous comparison. While lions refraining from predatory behaviour will surely die, political communities do not *need* to engage in predatory behaviour to survive. They may *choose* to invade others—and many do—but they always do so for reasons other than survival.

Second, the jungle analogy suggests that "state-eating" is a normal, commonplace, and everyday part of life in the international realm. In fact, despite the evidence noted above, throughout history, acts of predation leading to the submergence or elimination of political communities are relatively uncommon. In short, unlike wildebeests, penguins, field mice, or any other favourites of carnivores, political communities do not persistently face the danger of a threat to their survival from others.

### A "State of Nature"?

An equally common image used to try and capture the anarchical essence of international politics is the **state of nature**. The "state of nature" was a hypothetical construct used by early liberal political philosophers to explore the implications of what life would be like for human beings in a "natural condition"—in other words, without government or civil society. The most famous characterization of a "state of nature" was written by Thomas Hobbes in his treatise on politics and government, *Leviathan*, published in 1651. Hobbes suggested that life for humans in a state of nature would be disorderly, violent, and insecure. First, he argued that if they gave free expression to their natural rights, human beings would be

*"During the time men live without a common Power to keep them all in awe, they are in that condition which is called Warre...where every man is Enemy to every man."*

inclined to quarrel with one another and "invade" other humans. However, humans in such a condition would be essentially equal in both their vulnerability to the predations of others and their capacity to defend themselves against invasion. The result would be that, as Hobbes put it, "during the time men live without a common Power to keep them all in awe, they are in that condition which is called Warre...where every man is Enemy to every man."

# FOCUS

## *Brutal Predations: An Illustrative (But Not Exhaustive) List*

### MELOS

After its refusal to abandon its neutrality in the Peloponnesian War then raging, the colony of Melos was seized by Athenian forces in 415 BC. All Melian men of military age were put to death and all women and children were sold into slavery. Athenian settlers were sent to resettle the colony.

### CARTHAGE

In 146 BC, the end of the Third Punic War between Carthage and Rome was marked by the complete destruction of Carthage—with the victorious Romans spreading salt over the ruins and forbidding anyone to occupy the site for a generation.

### ROME

In 410 AD, the Visigoths, a Germanic tribe from the Danube River, captured and pillaged Rome, with large loss of life and considerable destruction. (The city was also taken by the Vandals in 455, but their "sack" of Rome was actually quite civilized: the tribe spent 14 days calmly emptying the city of all moveable wealth, with little destruction or loss of life. But for some reason "vandalism," not "visigothism," passed into modern European languages to describe acts of wanton destruction.)

### GOLDEN HORDE

Between 1237 and 1241, Batu Khan, grandson of the Mongol leader Ghengis Khan, led his Golden Horde (from the Tatar *altun ordu*, literally "golden army," after the golden tents used by Batu) across western Russia, Ukraine, Poland, and Hungary. Moscow, Kyiv, Kraków, and Lublin were laid waste, and thousands of their inhabitants put to the sword.

### DELHI

In the 14th century, Timur i Leng (or Tamerlane) established an empire that stretched from the Indian subcontinent to the Mediterranean Sea. His armies were notorious for their cruelty: when they sacked Delhi on 17 December 1398, over 100 000 were killed that night and the city was reduced to ruins.

### THE MASSACRES OF 1838

Efforts by Boers in South Africa to seize land from the Zulus in the 1830s resulted in mutual massacres: in February 1838, Pieter Retief, a Boer leader, and over 600 of his followers were killed by Zulu *impis*; their deaths were avenged at the Battle of Blood River on 16 December 1838, when Boers massacred 3000 Zulus.

### WOUNDED KNEE

The Plains Indian Wars resulted from the efforts of native Americans to halt the westward expansion of American settlement. The culmination of this struggle occurred on 29 December 1890, when U.S. troops opened fire on a Sioux encampment at Wounded Knee, South Dakota. Over 300 Sioux men, women, and children were killed; many of the 31 soldiers who died were shot by the indiscriminate shooting of their own colleagues.

### ARMENIA

In 1915, the Turkish government, as part of its efforts to consolidate control over Armenia, decided to deport the entire Armenian population to Syria and Mesopotamia. The forced removal of 1.7 million people was carried out with extreme barbarity: an estimated 600 000 Armenians died from disease or starvation or were massacred in the process.

### NANJING

On 13 December 1937, Japanese armies seeking to conquer China seized the capital, Nanjing. For the next seven weeks, Japanese troops indiscriminately raped and killed in an orgy of violence. Estimates of foreign observers were that some 20 000 Chinese women were raped, many of whom died after repeated assaults; 30 000 Chinese soldiers were killed; and 12 000 civilians were massacred. The capture of the city is still known as the "rape of Nanjing."

### TIMOR

In December 1975, Indonesian forces invaded the Portuguese territory of East Timor. Some human rights groups have estimated that over 100 000 Timorese died during the pacification campaign that ensued.

The "barbarian hordes" invading Rome. (See "Rome" in the Focus)

Second, Hobbes analyzed the consequences of having to "live without other security, than what their own strength, and their own invention shall furnish them withall." One of his more famous passages describes the impoverishment of life that inexorably results:

> In such a condition, there is no place for Industry; because the fruit thereof is uncertain; and consequently no Culture of the Earth; no Navigation, nor use of the commodities that may be imported by Sea; no commodious Building; no Instruments of moving, and removing such things as require much force; no Knowledge of the face of the Earth; no account of Time; no Arts; no Letters; no Society; and which is worst of all, continuall feare, and danger of violent death; And the life of man, solitary, poore, nasty, brutish, and short.[3]

This grim portrait of life without authority is frequently pressed into service as an appropriate way to describe international politics. In the international realm, just as in the state of nature, there is no "common power"—no Leviathan or government—to keep everyone, both individuals and their independent political communities, "in awe." Therefore, it is argued, international politics is just like a state of nature, with all states (to paraphrase Hobbes) in a state of war, with every state the enemy of every state.

Popular though the Hobbesian analogy remains in theorizing about international politics,[4] it is nonetheless entirely inappropriate to wheel Hobbes out as an international relations theorist, quoting snippets of Chapter 13 of *Leviathan* as though these were written as contributions to theorizing about world politics. First, *Leviathan* purports to provide a theory of peace, not *between* political communities, but *within* communities. As C.B. Macpherson reminds us, "Hobbes gave little thought to war between nations. His overriding concern was with civil war; its avoidance was for him the main purpose of political inquiry."[5] Rather, the "state of nature" was an imagined and hypothetical construct to demonstrate the logical (and largely negative) consequences of giving free rein to one's natural rights; it was never intended by Hobbes to be applied to politics among nations, as Michael C. Williams's careful analysis of Hobbes's work makes clear.[6]

Second, even if one ignored the philosophical purpose behind the "state of nature" and used it as an analogy for the international system, one would find it woefully inadequate. As Hedley Bull rightly notes, political communities are not at all like individual humans, and therefore the life of states in a state of nature does not resemble life of humans in a comparable state.[7] In particular, the various independent political communities which inhabit the international sphere are not equal in the vulnerability to attack and destruction assumed to exist among humans in a state of nature. Humans are vulnerable to attack because of their relative equality of strength, and in particular their equal need for sleep that is marked by prolonged periods of "deep" sleep. States have no such equality of vulnerability. Communities do not need sleep as an individual does; they can remain constantly vigilant against attack in a way that no individual human in a hypothetical presocial condition could. Moreover, communities come in vastly different sizes and with different power capabilities that stem from size. As a consequence, larger and more powerful political communities are always able (if not always prone) to dominate, exploit, or simply destroy the weaker.

Finally, the notion that the environment of international politics is like a "state of nature" is flawed in the sense that it is a poor description of reality. Life in a state of nature is supposed to be impoverished and uncivilized—"nasty, brutish, and short"—but we can readily observe that for at least the last ten thousand years, great civilizations emerged and flourished all over the globe. Likewise, if political communities were really in a state of nature, the development and growth of any kind of economy would be completely impossible. But it is clear that since antiquity there have been markets and an often vigorous cross-border trade in goods, often involving huge distances. (However, we should never lose sight of the fact that for many human beings, civilization has not necessarily meant a life free from nastiness or impoverishment; likewise, for the tens of millions of humans who perished in the wars that have swept across the globe during this time, life has all too often been short.)

I have argued to this point that the notions that international politics is like "the law of the jungle" or a Hobbesian "state of nature" are flawed. Nonetheless, one element of these analogies *is* useful for understanding international politics—the observation that in the lawless jungle or a state of nature there is no governing structure, no Leviathan, no "common power." International politics, in short, occurs in an anarchical environment.

Before exploring the implications of anarchy for world politics, it is important to discard the essentially negative view we tend to have about the word "anarchy," which we tend to associate with violence, chaos, and disorder. Partly this association is a legacy of the anarchist movement of the late 1800s and early 1900s. For anarchy not only describes a political *condition*, but also a political *ideal*: **anarchism** as a political philosophy envisions the possibility of a society without the coercive mechanisms of the state; anarchists advocate the dismantling of organized governmental structures. A century ago, some anarchists tried to advance their political goals by assassinating government leaders. In one seven-year period, the president of France, the president of the United States, the king of Italy, and the empress of Austria died as a result of anarchist assassinations. The anarchist campaigns of the last century gave the word a negative connotation that lingers, even if inchoately, down to the present. Moreover, this pejorative connotation has been encouraged by governments—not at all surprisingly, since governments have no interest at all in seeing an ideal so antithetical to their very existence flourish. Thus governments have been at the forefront of efforts to delegitimate anarchism, and indeed stamp out anarchists themselves, often ruthlessly.*

Mostly, our negative image of anarchy comes from observing what happens when *existing* governments have collapsed, and societies have been plunged into civil war where there is no government. Violence, chaos, and disorder have indeed ensued. England in the 1640s (about which Hobbes was writing); China in the so-called "warlord period" in the 1930s and 1940s; Lebanon in the 1970s; the former Yugoslavia, Somalia, and Rwanda in the 1990s—all demonstrated the terrible and bloody effects of the collapse of already existing governments.

Given this negative view of anarchy, it is not surprising that when the editors of the magazine *Atlantic Monthly* wanted to illustrate a grim examination of the future of world politics entitled "The Coming Anarchy"**—they chose photographs designed to deepen our tendency to connect "anarchy" and gruesome death. From Liberia, they chose a photograph of human skeletons on a road, rotting flesh still attached to the bones, and a picture of an executed soldier shackled to a post. From the former Yugoslavia came a picture of workers putting clear plastic body bags, stained an unmistakable red, into a mass grave in Bosnia, a gas mask providing a clue of the stench given off by the grave, and a picture of the body of a fighter in Vukovar, the bullet hole in his head still oozing blood. The images wordlessly reinforced the connection: anarchy is death.

But equating anarchy with disorder, chaos, brutality, and death in such an automatic fashion obscures an important point. There is nothing in the etymology of anarchy that suggests that a society without a ruler with the kind of authority and coercive power we normally associate with the state must always lead to disorder, violence, and chaos. Indeed, over the long span of history, there are numerous examples of societies which have existed, even flourished, without a state apparatus.

---

* Attempts to suppress anarchism were particularly pronounced in the United States. In the wake of the assassination of President William McKinley in September 1901 by an anarchist, stringent legislation was enacted outlawing anarchists, and thousands of anarchists were arrested in the early 20th century. Illustrative of the anti-anarchist mood was the case of Nicola Sacco and Bartolomeo Vanzetti, two immigrants from Italy. Sacco and Vanzetti were charged with a murder and robbery that had occurred in Massachusetts in 1920 and convicted on largely circumstantial evidence after a trial and appeals rife with bias. They were eventually executed in August 1927. It was widely believed that they were innocent and had only been condemned because they were strong anarchists. (Their names were eventually cleared by the governor of Massachusetts in 1977.)

** Robert D. Kaplan, "The coming anarchy," *The Atlantic Monthly* (February 1994), 44–76. While this widely-cited article has been reproduced in a number of edited collections, it is best read in the original, illustrated as it is with stark images of death and deprivation.

## Rethinking Anarchy

Over 30 years ago, Roger D. Masters argued that instead of embracing an "exaggerated" notion of anarchy as unmitigated chaos springing from the absence of a government apparatus with coercive powers, students of international politics might do well to consider the politics of those many groups of humans which existed for thousands of years without government.[8] Indeed, before the emergence of civilizations six to eight thousand years ago, all members of the species *Homo sapiens sapiens* lived and reproduced quite successfully for at least 100 000 years in **stateless communities**.

### Stateless Communities

Stateless communities are those polities that function without a formal government or state apparatus. Examples of stateless communities that were able to retain their patterns of politics well into the 20th century include the Nuer or Dinka of southern Sudan; the Ute of American midwest; many highland tribes in Papua New Guinea; groups of Khoi-San, such as the !Kung of the Kalahari desert region of southwestern Africa and Namibia; the Aeta of the Philippines; or the Mbuti of the Congo valley in central Africa. While such groups exhibit considerable differences in habitat, speech, and culture, all stateless communities have a number of common political characteristics.

**Absence of State Apparatus**   Obviously, what makes a stateless community stateless is the absence of a state apparatus to make and enforce rules for the entire community. There is no government to define what is right and wrong, to define what is just and unjust, to keep order, or to ensure compliance with the rules. There is no separate class of rulers or governors. There are no bureaucrats, tax-collectors, police officers, judges, or prisons.

**Sense of Community**   At the same time, however, there is a widespread recognition among the people of the group that they constitute a society or political community. They have a sense that they are different from other groups; they may have developed an identity and a separate culture.

**Law and Rules**   In communities without a state apparatus, there is no law as liberal philosophy understands that term, for there is no rule-enforcing apparatus to define what is just and what is unjust. But there is nonetheless an understood set of rules and taboos that govern relations among members of the community. Often unwritten, and usually derived from custom and bargaining among members of the community, the rules and taboos nonetheless exist to give shape to a sense of what is righteous behaviour—and what constitutes wrongful behaviour.

**Violence and Self-Help**   The final common characteristic of a stateless community is the reliance of individual members of the community on violence and self-help. In a state, when an individual breaks the law and harms another individual or the community as a whole, the state apparatus acts in an impersonal way to provide a corrective, right a wrong, restore order, impose a punishment, and maintain the peace. Indeed, the state has a highly bureaucratized system for this. It has separate agencies for formally accusing a law-breaker; depriving the accused of his or her liberty while the alleged violation is being considered; judging whether a violation did occur; and meting out a punishment if a violation of the law was deemed to have been committed. In such a system, the individuals who suffered at the hands of the law-breaker are specifically prohibited from "taking the law into their own hands" by trying to right the wrong by punishing those whom they believe offended them. Indeed, if they do so, the state will seek to punish *them* in order to entrench its own monopoly over these activities.

In stateless societies, individuals who have been wronged must use **self-help** to try to right a wrong or settle a dispute. Usually they are assisted by family or kin, or sometimes community elders. Self-help, as one might imagine, can easily turn violent. For example, consider the family who wished to avenge an assault on one of their members by inflicting a punishment on the individuals they believe to be the perpetrators. But what if the accused denied the allegation, and thus regarded efforts at punishment as inappropriate? In such circumstances, violence and feuding could easily break out, particularly since there is no institutionalized mechanism to prevent the outbreak of violence. And when dispute settlement turns violent, it is often the more powerful who prevail. Often, the weaker are forced to leave the community.

> *Communities that do not have a state apparatus do not necessarily exist in a (misconstrued) Hobbesian "state of nature."*

In short, communities that do not have a state apparatus do not necessarily exist in a (misconstrued) Hobbesian "state of nature." For all the absence of the state, there is still a sense of community; that community develops sets of rules about what is right and wrong; and the community settles its disputes in a way that may be violent and determined by power. Nonetheless, these communities perpetuate and reproduce themselves.

## Other Anarchical Systems

The same point about anarchy and order can be made by looking at other systems where there are none of the institutional arrangements for authority. The average maximum-security penal institution provides an illustration of how society can exist in an anarchical state. Of course, a prison is technically not an anarchy; there is a well-defined hierarchy of authority backed up by the coercive power of the state. On the other hand, the day-to-day reality for prisoners doing hard time is that they are members of a population that tends to be left to its own devices by the guards and the prison bureaucracy who generally turn a blind eye to all but a few key infractions (such as attempts to escape). Because of this, prison populations tend to develop clearly-identifiable societies. These societies have their own rules and taboos that coexist with the rules, both formal and informal, of the prison guards. Newcomers must learn these two sets of rules, often by trial and error. These societies have their own well-developed systems of right and wrong which often strike those on the outside as paradoxical. For example, in most prison societies, pedophilia is regarded as so heinous a wrong, even by those convicted of murder or sexual assault, that convicted pe-dophiles are routinely isolated from the general prison population for their own safety.

In prison societies, as in other anarchical communities, violation of the rules brings punishment from peers. Indeed, the violation of some rules (the taboo against snitching, for example) can often result in violent and bloody retribution. Raw strength is critical in all aspects of prison society, most brutally reflected in the enforced sexual subservience of the weak and the pervasiveness of male rape. Occasionally one group will dominate a prison population; more frequently different groups vie for dominance. For both groups and individuals, self-help is crucial for survival; running to the authorities will yield nothing but a deaf ear—and eventual retribution from one's fellow inmates for trying to rat them out.

Anarchical systems like prisons are, of course, very different from the stateless com-munities we discussed above. Prison societies are highly unnatural, artificially "constructed" of individuals who are forced to coexist with one another against their will; stateless com-munities, by contrast, comprise individuals who share numerous commonalities of inter-est. Unlike communities which lack a state apparatus, prison societies tend to be highly insecure places, even for the most powerful inmates. Unlike stateless societies, where the dis-satisfied can leave and establish a new village, prison societies offer no such escape. And un-like societies without a state, where the hard life of subsistence existence is leavened by the pleasures of family and community, the hard life of prison society is always lived in the shadow of the knowledge of life on the outside, and is marked by a tedium barely relieved by exercise, television, and periodic conjugal visits. But if life in prison is more raw than life in a stateless society, prisons nonetheless show us the relentless human propensity for social organization, even in conditions where life indeed tends to be nasty and brutish.

## CONCLUSION

In this chapter we have explored how we might think about world politics more system-atically. Pulling apart phrases, as we have done here, may seem like a exercise in hair-splitting, but its purpose was to try to be as clear as possible in the use of terms and language in order to lay out an understanding of world politics to guide our explorations.

The discussion of the anarchical nature of politics at a world level was likewise intended to demonstrate how easy it is to muddle thinking by the sloppy use of terms. Anarchy has been a central theme in thinking about international politics—quite appropriately—but this chapter shows how the anarchical idea has often been misused. Rethinking anarchy by drawing on the analogies of stateless communities and prison societies also allows us to think of the world as an anarchical community, a conception that is sketched out in more detail in the next chapter.

## Keyword File

| | |
|---|---|
| Foreign policy | Conflict |
| Supranational politics | Governance |
| Community | Power |
| Rules | Anarchy |
| Androcentrism | State of nature |
| Public | Anarchism |
| Private | Stateless communities |
| Economy | Self-help |
| Interests | |

## For Further Exploration

HARD COPY

Bull, Hedley. *The Anarchical Society: A Study of Order in World Politics.* London: Macmillan, 1977.

Buzan, Barry, Charles Jones, and Richard Little. *The Logic of Anarchy.* New York: Columbia University Press, 1993.

Doyle, Michael W. *Ways of War and Peace.* New York: W.W. Norton, 1997, Chapter 3: "Structuralism: Hobbes."

Kaplan, Robert D. "The coming anarchy," *The Atlantic Monthly* (February 1994), 44–76.

Lake, David A. "Anarchy, hierarchy, and the variety of international relations," *International Organization* 50 (Winter 1996), 1–33.

Masters, Roger D. "World politics as a primitive political system," *World Politics* 16 (July 1964), 595–619.

Oye, Kenneth A. "Explaining cooperation under anarchy," *World Politics* 38 (September 1985), 1–25; also published in: Oye, ed., *Cooperation Under Anarchy.* Princeton, NJ: Princeton University Press, 1985.

Waltz, Kenneth N. *Theory of International Politics.* Reading, MA: Addison-Wesley, 1979, Chapter 6: "Anarchic structures and balances of power."

Wendt, Alexander. "Anarchy is what states make of it: the social construction of power politics," *International Organization* 46 (Spring 1992), 391–425.

Williams, Michael C. "Hobbes and international relations: a reconsideration," *International Organization* 50 (Spring 1996), 213–36.

## WEBLINKS

**http://coombs.anu.edu.au/WWWVL–SocSci.html**

Home page of the Australian National University's Coombsweb WWW Virtual Library of social sciences resources

**http://osiris.colorado.edu/POLSCI/links.html**

University of Colorado at Boulder Political Science Resources

**http://www.library.ubc.ca/poli/**

University of British Columbia's Political Science Net Station of general resources in political science

**http://www.lsu.edu:80/guests/poli/public_html/research.html**

Site maintained by Louisiana State University Department of Political Science; key resources for research in political science

## *Notes to Chapter 3*

1. Harold Lasswell, *Politics: Who Gets What, When and How* (New York: McGraw Hill, 1936); David Easton, *A Framework for Political Analysis* (Englewood Cliffs, NJ: Prentice-Hall, 1965).

2. Joshua S. Goldstein, *International Relations*, 2d ed (New York: HarperCollins, 1996), 52; Jonathan Mercer, "Anarchy and identity," *International Organization* 49 (Spring 1995), 229.

3. Thomas Hobbes, *Leviathan, or the Matter, Forme, & Power of a Common-Wealth Ecclesiasticall and Civill* (London, 1651), ed. C.B. Macpherson (Harmondsworth, U.K.: Penguin, 1968), Chap. 13, pp. 62–63.

4. The use of the Hobbesian analogy is particularly endemic in international relations textbooks, with the vast majority of authors making a dutiful, if often only passing, mention of Hobbes. Indeed, one text is organized around the ubiquitous Hobbesian quote: Robert J. Lieber, *No Common Power: Understanding International Relations* (Glenview, IL: Scott, Foresman, 1988).

5. Macpherson, "Introduction," 9 (see Endnote 3).

6. Michael C. Williams, "Hobbes and international relations: a reconsideration," *International Organization* 50 (Spring 1996), 213–36.

7. Hedley Bull, *The Anarchical Society: A Study of Order in World Politics* (London: Macmillan, 1977), 49–50.

8. Roger D. Masters, "World politics as a primitive political system," *World Politics* 16 (July 1964), 595–619.

# *An* Anarchical Community: Imagining World Politics

**INTRODUCTION** The previous chapter outlined a multifaceted definition of world politics that focused on community, rules, conflict, governance, and power. It also looked at anarchy as the key environmental condition of politics at a world level, and examined how anarchy can be used (and misused) in thinking about global politics. In this chapter and the next, we seek to flesh out the various facets of the definition of politics, using an understanding of anarchy that we see in stateless communities. In this chapter we look at how community, rules,

conflict, and governance are manifested at a global level; in Chapter 5, we examine power in world politics.

This chapter, as the title suggests, tries to *imagine* world politics— providing an overall image for what most closely constitutes politics at this level. The overall image is that of an **anarchical society**, the image used by Hedley Bull, one of the leading scholars of the English School of international relations.[1]

## A GLOBAL COMMUNITY

Bull conceived of the world as a group of states which operate in an anarchic environment and construct what in essence is a society of states. But it can be argued that Bull did not go far enough in conceptualizing what is anarchical. His *society* consists only of states—governments which come together to form what is in essence a social organization. I argued in the previous chapter that one should not limit one's view of world politics to merely the interactions between 190 states. Rather, world politics might be better considered in broader terms—as a global society or community that goes beyond the 190 states that divide it.

### Society or Community? *Gesellschaft* and *Gemeinschaft*

What is the difference between "society" and "community"? The short answer is that not much distinguishes these words: **society** is from the Latin *socius*, companion; **community** is also from the Latin, *communis*, common. Both words imply a group of people ("companions") which have something in common. Other European languages also have two words for society and community, having the same Latin roots as their English counterparts: society (from companion) is *société* in French, and *Gesellschaft* in German; community (from common) is *communauté* in French and *Gemeinschaft* in German.

> Gemeinschaft *suggests that society is "something organic and traditional, involving bonds of common sentiment, experience, and identity. It is an essentially historical conception: societies grow rather than being made."*

But in German, the two words have acquired a special meaning in political science and sociology—they speak to the origins of societies. In the tradition of German sociology—widely embraced by English-speaking political scientists—a *Gesellschaft* understanding of the origin of society suggests that human societies are constructed and organized in a contractual way between individuals; atomistic (or separate) individuals come together and agree to form a society. By contrast, *Gemeinschaft* suggests that society is, in Barry Buzan's succinct formulation, "something organic and traditional, involving bonds of common sentiment, experience, and identity. It is an essentially historical conception: societies grow rather than being made."[2]

The use of "community" rather than "society" to describe world politics thus reflects a *Gemeinschaft* understanding of the origins of communities. That is not to say that a *Gesellschaft* understanding of society is not appropriate in some circumstances. As Rhoda E. Howard notes, a *Gesellschaft* understanding of community is often considered crucial for individualistic liberal society.[3] Prison societies are extreme cases of *Gesellschaft* societies—artificially thrown together, but societies nonetheless. The organizations and society-like structures and institutions that governments have created for themselves are examples of *Gesellschaft* "society-construction"; Bull was not wrong to describe this as an anarchical society.

But as noted in previous chapters, the view of world politics in this book seeks to extend beyond simply the interaction of 190 governments. We want to understand how political communities came to be and how the interactions between them created a broader community. Thus, an organic conception of political community, one that stresses the slow growth of bonds of commonality, seems to be preferable to one that focuses on the contractual and atomistic "state-eat-state" kind of anarchy examined in the previous chapter.

The historical record offers us many examples of people conceptualizing the existence of community at a level "above" their own political community, to see their polity as part of a broader community. For example, ancient Greeks believed that they comprised a single community—the Hellenes. Although divided into various *poleis*, or "city-states," they saw themselves as a united singularity against others, particularly Persians, and developed numerous community institutions. These included common spiritual institutions such as the oracle at Delphi; the inter-*polis* games held in four-year cycles at Olympia, Nemea, Corinth, and a site near Delphi; and a system of lawsuits for settling contractual disputes. *Poleis* would even hold civilized debates with one another about inter-*polis* affairs—before engaging each other in brutal and bloody wars. One cannot read Thucydides's account of the Peloponnesian wars without coming away with the sense that for all their warring, these *poleis* considered themselves as forming a single community.[4]

Likewise, we can point to Christendom in Europe during the feudal period or the conceptualization of "Europe" in the 17th century. As Kalevi J. Holsti points out,[5] phrases like "the tranquillity of Europe," "the health of the European community," and "*le repos général de la Chrétienté*" (the general repose of Christendom) dotted the discourse of international politics—at the same time that the armies of European kings and princes were fighting a series of destructive wars with each other.

In the contemporary period, we see a comparable tendency to conceptualize the world in community terms. Consider the widespread use of the phrase "the international community" by political leaders, the media, officials of nongovernmental organizations, and other elites. Today, "international community" is invariably used in a way that means much more than "190 governments and what they are doing." Rather, it usually refers to an inchoate unity—*all-governments-and-peoples-in-the-world*—a kind of unified proto-polity. It should be stressed that such a conceptualization is nothing close to a world-state or a global civil society. By the same token, however, when people use the term "international community" today, they have in mind something quite different from a "state of nature" in which 190 communities operate in wary fear of one another.

## RULES OF THE GLOBAL GAME

As in politics at other levels, global politics is also about rules. These rules include not only the formal and written rules—international law—but also unwritten understandings, norms, customs, and "ways of doing things." Both the informal and the formal "rules of the game" underwrite interactions at the global level. In other words, world politics is about the evolution of rules, laws, understandings, and taboos and how these evolve in an anarchical setting.[6]

### Informal Rules

The informal rules of the game come in such a variety of forms that it is virtually impossible to categorize them. Consider again the millions of daily global transactions noted in the introductory chapter. Such a huge volume of transactions simply could not be sustained without numerous sets of deeply embedded rules of the game. Some of these rules are formal and written, but most are informal.

All players in the international system have informal rules of the game—unwritten understandings, agreed-upon taboos—that guide behaviour. Many of the interactions of governments and their agents are based on informal rules. As we will see below, government leaders evolved a complex set of general rules that we know collectively as sovereignty.

Some informal rules can be quite specific, such as the contemporary "understanding" among leaders of governments that they will not try to assassinate one another. Note that this late-20th-century understanding is quite different from the rules that governed international politics in Renaissance Italy, when trying to kill the leader of another *città* was entirely *within* the bounds of acceptable behaviour.[7]

## Formal Rules and International Law

We are also interested in rules that determine what is considered "good" and "bad" behaviour for all international actors on a global level. It is true that "law" in an anarchical community does not exist as it does in a society which has developed a state apparatus that is able to impose its definition of right and wrong on all members of the community, by force if necessary. Yet written rules nonetheless exist. Highly developed sets of formal and written rules, constituting a body of **international law**, have been formulated to govern the global behaviour of individuals, groups, and even the governments of political communities. Again, the scope of international law is immense, covering everything from how prisoners of war and their captors must behave toward one another (international law gives prisoners a right to try to escape but prohibits them from killing their captors while trying to do so) to the air traffic control requirements for airports. Moreover, not only governments engage in writing such rules. The International Standards Organization (ISO) tries to create basic global standards for products. This private initiative, that has nothing to do with governments, has spread to the point that most inter-firm contracts now demand that parties meet ISO ratings. In short, all these laws and rules create a complex web of prohibitions against certain kinds of behaviour and an equally complex web of obligations to perform certain actions and meet certain standards.

There is a deep relationship between informal and formal rules. For example, the rules that have evolved to govern how diplomats deal with one another have not only developed over hundreds of years of informal understandings about what is acceptable and unacceptable behaviour. As well, the treatment of diplomats by everyone in the international community, governmental and nongovernmental actors alike, has been carefully codified in a number of international treaties and conventions.

The best illustration of the intimate connection between informal and formal rules can be seen in treaties between governments. In this area, an informal understanding underwrites formal contracts between governments: the widespread attachment to the principle of *pacta sunt servanda* (treaties are to be kept) allows governments to negotiate and sign formal treaties with one another with reasonable certainty that they will be honoured.

Like rules and laws at other levels, the informal and formal rules at the global level are sometimes deliberately broken. Sometimes drug runners double-cross their suppliers;

*But when rules are broken at other levels, we do not dismiss them as meaningless; therefore, we should not dismiss rules at the global level just because they are broken on occasion.*

sometimes government leaders try to liquidate an opponent; sometimes terrorists kidnap and murder a diplomat; sometimes officials stretch an understanding; sometimes intelligence agents kill someone they deem an unacceptable threat; sometimes a corporation tries to push the edge of the envelope in how it reports its international financial transactions; sometimes a government deliberately refuses to honour a treaty it has signed. In such cases, responses vary, for unlike rule-breaking at other levels, there are few enforcement mechanisms comparable to the justice systems most political communities have evolved. But when rules are broken at other levels, we do not dismiss them as meaningless; therefore, we should not dismiss rules at the global level just because they are broken on occasion.

## THE GLOBAL ECONOMY

Just as political communities have economic structures that are governed by the decisions and rules that people make about their economic lives, so too is there an economic structure at the world level. This structure differs considerably depending on time; place; level of technological development; and ideas about wealth and how it should be organized, created, and distributed.

### The Localized Economy

For much of the last 8000 years, the world was marked by a large number of different **localized economies**. These were largely self-contained systems of barter exchange that involved localities such as villages, towns, and even larger political units. Local economies almost always "nested" within a broader economic structure, however. Thus, for example, each Greek *polis* had its own economy, but each *polis* was intimately connected in a broader system of economic exchange between and among the *poleis* of Greece. Moreover, economic exchange between Greeks occurred in the context of a broader economic relationship that existed between the Greeks and their neighbours around the Mediterranean and the Aegean Seas.

Likewise, the economy of the Roman empire at the height of its prosperity in the century after the emperor Nero, who died in AD 68, was one that spread well beyond the Mediterranean. As the map in Figure 4.1 shows, a wide trade in a variety of goods was carried throughout the empire by both ship and road, requiring a huge network of individuals as producers, transporters, and consumers.[8]

The volume and variety of goods traded in the late 20th century would dwarf the trade of earlier eras. Most Roman cargo vessels were approximately 50 metres long and able to carry 250 tonnes of cargo. But sailings were few and depended on weather and winds: there was little traffic in the stormy winter months, and etesian winds made eastward voyages almost impossible during midsummer. By contrast, the carrying capacity of an average contemporary cargo vessel ranges from 12 000 to 30 000 deadweight tonnes (dwt);

*Figure 4.1* • **TRADE IN THE ROMAN EMPIRE, CIRCA 100 AD**

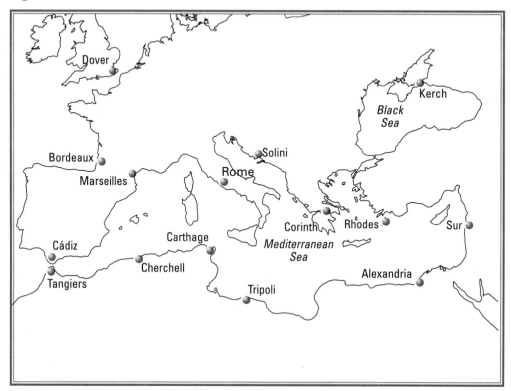

Principal ports, principal products. A variety of products came to Rome from the different parts of the Empire.

**Britain:** hides, slaves, dogs, silver, tin, lead
**France:** amber, slaves, furs, wine, silver, lead
**Spain:** gold, tin, lead, silver, timber, iron, grain, copper, olive oil
**North Africa:** timber, copper, marble, grain, olive oil, papyrus, granite, jewellery

**Middle East:** timber, wine, olive oil, silk, glass, dates, figs
**Greece:** wine, honey, diamonds, gold,
**Adriatic Coast:** silver, gold, grain
**Black Sea:** grain, slaves, fur, fish, timber, wine, marble

some container sea-barges can carry over 1600 standard 20' × 8' × 8' aluminum containers that are the staple of contemporary intermodal world trade. Moreover, the contemporary volume of sea-borne trade is staggering: at one port alone—Kwai Chung in Hong Kong, the world's busiest container port—over one million TEUs (twenty-foot-equivalent units, the measurement used for the container trade) are handled each month.

For all the differences, it is nonetheless instructive to reflect on the capacity of people in antiquity to organize moving desired goods to market, often over long distances. In the Bronze Age, some 5000 years ago, amber, which was used as both an ornament and a cure for illness, was regularly traded across the breadth of Europe. Two thousand years ago, an active trade carried worked gold, precious stones, silks, and spices from Asia to the Mediterranean and gold and silver back to Asia.

## The Interaction of Localized Economies

Until approximately 1500 AD, numerous local economies existed in different locations at the same time. In the 700s, for example, the local economies included a fragmented feudal economy in Europe, marked by subsistence farming and minimal commercial activity. In West Africa, the economy embraced the Ghanaian empire, which flourished in what is now Mali and Mauritania between approximately 400 and 1100, and neighbouring peoples along the Sénégal, Niger, and Volta rivers and in the interior desert. Ghana was essentially a trading community: gold, produce, textiles, tools, leather, jewellery, and salt were the main commodities. On the Yucatán peninsula, the various communities that we know as the Mayan civilization had an economy that was essentially agriculture-based. Trading in pottery, produce, and textiles occurred between tribes and towns using a money economy that used copper bells for currency. In the Middle East, the economy centred around the new capital of the Abbasid caliphate, Baghdad, and extended from Iraq to Egypt and the Arabian peninsula.

On the Indian subcontinent, the 700s were marked by intense political rivalries of three major political communities: the Pala dynasty in Bengal, the Rajputs in northwestern India, and the Rashtrakutas of the Deccan plateau. The impact on the economy was not unlike that in feudal Europe: the primarily agricultural economy continued to function despite the periodic conflicts of rival dynasts whose main aims were plunder and tribute. In East Asia, the Tang dynasty (618–907) saw commerce expand after a series of great canals were built, linking China's various regions. A tax system that guaranteed land to all farming families concentrated great wealth in local estates and Buddhist monasteries, which frequently acted as commercial lenders.

However, usually there was only minimal interaction between these economies. Between some there was none at all: as far as we know, no connection existed between the Mayans and the economies of Europe or Asia. In other cases there was some "inter-economy" trade, usually involving a small volume of luxury goods moved exceedingly long distances.

While most local economies had a few long tentacles into other economies, they remained primarily regional. A highly developed trade evolved in the Baltic and North seas in the 11th, 12th, and 13th centuries, but it centred on northern German towns such as Lübeck and Hamburg. These towns carried on trade in a network that extended from London and Brugge (in present-day Belgium) in the west, to Iceland and the Faroe Islands in the north, and to Reval (present-day Tallinn) and the independent city-state of Great Novgorod in the east. Members of the burgeoning merchant class in these towns began to organize trading associations with one another called *hanses*; their intent was to create and maintain monopolies in international trade. To this end, German merchants established trading posts in London, Flanders, and the Baltic countries, negotiating with local kings and lords for special trading privileges. In 1250, German merchants settled in London at the Steelyard, named for the device that measured the weight of the wool that was the primary English export at the time. With the approval of the English king, they established a monopoly trade that was one of the primary catalysts for the growth of the London economy in the declining years of the feudal period. Eventually these associations evolved from groups of merchants to associations of *Hansa* towns. The city-leagues of northern Germany not only grew wealthy but also powerful, fielding armies and deposing local lords. At the height of its power in the 13th and 14th centuries, the **Hanseatic League** consisted of over 200 towns that controlled the considerable Baltic and North Sea trade—but sought to go no further.

## The Internationalized Economy

Beginning in approximately 1500, we see the emergence of an **internationalized economy**—a single international marketplace connecting the different local economies of the world. European states expanded out into the world during the eras of mercantile imperialism and nationalist imperialism, fuelled by the technological innovations of the Industrial Revolution. European expansion consolidated regional economies into a single global economy that linked the centre, or metropole, in Europe and the United States with a vast periphery that extended around the world.

The descent of the world into a prolonged period of general conflict—marked by two world wars and an interwar period of economic and political crisis—strained the European-dominated international economy. Indeed, after the Second World War ended, the international economy enjoyed a period of considerable growth in the second half of the 20th century. And following the broad deregulation of the international economy after 1971, explored in Chapter 17, there was a massive expansion of economic activity, in both absolute and relative terms (see Figure 4.2). The expansion was reflected in all areas of the international marketplace: dramatic increases in trade in goods and services, investment, finance, agriculture, and other primary products.

*Figure 4.2* • **GROWTH IN WORLD TRADE OVER THE TWENTIETH CENTURY**

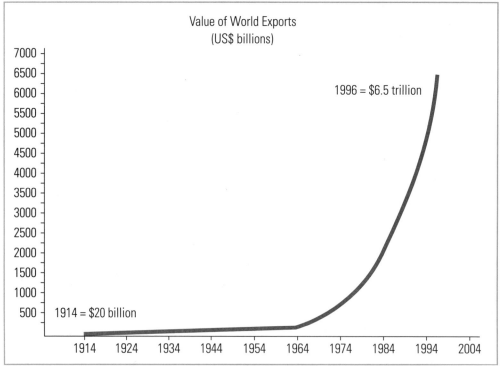

Sources: International Monetary Fund, *Direction of Trade Statistics Yearbook* (Washington: IMF, 1996); also World Trade Organization, Annual Report 1996 (http://www.wto.org/wto/intLTRAD/).

## The Globalized Economy

The changes in the international economy during the last quarter of the 20th century formed the beginnings of what some have called a **globalized economy**. No longer is the economy at the world level merely a marketplace for the exchange of goods and services between local economies; rather, all of the elements of wealth creation—finance, investment, production, distribution, marketing—are beginning to be organized on a global scale. The processes of globalization go well beyond merely economic organization, however.

*The economic structures at the global level are heavily determined by rules and ideas about the economy.*

Like their domestic counterparts, the economic structures at the global level are heavily determined by rules and ideas about the economy and the way economic exchange should be organized. In particular, through the ages, those who wielded political power and authority have sought to use the marketplace for political purposes. We will see in the chapters ahead how different conceptions of political power over the marketplace have given rise to different kinds of state—the mercantile state, the night-watchman state, the protective state, the welfare state, the competition state, and most recently, the service-station state.

The shape of the international marketplace and how it operates, the nature of wealth creation, and the complexity and dynamism of international exchange are all determined by rules made by the various communities that operate in the global arena. Economic rules determine allocations and thus influence who is rich, who is poor, who lives a marginal existence, who lives in luxurious splendour; we are thus interested in understanding how rules work in this area.

## INTERESTS, GOALS, AND CONFLICT

If conflict over the rules is endemic within political communities of thousands or millions of human beings, it should come as little surprise that there is considerable disharmony and incompatibility among the estimated six billion human beings inhabiting the planet at the beginning of the 21st century.

## Goals and Interests: Safety, Gain, and Reputation

What are the goals to which all human beings aspire? Political philosophers have long sought to identify universal political goals—what humans seek at all times and in all places. A classical trio of goals have been identified by a trio of classical writers: the goals are **safety** (security), **gain** (possessions or wealth), and **reputation** (honour and standing); the classical writers are the Greek historian Thucydides, the English philosopher Thomas Hobbes, and the American political scientist Hans J. Morgenthau.

This trio of goals made its first appearance when Thucydides put the words into the mouths of the Athenian representatives who participated in the debate being held in Sparta over whether Sparta should declare war against Athens in 432 BC. After delegations from Megara, Corinth, and other *poleis* had spoken bitterly against Athens during the debate, a group of Athenians who happened to be in Sparta asked to participate. They sought to defend their *polis* against the charges that they were being too aggressive against the members of their empire. "We have done nothing extraordinary," Thucydides has the Athenians say, "nothing contrary to human nature in accepting an empire when it was offered to us and then in refusing to give it up. Three very powerful motives prevent us from doing so—security, honour, and self-interest."[9] Such a trio of goals was echoed some 2000 years later in *Leviathan*, the book in which Thomas Hobbes sought to explain clearly the logical consequences of the natural equality of humankind. Arguing that there were three principal causes of quarrel between humans—competition, diffidence (or insecurity), and glory—Hobbes suggested that

> The first, maketh men invade for Gain; the second, for Safety; and the third, for Reputation. The first use Violence, to make themselves Masters of other mens persons, wives, children, and cattell; the second, to defend them; the third, for trifles, as a word, a smile, a different opinion, and any other signe of undervalue...[10]

(It might be noted that the echo should not be surprising: Hobbes's first published work was a translation of Thucydides into English, published in 1628.)

Hans J. Morgenthau, writing in the late 1940s, suggested that we could see international politics in terms of safety, gain, and reputation, though he used different terminology. He suggested that states pursued three different types of foreign policy: the policy of the status quo (which seeks to maintain the distribution of power which exists at a particular moment in history); the policy of imperialism (which seeks to overthrow the status quo); and the policy of prestige (which seeks social recognition from other states).[11] While the parallels are not exact, Thucydides and Hobbes are clearly echoed in Morgenthau's three "policies"—status quo/security/safety, imperialism/self-interest/gain; reputation/honour/prestige.

### Safety: Security in World Politics

The classic trio—and many others besides—assume that a key goal for all actors in world politics is security. Security is something highly subjective: it is that peace of mind that comes with a sense of safety, a freedom from threats of harm to all that one values. Insecurity is one's fear that harm will come to that which one values.[12] However, while that sense of safety is subjective, David A. Baldwin reminds us that in thinking about security and insecurity, we have to specify (i) *what* is to be made safe, (ii) against *what threat*, and (iii) *for whom* the security is to be provided.[13]

These different facets of security and insecurity must be analyzed on an *individual* basis. Individuals have markedly different conceptions of their own security, even when they occupy the same space at the same time. While individual definitions of security vary considerably, we can generalize about what is likely to create peace of mind in individuals. Firstly, security begins with a sense of personal safety: in other words, the ability to live in and move around one's own community without fear of being interfered with, mocked, hassled, robbed, assaulted, raped, taken away, imprisoned, expelled, "ethnically cleansed," or killed; or the assurance while in one's home that no one is going to break in and do the occupants harm. Security is also concerned with a sense of community safety—a sense that some other group is not going to try to seize the community's land, occupy its property, or imprison or harm the community in which one lives. Security involves a sense that one's property is safe against robbery, seizure, or destruction. Finally, security is a sense of well-being that can have economic, environmental, social, linguistic, or cultural dimensions.

Thus, threats to security come in a wide variety of forms—some natural, some as the consequence of human agency. Living on a geological fault line, in the shadow of a volcano, in a frequently deluged river delta, or at the fringe of a desert subject to desertification are examples of sources of natural insecurity. Insecurity can also result from the consequences of human action: not knowing where the next meal will come from; worrying whether one will be infected with HIV; living near a rickety Soviet-era nuclear power plant; or not knowing whether the fish stocks, on which one relies for a living, have been fished out. Insecurity can come from a fear about the future of one's language or culture threatened with being swamped in a larger cultural pool. Or insecurity can come from the behaviour of specific individuals: not knowing whether the young men approaching one's car, stopped for a light in Washington's southeast, intend one harm; not knowing whether the person standing next to you in a Tel Aviv mall is about to explode a suicide bomb strapped to his chest; not knowing whether the crowd of Hindus marching down a Mumbai street protesting the latest predations by Pakistan will turn on Muslims they might find in their path; not knowing whether the knock at the door at 3:00 a.m. is the secret police.

If we look at security in this multifaceted way, we can see that individuals can in fact have a mixture of insecurities and securities at the same time. Individuals may have secure employment, but live in neighbourhoods where personal insecurity is high; or they may live in a community that is completely free from any concern about being overrun by the country next door, but nonetheless may be worried about the fact that they are of a different religious faith than the majority of their neighbours who have shown a propensity to attack minorities. An individual may have no fear of his neighbours, but may worry that the state security forces will take exception to his union organizing. Or an individual may have no fear of any other member of the community, but may worry about the enmity of others across the border.

We can extrapolate these observations to different aggregates of individuals—families, groups, organizations, and even political communities. But with every aggregation, the complexity of the pattern of security and insecurity deepens. Consider the aggregation at the next level up, the family: the family-*qua*-unit might be declared "secure" by someone claiming to speak on behalf of the household, yet within that unit we might find a wife who is physically abused by her husband and thus has little sense of personal safety; we might find a teenage son who is shaken down for his lunch money every day by a gang at school; we might find a daughter who is convinced that, as a result of global warming, the city she lives in will be under a metre of water by the time she is an adult. In short, supposedly secure units can hide deep insecurities of members of the unit.

At the level of political community, the patterns of security and insecurity become even more deeply variegated.[14] Political communities, like individuals, generally try to create security for those who live within them—a sense of safety from attack from within or from outside and a sense that those things valued by individuals within the community will not suffer harm. Generally, it falls to the governing structure of the community— elders, emperors, kings or bureaucratic states—to provide this security.

Governments generally try to ensure that members of the community enjoy a certain level of security "inside." Indeed, members of those governing structures, as a "unit" within the community, carefully tend to their own security and well-being first and foremost. There are precious few examples in human experience of governors who are hungrier, poorer, less well housed, or generally less better off than the governed. Beyond their own well-being, governments normally try, at a minimum, to ensure that members of the community feel safe enough that they are not moved to run away or to rise up in revolt. To be sure, such efforts need not be extended to all the human beings living in that space. Sometimes governments purposely remove protections for certain groups or individuals within the community; the treatment of Jews by the Nazis is an extreme case. Frequently, governments try harder to create safety for some groups in some areas than others: there is generally more safety in places like Short Hills, Rosedale, Bowdon, Sandton, San Ángel, and Vaucluse than there is in East Orange, Jane-Finch, Moss Side, Soweto, Netzahualcóyotl, and Redfern.

> *There are precious few examples in human experience of governors who are hungrier, poorer, less well housed, or generally less better off than the governed.*

Governments generally try to ensure a comparable sense of safety for the political community *vis-à-vis* other communities. As a minimum, they seek to ensure that the community is not eliminated (as Melos was); destroyed (as Carthage was); devastated (as aboriginal tribes in Australia and the Americas were); overrun (as communities across Asia and Europe were by the Mongol Horde in the 13th century, or as Kuwait was in 1990); sacked (as Rome was by the Visigoths or as Delhi was by Tamerlane's forces); raided (as west African communities were by slavers in the three centuries after 1440); incorporated (as Nazi Germany incorporated Austria in 1938 and Luxembourg in 1942, and as Indonesia incorporated East Timor in 1976 following the December 1975 invasion); occupied (as France, Belgium, the Netherlands, and Denmark were by the Nazis, or as Afghanistan was by the Soviet Union); subjugated (as the peoples of Europe were by the Romans); colonized (as much of the world was by Europeans over the last five hundred years); or dominated (as the countries of Eastern Europe were after the Second World War).

But such efforts may or may not produce the desired result. Consider the huge failures of the Algerian government to provide for the safety of people against the GIA (*Groupe islamique armée*, Armed Islamic Group), who descend on villages in the dead of night and slit the throats of whomever they find there. Consider the number of women in India who after their marriage have gone to live with their husband's family and been killed for not being a sufficiently "good wife." Consider the incapacity of governments everywhere to create environments in which women feel safe, to protect their citizens against petty theft and crime, or to dampen economic or environmental insecurities felt by their citizens. Likewise, as the examples above indicate, communities are often incapable of defending themselves against the predations of others. They may lack the wealth, the technology, the numbers, the discipline, the will, or the skill.

Efforts by governments to keep their communities secure also produce some rich paradoxes. Consider the paradox of security during the Cold War era, when there was no way to provide safety for the citizens of a city targeted by nuclear weapons delivered by intercontinental ballistic missiles (ICBMs). The velocity of the warheads from a ballistic missile as they fell toward their target was simply too great and the size of the warheads too small. The only way to "defend" one's cities was to deter the would-be nuclear attacker by threatening to counter-attack with enough nuclear weapons that the costs of launching an attack would far out-weigh any benefits. In short, the logic of nuclear deterrence was to create a **balance of terror**, where paradoxically one created a sense of security by creating a huge sense of insecurity.[15]

Because the effects of even a limited nuclear exchange between the United States and the Soviet Union would not have been localized—as the Chernobyl disaster of 1986 showed*—all countries were affected by the balance of terror, even those which were not specifically targeted by nuclear weapons of the superpowers. Other countries chose different routes to try to defend themselves against the threat posed by nuclear weapons.

Some developed their own sizable nuclear arsenals. In the 1950s and early 1960s, Britain, France, and then China acquired their own nuclear weapons systems, with the French even pretending that their nuclear weapons were pointed *à tous azimouts* (in all directions). Numerous other governments also came to the conclusion that nuclear weapons would provide their communities with added security against their neighbours. Israel was reputed to have acquired several nuclear devices; South Africa experimented with nuclear devices in the 1970s and 1980s before renouncing the idea; India conducted a "peaceful ex-plosion" of a nuclear device in 1974; and the governments of Pakistan, North Korea, Iraq, and Libya have all been named as countries seeking to acquire nuclear weapons.

But the vast majority of governments did not try to develop nuclear weapons of their own. Some smaller non-nuclear states sought security by allying themselves with one of the superpowers, thereby sheltering (as it was commonly put) under their "nuclear umbrella." More often than not, however, other states simply suffered the insecurities created by the balance of terror in varying degrees of silence.

The insecurities created by nuclear weapons in the United States had another paradoxical effect. It can be argued that by the mid–1970s, a perfect balance of terror had been created—in the sense that both the United States and the Soviet Union had enough nuclear weapons to destroy each other many times over (known as **overkill** capability). But far from creating a sense of security—that the United States would be safe from a nuclear attack from the USSR—this actually created such insecurity that the governments of both the United States and the Soviet Union kept trying hard to find ways to defend their communities against a ballistic missile attack.

---

* On 26 April 1986, one of the four reactors at a nuclear power plant outside Chernobyl in northern Ukraine, then part of the USSR, went out of control and exploded. Before Soviet authorities could contain the damage, approximately 12 trillion Bq of radionuclides were released into the atmosphere and spread throughout western Europe.

In the United States, this gave rise to the **Strategic Defense Initiative** (SDI) of the 1980s. In the minds of those who dreamed up "Star Wars," as it was quickly dubbed, a set of space-based and ground-based weapons systems could be put in place that could destroy *all* ICBMs in the various phases of flight. First, space-based heat-guided lasers would try to destroy as many ICBMs as possible during the "boost phase"—in other words, as their rockets produced maximum thrust (and thus heat) and they rose slowly out of their silos. For those ICBMs that escaped, space-based "hunter-killer" satellites would try to destroy the "buses" that carried a number of warheads in "mid-course phase" orbit around the Earth. For those (few, it was hoped) warheads that made it through and descended to their targets in the "re-entry" or "terminal" phase, ground-based weapons, such as electromagnetic rail-guns, would be designed to fire a withering hail of coffee-can-sized projectiles at incoming warheads. This fantastic scheme caught the imagination of a number of political leaders, especially Ronald Reagan, the president of the United States, who touted SDI as the way to escape from the terror of a nuclear war. But Reagan's enthusiasm was not shared by the leadership in the Soviet Union. If the Americans could actually produce such a system, then the basis on which the USSR had built its own security would be rendered meaningless. Moreover, the Soviet leadership knew that they had neither the technical expertise to match the United States in such a venture, nor the economic capacity to build their own Star Wars defence umbrella. Thus SDI created considerable insecurity in the Soviet Union.

With the end of the Cold War, however, the intense rivalry that had marked relations between the United States and the Soviet Union faded. Some of the nuclear weapons of the great powers were destroyed, others decommissioned. By 1994, both Washington and Moscow had officially reprogrammed their arsenals so that they no longer targeted each other. The nuclear arsenals are thus still there, and their guidance systems could easily and quickly be reprogrammed. But despite this, the widespread insecurity associated with nuclear weapons has faded, demonstrating the importance of the subjective element of security.

During the Cold War era, the notion of security in international politics became intimately bound up in the rivalry of the USSR and the United States, with the result that it acquired almost a single dimension. With the passing of the nuclear threat, the notion of security in world politics has once again become quite multidimensional. Numerous scholars have devoted considerable energy to "rethinking" security in the post-Cold War era to capture that multidimensionality.[16] A common way is to adorn the word "security" with modifiers: global security, international security, national security, home security, personal security, common security, collective security, cooperative security, financial security, economic security, environmental security.[17] However, adorning security is useful only if, as Baldwin and Wolfers suggest, we continue to ask: "security for whom" and "security against what."

### Gain: Possessions, Wealth, and Welfare

The second goal assumed to be universal for all actors in world politics is gain—the desire of humans to possess and control. It can refer to the desire to own things of value and to accumulate desirable possessions (though exactly what is deemed worthy of collection is highly variable, and differs radically depending on culture and historical era). Gain also refers to the common desire of individuals, organizations, and political communities to provide for their "welfare," a sense of well-being that overlaps with notions of security. It is thus useful to define "gain" as widely as possible when thinking about what actors in world politics seek. In the chapters ahead we will come across a range of goals that reflect a desire for gain.

**Wealth**    Most commonly, we will see that actors seek wealth. Wealth can come in a variety of forms. Intimately connected to the structure and nature of local, international, and global economies, humans have sought wealth in numerous settings, exhibiting differing degrees of greed in that search, but often demonstrating considerable ingenuity and dedication in their efforts to provide consumers with products. Consider the early traders along the Silk Road who first connected the markets of China and Rome; the Portuguese who pushed around the west African coast; the Arab slavers who, together with their new buyers, the European imperial plantation owners in the Caribbean, moved some 15 million Africans to the New World in order to feed a growing European desire for sugar; the cod fishers who braved the storms and seas of the North Atlantic and fished the banks off Newfoundland; the Hanseatic traders of the Baltic; the Spanish explorers who pushed into Central and South America and discovered the riches of Aztec and Inca gold and silver; the settlers along the eastern seaboard from Virginia to New England and those who pushed westward into the heartland of the Americas; the inventors of the Industrial Revolution whose gadgets would transform the British, and then the European, economies; the imperial ocean-going European traders—British, French, and Dutch—who pushed into the Indies, China, and Japan; the 19th-century imperialists who carved up the continent of Africa and the islands of the South Pacific; and the 20th-century traders and managers of a dizzying array of companies, multinational corporations, and small firms—all seeking profit from operations both local and global.

We will see that most actors seeking wealth also sought to own and control land and territory, one of the dominant themes in the history of global politics. Often actors sought territorial control or ownership because the creation of wealth and the ownership of land were so intimately related historically. In this aspect of world politics, individuals have played a particularly important role. While much European settlement of the world beyond Europe that occurred after 1500 was sponsored by kings and governments, a great deal of settlement was the result of individuals searching for land. American pioneers, for example, pushed westward across the North American continent in search of land for agriculture. Dragging government after them to provide security against those they were displacing, these settlers would transform the politics not only of the Americas, but also—after the consolidation of the United States—politics at a world level. Settlers in Australia, Canada, New Zealand, Rhodesia, South Africa, and numerous other locations also sought land. Territorial claims were no less important to those lured from all over the world to the great gold rushes of the last two centuries—in California in the late 1840s, in Victoria in Australia in the early 1850s, in the Black Hills of South Dakota in the 1870s, in the Yukon in Canada and Kalgoorlie in Australia in the 1890s, and in the Amazon basin since the late 1970s.

However, it is not just individuals who have sought territorial gain. Throughout history, governors have despatched armies to conquer, occupy, and settle territory. European kings often sought to acquire new territorial possessions for no other reason than to expand their tax base—for territories were a source of income, a way to pay their troops, a means of staving off bankruptcy. Control of the Americas meant controlling the silver and gold deemed so important for mercantilist economies. The Japanese in the early 20th century believed that direct control of the natural resources of Manchuria were critical to fuel their industrial economy.

Wealth was not the only reason for seeking to expand territorial control. Often the desire for land and territory was an outgrowth of the national ideal. Sometimes it was a manifestation of other ideas about identity: Adolf Hitler and his followers conceived of territorial expansion as a natural consequence of the superiority of the Aryan race; the creation of *Lebensraum* (living room) for the Aryan race by conquering Eastern Europe and the Soviet Union was to be the natural manifestation of the superiority of Aryans over Slavs to the east. Sometimes the seizure of land has been for reasons of safety. In the chapters ahead we will examine numerous examples of governors who sought to increase the security of their communities by seizing the territory of others.

At times the seizure of land is for a mix of motives. For example, the Vietnamese seizure of Cambodia in early 1979 appears to have been motivated by a desire to extend Vietnam's political control and also to get rid of a regime whose internal policies were creating negative spillover effects down the Mekong River. Likewise, Joseph Stalin ordered the Soviet occupation and the deindustrialization of the countries of eastern Europe after the Second World War not only to compensate the Soviet Union for its wartime losses, but also to create a buffer zone against the possibility of another attack like the one inflicted by the Germans in June 1941.

**Welfare**   Such efforts to provide safety through gain can also be characterized as efforts to provide **welfare**, an objective that overlaps with both security and wealth. Welfare normally refers to a sense of well-being, usually having economic connotations—in other words, the provision of desired goods and services to both individuals (such as shelter, food, employment, education, and health services) and communities (such as institutions and infrastructure). However, welfare can also refer to the sense of well-being that comes from freedom from threats to one's security (economic, physical, environmental).

The various actors in world politics—individuals, organizations, and political communities—devote a great deal of energy to providing themselves with welfare. Individuals try to provide themselves (and their kin) with the necessities—and if possible the luxuries—of life; very basically, they seek a good life for themselves and a better life for their children. Organizations seek their own brand of welfare: an environment conducive to their operations, whether those operations involve making money or performing some other function. Finally, political communities, and particularly their governments, seek welfare. In general, governments look out for the welfare of the individuals and organizations which make up the political community. They not only seek security of all sorts for the community (physical, territorial, environmental, economic, and so on), but they also try to provide general well-being for the members of the community.

It must be stressed that this search for welfare can take hugely varied forms, depending on the cosmographic beliefs of the political community in question. Thus, for example, the rulers of Mayan cities like Copán and Tikal in the four centuries after 435 AD sought to ensure the welfare of their cities in ways that seem strange to us. The lords who ruled these cities sought to provide for the welfare of the community by waging incessant and bloody war on neighbouring communities in order to capture prisoners for sacrificial butchering. As Mayan art and sculpture so vividly show, the victims were often ritualistically bled, apparently sometimes for years; usually they were eviscerated or decapitated. These ritual sacrifices were believed to be necessary to satisfy the needs of the gods that blood be shed in order for the sun to rise each day. (These efforts to provide welfare would contain the seeds of the Mayan civilization's destruction. The lakes on which Mayan cities were built were believed to be the underworld, where sacrificial victims were believed to go after they had been despatched. The skulls and body parts were dumped into these lakes, eventually fouling the water and spreading disease. This contributed to the collapse of Tikal and Copán; around 830, the cities had to be abandoned.)

A more familiar pattern of welfare provision are the efforts of 20th-century governments to fulfil the requirements of the welfare state. In the 18th and 19th centuries, not much was expected of the so-called **night-watchman state**. In other words, the state was expected to provide basic security for members of the political community—defence against external threats through strong armed forces and security against internal disorder through a strong justice system. But anything else desired by individuals had to be provided either by themselves or by other community organizations, such as churches or voluntary groups. In the early 20th century, by contrast, we saw the rise of the idea of the **welfare state**, in which governments were expected to provide, through tax revenue and tax expenditures, a range of public services beyond the minimal services of the night-watchman state. The welfare state was expected to provide such varied services as public housing, public education, public health, public childcare, public libraries, public transit, and a range of urban services from utilities to sewage to water. The welfare state was also to be involved in the creation or encouragement of employment, either through state ownership of productive enterprises or through public spending and tax expenditures. There were few limits to the possible range and scope of the welfare state's responsibilities. Thus, even cultural pursuits were to be regulated and publicly funded: artists, poets, and writers; orchestras and musicians; ballet, opera, and theatre companies; radio, television, and film.

The demands on the welfare state meant that 20th-century governments tended to be deeply involved in the economic life of the political community. In their external involvements, governments were required not only to protect the welfare of the members of the political community, but also to protect their *capacity* to provide the services of the welfare state. Although by the end of the 20th century the welfare state is everywhere in retreat, we will see that the welfare aims of governments have not altered significantly.

## Reputation: Standing and Honour

The final goal in the classic trio is honour, reputation, or **prestige**. Hobbes assumed that all humans seek reputation as a goal: "For every man looketh that his companion should value him, at the same rate he sets upon himselfe: And upon all signes of contempt, or undervaluing, naturally endeavours, as far as he dares...to extort a greater value from his contemners, by dommage; and from others, by the example."[18] In other words, all humans want to be regarded by others as they regard themselves, and they tend to ensure that they secure that recognition by hurting those who hold them in contempt. By this action, they show others what happens when one is not held in proper regard.

In world politics, this goal manifests itself in different ways. The various actors at a global level—individuals, organizations, and communities—tend to be highly sensitive to what others think of them (including some of those who cultivate the appearance of studied indifference). In particular, these actors want to be well regarded by others and seen as legitimate, valued members of the international community. Individuals, organizations, and political communities thus tend not to take kindly to characterizations of themselves by others that are contemptuous or "undervaluing." They dislike being described in negative terms, and generally respond defensively to criticisms or insults levelled against them.

A good example is the American insult against the Soviet Union following its invasion of Afghanistan in 1979. Jimmy Carter's administration mounted an international effort to have the 1980 Olympic Games, scheduled to be held in Moscow, moved or cancelled. Washington argued that the USSR should be punished for the invasion; to allow the Games to go ahead would provide the Soviet Union with the same kind of international legitimacy that the Nazi regime of Adolf Hitler had reaped in 1936 when the Games were held in Berlin. The implication was clear: the Soviet Union was just like Nazi Germany. This was a deeply offensive charge, not only to the Soviet government, but to ordinary Soviets, millions of whose relatives had died fighting the Nazis in the 1940s. Not surprisingly, numerous Soviets were stung by this insult and by the subsequent boycott of the Games by 62 countries. The Soviet government tried its best to organize a comparable boycott against the 1984 Games, held in Los Angeles (even engaging in insults of its own against the United States, claiming that no right-thinking country would allow their athletes to go to such a smog-ridden and crime-infested city as Los Angeles).

The dispute over the 1980 Olympics demonstrates the degree to which ordinary people and governments alike are extraordinarily sensitive to negative comments about their political community by others. Nothing is surer to get an angry reaction than a foreigner's criticism of some aspect, practice, or feature of an individual's own community.

By the same token, however, the desire for standing may also prompt those actors widely regarded as **pariahs**, or outcasts, to change their behaviour to conform to emerging global norms and expectations. Pariahs can be individuals or entire countries. Thus, for example, slave-traders in the early 19th century were moved to abandon their trade in the face of increasing criticism and changing norms about slavery as an acceptable institution. The same dynamic occurred in the last half of the 20th century with apartheid in South Africa. In the 1950s, the racist policies of apartheid were not universally rejected: one could find people in liberal states, such as the United States, Britain, Australia, and Canada, willing to argue either that apartheid was not such a bad way of dealing with race, or that South African whites should be allowed to pursue their own path on this matter. However, with the passage of time, this support evaporated. By the 1980s, South African whites came to realize that the only people in the world who openly supported the racist policies of apartheid were discredited neo-Nazis from the white supremacist fringe. This overwhelming isolation, it has been argued, speeded the massive change of mind that was so much a feature of apartheid's end in the early 1990s.[19]

Reputation is not only a matter of responding to the perceptions of others. It also involves actors actively trying to cultivate a specific reputation. Nongovernmental organizations (NGOs) try to create different reputations for themselves. As we will see in Chapter 7, Greenpeace, an NGO engaged in pressing environmental issues at a global level, has sought to create a reputation for taking bold, irreverent, anti-establishment, and in-your-face actions in pursuit of its environmental goals. By contrast, Amnesty International, a human rights NGO, has cultivated a reputation for quiet, behind-the-scenes, and diplomatic appeals for victims of human-rights violations. But each NGO, in its own way, has found that its respective reputation has helped to advance its particular goals.

## Beyond the Classic Trio: Independence, Justice, Community

While much of the activity of global actors can be understood by reference to safety, gain, and reputation, the classic trio does not cover all the important goals and objectives of global actors. We need to look at their interests in independence, justice, and community.

### Independence

Actors in global politics seek **independence**. This word has a number of different meanings, all derived from "depend" (itself from the Latin *pendere*, to hang). Independence can mean the quality of being free from the control of others, having the ability to make one's own decisions. It can also mean not relying on anyone else, not being guided or influenced by the opinions of others (i.e., not having to "hang" on others). In the context of world politics, independence usually refers to the ability of a political community to govern itself rather than to be governed by others. The desire to be free of the control of others is related to, but qualitatively different from, the interests in security discussed above. When a community's security is threatened, its independence also tends to be threatened; but threats to independence do not necessarily involve threats to security. Hence we should treat them as separate goals.

As individuals, but particularly in collectivities, people seek to be independent. Examples of communities which have voluntarily and without coercion or duress decided to surrender their independence so that they could be ruled by other peoples are few: the Scottish parliament more or less voluntarily joined England in May 1707; on 29 December 1845, Texans gave up the independence they had gained from Mexico in March 1836 (though it can be argued that the similarities between Texans and those they joined were sufficiently great that this was not a surrender to another political community). In the contemporary era, Puerto Rico and Bermuda have decided as communities (in referenda or in regular elections) not to take up offers of independence.

But these are the few exceptions to an otherwise virtually universal norm that people prefer to govern themselves. "What nation likes to be oppressed by a stronger power?" asks one of the Dead Sea scrolls, written about 2000 years ago.[20] The question is rhetorical, for the answer—if human experience is any guide—must be "No nation." If much of world politics is about the struggle of some to oppress, dominate, and control others, for all the reasons we have surveyed above, then world politics is also about the intense struggle of people eager to escape the rule of others and establish their own independent existence. Certainly fights for independence have cost tens of millions of lives throughout the ages, as we will see in the chapters ahead.

Indeed, the histories of many communities revolve around the story of struggles for independence. From the 12th century until the 1989 elections, Poles suffered seven hundred years of periodic invasions by neighbours near and far, occasional outright elimination through partition, or domination by great powers. The efforts of Vietnamese to secure independence from China date back over two thousand years; in the 19th and early 20th centuries, the struggle was against French colonialism, but the Chinese "menace" was never far from the minds of Vietnamese. Thus, at the end of the Second World War, Ho Chi Minh, a Vietnamese leader, actually invited the French colonial forces back into Vietnam so that they would evict the Chinese troops occupying northern Vietnam. To his critics, Ho was blunt: "Better to sniff a bit of French shit briefly than eat Chinese shit for the rest of our lives."[21] His justification may have been crude, but it underscores nicely the visceral nature of the desire for independence.

*"Better to sniff a bit of French shit briefly than eat Chinese shit for the rest of our lives."*

Often, individuals will willingly die rather than surrender their independence. Consider the Melians, a colony of Sparta, who refused to join the Athenian empire in the great war between Athens and Sparta and their respective allies. In 416 BC, Athens demanded that Melos either surrender or be destroyed. As was usual in ancient Greece, Athenian representatives visited the *polis* of Melos to argue their case. In the ensuing debate, known to history as the **Melian dialogue**, the Athenians argued that "we want you to be spared for the good both of yourselves and of ourselves." The debate went on:

*Melians:* And how could it be just as good for us to be the slaves as for you to be the masters?

*Athenians:* You, by giving in, would save yourselves from disaster; we, by not destroying you, would be able to profit from you.

But in the end, the Melians decided to take their chances fighting, even though the Athenian forces were more powerful:

Our decision, Athenians, is just the same as it was at first. We are not prepared to give up in a short moment the liberty which our city has enjoyed from its foundation for 700 years. We put our trust in the fortune that the gods will send...and in the help of men—that is, of the Spartans; and so we shall try to save ourselves.

But the outcome was never in doubt: the numerically superior Athenians eventually forced the Melians to surrender. They killed every male and sold all the women and children into slavery.[22]

Comparable choices have been made by others. For example, for two years, 1000 Jewish Zealots held the fortress at Masada against a seige by Roman legions. When the Romans finally seized the fort, all but seven of the men, women, and children committed suicide rather than be enslaved by the Romans. When United States forces occupied the Japanese island of Okinawa in June 1945 during the closing stages of the Second World War, many Japanese chose suicide rather than surrender. Hundreds of men and women jumped to their deaths off the cliffs at the southern end of the island, many throwing their children off first, ignoring the frantic pleas not to jump being shouted in Japanese through megaphones by those in U.S. Navy vessels below. The grim and piteous scene was captured on film by U.S. military photographers. There are few more compelling testaments to the power of the idea of independence than those grainy images of hundreds of Okinawans tumbling into the sea to the sound of the entreaties of American sailors below.

## Justice

Economists argue that human beings seek only the concrete and the material; by contrast, political philosophers have long maintained that humans have a much wider and richer array of goals in life. In particular, humans tend to seek justice, or conceptions of the good. They will do this even when it is clearly not in their material or concrete interests to do so. Consider the favourite anecdote of Robert H. Frank, a rogue economist who rejects the dominant perspective of his discipline that seeks to reduce all human motivation to a rational search for concrete gain: Mr Jones owns a $200 leather briefcase; Mr Smith covets the briefcase. Using assumptions of rationality, Smith should simply steal the briefcase he covets so much. If (as economists predict) Jones is motivated by economic rationality, he would not object to the theft, because a calculation would quickly reveal that it would make more economic sense to simply go out and buy another briefcase. The time spent at the police station filling out reports, at the public prosecutor's office going over his testimony, and at court itself would clearly cost Jones far more in lost earnings than $200. Of course, we all know that human beings do not behave like this in the real world. We know that Jones is far more likely to become outraged at Smith's theft, and will spend not only a day's earnings, but a week's if necessary, to get his property back, and to see Smith punished for his wrongdoing.[23]

Frank's vignette reminds us that humans behave in ways that are not at all rational from a purely economistic point of view. It also highlights the importance of justice as an objective for actors everywhere, including at the level of world politics. Even at a cost to their material interests, actors want to see the "right thing" done; they want other actors to behave the "right way"; they want wrongdoers brought to justice.

But the desire of actors to see justice done creates conflict at the level of world politics. Definitions of "right" and "wrong"—in other words, definitions of justice—are always deeply contested, regardless of the level of politics we are looking at. For individuals are prone to come to different conclusions about matters of morality, notions of goodness, and righteous behaviour. Indeed, for political philosophers like Hobbes, that is why words like "right," "wrong," "justice," and "injustice" must be entirely devoid of meaning unless and until there is a "common power"—a Leviathan, a supreme authority, or a government. Hobbes's formula was succinct: without government, "nothing can be Unjust. The notions of Right and Wrong, Justice and Injustice have there no place. Where there is no common Power, there is no Law: where no Law, no Injustice."[24] But with a "common power," these words can be given meaning by defining *through law* what is right and what is wrong; with a common power, there is a means to insist that everyone abide by those laws.

*"Where there is no common Power, there is no Law: where no Law, no Injustice."*

In many political contexts, we do indeed have a Leviathan that makes laws defining wrong and right, and possesses the coercive power to try and impose those definitions on all those people under its authority. But at the level of global politics, there is no institution comparable to local or national governments that is capable of deciding what is right and what is wrong and then imposing its definition of justice on everyone.

Yet the absence of government at the level of global politics in no way dampens the concerns for justice. People push hard to see justice done, and actors, organizations, and institutions at the international level are concerned with the standard of justice. Individuals and governments do not hesitate to express themselves on their views of right and wrong. This has been particularly true on issues like human rights (including women's rights, children's rights, and the rights of aboriginal peoples), the economic and sexual exploitation of children, nuclear proliferation and disarmament, environmental protections of all sorts, slavery, the use of mercenaries, and global poverty.

Moreover, while there is no global Leviathan, nonetheless the search for justice at a global level has been considerably institutionalized. International organizations, such as the United Nations, have proved as willing as individuals to try and articulate commonly held views of justice and rightness on a range of matters. The International Court of Justice (ICJ) seeks to develop and apply the formal rules of the game we looked at above. Governments of countries bring disputes over what is just and unjust to the Court, and panels drawn from 15 judges (elected by the United Nations Security Council) hear cases and render their decisions based on the huge accumulated body of international law that has evolved over hundreds of years.

The ICJ deals only with governments of countries, but the international community also has institutionalized means for dealing with organizations and individuals. For example, those negotiating the Multilateral Agreement on Investment (MAI) in 1997 proposed that multinational corporations should have investment disputes with national governments submitted to panels of judges. Likewise, since 1950, individuals have had access to the European Court of Human Rights; its rulings are widely obeyed by governments of states, even when this has meant changing national laws.[25] The international community has also evolved means of dealing with individuals deemed to be international criminals. After the Second World War, the victorious powers established courts to try individuals accused of crimes against humanity. Following the civil wars in the former Yugoslavia and Rwanda in the 1990s, the United Nations established special International Tribunals to try individuals accused of war crimes.* Indeed, a group of jurists has recommended the establishment of an International Criminal Court (ICC) to deal with individuals accused of a specific range of crimes.

In addition, governments of countries often cooperate with one another in bringing individuals to justice. For example, elaborate rules and treaties govern **extradition**—the movement of those accused of wrongdoing from one jurisdiction to another. Likewise, there is considerable cooperation between police forces, not only through international organizations like Interpol, but also on a bilateral force-to-force basis.

> *"The standard of justice depends on the equality of power to compel...the strong do what they have the power to do and the weak accept what they have to accept."*

It is true that the search for justice at a global level is constrained by the absence of a global Leviathan to define right and wrong and impose that definition on all actors. As a result, the underlying *structure* of the search for justice at the global level has not changed much since Thucydides was writing 2500 years ago. At the outset of the Melian dialogue, discussed above, the Athenians claimed that they would use no "fine phrases" about rights in trying to persuade the Melians to surrender. Instead, they suggested that the Melians "look the facts in the face" and decide how to save their *polis* from destruction. "You know as well as we do," Thucydides had the Athenians say, "that, when these matters are discussed by practical people, the standard of justice depends on the equality of power to compel and that in fact the strong do what they have the power to do and the weak accept what they have to accept."[26]

And so it remains: justice everywhere and at all levels, national and international, is heavily dependent on the "equality of power to compel." We look at power in more detail below, but here it can be noted that the rich and powerful everywhere get a different brand of justice than the poor and marginalized. At the level of national politics, it is why lawyers and brokers who have bilked their clients of hundreds of thousands of dollars continue to drive about in their BMWs, while hard-time prisons everywhere are crowded with the poor who have, by contrast, netted only tiny amounts from their crimes.

At the level of world politics, the same dynamic obtains. The powerful usually manage to evade the mechanisms that exist to enforce rules; the less powerful "accept what they have to accept." Power explains why the individuals accused by the United States of blowing up

---

* The official name of the tribunal for Yugoslavia is the International Tribunal for the Prosecution of Persons Responsible for Serious Violations of International Humanitarian Law Committed in the Territory of the Former Yugoslavia Since 1991; it was established in May 1993. The International Tribunal for Rwanda was set up in November 1994.

Pan Am flight 103 over Lockerbie, Scotland, in December 1988 remain in Libya, while Manuel Noriega Morena, the former president of Panama, languishes in an American jail: Libya successfully resisted American demands that those accused of blowing up Pan Am 103 be extradited; Noriega, by contrast, had the misfortune to be captured by United States forces following the American invasion of Panama in December 1989, and forcibly taken to the United States to face charges of racketeering, drug smuggling, and money laundering.

Power is also why some of the individuals indicted by an international tribunal for war crimes in the former Yugoslavia in the early 1990s, like Radovan Karadzic, former president of the Serb republic in Bosnia, and Ratko Mladic, military commander of the Bosnian Serbs, remain free; while others, such as Dusan Tadic, a Bosnian Serb reservist and café owner, or Drazen Erdemovic, a Croat serving with the Bosnian Serbs, were prosecuted by the tribunal, found guilty, and sentenced to long prison terms for their crimes. Well might Tadic's lawyer describe his client as "a very small fish" when the crime for which he was convicted—slitting the throats of three Bosnian Muslim policemen—is compared with the mass killings of thousands of Bosnian Muslims cited in the indictments against Karadzic and Mladic.

And what is true for powerful individuals is also true for powerful communities. Countries like Cuba, Iraq, Myanmar, Nigeria, and North Korea—all small and relatively marginal actors in the international political economy—are inviting targets for international punishment. However, injustices by countries which are rather more central (and thus powerful) tend to go purposely unnoticed or unchallenged, while calls for justice go unheard.

## Community

If the world is seen in community terms, as I have argued, a logical extension of this is that actors in world politics seek to *create* community in world politics. In other words, as Chris Brown has argued, community becomes a goal of actors in world politics.[27]

Again it bears stressing that this does not refer to the idea of creating a single world-state, with a huge global Leviathan to create (and enforce) one set of laws over all the Earth. However, some support such a political project. For example, the World Federalist movement, begun during the Second World War, draws on the ideas outlined by the German philosopher, Immanuel Kant (1724–1804) in his treatise *Perpetual Peace*. Kant argued that if "one powerful and enlightened nation" started a federal association, one by one other countries would join up until the entire world was one big federation.[28] However, the World Federalists remain a tiny minority; the idea of a world federation commands virtually no support among the world's six billion human beings, for reasons that we will explore in the chapters ahead.

But if most people are not convinced by the idea of a world-state, they appear to be less hesitant about creating a world community. We can see the goal of community manifested in numerous ways, from the persistent efforts to organize, coordinate, harmonize, and regulate different aspects of human activity, to the equally persistent efforts to institutionalize political and economic interactions at a global level.

Indeed, a number of governments have explicitly embraced the notion of encouraging community in their foreign policies. For example, the Australian minister for foreign affairs from 1988 to 1996, Gareth Evans, consistently spoke of the importance of countries being "good international citizens." Likewise, many other smaller countries—often called **middle powers**—have focused their foreign policies on trying to create a sense of community at a global level.[29] The major powers—Britain, China, France, Germany, Japan, Russia—also actively seek to foster community (even if their attachment to community-creation tends to be less eager than it is in smaller countries). Even the government of the world's lone superpower—the United States—demonstrates such a commitment, despite the deep antipathy to the UN and notions of "international community" demonstrated by many Americans.*

### The Pursuit of Goals

In the chapters ahead, we will see how actors in world politics—individuals, groups, communities—try to pursue these six broad goals—safety, gain, reputation, independence, justice, and community. Most actors pursue a combination of these goals at the same time, and often engage in trade-offs between them. No goal is *absolute*, and most actors have a hard time creating a hierarchy of goals (in other words, ranking the goals and, for example, putting safety ahead of justice or independence ahead of reputation).

## A World of Conflict: The Clash of Interests

We have described a number of different goals, values, and objectives—commonly called **interests**—that individuals, groups, organizations, and communities have in world politics. What happens when these multifaceted goals and interests are actively pursued by six billion individuals, either individually or in groups? To answer this question, we need to think about the range of theoretical possibilities.

### The Intersection of Interests

When interests and goals are pursued by human beings, these interests can interact or intersect with one another in four possible ways.

The first possibility is that interests may not intersect at all. They may be **discrete interests**, in the sense that there is no contact between the interests as they are being pursued. For example, if some people have an interest in creating wilderness preservation areas and other people seek to market telecommunication services, it is unlikely that the two groups will intersect as each pursues its interests. There will be a number of "degrees of separation" between them.

---

* Such as Jesse Helms (Republican of North Carolina), the chair of the Senate Foreign Relations committee, who publicly suggested that the United States should withdraw from the UN if the world body did not "reform" to American satisfaction. See Jesse Helms, "Saving the U.N.," *Foreign Affairs* 75 (September 1996); also John Gerard Ruggie, *Winning the Peace: America and World Order in the New Era* (New York: Columbia University Press, 1996), 175.

Interests may complement each other. In other words, while interests may be different, there may be a considerable degree of overlap, and little incompatibility, between them. For example, if some people want to ensure that wilderness areas are preserved to maintain a harmonious natural environment, other people want to reduce deforestation in order to prevent the loss of species, and still others have an interest in lowering greenhouse gas emissions, we can call these **complementary interests**.

Interests may be **convergent**, with varying degrees of similarity that range from *identical* interests to *similar* interests. For example, if two people have an interest in logging, they have identical interests. If one person has an interest in logging and the other has an interest in clearing forest for agricultural development, their interests converge, and both people may be able to pursue their similar interests.

The final possibility is that interests, when they are pursued, may be **conflicting**. Consider again our wilderness preservation enthusiasts and how the pursuit of interests by others could conflict with their desire to pursue their interest. These others could include those who own forests and wish to log them; those who are employed by those logging companies; those who are employed by "downstream" industries which depend on logging, such as the pulp and paper industry; and those who have an interest in clearing forest for agricultural use. None of these groups could pursue their goals and objectives without coming into conflict with the wilderness preservationists.

### Harmonies and Disharmonies of Interest

When this framework is applied to the world level—and to six billion people—we can get some sense of the huge harmonies and disharmonies that are produced by the intersections of interests as people seek their goals. Individuals, groups, organizations, and communities all have their own conceptions of what their interests are, what they think is right and proper and just. Some of those interests will be discrete. One could easily conceive of hundreds of examples where the pursuit of interests by some people will not affect the interests of vast numbers of other humans.

Some of the interests will be complementary or convergent. As we will see, huge complementarities of interest underwrite international politics. Much of the cooperation that we see between individuals, groups, organizations, and political communities is driven by the complementarity of interests of those many actors who crowd the global marketplace. Indeed, that cooperation makes the contemporary international political economy possible. Likewise, we will see that there are deep bonds of complementary and convergent interests between actors both within and between political communities.

But we will also see that a great deal of world politics is marked by conflicts of interest between individuals, groups, and governments. Indeed, some of the disharmonies of interest are exceedingly deep. Consider those communities who claim the same piece of territory: unless they agree to share it, there is simply no way that one can overcome that incompatibility. Alexander Haig, the United States secretary of state, discovered this in April and May 1982, when he tried to negotiate a compromise after Argentina seized the Falkland Islands from the British. Or consider the huge disharmonies in interest that exist between those human beings whose lives are lived in deprivation and insecurity and those who live in luxury and security. Consider the disharmonies of interest about rules of the global game. Whether it be rules about land mines, investments, the "proper" role of women in society, human rights, or the flow of illegal drugs, there is considerable disagreement between individuals, groups, organizations, and communities. This facet directs our attention to conflicts at the global level, their sources, and, most importantly, their resolution.

## GOVERNANCE WITHOUT GOVERNMENT

In many political settings, conflicts of interest between people are mediated by the governing structure of the community. As we saw in the previous chapter, this structure can range from the community elders deciding which side in a dispute is right to the complex institutions of a 20th-century government. But regardless of structure, in all cases governance is designed to decide who is right, who is wrong, and whose interests will prevail. Normally, there is some mechanism to provide the governing structures with the ability to enforce their decisions on the members of the community in conflict.

However, as noted above, world politics occurs in an anarchical setting: there is no "government" of the whole world to enforce the rules of the global game. No global police force arrests offenders and no judicial system ensures that the interests of those in the right prevail.

### The Nature of Global Governance

But just as stateless communities engage in governance, so too does the world community. As we noted in the section on justice above, there are highly institutionalized methods for developing rules of the global game. Likewise, as we noted in the section on community, humans organized into different communities have persistently sought to make decisions on a global basis, and they have tried to resolve the conflicts, disharmonies, and incompatibilities that arise over these rules by fashioning institutions to assist in these efforts. In short, in the words of the Commission on Global Governance, **global governance** is "the sum of the many ways individuals and institutions, public and private, manage their common affairs. It is the continuing process through which conflicting or diverse interests may be accommodated and cooperative action may be taken. It includes formal institutions...as well as informal arrangements that people and institutions have either agreed to or perceive to be in their interest."[30]

### The Tragedy of the Commons and the Global Environment

In particular, we will want to explore how the international community deals with a dynamic known as the **tragedy of the commons**. In 1968, a biologist at the University of California, Garrett Hardin, published a long argument advocating that people give up their "freedom to breed" as a response to the global problems that he believed would come with population increases.[31] His argument about population, however, was grounded in an argument about the use of the "commons," the term given to land in medieval English villages that was set aside for common use, usually pasture where all farmers could send their animals to graze. Hardin noted that the idea of a commons works well enough if the number of animals owned by farmers is less than the "carrying capacity" of the land. But what happens when that carrying capacity is reached? Hardin notes that the benefits to an in-

*But the essence of tragedy is the remorseless and inevitable way in which that calamity unfolds.*

dividual farmer adding one animal to the common far outweighs the negative costs of overgrazing, because those costs are borne by all farmers using the land. Thus the rational farmer will add as many animals as possible. But, as Hardin notes, this conclusion is reached by all farmers. If they are all rational, they will all try to add animals, counting on the costs being borne by the collectivity. The result is that the commons is overloaded and overgrazed.

Hardin termed this a tragedy in two senses, firstly that the commons suffered a disaster. But more importantly, Hardin used the word in its literary sense: a tragedy is a form of drama in which the main character is brought to ruin or suffers extreme sorrow. But the essence of tragedy is the remorseless and inevitable way in which that calamity unfolds: the audience is gripped by an understanding that there is no way out for the central character, no escape from what they understand must be that character's fate.

For Hardin, the "tragedy of the commons" describes perfectly the dynamic of the global environment. All human beings, and each political community to which they belong, are like the farmer: they have every incentive to treat the "global commons" in a way that spreads the negative consequences of their treatment over the entire collectivity. This involves "taking out" of the commons (the way a grazing sheep takes out grass)—extracting non-renewable resources such as oil, gas, and minerals or renewable resources such as trees or fish, and decreasing biodiversity through development, such as urban growth. But it also means spreading the costs of what is "put into" the commons: the pollution, the effluent discharged into the water, and the noxious gases released into the air.

In the case of the global commons, the problem is exacerbated because of population pressures that spring from the reproductive strategy employed by the species *Homo sapiens sapiens*. Without birth control or other limits, a single *Homo* couple is capable of reproducing itself many times over, adding exponentially to the population of the species. Historically, however, population growth among humans was curbed in natural ways: disease, famine, and a hard subsistence existence took an exceedingly heavy toll. Death in infancy was common; childbirth itself involved a high risk of death for both mother and child. But with the progressive eradication of disease, improvements in diet, and other changes in the quality of life, the human population has increased dramatically. The global population, estimated at less than a billion before the 19th century, rose to 1.5 billion by the 1890s, 2 billion by 1930, 4 billion by 1970, and 6 billion by the mid-1990s. From a biological perspective, humans have a spectacularly successful reproductive strategy; in ecological terms, their reproduction poses a serious challenge to the carrying capacity of the ecosystem necessary to support human life.

The tragedy of the commons arises from the fact that the threats posed by overpopulation, overexploitation, and pollution are virtually impossible to deal with in the absence of an authority to dictate the behaviour of individuals in such matters—and the capacity to enforce those decisions. By definition, the globe does not have such an apparatus. Appeals to morality or conscience have limited effects: without the prospect of punishment, there will always be those who follow their interests, exploiting or polluting, and shifting the burden to the collectivity. Thus one is left with only one option: negotiation between the "users" of the commons with an eye to limiting use to the carrying capacity. As we will see in the chapters ahead, global governance also involves the attempts to grapple with this problem.

## CONCLUSION

In this chapter we have fleshed out a multifaceted definition of what politics at a world level involves. We have argued that world politics involves the building of community at a global level, the elaboration of rules of the game, the evolution of economic structures at a world level, and the interplay of different interests among global actors, giving rise to the need for global governance.

One element in the multifaceted definition, outlined in Chapter 3, still needs to be explored. One cannot understand any of the other elements of politics at a global level without examining power, sometimes called the master concept of political science. Power determines what shape global governance takes, which intersecting interests predominate, what economies look like, what rules are elaborated, and what kind of world community is built. We now turn to a consideration of power in world politics.

## *Keyword File*

| | |
|---|---|
| Anarchical society | Reputation |
| Society | Balance of terror |
| Community | Overkill |
| *Gesellschaft* | Strategic Defense Initiative |
| *Gemeinschaft* | *Lebensraum* |
| International law | Welfare |
| *Pacta sunt servanda* | Night-watchman state |
| Localized economy | Welfare state |
| Hanseatic League | Prestige |
| Internationalized economy | Pariahs |
| Globalized economy | Independence |
| Safety | Melian dialogue |
| Gain | Extradition |

Middle powers

Interests

Discrete interests

Complementary interests

Convergent interests

Conflicting interests

Global governance

Tragedy of the commons

## *For Further Exploration*

### HARD COPY

Baldwin, David A. "The concept of security," *Review of International Studies* 23 (January 1997), 5–26.

Barkun, Michael. *Law Without Sanctions: Order in Primitive Societies and the World Community.* New Haven: Yale University Press, 1968.

Buzan, Barry. "From international system to international society: structural realism and regime theory meet the English school," *International Organization* 47 (Summer 1993), 327–52.

Frank, Robert H. *Passions Within Reason: The Strategic Role of the Emotions.* New York: W.W. Norton, 1988.

Hardin, Garrett. "The tragedy of the commons," *Science* 162 (13 December 1968), 1243–48; widely reprinted, for example in David N. Balaam and Michael Veseth, *Readings in International Political Economy.* Upper Saddle River, NJ: Prentice-Hall, 1996, 361–73.

Howard, Rhoda E. *Human Rights and the Search for Community.* Boulder, CO: Westview, 1995.

Onuf, Nicholas G. and Frank Klink, "Anarchy, authority, rules," *International Studies Quarterly* 33:2 (1989), 149–73.

Wolfers, Arnold. "'National security' as an ambiguous symbol," *Political Science Quarterly* 67 (December 1952), 481–502; reprinted in Robert J. Art and Robert Jervis, eds., *International Politics*, 2d ed. Boston: Little, Brown, 1985, 42–54.

### WEBLINKS

**http://www.ecouncil.ac.cr**

Home page of the Earth Council, created by the Earth Summit in 1992

**http://www.isn.ethz.ch/**

Home page of ISN, the International Relations and Security Network, maintained by the Centre for Security Studies and Conflict Research

**http://lawlib.wuacc.edu/forint/forintmain.html**

Site maintained by Washburn University School of Law; links to international law resources, UN documents, and different countries

## Notes to Chapter 4

1. Hedley Bull, *The Anarchical Society: A Study of Order in World Politics* (London: Macmillan, 1977); Barry Buzan, "From international system to international society: structural realism and regime theory meet the English school," *International Organization* 47 (Summer 1993), 327–52.

2. Buzan, "The English school," 333.

3. Rhoda E. Howard, *Human Rights and the Search for Community* (Boulder, CO: Westview, 1995), 25-27.

4. Thucydides, *The Peloponnesian War*, trans. Rex Warner (Harmondsworth, U.K.: Penguin Classics, 1954).

5. Kalevi J. Holsti, *Peace and War: Armed Conflicts and International Order, 1648–1989* (Cambridge: Cambridge University Press, 1991), 45.

6. For a fuller exploration, see Nicholas G. Onuf and Frank Klink, "Anarchy, authority, rules," *International Studies Quarterly* 33:2 (1989), 149–73; F. Kratochwil, *Rules, Norms and Decisions: On the Conditions of Practical and Legal Reasoning in International Relations and Domestic Affairs* (Cambridge: Cambridge University Press, 1989).

7. For a good thumbnail sketch of the politics of the Italian peninsula during the 15th century, see K.J. Holsti, *International Politics: A Framework for Analysis*, 4th ed. (Englewood Cliffs, NJ: Prentice-Hall, 1983), 47–55.

8. See M. Cory and H.H. Sculland, *History of Rome*, 3d ed. (New York: St Martin's, 1976).

9. Thucydides, *The Peloponnesian War*, 80 [76 in original].

10. Thomas Hobbes, *Leviathan, or the Matter, Forme, & Power of a Common-Wealth Ecclesiasticall and Civill* (London, 1651), ed. C.B. Macpherson (Harmondsworth, U.K.: Pelican, 1968), 185 [62 in original].

11. Hans J. Morgenthau, *Politics Among Nations: The Struggle for Power and Peace*, 5th ed. (New York: Alfred A. Knopf, [1948] 1973), chaps. 4–6.

12. Barry Buzan, *People, States, and Fear: An Agenda for International Security Studies in the Post-Cold War Era*, 2d ed. (Boulder, CO: Westview, 1991).

13. David A. Baldwin, "The concept of security," *Review of International Studies* 23 (January 1997), 5–26.

14. See, for example, Arnold Wolfers, "'National security' as an ambiguous symbol," *Political Science Quarterly* 67 (December 1952), 481–502; reprinted in Robert J. Art and Robert Jervis, eds., *International Politics*, 2d ed. (Boston: Little, Brown, 1985), 42–54.

15. For an interesting discussion of nuclear weapons and nuclear deterrence that lives up to the claim in its subtitle, see Leon Wieseltier, *Nuclear War, Nuclear Peace: The Sensible Argument about the Greatest Peril of Our Age* (New York: Holt, Rinehart, and Winston, 1983).

16. See, for example, Richard H. Ullman, "Redefining security," *International Security* 8 (Summer 1983), 129–53; Jessica Tuchman Mathews, "Redefining security," *Foreign Affairs* 68 (Spring 1989), 162–77; J. Ann Tickner, "Re-visioning security," in Ken Booth and Steve Smith, eds., *International Relations Theory Today* (Oxford: Oxford University Press, 1995).

17. For a discussion, see Kim Richard Nossal, "Seeing things? The adornment of 'security' in Australia and Canada," *Australian Journal of International Affairs* 49 (May 1995), 33–47.

18. Hobbes, *Leviathan*, 185 [61 in original].

19. See Audie Klotz, *Norms in International Relations: The Struggle against Apartheid* (Ithaca, NY: Cornell University Press, 1995).

20. Quoted in Morgenthau, *Politics Among Nations*, 36.

21. Quoted in Stanley Karnow, *Vietnam: A History* (New York: Viking Press, 1983), 100.

22. Thucydides, *The Peloponnesian War*, 402, 407.

23. Robert H. Frank, *Passions Within Reason: The Strategic Role of the Emotions* (New York: W.W. Norton, 1988), x.

24. Hobbes, *Leviathan*, 188 [63 in original].

25. See Tina Rosenberg, "Tipping the scales of justice," *World Policy Journal* 12 (Fall 1995), 55–64.

26. Thucydides, *The Peloponnesian War*, 402.

27. Chris Brown, "International political theory and the idea of world community," in Ken Booth and Steve Smith, eds., *International Relations Theory Today* (University Park, PA: Pennsylvania State University Press, 1995), 90–109.

28. For a discussion of Kant, see Michael W. Doyle, *Ways of Wars and Peace: Realism, Liberalism, and Socialism* (New York: W.W. Norton, 1997), 251–300.

29. On middle powers and world politics, see Carsten Holbraad, *Middle Powers in International Politics* (London: Macmillan, 1984); also Andrew F. Cooper, ed., *Niche Diplomacy: Middle Powers in the Post-Cold War Era* (Basingstoke, U.K.: Macmillan, 1997). On Australia and Canada as middle powers, see Andrew F. Cooper, Richard A. Higgott, and Kim Richard Nossal, *Relocating Middle Powers: Australia and Canada in a Changing World Order* (Vancouver: University of British Columbia Press, 1993). On Australia as a good international citizen, see Peter Lawler, "Constituting the good state," in Paul James, ed., *Critical Politics: From the Personal to the Global* (Melbourne: Arena Publications, 1994).

30. Commission on Global Governance, *Our Global Neighbourhood* (Oxford: Oxford University Press, 1995), 2.

31. Garrett Hardin, "The tragedy of the commons," *Science* 162 (13 December 1968), 1243–48.

# C H A P T E R  ⑤

# Power *and*
# World Politics

**I N T R O D U C T I O N**   In Chapter 4, we looked at the elements of community, rules, governance, and conflict in world politics. Critical for notions of governance and the resolution of conflicts over the rules for the global community is power—its possession and its exercise. Much of the discussion in the chapters ahead will demonstrate that power helps explain the crucial differences that human beings experience in their conditions, and the conflicts that arise over the rules that govern the global community. Because power is so important for an understanding of world politics, it is necessary to look briefly at the nature of power and how it is exercised. That is the purpose of this chapter.

## THE NATURE OF POWER

**Power** is best defined as the ability to prevail over others in a conflict of interests—to get what you want when others want something else harmful to your interests. This understanding of power draws on the work of a British sociologist, Steven Lukes. His little book, *Power: A Radical View,*[1] presents an excellent dissection of **power analysis**, an analytical approach that attempts to eliminate what Stanley Hoffmann has called the elusiveness of power.[2] Definitions of power are usually phrased in terms of actor A, actor B and action X. Robert Dahl, for

*For Lukes, power is essentially negative: "A exercises power over B when A affects B in a manner contrary to B's interests."*

example, suggests that "A has power over B to the extent that he can get B to do something that B would not otherwise do."[3] But this formulation is too sloppy: consider the retailer who lowers the price of a product, prompting some people to do what they otherwise would not have done and buy the product. If we characterized the retailer as having "power" over these customers, it would violate the common understanding of the word. Clearly, therefore, power must be more than simply A getting B to do X. That is why Lukes's formulation is so useful. For Lukes, power is essentially *negative*: "A exercises power over B when A affects B in a manner contrary to B's interests."[4] In other words, what characterizes power is the degree to which there is a conflict of interests between the actors. When there is no conflict of interest between actors—when A gets his or her way by affecting B in a manner that is *not* contrary to B's interests—we cannot meaningfully talk about *power* being exercised; rather, getting one's way in such cases is **influence**, not power. Such a view of power also allows us to make important distinctions between the means by which actors are able to prevail in conflicts of interest.

## THE TECHNIQUES OF POWER AND INFLUENCE

Actors have numerous ways to try to get what they want, to ensure that their interests prevail. We can think of these as tools, in the sense that they are useful instruments for getting one's way. These tools include persuasion, inducement, manipulation, coercion, nonforceful sanctions, and force.

### Influence: Persuasion and Inducement

**Persuasion** is the ability to move others to change their conception of their interests so that it aligns with yours. Normally, persuasion involves discussion and argument, in which the superiority of one's logic moves others to change their minds (and hence their definition of their interests). Consider how minds were changed about such issues in world politics as slavery, apartheid, communism, land mines, drift-net fishing, and privatization. In each case, people who were persuaded to change their minds were moved to new ways of thinking by nothing more than exposure to argumentation.

Sometimes people can be moved to change their conception of their interests by an **inducement**—technically, the offering of a reward for doing something that they would not otherwise have done (or not doing what they otherwise would have done). Inducements include bribes offered to break the law; benefits, such as a reduction in price during a sale, as noted above; or concessions offered in a negotiation, where a benefit is offered in one area in return for a concession in another. Normally negotiations are marked by a *quid pro quo* (something for something), an inducement to move one's interests.

It should be stressed that when persuasion and inducement are used successfully, there is no conflict of interest between A and B. When A persuades or induces B to do something

(X) that is in A's interests, by definition it is also in B's interests to do X. (Otherwise, B would not have changed his or her mind or would not have agreed to the inducement.) Hence, when A gets B to do X by persuasion or inducement, *A has not exercised power, but influence.* The same, however, cannot be said about manipulation, one of the more complex tools in the exercise of influence and power.

## Influence and Power: Manipulation

Essentially, **manipulation** is the process by which A ensures that A's interests prevail over B's interests by structuring the environment to make B *think* X is in B's interests. The most common technique of manipulation is lying: if A persuades B to do X, and if A's arguments are based on lies, B was manipulated. The difficulty with manipulation is that we do not really know what B would have decided his interests to be. We often assume that if B knew the truth, he would have decided not to do X; but it must be admitted that B might have done X, even if he knew that A's arguments were based on lies. However, Lukes makes a compelling argument that because A does not give B an opportunity to know he is being lied to—and thus cannot make a calculation of his interests knowing the "real story," as it were—manipulation must be considered a form of power.

## Power: Coercion, Compellence, and Deterrence

**Coercion** involves the use of threats of harm to get one's way. A threatens to harm B either *if* B does X or *unless* B does X. The former is *deterrent coercion*, for A is seeking to deter, or prevent, B from doing something. The latter is *compellent coercion*: A seeks to compel B to do something. In each case, B is moved to comply with A's wishes out of a fear that A will do harm to something B values.

Measuring the success of deterrent coercion (or **deterrence**) is harder than of **compellent coercion**. For example, when the United States government threatened to boycott the Moscow Olympics in 1980 unless the Soviet Union had withdrawn its forces from Afghanistan by 20 February 1980, that is an example of compellent coercion: a harm will be inflicted unless you do what we want and bend to our interests. It was easy to measure the failure of that coercive diplomacy: on 21 February 1980, Soviet troops were still in Afghanistan.

But deterrence is more difficult. State A can issue a threat against State B—"If you cross this line, we will go to war against you"—but if B doesn't cross the line, it doesn't necessarily mean that it was because of A's threat. During the Cold War, did the Soviet Union not try to take over Western Europe because of NATO's soldiers stationed in Europe, or because Moscow did not want to launch such an invasion? Gwynne Dyer, a journalist who advocated Canadian withdrawal from NATO in the 1980s, compared the argument that American and Canadian troops were necessary to deter a Soviet invasion of Europe with the man travelling through Belgium on a train with his umbrella up. A puzzled fellow-traveller asks why he has an umbrella up inside the train. "To keep the elephants away," he replies. "But there aren't any elephants in Belgium," the other remonstrates. "See," the man with umbrella says, "It's working!"[5]

The same uncertainty underlay the balance of terror discussed in Chapter 4. **Nuclear deterrence** during the Cold War was based on mutual threats: each side threatened that if it were attacked, it would respond with a nuclear strike against the other side. But in such an event, both sides would suffer devastating destruction, since each side could survive a surprise attack long enough to launch a counter-strike—at least this is how the scenarios were played out in the surreal world of nuclear planning. Thus, both were mutually deterred from provoking a "hot war" during the Cold War by fear of mutual destruction. This power relationship was nicely captured in the purposely ambiguous acronym MAD, which could mean either **mutual assured destruction** or **mutual assured deterrence**. (MAD also provided a handy double entendre for antinuclear activists who took the view that keeping the peace by threatening hundreds of millions of people with nuclear death was indeed quite mad).

Nuclear deterrence was based on the creation of **terror**, or fear. The use of terror constitutes a special kind of coercion. As we will see in Chapter 7, in our discussion of those actors in world politics who use terror, the threat of violence is used to create fear; frequently, to create fear, violence itself is often used, sometimes (but not always) randomly.

## Nonforceful Sanctions

Coercion involves a threat of harm; the remaining tools—nonforceful sanctions and the use of force—involve the actual application of harm. A distinction is usually made between those harms that do not involve force and those harms in which violence is used. Nonforceful **sanctions** are any form of harm done to things B values: they can include a "time-out" imposed on a misbehaving child; a public denunciation of a wrongdoer; an interruption in the normal flow of economic exchange, such as a boycott or an embargo; a monetary fine or penalty; the loss of liberty involved in a prison sentence; or the loss of rights of membership in a political community that comes with being exiled.

In each case, harm is inflicted on B for a number of different reasons. The harm might be intended to punish B for a past infraction, X, with the idea that B will not do X again. It might also be intended not simply to teach B a lesson for doing X, but to ensure that C, D, and E, who see what happens to B, will not consider doing X.

## Force and Violence

**Force** has been called the *ultima ratio*—the last resort—in human affairs. Using violence against others to get our way is indeed the only technique available after all the others have been tried and failed. If A cannot ensure that his interests prevail over B's by the use of persuasion, inducement, manipulation, coercion, or nonviolent sanctions, then A can try to use force, either by inflicting such violent harms on B that B will be terrorized into surrendering and doing what A wants, or simply by killing B outright, thus solving the problem of B's resistance to A's demands.

Just as persuasion and inducement can never be considered tools of power, so too can coercion, terror, nonviolent sanctions, and the use of force never be considered tools of influence. Unlike persuasion or inducement, which *change* B's conception of interests to align with A's, these tools of power do not change B's interests at all; they only change the degree to which B will bend to A's desires out of fear of some harm. Thus, coercion, nonviolent sanctions, and force can never be anything other than techniques of power, always used by one actor to ensure that his or her interests prevail over another's.

## AUTHORITY IN WORLD POLITICS

Where does authority fit into this discussion? **Authority** is the capacity of A to get B to do X by the simple expedient of ordering him or her to do it. If A has authority over B, A does not have to engage in any of the other techniques. Efforts to persuade, or induce, coerce, or force B are not used; A simply orders B. B may submit to A's authority for a variety of reasons: B may have great respect for A's capacity to make decisions; B may believe that A is entitled to command as a result of occupying a particular position or office; or B may obey because of fears that A will use nonviolent sanctions or force if the orders are not obeyed (but note that in such circumstances, the fears are entirely perceived; A does not actually have to engage in coercion).

For this reason, Lukes rightly notes that authority may be an exercise in either influence or power. It depends on whether or not X is in B's interests. X, by definition, is always in A's interests, but it may or may not be in B's interests to obey. If B does not believe that X is in his or her interests, but nonetheless submits to A's authority (for whatever reason), then we can conclude that A has exercised power over B by using authority.

As we noted in Chapter 3, authority is crucial for the functioning of groups of humans, from families to political communities. It was also noted that usually world politics is conceived of as an environment where authority is simply absent: no one is entitled to command, and no one is obligated to obey. For this reason, political communities normally

*Authority is everywhere evident in the interactions of the numerous actors that crowd the world stage.*

object to being ordered around. For example, the government of the United States could try to assert its authority over the government of Myanmar (formerly Burma) by ordering it to hold free and fair elections. But if Washington tried to do so, the government in Yangon (formerly Rangoon) would reject outright the right of the United States to issue such orders. If the United States wanted the government of Myanmar to behave in a certain way, it would have to resort to other techniques.

But does this mean that authority is absent in world politics? Not at all: authority is everywhere evident in the interactions of the numerous actors that crowd the world stage. It is evident in the governance of the numerous political communities—nation-states and local communities. It is evident in the vast number of organizations—states and state agencies, firms of all sizes, nongovernmental organizations (NGOs), and intergovernmental organizations (IGOs)—that operate in the international sphere.

Moreover, in the chapters ahead we will see that governments of sovereign states, supposedly those most resistant to authority, frequently submit to the authority of international organizations. The governments of the European Union routinely accept the decisions of the EU authorities in Brussels; the governments which are members of the World Trade

Organization routinely accept the decisions of WTO dispute resolution panels; and, as noted in Chapter 4, states routinely accept the findings of the International Court of Justice and the European Court on Human Rights.

To argue, as some do, that authority is lacking at the level of world politics because one does not *have* to accept these decisions is to miss the point about authority: no one at any level, domestic or international, *has* to accept authority if they do not want to. They can simply refuse to obey orders, forcing the "authorities" (who, by the way, lack authority at that point) to try to use other means to secure compliance (such as persuasion, inducement, coercion, sanctions and even force). But the moment that other means must be tried, this is no longer authority. Thus authority rests on an exceedingly thin and fragile basis, and can disintegrate with amazing speed—as many high-school teachers and parents of teenagers have discovered. In the political realm, the disintegration of authority can be no less dramatic: Muhammad Reza Shah Pahlavi, the shah of Iran, was swept from power in 1979 within weeks. A decade later, the communist regimes of Eastern Europe simply crumbled in a comparable fashion. Thus, it is true that governments do not have to comply with authoritative decisions of international organizations; but the fact is that they do. Hence we can meaningfully speak of authority at the level of world politics, even for states.

## THE "TOOLS OF STATECRAFT"

At this point, it should be noted that the instruments discussed above are used by *all* actors in world politics, as we will see in Chapter 7. Individuals and collectivities of all sorts (such as organizations, firms, governments, and states) try to get their way by using the tools of power, influence, and authority. In other words, it is not just governments which engage in persuasion, inducement, coercion, manipulation (subversion, spying, propaganda, disinformation), nonviolent sanctions, and the use of force.

However, when governments use these tools to try to get their way, we give them a special name. Used by governments, these become **tools of statecraft**—in other words, instruments used by states to ensure that their interests prevail. The study of statecraft occupies a special place in the analysis of world politics; a considerable literature has grown up that examines each of these tools.[6]

### Diplomacy and Negotiation

Governments most frequently use the tools of persuasion and bargaining with one another. **International negotiations** occur in countless forums, over a wide variety of issues. Sometimes the negotiations can be informal, such as the routine phone conversations between leaders of countries, sometimes known as **Rolodex diplomacy**; or talks between diplomats in the Delegates' Lounge at the United Nations over the wording of a General Assembly resolution. Sometimes the forum is grand and formal, involving every government in the international community.[7]

### Propaganda

Governments also use a wide variety of **propaganda** tools to persuade or manipulate others. The range of government propaganda is considerable. Mostly it involves **spin-**

**doctoring**—trying to put the best "spin" on one's position. For example, the Canadian government's efforts to combat acid rain in the 1980s included giving pamphlets to visiting Americans that outlined the damage being done to Canada by polluters in the United States. The Australian prime minister tried to influence French opinion by writing articles for French newspapers outlining Australian objections to nuclear testing in South Pacific. But on occasion, propaganda includes outright lying and manipulation, called **disinformation**, a word that entered the language in the late 1930s from the name of the Soviet bureaucracy set up by Joseph Stalin to spread false rumours and lies.

## International Sanctions

**International sanctions**—nonviolent but harmful measures imposed by governments or IGOs against other governments or states—are an immensely popular tool of statecraft. International sanctions are measures that try to disrupt the normal relations between states. They thus come in a wide variety of forms: government bans on trade or investment, seizures of financial or other assets, bans on sporting or cultural contacts, or restrictions on flights in and out of the sanctioned country. Because sanctions are measures aimed against an entire national economy, they end up doing considerable harm to the poorest members of a sanctioned state. As a result, efforts are sometimes made to employ "surgical sanctions" or "smart sanctions" that hit only some groups, particularly the elite rather than the poor. Margaret Doxey has called these **designer sanctions**, to underscore that they are not only designed to act on certain segments of the population, but also targeted against those most likely to be wearing designer clothes.[8]

## War and the Use of Force

On occasion, governments use force to prevail in a conflict of interest in world politics. Again, the spectrum is a wide one. Some uses of force are limited in scope and entirely non-lethal, such as when the Canadian government forcibly arrested the Spanish fishing trawler *Estai* outside Canada's 200-mile limit.[9] Some involve skirmishing, for example, when Soviet and Chinese soldiers fought one another with water cannon in the initial stages of the Ussuri River dispute in 1969. Others involve limited military attacks designed to intimidate or harass, such as the periodic Syrian shelling of Israeli settlements from the Golan Heights (that prompted the Israeli government to keep the Heights after the Six Day War in 1967), or the occasional exchange of artillery fire across the border between India and Pakistan. On occasion, a government will use force simply to punish another government, as China did when it briefly invaded Vietnam in February 1979 in response to Hanoi's mistreatment of Vietnamese of Chinese origin.

Sometimes governments will invade another country to remove a government they do not like: the Soviet Union invaded Hungary in 1956 to remove a reform-minded government and did the same in Czechoslovakia in 1968 for the same reason; in December 1978, Vietnam invaded Cambodia; Tanzania invaded Uganda in April 1979; the USSR invaded Afghanistan in December 1979; and the United States invaded Grenada in October 1983 and Panama in December 1989.

Sometimes force is used to retake land that a state claims has been wrongfully taken from it. India used force to take the Portuguese colony of Goa in 1961; Indonesia seized East Timor from Portugal in December 1975; Argentina took the Falkland Islands in April 1982. Sometimes a state simply seizes territory because it wants to make use of it: in the modern era the signal example is the seizure of Kuwait by Iraq in August 1990, one of only two cases in the post-1945 period where an existing state has been totally extinguished by an invader (the other was Tibet, invaded by China in October 1950).

It is important to realize that the use of force may or may not result in **war**, in which two sides engage in organized violence against each other. Thus, the uses of force in Goa, Timor, Tanzania, Grenada, and Panama did not result in war; the uses of force in Cambodia, Afghanistan, the Falklands, and Kuwait did. Thus, to analyze the use of force, one must look not only at why a government decided to use force in a particular situation, but also at why those against whom force was used either chose not to respond with violence, or chose to fight back, precipitating a war.[10]

## POWER RESOURCES

One reason why we tend to differentiate between the use of influence, power, and authority by governments on the one hand, and by all other actors on the other, is because governments generally have more access to **power resources** than other actors.

In order to exercise influence, power, or authority, one must have resources. To exercise authority, for example, one must have position or office that entitles one to command. But office is neither necessary nor always sufficient for the exercise of authority. Many political leaders exercise widespread authority without actually holding political positions. For example, Chinese communist leaders such as Mao Zedong and Deng Xiaoping commanded great authority but did not occupy a senior office in the Chinese state apparatus; Ruhollah Khomeini, a religious scholar who earned the title ayatollah in the Shi'ite sect of Islam, commanded considerable political authority in Iran, eventually challenging the shah himself. Indeed, the same dynamic is evident everywhere in human groups, from families to large bureaucratic organizations. Likewise, merely holding office does not guarantee authority, as the numerous deposed leaders of states, governments, firms, and organizations will attest.

To use the techniques of influence—persuasion or inducement—one also needs resources, both financial and nonconcrete resources such as rhetorical or leadership abilities. To use coercion, one must have access to even more resources, to ensure that if the target of coercion does not submit from fear of threats of harm, then that harm can actually be applied. Sanctions and force require the most resources of all. To use force, one needs not only the financial resources to equip individuals with the weapons needed to harm and kill others; one also needs to recruit, train, house, provide for, and sustain the morale of these individuals.

It bears mentioning that merely having the power resources does not automatically provide one with power (i.e., the ability to prevail in a conflict of interests). It is common for people to speak of power as the "currency of politics." But the reality is, as David

Baldwin so rightly points out, rather different.[11] Currency is highly *fungible*—in other words, changeable or convertible: indeed, its very purpose is to provide an effective means for exchange. By contrast, power resources in world politics are highly infungible. What A uses to exercise power over B in one area cannot simply be converted (as currency is) to exercise comparably successful power in another area or against other actors. For example, an NGO may discover that its power resources—a mix of solid technical arguments, well-honed public relations capabilities, and a receptive audience—are highly successful in preventing multinational corporation R from investing in country S, in which the government is engaged in human rights violations. But that NGO may discover that when it tries to deter multinational corporation T from investing in country U, it meets with little success. This is particularly true of governments, which have the widest range of power resources at their disposal. An army and an air force, equipped with the state-of-the-art weapons systems, may be a most effective resource against invasion by another state. However, well-equipped armed forces are entirely useless as a means of getting a state to cease subsidizing a protected industry, or getting that state's government to vote in favour of a resolution in the United Nations Security Council.

## THE SPECTRUM OF POWER

One might think of the means by which individuals and collectivities exercise influence and power as existing on a spectrum that ranges from the benign means of persuasion to the lethal tools of force. As one proceeds down the spectrum, however, two important changes occur. The first, and most obvious, is that the costs associated with each tool increases. It costs relatively little to try to move others to your way of thinking (though the costs can mount when one is trying to persuade millions of people). Inducements, by contrast, are slightly more costly, since what people regard as benefits to be traded for changing their conception of interest must of necessity be in short supply. Manipulation is normally a more expensive tool than inducement, since a great deal must normally be spent on the mix of hidden persuasions and inducements necessary for successful manipulation.

It is true that coercion can be done very cheaply. One can threaten to do harm without actually having the means to inflict harm; it is enough for the target of one's coercive efforts to *believe* that one has those means—and thus complies with one's threat—for coercion to be successful. But what if the target calls one's bluff and reveals the emptiness of the threat? Consequently, coercion must normally be backed up by the means to inflict harm—and those resources tend to be expensive.

Finally, the actual infliction of harm—whether by sanctions or the use of force—involves considerable costs. One must be willing to devote considerable treasure to nonviolent sanctions or the use of force. For example, one must be willing to purchase or develop weapons. But the "costs" go well beyond the financial. One must also convince those who apply the force to put themselves in harm's way, which in itself can be hugely expensive.

The second effect is that the predictability of the consequences of using each tool decreases as one moves along the spectrum. If one uses persuasion, for example, the range of outcomes is relatively small: the target of persuasion can say yes or no. But at the more lethal end of the spectrum, employing these tools generally involves a leap into the dark where the range of possible outcomes widens considerably. The use of coercion, sanctions,

*The use of coercion, sanctions, and force sets in motion a sequence of events whose outcome tends to be highly unpredictable.*

and force sets in motion a sequence of events whose outcome tends to be highly unpredictable. For example, as we will see in Chapter 14, those who enthusiastically marched off to war in August 1914 had no idea of what they were setting in train. Likewise, the use of force at Pearl Harbor by the Japanese government in December 1941 brought a reaction from the United States that was, from the Japanese

perspective at least, highly unpredictable. In the Japanese view, the Americans *should not have acted that way*; they should have rolled over in the face of violence and meekly surrendered. As we will see in Chapter 15, the use of force by the North Korean government in June 1950 produced a series of far-ranging consequences that Kim Il Sung, the leader of North Korea, could not have imagined as he gave the order to attack.

## CONCLUSION

In the previous two chapters, I have tried to define world politics in such a way as to be as explicit about the assumptions that might be used to analyze its scope and domain. I have focused in particular on the themes of community, rules, economic structure, conflict, governance, and power. Much of this has been in the form of a preview, for in the chapters that follow we will attempt to flesh out these different elements as they are revealed in the practices of world politics: we will look at the conflicts that divide people; we will

*Figure 5.1* • **THE SPECTRUM OF POWER**

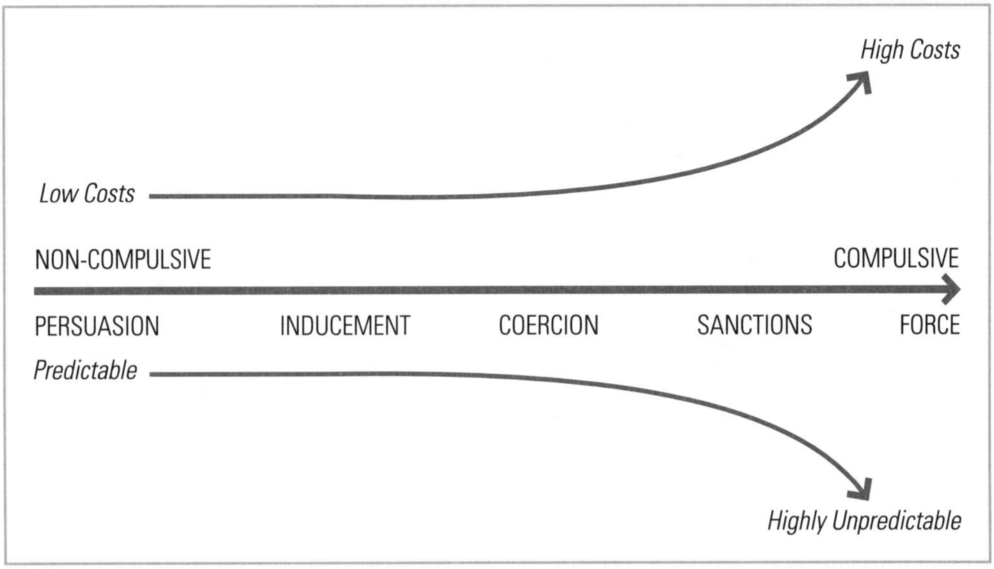

examine how they pursue their interests; and we will determine how the "rules" of the international community are established. But first we have to look at how we analyze world politics, and in particular who the actors in world politics are.

## Keyword File

| | |
|---|---|
| Power | Force |
| Power analysis | Authority |
| Influence | Tools of statecraft |
| Persuasion | International negotiations |
| Inducement | Rolodex diplomacy |
| Manipulation | Propaganda |
| Coercion | Spin-doctoring |
| Deterrence | Disinformation |
| Compellent coercion | International sanctions |
| Nuclear deterrence | Designer sanctions |
| Mutual assured destruction/deterrence | War |
| Terror | Power resources |
| Sanctions | |

## For Further Exploration

### HARD COPY

Baldwin, David A. *Paradoxes of Power*. Oxford: Oxford University Press, 1989.

Craig, Gordon A. and Alexander L. George. *Force and Statecraft: Diplomatic Problems of Our Time*. Oxford: Oxford University Press, 1983.

Doxey, Margaret P. *International Sanctions in Contemporary Perspective*, 2d ed. London: Macmillan, 1996.

Kagan, Donald. *On the Origins of War and the Preservation of Peace*. New York: Doubleday, 1995.

Lukes, Steven. *Power: A Radical View*. London: Macmillan, 1974.

McNeill, William H. *The Pursuit of Power: Technology, Armed Force, and Society*. Chicago: University of Chicago Press, 1982.

### WEBLINKS

### http://nuke.handheld.com/

A good source for all aspects of nuclear technology, including nuclear weapons and nuclear power

**http://www.sipri.se**

Stockholm International Peace Research Institute home page; information on peace and security issues, including nuclear weapons

**http://ssdc.ucsd.edu/ssdc/conf.html**

University of California, San Diego; Studies for Conflict, Aggression, and War home page

## Notes to Chapter 5

1. Steven Lukes, *Power: A Radical View* (London: Macmillan, 1974).

2. Stanley Hoffmann, "Notes on the elusiveness of modern power," *International Journal* 30 (Spring 1975), 184–87.

3. Robert A. Dahl, "The concept of power," in Roderick Bell, David V. Edwards and R. Harrison Wagner, eds., *Political Power: A Reader in Theory and Research* (New York: Free Press, 1969), 80; Hoffmann, "Elusiveness of modern power," 188.

4. Lukes, *Power*, 27.

5. See, for example, Tina Viljoen and Gwynne Dyer, "Neutrality: a choice Canada can make," *Compass* 5 (January 1988), 6–8.

6. For an excellent survey of these techniques, see Kal J. Holsti, *International Politics: A Framework for Analysis*, 7th ed. (Englewood Cliffs, NJ: Prentice Hall, 1995), chaps. 6–10.

7. See Fred Iklé, *How Nations Negotiate* (New York: Harper Row, 1964); Gilbert Winham, "Negotiation as a management process," *World Politics* 30 (October 1977), 1–20.

8. See Margaret P. Doxey, *International Sanctions in Contemporary Perspective*, 2d ed. (London: Macmillan, 1996); Kim Richard Nossal, *Rain Dancing: Sanctions in Canadian and Australian Foreign Policy* (Toronto: University of Toronto Press, 1994).

9. This case is explored in Andrew F. Cooper, *Canadian Foreign Policy: Old Habits and New Directions* (Scarborough, ON: Prentice Hall Allyn and Bacon Canada, 1997), chap. 4.

10. On war and the use of force, see Gordon A. Craig and Alexander L. George, *Force and Statecraft* (New York: Oxford University Press, 1983); Kalevi J. Holsti, *Peace and War: Armed Conflicts and International Order, 1648–1989* (Cambridge: Cambridge University Press, 1991); Donald Kagan, *On the Origins of War and the Preservation of Peace* (New York: Doubleday, 1995).

11. David Baldwin, "Money and power," *Journal of Politics* 33 (August 1971), 578–614.

# "Inside" *and* "Outside": Analyzing World Politics

Chapter 3 argued that politics at the world level should logically be concerned with the same phenomena as politics at other levels. This is a relatively uncommon view. More commonly, "world politics" is seen as occurring in a completely different sphere than politics at other levels. Politics at other levels is known as "domestic" politics—the politics *within* the different communities that dot the globe. Politics *between* these different communities, by contrast, is said to be fundamentally unlike domestic politics. R.B.J. Walker has demonstrated the important philosophical implications of making such a dichotomous distinction between politics "inside" and politics "outside." In the **inside/outside dualism**, domestic politics—"inside" the political community—envisages the possibility of law, justice, and social progress. By contrast, international politics—or politics "outside"—is actually the *negation* of the political. Using the kind of misconstrued notions of anarchy examined in Chapter 3, international politics becomes just the endless and repetitive clash of wills in which neither justice nor progress is possible.[1]

However, constructing domestic politics/world politics as an inside/outside dualism also has empirical implications—in other words, it affects how we *analyze* politics "inside" and "outside." In this chapter, I want to look at how we create "insides" and "outsides" when we look at world politics, and examine the way in which seeing politics "inside" and "outside" affects our analysis of how politics works itself out globally and locally.

## ANALYZING POLITICS "INSIDE" AND "OUTSIDE"

Although politics at a world level should logically be analyzed using the same framework for analysis that we use to analyze politics at other levels, we tend to treat politics at a world level differently. We use one set of assumptions to analyze politics *within* political communities, and entirely another set of assumptions to analyze politics at the world level.

### "Inside": Assumptions of Pluralism and Contention

When we analyze **domestic politics**, we commonly focus on division and pluralism within the community; on conflict between different groups; and on the exercise of power, influence, and authority among the different individuals and groups that comprise the political community. In other words, our analysis assumes that the politics of the community is about the interaction of the *individuals* and *groups* that comprise the community. Our analysis examines the often sharp **political cleavages** that appear *within* political communities because of the different attributes of the human beings residing within those communities. Thus we look at the political impacts of cleavages based on age, gender, marital status, sexual orientation, tribe, ethnicity, race, national background, language, accent, dialect, religious beliefs, political views, caste group, class, occupation, region, and education. Analyzing any one of these attributes—and more commonly a complex of them—is necessary to make sense of politics within a community. While some cleavages are important in all communities—age and gender, for example—the salience of the cleavages varies with the polity and the historical period.

In most communities, there are differences between those who live in cities and those who live on and work the land, raising crops or livestock, or who are engaged in other primary pursuits, such as mining, logging, or fishing. Sometimes that urban/rural cleavage leads to conflict. Occasionally it may even lead to the kind of genocidal war between town and country that we saw in Cambodia in the 1970s, when under the leadership of Pol Pot, the poor rural peasant soldiers of the Khmer Rouge tried to abolish the cities that they blamed for their poverty. All of Cambodia's cities were evacuated. Their residents were forced at gunpoint into massive marches into the countryside, which, not surprisingly, was unable to sustain such large numbers. Hundreds of thousands of Cambodian city-dwellers died as a result.

In most communities, contending religious beliefs are a source of division that play themselves out in numerous and often subtle ways in the politics of the community. While tolerance of religious differences has been a frequent feature of politics, religious intolerance is just as widespread. In numerous instances people have been killed because of their religious affiliation or beliefs: the Huguenots in France or Calvinists in the Netherlands in the 1570s; Catholics in Ireland in the 1650s; Baha'is in Persia in 1852; Jews in central Europe in the 1940s; animists in southern Sudan or Sikhs in India in the 1980s; Shi'ite Muslims in Iraq or Muslims in the former Yugoslavia in the 1990s. Some communities have been periodically rent by bloody clashes: Muslims and Hindus in India, or Catholics and Protestants in Northern Ireland, or Sunni and Shi'ite Muslims in Pakistan. Other communities are divided by rival interpretations of the same set of beliefs. Thus Jews in Israel are divided over religious observance, and in predominantly Muslim Algeria, a grisly war of assassination and civilian slaughter erupted after the army cancelled the 1992 elections that was about to bring the Islamic Salvation Front to power.

Not all attributes are politically important everywhere. Caste group politics exist in India but not in New Zealand; one's accent is more important in England than in Australia; tribal affiliation is important in Nigeria and Sudan, but not in the Netherlands or Sweden; language is political in Belgium and Canada but not in Japan; ethnicity remains political in South Africa or Fiji but not in Iceland; race suffuses politics in the United States, but is not an issue in Thailand. Some societies may be cleaved by profound regional differences, while others may be cleaved by competing nationalisms. Some variations may be quite idiosyncratic: for example, in most communities, variation in eye and hair colour has little political significance; but for the Nazis during the Third Reich in Germany from 1933 to 1945, these attributes served as an important mechanism for discrimination.

In short, when we analyze "domestic" politics, we tend to look for the political fault lines based on attributes that differentiate individuals; we have no difficulty in conceiving politics "inside" the political community in highly fragmented terms.

## "Outside": Assumptions of Singularity and Unity

At the global level, an interesting transformation tends to occur in our analysis. The contentions and cleavages that are so important in analyzing "domestic" politics simply disappear; the political community becomes, almost as if by magic, a united singularity, a single actor, speaking with one voice. We focus on the **foreign policy** of each state, in others words examining the actions of each government in the international sphere. World politics—the politics "outside"— is then analyzed as if it were occurring between these singular political actors. In this view, the political realm is reduced from the interactions of the six billion human beings who inhabit the planet to the foreign policies and interactions of approximately 190 political communities that we call states.

*In this view, the political realm is reduced from the interactions of the six billion human beings who inhabit the planet to the foreign policies and interactions of approximately 190 political communities that we call states.*

## The Convenience of Code

Our tendency to think about the politics of individual states in the singular stems in part from our use of codes, a type of shorthand to describe phenomena around us. We tend to think—and talk—about countries in terms that are either *reified* (treating these abstractions as though they were concrete or material) or *personified* (treating them as though they were persons). We attribute human emotions to countries (Germany was angered, France was pleased, Britain was hopeful); we attribute actions to countries (Iraq invaded Kuwait, Britain handed Hong Kong back to China); we attribute attributes to countries (China is powerful, Mongolia is remote, Lesotho is weak). We use capital cities to mean countries (Beijing negotiated with Moscow, Stockholm changed its position) or international organizations ("Brussels" to mean the European Union, for example). We even use buildings, addresses, and nicknames—such as "the White House"—as shorthand, or **metonyms**, the technical term for such figures of speech (see Focus on p. 105).

A moment's reflection reveals how impossible much of our shorthand code is if taken literally: sentences like "France was pleased" or "Stockholm changed its position" do not make any sense. Likewise, for "Iraq"—434 000 square kilometres of territory and 21 million people—to "invade" "Kuwait"—17 800 square kilometres and 1.7 million people— would be a geological, geopolitical, and sociological impossibility.

Of course, we all know that such sentences are not to be taken literally; that this is shorthand for a more complex reality. We know that "the White House" really means "the individual who occupies the office of the president of the United States or anyone authorized to speak in the president's name." Likewise, we know that "Iraq invaded Kuwait" is a more economical, even if less precise, way of saying: "Saddam Hussein, the leader of the governing apparatus of the political community we call Iraq, issued orders to soldiers of the organization known as the Iraqi army to travel to Kuwait City, detain or kill those individuals

"Westminster" is the shorthand code used to refer to the British Parliament.

## FOCUS

### IR Code: Buildings, Place Names, and Addresses as "Metonyms" or Shorthand

| Name/Address | Shorthand code for: | | |
|---|---|---|---|
| The Kremlin | Russian government | Elysée Palace | French president's office |
| The White House | in Russia, the legislature; in the United States, the president's residence or the presidency | Quai d'Orsay | French foreign ministry |
| | | 10 Downing St | British prime minister's residence |
| Capitol Hill | U.S. Congress | Whitehall | British government offices |
| The Pentagon | U.S. Department of Defense | Westminster | British Parliament |
| Langley | U.S. Central Intelligence Agency | Los Pinos | Mexican president's office |
| Foggy Bottom | U.S. Department of State | 24 Sussex Drive | Canadian prime minister's residence |
| Zhongnanhai | The walled park in central Beijing where all senior officials live: i.e., the Chinese leadership | Pearson Building | Canadian foreign ministry |
| | | The Lodge | Australian prime minister's residence |
| Die Kanzlerei | (The Chancellory) German chancellor | Casey Building | Australian foreign ministry |

who called themselves the government of Kuwait, take control of the government buildings, establish positions of control in the city, and shoot anyone who shows any opposition; these orders were obeyed and successfully carried out."

While this reductionism is entirely understandable—imagine how long the nightly news would take to read without metonyms—it often obscures some important realities of politics at a global level. Recall the discussion of security in Chapter 4, and the difficulty of combining numerous individual patterns of security and insecurity into a single conception of "national security." The same process occurs with the use of code. Code fuses, for example, the one billion people living in India and the 270 million people living in the United States into two single political entities. It rumbles, steamroller-like, over the sharp divisions occurring *within* political communities that can have an impact on global politics; instead, the steamroller flattens each political community into a nice seamless unity that can then "act" in the singular in international affairs.

### Steamrolling Countries: A Comparison

Such a steamroller approach deeply affects how we analyze world politics. Consider the two political communities mentioned above, India and the United States, and reflect on how we usually see these two supposedly single-entity actors in world politics. Flattened down, this thing we call the "United States" becomes "rich," "secure," "powerful," the "world's only superpower"; this thing we know as "India," by contrast, is seen as "poor," "insecure," "weak," and a "regional power" at best.

If we see these countries as united singularities in this fashion, our vision becomes seriously distorted, for we overlook the deep cleavages *within* each of these communities. Divisions of race, wealth, language, religion, caste grouping, and ideology make the idea of singularity exceedingly problematic. We overlook the paradox that while "the United States" might be considered secure and rich as a political community, the day-to-day reality for

> *We overlook the paradox that while "the United States" might be considered secure and rich as a political community, the day-to-day reality for millions of Americans is that they are not at all rich or powerful or secure.*

millions of Americans is that they are not at all rich or powerful or secure. On the contrary: millions of Americans live in grinding poverty; the lives of many Americans are marked by powerlessness and marginalization; many are caught in an underclass existence of welfare dependence, gang warfare, crime, crack addiction, and an almost casual disregard for human life; and many Americans, both rich and poor, live in considerable day-to-day insecurity that comes with having one of the highest murder rates in the developed world. By the same token, we may regard India as "poor," but the reality is that many Indians are exceedingly rich. Indeed, India's burgeoning middle class numbers approximately 260 million—close to the entire population of the United States. And the rich of Delhi, Calcutta, or Madras are probably more secure than those Americans who drive home at night to their wealthy gated communities in Miami, Houston, or Los Angeles, their Second Amendment .38 Specials tucked into their glove compartments. Statistically at least, one is less likely to be shot to death in India than in the United States.

Moreover, considerable similarities between the two communities are hidden by a single-entity perspective. Those Americans who live in the bleak decrepitude of Chicago's public housing projects, sleep in cardboard cartons tucked under the El, or eke out a living squeegeeing windshields in the shadow of the Wrigley Building, have lives not much different from those Indians who live in areas like Mumbai's Dharavi district, often called the worst slum in Asia. Many in the United States who happen to be Hispanic or African American face discrimination in their daily lives not dissimilar to that encountered by members of the *dalit*, or "untouchable," caste groups in India, whose very presence is considered to be polluting by many of those belonging to putatively "higher" caste groups.

Or consider the militia movement in the United States. Groups such as the Michigan Militia Corps, the Militia of Montana, and the Aryan Nations refuse to accept the authority of the federal government in Washington. This view has prompted many militia members to wage a sporadic war against that government, such as the bombing of the federal building in Oklahoma City in April 1995 that killed 168 people. This is not dissimilar to the Hindu supremacist group, *Rashtriya Swayamsevak Sangh* (RSS—National Volunteer Corps), whose members do not accept the legitimacy of the government in New Delhi. The RSS refused to accept the partition of the subcontinent and remains committed to the suppression of Muslims. On 13 January 1948, one of its members, Nathuram Godse, was implicated in the assassination of India's foremost advocate of independence, Mohandas Gandhi. Members of the RSS destroyed a mosque in Ayodhya in 1992, sparking communal riots across India. Hit squads said to belong to the RSS operate in a number of Indian cities, targeting Muslims: in Mumbai in 1993, 1400 Muslims were killed by Hindu hit squads. On a number of occasions, the RSS has been banned by New Delhi for allegedly trying to overthrow the government.

In short, erasing domestic politics and presenting political communities as singular entities creates a certain blurring of analytical vision. It not only obscures differences and similarities between communities, but it also blinds us to the important analytical implications of seeing politics in holistic terms, rather than inside/outside terms.

## LOCAL DIVISIONS, GLOBAL POLITICS

When analyzing politics at the international level, we should be sensitive to the kinds of cleavages that we see on the "inside": gender, class, ethnicity, religion, and so on. A focus on the attributes that divide individuals *within* communities can also help explain divisions and similarities *between* communities, as the following examples of gender and age suggest.

### Gender

Focusing on gender divisions *within* states helps us understand why so much of world politics is so deeply gendered. The gendered nature of world politics comes in a number of forms. First, in a most basic sense, politics works in ways that leave women in an unequal position to men. The **gender inequality** is both global and national. As the United Nations Development Program (UNDP) put it succinctly, "no society treats its women as well as its men."[2] Globally, female access to education and literacy rates are well below those of males. In some societies, female children are less valued than males; in China, for example, where the state disapproves of more than one child per family, there have been reports of girls being killed so that parents can try again for a male. In affluent countries of the industrialized world and nonaffluent countries alike, men receive the larger share of income and recognition for their economic contributions. Most women's work in the **formal economy**—those economic activities that are counted by national statisticians—remains undervalued. Virtually all women's work in the **informal economy**—the economic

*"In most societies in the world, [women] first feed the men, then their children; only then do they eat what—if anything—remains."*

activities that tend not to be "counted"—remains invisible. Much of their work is unpaid and unrecognized. Unpaid work can include child-rearing, food-gathering and/or production, fuel-gathering, caring for the sick and/or the elderly, and other time-consuming work necessary for the maintenance of a household, such as cleaning and laundering. Moreover, even when women are employed in the paid labour market they generally play a double role, performing more than an equal share of household and domestic activities, such as child-rearing, shopping, food preparation, cleaning and laundering.

Gender inequality tends to be more pronounced in poorer countries, particularly in the pattern of intrahousehold food distribution which often favours men over women. "In most societies in the world," Catherine Bertini, executive director of the UN World Food Program (WFP), has written, "[women] first feed the men, then their children; only then do they eat what—if anything—remains."[3] Moreover, the tendency of women and girls to eat last—and least—affects not only women who are pregnant or lactating, but also their fetuses and infants, whose health is seriously at risk because of the malnutrition of their mothers.[4]

As gender politics have become more important in domestic politics in some countries, gender issues have increasingly made their way to the international agenda. A generation ago, there was virtually no international discussion of women's issues, either in the study of international relations or its practice. Today, by contrast, there is a burgeoning IR literature, as we noted in Chapter 2. That literature explores the gendered nature of the IR discipline, including empirical issues such as the impact on women of the location of military bases or the use of particular ports for R&R (rest and recreation); the impact of the World Bank's structural adjustment programs (SAPs) on women; or the gendered effects of international sanctions.[5] (Sanctions normally disrupt supplies of food, fuel, and medicines, affecting what in many societies is predominantly a female sphere of activity.)

In addition, feminist issues such as demands for a Japanese apology for the enslavement of some 200 000 Koreans as "comfort women"—as the Japanese imperial army euphemistically called them—for troops during the Second World War; the widespread use of rape as a weapon of war, particularly in the former Yugoslavia in the 1990s; and the thriving international market in prostitution have all been raised at the international level.[6] Likewise, international organizations have paid increasing attention to women's issues since the early 1970s: a UN Decade for Women was declared in 1975, and in 1981 the Convention on Elimination of All Forms of Discrimination Against Women (CEDAW) came into force. An International Women's Year conference was held in Mexico City in 1975, a review conference in Nairobi in 1985, and a United Nations Conference on Women in Beijing in 1995. Women have received greater attention in development projects and programs. However, for all this increased attention and concern, Kathleen Mahoney argues that there has been a "significant lack of measurable progress for women worldwide."[7]

Finally, world politics are gendered in the sense that, by and large, women are simply not players in the processes that determine international politics. Although women constitute half of the species, one would never know it looking at global politics. Governments of states are overwhelmingly dominated by males. In many countries women are not even represented around the cabinet table, and often when they are, they are given highly gendered portfolios like "women's affairs" or "childcare." Most leaders in the international system are male, although a number of women have risen to positions of national leadership in the last 50 years. These include Sirimavo R.D. Bandaranaike in Sri Lanka, Golda Meir in Israel, Isabel Martínez de Perón in Argentina, Indira Gandhi in India, Margaret Thatcher in Britain, Vigdis Finnbogadottir in Iceland, Gro Harlem Brundtland in Norway, Corazon Aquino in the Philippines, Benazir Bhutto in Pakistan, Mary Robinson in Ireland, Violeta Barrios de Chamorro in Nicaragua, Begum Khaleda Zia in Bangladesh, Kim Campbell in Canada, Tansu Çiller in Turkey, Biljana Plavsic in Republika Srpska (the Bosnian Serb republic), and Jenny Shipley in New Zealand.

Likewise, a number of women have been appointed foreign ministers and thus responsible for their country's international relations: Janet Bostwick in Bahamas, Billie Miller in Barbados, Flora MacDonald and Barbara McDougall in Canada, Maria Emma Mejia in Colombia, Tarja Halonen in Finland, Gladys Sánchez de Vielman in Guatemala, Claudette Werleigh in Haiti, Susanna Agnelli in Italy, Roza Otunbayeva in Kyrgystan,

Andrea Willi in Liechtenstein, Gabriele Gatti in San Marino, Danielle de St Jorre in Seychelles, Lena Hjelm-Wallén in Sweden, and Madeleine K. Albright in the United States. But set against the universe of political leaders and foreign ministers in 190 countries over the last five decades, these are relatively small numbers.

The numbers get even smaller, relatively speaking, when one looks at the diplomatic officials that keep the wheels of interstate relations turning—the ambassadors and their staffs that 190 countries send abroad to other countries and to international organizations. The world of interstate diplomacy is predominantly male. As well, women are deeply underrepresented in the senior ranks of the world's international organizations, the world's major corporations, and other nongovernmental organizations in international affairs.

Much of the invisibility of women's concerns or of women themselves is a function of how gender politics plays itself out differently within different communities. Women will be less visible at the international level if they are less visible at the national level. Likewise, differences in the development of gender politics within political communities may also have an important impact on how an issue may play out internationally. A good example is the practice in some Islamic communities in Africa and the Middle East of performing **female genital alteration** on young girls before or at puberty—most commonly the excision of the clitoris (clitoridectomy), but also the removal of some or all of the external genitalia and labial tissue (infibulation), and even in some instances the sewing up of the vaginal opening. This traditional ritual, which the World Health Organization estimates has been performed on 100 million women worldwide, is designed mainly to permanently remove sexual desire (thus increasing the chastity of women both before and after marriage); partly to be able to demonstrate an unmarried woman's chasteness (thus increasing the "bride price" often paid at marriage); and partly for aesthetic reasons. In some countries, these ritual genital alterations are performed in less than sanitary conditions; as a result, infection and death are common.

This practice generates considerable difference of opinion in the international community. In the industrialized world, the practice is almost universally condemned as a ritual designed purely for the benefit, pleasure, and interests of men—a "cruel and barbaric practice" was how the Federal Court of Canada put it in 1995 when it upheld the right of a Ghanaian woman to seek refugee status on the grounds that she faced genital alteration if she returned to Ghana. The elimination of sexual pleasure is decried as the removal of an essential part of being human. The terms "female circumcision" or "genital alteration" are denounced as euphemistic; the term of choice is "genital mutilation," which underscores the essential difference between this practice and other forms of (often painful) alteration of the human body that are designed to enhance beauty (such as piercing, neck rings to elongate the neck, lip plugs, or scarification).

However, when women's groups from the industrialized world projected their anger over this ritual into the international sphere in the 1980s, demanding an end to the practice and the "liberation" of women's sexuality, women's groups from Islamic countries strongly rejected these demands and denounced women's groups from Europe and the United States as imperialists for trying to impose their morality on others.

By the early 1990s, women's groups from the industrialized world had changed tack: they decided to focus on the health risks posed by female genital alteration rather than portraying it as an issue of sexuality. The result was that many more women's groups from Africa and the Islamic world joined the call for an end to the practice. In some countries the issue has been put on the national agenda. In Egypt, in response to a campaign organized by the Egyptian Organization for Human Rights, the minister of health, Ibrahim Sallam, issued a decree banning the practice in 1996. The ban aroused the anger of doctors (who perform the operations). It has provoked a debate between those Muslims who argue that the Prophet Muhammed favoured the practice, and those, such as Muhammed Sayyed Tantawi, the head of the al-Azhar Institute, who argue that the saying of the Prophet in question is unauthenticated and that the practice is therefore un-Islamic. The case has made its way to the Egyptian courts: a lower court ruling in June 1997 that the ban was illegal was subsequently overturned by a higher court.

## Age

An "age-ist" analysis of world politics focuses on how intergenerational politics affects international relations. War and the issue of age provide a good example. Although wars are inevitably started by older members of the community, it is the young who tend to make up the bulk of regular armies, and it is the young who tend to die in the largest numbers when those armies go to war.* Millions of young soldiers were killed in the various major wars of the 20th century or in the hundreds of other smaller wars, *coups d'état*, skirmishes, and battles. The young have always served as cannon fodder (as infantry began to be known in the late 19th century). Occasionally they are used in self-consciously brutal ways by their high commands: during the Iran-Iraq war of 1980–88, for example, young Iranian boys, inspired by the belief that death on the battlefield would lead them immediately to the rewards of heaven, marched into the minefields protecting Iraqi positions, acting as human mine-sweepers and thus clearing the way for regular soldiers advancing behind them.

Youths are often just as important for irregular armies. The Khmer Rouge armies that swept out of the Cambodian jungles in 1975, seizing the cities and evacuating them by force, killing hundreds of thousands in the process, were dominated by young boys. The *mujahideen* who fought Soviet troops in Afghanistan in the 1980s recruited both girls and boys to its ranks. Many of the soldiers who marched through Zaire in 1997, forcing Mobutu Sese Seko from power, were teenagers.

Young people also tend to be at the forefront of political violence (to be contrasted with the criminal violence of youthful gangs, which generally does not have any overt political

---

\* Indeed, in most jurisdictions "age of majority" laws tend to be an illogical and inconsistent jumble. There are different "ages" for having sex legally, getting married, leaving school, buying cigarettes, getting conscripted into the military, consuming alcohol, working full-time, driving a car, being prosecuted for a crime in adult court, and voting. In some jurisdictions, it is possible for young people to be conscripted to die for their country two or three years before they are legally allowed to drink alcohol.

content). Sometimes this political activity is organized and encouraged by adults; sometimes it occurs despite the opposition of adults. The Red Guards, a youth organization of the Chinese Communist Party, carried out much of the political violence of the Cultural Revolution in China between 1966 and 1969, during which thousands of "rightists" were killed. During the "Troubles" in Northern Ireland, young people on both sides of the Protestant/Catholic divide have always been actively involved, often opposing equally youthful British soldiers. During the unrest that broke out in the townships of South Africa in the mid-1980s, teenagers enthusiastically engaged in the "necklacing"* of informers or collaborators. In the Palestinian *intifada* ("uprising") in the territories occupied by Israel in the late 1980s, children as young as nine or ten participated in the demonstrations against Israeli troops, throwing stones and taunting soldiers. In Sierra Leone, young soldiers staged a *coup d'état* in April 1992, bringing to power Capt. Valentine Strasser, at 27 the world's youngest head of state. Youthful exuberance at having seized the state manifested itself in a variety of ways—for example, soldiers reportedly took the government fleet of Volvos, BMWs, and Mercedes out on joyrides and purposely wrecked them.[8]

The young, in short, tend to be highly visible in these violent spheres. But their roles tend to be deeply age-determined. As a rule, governments are dominated by older people. Leaders in most countries tend to be in their fifties or sixties, making someone like Strasser in Sierra Leone a clear exception. More importantly, young people are rarely included in the councils where the elders of a community decide the questions of war and peace that determine whether the country's young will be put in harm's way. By the same token, it has become relatively rare for the elders of a community to participate in actual war-fighting. Numerous medieval European kings lost their lives on the field leading soldiers into battle; few leaders of contemporary states actually fight—the fantasies of *Independence Day* or *Air Force One* notwithstanding.

The issue of **child labour** provides another illustrative example of how age manifests itself in world politics. In most pre-industrial societies, children joined their parents in agricultural production, hunting/gathering, or cottage production as soon as they could perform simple tasks. With industrialization in the latter part of the 18th century came the employment of children in factories and in mines. The conditions of that industrial work led to increasing efforts by the state in both Britain and the United States to regulate the labour of children, though it was not until 1878 that the minimum age of employees in Britain was raised to 10, and not until the early 1940s that the United States finally managed to pass comprehensive child labour legislation. However, changing norms about children—that they should be educated in a universal, publicly funded school system and that employment, particularly employment in manufacturing or hazardous occupations, should not interfere with that education—spread rapidly throughout the industrialized world. A key actor in the spread of these norms has been the International Labour Organization, an

---

* The "necklace" is a car tire, filled with gasoline, jammed down over the victim's shoulders, and set alight. Death comes slowly, the victim succumbing to a combination of burns from flame and melting rubber, and asphyxiation from acrid smoke.

international body established in 1919. Members of the ILO have passed a number of conventions covering such issues as minimum age for employment and the regulation of night work.

The spread of these norms about children has not been universal, however, as Figure 6.1 shows. In many communities, the income provided by children's employment remains integral for family survival. The problem is particularly acute in many industrializing states, where there is often a powerful incentive for parents, employers, and governments to turn a blind eye to the international conventions of the ILO, and where very young children are involved full-time in carpet-weaving, match-making, and other strenuous work.

Child labour issues of a different kind are evident in the persistence of female bondage. Much of the **sex trade** in very young girls is driven by the tendency of many to regard their daughters as chattels—goods to be sold or traded on the open market. For example, many of the prostitutes in the brothels of Bangkok frequented by "sex tourists"—mostly middle-aged men from Japan, Europe, Australia, and North America—are very young village girls who have either been sold outright to sex-traders, or "leased" into bondage, by their own

*Figure 6.1* • **"ECONOMICALLY ACTIVE CHILDREN": CHILD LABOUR IN SELECTED COUNTRIES**

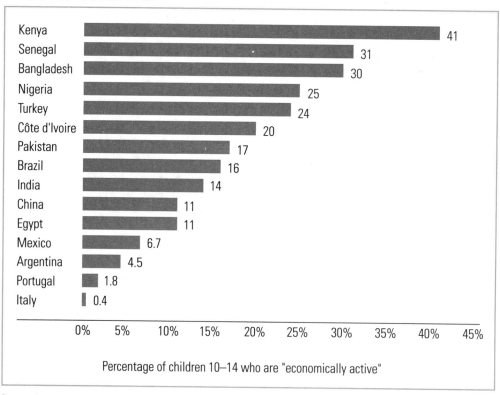

Percentage of children 10–14 who are "economically active"

Source: International Labour Organization, *Child Labour: Targeting the Intolerable* (1997); UNICEF, *State of the World's Children, 1997* (New York, 1997), http://www.unicef.org

parents. Likewise, some Ewe families in Ghana continue the practice of atoning for crimes committed by a family member by giving one of the family's young girls to a religious shrine, assigned to a priest as a *trocosi* ("slave of the gods"), to be used as the priest wishes and only to be freed if the priest consents.

There are clear differences in how the politics of child labour is played out in different communities. In industrialized countries, putting very young children to work in factories is widely seen as a violation of the rights of children, and while teenage prostitution does exist in cities, prostitution involving very young girls occurs on the fringe; actively selling or giving daughters into bondage or slavery is virtually unknown. In other countries, by contrast, the politics play out differently: efforts by the central government to erase *trocosi* bondage in Ghana, or to clamp down on the sex trade in very young girls in Bangkok, tend to run into opposition. In many countries, support for the kind of child welfare laws that are common in the industrialized world is not widespread. In many of these countries, there simply is not the wealth to fund a public education system from kindergarten to the end of high school.

The differential we see on these issues is intimately related to world politics: the pattern of wealth distribution in the contemporary system and the differences in norms and ideas. Much of the differential comes from differences in wealth. Many children in industrialized countries have the luxury of being able to regard paid employment as their own personal income rather than a necessary part of family income necessary for survival. And even for the poor in the industrialized world, there is a social-welfare safety net that is simply unknown in much of the rest of the world. By contrast, in much of the world, the collapse of traditional agricultural economies and the rise of urbanization has meant that for many, the work of the children is crucial for the economic survival of the family. As a consequence, in many countries today we see the same coincidence of interest between parents, factory owners, and state officials that kept young children at work in the mills of Manchester and the coal mines of Newcastle two hundred years ago.

Moreover, there is the additional problem of differences in outlook and philosophy. First, and most important, conceptions of family differ. The dominant conception of the family in the industrialized world tends to be atomistic (in other words, separate and self-contained), a reflection not only of liberal conceptions of the individual, but also of the essential separation of work/occupation from the family unit that has come with urbanization and industrialization. As a result, the notion that young children should have their education put aside so they can work full-time to help support the family is regarded as quite alien, and is reflected in the laws prohibiting it. By contrast, the dominant conception of family (or, more broadly, kinship group) in many other places in the world tends to remain more organic and holistic—in other words, more pre-industrial. From such a view, the notion flows naturally that all members of the family should participate in the sustenance of the family.

This difference in outlook tends to be exacerbated by the fact that in many places, people simply have not accepted the liberal notion that each human being has a set of inalienable rights. As noted above, children, like women, are often seen merely as chattels, things that are "owned," and thus can be "disposed of" as the adult sees fit.

## CONCLUSION

We have looked at only two of the cleavages "inside" (gender and age) that have an impact on politics "outside," and how politics "outside" affects those cleavages. One could explore a range of other attributes—religion, class, or race—that help illuminate some of the paradoxes and contradictions of international affairs. Looking at world politics through such a lens helps us understand, for example, why in the midst of a famine that was killing thousands of people daily in 1984 and 1985, the government of Ethiopia spent millions of birr hosting a summit meeting for the Organization of African Unity, with groaning boards of food for the assembled diplomats and a freshly purchased fleet of Mercedes-Benzes to whisk them around Addis Ababa. Or why the United States government spends billions of dollars each year in military aid to other countries to improve the economic welfare and security of their elites, while millions of others in those countries (and in the U.S. itself) live in poverty and insecurity. In short, perhaps we can understand why politics "inside" and politics "outside" are deeply intertwined, and why it makes little sense to treat them as though they occurred in separate and distinct spheres.

Furthermore, erasing domestic politics and treating countries as though they were united singularities causes us to lose sight of who the actors and agents in world politics are: we end up thinking about world politics as simply the behaviour of 190 reified names instead of conceiving of world politics as a realm in which there is a huge panoply of actors. To this issue we now turn.

## *Keyword File*

Inside/outside dualism

Domestic politics

Political cleavages

Foreign policy

Metonyms

Gender inequality

Formal economy

Informal economy

Female genital alteration

Child labour

Sex trade

## *For Further Exploration*

### HARD COPY

Bonnet, Michel. "Child labour in Africa," *International Labour Review* 132 (1993).

Jones, Adam. "Does 'gender' make the world go round? Feminist critiques of international relations," *Review of International Studies* 22 (October 1996).

Mahoney, Kathleen E. "Human rights and Canada's foreign policy," *International Journal* 47 (Summer 1992).

Walker, R.B.J. *Inside/Outside: International Relations as Political Theory.* Cambridge: Cambridge University Press, 1993.

Zalewski, Marysia. "'Well, what is the feminist perspective on Bosnia?'" *International Affairs* 71 (1995).

## WEBLINKS

**http://www.unicef.org/**

Home page of UNICEF, the United Nations Childrens Fund, including *State of the World's Children, 1997*

**http://www.undp.org/fwcw/daw.htm**

Site of the UN's Division for the Advancement of Women

## *Notes to Chapter 6*

1. R.B.J. Walker, *Inside/Outside: International Relations as Political Theory* (Cambridge: Cambridge University Press, 1993); for a useful overview of Walker's approach to IR, see Lene Hansen, "R.B.J. Walker and international relations: deconstructing a discipline," in Iver B. Neumann and Ole Wæver, *The Future of International Relations* (London and New York: Routledge, 1997), 316–36.

2. UNDP, *Human Development Report 1996* (Oxford: Oxford University Press, 1996), 32.

3. Catherine Bertini, "To feed the world, get the food to the women," *New York Times News Service*, 12 November 1996.

4. Phillips Wayne Foster, *The World Food Problem: Tackling the Causes of Undernutrition in the Third World* (Boulder, CO: Lynne Rienner, 1992).

5. For good overviews of the feminist approach to international politics, see Marysia Zalewski, "'Well, what is the feminist perspective on Bosnia?'" *International Affairs* 71 (1995); and J. Ann Tickner, *Gender in International Relations: Feminist Perspectives on Achieving Global Security* (New York: Columbia University Press, 1992). Adam Jones provides a useful constructive critique in "Does 'gender' make the world go round? Feminist critiques of international relations," *Review of International Studies* 22 (October 1996). Cynthia Enloe's books—*Bananas, Beaches, and Bases: Making Feminist Sense of International Politics* (Berkeley: University of California Press, 1990) and *The Morning After: Sexual Politics at the End of the Cold War* (Berkeley: University of California Press, 1993)—explore ways in which international politics is gendered. For more advanced scholarly perspectives, see V. Spike Peterson, ed., *Gendered States: Feminist (Re)Visions of International Relations Theory* (Boulder, CO: Lynne Rienner, 1992) and Rebecca Grant and Kathleen Newland, eds., *Gender and International Relations* (Indianapolis: Indiana University Press, 1991). For empirical studies, see Sandra Whitworth, "Theory as exclusion: gender and international political economy," in Richard Stubbs and Geoffrey R.D. Underhill, eds., *Political Economy and the Changing Global Order* (Toronto: McClelland and Stewart/London: Macmillan, 1994); and Lori Buck, Nicole Gallant, and Kim Richard Nossal, "Sanctions as a gendered instrument of statecraft: the case of Iraq," *Review of International Studies* (1998).

6.  L. Reanda, "Prostitution as a human rights question: problems and prospects of United Nations action," *Human Rights Quarterly* 12 (May 1991).

7.  Kathleen E. Mahoney, "Human rights and Canada's foreign policy," *International Journal* 47 (Summer 1992), 568.

8.  Robert D. Kaplan, "The coming anarchy," *The Atlantic Monthly* (February 1994), 44–45.

# PART 3

# Actors *and* Agents *in* World Politics

C H A P T E R  7

# "Onstage" *and* "Offstage": Defining *the* Players

**I N T R O D U C T I O N**

In the previous chapter we examined how the inside/outside dichotomy affects our analysis of world politics. In this chapter, we examine another problem created by our tendency to view world politics as though it were the politics between 190 states: the difficulty of determining who are the "actors" on the "stage" of world politics. Who do we define as "onstage" and who do we define as "offstage"?

## DEFINING THE ACTORS

There are three different ways to look at the actors in world politics. One is the state-centric view, which argues that world politics is about the behaviour and interactions of states, or, more precisely, of the governments of states. A second view accepts the importance of states, but divides the world into two groups of actors, states and nonstate actors. These two state-centric approaches encourage the view that international politics is exclusively concerned with the foreign policies of states. There is, however, a third approach, which looks at the issue of actors and agents in world politics using a more holistic perspective.

## The State-Centric View

A common way of thinking about actors in world politics flows directly from the steamroller method discussed in the previous chapter: the actors in world politics, many students of IR suggest, are governments. According to the **state-centric model**, world politics is concerned with how these governments behave toward each other, what policies they embrace, what objectives they pursue. The proper focus of world politics, in other words, is the state, as Figure 7.1 suggests. In this approach to international politics, all 190 states are "onstage" as the principal actors; and everyone (and every-thing) else is "offstage."

## The State-Centric Corollary: Nonstate Actors

The obvious difficulty with the state-centric view of international politics is that it does not square with ordinary and common-sense observations of the world around us. The state is clearly not the only actor on the world stage: that stage is crowded with many more actors, not all of them states. From such observations was born the idea of dividing the world into two kinds of global actor—the state, or government, and all others, which are clumped together as **nonstate actors**.[1]

In this view, as Figure 7.2 suggests, the state shares the stage with nonstate actors. It is often constrained by them and always feels the need to manage them. Joseph S. Nye, Jr., and Robert O. Keohane pointed to the different transborder interactions that could result by admitting nonstate actors to the cast: world politics is not only about interstate relations, but also about relations among **transnational actors** (groups in different countries), and **transgovernmental actors** (different subunits of different governments).[2]

However, in this view, governments of states are still the most important actors. States may share the stage, but they dominate it. After all, governments of states plunge the world into war or keep it at peace; governments negotiate the conditions of peace and prosperity.

*Figure 7.1* • **THE STATE-CENTRIC MODEL**

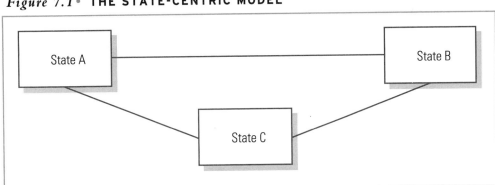

*Figure 7.2* • **THE STATE-CENTRIC COROLLARY: NONSTATE ACTORS**

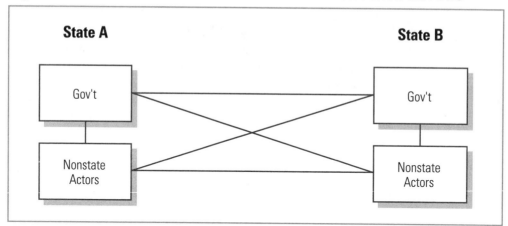

## The Foreign Policy Approach to IR

The above models encourage us to concentrate on understanding the behaviour of governments in international affairs. Every government has a **foreign policy**, best defined by Steve Smith and Michael Smith as "an umbrella term for attempts by governments to influence or manage events outside the state's boundaries."[3] **Foreign policy analysis** examines a particular government's decisions about the outside world and its relations with other actors.

### Determinants of Foreign Policy

The sources, or determinants, of a country's foreign policy are found within three different political environments—the external, the domestic, and the governmental.[4] The **external sources of foreign policy** are those influences on a government's behaviour that come from the international system. These influences arise from a state's geographic and strategic location, its power, its linkages to the international economy, and its trade and investment ties with other states. External factors include the impact that other actors have on the government through the exercise of influence and power.

By contrast, the **domestic sources of foreign policy** are those that come from within the community. Domestic sources include a country's political culture, and the ideas, attitudes, and perspectives that are dominant in that society. They include a country's economic structure, which inexorably exerts a dominant influence on how a government acts in the international system. One also must examine the political actors within the community: politicians, political parties, interest groups of all kinds, unions, nongovernmental organizations, and unorganized interests. Of considerable importance in many countries is the electoral connection—the impact of electoral politics on the external decisions and behaviour of the state.

The **governmental sources of foreign policy** are the determinants that spring from within the state apparatus itself. Foreign policy decisions are the result of a process of consideration about how to act (or not act) that occurs within an organizational setting. Thus to understand a state's foreign policy, one must look at the politics within the state apparatus itself. One must examine the leaders, their attitudes and views on politics, and the impact that different organizations and individuals within the state may have on their decisions. One should study the system of government, for how different countries organize their governments has an important impact on how policy is made and how important different organizations are. For example, the legislature is more important in some systems than others. In countries where the legislature is appointed by the state leader, it likely has minimal importance in shaping that country's foreign policy. By contrast, in the United States, where the presidency is purposely separated from the legislature, one cannot understand American foreign policy without looking at the role of the United States Congress in the shaping of decisions. In federal countries, the government's foreign policies may be shaped by the intergovernmental politics between the central government and the governments of the constituent parts of the federation.

## A World of 190 Foreign Policies

Each of the world's 190 governments has a distinctive foreign policy, shaped by the particularities of domestic politics, economic structure, personalities, and history. Moreover, a considerable literature exists on each country's foreign policy, as the small sampling presented in the Focus on p. 122 suggests. Getting to know the foreign policies of even a small number of countries is a daunting task. However, it is important for an understanding of the role of particular states and governments in world politics.

## An Alternative View: The Inclusive Cast

State-centric approaches are useful for examining a particular state's foreign policy; but they do not provide a broad perspective on IR. An alternative view is suggested by the same assumptions that we use to analyze politics at other levels. When we want to understand the politics of a city or a country, we look at the attributes and behaviour of the individuals who comprise that polity. We would not think of trying to understand politics at any other level by ignoring individuals and only focusing on governments. Consider what an odd picture we would have if we proceeded on the assumption that "American politics" consisted of the relations of the 50 state governments and the federal government in Washington. So too in world politics: we should not think of trying to understanding politics at the world level by ignoring all of the human beings whose behaviour, both individually and within organizations, creates politics at this level.

*Consider what an odd picture we would have if we proceeded on the assumption that "American politics" consisted of the relations of the 50 state governments and the federal government in Washington.*

## INDIVIDUALS

We should think about every human being as a potential actor in world politics: actors whose daily decisions affect politics at a world level and whose lives are, in a circular fashion, affected by the currents of world politics. That means thinking about the behaviour of individuals in a vast complex of settings and interactions.

## FOCUS

### Foreign Policy Analysis: Introductions to the Foreign Policies of Selected States

**AUSTRALIA**

Gareth Evans and Bruce Grant, *Australia's Foreign Relations in the World of the 1990s*, 2d ed. (Carlton, Vic: Melbourne University Press, 1995)

T.B. Millar, *Australia in Peace and War*, 2d ed. (Canberra: Australian National University Press, 1991)

**BRITAIN**

Michael Smith, Steve Smith, and Brian White, eds., *British Foreign Policy: Tradition, Change and Transformation* (London: Unwin Hyman, 1988)

**CANADA**

Tom Keating, *Canada and World Order: The Multilateralist Tradition in Canadian Foreign Policy* (Toronto: McClelland and Stewart, 1993)

Andrew F. Cooper, *Canadian Foreign Policy: Old Habits and New Directions* (Scarborough, ON: Prentice Hall Allyn and Bacon Canada, 1997)

**CHINA**

Thomas W. Robinson and David Shambaugh, eds., *Chinese Foreign Policy: Theory and Practice* (Oxford: Clarendon Press, 1994)

Samuel Kim, ed., *China and the World*, 3d ed. (Boulder, CO: Westview, 1994)

**INDIA**

Harcharan Singh Josh, *India's Foreign Policy: Nehru to Rao* (New Delhi: Indian Council of World Affairs, 1994)

Ramesh Thakur, *The Politics and Economics of India's Foreign Policy* (London/New York: Hurst/St Martin's, 1994)

**IRELAND**

Paul Sharp, *Irish Foreign Policy and the European Community* (Aldershot, U.K.: Dartmouth, 1990)

**JAPAN**

Inoguchi Takashi, *Japan's Foreign Policy in an Era of Global Change* (New York: St Martin's, 1993)

**NEW ZEALAND**

Malcolm McKinnon, *Independence and Foreign Policy: New Zealand in the World since 1935* (Auckland: Auckland University Press, 1993)

**RUSSIA**

Nicolai N. Petro and Alvin Z. Rubinstein, *Russian Foreign Policy: From Empire to Nation-State* (New York: Longman, 1997)

**SOUTH AFRICA**

Walter Karlsnaes and Marie Muller, eds., *Change and South African External Relations* (Johannesburg: International Thomson, 1997)

James P. Barber and John Barratt, *South Africa's Foreign Policy: The Search for Status and Security, 1945–1988* (Cambridge: Cambridge University Press, 1990)

**UNITED STATES**

Stephen E. Ambrose, *Rise to Globalism: American Foreign Policy since 1938*, 6th ed. (New York: Penguin, 1991)

Walter LaFeber, *The American Age: United States Foreign Policy at Home and Abroad, 1750 to the Present*, 2d ed. (New York: Norton, 1994)

## Individuals as Purposive Global Actors

Most individuals, as they live their lives, do not consciously intend to have an impact on global politics. But some individuals do set out to try to make a difference. For example, in the 1860s, Jean Henri Dunant pressed for the establishment of an agency to care for the wounded in war; this agency became the Red Cross (examined in more detail below). Gavrilo Princip, a Serbian nationalist, assassinated the Archduke Ferdinand on 28 June 1914, setting in motion a chain of events that led to the Great War. Oskar Schindler, a German industrialist, saved over a thousand Polish Jews from the gas chambers at Auschwitz concentration camp. As a young boy in the late 1940s, Sabry Khalil al-Banna saw the new state of Israel seize his father's wealth and drive his family into the poverty of refugee camps; 20 years later he waged a war of terror against Israelis using the *nom de guerre* Abu Nidal. Bob Geldof, the lead singer of the Boomtown Rats, organized a worldwide rock concert, Live Aid, for African famine relief in July 1985. Archbishop Desmond Tutu, head of the Anglican church in South Africa, led nonviolent opposition to apartheid. Rigoberta Menchú Túm of Guatemala campaigned on behalf of indigenous peoples, for which she was awarded the 1992 Nobel Peace Prize. Before her death in September 1997, Diana, Princess of Wales, gave an important impetus to the campaign for the abolition of antipersonnel land mines. In October 1997, Ted Turner, the owner of CNN, made a personal donation of US$1 billion to the United Nations, an amount about equal to the dues owed the UN by the United States government.

But even the "little" actions of individuals can have consequences. Consider those who signed a petition urging a firm to improve the labour conditions in its factories around the world; or demonstrated at a foreign embassy or consulate; or refused to buy products from a foreign country as a protest; or wrote to a foreign leader on behalf of a prisoner of conscience; or refused to report for military service; or gave a donation to any one of the thousands of organizations delivering development assistance to the poor. Or consider those four million people who bought *We Are the World*, the 1985 multi-platinum song recorded to assist victims of the Ethiopian famine. These are purposive individual acts—not taken on behalf of any organization or firm—that are designed to effect change in politics at the world level.

And some individual action, when aggregated, can affect world politics. For example, animal rights activists, centred mainly in the United States, objected to the large number of marine mammals, particularly dolphins, killed in the purse seines and drift nets used by tuna fishing fleets in the Pacific. In 1972, in response to this pressure, the United States government imposed limits on the number of dolphins that could be killed in this way by American fishing fleets. However, this action had no impact on fishing fleets from Japan and other Asian countries, which continued to use drift nets. In the 1980s, a consumer protest began, focusing not so much on the Asian trawlers—on which individual consumers could have little impact—but instead on American firms selling processed and canned tuna purchased from boats using these harvesting methods. The pressure eventually had an impact: in 1990, the three largest American firms began demanding that fishing boats supplying them with tuna certify that the fish had not been caught in purse seines or drift nets; in 1992, the United States Congress banned the importation of fish caught in drift nets. Eventually Japanese fishing fleet owners announced that they were giving up drift net methods.[5]

Likewise, the worldwide campaign urging Nike to improve the working conditions at its factories had an impact: Nike chose to undertake a massive advertising campaign to assure its customers—and would-be customers—that it was moving to meet the criticisms about labour conditions at its factories in poor countries.

Or consider the impact of individuals in the case of the American war in Vietnam in the 1960s, explored in more detail in Chapter 15. This war became increasingly unpopular in the United States, the opposition taking the form of large-scale demonstrations on university campuses and quieter forms of protest, such as young Americans who either dodged the draft or deserted, moving to Canada or Scandinavia. More importantly, parents of young Americans—seeing the war bloodily unfold on their television screens each evening—began registering their dismay at the Johnson administration's Vietnam policy, a message quickly picked up by members of Congress.

The reaction of ordinary Australians to the resumption of French nuclear testing shows how individual actions can aggregate. In June 1995, the French government of Jacques Chirac announced that it was planning to resume underground testing of its nuclear weapons at the French testing site on the South Pacific atolls of Mururoa and Fangataufa. This announcement produced a wave of public protests throughout the Asia-Pacific. But nowhere was the anger more fierce than in Australia.[6] Thousands took to the streets. The French embassy in Canberra was inundated with 13 000 letters of protest in two months; French diplomatic missions could not use their phone or fax lines because they were constantly jammed by crank callers. French goods and services and even French restaurants were boycotted. A billboard appeared in the heart of Melbourne's central business district featuring a woman, whose bare bottom was painted in the French tricolour, giving Chirac the finger with the message: "Language is *no* barrier to our anger Mr Chirac." Unions imposed rolling "black bans" on mail and telephone services to French diplomatic missions; services to Air France aircraft, French air cargo, and French ships were withdrawn. The president of the Australian Council of Trade Unions (ACTU), Martin Ferguson, endorsed a national boycott of all French products. A truckload of manure was dumped on the driveway of the French embassy in Canberra. French cars had their tires slashed. The premises of the honorary consul of France in Perth were firebombed.

The vehemence of the Australian protests surprised the French government, which watched as its relationship with Australia deteriorated dramatically. The individual acts of protest had an impact: the French government decided to reduce the number of tests and then close the South Pacific testing facilities for good.

In addition to such higher profile cases, we should not forget the more routine, and thus less celebrated, cases where individual actions have an effect. In many cases, the intervention of ordinary individuals writing to foreign leaders on behalf of Amnesty International's prisoners of conscience has secured their release; in other cases, individual donations of money or labour have ameliorated conditions in poorer localities.

## Individuals and the Global Economy

While we can point to some acts where individuals act purposefully to influence world politics, most individuals, most of the time, are in fact not purposive actors in world politics. In other words, they are not thinking about the impact their decisions may have on politics at a world level. This is perhaps best seen by examining the participation of most people in the global economy.

Simply trying to conceive of the billions of daily human interactions that constitute the contemporary global economy is a vast task, rather like trying to imagine the synaptic operations of the human brain. But it is worth reflecting on the vastness of that network, and the degree to which world politics is both a reflection of, and a contributor to, that huge number of interactions.

Consider, for example, the extent of the global economy and the number of individuals who take part in that economy by pursuing their particular economic interests in their day-to-day activities. But how many of those individuals, as they go about their daily lives, are conscious of the political effects of their individual economic decisions and actions? How many people are aware of the degree to which individual patterns of consumption, for example, affect what goods are manufactured, what crops are raised, what animals are bred, what clothes are made, and where?

But even if no purposive action is intended, these millions of little economic decisions have a collective impact. Consider how many individual actions, decisions, interactions, agreements, payoffs, payouts, and exchanges are needed to get a pair of sneakers on one's feet, food on one's table, music in one's Walkman, or the World Wide Web on one's computer.

Consider too those whose willingness to supply labour for the functioning of the global economy keeps that economy working. Whether it be in primary or secondary manufacturing industries, the service or "knowledge" sectors, or any one of a hundred thousand occupations, those who are employed in the global economy are purposive and important actors in world politics. We must include as global actors all those throughout history who moved to new lands to find a better life for themselves, their families, or their community.

Or consider the hundreds of thousands of individual owners of capital, each engaging in microdecisions about where to invest their money in a way that maximizes their return on investment. The millions of decisions they make each day—or perhaps more commonly the decisions of their agents taken on their behalf—give shape to the contemporary global economy, causing the markets to rise or fall and causing interest rates, exchange rates, and the value of a hundred currencies to fluctuate. With these fluctuations, personal, corporate, and national fortunes rise and fall.

This intimate relationship between the pursuit of economic interest and global politics is not just a contemporary phenomenon, even though it is often portrayed as an artifact of the modern global capitalist economy that emerged from the feudal economy of Europe. In fact, throughout history individuals have pursued their economic self-interest by bartering; exchanging; buying and selling; and moving labour, goods, services, capital, technology, and ideas around the world.

## Individuals as Agents

Individuals do not only act on their own behalf. They also act on behalf of their family, clan, tribe, or community, or on behalf of some organization. The broker acting for a investment consortium; the diplomat negotiating for a national government; the soldier patrolling a ceasefire line for an international organization; the missionary intent on bringing the word of God to the world on behalf of a religion; the lobbyist pressing the interests of a foreign client to local politicians; the American communist passing atomic secrets to his Soviet "handler"; the terrorist exploding a bomb on a busy street on behalf of a revolutionary organization; the explorer venturing into uncharted waters on behalf of a king or a corporation; the advocate speaking out on human rights violations in a foreign country on behalf of a non-governmental organization; the foreign correspondent reporting the news for a television network; the president or prime minister attending an international summit on behalf of his or her country; the official of an intelligence agency booby-trapping a foreign leader's cell phone so that it will explode when used; the pilot of a small plane delivering a consignment of illegal narcotics on behalf of any number of organized crime syndicates—these are examples of individuals whose actions change the shape of politics at the world level as profoundly as any of the hundreds of billions of daily decisions of individuals.

## ORGANIZATIONS

Organizations are collectives of individuals who work on behalf of the group. The numerous group actors and agents in world politics include economic organizations, both legal and illegal; the global media; nongovernmental organizations (NGOs); political movements of all sorts; governments of all kinds; and intergovernmental organizations (IGOs).

### Organizations in the Global Economy

In its totality the global economy comprises the interaction of hundreds of millions of producers, consumers, and those who connect them. But much of this activity is generated by organizations of different kinds.

#### Businesses: *Societas*, Guilds, Corporations, Multinationals

Those who own, organize, manage, administer, and finance patterns of production and consumption are critical actors in world politics. Economies invariably comprise individuals, families, and groups who provide the labour necessary to move and process products for market. Invariably, political authorities (governments or the state) and other large organizations (such as corporations) play a crucial role in organizing and financing such operations. Over the years, these organizations have had different attributes and played different roles in the economy depending on time and place. For example, in imperial Rome, one of the important economic actors was the *societas*, associations of those members of the commercial class, the *publicani*, who were contracted by the government to provide goods or services. In northern Europe during the feudal period, commerce was dominated by the merchant guilds of the Hanseatic League, as we saw in Chapter 4. In the mercantile age— discussed in Chapter 9—the primary catalysts of the internationalization of trade were the great **monopoly trading corporations**, such as the different East India Companies formed to develop trade with the countries of the Indian Ocean. In England, the trading companies were "chartered" by the government: the Muscovy Company, the Governors and Company of Merchants of the Levant, the Merchant Adventurers (who sought to challenge Hanseatic dominance in the wool trade), or the Hudson's Bay Company.

The rise of trade between Europe and imperial China saw the Chinese government organize special trading companies, called *cohongs*, to trade with Europeans. The growth of the joint-stock company in Britain in the 19th century, and of the corporation in the United States in the late 1800s and early 1900s, would transform business organization and promote, in symbiotic fashion, the growth of urban markets. Often these firms created subsidiaries in other countries behind the tariff and regulatory walls that, as we will see in Chapter 12, marked the predominant economic organization of this era.

In the latter half of the 20th century, the global economy is dominated by an internationalized and bureaucratized version of the 19th century company, the **multinational corporation** (MNC), sometimes called a **transnational corporation** (TNC).* The modifier points to the nature of this economic actor: unlike the trading corporation of the mercantilist period or the foreign subsidiary of the early 20th century, the MNC is not simply a domestic corporation operating outside the borders of its "home" state; rather, the MNC is organized to operate *across* borders in a number of different nations. While MNCs continue to have clearly defined corporate "nationalities" and maintain head offices located in a particular nation, they organize supply, production, assembly, distribution, and marketing on a global basis, seeking to take advantage of differential rates of wage labour, working conditions, government regulations, and rates of education and literacy, to rationalize production and maximize return on investment.

The pervasiveness of this form of economic organization in the contemporary economy can be seen from the numbers. There are some 40 000 multinational corporations, the vast majority headquartered in the United States, Japan, and the countries of the European Union. The economic activity of the "Fortune 500"—the 500 largest corporations listed by *Fortune* magazine—employed some 35 million workers worldwide and had sales of over $10 trillion.

As will be evident from these raw figures, the MNC has considerable capacity to influence world politics; as Robert T. Kudrle has noted, the MNC presents several faces to the global political system.[7] Decisions made by MNC managers influence patterns of investment, supply, production, and service, and thus can have crucial effects on employment and wealth generation in particular countries. MNCs are relatively mobile and can move around the international community with considerable ease. While few corporations are keen to abandon productive sites in which they have sunk considerable investment, MNCs will rationalize production and close plants when it is in their interests to do so. MNCs are also sensitive to unstable political conditions: the withdrawal of some MNCs from a market may precipitate **capital flight**, large-scale withdrawals of investment. Consider the huge flight of MNC capital from South Africa during the unrest of the late 1980s. Likewise,

---

* Paul Hirst and Grahame Thompson make a case for distinguishing between an MNC, which has a national home, and a TNC, which would be "genuine footloose capital" without a national home, able and willing to locate anywhere in the world. Hirst and Thompson argue convincingly that such "stateless" corporations are actually very rare. See *Globalization in Question: The International Economy and the Possibilities of Governance* (London: Polity Press, 1996), 11–13.

Jardine-Matheson, one of Hong Kong's oldest firms, decided to relocate its head office before the colony was passed back to China in 1997. But MNCs are quite responsive to efforts by governments to make locating in a particular jurisdiction attractive: the liberal incorporation laws of the state of Delaware, for example, is the reason why over half the Fortune 500 is officially incorporated there (even if they maintain their headquarters elsewhere). Thus governments are consistently trying to woo the kind of investment—and employment—that multinationals bring with them.

Governments also struggle with some of the negative consequences of the increasingly global organization of enterprise. MNCs pose both macroproblems and microproblems. For example, at the macro level, the mobility of MNCs make national governments extraordinarily sensitive to the consequences of decisions that are made about their country and their jurisdiction around a boardroom table in Hong Kong, London, New York, Paris, or Tokyo. MNCs also need micromanaging: for example, most corporations engage in **transfer pricing** practices that tend to minimize their tax liability. In such schemes, subsidiaries of a company located in different countries will trade products between each other at prices determined by the MNC, not the market. In this way, MNCs can arrange to have a subsidiary in a high-tax jurisdiction pay an artificially high price for supplies purchased from another subsidiary in a different jurisdiction, writing off the (high) cost of goods against tax owing.

## Financiers, Bankers, Brokers, and Currency Traders

Among the most important international actors are the financiers of the global economy—those who provide the funds that underwrite economic growth. These have included public authorities, such as the imperial Roman *aerarium*, or public treasury, which loaned large sums to finance public projects undertaken by individual contractors and *societas* at rates of interest established by the imperial Senate. Likewise, much of the transoceanic exploration undertaken by Europeans in the middle of the millennium was financed by the treasuries of kings.

Private arrangements for financing the international economy have varied over time. For example, in imperial Rome, *negotiatores* sold *partes*—shares—in what today we would call joint-stock ventures to raise funds for both public and private projects. The goldsmiths of 17th century England came to the banking business only because King Charles I seized all the bullion that merchants had put on deposit at the Royal Mint and the merchant class needed strongboxes to store their money. In the 19th century, commercial banking houses emerged which specialized in directing the funds of "savers" in the burgeoning corporate world to investments. In the 20th century, we have seen the growth of international lending institutions underwritten by the power and wealth of states: the International Monetary Fund (IMF) and the International Bank for Reconstruction and Development (the World Bank). We must see the stock exchanges of the world—the exchanges themselves, the governments which regulate them, the various brokers who work them, and the merchant bankers who underwrite their activities—as global actors, for the interactions that occur in that marketplace can have profound consequences for global politics.

Private financial organizations also finance state activity in the global realm. Because all government projects—whether the waging of war, the encouragement of industrial activity, or efforts to develop the economies of others—are essentially economic projects, they must be financed either directly through taxation, or through loans, bonds, or debentures. Financial organizations can play a crucial role in generating capital for successful government projects in those cases where annual expenditures exceeds annual income. On occasion, governments, like individuals, will find their credit maxed out. When governments are no longer able to generate funds by mortgaging future tax revenues, no matter how high the interest rate offered, they must declare bankruptcy (as, for example, Spanish kings were obliged to do on six occasions: in 1557, 1575, 1576, 1607, 1627, and 1647). As we will see below, liquidity crises are a recurring pattern of world politics.

The organizations which make up the international monetary system are also international actors. The currency markets electronically move huge amounts of money—well over $1 trillion—around the international system each day.

*"The financial casino has everyone playing the game of Snakes and Ladders. Whether the fall of the dice lands you at the bottom of a ladder, whisking you up to a fortune, or on the head of a snake, precipitating you to misfortune, is a matter of luck."*

Susan Strange has described those who play (and thus comprise) the currency market—private traders, bankers, and the central banks of governments—as players at a casino, watching their computer screens flickering with changing prices no less intensely than gamblers watching the rotating cylinders of the slots. But, as Strange notes, while you can choose not to go to a casino, those who play **"casino capitalism"** trap all of us into playing the game quite involuntarily. Changes in the value of national currencies have profound effects, as do changes in interest rates; workers, managers, farmers, exporters, importers, consumers are all affected. Yet all these changes depend entirely on serendipity: "The financial casino has everyone playing the game of Snakes and Ladders. Whether the fall of the dice lands you at the bottom of a ladder, whisking you up to a fortune, or on the head of a snake, precipitating you to misfortune, is a matter of luck."[8]

## Organizers of the Global Economy: States and Markets

Those who try to *organize* the world economy to their liking are global actors. Although the market is often characterized as a site of economic exchange that operates best without governments trying to regulate it, in fact markets are heavily determined by the most powerful actors who operate in them—governments and firms. The most potent of these organizations are governments of all sorts. While we will look at governments separately below, it should be noted in this context that throughout history, governments have always sought to regulate, control, and most importantly, profit from the economic activities of ordinary folks—in a dizzying array of ways. Such efforts have included imposing duties and tariffs on goods coming into, or even just passing through, territories they controlled; prohibiting the export of certain products considered vital; trying to ensure the cheap supply of needed goods (grain from Egypt in the case of Rome during imperial times, bullion from the New World in the case of Spain in the 16th century, oil from the Middle East in the case of the industrialized world in the 20th century); trying to create monopolies on the supply of highly valued goods; trying to limit the spread of technology or knowledge to competitors; trying to encourage investment in some industries; and trying to put competitors out of business.

But governments have also shown a propensity to try and organize the international economy for what they see as the benefit of the world community as a whole. Consistent efforts are made to manage the contemporary world economy. Governments do it, through a variety of mechanisms that range from informal contacts at the bureaucratic level to summit meetings of political leaders. Central bankers do it, by strategic interventions in the currency market and through their international organization, the Bank for International Settlements (BIS). International organizations, ranging from the IMF and the World Bank to regional development banks, do it. Even institutionalized groups of individuals try to influence the direction of thinking about the world economy. Each year at the World Economic Forum in Davos, Switzerland, hundreds of the world's economic and political elite converge to discuss the world economy, and the Trilateral Commission, a group of business people, intellectuals, and former government leaders from Western Europe, North America, and Japan, regularly meet to exchange ideas about the world economy.

## Rougher Trade: The Global Economy's Other Face

Most discussions of the international political economy (IPE) focus on flows of debt, investment, trade, and services between communities; squabbles over imbalances in trade; the influence of business associations; the inner workings of central banks; the impact of the product cycle on national wealth; negotiations among agricultural traders; patterns of dependency of poor states; the organization of large firms in capitalist systems; the globalizing influence of American television; and the intricacies of protecting intellectual property rights. Likewise, the actors talked about in IPE come from society's elites: political leaders, government officials, central bankers, managers of multinationals, brokers, traders, and union officials.

Notably absent in such portraits are discussions of the other side of the international political economy: smuggling, slaving, prostitution, drug-running, arms-dealing, money-laundering, racketeering, extortion, bribery, and kick-backs.* We must include as international economic actors Afghani brigands, Japanese *yakuza*, Hong Kong triads, Sicilian *mafiosi*, Southeast Asian pirates, Québec bikers, Jamaican posses, Russian *Mafia*, Colombian cartels, and the smugglers, racketeers, thieves, con artists, and criminal organizations operating in

---

* There are exceptions: Susan Strange, in collaboration with Letizia Paoli, has written on the mafias: see Strange, *The Retreat of the State: The Diffusion of Power in the World Economy* (Cambridge: Cambridge University Press, 1996), 110–121; see also Richard Stubbs and Geoffrey R.D. Underhill, eds., *Political Economy and the Changing Global Order* (London: Macmillan, 1994). By contrast, the seamier side of IPE is not mentioned at all in Joan Edelman Spero and Jeffrey A. Hart, *The Politics of International Economic Relations*, 5th ed. (New York: St Martin's, 1997) or David N. Balaam and Michael Veseth, *Introduction to International Political Economy* (Upper Saddle River, NJ: Prentice Hall, 1996).

every jurisdiction. International political economy is as much about the flows of cocaine from the fields of Colombia to the noses of New Yorkers as it is about the flows of foreign direct investment; as much about money-laundering schemes run by shell companies in the Cayman Islands as it is about the debts of governments. We have to look at a fuller range of global economic activities, such as the movement of illegal aliens into the United States by smugglers (known as "snakeheads" if they are moving people from China or "coyotes" if they are smuggling Mexicans); the gun-running down the east coast of Africa; or the sex-tourist trade of Southeast Asia.

### Pirates

**Piracy** was a persistent problem in international commerce down to the 19th century, when it was largely eliminated with the invention of the telegraph and the advent of modern navies. Although piracy is no longer as widespread as it once was, it is still enough of a problem that the International Chamber of Commerce maintains an International Maritime Bureau (IMB), based in London, to monitor the problem; likewise, the International Transport Workers Federation in London maintains a piracy response group. According to the IMB, there were a total of 224 attacks on shipping by pirates in 1996; in the first six months of 1997, seven people had died in 79 attacks and five ships in the Asia Pacific simply disappeared, presumed taken by pirates. So frequent were the attacks in the Straits of Malacca, the major trade route linking Asia and points west, that the IMB established a regional piracy centre in Kuala Lumpur in 1993.

### Slavers

As international actors, slavers were more important in history than at present. In the chapters ahead, we will see how slavery played a critical role in the evolution of European imperialism after the first European slave trade was recorded in 1442. The **slave trade** was abolished in the 19th century, and slavery as an institution was abandoned by all governments (though the Nazis in Germany resurrected a form of slavery during the Second World War). As we saw in Chapter 6, forms of slavery do continue to exist, mainly involving girls and women, but mainly on the fringes of local economies. Some women from Southeast Asia who have voluntarily taken positions as domestics overseas have discovered that they are kept in slave-like conditions.

### The Sex Trade

One aspect of international slavery that persisted into the late 19th and early 20th century, called **"white slavery,"** involved the abduction of young girls who were shipped to other countries and sold into prostitution. In the 1870s and 1880s, campaigns were organized in Europe and North America to stop this trade; the United States passed legislation banning it; international conferences were held. However, the white slavery campaigns, as Deborah Stienstra has pointed out, were little more than an often highly gendered effort to suppress and regulate prostitution,[9] for there was in fact little evidence that children, white or any other colour, were being abducted and sold into slavery. Most of the international movements of supposed "white slaves" were young prostitutes who were quite willingly moving to take up employment in other cities.

Unlike the white slavery scares of the late 19th century, white slavery at the end of the 20th century is very real. It has two dimensions. One involves so-called "sex slavery" rings that promise young Asian women—typically from Thailand and Malaysia—a new and rich life in North America. Lured by the prospect of massive wealth, the women are "lent" the supposed cost of bring them to North America, as much as US$40 000. They are then flown to Vancouver, Los Angeles, San Diego, or Toronto, where they are "sold" by middlemen to a local brothel for between $5000 and $10 000. The brothel owners demand immediate repayment of the cost of her purchase, which usually requires many weeks of turning tricks; to ensure compliance, they normally take away the young girl's passport. While many of the women know full well what they are signing up for, their treatment by brothel owners constitutes a form of bondage that makes the term slavery not at all inappropriate. Moreover, should they be caught by authorities in the United States or Canada and returned to Asia, they face an even greater problem: they (and often their families) remain formally indebted to the ring organizers, with an amount that is impossible to pay off in Thailand or Malaysia.

A second type of white slavery involves very young children in international prostitution, particularly in Asia. This trade has been internationalized as a result of firms in Europe, Japan, North America, and Australia offering "sex tours" to countries like Thailand, where men are able to use very young boys and girls for sexual pleasure. While some teenage prostitutes in Bangkok ply their trade by choice, many of the preteenage boys and girls routinely used by middle-aged men have been sold into servitude to brothels, often by their own families.

While the international sex trade does not have the same kind of economic impact as other illicit areas of the international economy, prostitution nonetheless can produce considerable local social and highly gendered effects, such as the deep institutionalization of the exploitation of women, the spread of infectious diseases such as AIDS and other sexually transmitted diseases, and the rise of organized crime. It can also affect urban development. For example, the million or more young American GIs who passed through the countries of the Asia-Pacific during the Vietnam war had a visible impact on the social landscape at the time: Cholon in Saigon, Sukhumvit Road in Bangkok, Wanchai in Hong Kong, and King's Cross in Sydney were all marked by the demand for bars and prostitutes from Americans on R&R (rest and recreation). Indeed, in some cases, the GIs left a more permanent legacy: in Vietnam, there are hundreds of thirtysomething Eurasian men and women who suffer persistent discrimination on account of the miscegenation of American GIs and Vietnamese prostitutes in the 1960s; indeed, in the 1980s, the Vietnamese government in Hanoi routinely demanded that the United States accept every Eurasian it had "left behind."

### Smugglers

**Smuggling** involves illegally moving items between jurisdictions. The smuggled items and those who engage in all phases of smuggling—from those who sell the items, to those who carry them across borders, to those who arrange for their sale, to those who buy them—ranges widely. Rhino horns and seal penises are moved to Southeast Asia, commanding a high price because of a widespread belief that these products enhance potency. There is an intercontinental smuggling trade between Africa, Asia, Europe, and North America in prohibited live birds, skins of endangered species, and ivory. Small arms and larger weapons systems are bought and sold on a black market that is worth an estimated US$9 billion a year. This market showed a particular increase after the collapse of the Soviet Union in 1991, when large numbers of Red Army officers apparently sold weapons under their command and control. We should also include the smuggling in people, particularly smugglers who charge to get people into the United States. For example, snakeheads can charge up to $30 000 to smuggle a single Chinese person into the United States. Some smuggling crosses borders but is essentially local: the lively trade in stolen Toyota Crowns, whisked from Hong Kong to the Chinese mainland in *tai fei*, high-powered speedboats; and the smuggling of cigarettes by native peoples across the Canadian-American border using the special legal status of reservations to get around high Canadian taxes on cigarettes (eventually the government in Ottawa was prompted to abandon its taxes).

### Drug-Runners

The **drug trade** moves the goods most smuggled in the contemporary international system—illegal narcotics, primarily the by-products of the opium, Indian hemp, and coca plants: heroin, hashish, marijuana, cocaine, and crack. Heroin comes from the Golden Triangle, where China, Laos, Myanmar, and Thailand meet; the Golden Crescent (Afghanistan, Iran, and Pakistan); and Mexico. The main coca producers are in Latin America: Bolivia, Brazil, Colombia, Ecuador, Peru, and Venezuela. Marijuana is grown widely throughout Africa, Latin America, Asia, and North America, though the most significant producers for the world market are Belize, Colombia, Jamaica, Mexico, and the United States.

*A farmer in Myanmar receives approximately US$700 for a kilo of heroin; that single kilo of heroin will eventually net US$750 000 on the streets of American cities.*

Although these drugs are consumed in most countries around the world—for example, Australia has roughly the same number of heroin addicts as the United States on a per capita basis—the primary consuming market is the United States. Official estimates put consumption by Americans at more than six tonnes of heroin, 175 t of cocaine, and over 9000 t of marijuana a year. The annual value of the cocaine consumed by Americans annually is estimated at some US$17 billion.[10]

The huge demand for these drugs in the United States and the fact that they are all illegal combines to produce exceedingly high prices at the consumer end. Enough money can ripple backward to all those who handle these products that the organizers of the drug trade are able to purchase an exceptionally smooth flow from farmer's field to the final high. By way of illustration, consider the degree of value added to a kilogram of heroin: a farmer in Myanmar receives approximately US$700 for a kilo of heroin; shipped to a centre like Bangkok for processing, that kilo, refined, is now worth US$10 000. Cut and shipped to the United States, usually through Hong Kong and its massive container port, that single kilo of heroin will eventually net US$750 000 on the streets of American cities. With profits like this, it is little wonder that it is so easy to smooth the way by bribery.

In addition to all those involved in the organized drug trade, we have to include all those who launder the profits created by the relentless demand of Northerners for psychotropic substances. It is estimated that approximately US$300 to US$500 billion in drug money is laundered annually by banks, legitimate firms, and illegal front organizations. Much of the Golden Triangle cash is laundered through what is known colloquially as the "Chinese Laundry," or the "Chinese Underground Bank"—a worldwide network of overseas Chinese who will move large sums of money on trust alone, thus eliminating a paper trail.[11] The laundering is spread widely over the international system: an investigation by the Bureau of International Narcotics Matters of the United States Department of State revealed that the Cali and Medellín cartels had financial operations in some 40 countries.[12]

### Mercenaries and Transnational Security Corporations

Throughout history, governments and peoples have employed **mercenaries**—those who fight other people's wars for profit—to fight their wars. The Persians used mercenary Greek *hoplites* (foot soldiers who carried spears) to stop Alexander the Great in 334 BC, mercenaries provoked the First Punic War between Rome and Carthage (264–241 BC), and German mercenaries helped defend the Roman empire in the second century. In the 15th and 16th centuries, European wars were often fought by *condottieri*, mercenaries who were so skilled in "fighting" each other that battles would often be fought without anyone being killed except by accident. During the American revolutionary wars, the British augmented their own forces with 8000 German mercenaries.

The use of mercenary troops waned considerably with the rise of the nation-state. War fought for religion or for nation put mercenaries at a distinct disadvantage. Mercenaries, who fight for money, fight in such a way as to live another day to enjoy the spoils of war; those who fight for a cause have a different agenda. Thus, after the French Revolution and the Napoleonic Wars which followed, mercenary armies tended to be eclipsed by national armies.

With the rise of national armies, mercenaries acquired an increasingly negative connotation. Individual mercenaries, termed **"vagabond mercenaries"** by Anthony Mockler,[13] have persistently made an appearance in contemporary international politics. They were active in the Congo crises of the early 1960s. Mercenaries fought in the Nigerian and Sudanese civil wars. When foreign mercenaries recruited to fight in the Angolan civil war in 1975 were captured by the Angolan government, they were put on trial; three Britons, and an American who had joined up to pay medical bills for his family, were eventually executed on 10 July 1976. Coups or attempted coups staged by mercenaries have occurred in the Seychelles in 1977 and in November 1981; in the Maldives in 1988; and in Comoros in May 1978, November 1989, and September 1995.

In the 1990s, mercenary activity has been increasingly corporatized. There are now companies that will, for a price, contract with governments, multinationals, and international organizations to provide a range of security services: basic security protection; infantry, artillery, and airborne training; intelligence-gathering; covert operations; counter-espionage operations; and warfare of all sorts. A number of firms offering these services have emerged. Many of them are located in South Africa, including Strategic Concepts, Omega Support, and Executive Outcomes. Other firms offering similar services include Military Professional Resources Inc. (MPRI), based in MacLean, Virginia; Falconstar and Intersec in Britain; and Alpha Five, a firm founded by a group of former Soviet intelligence officers.

These **transnational security corporations** have played an important role in world politics.[14] For example, Executive Outcomes (EO) was contracted by the government of Angola to protect oil facilities at Soyo and to train units of the Angolan army to fight against a rebel group that controlled key Angolan diamond fields. In 1995, EO was hired by the government of Sierra Leone to deal with a threat from a rebel army, the Revolutionary United Front (RUF). Based on its success in Sierra Leone, EO was subcontracted to secure a copper mine held by rebels on the island of Bougainville in Papua New Guinea (PNG) in 1997 (a rebellion we examine in more detail in Chapter 11). However, as a result of opposition from the Australian government of John Howard and objections from the Papua New Guinea Defence Force (PNGDF), the mercenaries were expelled from PNG and the prime minister, Sir Julius Chan, was forced to step down temporarily while an investigation was held.

## The Media: Global Reach/Local Vision

The global media is a special actor in world politics. Privately owned newspapers, magazines, television networks, radio networks, and cable and satellite television systems are businesses like any other, seeking to generate profits for owners and shareholders. Publicly owned media are increasingly expected by governments to operate as businesses. In the search for profits, media organizations seek viewers, listeners, readers, and subscribers, for those numbers determine how much they can charge advertisers. And yet the activities of the media arguably produce far deeper political and cultural effects on the global system than any other single "industry."

### The "CNN Factor": The Political Impact of the Media

Three general political effects of the media can be identified. First, the media defines what we see of the world—and what we do not see. Second, it creates a world. And third, it shapes politics at a global level.

**Defining the World**    What we see on television and read in newspapers are the result of a process of filtering that gives us a partial view of the world around us. Some conflicts are chosen over others, the pronouncements of some individuals are favoured over others, some events are considered more important than others, some interpretations are privileged while other interpretations are excluded. As a consequence, the media does *not* present a great deal of the world to us.

Some of the filtering is the result of the narrowness of the media's vision. It is a paradox of the media that its coverage extends over so much of the Earth, and yet in its day-to-day operations, the supposedly "global" media is relentlessly parochial and local in its vision. For the vast majority of editors and producers, the news is like a stone rippling the water: what is deemed important is that which touches the local community, followed by the national community. As the ripples extend from the epicentre, the importance of what happens "out there" diminishes dramatically.

Some of the filtering results from the patterns of media ownership, though often news-room decisions are determined not so much by the direct intervention of owners, but rather by the **rule of anticipated reaction**. Editors and producers ask themselves what the consequences of a story will be for the owner; if they judge that the consequences will be negative, they "spike" (or kill) the story.[15]

However, the process of "defining" the world is not always the result of careful calcu-lation. The images that the media offers us of the world emerge from a process of individual decisions of thousands of editors and producers: decisions that are often far more haphaz-ard than we might think. These decisions are often the result of pragmatic considerations—do we have someone on site, and if not, how quickly can we get someone there? Can our budget afford US$25 000 to put a team onto a story for three days? Or can we make do with a cheaper feed from the wire services? Such choices are often driven by a not-very-scientific process of second-guessing others: what will the competition be doing with this story? is this story *really* that significant? what do our readers, viewers, or listeners want?

As a result, there is a tendency toward commonality in the way in which newspapers and TV news programs treat international stories. Editors and producers who consistently choose stories that are not chosen by other outlets, or in which readers or viewers show little interest, discover that circulation or ratings fall—and that they are out of a job.

**Creating a World**   Not only does the media help *define* our world through the choices of individual editors, producers, and owners. The contemporary global media also *creates* a world. This is particularly true for television, which since the early 1960s has had the capacity to broadcast live to increasingly large numbers of communities, particularly with the advent of satellite relay systems.

Access to real-time images creates a world in a number of ways. Most importantly, it communicates images of life, politics, and culture in a more compelling way than print or sound, and in a more immediate way than the movies. Moreover, because of the fundamentally parochial nature of the media, these images are essentially homogenizing, in the sense that television viewers are exposed to a relatively homogenous (and Euro-American) image of life: a world of suits (and, in the case of *Baywatch*, the world's most-watched television show, swimsuits), cars, cities, cell-phones—in other words, secular bourgeois consumerism. Exposure to such images does not mean that everyone automatically turns into an urbanized, secu-larized, and bourgeois American, or begins yearning for a lithe and tanned life in a red lycra swimsuit on a California beach. Rather, the homogeneity manifests itself in an essentially glob-alized set of expectations about how to define wealth and convenience.

The media also create a world in the sense that through contemporary technology, people in all parts of the world are able to participate in what can best be described as **global occasions**, when large numbers of people around the world tune in to television broadcasts of events that transcend their locality and become occasions to be celebrated— or mourned—as part of a global community as a whole. Such a dynamic could be seen in its infancy in November 1963. Following the assassination of John F. Kennedy, a live broadcast captured the image of his accused assassin, Lee Harvey Oswald, being gunned down in a Dallas police station. Kennedy's funeral was an event watched by millions of people around the world. The first truly global event caught in real time was the landing of Apollo 11 on the moon on 20 July 1969, which was broadcast live from the moon and beamed around the world. Since then, significant global events have drawn people together: the Challenger disaster on 28 January 1986, when an American space shuttle exploded minutes after take-off; the quadrennial opening and closing celebrations of the Olympic Games; and the funeral of Diana, Princess of Wales, on 6 September 1997, which drew nearly three billion viewers, almost half the people on the planet.

**Shaping—And Being Shaped by—Politics**  The filtering process by the media is important, because it can give shape to politics both within political communities and at the world level. Media choices, by defining issues, can influence political outcomes. The so-called **CNN factor**—named after the Cable News Network of Atlanta—describes the impact that the television networks can have on the evolution of policy.

Sometimes the media will galvanize an issue, either within a single country, or more broadly. For example, a severe famine had been plaguing Ethiopia since the early 1980s. But it was not until a camera crew from the British Broadcasting Corporation (BBC) toured a refugee camp in 1984, capturing images of children dying of hunger, that a massive international operation was begun to send food to Ethiopia. Likewise, when the Iraqi government resumed its attacks on Kurds following the Gulf war of 1991, tens of thousands fled into the mountains in northwestern Iraq. Large numbers began dying of cold and lack of food. While in the past the plight of the Kurds had not stirred much concern in Europe or North America, the live coverage of hundreds of thousands of Kurds huddled on cold and barren mountaintops prompted the British, French, and American governments to organize a massive relief effort. We can see the same kind of dynamic at work in the coverage that the media gave to Diana, Princess of Wales, on her visits to land-mine victims in Angola and Bosnia in 1997. Her involvement radically transformed the campaign to ban this weapon: even the United States government, which had steadfastly resisted such a ban, was moved to alter its position slightly.

The same dynamic can work within a single country. For example, the Australian media played a critical role in galvanizing public opinion against French nuclear testing in 1995. The newspapers, television networks, and radio talk-shows did not so much *create* the mood of protests, but the willingness of the media to act as a transmission belt for protests— and indeed in some cases to act as a protestor in its own right—was important for promoting that protest.

Because of its powerful impact on the political realm, the media are often used by other actors for their own purposes. For example, during the French testing issue in 1995, Greenpeace International sent a ship, the *Rainbow Warrior II*, to the testing site, making sure that the ship arrived at the exclusion zone on 10 July 1995, exactly ten years to the day after French intelligence agents blew up the original *Rainbow Warrior* in Auckland.*

> *"[W]e clearly plan whatever we're doing to make it safe for the participants, and effective, but also visually interesting, particularly for television and, in terms of photographs, for newspapers."*

Greenpeace understood the important role of the media. Its public relations campaign coordinator, Toby Hutcheon, stated that "when we do any of our direct actions, we clearly plan whatever we're doing to make it safe for the participants, and effective, but also visually interesting, particularly for television and, in terms of photographs, for newspapers."[16] That is why Greenpeace ensured that when *Rainbow Warrior II* left Tahiti, it carried a number of journalists and a team from an Australian television show, the Nine Network's *A Current Affair*.

As the *Rainbow Warrior II* approached the exclusion zone, a French warship rammed it and French commandos, dressed in black helmets and black jumpsuits, boarded the ship. They used sledge-hammers to break into the wheelhouse, spraying those inside with glass. Three others remained locked in the radio room, including Stephanie Mills, a Greenpeace spokeswoman, who was being interviewed live by a New Zealand radio station. Commandos smashed the portholes and threw in tear gas. Mills's frantic cries—"They've thrown something like tear gas...Stop it, stop it"—were caught live before commandos disabled the radio. Nine Network cameras were also rolling, beaming footage of the incident live to Australia via satellite uplink. The following day, images of the ship being swarmed by black-suited French commandos, only their eyes visible, were broadcast (and rebroadcast) around the world. The event was constructed, as Stewart Firth put it, "as a clash between the David of world public opinion and the Goliath of an arrogant French state."[17] But without the crucial role played by the media in transmitting these images, there would have been little impact. (This the French belatedly realized: in September, 1995, French authorities seized and confiscated both Greenpeace vessels in the South Pacific, thus denying Greenpeace its most effective platform for operations.[18])

The media is also used by governments, for example, to make announcements, float ideas, control damage, put out negotiating positions, leak information, discredit opponents, and spin an event in a particular way. With the advent of CNN, and related networks such as CNN International and CNNE (*CNN en Español*), there is a 24-hour-a-day global

---

* Greenpeace protests against nuclear testing in the Pacific prompted the government of President François Mitterrand to authorize French intelligence agents to blow up Greenpeace's ship, *Rainbow Warrior*, when it was in Auckland. On 10 July 1985, the vessel was blown up, killing a Greenpeace photographer. Two French agents were arrested, put on trial, convicted of manslaughter, and sent to jail. The government in Paris demanded that they be released to serve their time in French jails. When France threatened New Zealand with economic sanctions, Wellington backed down: the agents were released to French custody. After a brief time in French prisons, the agents were released, and one was decorated for meritorious service.

news network beamed into the vast majority of cities on the planet. Importantly, this network can be used as a common means of indirect communication between political elites. For example, when the Iranian president, Mohammed Khatami, wanted to open a dialogue with the United States government in January 1998, he gave an interview on CNN. This assured that his conciliatory message would be widely heard in the United States, and force the administration of Bill Clinton to respond.

### Politics, the Media, and War

Nowhere is the symbiotic relationship between the political realm and the media more evident than during war. Governments want to use the media to generate support and to put a particular "spin" on war-fighting; that requires considerable control. For its part, the media wants access to "the story" and to be able to report news (and increase circulation or viewership). The resulting relationship is an uneasy one, as the following cases show.

During the war in Vietnam, the United States government made little effort to control the media. As increasing numbers of photographers and correspondents were deployed to cover the conflict, the more accessible the war became. As a result, there was a relatively free flow of images and stories about the fighting; soldiers were interviewed, their battlefield experiences and opinions broadcast or reported uncensored. It became, in Michael Arlen's phrase, a **"living-room war."**[19]

But the images of that war, broadcast to the living-rooms of the United States, eventually affected how that war was fought. The pictures of young GIs, bloody and bandaged, being brought back from firefights; the stories about the nature of guerrilla war, with its gruesome bamboo booby-traps, the narrow tunnels, and grenade attacks by children and civilians— these had an important impact on the "home front," providing a grisly reminder to draft-age American boys (and their parents) of what lay in store for them should they be drafted. At the same time, American government officials were having an increasingly hard time justifying the war. The daily rituals of the military briefing, in which the "body count" of the Vietnamese communists, or Viet Cong, killed was dutifully recorded as an indication that everything was going well, sat uneasily with the escalating demands for more and more American troops.

By 1967, public support for the war, and for President Lyndon B. Johnson himself, was declining dramatically. But the crucial turning point came during the lunar new year festival, called Tết, in 1968. Because the Viet Cong had declared a ceasefire for the holiday, South Vietnamese and American soldiers were given the holiday off. The ceasefire was a ruse: on 31 January, communist forces launched the **Tết offensive** against Saigon (as Ho Chi Minh City was known) and virtually every other South Vietnamese city. The Viet Cong and the North Vietnamese troops operating with them advanced as far as the grounds of the United States embassy, killing five embassy personnel. The offensive and its aftermath filled American newspapers, newsmagazines, and television screens; the media was transfixed by the huge number of American soldiers bleeding and dying. The images stunned Johnson, who eventually announced that he would not seek reelection. However, the focus on bleeding Americans prompted everyone to overlook the fact that the offensive had left the communists severely weakened. General Tran Van Tra, a senior communist commander, admitted after the war that had the United States counter-attacked, the Viet Cong would have collapsed.[20]

Such lax control over the media during wartime was not repeated when the British sent a military force to recapture the Falkland Islands after Argentina seized them in April 1982. The media was strictly and tightly regulated. A **media pool**\* was used, and only British reporters were allowed to accompany the task force; copy was controlled; and video images were tightly regulated. Whatever blood was spilled in the retaking of the islands was not seen on the television news. Despite the restrictions imposed on it, the British press nonetheless played a role in encouraging support for the war. The *Sunday Times* called it "the war that had to be," and the tabloid press was jingoistic: "Gotcha!" was the full-page banner headline of *The Sun* following the sinking of the Argentinean ship *General Belgrano* on 3 May 1982, with a loss of some 350 lives. The press was also used for military purposes: the Ministry of Defence put out rumours that a Royal Navy nuclear submarine, *HMS Superb*, was in the South Atlantic when in fact it was not. The press dutifully reported these stories, with the result that the Argentinean navy was hesitant to venture out of port in the early days of the conflict.

A slightly different tack was taken during the Persian Gulf War of 1991. In that conflict, the media was carefully played by the United States Department of Defense (DoD). Immediately after Iraq's invasion of Kuwait on 2 August 1990, the media was used (or allowed itself to be used) as an adjunct to the efforts of the administration of President George Bush to reverse the invasion. It was known that Saddam Hussein watched CNN, and so the administration sought to use that network as a channel for signalling to the Iraqi government before the war began.

*The Gulf War was quickly dubbed the "video game war," obviously by someone who had not been to an arcade since the late 1970s.*

After the start of the war itself, video images taken from American weapons systems were carefully fed to the media, and most of the military briefings revolved around the images of Iraqi buildings, bridges, and tanks being destroyed. Because of the widespread use of these nose-cone videos, the conflict was quickly dubbed the **"video game war,"** obviously by someone who had not been to an arcade since the late 1970s.\*\*

During the Gulf War, the media was also used for propaganda purposes. Kuwait hired a public relations firm to organize an anti-Iraqi campaign in the United States. The firm sent

---

\* A media pool is an arrangement used when it is impossible for a crowd of reporters and photographers to cover an event. Instead, one or two journalists are selected by their colleagues to report for the entire group; it is understood that those representing the pool will not try to score an exclusive "scoop," but will first report back to the group.

\*\* The Gulf War images were bloodless and sanitary: they showed buildings and tanks exploding, but the Iraqis being blown apart in these attacks were never visible. They were just like video games when they were in their infancy: Missile Command and Galaga were entirely bloodless. By contrast, video games today revel in their ability to portray as realistically as possible what actually happens to individuals engaged in Mortal Kombat—all severed limbs and decapitated heads, cheerfully spurting buckets of blood.

a young Kuwaiti girl to testify anonymously before the United States Congress that she had seen Iraqi troops commit atrocities in Kuwait City hospitals, dumping newborn babies out of their incubators. Her testimony was accepted by all of the Americans networks without question and was constantly repeated as evidence of Iraqi brutality. However, it later turned out that the girl was in fact the teenage daughter of the Kuwaiti ambassador to the United States and had been nowhere near Kuwait City in August 1990; her stories were fabrications.[21] For his part, Saddam Hussein also tried to use the media for propaganda purposes of his own, most of which backfired. When he paraded some of the women and children he was holding as hostages in front of the cameras, patting one young boy on the head, it merely fuelled foreign anger at the hostage-taking. Likewise, he allowed the cameras to tour a factory that the United States claimed was engaged in making explosives, but which the Iraqi government claimed was making baby formula. Any doubts about the American claim were laid to rest when the cameras showed crude cardboard signs hung around the factory, and workers with the English words "Baby Milk Factory" stencilled rather too obviously on their clothes.

## Nongovernmental Organizations

Another kind of organization active in world politics is the **nongovernmental organization** (NGO). It might be assumed that all the organizations we have examined to this point—the economic firms and media outlets—are NGOs: they are organizations and not "governmental." However, NGOs, as that word is used in world politics, are those organizations that are institutionally separate from governments and operate on a not-for-profit basis.[22] NGOs can be organized nationally, globally with national chapters, or globally, but any kind of NGO can play a role in world politics (in other words, NGO actors in world politics are not limited to those NGOs organized on an international basis).

The range of issues, objectives, and concerns of NGOs is massive. The landscape of politics in most communities is marked by individuals who come together to advance their interests in an organized way. In the United States, thousands of NGOs exist to press commercial or economic interests (such as business or industry associations, both at a federal level and in all 50 states); social issues (such as Mothers Against Drunk Driving); moral concerns (groups on either side of the abortion and capital punishment issues); environmental issues (such as the Sierra Club, Greenpeace, Friends of the Earth, and numerous others); issues of race (whether seeking racial equality, such as the National Association for the Advancement of Colored People, or seeking the opposite, such as the White Citizens Council or the Knights of the Ku Klux Klan); or a vast array of political issues, ranging from the National Rifle Association lobbying to allow the unrestricted import of semiautomatic weapons into the United States to the National Organization of Women organizing support at the Democratic National Convention in 1984 for the nomination of Geraldine Ferraro as vice-presidential candidate.

Some of these domestic groups try to have an impact on politics outside the United States. For example, the peak American union organization, the AFL-CIO (American Federation of Labor-Congress of Industrial Organizations), lobbied against the ratification of the North American Free Trade Agreement in 1993: Lane Kirkland, its president, called NAFTA "a poison pill."[23] The KKK sought to expand its operations beyond the United States, opening an office in Toronto in 1980. Some American environmental groups have protested the environmental practices of peoples and governments outside the United States. In 1994–95, the Rainforest Action Network protested the logging policies of the British Columbia government by running an ad campaign mimicking the province's tourist slogan—"Visit Beautiful British Columbia"—with the additional admonition to "Picnic in the clearcut forests. Hike the eroded hillsides. See the dried-up salmon streams."[24] In a similar vein, American ethnic interest groups lined up to pressure the United States Congress to approve the admission of new countries to NATO: the Polish American Congress, the Hungarian American Coalition, and the American Friends of the Czech Republic all applauded the July 1997 decision to admit Poland, Hungary, and the Czech Republic.

The activities of NGOs in one country often have an impact on politics elsewhere through **policy convergence**—where ideas from one jurisdiction are picked up by others and copied.[25] Thus, Mothers Against Drunk Driving began in the United States, but the idea of organizing a national protest movement against driving while under the influence of alcohol has spread to many other countries.

Some NGOs are organized on an international level; it is estimated that there are some 5000 NGOs active in contemporary international politics. The range of their concerns is no less catholic than one finds at the level of national politics. A full survey would be impossible. The following is an illustrative rather than exhaustive survey of some of the NGOs active in world politics.

## Humanitarian Groups

The desire to alleviate human suffering has been a powerful motivator for NGO activity. One of the oldest **humanitarian NGOs** is the International Red Cross and Red Crescent Movement, a group of NGOs dedicated to alleviating the suffering of those afflicted by war or disaster. It began when Jean Henri Dunant (1828–1910) came across the aftermath of the battle of Solferino in June 1859 during the Franco-Austrian war. There were some 40 000 casualties during that battle, and thousands lay untreated on the battlefield. Dunant helped organize emergency aid to the wounded, and subsequently wrote a book describing the horror of those who did not have proper care. He proposed the formation of a society in every country that would aid the wounded during war. Four years of persistent campaigning paid off: in October 1863 representatives from 16 countries met and agreed to form the Red Cross. (Although Dunant went bankrupt soon after and lived the next 40 years in poverty and obscurity, he was "rediscovered" by a newspaper reporter in the 1890s and propelled to celebrity status, being a co-recipient of the first Nobel Peace Prize in 1901.)

From those modest beginnings, the Red Cross (and in Muslim countries, the Red Crescent) grew into a worldwide network of national societies, whose work is coordinated by the International Committee of the Red Cross (ICRC) and the International Federation of the Red Cross and Red Crescent Societies. Beginning with the Dano-Prussian War of 1864, the Red Cross has provided care to the wounded, ambulances, canteens, rest homes for convalescing soldiers, and assistance to prisoners of war. National societies provided assistance to their own combatants, and the Geneva-based organizations—taking advantage of the perpetual neutrality of the Swiss government in all wars—helped to organize international cooperation. The activities of the Red Cross and Red Crescent also extend to relief operations in the wake of natural disasters.[26]

The many relief organizations established by various Christian churches in the 19th century—often outgrowths of the missionary impulse, discussed at more length below—also fall into the category of humanitarian NGOs, as would contemporary groups like *Médecins sans frontières* (MSF, or Doctors without Borders), which organizes volunteer medical units to provide services in war zones or areas hit by natural disasters.

## Human Rights Groups

The spread of the idea that human beings are endowed with certain rights has led to a concern over how humans everywhere are treated and whether their rights are being respected. **Human rights NGOs** are a natural outgrowth of this concern. For example, Amnesty International was founded in 1961 by a British lawyer, Peter Beneson, to press for the humane treatment of political prisoners overseas. Since then, it has expanded dramatically: AI chapters in more than 150 countries now boast more than a million members. AI "adopts" political prisoners and presses foreign governments for their release or humane treatment: since 1961, AI has intervened on behalf of more than 35 000 prisoners in more than 100 countries. And because AI is selective about whom it adopts—only those who do not advocate violence, for example—and is unfailingly polite in letters written to foreign governments, its "success rate" has been high. Indeed, AI's impact on world politics was recognized by being awarded the Nobel Peace Prize in 1977.

While Amnesty International is one of the largest human rights organizations, there are numerous groups—some organized nationally, others organized internationally—which monitor human rights concerns. Some, such as the "three watches"—Americas Watch, Africa Watch and Asia Watch—limit their focus to a particular region; some focus on one country, such as the East Timor Alert Network. Some focus on the rights of particular groups of individuals: the Writers-in-Prison Committee of International PEN, a worldwide association of writers, or the multinational NGO, End Child Prostitution in Asian Tourism, in Bangkok. Some emerge from a particular episode in a country's politics: the Mothers of the Plaza de Mayo gathered in the Plaza de Mayo in the centre of Buenos Aires to protest against the Argentinean junta for "disappearing" their sons and daughters during the "Dirty War" against leftists after the *coup d'état* in 1976.

## Environmental Groups

Concern over environmental degradation has also given rise to numerous **environmental NGOs**. Greenpeace is perhaps the best known of the contemporary NGOs which focus on the global environment. Like Amnesty International, it began as a local movement and expanded worldwide. It had its origins in Canadian protests against United States plans in 1971 to conduct underground nuclear tests on the island of Amchitka, at the western edge of the Aleutian chain. There was a fear that the tests would trigger tidal waves or earthquakes along the west coast; Canadian protests were loud and vociferous.[27] One of the west coast protest groups, the Don't Make A Wave Committee, later evolved into Greenpeace, an international organization with offices in 40 countries, a headquarters in Amsterdam, and a worldwide membership of more than three million people.

Unlike Amnesty International, however, Greenpeace is not at all polite in its approach to environmental politics. As we noted above, Greenpeace actively sought confrontation with the French authorities around Mururoa Atoll. This was typical of its tactics, which have featured civil disobedience, confrontation with authority, and feats of daring designed to capture media attention—and people's imaginations. Greenpeace has disrupted whaling operations, the harvest of harp seal pups on Canada's east coast, the planned sinking of an oil rig in the Atlantic, and nuclear testing. Its members have scaled corporate headquarters buildings and factory smokestacks to hang banners of protest.

Greenpeace's stridency is unusual. Other environmental groups, both nationally and internationally, work more quietly for environmental causes, often seeking to ensure that governments incorporate into their policy planning the notion of sustainable development— economic growth that maintains itself without exhausting resources or harming the natural environment. In this regard, we should also include the various Green parties around the world which are committed to an environmentally sensitive politics; however, because political parties are organizations that are connected to the state and thus not "non-governmental," we look at the Greens under the section on movements, below.

### The Impact of NGOs

Nongovernmental organizations have an important impact on the patterns of world politics. The founding of the Red Cross prompted a diplomatic conference in 1864 attended by 26 governments; it resulted in the first Geneva Convention regarding the care of those wounded in battle. A second convention in 1907 extended the principles to naval battles. A third convention in 1929 codified understandings on the rights and responsibilities of those taken as prisoners of war. And in 1949, a fourth convention outlined measures that were to be taken to protect civilians in times of war. Importantly, the various Red Cross and Red Crescent societies at the national level, and their International Committee in Geneva, play a critical role in upholding and maintaining the norms and standards agreed to in the various Geneva Conventions. In this way, NGOs have played an important role over the last century in making the dehumanizing nature of modern war-fighting slightly more humane.

NGOs have played a critical role in the politics of postwar reconstruction. Whether after an international war, such as the Second World War in Europe or the Korean War in the early 1950s, or after a civil war, such as in Cambodia in the early 1990s or Rwanda in the middle of the decade, NGOs have been active in moving supplies, providing assistance, rebuilding institutions, establishing medical convalescent services, and defusing mines— often with the assistance of governments.

Governments and NGOs often work together, as the case of the Red Cross suggests. Reconstruction after a war and even the delivery of development assistance rarely involves just the community of NGOs, but governments as well. And, as Kathryn Sikkink argues, interaction between governments and NGOs has been crucial for the development of human rights practices, from inclusion of human rights in the United Nations Charter in the 1940s to the pursuit of human rights in Latin America in the 1980s.[28] Indeed, efforts to monitor human rights are often met with cooperation by governments: Tung Chee-hwa, the chief executive of the Hong Kong Special Administrative Region, meets regularly with members of Human Rights Monitor to discuss human rights in the HKSAR. Even those accused of human rights violations cooperate on occasion: the Chinese government allowed groups of French and Australian parliamentarians to tour China on human rights missions in the early 1990s.

One measure of the importance of NGOs is the number of governments which have moved to involve them in policy development. Governments routinely consult NGOs, both formally and informally, and NGO representatives are frequently included on national delegations—a process that Denis Stairs has termed the **domestication of foreign policy**.[29] Governments do this for two primary reasons. First, consultation allows governments to tap into the considerable expertise that NGOs tend to develop. Second, consultation allows governments to engage in the intricate game of **stakeholder politics**, which involves drawing various "interested parties" into the process of policy-making (thus assuring, if nothing else, that NGOs which have been consulted by government are less able to criticize policy that emerges from that process).

For similar reasons, international organizations have included NGOs in their activities, and in some international organizations, NGOs have special rights of participation and consultation. NGOs have become so embedded and institutionalized in contemporary international politics that NGO forums are now held whenever the United Nations holds its major World Conferences on specific issues. While the representatives of the world's 190 governments discuss an issue in an intergovernmental setting, delegates from NGOs hold their own conference, often issuing an Alternative Declaration to the one issued by the intergovernmental conference.[30]

Frequently, however, there is tension between governments and nongovernmental organizations. For example, a coalition of 45 NGOs, including the International Rivers Network and the Sierra Club, organized transnational opposition to the Three Gorges Dam on the Yangtze River in China. The project is massive: costing over US$25 billion, the dam will be 200 metres high, creating a lake over 640 km in length and an average of 2 km wide. Over 1.2 million people will be forced to moved and numerous cities will be inundated. Over 18 200 megawatts of electricity a year will be generated by the hydro-electric generating stations—over a tenth of China's output. But the environmental costs have pitted NGOs against the Chinese government, making the project politically sensitive abroad: government institutions, such as the Export-Import Bank in the United States, international financial institutions such as the World Bank, and even private investment houses, have refused to provide financing for the project, forcing the Chinese government to seek private financing through bonds issued by the State Development Bank of China.

However, even when NGOs and governments seek to cooperate, there can still be problems. As Leslie A. Pal has shown on the issue of human rights,[31] governments and NGOs often speak a different language, have different assumptions about what is important, and often have radically different objectives. At the United Nations World Conference on Women in September 1995, the Chinese government located the NGO forum in Huairou, a town some 50 km from Beijing. The Chinese government claimed locating the conference there was necessary because the capital could not accommodate both the intergovernmental conference and the 30 000 delegates at the NGO forum; critics claimed that the NGO forum was located well out-of-town to limit the exposure of Beijing women to the ideas and views being expressed by NGO delegates.

## Movements

A **social movement** is a very loosely organized collection of individuals who pursue the same set of political or social goals. Strictly speaking, a movement is not a political "actor"; only those individuals who embrace the ideals of the movement and seek to advance it by political action are the "actors." Our task here is to identify a number of movements that have been important in galvanizing activity at a global level.

### Religious Movements

The desire to propagate particular religious beliefs has always been a powerful driving force in world politics. **Missionary religions** are those whose members seek to convince others to embrace their conception of the divine. Three of the world's dominant religions—Buddhism, Christianity, and Islam—have always been missionary religions; in antiquity Judaism was more missionary than at present; and Hinduism became more missionary only in the last century. Buddhism is the oldest missionary religion, beginning its spread under the Mauryan king Asoka in the third century BC.

Christianity spread from its origins in the Roman province of Judea throughout southern and northwestern Europe in the first millennium after Christ, as far west as Ireland and as far east as China (where it flourished in the imperial capital before being eliminated by persecutions beginning in 845). When European sailors began their world explorations in the 15th century, they were accompanied by clergy eager to bring new souls into the Christian fold. The age of European imperialism was thus also an age of Christian missionary expansionism. The legacy of that activity remains today, as Christian churches maintain a network of missions around the world that continue to engage not only in evangelizing, but also in a variety of social, political, and development activities.

Of all the Christian denominations, the Roman Catholic church remains the most visible international actor. It intervened at the United Nations Conference on Population held in Cairo in 1994 to oppose birth control.[32] Pope John Paul II has played a prominent role in international politics, travelling widely and taking positions on international issues. A Pole by birth and a former archbishop of Kraków, he championed the cause of freedom from the USSR in Eastern Europe with such vigour that it was widely believed that the Soviet Union was behind the attempt on his life on 13 May 1981 by Mehmet Ali

Agca, who worked for the Bulgarian secret service. John Paul II also closed down much of the political activity by radical priests in Latin America and Africa, forbidding priests from engaging in political activities or from holding public office.

The teachings of the Prophet Muhammad were also spread throughout the international system. From the Arabian peninsula in the seventh century, the military victories of the Islamic caliphate in northern Africa and the Middle East brought Islam to millions of people, as we will see in the next chapter. Beyond these lands, individual merchants, travellers, and traders to the countries of Africa and Asia spread Islam as far east as Indonesia and as far west as Cap Vert in Senegal. But it was not until the 19th century, and the formation of the Ahmadiyya movement in 1889, that there was an Islamic missionary organization similar to those of Christian churches.

### Ideological Movements

An **ideology** is a comprehensive set of beliefs about the political world. Ideologies provide not only a way of understanding the world, but also a blueprint for a creating a better world. We will see in the chapters ahead the profound impact that ideas can have on international politics.

Because they purport to offer the Truth, ideologies tend to encourage a missionary zeal in some of their adherents, a desire to spread the "good word" to others. For example, we will see in Chapter 12 that the ideas of Adam Smith did not simply propagate themselves through sales of *The Wealth of Nations*; his ideas were pushed by those who believed in his critique of mercantilism. Even then, it took nearly three generations for his ideas to be incorporated into English policy.

**Organized Ideological Movements: The Case of Communism**    Some ideological movements are organized into transnational "internationals"—organizations that link political parties of similar persuasion. These include the Christian Democrat International (CDI); the International Democrat Union, which attracts centre-right and conservative parties; the Liberal International; and the Socialist International.

The various "Internationals" that today link political parties with similar ideological persuasions are derived from an earlier effort to organize the spread of the ideology of **communism** internationally. Karl Marx (1818–1883) and Friedrich Engels (1820–1895) were not content to depend on natural propagation of their ideas about history and politics. Rather, they tried to translate their understanding of scientific socialism into political action. What they saw as the inevitable clash between the capitalist bourgeoisie and the working class, or proletariat, was not of mere academic or scholarly interest, but rather the basis for political action. Both were active in the Communist League which commissioned them to write a statement of principles and objectives. The *Communist Manifesto* was published just before the great revolutions which swept across Europe throughout 1848. This document was the central statement of a movement that tried to create a supranational solidarity among members of the working class. This movement was institutionalized in 1864 in the International Workingmen's Association in London, also known as the First International, which collapsed in internal bickering between communists and anarchists. In 1889, the centenary of the French Revolution and a year after Marx's death, a Second International was formed. This organization of socialists eventually established a coordinating office in Brussels in 1900; this International Socialist Bureau was charged with the propagation of class solidarity across borders. But the Second International abandoned the idea of revolution, instead seeking to work within the existing political systems for reform. It came to an end with the outbreak of the Great War in 1914, when national loyalties proved more durable than class loyalties, and socialists across Europe ended up supporting their nations in that conflict.

The **Bolshevik revolution** in Russia in 1917, examined in more detail in Chapters 14 and 15, was organized by Vladimir Ilich Lenin (1870–1924). Lenin was a Marxist political theorist in his own right, who contributed to a debate on the origins of European imperialism. He was also a strategist—his 1902 book, *What Is To Be Done?*, explains the principles of revolution based on the necessity of a highly organized professional group that would act as the "vanguard" of the working class. In 1919, Lenin organized the Third International, usually known as the Communist International or Comintern. The purpose of this organization was to propagate the ideas of Marxism-Leninism—the notion of a Marxist state brought about by a Leninist revolution carried out by a vanguard. Lenin's successor, Joseph Stalin, dissolved the Comintern in 1943. It was replaced in 1947 by the Communist Information Bureau or Cominform, which was supposed to act as a coordinating mechanism for communist parties around the world, but it too was dissolved in 1956.

After 1919, the Communist International ceased to be a truly transnational movement. Instead, it was controlled by the Communist Party of the Soviet Union (CPSU)—and hence can be seen more properly as an agency of the Soviet state. However, while the Internationals eventually collapsed, they were nonetheless important in spreading communism. Millions of people came to believe in the communist ideal, including those whose political leadership would deeply affect global politics in the period after the Second World War—Mao Zedong, Zhou Enlai, and other Chinese leaders; Kim Il Sung in Korea; and Ho Chi Minh in Vietnam.

Many people in capitalist societies in the period between the two world wars were enamoured with the Soviet Union as the world's only "worker's paradise." These enthusiasts tended to overlook some of the grimmer features of Marxism-Leninism as practised by Stalin: the collectivization of farming that led to a famine in the Ukraine in 1932 and 1933, killing approximately seven million people; and the **Great Terror**, the name given to the ruthless extermination of anyone vaguely suspected of posing a threat to Stalin or the regime. Soviet intelligence agents were particularly skilled at capitalizing on these sympathies. In the interwar period, numerous individuals joined communist parties in their countries; some were recruited as spies and agents of influence for the USSR. The most successful operation was at Cambridge University, where Guy Burgess, Kim Philby, Anthony Blunt, and Donald Maclean were recruited as double agents to spy for the USSR. Philby went to work for MI6, the British secret intelligence service, rising through the ranks to become head of the anti-Soviet section and then chief intelligence liaison with the United States—all the while passing information to Moscow.

But there were other operations: in 1945, a cipher clerk at the Soviet embassy in Ottawa, Igor Gouzenko, defected, revealing a communist spy ring that included a McGill University scientist and the only Marxist member of Parliament, Fred Rose. In the United States, Julius Rosenberg, a member of the Communist Party of the United States, passed information about the construction of atomic weapons to the Soviet Union. In 1951, he and his wife Ethel were charged under the Espionage Act of 1917, convicted, and executed in 1953. Because of cases such as these, even those who had been members of the Communist Party were unable to shake the suspicion that they were Soviet agents. For example, E. Herbert Norman, who had been a communist sympathizer during his Cambridge University days in the 1930s before joining the Canadian diplomatic service, was publicly accused by the United States Congress in the 1950s of being a Soviet spy. Although he was cleared by internal investigations, the charges continued into the mid-1950s; finally, in April 1957, Norman, who by that time was Canada's ambassador to Egypt, jumped to his death from his Cairo apartment building.

By the centenary of the Second International in 1989, the communist movement had collapsed. In China, protests by students and workers against corruption in the Chinese Communist Party were put down with great brutality in Tiananmen Square in June; in November, protests against the communist regime in East Germany led to the breaching of the Berlin Wall that had been erected in August 1961; in December, demonstrations in Romania led to the toppling of the regime and the execution of the president, Nicolae Ceausescu and his wife Elena on 25 December. Within two years, the Soviet Union itself would be declared at an end.

The case of communism provides a good illustration of the range of global actors that can be involved in ideological movements: university students, who are testing ideas and challenging authority; workers moved by the power of ideas; and academics and others who move ideas across borders. And in this case, we have to include spies and intelligence agents, whose job is to ferret out information and if necessary to "turn" individuals to work for the cause. But if we look at the transnational spread of other ideological movements—whether it be fascism in the 1930s or neoconservatism in the 1980s—we will see a similar range of actors and agents trying to spread the "good word."

### Social and Political Movements

Some movements are not highly ideological, but nonetheless have political or social goals. The anti-slavery movement, the human rights movement, the environmental movement, and various peace movements are examples of social and political movements that have had an impact on international politics. Although some would argue that there is an ideological component to these movements, in fact they tend to be united by sets of ideas that are often only loosely connected.

For example, the **environmental movement** is not based on an ideology, but rather ideas that tend to unite environmentalists: sustainable development, minimal pollution, minimal interruption to the ecology, maximum conservation of energy, and zero population growth. In many countries **green parties**—green being the acknowledged colour of the environmental movement—have emerged as the standard bearers of the environmental movement at election time. Most of today's green parties did not begin life that way. The United Tasmania Group was organized to contest state elections in the early 1970s on the issue of the flooding of Lake Pedder for hydroelectric development. This first green party was copied in New Zealand, spread to Britain in 1973, and then to Germany, where in January 1980, a number of environmentalist parties met to form *Die Grünen* (the Greens), some of whom were eventually elected to the *Bundestag* in the 1983 elections. Since then, most environmental parties have adopted the name Green (though some, such as Belgium's Agalev—*Anders Gaan Leven*, or Live Differently Party—retain their original names).

## Think Tanks

The spread of ideas transnationally has been important for movements of all kinds. Ideas move through interpersonal meetings, by the media, by mail, by phone, and over the Internet. In the spread of ideas, think tanks also play an important role. As the name suggests, a **think tank** is an institution, usually but not always a not-for-profit nongovernmental organization, that exists primarily to engage in research and thinking about policy questions. Invariably they have as their mission the encouragement of discussion about international affairs and the dissemination of knowledge. Thus, they fall into a special category: they have some of the characteristics of an NGO and can play an important role in ideological or social movements.

Some think tanks focus on broad foreign policy matters and the encouragement of public discussion of international affairs. Most countries have an institute modelled on the Royal Institute of International Affairs (RIIA) in Britain or the Council on Foreign Relations in the United States, such as the Australian Institute of International Affairs and the Canadian Institute of International Affairs. In some countries, institutes of international affairs are private not-for-profit organizations; in others, these institutes are run out of the country's foreign ministry. These organizations usually publish a journal, host public conferences, and may run a research and publication program. In some cases, these institutions are important venues for what is known as **track-two diplomacy**—where nongovernmental actors are used by governments to engage in talks or relations that might be considered too sensitive or politically difficult for governments (which operate on "track one"). Thus, for example, in the late 1980s and early 1990s, a Malaysian think tank, the Institute of Strategic and International Studies (ISIS), played a critical role in bringing together nongovernmental actors from countries around the Asia-Pacific for discussions on security matters that could never have occurred between government officials of those countries, and laid the foundation for a "track one" organization, the ASEAN Regional Forum (ARF).[33]

Some think tanks are primarily research institutions: the Rand Corporation, the Hudson Institute, and the Brookings Institution in the United States, and the International Institute for Strategic Studies (IISS) in Britain focus on strategic policy matters, and the World Resources Institute, a "green" think tank, does research on sustainable development.

Think tanks are important global actors because they have the capacity to shape global debates through the process of policy convergence discussed above. Many of the neoconservative ideas that were embraced by governments in the 1980s and 1990s, such as privatization and deregulation, were spread throughout the international system by neo-conservative think tanks like the Heritage Foundation and the Cato Institute, and even by "think tank clubs" like the Atlas Foundation, which tries to bring together the world's neo-conservative think tanks.[34]

## "Terrorists"

What is a "terrorist"? The word has been so overused—and cynically and hypocritically abused for political purposes—that it has lost much of its meaning. In particular, political leaders and the media tend to brand as a "terrorist" anyone who uses violence for political purposes that they do not agree with; by contrast, those who use violence for "good" objectives are given another, more exculpatory, name such as "freedom fighter." As Ian Smart has observed, "'terrorist' has become a term of glib abuse, intended to express contempt."[35] Virtually any form of political violence, such as an assassination, a targeted killing or bombing, or a kidnapping, becomes a "terrorist" act.

> "'Terrorist' has become a term of glib abuse, intended to express contempt."

A more precise way of thinking about terrorists and **terrorism** is to keep in mind that terror is a political tool. As we saw in Chapter 5, one of the ways of wielding power and ensuring that one's interests prevail over those of others is by the use of terror; thus, strictly speaking, *anyone* who uses terror as a political instrument is a terrorist.

Normally terror is created by using violence, since human beings fear pain and death. But it is important to remember that not every act of violence is designed to create terror; it is misleading simply to equate violence with terror. Moreover, it is equally important to remember that one can create terror by means other than violence. For example, we will see in Chapter 9 that the Church in Rome used the **interdict** as a weapon against rebellious kings. When a country was placed under an interdict, no one was permitted to receive any of the Christian sacraments. This was a frightful situation for those who believed that without the sacraments they would suffer hellfire for all eternity; the interdict was nothing less than a terrorist act.

If measured purely in terms of the number of people who have been terrorized, or actually killed or injured by attempts to create terror, the most common terrorists in world politics are governments and their agents: members of armed forces, secret intelligence services, internal security forces, public safety agencies, and police, and of course those politicians and political leaders who direct their activities, approve their operations, or simply choose not to know what their agents are doing.

The largest-scale terrorist operation known to history was the use of nuclear weapons during the Cold War. Both the United States and the Soviet Union targeted their nuclear warheads against the other country's cities, and thus held the other side's population hostage. There was widespread fear of nuclear attack, the horrible effects of which were seen after the United States dropped atomic bombs on Hiroshima on 6 August 1945 and Nagasaki three days later. Each side depended on the fear of nuclear attack to deter the other side from trying to dominate, a process entitled (none too delicately but quite appropriately) the **balance of terror**. This terror was created entirely by *deploying* huge nuclear arsenals, not by actually using them.

Governments also try to create terror by inflicting pain and death. When governments bomb cities during war, these are quite self-conscious acts of terror: the purpose of city-bombing is to kill and maim indiscriminately, and by doing so to instil in the civilians who remain alive a fear that they and their loved ones may be next. Of course the creation of such fear is not an end in itself: the instrumental purpose of fear is to weaken the will to fight, to sow the seeds of disaffection, and to encourage the dispirited to bring the war to an end.

Likewise, when agents of a security force knock on someone's door at 2:30 a.m., rouse everyone from their sleep, and hustle the arrested person off to a headquarters from which they may not return, the purpose is not simply to take that particular individual into custody. It is also to create fear in all those who are watching from behind their curtains: they could be next.

Terrorist acts by government agents have killed of millions of people over the course of the 20th century. Consider the number of people killed by Soviet security forces during the Great Terror in the 1930s, either by firing squad or by being sent to the system of prison camps known as the Gulag (from *Glavnoye upravlenie lagereiy*, Chief Administration of Camps). Some estimates put the number of those who died in this fashion at 30 million; many of these would have been killed purely as an example. Or consider the use of terror by the Nazi regime in Germany: the random killings in both the ghettoes and the concentration camps that were designed to keep people in fear while the regime found ways to exterminate them (an act of violence that was, by contrast, *not* an act of terrorism, but pure instrumentalist genocide). Consider the number of people, many of them totally innocent children, who died when governments used city-bombing to try to destroy civilian morale: during the Spanish civil war in the 1930s; by the United States, Britain, and Germany during the Second World War; by the United States during the Vietnam War in the 1960s and early 1970s; by the Soviet Union during the war in Afghanistan in the 1980s; or by the United States and other members of the international coalition during the Persian Gulf War in 1991.

Terrorism is frequently used by governments in countries that have dissolved into civil war, often in response to the use of similar tactics by opponents. For example, thousands of Algerians died during the war of independence at the hands of French forces who imposed collective punishments against communities suspected of harbouring guerrilla fighters; sometimes entire villages were slaughtered, partly in retribution, but also partly to instil fear in others. Thousands of people died at the hands of security forces in Argentina during the **Dirty War** in the 1970s. Many leftists, real or imagined, were "disappeared" by security forces, many of them dropped alive out of helicopters into the South Atlantic after having been tortured, tales of their fate purposely spread through Argentinean society to create fear. Security forces have used violence to create terror in Chile, China, East Germany, India, Indonesia, Iran, Iraq, Libya, Pakistan, apartheid South Africa, the former Soviet Union, Sudan, Syria, and Uganda.

Governments also routinely support others in the international system who use terror tactics; they run training courses on the use of torture. The United States government trained officers of Savak, the secret police of Reza Shah Pahlavi of Iran. Washington also provided support for the Chilean security forces after the September 1973 *coup d'état* in which Salvador Allende Gossens was overthrown and murdered, and which brought Gen. Augusto Pinochet Ugarte to power. It supported the South African apartheid regime and its Bureau of State Security (BOSS). Torture was routinely used in Iran, Chile, and South Africa to create terror. American-made electroshock equipment has been exported to governments around the world for use in torturing their citizens. During Ronald Reagan's presidency, the United States supplied the *contras* who were fighting the Sandinista regime in Nicaragua and the *mujahideen* fighting the Soviet invaders in Afghanistan. Both *contras* and *mujahideen* routinely used terrorist tactics: indeed, the *mujahideen* purposely inflicted the most horrible tortures on the young Soviet conscripts they captured for the sole purpose of weakening the Soviet will to fight in Afghanistan.

But the United States government is by no means alone in its support for terrorists. During the Cold War, the Soviet Union not only inflicted terror on its own citizens, but also encouraged the use of terrorist tactics by others—by governments in Eastern Europe and by other groups in the international system. In the 1980s, the Syrian government of Hafez Assad supported terrorist attacks against American, European, and Israeli targets so openly that the media did not even have to depend on clandestine sources in intelligence agencies to put together stories linking the Syrian government to a long list of attacks.[36] In addition, Algeria, Bulgaria, Cuba, Czechoslovakia, East Germany, Hungary, Iran, Iraq, Lebanon, Libya, North Korea, and South Yemen all provided either training facilities, arms, or money to groups that engaged in terrorist activities. In the post-Cold War period, government support for terrorist activities diminished somewhat, although a number of countries—Iran, Iraq, and Sudan—are associated with support for nongovernmental terrorist groups.

**Nongovernmental terrorism** tends to take a different form than the use of terror by governments. Governmental terror tends to be routinized, highly bureaucratized, and institutionalized. Well-developed bureaucratic systems and a large number of government employees are needed to send a United States Air Force B-52 bomber on a raid to terrorize the residents of a suburb of Hanoi or Baghdad. By contrast, nongovernmental groups which resort to terror tend to employ rather different tactics, usually dramatic and violent bombing attacks, often utterly random.

Of course, the actual results of attacks by governments and nongovernmental groups do not differ at all. The milk-churn bombs that were set off in the King David Hotel in Jerusalem on 22 July 1946 by an Irgun terror squad under the direction of Menachem Begin* had exactly the same effects as the high-explosive bomb dropped by the United States Air Force, acting on the authority of President George Bush, on an air raid shelter in

---

* Begin's terrorism as a 32-year-old did him no long-lasting political damage. He eventually served as Israel's prime minister from 1977 to 1983, and in that role was often openly welcomed by the same leaders who routinely denounced exactly the kind of political violence that he had perpetrated in 1946.

Baghdad on 13 February 1991. In both cases, large numbers of people were killed: the bombs detonated on Begin's orders killed 91 people, including 17 Jews; the bomb dropped on Bush's orders killed an undetermined number of people, estimated to be between 300 and 500. And the physical effects were precisely the same: the pressure created by such explosions caused internal organs such as hearts, lungs, and livers to burst; flesh and bone close to the blast was vaporized, the victims literally disappearing without a trace; and building material, furniture, bomb fragments, and shrapnel ripped apart those who were not at the centre of the blast.

And the purpose of such attacks do not differ much either. Governments use terrorism to create a climate of fear that will cause people to bend to their will; nongovernmental groups also use terrorist tactics to create fear for political purposes. At times, they try to do this by engaging in singular acts of random violence on innocent people. These attacks are not intended to kill large numbers, but instead are designed to have ripple effects on those who witness the violence. As Brian Jenkins has said, "Terrorists want a lot of people watching, not a lot of people dead."[37] Thus, in Egypt in the mid- and late-1990s, when militant opponents of the regime targeted foreign tourists, they actually killed relatively few foreigners. But their campaign weakened the Egyptian tourist industry. At other times, the intent is to create terror *and* to kill large numbers of people. That was clearly the case with the poisonous nerve gas released in the Tokyo subway system in March 1995 by members of Aum Shinrikyo, a religious cult. While only 11 people died, more than 5500 were injured.

*"Terrorists want a lot of people watching, not a lot of people dead."*

However, the Aum Shinrikyo attack was relatively unusual. More common has been the use of widespread violence to both create terror and eliminate the terrorized. Thus, for example, when the Vietnamese communists decided in 1959 to try to destabilize the government of South Vietnam, they targeted local village chiefs and school teachers who were loyal to the regime in Saigon. During the assassination campaign, 4000 South Vietnamese government officials were killed each year. Likewise, immediately after the elections set by the Islamic Salvation Front were cancelled in January 1992, militant Islamic groups such as the GIA (*Groupe islamique armée*, Armed Islamic Group) targeted foreigners, journalists, and ordinary Algerians: tens of thousands of men, women, and children have been killed, usually by having their throats slit. In each of these cases, the purpose was to terrorize a specific group of individuals—and to kill as many of them as possible.

Often, acts committed by the same group may have very different purposes that tend to be obscured when we call every act by that group "terrorist." For example, for nearly three decades Palestinian groups such as the Popular Front for the Liberation of Palestine, Black September, the Revolutionary Council of Fatah, *Hamas* (Islamic Resistance Movement), and *Hezbollah* (Party of God) carried on a war against Israel that featured random acts of violence directed against Israelis, Americans, and Europeans. Much of the violence directed at Americans and Europeans in the 1980s—the hijacking or bombing of aircraft, the machine-gun attacks at Rome and Vienna airports in December 1985—was designed to weaken the support of those countries for Israel. By contrast, the violence inflicted on

Israelis, such as *Hamas* suicide bombings in Tel Aviv and Jerusalem, had a range of purposes besides creating terror among Israelis, from retaliation to highly specific political ends, such as disrupting the peace process.

So too in the case of other groups, such as the Irish Republic Army, the Liberation Tigers of Tamil Eelam (LTTE) in Sri Lanka, or the ETA (*Euzkadi ta Azkatasuna*, or Basque Homeland and Liberty) in Spain: while some of the actions of these groups clearly have been designed to create terror, much of their killing was more properly assassination than terrorism.

In short, when we identify as terrorists just a small group of the actors who use terror, we lose sight of the fact that the violence perpetrated by some "terrorist" groups is not at all designed to create terror. We also lose sight of the fact that some actors whom we do not usually think of as terrorists (such as agents of legitimate governments or medieval popes) are very much in the business of seeking to advance their political goals by the creation of terror.

## Governments

The stage of world politics is crowded by those who claim to act on behalf of, and in the name of, different political communities. While these actors are called "governments," it is for convenience only: for the precise nature of these "government" actors varies greatly depending on the era. At times, we may be looking at emperors, kings, princes, members of their courts, and their armies; at other times, we may be looking at leaders of large armed nomadic bands. In the contemporary period, "governments" consist of the agents of the modern state—a political formation we look at in more detail in Chapter 9. However, at all times and in all places, we want to see how the interaction of the agents of political communities influences politics at a global level.

The discussion in Chapter 6 about code also applies here: when we speak of *governments* acting in international politics, we really mean those individuals who occupy positions as political leaders (emperors, kings, presidents, prime ministers, premiers, foreign ministers, cabinet ministers) and their various and sundry agents. As a consequence, we need to consider the full panoply of individuals who act on behalf of the political community and in the name of its government: political leaders, parliamentarians, diplomats, soldiers, spies, and other bureaucrats in the state apparatus.

### The Political Leadership

Virtually all political communities known to history have leaders—individuals who are recognized as able to speak for the political community, to lead it, to make decisions in its name. Over time the names of these positions change, as does how individuals come to these positions, and what range of powers they may exercise. But there are some key commonalities for the purpose of our exploration into world politics: in relating with other peoples and other communities, the **political leadership** commonly personifies the community and acts on its behalf and in its name; leaders, because of their positions *within* the community, are also well placed to try and galvanize the energies of the community *vis-à-vis* other communities. For this reason, political leaders are crucial actors in international relations: the decisions they make can have a profound influence on the course and nature of politics at a global level.

This is not to suggest that world politics is simply the outcome of the decisions and actions of the men and women who occupy leadership positions in 190 states today. On the contrary: as we have suggested above, world politics is shaped by numerous actors and forces. And leaders themselves are pushed and pulled in a variety of directions by different forces. They are constrained by constitutional limits on their authority; they are impelled by the demands of politics within their community; they are moved by ideas and perceptions of what is the "right thing" to do in a given situation. Strong systemic forces, internal and external, influence the decisions all leaders make daily.

That being noted, there can be little doubt that individual leaders matter. They may be "shaped" by systemic forces, and they may be bound by numerous constraints, but individual leaders can make a difference. Again using the notion of contingency and path dependency discussed in Chapter 2, we can get a sense of the importance of leadership by considering how differently world politics would have played out had Joseph Stalin suffered a massive coronary at the age of 40 in 1919; or had Mao Zedong died of disease on the Long March in the winter of 1934; or had Franklin D. Roosevelt adhered to the norm set by George Washington and not sought a third term in the summer of 1940, but had instead left the Democratic nomination for the isolationist John Nance Garner; or had Richard M. Nixon been more confident in his chances for reelection in 1972 and not bothered to engage "plumbers" to burgle and wiretap the campaign headquarters of the Democratic party at the Watergate Hotel that eventually forced his resignation; or had the Provisional Irish Republican Army bomb that blew up the Grand Hotel in Brighton in October 1984 caught Margaret Thatcher in its blast; or had P.W. Botha not suffered a stroke in January 1989 and F.W. De Klerk remained the South African minister for education; or had Nelson Mandela suffered a fatal beating at the hands of a jailer at Robben Island maximum security prison in 1966.

In each of these counterfactual situations, other names would surely have filled the empty spaces, but the resulting pattern of politics would surely have differed. For there is nothing automatic about the flow of events which individuals do so much to shape. For example, in the absence of a De Klerk and a Mandela, who is to say how the end of apartheid in South Africa might have come about?

Political leaders act out their parts in world politics in a constant and complex whirlwind of carefully choreographed activities. They make hundreds of routine decisions on matters of state that touch on world affairs; they give numerous speeches outlining their views on international questions that are thus the views of the governments they head; they host visitors from overseas; they themselves frequently visit other countries; they make countless telephone calls about global issues to other leaders and to domestic actors; and their calendars are organized around a circuit of **summit meetings**, as meetings of political leaders are called.

In the category of political leadership we also need to include **legislators** or parliamentarians—the elected representatives of the political community. Most parliamentarians are active players on the stage of world politics: their debates and decisions affect political outcomes; the interparliamentary meetings they attend are another important form of international communication; and the trips they take abroad tend to influence their attitudes toward global issues. Some legislators are more important than others: in Westminster-style systems, those Members of Parliament who sit in cabinet are considerably more important than those who remain on the government and opposition backbenches. In the United States, where the separation of powers provides the Congress with immense power over foreign affairs quite independent of the president, legislators are crucial players. The attitudes and policy behaviour of members of Congress are of great importance, particularly the leadership of the Senate and the House of Representatives, and the leadership of key committees such as the chair of the Senate Committee on Foreign Relations.

### Government Agents: Diplomats, Soldiers, Spies, Traders

Presidents, prime ministers, premiers, foreign ministers, and other cabinet ministers make decisions on behalf of governments, but the actual behaviour of governments are the actions of the hundreds of thousands of agents of different governments acting on orders, general or specific, from their political leaders. We can classify these agents into four major groups.

**Diplomats**    **Diplomats** are the agents responsible for conducting and maintaining relations between political communities. The bureaucratic arm of a government responsible for these relations is generically known as a **foreign ministry**, usually with names like Department of Foreign Affairs.* Diplomats have a number of different functions. Posted to a foreign capital, they *represent* their government in other countries, explaining and pressing the interests of their government to other governments. Diplomats are the main way in which governments *communicate* with one another. While political leaders pick up the phone and chat with one another and meet one another at summit meetings, most of the business between governments is handled by diplomats. Diplomats *negotiate* on behalf of their government, in both bilateral negotiations (with only two sides) and multilateral negotiations (in which a number of governments are negotiating). Indeed, much of the interaction between diplomats is highly routinized: just as government leaders have regular summits to discuss matters, so too do bureaucrats have their own summits, usually known as Senior Officials Meetings (SOMs). Diplomats *gather intelligence* about the country they are posted to: they try to get to know the personalities, the local customs, the local politics, and local issues. They also *perform consular services*: they handle requests for visas and provide services to the citizens of their own country who are travelling abroad and have run into trouble. Diplomats also have a policy-making function: they *provide advice* to their political leaders. Finally, one of the functions of diplomats is to *be diplomatic*—in other words, to try to minimize frictions between societies and governments.

---

* In the United States, the foreign ministry is called the Department of State; in Britain, it is the Foreign and Commonwealth Office (FCO). In some countries, the ministry of foreign affairs and the agency responsible for international trade have been merged, for example, the Australian Department of Foreign Affairs and Trade (DFAT) and the Canadian Department of Foreign Affairs and International Trade (DFAIT).

**Soldiers** Members of a government's **armed forces** are agents in world politics of a different sort. Armed forces include all those agents of a political community who are organized to kill other human beings on command. Armed forces vary according to the period in history and the technology available. They can include such groups as infantry, archers, cavalry, charioteers, artillery, armour, marines, navy, air force, and whatever state agency controls nuclear weapons and space-based weaponry, together with all those in support roles: those who provision armed forces, provide logistics, and administer everything from supplies to pension plans. And we have to include those "private" armed forces hired by the state—whether the privateers of old, licensed by monarchs to go marauding; classical mercenaries; or forces put together by transnational security corporations.

Armed forces are used in a variety of ways that affect world politics. Political communities use them to defend themselves against the predations of others, to seize or enslave other communities, or to dominate others or bend them to one's will through coercion. Stationed on the soil of friends, they can be used to deter attack, prop up a shaky regime, or provide a visible symbol of one country's commitment to another; stationed on the soil of enemies, they can be used to plunder or keep that country weak. Armed forces can be used to separate enemies (for example, in peacekeeping operations), to try to restore order in civil war situations (peacemaking operations), or even to help create civil institutions (peacebuilding operations).

**Spies and Secret Services** As the above discussion of ideological movements suggested, many political communities maintain agencies to provide a range of security services for the state beyond military activities. Many governments maintain counterterrorist units; some state agencies are organized to defend against espionage, subversion, and terrorism by other states—and to conduct espionage, subversion, and terrorism against others. Secret services that operate outside the country against other countries are called **offensive intelligence agencies**; those which only conduct operations within their own countries are termed **defensive intelligence agencies**.

Most large countries maintain both kinds of agencies. The United States, for example, has a large number of different intelligence agencies, but the primary external agency is the Central Intelligence Agency (CIA) and the internal agency is the Federal Bureau of Investigation (FBI). The Soviet Union had the KGB (*Komitet gosudarstvennoy bezopasnosti*, Committee on State Security). After the collapse of the USSR in 1991, the KGB was reorganized into the Russian Foreign Intelligence Service (FIS), which operates abroad, and the FSB (*Federalnaja Sluzhba Besopasnosti*, Federal Security Service), which operates in Russia itself. The British intelligence services emerged from sections of wartime Military Intelligence; Section 5 (MI5) was responsible for domestic operations and Section 6 (MI6) for external operations. The French agency is the *Direction générale de la Sécurité extérieure* (DGSE). The People's Republic of China has one agency, the Ministry of State Security, for both internal and external operations; external operations are run out of three bureaux: Foreign Affairs, Overseas Chinese, and Taiwan.

Smaller countries also have such agencies. Israel's external intelligence agency is known as Mossad (after *Mossad Merkazi Le Modin Uletafkidim*, Central Institute for Intelligence and Special Missions). The Canadian Security and Intelligence Service (CSIS) and the

Australian Security Intelligence Organisation (ASIO) are defensive agencies, while the Australian Secret Intelligence Service (ASIS) is permitted to conduct offensive operations.

Agents of secret services spend a great deal of time recruiting people in other countries to work for them as moles or "turning" agents of other services to work as double agents. Some double agents, like Philby and his Cambridge colleagues, willingly turned because of ideological sympathy. Others, like Aldrich Ames, worked purely for the money. A CIA officer, Ames, was convicted in April 1994 of selling secrets to the USSR over a decade for approximately $2 million. During that time he had compromised numerous CIA operations and exposed the identities of the double agents that the CIA was running in the Soviet Union; at least 38 of these agents were subsequently executed.

But secret services do more than recruit for the cause. Like diplomats, intelligence officers gather information. Unlike diplomats, they gather intelligence in a variety of ways. Some intelligence is gathered openly. But some is gathered by bribery, some by extortion, and some by outright thievery using the same methods as any ordinary break-and-enter artist.

Secret services may organize transnational kidnappings, or **snatch operations**, crossing borders without the permission of other governments, grabbing someone, and spiriting them back home. For example, Israeli intelligence agents kidnapped Adolf Eichmann from Argentina in 1960 and returned him to Israel to stand trial for his role as the organizer of the "Final Solution" of transporting Jews from across Europe to the death camps for extermination. He was found guilty of crimes against humanity and eventually executed in 1962. A similar kidnapping operation occurred in 1997, when United States intelligence operatives kidnapped Mir Aimal Kansi in Pakistan and brought him back to stand trial in the United States for his role in the murder of two CIA officials. (See the Focus on p. 161.)

Agents of secret intelligence services may also try to destabilize or overthrow "unfriendly" governments or organize *coups d'état*. Assassination and murder are, as we saw in Chapter 5, key tools for intelligence agencies. For example, as we noted above, the KGB is widely believed to have helped the Bulgarian secret service organize the assassination attempt on Pope John Paul II in March 1981. Sometimes secret services may propose bizarre ways of killing opponents, as the CIA did in the early 1960s when a plan to poison Fidel Castro's wetsuit was allegedly circulated around the agency. Sometimes they actually use those bizarre methods. In the 1980s, the Bulgarian secret service assassinated opponents of the regime by pricking them on the streets of London with umbrellas that had poisoned tips. In September 1997, Israeli agents crossed into Jordan and tried to kill Khaled Meshal, one of the leaders of *Hamas*, a Palestinian group responsible for suicide attacks in Tel Aviv and Jerusalem that killed scores of Israelis. They managed to hit Meshal with a poisonous compound that left no traces, making it look like a natural death. But two agents were caught in the act and arrested. King Hussein of Jordan demanded that Israel provide him with the antidote to the poison; Meshal survived.

Assassination has been a favourite tool for Israeli intelligence. After members of a Palestinian group, Black September, murdered 11 Israeli athletes at the Olympic Games in Munich in 1972, the Israeli government authorized Mossad to hunt down and kill those

*Figure 7.3*

Map of Pakistan, showing where the CIA intercepted Mir Aimal Kansi. See the Focus on p. 161.

responsible. Teams from a special Mossad section spent seven years tracking down and killing all those Palestinians who had participated in the 1972 massacre, including the organizer, Ali Hassah Salameh, who was killed by a car bomb in Beirut in 1979. (They also murdered at least one innocent person: in 1973, a Moroccan waiter walking home from work was killed on the streets of Lillehammer in Norway).

The fate of Gerald Bull shows us how deadly espionage can become. Bull was an engineer at McGill University in Montréal who became fascinated with the idea of producing a **supergun**.[*] In the 1960s, his research into superguns was supported by both the Canadian and American military, but when his funding was terminated, Bull moved to the United States, became an American citizen, got involved in arms sales to South Africa, and eventually spent time in prison for violating American export regulations. However, he retained his interest in superguns. In 1988, he approached Saddam Hussein, president of Iraq, who was interested in acquiring the kind of artillery capability that Bull was promising. Working from Brussels, Bull began putting together a supergun for Hussein. He subcon-

---

[*] Superguns are long-range cannon like the one produced during the First World War by *Krupp-werke*, at the time the prime arms manufacturing firm in Germany. The English nicknamed this gun "Big Bertha," after the head of the firm, Bertha Krupp; the Germans called it the *Pariskanone*, for with it they could bombard Paris from more than 120 kilometres away.

## FOCUS

### The Long Reach of United States Intelligence: The Case of Mir Aimal Kansi

On 25 January 1993, two agents of the United States Central Intelligence Agency were gunned down as they arrived for work at the agency's headquarters in Langley, Virginia. The prime suspect was a 29-year old Pakistani national residing in the United States, Mir Aimal Kansi (also spelled Kasi). According to some stories, his family in Pakistan worked for the CIA in the 1980s, running guns to the *mujahideen* fighting Soviet forces in Afghanistan; Kansi told his friends that the CIA had betrayed his father. Following the murders, Kansi managed to elude local police and Federal Bureau of Investigation (FBI) officials and fled to Quetta, his home in western Pakistan. The director of the Central Intelligence Agency, James Woolsey, publicly vowed to track Kansi down wherever he was in the world.

Under the authority of a 1995 presidential directive authorizing American officials to forcibly seize those accused of terrorism against the United States anywhere in the world (even in the absence of local cooperation), officials from a number of American agencies—the Drug Enforcement Agency (DEA), the FBI, the CIA, and the U.S.

Army's counter-terrorist force, Delta Force—tried to capture Kansi for four years. On one occasion, Pakistani police raided his family's compound in Quetta and seized what turned out to be a relative who resembled Kansi; on another, Kansi was almost captured by American agents inside Afghanistan. Finally, the CIA offered a reward of US\$3.5 million for his capture—a sum so large that Kansi's own bodyguards betrayed him.

On 15 June 1997, the FBI and CIA snatched Kansi at a hotel in Dera Ghazi Khan in central Pakistan. The local police, who had not been informed of the operation, chased the Americans through the streets of Dera Ghazi Khan but a helicopter picked up the agents and their captive and flew them to Islamabad. There, the United States officials were detained by Pakistani customs agents. Not until the United States secretary of state, Madeleine K. Albright, phoned the prime minister of Pakistan, Nawaz Sharif, were the Americans allowed to fly Kansi back to the United States to stand trial. He was found guilty of murder in November 1997 and sentenced to death.[38]

tracted his work so blatantly in Europe that the project came to the attention of the Israelis, whose security would be most threatened by an Iraqi supergun. Bull told his son that agents from Mossad warned him to stop working on the project, a warning which he chose to ignore. On 22 March 1990, Bull's body was found outside the door of his Brussels apartment, riddled with five bullets. No one was ever charged with the murder, though it probably pleased Israeli intelligence that they were widely credited with the killing. Even if Mossad had had nothing to do with Bull's death, the mysterious killing would doubtless cause others who were considering messing with Israeli security to have second thoughts.

It should be noted that spying on friends is as common as spying on enemies, and all the major intelligence agencies run spying operations of some kind in friendly countries. The Israelis recruited an American naval analyst, Jonathan Pollard, to spy for them. In February 1995, the French government publicly accused the CIA of industrial espionage—bribing French civil servants to reveal French government negotiating positions and trying to buy technical secrets from the state telecommunications firm. As we saw above, on one occasion, agents even engaged in a bombing attack in a friendly country: in July 1985, DGSE agents bombed the Greenpeace ship *Rainbow Warrior* while it was in Auckland, killing a photographer.

**Traders**  Most governments have used agents to encourage international economic relations. As noted above, "traders" include those merchants and explorers commissioned by kings and emperors during the age of imperialism and the monopolistic trading companies created during the mercantilist period. Many contemporary governments have agencies devoted to the encouragement of trade and commerce. Governments use the agents essentially as commercial diplomats: representing the commercial interests of the state abroad, gathering commercial intelligence, negotiating commercial matters, and identifying commercial opportunities for producers located in their home country.

Traders include those individuals who have a specialized knowledge of the international trading system and are used by their governments to engage in bilateral or multilateral trading negotiations. With the progressive institutionalization of the trading system over the second half of the 20th century, this group of agents has become increasingly important in interstate diplomacy.

## Noncentral Governments: Cities, Provinces, Cantons, States

Our discussion to this point has focused on national governments, but most political communities also have governments at different levels. Federations include a central national government plus governments of all the constituent parts. In unitary systems, there may be governments for particular regions or administrative divisions. And most cities have municipal governments. Brian Hocking suggests that we call these various types of governments **noncentral governments** to distinguish them from "central governments."[39]

Noncentral governments also engage in international politics. Such engagement may take different forms: Victoria grappling with pressure to cancel contracts with French firms to protest nuclear testing in the Pacific; Maryland imposing sanctions against South Africa during the 1980s; New South Wales embarking on a policy to increase trade relations with China in the 1980s; Georgia trying to secure the approval of the International Olympic Committee (IOC) for Atlanta as the site of the 1996 Olympic Games; Hong Kong lobbying members of Congress in Washington in the early 1990s on the issue of Most-Favoured-Nation status for China; Catalonia undertaking an advertising campaign to attract foreign investment; or Baden-Württemberg undertaking active development assistance policies during the 1980s.

Noncentral governments seek to "go international," as John Kincaid put it,[40] for numerous reasons. First, this activity reflects the increasing globalization of the economy—a process marked by the growing integration of international markets, the internationalization of trade and investment, and the growing importance of tourism. Noncentral governments are just as eager as national governments to maintain their economic competitiveness and hence the economic security of their citizens. They respond to globalization by extending their reach out into the international sphere, searching for new markets for their products, new sources of investment, and an increase in economic interchange of all kinds, from tourism to high-profile events like Olympic Games or international expositions.

Noncentral governments are impelled to involve themselves in international issues in response to demands from their citizens who expect their governments, even if they are local, to respond to global issues. In the late 1980s, numerous noncentral governments embraced sanctions against South Africa to protest apartheid: government-run liquor stores refused to stock South African wines and liquor; prisons were forbidden to purchase South African canned fruit to serve to prisoners; and government-run pension funds divested stocks of companies doing business in South Africa. Some municipalities such as Boston have embraced similar sanctions against Myanmar. In Australia, governments of many cities, all six states, and the Northern Territory added their voices to the protests against French nuclear testing in the Pacific in 1995. After Nigeria executed Ken Saro-Wiwa in November 1995, Toronto imposed sanctions against Shell Canada because Shell International maintained investments in Nigeria.

Third, noncentral governments engage in international activities to protect local interests. Noncentral governments played a role in the **acid rain**★ dispute between Canada and the United States in the 1980s. On the one side, Canadian provinces and American states being hurt by acid rain actively pressed the administration of Ronald Reagan to support legislation to reduce emissions. On the other side, state and local governments which stood to lose economically if heavier environmental controls were introduced—Michigan, Ohio, and West Virginia—were equally vociferous in opposing these initiatives. Likewise, the governments of Alaska, British Columbia, and Washington all played an important part in the dispute over the salmon fishery on the west coast in 1997.

Finally, noncentral governments "go international" as part of a desire to become sovereign. Québec is propelled into the international sphere for all the reasons noted above. But it has an additional purpose, particularly in those periods when Québeckers have elected *Parti québécois* (PQ) governments. The PQ has an interest in showing the world that Québec is a state-in-waiting, ready and willing to join the international community as a fully fledged member once independence from Canada is achieved. Such efforts have occasionally been encouraged by the government of France, much to the on-going chagrin of the federal government in Ottawa.[41]

## Intergovernmental Organizations

The final set of actors in world politics are **intergovernmental organizations** (IGOs). Political communities have often found it useful to create forums in which leaders can

---

★ Acid rain is the process that occurs when nitrogen oxides ($NO_x$) and sulfur dioxide ($SO_2$) are released into the atmosphere and combine with moisture to form acids. These acids may be carried long distances by prevailing winds before returning to earth as rain, snow, or fog. Because of its high acidic content, acid rain kills life in lakes and damages sandstone buildings, trees, and crops. In Germany, acid rain has damaged parts of the Black Forest; in North America, acid rain has damaged sport fishing and the maple syrup industry in central Canada and New England. See Don Munton and Geoffrey Castle, "Reducing acid rain, 1980s," in Munton and John Kirton, eds., *Canadian Foreign Policy: Selected Cases* (Scarborough, ON: Prentice-Hall Canada, 1992), 367–81.

meet and discuss matters of contention. The conferences held at the end of major wars were often common meeting points. But these were only temporary: leaders gathered, signed treaties, and then dispersed. Not until the early 19th century did the idea of creating a more permanent forum emerge.

*"...the High Contracting Parties have agreed to renew, at fixed periods...reunions devoted to the great common interests..."*

### Early Prototypes: The Quadruple Alliance to the League of Nations

The **Quadruple Alliance** was signed in the aftermath of the Napoleonic Wars at Paris on 20 November 1815 by Austria, Britain, Prussia, and Russia. It reaffirmed the Treaty of Chaumont of March 1814, which had created a 20-year alliance to ensure that Napoleon Bonaparte would never return to France. But Article VI of the Quadruple Alliance put in place a mechanism not before seen in world politics: a regular "reunion" of governments for the management of problems. The text of Article VI provides a flavour of the thinking of the leaders:

> To consolidate the intimate relations which today unite the 4 Sovereigns for the good of the world, the High Contracting Parties have agreed to renew, at fixed periods...reunions devoted to the great common interests and to the examination of measures which, at any of these periods, shall be judged most salutary for the repose and prosperity of the peoples, and for the maintenance of the peace of the State.[42]

This organization did not survive even a decade: by 1823, Britain had withdrawn, and no further conferences were held after 1825. But the idea of *institutionalizing* intergovernmental relations, once thought of, remained as a guide to action.

Over the next century, small steps were taken, particularly in those areas where an element of cooperative management between governments was necessary for the successful functioning of systems. This was particularly true in the areas of transportation and communications. For example, the Congress of Vienna created a regime for the joint management of navigation on the various rivers that were becoming increasingly important for European industry—the Rhine, Danube, Elbe, and Oder. These rivers were declared to be international rivers, with their waters remaining under national control, but with vessels being free to transport goods and persons. This gave rise to the first international organizations: the Central Commission for the Navigation of the Rhine, created in 1815, was responsible for the coordination of works on the river and the maintenance of free navigation; in 1856, the Treaty of Paris that brought the Crimean War to an end established an eight-member European Commission of the Danube, headquartered in Galati in Romania.

Following the invention and perfection of the telegraph in the 1840s and its increasing commercialization in the 1850s, an international conference at Paris met in 1865 to institutionalize cooperation for the wiring and laying of the cables necessary to connect different centres. The result was the *Union télégraphique internationale* (UTI). The General Union of Posts was created in October 1874, and its name was changed to Universal Postal Union (UPU) in 1878.

Although international agencies were created in functional areas, the notion of an international institution for the management of political relations between governments was not resurrected until after the next general war, the Great War of 1914–1918 (discussed in Chapter 14). The League of Nations, created by the Treaty of Versailles of 1919 which brought that war to an end, was designed to provide a permanent and institutional forum for the discussion and management of international political affairs, and in particular the preservation of peace. We will see that the League failed to live up to the high expectations of its founders; but the lasting significance of the League is that it entrenched the idea of a permanent intergovernmental organization that had been introduced in 1815 by the Quadruple Alliance. Today, there are over 1,100 intergovernmental bodies. For the purposes of this survey, they can be divided into two different types—universal and exclusive.

## Universal IGOs: The United Nations System

Universal IGOs are designed to be open to all governments in the international community. The key **universal IGO** is the United Nations. It emerged from the wartime alliance of Britain, France, the United States, the Soviet Union, and 22 other countries which signed a pledge on 1 January 1942 not to make a separate peace with Germany, Japan, or Italy. In April, May, and June 1945, the "United Nations," by then 50 in number, negotiated a Charter at a conference in San Francisco. The preamble of the Charter outlined the essential aims of the organization:

> We the peoples of the United Nations
>
> determined
>
> to save succeeding generations from the scourge of war, which twice in our lifetime has brought untold sorrow to mankind, and
>
> to reaffirm faith in fundamental human rights, in the dignity and worth of the human person, in the equal rights of men and women and of nations large and small, and
>
> to establish conditions under which justice and respect for the obligations arising from treaties and other sources of international law can be maintained,
>
> and to promote social progress and better standards of life in larger freedom...
>
> have resolved to combine our efforts to accomplish these aims.

The Charter was signed on 26 June 1945, and came into force on 24 October 1945 after a majority of signatories ratified it. President Harry S Truman invited the new organization to establish its headquarters in the United States, and on 10 January 1946, the first General Assembly was convened.

The UN also incorporated the functional IGOs that had been connected with the League of Nations, such as the UPU, the International Telecommunications Union, the International Meteorological Organization (established in 1878), the International Labour Organization (created in 1919), and the Permanent Court of International Justice (created in 1920). In the years since 1945, the UN has also created a large number of organizations, bodies, and agencies. It has also organized well over 100 world conferences, which are institutions in themselves. The UN thus constitutes a "family" of universal IGOs, as Table 7.1 suggests.

*Table 7.1* • **THE UNITED NATIONS "FAMILY"**

### Principal Organs

General Assembly
Security Council
Economic and Social Council (ECOSOC)
Trusteeship Council[a]
International Court of Justice (ICJ)
The Secretariat

### Subsidiary Organs

General Assembly (year of GA approval):
    UNICEF: UN Children's Fund (1946)[b]
    UNHCR: UN High Commissioner for Refugees (1949)
    UNRWA: UN Relief and Works Agency for Palestine Refugees in the Near East (1949)
    UNITAR: UN Institute for Training and Research (1963)
    UNRISD: UN Research Institute for Social Development (1964)
    UNCTAD: UN Conference on Trade and Development (1964)
    UNDP: UN Development Program (1965)
    UNFPA: UN Population Fund (1967)[b]
    UNU: UN University (1972)
    UNEP: UN Environment Program (1972)
    WFC: World Food Council (1974)
Security Council:
    All Peacekeeping Forces (approximately 16 active, as of 1997)
ECOSOC:
    Functional Commissions (Crime Prevention, Human Rights, Narcotic Drugs, Population and
        Development, Science and Technology for Development, Social Development, Status of
        Women, Sustainable Development)
    Regional Commissions (Africa, Europe, Latin America and the Caribbean, Asia and the Pacific,
        Western Asia)

### Specialized Agencies (year of foundation[c])

FAO: Food and Agriculture Organization (1945)
IBRD/World Bank: International Bank for Reconstruction and Development (1944)
ICAO: International Civil Aviation Organization (1944)
IDA: International Development Association (1960)
IFC: International Finance Corporation (1955)
IFAD: International Fund for Agricultural Development (1974)
ILO: International Labour Organization (1919)

IMO: International Maritime Organization (1958)

IMF: International Monetary Fund (1944)

ITU: International Telecommunication Union (1865)

UNESCO: UN Educational, Scientific and Cultural Organization (1945)

UNIDO: UN Industrial Development Organization (1966)

UPU: Universal Postal Union (1874)

WHO: World Health Organization (1946)

WIPO: World Intellectual Property Organization (1967)

WMO: World Meteorological Organization (1951)

## Related Organizations

GATT: General Agreement of Tariffs and Trade (1947)

IAEA: International Atomic Energy Agency (1956)

WTO: World Trade Organization (1995)

## UN Conferences *(Selected Only)*

Since 1946, some 120 world conferences have been held under UN auspices on a wide variety of topics and issues.

Conference on the Human Environment, Stockholm (1972)

UNCLOS III: Third UN Law of the Sea Conference (1973, 1982)

World Conference of the International Women's Year, Mexico City (1975)

World Assembly on Aging, Vienna (1982)

World Conference to Review and Appraise the Achievement of the UN Decade for Women, Nairobi (1985)

World Summit for Children, New York (1990)

UNCED: UN Conference on Environment and Development, Rio de Janeiro (1992)

World Conference on Human Rights, Vienna (1993)

International Conference on Population and Development, Cairo (1994)

World Conference on Women, Beijing (1995)

UN Conference on Climate Change, Kyoto (1997)

## Notes

[a] The UN Trusteeship system is discussed in Chapter 13; the Council suspended its activities in 1994 when the last trust territory, Palau, received independence.

[b] The UN International Children's Emergency Fund was changed to UN Children's Fund in 1953 but retained the abbreviation UNICEF; the name of the UN Fund for Population Activities changed to the UN Population Fund in 1969 but retained the abbreviation UNFPA.

[c] Dates are those when the organization was agreed to; normally agreements came into force at a later date. Many organizations were not immediately approved as "UN Specialized Agencies."

The distinguishing feature of the UN is the universality of its membership. Only six states are not members: the South Pacific countries of Kiribati, Nauru, Tonga, and Tuvalu; the Vatican (Holy See); and Switzerland. However, both the Holy See and Switzerland are observers and maintain permanent missions at UN headquarters.

### Exclusive IGOs: Regional and Functional Organizations

While universal IGOs are designed to be open to all, **exclusive IGOs** have restricted memberships depending on their purpose. Some IGOs are regional in focus: the Organization of American States (OAS), the Organization of Eastern Caribbean States, the Nordic Council, the Gulf Cooperation Council, the Organization of African Unity (OAU), South Asian Association for Regional Cooperation (SAARC), the Association of Southeast Asian Nations (ASEAN), and the South Pacific Forum. In addition to these organizations, there is an extended "European family" of IGOs, some of which we will examine in more detail in Chapter 17. In the Asia Pacific, the Asia Pacific Economic Cooperation (APEC) forum has some similarities to a regional organization, but its members come from around the Pacific littoral, and thus APEC might be more appropriately thought of as a transregional IGO. In regional IGOs, governments from "outside" the region are generally not welcome as full members (though they may be welcome as observers). In addition, there are regional development banks and regionally based economic cooperation organizations such as the Southern African Development Community (SADC), the Common Market of the Southern Cone (MERCOSUR), the Caribbean Community and Common Market (CARICOM), and the Black Sea Economic Cooperation forum.

Some intergovernmental organizations are constructed around former empires. The Commonwealth is an association of states that grew out of the transformation of the British Empire in the early part of the 20th century, examined in more detail in Chapter 13. Global issues are discussed at a summit meeting, the Commonwealth Heads of Government Meeting, or CHOGM (pronounced either CHO-gum or CHOG'm), held in different capitals every two years. While the vast majority of Commonwealth members were at one time self-governing dominions, colonies, or dependencies of Britain, other states with no historical connection to Britain, such as Mozambique, have been admitted; the only requirement for membership is that governments must acknowledge the British Crown as the head of the Commonwealth.

The French and Canadian governments have also taken the lead in creating a Commonwealth-like association of French-speaking countries. While a francophone cultural and technical cooperation association existed, it was not until February 1986 that 41 leaders of countries with a French connection in their past—including Egypt and Vietnam—met in Paris for the first francophone summit. Since then, the *Conférence des chefs d'État ayant en commun l'usage de français* (Summit of Heads of State and Government having the Use of French in Common)—or, more colloquially, *la francophonie*—has met every two years.

Some IGOs are organized around specific commodities; they exchange scientific and commercial information and coordinate marketing, trading, and pricing arrangements. Such commodities include bananas, bauxite, cocoa, cotton, coffee, copper, groundnuts, iron-ore, lead, natural rubber, olive oil, petroleum, sugar, tin, whales, wheat, and wool. In many of these IGOs, countries that are large consumers of the commodity are also members of the organization. Some of these IGOs, however, retain their exclusivity: all 12 members of the Organization of Petroleum Exporting Countries (OPEC) are petroleum exporters.

Some IGOs were created to coordinate military activities for members of alliances. In Chapter 15 we will discuss the North Atlantic Treaty Organization (NATO), the intergovernmental organization created to coordinate the military efforts of the various governments which signed the Treaty of Washington on 4 April 1949. This treaty, more commonly known as the North Atlantic alliance, commits all signatories (particularly the United States) to come to each other's aid if any one of them (particularly those in Western Europe) should be attacked by another power. It was originally aimed at the Soviet Union and its allies in Eastern Europe, and thus the end of the Soviet Union in 1991 meant that the original *raison d'être* of the alliance disappeared. Numerous governments from the former Soviet bloc asked to be admitted to NATO, in the hope that the security umbrella that the United States extended to the smaller Western European states would be extended to them against Russia in the post–Cold War period. NATO invited three of these countries—Poland, Hungary, and the Czech Republic—to join in July 1997.

Some IGOs have a highly limited membership. For example, the Mano River Union has three members—Guinea, Liberia, and Sierra Leone—as does ANZUS, the alliance that links Australia, New Zealand, and the United States (though in the 1980s, New Zealand was effectively frozen out of the association as a result of its policy barring the entry of nuclear-powered ships into its harbours). And there are even binational IGOs: Canada and the United States maintain a number of organizations, including a joint aerospace command (NORAD) and a binational organization for the management of boundary waters, the International Joint Commission (IJC).[43]

### IGOs as Autonomous Actors?

Although we talk of "the UN doing this," or "NATO deciding that," in fact intergovernmental organizations are not fully autonomous actors in international politics. The preamble of the UN Charter may begin "We the peoples of the United Nations," but the use of the word "people" in this context is entirely metaphorical. All intergovernmental organizations, just as the name suggests, are organizations created by governments, run by governments, paid for by governments, and, in the end, controlled by governments.

It is true that IGOs are not always and everywhere totally dominated by the state governments that gave them life. A number of nongovernmental organizations are permitted to participate in the activities of many IGOs—for example, representatives of the Sami (or Lapp) parliaments in Finland, Sweden, and Norway are observers in the Nordic Council. The Canadian government includes in its delegation to the Arctic Council members of the nongovernmental Inuit Circumpolar Conference (a body that includes native peoples from Alaska, Canada, and Greenland).

It is also true that one does not even have to be a central government to participate in intergovernmental organizations. The Hong Kong Special Administrative Region (HKSAR) government is a member of numerous intergovernmental organizations, operating as "Hong Kong, China," an actor separate and autonomous from the central government in Beijing. The governments of the Canadian provinces of Québec and New Brunswick both participate in *la francophonie*, again autonomously from the federal Canadian government in Ottawa.

Moreover, intergovernmental organizations, like all organizations, acquire a certain "life of their own"—separate and distinct from the dictates of their constituent members. After all, governments simply cannot control the day-to-day activities of the huge number of international civil servants employed by IGOs around the world, or of the equally large number of national bureaucrats who are seconded from their national governments to work in IGOs.

However, it is important to recognize that IGOs have only limited independence and autonomy from the states which sustain them. The major international financial institutions, such as the World Bank and the International Monetary Fund, have little capacity to develop positions autonomously from the governments which fund their activities and nominate officials to run them. Perhaps the sharpest reminder of the essential subservience of IGOs to the wishes of state governments came in late 1996, when the UN secretary-general, Boutros Boutros-Ghali, indicated that he would like to seek reelection to the position. The United States government, including President Bill Clinton, Secretary of State Warren Christopher, and leading members of the United States Congress, were all of the view that the UN under Boutros-Ghali had become too independent. The United States resolved that he would not get a second term, and from that position it never wavered, even though it was the only one of the UN's 185 members to formally object. Eventually, when it became clear that the United States would not move, Boutros-Ghali had little choice but to give in; Kofi Annan of Ghana was selected as the seventh UN secretary-general.

## ANOMALOUS ACTORS: THE NOBEL PEACE PRIZE COMMITTEE

In any attempt to list different types of actors in global politics, there will always be some who defy easy categorization. A good example would be the five members of the Norwegian *Storting*, or parliament, who each year decide on a winner of the **Nobel Peace Prize**. They meet to fulfil the wish expressed in the last will and testament of Alfred Nobel (1833–1896), a Swedish chemist and inventor, who amassed a sizeable personal fortune after he invented dynamite. On his death he directed that a number of prizes bearing his name be created. One of them was to be given, in the words of his will, "to the person who shall have done the most or the best work for fraternity between nations, for the abolition or reduction of standing armies and for the holding and promotion of peace congresses."[44] While all the other Nobel Prizes are decided in Sweden, the Peace Prize is awarded by the five-person committee of the *Storting*.

The five individuals who award the annual Nobel Peace Prize are officials of the Norwegian state—but in this role they are not acting as part of, or on behalf of, the

Norwegian government in Oslo, and thus not exactly like governmental actors or agents we looked at above. Yet their choice of nominee is deeply *political*. For when they award the prize to an individual or an organization, the members of the committee confer political legitimacy on an individual or group, and in particular the cause they espouse. A full list of Nobel Peace Prizes awarded in the last 30 years appears in Table 7.2.

As is evident from the table, the prizes are awarded for different reasons. Sometimes it is to signal the importance to global order of NGOs such as the International Committee for the Red Cross (1917, 1944, 1963), or the Pugwash Conferences (1995), or Amnesty International (1977); or IGOs such as the UN High Commissioner for Refugees (1954, 1981), the UNICEF (1965), the International Labour Organization (1969), or UN peace-keeping forces (1988). Sometimes it is to recognize selflessness in helping others, such as Albert Schweitzer of France (1952) or Mother Teresa of India (1979). Sometimes the committee honours the contributions of individual political leaders whose personal interventions promoted peace: Aristide Briand of France and Gustav Streseman of Germany (1926); Cordell Hull of the United States (1945); Lester B. Pearson of Canada (1957), for his role in the Suez crisis; Henry Kissinger of the United States and Le Duc Tho of North Vietnam (1973), for their role in bringing the Vietnam War to an end (Le Duc Tho declined the award); Mikhail S. Gorbachev of the USSR (1990), for his contribution to the end of the Cold War; and Nelson Mandela and F.W. de Klerk of South Africa (1993), for their role in bringing apartheid to a peaceful end. Twice the award has gone to leaders who have tried to bring peace to the Middle East: in 1978 to Anwar al-Sadat of Egypt and Menachem Begin of Israel, and in 1994 to Yasir 'Arafat of the Palestine Authority, and Shimon Peres and Yitzhak Rabin of Israel.

Sometimes the Nobel Peace Prize is given for work in human rights: Albert John Luthuli of South Africa (1960); Martin Luther King, Jr. of the United States (1964); Andrei Sakharov of the USSR (1975); Lech Walesa of Poland (1983); Archbishop Desmond Tutu of South Africa (1984); Daw Aung San Suu Kyi of Myanmar (1991); Rigoberta Menchú of Guatemala (1992); or Bishop Carlos Belo and Jose Ramos-Horta of East Timor (1996).

The increasing propensity of the Nobel committee to legitimize human rights activists means that the October announcement of the award can produce heartburn for regimes that have tried hard to squelch activists. The Polish regime of Gen. Wojciech Jarulzelski was not at all pleased when the 1983 prize was awarded to Lech Walesa, head of the Solidarity trade federation that challenged the power and authority of the communist regime. Nor was the government of the People's Republic of China pleased when the Dalai Lama of Tibet was honoured in 1989—Beijing redoubled its efforts to marginalize this religious leader. The junta in Myanmar was upset when the prize was awarded to Daw Aung San Suu Kyi, whom they had placed under house arrest in 1989. Indeed, so upset was President Suharto of Indonesia when Bishop Belo of East Timor was a corecipient of the 1996 prize that he pointedly refused to even mention the honour when he met the bishop on a visit to Dili in October 1996.

*Table 7.2* • NOBEL PEACE PRIZE WINNERS, 1967-1997

| | Name | Country | Cause |
|---|---|---|---|
| 1967 | Not awarded | | |
| 1968 | René Cassin | France | Declaration on Human Rights |
| 1969 | International Labour Organization | | Worker's rights |
| 1970 | Norman Borlaug | United States | Agricultural improvements |
| 1971 | Willy Brandt | West Germany | East-West détente |
| 1972 | Not awarded | | |
| 1973 | Henry A. Kissinger | United States | } Peace in Vietnam |
| | Le Duc Tho (declined) | Vietnam | |
| 1974 | Seán Mac Bride | Ireland | Peace in Northern Ireland |
| | Sato Eisaku | Japan | Nuclear nonproliferation |
| 1975 | Andrei Sakharov | USSR | Human rights |
| 1976 | Mairead Corrigan | Northern Ireland | } Peace in Northern Ireland |
| | Betty Williams | Northern Ireland | |
| 1977 | Amnesty International | | Human rights |
| 1978 | Menachem Begin | Israel | } Peace in Middle East |
| | Anwar al-Sadat | Egypt | |
| 1979 | Mother Teresa | India | Humanitarianism |
| 1980 | Adolfo Pérez Esquivel | Argentina | Human rights in Latin America |
| 1981 | UN High Commissioner for Refugees | | Refugees |
| 1982 | Alva Myrdal | Sweden | } Disarmament |
| | Alfonso García Robles | Mexico | |
| 1983 | Lech Walesa | Poland | Human rights in Poland |
| 1984 | Desmond Tutu | South Africa | Human rights in South Africa |
| 1985 | International Physicians for the Prevention of Nuclear War | US and USSR | Nuclear disarmament |
| 1986 | Elie Wiesel | United States | Human rights |
| 1987 | Oscar Arias Sánchez | Costa Rica | Peace in Central America |
| 1988 | UN Peacekeeping Forces | | Peacekeeping |
| 1989 | Dalai Lama | Tibet | Nonviolent opposition to Chinese rule in Tibet |
| 1990 | Mikhail S. Gorbachev | USSR | Ending Cold War |
| 1991 | Daw Aung San Suu Kyi | Myanmar | Human rights in Myanmar |
| 1992 | Rigoberta Menchú Túm | Guatemala | Rights of aboriginal peoples |
| 1993 | Nelson Mandela | South Africa | } Peace in South Africa |
| | F.W. de Klerk | South Africa | |
| 1994 | Yasir 'Arafat | Palestine Authority | } Peace in the Middle East |
| | Shimon Peres | Israel | |
| | Yitzhak Rabin | Israel | |
| 1995 | Joseph Rotblat and Pugwash Conferences | | Nuclear disarmament |
| 1996 | Bishop Carlos Belo | East Timor | } Human rights in Timor |
| | Jose Ramos-Horta | East Timor | |
| 1997 | Jody Williams | United States | Abolition of land mines |

## THE RELATIVE IMPORTANCE OF GLOBAL ACTORS: AN ASSESSMENT

This chapter has presented a broad survey of the many actors and agents that one finds in world politics. However, it can be asked whether all these actors play an equally important role. Those who see world politics through a state-centric lens would take the view that it is erroneous to lump government actors in with "nonstate" actors. They argue that governments *must* be more important than nonstate actors, if for no other reason than they are able to exercise considerable power over all other actors; they have raw and coercive power behind them. State-centric enthusiasts argue that states remain dominant.

But clearly governments are not all-powerful. They have problems exerting control over nongovernmental actors; markets are notoriously resistant to state control; and ordinary individuals can and do have an impact on world politics. In short, the panoply of global actors we have surveyed in this chapter are all seeking to exercise political power over each other to further their own interests. And, as in all exercises of power, outcomes tend to be uneven and unpredictable. Even those players in whose favour the dice tend to be heavily loaded—the governments of states and the huge coercive and destructive power of their security forces—are not always assured of a "win." To be sure, in contests between governments and nonstate actors, governments frequently "win."

Rather than simply assuming that governments always win and nonstate actors always lose (or even assuming the opposite), one should look at the interplay of the various actors on the world stage, recognize the exercise of power everywhere, and always try to assess in whose interests the outcomes of these clashes tend to be. That is why this chapter has stressed the importance of going beyond the state-centric assumption that world politics is only about states. It has even argued that the nonstate actor corollary, which insists on the primacy rather than the exclusivity of the state, does not adequately reflect the realities of world politics, either today or in the past. Rather, in the chapters ahead, we will see that the stage of world politics—if it can be conceived of in such terms—has always been crowded with a huge and complex cast, as Figure 7.4 attempts to portray graphically.

## CONCLUSION

This chapter has focused on the individuals and organizations involved in world politics. We have looked at these actors in atomistic fashion, examining individuals and organizations in sets for the purpose of analysis. However, it is critical to keep in mind that individuals and the multiplicity of organizations to which they belong—from businesses to NGOs to governments—do not interact with one another atomistically. Rather, all these individuals and all the organizations examined in this chapter interact with one another in the context of their membership in *political community*. Thus, in order to make sense of the interactions of individuals and organizations on the world stage, we have to look at the political communities into which humans have divided themselves. The next two Parts of this book explore political community in world politics.

*Figure 7.4* • **THE ACTORS IN WORLD POLITICS: A HOLISTIC CAST**

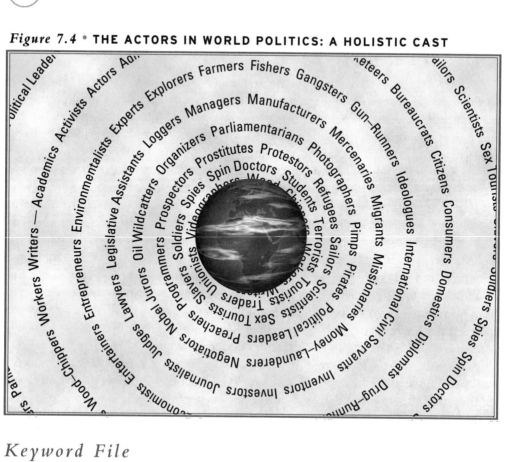

## Keyword File

| | |
|---|---|
| State-centric model | "Casino capitalism" |
| Nonstate actors | Piracy |
| Transnational actors | Slave trade |
| Transgovernmental actors | White slavery |
| Foreign policy | Smuggling |
| Foreign policy analysis | Drug trade |
| External sources of foreign policy | Mercenaries |
| Domestic sources of foreign policy | "Vagabond mercenaries" |
| Governmental sources of foreign policy | Transnational security corporation |
| Monopoly trading corporation | Rule of anticipated reaction |
| Multinational corporation | Global occasions |
| Transnational corporation | CNN factor |
| Capital flight | "Living-room war" |
| Transfer pricing | Têt offensive |

Media pool

"Video game war"

Nongovernmental organization

Policy convergence

Humanitarian NGOs

Human rights NGOs

Environmental NGOs

Domestication of foreign policy

Stakeholder politics

Social movement

Missionary religions

Ideology

Communism

Bolshevik revolution

Great Terror

Environmental movement

Green parties

Think tank

Track-two diplomacy

Terrorism

Interdict

Balance of terror

Dirty War

Nongovernmental terrorism

Political leadership

Summit meeting

Legislators

Diplomats

Foreign ministry

Armed forces

Offensive intelligence agencies

Defensive intelligence agencies

Snatch operations

Supergun

Noncentral governments

Acid rain

Intergovernmental organizations

Quadruple Alliance

Universal IGOs

Exclusive IGOs

Nobel Peace Prize

## For Further Exploration

HARD COPY

Combs, Cindy C. *Terrorism in the Twenty-First Century*. Upper Saddle River, NJ: Prentice Hall, 1997.

Hocking, Brian. *Localizing Foreign Policy: Non-Central Governments and Multilayered Diplomacy*. Basingstoke, U.K./New York: Macmillan/St Martin's, 1993.

Johnston, Douglas and Cynthia Sampson. *Religion: The Missing Dimension of Statecraft*. Oxford/New York: Oxford University Press, 1995.

Leyton-Brown, David. "The roles of the multinational enterprise in international relations," in David G. Haglund and Michael K. Hawes, eds. *World Politics: Power, Interdependence and Dependence*. Toronto: Harcourt Brace Jovanovich, 1990, 224–41.

Luard, Evan and Derek Heater. *The United Nations: How It Works and What It Does*, 2d ed. New York: St Martin's, 1994.

Neumann, Johanna. "The media's impact on international affairs, then and now," *National Interest* 16 (Winter 1995–96), 109–23.

Riddell-Dixon, Elizabeth. "Social movements and the United Nations," *International Social Science Journal* 144 (June 1995), 289–303.

Sterling, Claire. *Thieves' World: The Threat of the New Global Network of Organized Crime.* New York: Simon and Schuster, 1994.

Strange, Susan. *Retreat of the State: The Diffusion of Power in the World Economy.* Ithaca, NY: Cornell University Press, 1996.

Utley, Garrick. "The shrinking of foreign news." *Foreign Affairs* 76 (March/April 1997), 2–10.

WEBLINKS

**http://titsoc.soc.titech.ac.jp/titsoc/higuchi-lab/icm/ngo/cafe-flier.html**

The NGO Cafe: information about and links to different non-governmental organizations

**http://www.amnesty.org**

Home page of Amnesty International

**http://www.earthtrust.org/dnpaper/contents.html**

Paper on driftnet fishing by Earthtrust

**http://www.eo.com**

Home page of Executive Outcomes, a transnational security corporation

**http://www.greenpeace.org**

Home page of Greenpeace International

**http://www.hrw.org**

Home page of Human Rights Watch

**http://www.keele.ac.uk/depts/po/official.htm**

Official sites of different governments of the world. Maintained by the Department of Politics at the University of Keele, this is a good jumping-off point to various government home pages.

**http://www.loyola.edu/dept/politics/intel.html**

Site maintained by Loyola College providing full information on many of the world's intelligence agencies

**http://www.nobel.se/**

Home page of the Nobel Foundation; information about the Nobel Peace Prize

## Notes to Chapter 7

1. Elizabeth Riddell-Dixon, "Social movements and the United Nations," *International Social Science Journal* 144 (June 1995), 289–303.

2. Joseph S. Nye, Jr. and Robert O. Keohane, "Transnational relations and world politics," *International Organization* 25 (Summer 1971), 721–34; also Keohane and Nye, *Power and Interdependence: World Politics in Transition* (Boston: Little, Brown, 1977).

3. Steve Smith and Michael Smith, "The analytical background: approaches to the study of British foreign policy," in Michael Smith, Steve Smith, and Brian White, eds., *British Foreign Policy: Tradition, Change and Transformation* (London: Unwin Hyman, 1988), 15.

4. Kim Richard Nossal, *The Politics of Canadian Foreign Policy*, 3d ed. (Scarborough, ON: Prentice Hall Canada Inc., 1997), 7.

5. For further information on driftnet fishing, see the Weblinks at the end of this chapter.

6. See Kim Richard Nossal and Carolynn Vivian, *A Brief Madness: Australia and the Resumption of French Nuclear Testing*, Canberra Papers on Strategy and Defence 121 (Canberra: Strategic and Defence Studies Centre, Australian National University, 1997); Ramesh Thakur, "The last bang before a total ban: French nuclear testing in the Pacific," *International Journal* 51 (Summer 1996), 466–86; and Stewart Firth, "The road to the Comprehensive Test Ban Treaty: responses to French nuclear testing during 1995," *Australian Quarterly* 68 (Autumn 1996), 77–87.

7. Robert Kudrle, "The several faces of the multinational corporation," in W. Ladd Hollist and F. Lamond Tullis, eds., *An International Political Economy* (Boulder, CO: Westview Press, 1985).

8. Susan Strange, *Casino Capitalism* (New York: Basil Blackwell, 1986), 2.

9. Deborah Stienstra, *Women's Movements and International Organizations* (New York: St Martin's Press 1994). These campaigns were gendered in the sense that they focused on the behaviour of women rather than the men who paid for the services of prostitutes.

10. Ivelaw L. Griffith, "From Cold War geopolitics to post–Cold War geonarcotics," *International Journal* 49 (Winter 1993–4), 3.

11. Peter Chalk, "The Golden Triangle and heroin: a growing challenge," *CANCAPS Bulletin* 14 (August 1997), 7–8.

12. See Gerald Mobius, "Money laundering," *International Criminal Police Review* 440 (January-February 1993), 2–8.

13. See Anthony Mockler, *The New Mercenaries* (London: Sidgwick & Jackson, 1985).

14. See William Reno, *Warlord Politics and African States* (Boulder, CO: Lynne Rienner, 1998); Kim Richard Nossal, "Roland goes corporate: mercenaries and transnational security corporations in the post–Cold War era," *Civil Wars* 1 (1998).

15. For a discussion of this in the case of reporting on China, see Garrick Utley, "The shrinking of foreign news," *Foreign Affairs* 76 (March/April 1997), 9.

16. *Sydney Morning Herald*, 10 July 1995.

17. Stewart Firth, "The road to the Comprehensive Test Ban Treaty: responses to French nuclear testing during 1995," *Australian Quarterly* 68 (Autumn 1996), 80.

18. Nossal and Vivian, *A Brief Madness*.

19. Michael Arlen, *The Living-Room War* (New York: Viking, 1969).

20. Stanley Karnow, *Vietnam: A History* (New York: Viking, 1983), 544.

21. John R. MacArthur, *Second Front: Censorship and Propaganda in the Gulf War* (New York: Hill and Wang, 1992), 53–77.

22. This definition follows Kenneth D. Bush, "NGOs and the international system: building peace in a world at war," in Fen Osler Hampson and Maureen Appel Molot, *Canada Among Nations, 1996: Big Enough to be Heard* (Ottawa: Carleton University Press, 1996), 267, fn 1.

23. See, for example, Robert A. Pastor, *Integration with Mexico: Options for U.S. Policy* (New York: Twentieth Century Fund Press, 1993).

24. *The Globe and Mail*, 21 March 1994, B3; *Toronto Star*, 28 May 1995, F5.

25. Colin J. Bennett, "What is policy convergence and what causes it?" *British Journal of Political Science* 21 (April 1991), 215–33.

26. David P. Forsythe, *Humanitarian Politics: The International Committee of the Red Cross* (Baltimore: Johns Hopkins University Press, 1977).

27. See the account in Peter C. Dobell, *Canada in World Affairs*, vol 17: *1971–1973* (Toronto: Canadian Institute of International Affairs, 1985), 116–17, 400–401.

28. Kathryn Sikkink, "Human rights, principled issue-networks, and sovereignty in Latin America," *International Organization* 47 (Summer 1993), 411–41.

29. For an application in the Canadian case, see Denis Stairs, "Public opinion and external affairs: reflections on the domestication of Canadian foreign policy," *International Journal* 33 (Winter 1977–8), 128–49.

30. See, for example, the contributions in Thomas G. Weiss, ed., *NGOs, the United Nations, and Global Governance* (Boulder, CO: Lynne Rienner, 1996).

31. Leslie A. Pal, "Competing paradigms in policy discourse: the case of international human rights," *Policy Sciences* 25 (1995), 185–207.

32. George D. Moffett, *Critical Masses: The Global Population Challenge* (New York: Viking, 1994), 248–49.

33. Muthiah Alagappa, "Managing security in Southeast Asia: existing mechanisms and processes to address regional conflicts," *Australian Journal of International Affairs* 47 (October 1993), 210–20; Desmond Ball and Pauline Kerr, *Presumptive Engagement: Australia's Asia-Pacific Security Policy in the 1990s* (Sydney: Allen and Unwin, 1996).

34. For overviews, see Diane Stone and Richard Higgott, "The limits of influence: foreign policy think tanks in international relations," *Review of International Studies* 20:1 (1994), 15–34; also Donald Abelson, *American Think Tanks and their Role in US Foreign Policy* (New York: St Martin's 1996).

35. Ian Smart, "International terrorism," *Behind the Headlines* (February 1987), 4.

36. The most famous of these is the *US News and World Report* story of 10 November 1986 outlining in detail the links between the groups claiming responsibility for attacks and the Syrian government.

37. Quoted in Cindy C. Combs, *Terrorism in the Twenty-First Century* (Upper Saddle River, NJ: Prentice Hall, 1997), 133.

38. See *Christian Science Monitor*, international edition, 11–17 July 1997, 3; *Newsweek*, 11 August 1997, 37.

39. Brian Hocking, *Localizing Foreign Policy: Non-Central Governments and Multilayered Diplomacy* (New York: St Martin's Press, 1993). There is a large literature on noncentral governments: see, for example, Hans J. Michelmann and Panayotis Soldatos, eds., *Federalism and International Relations: the Role of Subnational Units* (Oxford: Clarendon Press, 1990); Earl Fry, "The impact of federalism on the development of international economic relations: lessons from the United States and Canada," *Australian Outlook* 43 (1989); Hans J. Michelmann, "Federalism and international relations in Canada and the Federal Republic of Germany," *International Journal* 41 (Summer 1986), 566–67; Uwe Leonardy, "Federation and *Länder* in German foreign relations: power-sharing in treaty-making and European affairs," in Hocking, ed., *Foreign Relations and Federal States*, 236–51; and Kim Richard Nossal, "Anything but provincial: the provinces and foreign affairs," in Christopher Dunn, ed., *Provinces: Canadian Provincial Politics* (Toronto: Broadview Press, 1996), 503–518.

40. John Kincaid, "State and local governments go international," *Intergovernmental Perspective* 16 (Spring 1990), 6.

41. For a survey of the politics of the Québec–Ottawa–Paris triangle, see Nossal, *Politics of Canadian Foreign Policy*, Chap. 12.

42. Quoted in Hans J. Morgenthau, *Politics Among Nations: The Struggle for Power and Peace*, 5th ed. (New York: Alfred A. Knopf, 1973), 437fn.

43. On Canada–United States institutions, see William R. Willoughby, *The Joint Organizations of Canada and the United States* (Toronto: University of Toronto Press, 1979).

44. Nobel's will is reproduced at http://www.nobel.se/alfred/will.html

# PART ④

# A World
## *of* Boundaries

# CHAPTER ⑧

## *A* Species Fragmented:
## *How* Humankind
## Divides *Itself*

**INTRODUCTION**

I have argued that treating world politics and domestic politics as though they occurred in distinct and separate spheres—what R.B.J. Walker calls "insides" and "outsides" in world politics—yields a distorted analysis of politics at the world level. Chapter 7 suggested that trying to exclude some actors from the "stage" of world politics results in a no less distorted view. At the same time, however, we cannot deny that human beings each *create* their own "insides" and "outsides" in how they think about the world, their community, and their own relationships with their community and the world. Also, many of the actors surveyed in Chapter 7 define themselves and the groups to which they belong as "inside," and others as "outside." This chapter explores the ways in which humans have sought to divide the world into a series of dualities to create a distinct **identity** for themselves—and for others: defining who is "inside" and who is "outside," who is "here" and who "there," who is "us" and who is "them" or "other," who is "civilized" and who is not. Just as local divisions are necessary for an understanding of world politics, so too do these global divisions have an impact on local politics.

## A SPECIES-LEVEL IDENTITY?

Although all humans who have lived for the last 100 000 years or more are members of a single species, *Homo sapiens sapiens*, human beings rarely see themselves in species terms. It

*"As a woman I have no country. As a woman I want no country. As a woman my country is the whole world."*

is true that there is a long philosophic tradition that values the universality of humankind and condemns efforts to create artificial political barriers between people. Alexander the Great rejected the view common in the Greek *polis* that non-Greeks were barbarians to be enslaved. He conceived of leading a *cosmopolis*—a "world-polity"—in which Greek and non-Greek alike would be equal—hence **cosmopolitan**. The Stoic philosophers also embraced cosmopolitanism. The Christian tradition stresses the oneness of humankind under God: "There is no room for distinction between Greek and Jew..." St Paul wrote (Col. 3:11), "or between barbarian and Scythian, slave and free man."

Over the years, numerous individuals have been prone to deny any local identification and proclaim a more global affiliation. We can start with the claim attributed to Socrates: "I am a citizen, not of Athens or Greece, but of the world." He was not to be the last, as over the ensuing millennia the same thought has been put both ways: "My country is the world," Thomas Paine wrote in *The Rights of Man* in 1792; the Canadian poet F.R. Scott put it the other way in 1964: "The world is my country." In 1929, Virginia Woolf expressed it this way: "As a woman I have no country. As a woman I want no country. As a woman my country is the whole world."

But these are untypical views—and indeed they are remembered and repeated over the years precisely because they are so exceptional. The more common view over the last 5000 years is precisely the opposite. Humans may conceive of "the world" as a singular entity of all human beings as a biological abstraction ("we are all members of the species *Homo sapiens*"), a religious notion ("we are one people under God"), a philosophical transcendence ("we are the world"), a geopolitical fancy ("we are all members of the global village"), a protopolitical idea ("we are members of the international community"), or the view inspired by photographs of the planet taken from space ("we are all travelling together on Spaceship Earth"). But when it comes to actually living out a day-to-day existence, humans by and large have operated on quite a different set of assumptions. They have opted to divide themselves from other human beings, and, as we will explore in detail below, to entrench and maintain those divisions in a set of deeply rooted practices.

## TERRITORIAL DIVISIONS? THE REAL ESTATE APPROACH

The easiest way to get a sense of the intraspecies divisions that humans have created is simply to look at a contemporary map of the world. There one will see the clearest representation of human division: that map will show that, with the exception of a part of Antarctica, all land above sea level in the world is divided up between 190 or so separate countries; not even the most barren and uninhabited rocky outcropping in the middle of the ocean lies outside this division. Each of these countries has its own name, and clear territorial boundaries mark each one off from the other.

But to map the 190 states like this provides a distorted image of political reality. First, it implies that the divisions between people are mainly territorial. It suggests that all one has to do is survey a line on the ground between this space A and that space B; put in a set of boundary markers with a corresponding line on a map, and presto: all those on one side of the line are the people of A, and all those on the other side are people of B.

One can draw the lines and divide the world in such a fashion, but doing so tells us little about the political divisions that mark world politics. It tells us little about *how* people divide themselves, or *why*. There are many hooks on which one can hang a separate identity that creates an "us" on the one hand and a "them" on the other, and a real estate definition— by itself—is probably the least important. Indeed, it could be argued that a line-drawing approach to human division masks a number of the realities of divisions that simply do not conform to the lines on the map, as the case of North America suggests.

## Colouring Outside the Lines: The Case of North America

A map of North America shows the continent neatly cleaved into three: Canada, the United States, and Mexico. But do those dividing lines accurately reveal the range of "we/they" divisions among the almost 400 million people living in the area we call North America?

Does drawing a borderline between Tijuana and Matamoros and stringing miles of border fencing, carefully guarded by a border patrol, neatly separate all "Mexicans" on the south side from all "Americans" on the north side? In fact, despite the fences and the border guards, the Mexican-American border has been so porous that there are similarities of identity that extend *across* the border. Large numbers of those physically in the United States have ties of language, family, and identity with Mexico: of the estimated 27 million Hispanics in the United States, some 18 million are of Mexican origin. Some are physically in the United States but are not there legally; illegal aliens lead their lives in the shadows, always in fear of a raid by agents of the United States Immigration and Naturalization Service (INS). Some live a transborder existence: many owners or managers of the *maquiladoras*—twin-plant assembly systems where components made in the United States are assembled in Mexico and shipped back across the border—work in Tijuana or Nuevo Laredo by day, but at night and on the weekend, they live across the border in the suburbs of San Diego, California or Laredo, Texas. About 750 000 people move across the Mexican-American border each day. In short, Hispanics have become so numerous that they are changing the linguistic and demographic, and hence the political, dynamics of many southern American states. Some have even argued that the border area, differing as it does from the rest of Mexico and the rest of the United States, should be considered a separate nation.[1]

The two international borders that seemingly cleave North America so cleanly also do not help us understand important "we/they" constructions of political identity *within* those borders. For example, identity based on race manifests itself in countless everyday ways between African-Americans, Hispanics, Asians, and whites in the United States, and occasionally bubbles into overt violence, such as the urban riots in the mid-1960s or the Los Angeles riots of May 1992. Or consider identity based on ancestry, which is politically important in Mexico, where the broad three-fold division of those of European descent, native peoples, and *mestizos* (those of mixed ancestry) can be further subdivided by numerous native tribal divisions and dialects inherited from a Mayan or Aztec past. Or identity can be defined by nation: *québécois*, native Americans, aboriginal Canadians, native Hawai'ians, aboriginal Mexicans. Or identity is often based on one's region, state, or province: consider the strong state identities of Texans or Californians; the regional identities of those from the south, the southwest, the northwest, the mid-west, the northeast, or broader coastal identities—east coast and west coast; Central Canadian and those from the north, the west, and the east; Newfoundlander and those from "away" (from the mainland); or in Mexico the regional distances felt by those in Baja California Sur or Chiapas from *el DF*—the *Distrito Federal* in which Mexico City is located.

Likewise, drawing borderlines do not enable one to map accurately the divisions of political identity within Canada between those who want to form their own separate country, Québec, and those who want the entity they call Canada to remain as it is. The Québec **sovereigntists**—those who want Québec to become a separate country—try to solve the problem by the simple expedient of saying that the borders of an independent Québec would be the borders of the present-day province. But this too masks realities of identities: what about the people who live within those territorial boundaries who identify themselves as Canadians rather than *québécois* and do not want to leave Canada? Or what about those in the northern part of Québec who identify themselves politically as part of the Cree nation, but who want that nation to remain under the umbrella of Canada?

Painting Mexico as a single undifferentiated entity is no less problematic. Borderlines do not reveal the differences in language, race, class, and region that divide Mexico. On occasion, these cleavages have led to violence. In January 1994, a group of native Mexicans in the poor

*Identity not only involves seeing oneself as part of a group; it also means defining others as not being part of that group—even those who live within the territorial boundaries of the community.*

southern state of Chiapas organized the *Ejército Zapatista de Liberación Nacional* (EZLN, Zapatista National Liberation Army) and, under the command of a leader known only as "Subcommandante Marcos," launched an armed uprising against the federal authorities. This has provoked the often brutal use of force by government forces against armed rebels and unarmed civilians alike: for example, in December 1997, 45 native Mexicans in the Chiapas village of Acteal were massacred; it was widely believed that their killers were individuals connected to the governing party, *Partido Revolucionario Institucional* (Institutional Revolutionary Party, or PRI).

Nor does line-drawing help us to understand the reverse side of identity creation: the identifying of some people *out* of one's community. Identity not only involves seeing oneself as part of a group; it also means defining others as *not* being part of that group—even those who live within the territorial boundaries of the community. For example, some *québécois* consider those who are not **pure laine** ("pure wool"—in other words, descended from the original settlers who occupied New France before it was seized by the British in 1759 and 1760), or those who do not speak French, as "outsiders," even though they may live in Québec. Likewise, those in the United States who belong to groups such as the Christian Identity Movement, the Aryan Nations, or the Ku Klux Klan tend to define blacks, Jews, and many others as being outside their conception of political community. And in all three countries, native peoples get "defined out" in a variety of ways, frequently occupying the socioeconomic—and hence the political—margins of society.

Immigrant groups can also get "defined out." The immigrants from different countries who have come to Canada and the United States in waves over the past century and a half—Irish, Germans, Swedes, Poles, Ukrainians, Italians, Portuguese, Chinese, Japanese, South Asians, Vietnamese, Russians—have all discovered what being an "outsider" means. Some have experienced it in the extreme: after war was declared against Japan in December 1941, both the American and Canadian governments rounded up all those of Japanese ancestry, confiscated their property, and shipped them off to internment camps. In the United States, it was to prevent sabotage and subversion; in Canada, the internment was prodded by fear that the presence of Japanese would provoke other British Columbians into the kind of anti-Asian riots that had marked that province's history. In both countries, citizenship did not matter; it was enough to just *look* Japanese. Of the 112 000 Japanese-Americans interned, fully 70 000 of them were bona fide United States citizens.

But this is a never-ending process. The defining out of one group is replaced by the defining out of another. Discrimination against Irish Catholics, endemic in North American cities in the 19th century, has declined in the 20th. When Vietnamese who immigrated to the United States after the end of the Vietnam war in 1975 bought shellfish boats on the Gulf coast, they were shot at, and some were killed, by fishermen in Mississippi who claimed that they were taking away jobs from "Americans." Twenty years later, there is peace on the Gulf coast.

Today we continue to see the dynamic at work. For example, in the 1994 elections, Californians were asked to decide on Proposition 187, a measure designed to deny education, health, and welfare benefits to illegal aliens. However, those Californians who voted for Proposition 187 seemed unconcerned that, in practice, this measure would put the onus on people who simply looked Hispanic or had Hispanic names to prove that they were legal residents (or "real" Americans), a requirement not faced by whites, blacks, or Asians. Some British Columbians do not consider immigrants from Hong Kong arriving in Vancouver to be "real" Canadians. Sikhs in Canada continue to struggle for common (and legal) acceptance of the distinctive religious symbols required by strict observance, particularly the carrying of the *khanda* (or small dagger) or the wearing of turbans.

In short, the lines on the map of North America are quite deceptive. Moreover, the North American example is not at all unique. One could perform a similar analysis on lines drawn virtually anywhere in the international system. Very often, the line drawn simply does not perfectly fit divisions of political identity. In other words, one cannot understand human divisions by looking at territorial boundaries alone.

## IDENTITY DIVISIONS: "SELF"/"OTHER"

A much clearer picture is obtained if we do not look for political divisions based on real estate, but rather those based on how people define themselves (and others) as members of an identifiable group, "us" and "them." As psychologists, anthropologists, and sociologists remind us, engaging in such definitions is ubiquitous in the human experience.[2] Indeed, we often do it quite subconsciously. At the most superficial—but nonetheless quite illustrative—level, consider the dynamics of how (and why) people side with sports teams, happily wearing scarves, hats, or other symbols that mark supporters of "our" team from supporters of "their" team. This form of dualistic identification is everywhere evident. We define family in these terms, even making fine distinctions between the nuclear, immediate, or extended families. **Kinship ties** appear to be a universal source of loyalty and love, and most people are willing to put themselves in harm's way to protect those ties. Consider how many parents assess their marriageable children's proposed choice of partner in largely "we/they" terms. Think how easily we fall into we/they definitions when it comes to religious or political beliefs. Or how readily we classify ourselves and others on any number of other sociopolitical attributes, such as gender, class, race, age, or background.

That same process of defining "self" and "other" in such a fashion is evident at the level of political community. In other words, we should look for divisions based on definitions of a political **in-group**. The in-group defines who "we" are: those we identify with, are loyal to, love, and (if necessary) will fight and die for. Likewise, because people tend to define who they are by what they are not, as social psychology reminds us, that means also looking for definitions of an **out-group**—those who are deemed *not* members of the group. This is who "they" are, the "Other" with a capital O.

It should be noted that simply defining **Otherness** is to say nothing about how that Other is regarded. All too often, we forget that the Other is, at bottom, nothing more than a definition of "not us." As such, Otherness can arouse the full range of human emotions—positive, negative, and neutral. Thus, "we" can feel admiration, warmth, kinship, loyalty, pity, sympathy, or friendship for the Other "them." On the other hand, we can mock, scorn, or patronize the Other; we can also envy, fear, or—especially—hate the Other, sometimes with enough fury that we have no difficulty with the idea of harming or even killing them. Or, alternatively, we can be utterly indifferent, literally not caring one way or another about all those human beings we define as "outside" the in-group.

### The Roots of Identity? Tales from the Paleolithic

We can see these tendencies as far back as humans have recorded their history. Indeed, some might be tempted to delve back even further, into prehistory, when *Homo sapiens sapiens* was overspreading the Earth during the **Paleolithic Era** (or Old Stone Age). This era spans about two million years—to the end of the last Ice Age, approximately 11 000 years ago. During this time humans developed chipped stone tools and hunted and gathered their food. The next phase is called the **Neolithic Era**, or New Stone Age. Technically, Neolithic refers to the use of polished stones rather than chipped ones, but more commonly it describes that period when societies began to develop agriculture and domesticate animals—necessary conditions for the evolution of what we term civilization.*

Going back to the Paleolithic has some advantages, for at this time—before the emergence of civilization or the conditions necessary for civilized life—all human beings lived virtually identical existences. Some demographers have estimated that by 10 000 BC, there were only 10 to 15 million humans, spread over all the continents save Antarctica. Climatic and geographic conditions had produced specialized differences among humans in bone structure, skin pigmentation, hair colour and form, and other features. But the major racial divisions of the species—the Mongolians of East Asia, the Caucasians of the Mediterranean, the Americans of the western hemisphere, the Malayans of Australia and the South Pacific, and the Ethiopians of subsaharan Africa—did not in any sense mitigate the sameness of their existence. All humans eked out a subsistence existence, based on hunting and gathering, in small bands of 30 to 100 people. They used rudimentary implements, controlled fire, and lived in rude shelters, often in caves. To that point no society of human beings had extended beyond the hunter-gatherer phase.

How did the vast number of little groups of human beings, spread across the world, organize themselves during this era? The short answer is that we do not know. Much of our knowledge about human existence in prehistory must be based on inference and conjecture, for these groups left little concrete evidence about how exactly they organized themselves. However, we do know from cave paintings and burial sites that prehistoric groups tended to have identifiable cultures. We may infer that many bands might have had myths, developed or inchoate, about the origins of the Earth or even their particular band. We may infer that in each group, language evolved in idiosyncratic ways, with vocabulary suited to particular local conditions. We may even infer that the contact between groups was limited: given the amount of land needed to sustain a hunter-gatherer band, it has been hypothesized that members of some bands might have lived their entire lives without coming into contact with another group of humans.

Most importantly for our discussion here, the dynamics of group identity are unclear. Did these bands have a sense of "self"—an identity that set the band off from others, most evident in giving themselves a name? Did the *idea* of the band command love and loyalty from its members? We know that people in prehistorical bands fought and died in wars with one another: would it be appropriate to infer that band identity prompted them to put themselves in harm's way, or lay down their lives for the band and its members?

We cannot know the answers to such questions. We can, however, speculate that if it is true that some bands simply did not come into contact with others, then it would be unlikely, in the absence of others, for such a group to have developed a sense of itself as something

---

* It should be noted that it is impossible to date this period in human development exactly, for emergence from the Neolithic has been highly variable. Some human societies—for example, those in northern Africa, the Middle East, and east Asia—developed civilizations some 6000 years ago. For others, by contrast, the Neolithic ended much later: in Central America, for example, prehistory did not end until 200 BC, and in South America not until 1500 AD, just before the Spanish conquest. And many peoples were still living an essentially prehistorical existence when "discovered" by Europeans in the contemporary era.

identifiable from others. Likewise, we can surmise that as different groups, speaking different languages, came into contact with one another, they would have tended to develop such a sense of "us" and "them." They might even have developed names for their band and the others. But we cannot know this definitively, for the simple reason that Neolithic groups left us no evidence of how they saw themselves.

By contrast, we have considerable evidence from the **civilizations** that evolved from prehistory following the discovery of agriculture, the domestication of animals, the invention of metal-working, and, most importantly, the invention of writing. The civilizations that began to emerge from the progressive agglomeration of small groups in the river valleys of the Tigris, Euphrates, Nile, Indus, and Yellow (or Huanghe), around six to eight thousand years ago, demonstrated a well-developed sense of communal identity.[3]

## Identifying Divisions: Naming "Us," Naming "Them"

Perhaps the clearest indication of the development of such a sense of "communal self" is the practice that appears to be a universal feature of human societies after the Neolithic: giving themselves—and others—a name. The ancient Egyptians, for example, had names for their land. They did not use the word "Egypt," which is a modern European word derived from the Greek *Aigyptos* (itself likely a corruption of one of the names of the city of Memphis, where the god Ptah, creator of the Earth, was worshipped: Hikuptah, "house of the soul of Ptah"). Nor did they use Misr, the Arabic word that present-day Egyptians use to refer to their country. Rather, ancient Egyptians referred to their land as Keme, the Black Land—a reference to the fertile soil of the Nile valley and delta that separated them from the "Red Land," in other words the inhospitable surrounding desert. Egyptians also distinguished between the land of the delta and the land of the Nile valley: Egyptian rulers proclaimed that they were "kings of the two lands." Pharaohs wore a double crown, white for the south, red for the delta, and their tiara featured the head of a cobra, which symbolized a different god in each region.

As importantly, Egyptians had names for others. When a nomadic tribe invaded from the north in 1720 BC, capturing Memphis and installing themselves on the throne for a hundred years before being expelled, the Egyptians called them the Hyksos. This is how they are remembered in history, though it is not a name that the Hyksos would likely have called themselves, for it means "foreign rulers." Likewise, the word Habiru ("those who pass from place to place") appears in Egyptian records as the name of a small nomadic band from the northeast who settled in Egypt at the time of the Hyksos and were persecuted after the Hyksos were expelled in 1570 BC. Habiru is a term that those people—who called themselves the people of Israel—eventually applied to themselves. Egyptian records persistently refer to the Sea People, who were probably a number of different nomadic groups, most likely from the Balkans, which moved south around the eastern Mediterranean coast about 1200 BC, attacking the great empires of the Hittites, the Assyrians, and the Egyptians themselves.

The Egyptian example demonstrates a number of aspects about how peoples are named. First, throughout recorded history we can identify distinct societies with individual characteristics and a sense of identity that mark their communities as distinct from others.

Often symbols were used to reinforce this identity, suggested by the use of colours and cobra to signify the unity of two different parts of Egypt, the Japanese chrysanthemum, the Chinese dragon, the Roman eagle, the English lion, or the French *fleur de lys*. The sense of communal self became particularly pronounced after the "invention" and subsequent spread of civilization. As different civilizations—with their different languages, cosmologies, religious beliefs, cultural rituals, and governmental practices—developed in different parts of the world, the patterns of human existence began to diverge dramatically from the essential sameness of life in prehistory.

The forms of political identification vary widely. Great civilizations, empires, or kingdoms are not the only political formations that attracted or commanded love and loyalty. On the contrary: political identification can take many different forms. For example, we must include notions of personal identification, in which the political identity begins by being fixed on a single individual who is able to gather followers and create a new political community. History abounds with examples, though a particularly spectacular case of a political community that was created from a tiny band under the charismatic leadership of a single individual was the vast empire created by Genghis Khan. In only 16 years (1206–1222), his empire spread from Korea in the east to Russia in the west.

A special kind of personalized political identification and political loyalty can be found during the period of **feudalism** in medieval Europe. Feudalism was a set of overlapping political relationships that linked suzerains, barons, and knights in a system of vassals, fiefs, fees, and pledges of fealty (loyalty by a vassal, or peasant, to his feudal lord). Indeed, so complex were these socio-political relations that trying to discover political identity in a feudal context can be a distinct challenge. The social unit of greatest importance was the **feudal domain**—the estate, land, and serf labour which was the "fee" (or *feudum*) that a lord gave to a lesser vassal in return for a pledge of personal fealty. As Maurice Keen puts it succinctly, government in Europe during feudal times was little more than "the patrimony of powerful men." The basis of political identification "was not a sense of obligation to a 'common weal' (or commonwealth), but the personal oaths of individual men to individual lords."[4]

In this context, we should not forget **dynastic identity**. In such cases, identity and loyalty are focused on a dynastic family (such as the Umayyad and Abbasid families in the Muslim world, or the Tokugawas in Japan), sometimes styled a royal "house" (such as the house of Savoy, the house of Windsor, or the house of Saud). The Wars of the Roses in England between 1455 and 1485 evolved from rival claims to the English throne between the House of Lancaster, which used a red rose as its emblem, and the House of York, which used a white rose.

Tribes, large and small, also developed identities, even if they may not have had other attributes of civilization, such as literacy or urbanization. For example, when Europeans arrived in southeastern Australia in the 1780s, they discovered numerous groups of Aboriginals, each with a well-developed sense of identity, and sufficient contact between the various groups that bilingualism and multilingualism was common.

Likewise, larger tribes, or peoples, have always had a sense of identity. Much of the long history of world politics is about peoples and their movements, often over large

*Much of the long history of world politics is about peoples and their movements, often over large distances.*

distances. Consider, for example, the land between the Tigris and Euphrates rivers, that area of the world that the Greeks called Mesopotamia ("between two rivers"), where the first human civilization arose in the fourth millennium BC. For fully 4700 years—from the time that Etana, king of Kish, established a Sumerian polity around 2800 BC to the formation of Iraq as an independent country in 1932—this land was controlled by a succession of tribes and peoples who moved in, raided, conquered, overthrew the existing order, settled, and were then in turn overthrown by newcomers. The list begins with Sumerians and ends with the British, who seized the area during the course of the Great War. In between came Akkadians, Gutians, Elamites, Babylonians, Hittites, Kassites, Hurrians, Assyrians, Chaldeans, Seleucids, Parthians, Sassanids, Arabs, Mongols, Bedouins, and Turks.

That same pattern is evident in many parts of the world. Consider the numerous tribes and peoples that appear in the accounts of the Old Testament. Or the waves of conquering peoples that gave shape to ancient Greece and Rome. Or the *Völkswanderung* ("nomadic peoples") of Europe, sweeping across the continent and around the Mediterranean Sea in the first millennium AD: Vandals, Jutes, Angles, Saxons, Burgundians, Suevi, Alans, Visigoths, and Ostrogoths; or a miniature version of the broader European pattern playing itself out in Britain between Picts, Scots, Celts, Britons, Romans, Angles, Saxons, Danes, and Normans. Or the struggles of the Kanuri, Bulala, and Fulani peoples which so altered the shape of the Kanem-Bornu empire of West Africa over its 1000-year existence.

We should always remember that the names we use to identify peoples are not necessarily the names they give themselves. For example, Greeks have never called themselves "Greeks" (unless, of course, they are speaking English); they were and are Hellenes (and remain so today as Elleniki Demokratia, the Hellenic Republic), and their country is Hellas. Graecia was the Latin name Romans gave to Epirus, the small Hellenic tribe with whom they first had contact. Likewise, the people we know as the Incas were so named by Spanish invaders, who called the entire people after the Quechuan word for king or prince, *inka*. For their part, the "Incas" called their community Tahuantinsuyu, "land of the four quarters." The Crees, observing the dietary habits of their northern neighbours, provided the phrase by which the peoples of the Arctic region were known for many years: *askimowew*—"he eats it raw." But the word the Arctic peoples use to describe themselves is Inuit, which is the plural of *inuk* (person); it means, simply, "the people." The word we use today to identify the Sioux is a short-form corruption of Nadouessioux, a name given to the tribe by their enemies, the Ojibwa. French missionaries shortened it, ignoring the fact that the Sioux called themselves the Dakota, meaning "ally." When Europeans first visited Korea, they called the country by the name of one of the political communities that had unified the peninsula between 918 and 1392, Koryo; the name Koreans give their country is Choson, meaning "morning calm."

In short, the emergence of naming political communities is an important step in the creation—and maintenance—of the essential we/they dualities that mark world politics. However, this is not to imply that such a sense of identity was widespread among all those who lived in these historical polities. On the contrary: it is likely that in many cases, the sense of identity with the political community was limited to the ruling, priestly, and warrior classes. The vast majority probably lived out their lives unaware of the larger political community of which they were nominally members. In other words, the political horizons of most people most of the time remained limited to their own village; they would not understand that those in the next village belonged to a broader political community. For many people, the wider political community made its presence known only when the tax collector came, when labour for public works was required, or when soldiers were needed to fight invaders (or to go invading).

One should not be too categorical about this, however. Clearly the sense of community was keener and better developed in some polities than others. For example, it is likely that a sense of political identity was more widespread in the average Greek *polis* in the fourth century BC than, for example, in the average village in one of the large empires in the same era—China or Persia. Likewise, it is probable that a sense of community was more widespread among the members of large nomadic groups—and those with whom they fought. Consider the great Vandal sailing of May 428. In that month, the Vandal king Gaiseric assembled the entire Vandal tribe on the shores of Andalusia. Every male, adult and child, was counted (there were 80 000 males and an untold number of females), and then the entire community was transported to North Africa in ships in order to attack Roman cities there. It is difficult to believe that a sense of tribal identity was not imparted to all those who took part in this great movement of people.

While in many historical contexts there might have been only a limited and partial sense of identity *with* other people who lived in the same community, people appeared to have a universal tendency to recognize those who were *not* part of the community. In other words, people might not have known who all the members of the in-group (or "we") were, but they surely knew who was *not* part of the group—who "they" were. Most languages have words to describe the nonmember, the out-group "Other" who does not belong. In an historical context, these people stood out. Their clothing, for example, would immediately mark them as outsiders, for dress in most historical communities was used as a means of distinguishing one's place in society (much more so than the universal and essentially egalitarian dress patterns we are familiar with today). But other attributes—looks, skin colour, language, habits, ways of thinking, or religious beliefs—would also mark them as outsiders, outlanders, strangers, foreigners, aliens, or enemies.

Because of this, it is perhaps not surprising that the words we use for "foreigner" are invariably the same as the word for strange or unusual. In French, for example, *étranger* used as a noun means foreigner or outsider; as an adjective it means foreign, strange, unknown, or irrelevant. Likewise, in Russian, the various words for foreigner, stranger, alien, interloper, and "belonging to someone else" all use the root *chuzh*. In German, *Fremde* means a foreign country; the adjective *fremd* means strange, alien, unknown, unusual, peculiar, or exotic. English is no different: we derive "foreign" from the Latin *foris*, outside, an adverb occasionally used by the Romans to mean outside Rome; but in English, foreign does not only mean outside, but also "not belonging." Other words underscore the peculiarity of the foreigner: for example, we use "outlandish," from outlander (itself from the Dutch *uitlander* and German *Auslander*), to describe dress or behaviour that is bizarre or unconventional. In Italian, stranger is *forestiere*, "out of the forest."

## CIVILIZATIONAL DIVISIONS: CIVILIZED "SELF"/BARBARIAN "OTHER"

Some definitions of in-group/out-group went beyond merely identifying the foreigner as a stranger with unusual characteristics who did not belong. Rather, in some cases, the division between "we" and "they" acquired a highly value-laden assessment that divided the civilized "Self" from the uncivilized "Other," a sense of superiority attached to one's in-group, and inferiority imputed to the out-group. In particular, superiority was attached to the way in which the civilized Self organized its political, economic, social, or cultural lives as against the practices of Others.

There are a number of examples of such a civilized/uncivilized duality. We can usefully begin with what is perhaps the most self-conscious civilizational division—that of imperial China. As we saw in Chapter 2, the Chinese conceived of their country as *Jungguo* (middle country or kingdom). But we must see this name in the context of the unique Chinese conception of themselves in the world. Those schooled in the Confucian tradition did not conceive of *China* as a political community that existed separately from others. Rather, they conceived of the world as a single entity, full of peoples and lords over whom the Chinese emperor, or *huangdi*, was indeed "lord of all lords." The emperor was *Tianzi*, "Son of Heaven," the intermediary between heaven and Earth; the emperor's right to rule over the entire world and all its people was derived from *Tianming*, the **Mandate of Heaven**. That mandate required the emperor to order the world, including extending the benefits of civilization to all people (*ren*). In such a worldview, there could be no duality between Chinese and *foreigner*.[*] Rather, this worldview cleaved the world's people into two states-of-being: *huaren* (literally, "splendid people"), who enjoyed the refinements of Chinese

*"The yiren cannot be governed in the same way as China is governed. That is to say, to seek good government among animals will inevitably lead to great confusion."*

culture and civilization, and *yiren*, people who lived beyond the civilized environs of the imperial centre. A common English translation for *yiren* is "barbarian people," but that word does not adequately capture the essence of the duality between *huaren* and *yiren*.

There can be little doubt that classical Chinese regarded the *yi* as uncivilized—culturally and morally impoverished. Such people were not very different from animals: as a Song dynasty official wrote in the 11th century, "The *yi* cannot be governed in the same way as China is governed. That is to say, to seek good government among animals will inevitably lead to great confusion."[5] But translating *yi* as "barbarian" implies that the Chinese saw them

---

[*] It should be stressed that this discussion concerns classical Chinese thought. Chinese have long abandoned notions of universal empire, and today make more conventional distinctions between themselves and "foreigners," or *waiguoren* (outside-country people).

as people beyond the civilized pale, to be shunned; this was not the case, however. The Chinese worldview of a single universal polity demanded that those unfortunate enough to have been born *yi* be brought the benefits of Chinese civilization; that was what the Mandate of Heaven was all about. Thus, we can say that the *yiren* were not so much "barbarian people" as they were "people yet to be civilized."

By contrast, when the ancient Greeks divided the world into the civilized Hellenes and the uncivilized barbarians, they had no such civilizing aspirations. They employed a more conventional civilizational division, in which a barbarian really was a barbarian—and would remain one. The word did not begin life that way, however: the ancient Greeks originally used the word *barbaros* (βαρβαρος) as nothing more than an onomatopoeic device to describe the speech patterns of the Carians, a people who occupied what is now the southwestern coast of Turkey; the word initially was used to describe non-Greek speakers. Gradually, however, the word acquired a politico-cultural meaning rather than just a linguistic one: **barbarians** came to include all those outside the civilized orbit of the *poleis* of Hellas. It was applied especially to the Persians, but also eventually even to some who spoke Greek, such as the Macedonians. Barbarians were, in this view, people of uncultivated roughness, without the virtues imparted by the civilized Hellenes. Aristotle, for example, noted the common Greek view that barbarians were little different than slaves—in other words, it was right and proper for Hellenes to treat barbarians as they treated slaves.[6] But there was little desire, unlike in China, to bring the barbarians into the civilized orbit of the Hellenic *polis*.

For their part, the Romans adopted both the word and its usage, though for Romans the civilizational division involved a tip of the hat to the civilizing influences of the Greeks. In Latin, *barbaria* meant any foreign country other than Rome or Greece, and *barbarus* referred to any foreigner other than a Roman or a Greek, and likewise implied a certain savagery.

## RELIGIOUS DIVISIONS: TRUE BELIEVER/HERETICAL INFIDEL

The word barbarian then made its way into most European languages, where it was quickly employed to describe another kind of civilizational duality, that of religion, and the dichotomy between believer and infidel (nonbeliever). Over the course of the first millennium after the death of Jesus Christ, two great religions spread around the Mediterranean—and into many lands beyond. Christianity spread westward across the northern coast, and thence northward into Europe; after Muhammad's death in 632, Islam spread from Arabia across North Africa, into parts of Sicily and Spain in the west, to some African communities south of the Sahara, and in the east all the way to the Malay peninsula. Both Christians and Muslims were inclined, each in their own way, to create dualities that distinguished believers from nonbelievers.

### Christian "Insides" and "Outsides"

Most European Christians in the Middle Ages appear to have forgotten St Paul's conception of a universal church; instead they preferred to divide the world into Christendom, the collectivity of all true believers in Christ, and the world of the anti-Christian heretic and non-Christian infidel. This simple dualism explains the huge enthusiasm that Europeans showed for the idea of the **Crusades**, a series of military campaigns undertaken in the 11th, 12th and 13th centuries by Christian Europeans against unbelievers of all sorts, heretics inside Christendom and infidels outside.

Inside, the heretics were mainly the Cathari, the Waldenses, and other sects. The Cathari (or the "purified") comprised different sects who believed in the existence of two gods, one of goodness and one of evil. This sect spread through southern France in the 11th and 12th centuries; adherents were known as Albigenses, because they were centred in the French town of Albi. The Albigenses were regarded as heretics by the Church, and Pope Innocent III (pope from 1198 to 1216) launched a crusade against them in the early 13th century, brutally repressing the movement and forcing adherents into isolated areas. Pope Gregory IX (pope from 1227 to 1241) decided to pursue the remainder, and in 1231 institutionalized the prosecution of heretics directly under papal control by putting into place the mechanisms of the Inquisition. Other persecuted groups included the Waldenses, followers of Peter Waldo of Lyon. This Christian sect, which emerged in the late 1100s, opposed the opulence of the Church; for that reason, the Church moved to eradicate them by Inquisition and a crusade, organized by Pope Innocent VIII as late as 1487.

The other nonbelievers who lived in Christian Europe were the Jews, widely despised and discriminated against for their purported role in Christ's death. For example, true believers and infidels were not permitted to live together, according to a Lateran Council decision of 1179. In many European countries, Jews were forced into segregated areas (eventually institutionalized after 1555 as the *Ghetto* in Italian cities, the *Judengasse* in German cities, and the *carrière des juifs* in France).

Outside Christendom, the world was deemed to be occupied by pagans and heathens whose religious beliefs were uncivilized, or by infidels who rejected the Word of God. The prime target of Christian antipathy were Muslims, who fervently denied the sonship of God that lay at the heart of Christian beliefs. Muslim lands in North Africa were given the pejorative term Barbary, with the clear implication that those who inhabited such lands were barbarians.[*] To be sure, it might have been incongruous for Europeans, whose civilizational accomplishments in the latter part of the first millennium were both slim and rude, to use "barbaric" to describe a people whose achievements were considerable, particularly in the sciences, business, mathematics, art, architecture, and literature. But European Christians were more concerned with what they saw as the heresies of Muhammad and what were inevitably described as his "infidel followers" than in the achievements of the Islamic civilization that flourished under the Abbasid caliphate in the eighth and ninth centuries.

---

[*] It should be noted that large sections of North Africa were populated by a non-Arabic tribe whom Arabs called Berbers, from the Arabic *barbara*, to talk noisily and confusedly. We cannot know whether the Arabic verb is related to the onomatopoeic *barbaros* of the Greeks; but we do know that the use of Barbary by Europeans derives from the Latin and Greek meaning of land of barbarians rather than land of Berbers.

*The Crusaders saw no difficulty at all with the idea of killing in the name of Christ. Indeed, they frequently did so with great and bloody abandon.*

Given such views, it is not surprising that Europeans were fired by a desire to throw the Muslims out of Palestine, considered the Holy Land by Christendom. The First Crusade was organized to "liberate" Jerusalem and return it to Christian control. The Crusaders saw no difficulty at all with the idea of killing in the name of Christ. Indeed, they frequently did so with great and bloody abandon: on 15 July 1099, for example, the Crusaders captured Jerusalem and slaughtered virtually every inhabitant in a single day of human butchery, claiming afterward that the blood of the infidels had "purified" the city.

## Muslim "Insides" and "Outsides"

For their part, Muslims were constrained by their faith to divide the world into believers and nonbelievers: *dar al-Islam*, the abode or "house" of Islam—those who have surrendered to the will of God (*islam* in Arabic means submit)—and *dar al-harb*, the abode of war, the world of the nonbeliever. Islamic law took the different injunctions in the Qu'ran to fight nonbelievers—under certain conditions to the death—and institutionalized these as the **jihād**.[7] The word, which means "striving," is commonly translated by non-Muslims as "holy war," and it is often assumed that the purpose of the *jihād* was to spread Islam. However, there is nothing in the Qu'ran or Islamic tradition that supports such a view; more accurately *jihād* refers to the permanent obligation of every Muslim to ensure the spread of *Muslim rule*, not *Islamic faith*, over all the Earth.

Because of this, there were considerable differences in how the believer/nonbeliever duality worked in the case of Islam. Under Islamic law, not everyone had to surrender as Muslims expanded *dar al-Islam*. Instead, conquered peoples were divided into two categories. Those who were "possessors of scripture" were *ahl al-Kitāb*, "people of the Book"—Jews, Christians, and the Zoroastrians of Persia—and they were given three choices when Muslims seized their community. They could convert to Islam; they could fight (though if they fought and lost, they could be put to death, their families could be enslaved, and their property seized); or they could submit to Muslim rule and, as a symbol of their submission, pay a special tax as *dhimmis* or "wards" who enjoyed the protection of the authorities and could continue to practise their faith. By contrast, polytheist disbelievers (*kufr*), such as Hindus or Buddhists, had only two choices: conversion to Islam or death.

In practice, these divisions had important consequences for nonbelievers under Muslim rule. For example, when Mahmud of Ghazni, in what is now Iran, seized northwestern India in the early years of the 11th century, his armies massacred Hindus by the thousands, plundered and destroyed temples, and sacked entire cities. By contrast, Christians and Jews in Muslim-ruled lands were treated very differently. True, the *dhimmi* did not enjoy all the rights and privileges of Muslims: they had to ride donkeys instead of horses, they could not build their houses as high as Muslims, they had to wear distinctive clothing in the streets, and they paid higher taxes than Muslims. But they were never despised by Muslims in the same way that Jews and Muslims were despised by European Christians: they were never confined to ghettoes, and they were in general not treated as contemptible outsiders. On the contrary: many Christians and Jews played important roles in Muslim society as physicians, bureaucrats, traders, and bankers. Some even became viziers, the senior officials of the caliphate.

## CONCLUSION

To this point, we have surveyed the tendency of human beings to divide themselves through identification with political community, broadly defined as including all kinds of polities, from small villages to large civilizations. However, this analysis of human division has not mentioned either "states" or "nations." Avoiding these terms to describe the political communities discussed above was both conscious and purposeful. The simple reason is that *states* and *nations* are both relatively recent human inventions, and thus it would be inappropriate and anachronistic to apply such terms backward in history to political formations that might have looked like nations or states, but in fact were neither.

But there can be little doubt that each separately (and both together, as the *sovereign nation-state*) have been important sources of division between human beings over the last two centuries. In that time, the sovereign nation-state has indeed been all-consuming: billions of human beings have organized their political loyalties around it; tens of millions of lives have been lost fighting in its name; and trillions of dollars have been devoted to promoting, advancing, maintaining, and defending it. However, to get a full sense of how it is that the triplet of territory, sovereignty, and nationality have come to be such a potent source of political division between human beings, we need to explore the emergence of the sovereign nation-state in more detail. To that issue we turn in the upcoming chapters: Chapter 9 focuses on the state; Chapters 10 and 11 examine the notion of sovereignty. Part V—Chapters 12 to 14—looks at the nation, nationalism, and the nation-state.

## *Keyword File*

| | |
|---|---|
| Identity | Paleolithic Era |
| Cosmopolitan | Neolithic Era |
| *Maquiladoras* | Civilization |
| *Mestizo* | Feudalism |
| Sovereignists | Feudal domain |
| *Pure laine* | Dynastic identity |
| Kinship ties | Mandate of Heaven |
| In-group | Barbarian |
| Out-group | Crusades |
| Otherness | *Jihād* |

## For Further Exploration

HARD COPY

Erdmann, Carl. *The Origin of the Ideal of Crusade.* Princeton, NJ: Princeton University Press, 1978.

Harrison, John A. *The Chinese Empire.* New York: Harcourt Brace Jovanovich, 1972.

Keen, Maurice. *The Penguin History of Medieval Europe.* London: Penguin, 1968.

Romer, John. *Ancient Lives: Daily Life in Egypt of the Pharaohs.* New York: Holt, 1990.

Roux, George. *Ancient Iraq.* Harmondsworth, U.K.: Pelican, 1980.

WEBLINKS

**http://cedar.evansville.edu/~ecoleweb/documents.html**

Ecole Initiative Early Church Documents: resources on early Christianity, including the sects discussed in this chapter

**http://www.bnf.fr/enluminures/themes/t_1/st_1_02/a102_006.htm**

Display of contemporary prints of the Crusades from the *Bibliotèque nationale de France*

**http://www.orb.rhodes.edu/default.html**

Site of Online Reference Book for Medieval Studies; essays, bibliographies, and primary documents for Middle Ages

**http://www.ummah.org.uk**

Home page of Islamic Gateway, with connections for Islamic history

## Notes to Chapter 8

1. See, for example, Joel Garreau, *The Nine Nations of North America* (New York: Avon, 1982).

2. Rhoda E. Howard, *Human Rights and the Search for Community* (Boulder, CO: Westview, 1995), 137–38.

3. On the rise of civilizations, see: William H. McNeill, *The Rise of the West: A History of the Human Community* (Chicago: University of Chicago Press, 1963); Fernand Braudel, *History of Civilizations* (New York: Penguin, 1994).

4. Maurice Keen, *The Penguin History of Medieval Europe* (London: Penguin, 1968), 52–60.

5. Immanuel C.Y. Hsu, *China's Entrance into the Family of Nations: The Diplomatic Phase, 1858–1880* (Cambridge, MA: Harvard University Press, 1960), 7.

6. Aristotle, *The Politics*, book 1, *The Complete Works of Aristotle*, ed. and trans. Jonathan Barnes (Princeton: Princeton University Press, 1984).

7. "Then fight them until there is no persecution and religion is held wholly for the sake of Allah" (*Holy Qu'ran*, 8:39–41); and "Fight those who believe not in Allah nor the Last Day" (9:29). On the conditions under which idolators may be killed, see 9:3–6; also 47:5–12. Likewise, the Qu'ran promises a "great reward" for anyone killed in the cause of Allah (4:75). See also Rudolph Peters, *Jihād in Medieval and Modern Islam* (Leiden, Netherlands: E.J. Brill, 1977).

# C H A P T E R ⟨ 9 ⟩

# Dividing *the* World:
# *The* State

**I N T R O D U C T I O N**
In the last chapter we looked at the way in which human beings have divided the world since the times of antiquity on the basis of political identity. In their definition of political community, they created "insides" and "outsides" on the basis of tribe, race, language, empire, civilization, and religion, persistently avoiding species-level identifications in their actual day-to-day political behaviour (despite the species-level rhetoric of many).

In this chapter we begin to explore a more recent source of political division, the sovereign nation-state. More accurately, I want to examine all three components—sovereignty, state, and nation—separately in order to show their intimate relationship with one another. This chapter therefore first looks at the idea of "the state" as it evolved out of the feudal estate and consolidated as the sovereign state. Chapters 10 and 11 then survey the related idea of sovereignty and examine how the sovereign state helps entrench divisions among humankind. In Part V (Chapters 12–14), we look at the notion of nation, which like the state and sovereignty, was an idea that was invented relatively recently. As we will see, all three ideas are related to one another: state, sovereignty, and nation evolved in a way to create the deepest and most pervasive source of political identity.

## FROM "STATUS" TO "LO STATO": THE EMERGENCE OF THE STATE

The state is a relative latecomer to the various kinds of political communities that populate the world stage. Although many people commonly use the word "state" to refer to earlier political formations, such as *poleis*, empires, kingdoms, or duchies, such usage is in fact highly anachronistic. The state as an identifiable political formation emerged in a particular historical context, with the result that those polities existing before it cannot with any accuracy be called states.

The state did not simply appear suddenly in international politics. Many scholars argue that the modern state system was created by the Peace of Westphalia in 1648 that brought the Thirty Years' War to an end; in fact the state was an idea that had been slowly emerging over the previous centuries and was well entrenched in many parts of Europe even before the Thirty Years' War broke out in 1618. In this section, we look at the emergence of the state as an idea and as a way of organizing political authority. However, the evolution of the idea of the state was slow, accompanying as it did the collapse of European feudalism and the transformation of European Christendom.

### The Collapse of Feudalism

In brief, the idea of the state emerged out of the slow collapse of the **feudal system** in Europe. This system was based on the *estate* (from the Latin, *status*, or standing), the etymology underscoring the intertwined nature of property and standing—in the European Middle Ages, one's social standing depended heavily on property. The idea of the state also arose out of the dissolution of the universal Christian cosmology that underwrote the feudal system. The complexity of the many interrelated factors that brought about the transformation of medieval Europe between 1000 and 1600 cannot be compressed even into a brief summary, but we can note a number of broad trends.

### The Transformation of the Feudal Economy

Profound changes began to undermine the economic order of feudal Europe after 1200. The estate, with its subsistence mode of production, increasingly gave way to urbanization as agricultural production shifted. There were sharp swings in population, including a dramatic population decrease in the 14th century, a demographic disaster that was a consequence of a succession of epidemic diseases (including the Black Death of 1348–50). Disease and crop failures brought in their wake a sudden reduction of the labour force, and an equally rapid emergence of a money economy. There was an increase in trade, both within Europe and between Europe and elsewhere, a trend accelerated by the rise in European maritime exploration of Africa, the Americas, and Asia and the rise of a wealthy merchant class.

At the same time, we see some changes in the very notion of property itself. During the feudal period, land was the primary source of wealth, but land could only be held, not owned. The only owners of land, in the contemporary sense of the word, were kings and the Church. With the rise of a merchant class, however, new forms of property appeared—revenue-producing stocks, for example. It would not be until the 17th century that we would see the full effects of these changes, notably the emergence of the liberal ideas of **possessive individualism**—the notion that each human being was an individual and could possess property.[1] However, at the end of the feudal period, we can nonetheless see the idea that land was just another commodity to be bought and sold. This process is known as the **commodification of land**.

Finally, the feudal economy was transformed by shifts in military technology. Gunpowder made its way to Europe from China; new cast-iron cannons were capable of demolishing the thick walls of the castles that were at the centre of the feudal estate; and steel cross-bow bolts were able to pierce the armour of the mounted knight who was the mainstay of the typical army of the Middle Ages. Armed with this new technology, local rulers were able to dramatically increase their spheres of military control, dominating, and progressively eliminating, the feudal estates.

### Changes in Religious Belief

Changes in thought and practice in religious beliefs also began to undermine the universal Christian cosmology on which the hierarchical feudal order during the Middle Ages was largely based. Medieval Christendom was marked by a belief in the essential unity of the people of the faith, an understanding that all power on Earth derived from God. Political authority, both the authority of the Church and the *majestas* (majesty, or greatness—from the Latin *magnus*, great) of lay rulers, came from Jesus Christ, as Son of God, who established the Church on Earth under St Peter, the first bishop of Rome. Kings, queens, and princes may have ruled on Earth, but they did so *Deo gratia*—by the grace of God. They may have asserted that their right to rule came from God (which would by the 17th century metamorphose into the doctrine of the **divine right of kings**, in which the king became a kind of mortal God); but like all other Christians, they were subject to the overarching authority of the bishop of Rome, or, as he was called after the eighth century, pope (or *papa*, Latin for father). The "secular arm" of the Church was the **Holy Roman Empire** (*sacrum Romanum imperium*), which began its life on Christmas Day, 800, when Pope Leo III crowned Charlemagne emperor, thereby asserting the right of the pope to determine the earthly ruler for all Christendom.

Such a system was precarious, for it involved two sets of political authorities operating in the same physical area, ordering around and taxing the same group of people. The *imperium* was the temporal authority of empire and the *sacerdotium* the priestly authority of those who defined themselves as having a direct link to God. The system worked, but only as long as the *imperium* was willing to obey the *sacerdotium* and thereby maintain the theoretical unity of Christendom.

But all too often, the two authorities clashed. Consider the cases of two kings of England, King Henry II, who reigned from 1154 to 1189, and John, one of his sons, who ruled from 1199 to 1216. Both quarrelled with the Church. For his part, Henry disliked the idea of his royal courts being subservient to the courts of the Church. However, when he tried to assert royal dominance over ecclesiastical courts in 1164, the archbishop of Canterbury, Thomas à Becket, strongly resisted, provoking a six–year–long quarrel between the Church and the king that ended with Becket's murder in his own cathedral in 1170. John was no less quarrelsome: in 1207 he refused to recognize the election of Stephen Langton, a confidant of Pope Innocent III, as the archbishop of Canterbury. Innocent immediately excommunicated John, and put all of England under **interdict**. This meant that none of the sacraments could be administered to any of John's subjects: no one could have their children baptized, or have their sins absolved, or be married, or receive the last rites before death. As we noted in Chapter 7, this was a form of terror: people believed that without the grace of the sacraments they would burn in hell for all eternity. The interdict was frightening (as indeed it was meant to be). John found it prudent to relent and bow to papal authority.

*People believed that without the grace of the sacraments they would burn in hell. The interdict was frightening (as indeed it was meant to be).*

The tensions in the system were not helped by the fact that a succession of popes persistently tried to widen the scope of their temporal power. Increasingly, these efforts were resisted, then rejected outright. Kings and other temporal leaders grew more and more annoyed at the intrusion of the pope's authority into what they regarded as their own affairs, and kings grew equally concerned about the willingness of the Church in Rome to levy taxes and control the use of land in what they saw as their own domains.

Increasingly, these quarrels helped to galvanize the idea of dynastic interest that often conflicted with the interests of the Church. For example, for much of the 13th century, the Capetian kings of France and the Church in Rome were close allies. The Church was useful for French kings, supplying the royal bureaucracy with literate clerks and the king with occasional military support and considerable legitimacy in the eyes of vassals. However, the French king was no less useful for the Church, providing political support against enemies without and heretics within. But the alliance fell apart. Philip the Fair of France wanted to seize Aquitaine from English control, and in 1294 taxed the churches in his realms to raise the army. The pope, Boniface VIII, objected to these taxes on the grounds that this was not a war of self-defence nor did it involve defending the faith. A sustained conflict ensued. When Boniface issued a papal bull in 1302 reasserting the supremacy of the Church over secular authority, Philip cheekily responded that since there had been kings before popes, popes could not possibly be superior to kings. It was, as Hendrik Spruyt put it, the end of a beautiful friendship,[2] wrecked by the assertion of dynastic interests.

*Philip cheekily responded that since there had been kings before popes, popes could not possibly be superior to kings.*

The annoyance of kings during this period was mirrored by the disaffection of the faithful, particularly over what was widely seen as the moral decay and open greed of many Church officials—most dramatically reflected in the sale of **indulgences** (see the Focus). Moreover, the tax-free status enjoyed by the Church in most domains in feudal Europe created considerable resentment among the heavily taxed peasants and burghers. Finally, the Church itself presented an essential contradiction to the faithful: by the late

# FOCUS

## *Indulgences and the Transformation of the Church*

An indulgence, in ecclesiastical practice, was intimately linked to the sacrament of confession of sins as practised by the Church of Rome. Sinners might confess their sins and their guilt might be absolved, but the sinner still owed a punishment, or penance, which was established by canonical law. However, one could satisfy these fixed penances by securing an indulgence (from the Latin *indulgere*, to allow or permit), which remitted the penance, either in full or in part. Originally, one could gain an indulgence by substituting periods of fasting, a pilgrimage, or alms to the poor.

In the 11th and 12th centuries, however, the Church began to accept direct monetary payments to "good works" as the means of gaining indulgences. Using this highly effective method of extracting money from a constantly sinning population, the Church was able to finance the construction of cathedrals, churches, universities, bridges, and hospitals throughout Europe. Proceeds from indulgences were, however, also used to sustain an increasingly opulent and decadent lifestyle for many of the Church's greedy and corrupt officials: indeed, we come by the modern meaning of "indulgent" from the ecclesiastic corruption during this era.

medieval period, the Church had become a huge bureaucracy, creating magnificent public works and exercising the power of empire across Europe; yet the fundamental purpose of the Church was to spread the message of Christ, a message that championed the poor and the meek.

## Intellectual Changes: The Renaissance

The growing annoyance at the Church was accelerated by other factors. The inventions of moveable type and the printing press meant that the Bible could be translated from Latin into the vernacular and distributed cheaply throughout Europe. All of a sudden, the Word of God, instead of being limited to a few laboriously hand-written Latin editions located in regional cathedrals, was now available to every lowly parish priest and to anyone else who could read.

As importantly, the ideas of the intellectual movement that we now call the **Renaissance** could be spread more easily. This "rebirth"—the rediscovery of the Greek and Roman classics, and their translation into the vernacular—had a profound and often subversive impact on people's understanding of the world around them. In particular, the dominant Christian cosmology was challenged by the resurgence in such humanist views of history and politics as those of Aristotle. Aristotle stressed that *Homo sapiens sapiens* was a "political animal," capable of reasoning about how to organize social life. In such a conception of politics, authority flowed *upward*: humans, not gods, created political authority.[3] The dominant notion that political authority flowed *downward* from God was fundamentally incompatible with Aristotelian thought.

Such a humanist view was at the heart of the writings of one of the foremost political theorists of the Renaissance, Niccolò Machiavelli, a senior official in the Florentine Republic which flourished briefly from 1494 after the Medici family, which had ruled Florence since 1434, was overthrown. When the Medicis were restored in 1512 by a Spanish army, Machiavelli was briefly imprisoned and tortured, and then forced into retirement, where he wrote. In *The Prince* and *The Discourses on the First Ten Books of Titus Livy*, he laid out a radically different understanding of political community than the one prevailing in Christian Europe at the time. Machiavelli drew on the work of Greek and Roman political theorists and historians—Aristotle, Cicero, Polybius, and Livy—to portray the basis of political authority in essentially humanist and secular terms, rather than in the universal Christian notions of authority derived from God.

As a result of these various factors, political authority in the European context underwent a slow but steady transformation. The stunted subsistence economy of the feudal estate was being transformed by the emergence of new forms of economic production and organization, particularly the rise of a money economy. The dominance of the rural economy was often eclipsed by the rise of cities; the landed gentry was being challenged by a growing urban middle class; and new ways of thinking about property were changing the view of land. The pyramid-like structures of vassalage and fealty that marked feudal politics were yielding to new definitions of dynastic interest being pushed by kings eager to expand their spheres of rule. The local castle, the stronghold of the estate, was no longer immune to cannon. And there was an increasing willingness to challenge the authority of the Church in Rome (and thereby the universality inherent in Christendom): no longer were people deterred by fear of excommunication or the interdict. By the 16th century, measures that had so terrified English people in 1206 had simply lost their terroristic thrall.

## The Reformation and Political Authority

The final collapse of the European feudal order came with the protest movement against the Church in Rome we know as the **Reformation**. This sparked division within all western European countries and escalated to gruesome wars, both civil and international, fought between Catholics and Protestants. But the Reformation would give rise to the idea of sovereignty.

### The Reformation

The signal event in the increasing disaffection of many Europeans for the Church in the late 15th and early 16th century came in October 1517, when Martin Luther, a priest who held the chair of biblical theology at the University of Wittenberg in Germany, published a wide-ranging criticism of the Church in Rome. In particular, he attacked the misuse of indulgences. The response of the Church was to order Luther to submit to papal authority; when that failed, he was excommunicated. Luther continued to outline a program of ecclesiastical reform, including the elaboration of an idea that earthly rulers should be independent of supervision by the Church. This gained him considerable support from princes and kings. Lutheran protests spread northward to Scandinavia, where the challenge to the authority of what was becoming known as the Roman Catholic Church was led by the king of Denmark (which included Norway and Iceland) and the king of Sweden.

At the same time, movements grew up in other countries around the preachings of other reformers. In Switzerland, Protestant movements centred on Huldreich Zwingli and John Calvin. In France, Calvinists were known as **Huguenots**. In the Netherlands, Charles V, emperor of the Holy Roman Empire, tried to stamp out the spread of Protestant ideas by having Luther's books burned in 1522, but Calvinist Protestantism spread there nonetheless. In Scotland, the movement was led by John Knox. By 1560 the Scottish parliament officially embraced Calvinism; not even the opposition of the Roman Catholic queen, Mary, Queen of Scots, could overcome the hold that Calvin's ideas had.

There was also an English dimension to the Reformation, but there the pressure to break with the papacy came from the king rather than from the faithful. Moreover, the break was not inspired by differences in religious dogma. The origin of the dispute lay in the desire of Henry VIII to father a male heir so as not to plunge England into the kind of conflict over succession that had embroiled the country during the War of the Roses in the latter part of the 15th century. Unfortunately for Henry, Catherine of Aragón bore him a number of children, but only one, a daughter, survived infancy. When he sought to divorce Catherine and marry Anne Boleyn, Pope Clement VII refused to grant his request. Henry's response was to assert his right to exercise supremacy over the church in his domain. He created a Church of England, with the monarch as its head. Because Henry's church did not involve any change in dogma or religious practice—in other words, during Henry's time it was essentially Catholic in all but name—there was considerable public support for the move in England at the time.

**Wars of Religion**

By the middle of the 16th century, the supposed universality of Christendom lay in tatters as divisions between Protestants and Roman Catholics hardened and developed into war, both civil and international. In France, eight civil wars were fought between 1562 and 1598, including the St Bartholomew's Day Massacre on 24 August 1572, when in a single night of bloodshed thousands of Huguenots were massacred by Catholics throughout France. In the Netherlands, the appeal of Calvinism was twinned with a deep-seated antipathy toward the Roman Catholic ruler, Philip II of Spain, who was intent on crushing the heresy of Protestantism in his realms. In August 1566, riots occurred in Antwerp and a number of other cities, and several churches were destroyed. Philip sent in an army under Fernando Álvarez de Toledo, who executed hundreds of the rioters. By 1572, a full-scale rebellion was underway, which the Spanish proceeded to try and suppress with much brutality. The cities of Malines and Zutphen were sacked; the entire population of Naarden was massacred; and Haarlem was besieged for months. When it fell in 1573 all of the defending soldiers were slaughtered. In the end the Spanish armies were unsuccessful: the northern Protestant provinces declared themselves united in January 1579, and in July 1581 declared that they were no longer bound by allegiance to Philip. The struggle of Holland to free itself from Spanish rule continued for 30 years, eventually involving a number of other European rulers, until a truce was arranged in 1609.

In Germany, the division between Catholics and Protestants also led to war. Protestant princes met in Schmalkalden, Thuringia, and organized themselves into a defensive alliance. Eventually the Holy Roman Emperor, Charles V, went to war with the **Schmalkaldic League**. The result was the Peace of Augsburg, signed in 1555; its most significant provision was that German princes were granted the right to select the religion of their particular lands.

Thus, what was emerging in Europe over the course of the 16th century was a radically different idea about governance that would bring an end to the overlapping and ill-defined boundaries of authority inherent in feudalism. This was the idea of *lo stato*, the state: not some ruler's *stato*, which is how Machiavelli used the word, but *lo stato*, a more impersonal conception of *the state* as not necessarily attached to a single individual.[4] Rather, *lo stato* came to mean a territory where the local ruler, not some authority elsewhere, was the supreme political authority. That notion—that a ruler could rightfully claim to be supreme within a particular defined territory—was given a name: **sovereignty**.

## The Growth of the Sovereign Idea

The state, Michael Walzer once argued, "is invisible; it must be personified before it can be seen, symbolized before it can be loved, imagined before it can be conceived."[5] Walzer is

> *"The state is invisible; it must be personified before it can be seen, symbolized before it can be loved, imagined before it can be conceived."*

right to point out that the sovereign state is first and foremost an *idea*, a way of conceiving how to organize political authority. But this leaves the impression that the idea preceded the practice—that the idea of the sovereign state was dreamed up by some thinker and then adopted by rulers who liked the idea. In fact, the evolution of the idea of state sovereignty was much messier: in symbiotic fashion, the practices of rulers influenced the development of the idea in the minds of thinkers, and the writings of thinkers influenced the practices of kings.

### Jean Bodin and the Seigneuries Souverains

We derive "sovereign" from the Old French, *souverain*, used to describe kings or those in a superior position; the French is itself believed to come from the medieval Church Latin word *superanus*, or superior; there is no imperial Latin word that comes close to "sovereign."* Thus, when "sovereignty" was translated "backward" into Latin, Europeans used the word *majestas* (majesty).

Until the end of the 16th century, sovereignty was an idea that tended to be linked to the individual sovereign rather than to the larger political community. The word first appears in English in 1297 to describe the recognized ruler of a country, and that remained its primary meaning for the next 200 years. Indeed, in 1503, Henry VII of England decided to call one of the coins in circulation a sovereign, ensuring that the linkage would be made in everyday life.

---

* However, the Romans did have a full vocabulary for describing political authority and political power. In Latin, the *regis* (king), *principes* (leading statesmen), or *imperator* (emperor) exercised *potestas* (political power) and obtained his *imperium* (the right to command) by constitutional means or even brute force.

Certainly it was this meaning that Jean Bodin, a French lawyer and philosopher, attached to *souverain*. Bodin is usually associated with enunciating the first clear statement of sovereignty as supreme political authority in *Six livres de la république*, published in 1576. Writing in the shadow of the religious conflicts sweeping across France, Bodin wanted to show why political authority should not be divided within a territory, for that division had brought the massacres of the **Wars of Religion**. Instead, he was concerned with constructing a theory of royal absolutism that would justify strong and *indivisible* rule that could bring anarchy to an end.

But Bodin provided what Julian H. Franklin has termed a theory of "ruler sovereignty" rather than state sovereignty.[6] This is more clearly seen in the translation Bodin did of his own work into Latin in 1583 than in the French original. In French, sovereignty was defined as "the absolute and perpetual power of a commonwealth." In Latin, however, Bodin rendered this as *Majestas est summa in cives ac subditos legibusque soluta potestas*, literally "Majesty [i.e., sovereignty] is supreme and legally unbound political power over citizens and subject peoples." Most students of Bodin have focused on the implications of this definition for our understanding of the role of the sovereign in *internal* politics—the idea that there should be a single and supreme power within a state, suggested by invoking the phrase *legibus solutus*.[*] Indeed, Bodin sought to show that political authority should not be divided within a state, that one had to be able to locate one source of supreme political authority.

But there is also an important *external* element of Bodin's definition. For Bodin was not only seeking to define the sovereign as "legally unbound" *from within* (however constrained by natural and divine law the sovereign might be), but also "legally unbound" *from without*. In other words, Bodin's theory supported the idea that *seigneuries souverains* (sovereign lordships) were not bound by the laws of other sovereigns. In this usage, sovereignty more closely reflected what in fact many kings and princes in Europe were trying to accomplish in the 16th century: to rule supreme in their own lands and be bound by no one else's law, particularly not the law of the Church in Rome.

### State Sovereignty and the Thirty Years' War

By the early 17th century, we see the emergence of another understanding of the term. While still retaining its meaning as supreme rule, sovereignty starts to be attributed to an impersonal state rather than to an individual sovereign. In English, the term "soueraigne state" first appears in William Shakespeare's *The Life and Death of King John*, written in 1595: Lewis, the dauphin, or eldest son of the French king, says (Act V, ii, 79–82):

---

[*] In imperial Roman law, this was the doctrine that the ruler was the source of law: the emperor was *legis lator*, proposer of law, and was thus *legibus solutus*, "legally not bound." Bodin's *summa…legibusque soluta potestas* is often translated as "supreme power unrestrained by law," or "absolute power": see, for example, Andrew Vincent, *Theories of the State* (Oxford: Basil Blackwell, 1987), 34, 198. Some have argued therefore that Bodin was trying to justify an absolutism whereby *nothing at all* should stop the sovereign from doing whatever he or she wanted. This, however, was not the case: Bodin believed that sovereigns had to be constrained by some basic rules derived from God, natural law, and the laws of their own states. See Jean Bodin, *On Sovereignty: Four Chapters from the Six Books of the Commonwealth*, ed. and trans. Julian H. Franklin (Cambridge: Cambridge University Press, 1992), xiii; also Jens Bartelson, *A Genealogy of Sovereignty* (Cambridge: Cambridge University Press, 1995), 141–42.

I am too high-born to be propertied,
To be a secondary at control,
Or useful servingman and instrument,
To any soueraigne state throughout the world.

The difference is important, for it means that the idea of sovereignty becomes not something personal, attached to a sovereign, but something essentially impersonal, a condition that can be attached to the state (as a territory over which a sovereign—either a monarch or a republican government—has supreme authority). In this formulation, the sovereign and the state are both separated (*lo stato* is no longer the personal *status* of a king ruling by divine right) and yet deeply intertwined, with one no longer possible without the other: "What makes the state a state is the presence of a sovereign; what makes the sovereign sovereign is the presence of a state."[7] *Sovereignty* attaches to both: the government is sovereign *within* the state; the state and its government are sovereign *vis-à-vis* other states.

> *"What makes the state a state is the presence of a sovereign; what makes the sovereign sovereign is the presence of a state."*

As with many ideas, the notion of sovereignty evolved in the context of the contemporary politics of the early 1600s. The religious wars within the territories of European rulers that had marked the Reformation gave way to a series of wars of religion *between* European rulers that lasted between 1618 and 1648. We know these wars today as a singular whole—the Thirty Years' War—but they were in fact a series of wars and military campaigns that involved different combatants at different times over these three decades.

The origin of the war, however, was religious friction in Germany and the disaffection caused by Rudolph II, the Holy Roman Emperor from 1576 to 1612. Under Rudolph, Protestants suffered the destruction of their churches and increasing restrictions on their rights of worship, and saw the resurgence of Roman Catholic power. Protestants organized a defensive Evangelical Union in 1608; Catholics responded by organizing a Catholic League the following year, and tensions escalated over the following decade. The spark came in May 1618, when Bohemian Protestants, angered by the anti-Protestant policies of their Roman Catholic Hapsburg king, stormed the royal palace and threw two of his ministers out the window to their deaths. The **Defenestration of Prague**, as it came to be known, set off a rebellion that quickly spread to other Hapsburg lands. Although these rebellions were quashed by force, the conflict spread when Christian IV, the king of Denmark and Norway, weighed in on the side of the Protestants in 1625, followed by Gustav II Adolph of Sweden in 1630. Both were defeated by the Catholics: Christian was forced to settle in 1629; Gustav was killed leading his armies in battle in November 1632 and the Swedish forces were routed in September 1634. The final phase of the war was not inspired by religious conflict, but dynastic interests in territory and control. It became a general European conflict, with the French declaring war on the Spanish and Austrian Hapsburgs, the Swedes, and numerous German principalities.

After nine years of general war, the protagonists began to conduct peace negotiations in the Westphalian towns of Münster and Osnabrück in 1644, even though the fighting continued until May 1648, when a series of defeats prompted the Hapsburgs to sue for peace. On 24 October 1648, the Holy Roman Empire signed two peace treaties: one with France at Münster, the other with the Swedes and the German Protestant states at Osnabrück. Much of the **Peace of Westphalia**, as these two treaties are known, was devoted to rewarding the winners with territorial spoils, stripping the Hapsburgs of power, and increasing French dominance on the continent. The peace treaties also addressed religious issues, confirming, for example, the rights of private worship, liberty of conscience, and emigration in some lands.

But most importantly, the Peace of Westphalia institutionalized the changes in state sovereignty that had been in train for the previous century and a half. By its terms, the authority of the Catholic Church to intervene in German affairs was dismissively rejected. The notion that states were something that existed separate and apart from the individual sovereigns that governed them was underscored by the provision that if a prince changed religion, he would have to forfeit his lands. While this provision was included in order to slow the spread of Protestant ideas and encourage religious stability, it also legitimized the idea of the impersonal state.

In addition, the sovereignty of all states was formally recognized. This meant that approximately 300 German princes were suddenly the supreme authorities in their lands. In addition, both Switzerland and the United Provinces of the Netherlands were recognized as independent and sovereign states.

## The Rise of the Mercantile State

The story of the rise of the sovereign state cannot be disentangled from the economic developments of this era. In symbiotic fashion, the changing economy made the rise of the sovereign state possible; but the rise of the sovereign state also brought about significant changes in economic structure. Three strands are important for an understanding of the development of the sovereign state: the exploration of the oceans by Europeans that began in the 15th century, the progressive colonization of the non-European world, and the impact that exploration and colonization had on the European economy and state behaviour.

### The Age of Exploration

The state arose at a time when Europeans began to explore beyond their immediate neighbourhood. Borrowing from Arabic knowledge and sailing skills, European sailors began sailing beyond the Mediterranean and northwestern Europe: first down the coast of Africa, and then across the Atlantic Ocean. Spearheaded by Portuguese, Italian, and Spanish explorers, the **age of exploration** resulted in a rapid expansion of European knowledge of the world beyond Europe. In only 50 years, European sailors explored and mapped the Atlantic coast of what came to be known as the Americas (after one of the explorers, Amerigo Vespucci, was lucky enough to have his explorations published by a German geographer who decided to name the "new world" after him, a name that stuck). By 1519, both the Cape of Good Hope and the cape named after Ferdinand Magellan had been rounded, and indeed Magellan had crossed the Pacific Ocean, reaching what are now the Philippines.

These explorations must be seen in the broader context of the Renaissance, which helped to inspire exploration of the unknown for its own sake. But the enthusiasm for

*"To serve God and his Majesty, to give light to those who sat in darkness and to grow rich as all men desire to do."*

exploration was also driven by a number of very concrete goals. As one Spanish explorer put it, he had searched for the Indies "to serve God and his Majesty, to give light to those who sat in darkness and to grow rich as all men desire to do."[8] The primary goal was a sea route to the east and access to luxury goods like spices and silks. These items had been imported to Europe during the feudal era, but only in a trickle because of the limited wealth of feudal Europeans and the high cost of transporting these goods overland. This began to change: not only were Europeans wealthier, but transportation costs by ship were much lower. For example, the spices that Magellan's ship, the *Victoria*, brought back from its round-the-world voyage in September 1522 more than covered all the expenses of the five ships that had departed from Spain in September 1519.

These explorations were thus financed either by merchants or by dynasts eager to increase their wealth; the lands "discovered" would inexorably be claimed in the name of which monarch was sponsoring the voyage. Thus the Portuguese explorer Magellan, who was financed by the Spanish king, claimed the islands he came across in the Pacific for the Spanish crown. Eventually they were named after the heir to the throne, Philip, and remain today the Philippines. The Venetian John Cabot claimed what he discovered—what is now Newfoundland and Labrador and the New England coast—for his royal sponsor, Henry VII of England.

Giving "light to those who sat in darkness" was no less important. As European explorers ventured across the oceans, claiming more land for their sponsor-kings, they also tried claiming more souls for their church (not always successfully: Magellan was killed in 1521 trying to extend Christianity to the Mactan people in the Philippines). Indeed, the New World offered the prospect of so much territory to be claimed, and so many potential souls to be saved, that the Portuguese and Spanish kings went to the pope to arbitrate: in May 1493, Pope Alexander VI drew a north-south Line of Demarcation running 100 leagues (about 500 km) west of the Cape Verde Islands, and assigned any newfound land east of the line to Portugal and west of it to Spain. When John II of Portugal realized that this line would net Portugal a lot of ocean and not much else, he sought a new line, which was then set at 370 leagues west of the Cape Verde Islands, giving Portugal what is present-day Brazil.

## The Age of Empire

But it was not the souls awaiting salvation that helped transform the European economy—and thereby the state system—in the 16th century. Rather it was what the new **empires** (the territories occupied and then settled by Europeans) yielded for consumers that helped accelerate economic growth in a post-feudal Europe: bullion and agricultural produce.

Massive quantities of gold and silver were discovered after Hernán Cortés conquered the Aztecs in Mexico and Francisco Pizarro conquered the Incas in Peru. This was shipped back to Spain as **bullion**, with the result that in the 16th century the European economy was infused with huge amounts of these precious metals: in the 150 years after the voyages of Christopher Columbus, some 14 000 tonnes of silver and more than 2000 tonnes of gold, approximately 35 per cent of all world production at the time, were shipped to Europe. This massive infusion had a number of important effects. First, it accelerated the decline of the feudal economy we noted above, particularly the move from a barter-dominated economy to a money-based system of exchange. Second, the bullion that flowed into Spain and Portugal proved to be crucial for paying the bills associated with war-fighting. Charles V, the first Hapsburg king of Spain, managed not only to increase the prosperity of his subjects but also to wage a series of long wars against the French that would have been punishing to any treasury that was not receiving such an annual inflow.

But the impact of the agricultural produce of the new settlements was equally important. Europeans decided that they liked the hardwoods, the coffee, and particularly the sugar brought back from the new world. But these products required plantations, and plantations required labour; and neither of the primary imperial powers of the time, Portugal or Spain, had the labour. Indeed, Portugal had already tried to meet labour shortages in the 15th century by importing slaves captured as Portuguese explorers travelled down the west African coast. A large-scale **slave trade** grew up to supply the new plantations in the New World. For many years, Portugal managed to hold a monopoly on slaves provided through its slaving stations in Africa, where slaves were purchased from African and Arab slavers and transported to the Americas.

These interrelated developments would have a major impact on patterns of European settlement overseas. In the western hemisphere, the increasing importance of bullion and plantation produce in the 16th century encouraged the immediate colonization and settlement of the newfound territories and the expansion of European rule. The transfer of massive wealth across the Atlantic attracted the attention of fleets of others with sea-faring capability. English, Dutch, and French ships began plundering the Spanish fleet, and English, Dutch, and French settlements began appearing in the northern half of the Americas. Some settlements, like the territory of Virginia named for the "virgin queen" of England—Elizabeth I—proved highly profitable for the customs revenues secured by its tobacco.

In the Indian Ocean the pattern of European imperialism differed considerably. In the 16th century, the Portuguese dominated trade along the west African coast and into South and Southeast Asia. But Portugal established a series of trading stations—outposts in other communities usually obtained through negotiations with local rulers, at times under the duress provided by superior Portuguese gunnery. Japan, China, Macao, Goa, and Calicut were all opened to Portuguese traders. However, when Portugal and Spain were joined in 1580 and war eventually broke out between Spain and the Dutch, Portuguese dominance in the Indian Ocean faded as the Dutch seized Portuguese trading stations over the course of their 80-year war with Spain. England, an ally of the Dutch, also joined in the attacks on Portuguese trade around the Indian Ocean.

Both the Dutch and English governments used much the same technique to expand trade: **monopoly trading corporations**—private companies which were granted a government-backed monopoly charter. The English East India Company was given its charter by Elizabeth I in 1600; the Dutch East India Company was granted its monopoly by the States General, the government of the United Provinces, in 1602. Both companies began competing with the Portuguese and with one another in the Indian Ocean market, with the Dutch able to dominate the spice trade in the Netherlands East Indies, and the English left to the Indian coast, trading in coffee and textiles.

It was not until well into the 18th century—in 1764, at the end of the Seven Years' War between Britain and France—that direct English control would be established over India. In that year, the English East India Company became the formal ruler of Bengal, prompting the British government to turn it into a semi-official government agency in 1773. (It was not until 1858, after the Sepoy Mutiny, that the British government transferred the administration of India from the East India Company to the Crown.) By 1800, the essential patterns of European empire had been established, with Europeans controlling all of the western hemisphere; key points along the African coast; much of India; and, after the First Fleet landed in 1788, Australia.

The state as it was emerging in the 16th and 17th centuries was key in providing the framework, if not the impetus, for empire. Dynastic interest, which we saw emerging toward the end of the feudal period, segued smoothly into state interests as the economies of European states expanded and grew increasingly dependent on a burgeoning trade with the world. And this world was increasingly governed by Europeans in the metropole, or imperial centre.

## The Mercantile System and State Policy

Those who governed the states that were developing during the 16th and 17th centuries were much influenced by a set of understandings about the economic world that we have come to call **mercantilism** or the mercantile system. This set of understandings would shape the governors' approaches to international trade and the acquisition of overseas territories.

The mercantile system was marked by a set of interrelated beliefs about how a state's economic strength should be encouraged. First, it was deemed important to own large amounts of precious metals like gold and silver, for this, it was believed, was the key to wealth. Second, it was important to encourage exports rather than imports, and to encourage the growth of industries that added value to materials. Third, a large and dense population was seen as important for state strength. Finally, it was right and proper for the government of a state to actively work to achieve the other three objectives.

Mercantile beliefs were manifested in a number of ways. States encouraged urban industry rather than agriculture, for exports of manufactured goods proved more valuable than agricultural produce, and thus added to both state revenues and the country's net holdings of bullion. States began to regulate industries to keep quality high and prices low, so as to maximize the attractiveness of products on the international market; again, the goal was revenue generation for the state and bullion generation for the country. High duties were placed on imports, partly for the revenues they generated for the state, but also because they discouraged domestic consumption of foreign goods, thereby maintaining a favourable balance of trade and thus maximizing the holdings of bullion. Moreover, high import duties provided a form of protection for domestic industries.

In the mercantile system, the acquisition of **colonies** was particularly favoured. They were seen as ready sources of public revenue and raw materials for processing by industries in the metropole and as customers for the metropole's products. In fact, colonies were prohibited from trading with anyone other than the "parent country," and little effort was made to encourage industry in the colony. Instead, colonies were seen by the metropole to be little more than the Gibeonite slaves were in ancient Israel: "hewers of wood and drawers of water" (Joshua 9:20–21). (Indeed, such a view would lead directly to the loss of one set of colonies in the 1770s.)

In short, the sovereign state emerged in the 16th and 17th centuries as a consequence of a conjuncture of different forces at work. The relationships between the intellectual, religious, political, sociological, and economic forces are deeply embedded and cannot easily be pulled apart. Together, these forces interacted to create a political form that would deeply entrench geopolitical divisions, not only in Europe, but throughout the world.

## HOW THE CONTEMPORARY STATE DIVIDES THE WORLD

The idea of the state, which began life as a European idea that emerged from the conjunctures of European politics and economics, spread throughout the world in the 350 years after the Peace of Westphalia. Every political community would come to embrace the state form of political organization (even if some managed better than others to actually achieve it in practice). All the new polities "founded" in the process of European exploration and colonization would fashion states modelled on their European "mother countries"; all the polities that eventually returned by decolonization to indigenous rule would adopt the European state form; even those political communities whose roots long antedated the rise of European power would, by revolution or evolution, change their traditional patterns of ruling and embrace the state form. As a result, the state is today a political formation that is both *ubiquitous* and *homogenous*. The state is, quite literally, everywhere: all human beings alive today live in one of the 190 or so states spread around the globe. And the state, as a form of political organization, manifests an arresting sameness wherever it occurs.

However, what constitutes the state in contemporary international politics must always be seen in the context of the slow evolution of the idea of the sovereign state and its eventual entrenchment in the Peace of Westphalia. The story of that evolution does not, of course, end abruptly in October 1648, for the idea of sovereignty continued to evolve.

For example, increasingly, kings were no longer seen as the locus of supreme political power within the state. In England, king and Parliament vied for supreme political power. That struggle plunged the country into civil war and revolution, cost one king his head and another his throne, and gave the country Oliver Cromwell, its only Lord Protector. It was nearly 50 years before Parliament emerged supreme following the **Glorious Revolution** of 1688, which established parliamentary supremacy. Almost a hundred years later, another revolution in the Americas would locate sovereignty elsewhere—in "the people"—a theme which was echoed in the French Revolution of 1789.

Sovereignty, it was also discovered, could be indivisible and divisible at the same time. The present Constitution of the United States, conceived in 1787, manages quite successfully to divide "supreme authority" numerous ways. The embrace of the notion of the

**separation of powers** between the three branches of government meant that no one in the United States government had truly supreme authority. Likewise, the embrace of **federalism** also divided sovereign authority between the central government and the governments of the different states of the union—in different spheres of jurisdiction.

Finally, sovereignty would increasingly become intertwined with the rise of the bureaucratic state in the 19th and 20th centuries. The ability of the burgeoning bureaucracies of the modern state to direct the economic and political affairs of the community depended heavily on the ability to exert political power as well as authority. Increasingly, sovereignty came to be equated with the ability of the state apparatus to exert exclusive dominance within the state. As the German scholar Max Weber (1864–1920) put it succinctly, a sovereign state must "successfully claim the monopoly of the legitimate use of physical force within a given territory."[9]

Despite all these major developments, however, the essential attributes of the **sovereign state** have remained remarkably constant since the Peace of Westphalia. In particular, states in the contemporary international system have four attributes that entrench the divisions between people and political communities. These attributes have been codified, most explicitly by the Convention on the Rights and Duties of States, signed in December 1933 at the Seventh International Conference of American States, in Montevideo, Uruguay. Three of the attributes are *objective* or *empirical*, in the sense that they can be readily observed: *territory*, *population*, and a *government*. The fourth attribute is *sovereignty*; its "existence" is more difficult to determine.

## Territory

As noted above, changes in the creation of wealth during the feudal period had a pronounced impact on people's understanding of land. Not coincidentally, the rise of the territorial state occurred at the same time that this philosophical shift was taking place in how property was perceived in Europe. The commodification of land required that owners describe precisely what it was that was being sold; buyers had no less need to know what they were buying. More precise definitions of "territory" were the logical result. Advances in surveying techniques—the use of plane tables and triangulation—meant better mapmaking. The same techniques that were increasingly being used to establish property rights *within* states were also being used *between* states to demarcate territory.

### Marking Territory

With but a few exceptions, a state's borders are formally demarcated and carefully surveyed, with border markers, or monuments, erected to indicate the territorial division. In some cases, one can actually see the results of this exercise: for example, sections of the Canada-United States border running through the Maine/New Brunswick bush are clearly visible from the air because of the seven-metre clearcut "vista" maintained by the Canada-United States International Boundary Commission.

It should be noted that surveying and demarcation is not always perfect. For example, in 1906, the Québec-Maine border around the St Francis River was resurveyed. An error was discovered, with the result that the new boundary cut through part of the town of Escourt, Québec, that had grown up inside the old boundary. Escourt Station, Maine, is the name of the resulting American settlement, which numbers several French-speaking families (but has to get United States Mail delivered through Canada). Another example is the luxury hotel on a beach in Taba, adjoining the southern port of Eilat. The hotel had been built by an Israeli in the 1970s, on the Israeli side of what was assumed to be the Egyptian-Israeli border. In 1906, the Ottoman Empire and the Anglo-Egyptian government had agreed that the border would run through Taba. However, a British military survey in 1915 got it wrong, and put the boundary markers a kilometre away. The discovery of another boundary marker close to the beach prompted the Egyptian government to press for a resurveying of the border. The Israeli government agreed to submit the case to arbitration in 1986, and a tribunal supported the Egyptian claim. The border was redrawn, and the luxury hotel and the beach are now in Egypt (the Israeli owner having been compensated for his loss).

Only where the land is utterly inhospitable have states foregone the rituals of formally defining their borders with careful surveys. For example, the border between Saudi Arabia and its neighbours, the Yemen Republic and Oman, runs through a vast hot and uninhabited sand-dune desert that is simply known as *Rub' al Khali* (or Empty Quarter). Boundary markers would simply be lost in the shifting sands; a dotted line on a map is used to approximate where the borders might be—if anyone were there to notice.

Precise definitions of territory were the necessary result of the Peace of Westphalia: kings and republics alike needed to know the exact limits of their sovereign authority, both for ascertaining the divisions of religious affiliation and for the purposes of taxation. Thus border-drawing was an activity that consumed a great of energy (and not a few conflicts) in the three centuries after the Peace of Westphalia, as states consolidated, or were founded, or colonized others.

### The Evolution of Borders

The borders of many contemporary states reflect the historical evolution of the divisions between communities created by the natural phenomena of geography: seas, bays, estuaries, rivers, lakes, marshes, deserts, mountain ranges, forests, and jungles. Other borders reflect the uneven historical allegiances, religious affiliations, or languages of different towns around which borders were subsequently drawn. Hence they are called **subsequent boundaries** by political geographers, as opposed to **antecedent boundaries** that were drawn before widespread settlement (such as most of the boundaries in British North America in the 18th century), or **superimposed boundaries** that are drawn after political communities developed (such as the boundaries imposed on central Europe after the Second World War).[10]

A good example of a subsequent border is the Franco-Belgian frontier, which twists and turns across the coastal plains of Flanders into the forested hills of the Ardennes. It features a finger of French territory that juts deep into present-day Belgium, at the tip of which is located Givet, a town on the Meuse River. This border is a reflection of 17th-century

*Figure 9.1* • **THE FRANCO-BELGIAN BORDER**

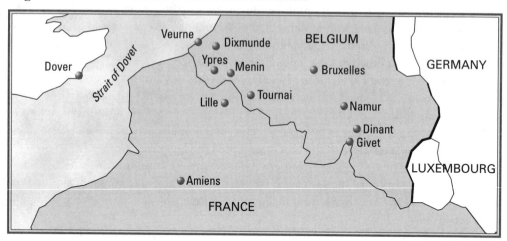

dynastic quarrels between Louis XIV of France, the Hapsburgs, England, and the United Provinces of the Netherlands over the Spanish Netherlands (the area from which Belgium was eventually carved as an independent state in 1830). By the late 17th century, the French sought to consolidate its control of this territory won from the Dutch by fortifying a series of towns across the southern reaches of Belgium. When France suffered several defeats during the War of the Spanish Succession (1701–1714), the Dutch sought to turn the tables and garrisoned these forts with their own troops, thereby erecting a defence barrier against France. The so-called Barrier Treaties of 1709, 1713 and 1715, signed as part of the peace settlement that brought the war to an end, gave the Dutch the right to maintain a string of fortified towns in Spanish Netherlands. The string of fortifications that ran from the sea to the Meuse River—Veurne, Dixmunde, Ypres, Warenton, Menin, Tournai, Namur, Dinant—in essence defined the frontier, giving the border its present sinuous contours.

However, some borders are simply straight lines that run across a map, reflecting the fact that convenience and simplicity were often used as the over-riding criteria in defining

*Some borders are simply straight lines that run across a map, reflecting the fact that convenience and simplicity were often used as the over-riding criteria in defining state borders.*

state borders. The vast majority of the Canada–United States frontier consists of straight lines, making it the longest straight-line border in the world. Straight lines cleave New Brunswick and Maine close to the 68th parallel west; Québec, Vermont, and New York along the 45th parallel north; Yukon and Alaska up the 141st parallel west from the Panhandle to the Beaufort Sea; and of course the border running from Lake of the Woods to the Strait of Georgia along the 49th parallel. These lines were drawn during several sets of negotiations between British and American officials that were not finalized until 1846. The degree to which this exercise was entirely theoretical—the result of negotiators sitting in Washington marking lines on maps that were not terribly exact—can be seen by the real-life impact of the diplomats' line-drawing. One example is the Halfway House, a pub that happened to be built precisely on the 45th parallel, and thus is half in Dundee, Québec and half in Fort Covington, New York; its bar and pool area has the international border prominently marked down the middle.

Another example is the anomaly of Point Roberts. The American and British negotiators meeting in 1846 drew the line from the Rockies to the middle point in the Strait of Georgia (instead of simply the Pacific shore, which is located at Blaine, Washington). As a result, the tip of a little peninsula which extends down from British Columbia happens to be south of the 49th parallel, and thus is United States territory. The tiny community of Point Roberts is physically cut off from the rest of Blaine County in Washington state, posing considerable problems for the residents: students bussed to high school, for example, have to cross two international borders.

Many of the borders that now divide countries were drawn by colonial administrators during the period of European imperialism. The borders of contemporary African states are inherited from the era of imperialism, which we examine below in Chapter 13. This was the so-called "Scramble for Africa," when in the last two decades of the 19th century European powers scrambled to secure colonies in Africa. In the process, they carved up virtually the entire continent. Of all indigenous African peoples, only the Liberians and the Ethiopians were successful in retaining independence during this period. As Europeans consolidated their control, they applied the same line-drawing techniques to Africa as were being used in the Americas, often dividing tribal communities between different colonies, or including numerous different African communities within the same colony. Some borders that divide states today were internal colonial borders. For example, the borders that divide Mauritania, Algeria, Mali, and Niger across the Sahara desert are the straight lines drawn for convenience by colonial administrators to mark the internal divisions of the vast French holdings in Africa in the 19th and early 20th centuries—the colonies of Algeria and French West Africa.

Colonial borders in Africa persist to the present day. When African states began to secure their independence in the 1950s, there was general agreement among African leaders that however illogical the borders drawn by Europeans may have been, reopening border questions would lead to too many debilitating conflicts. African borders became sacrosanct, untouchable. Even when African states quarrelled over ownership of territory—as Mauritania and Morocco did over the former Spanish Sahara in the late 1970s—the protagonists left the lines drawn by Europeans alone. Only twice since decolonization began in the 1950s have African borders undergone major revision, most recently when Eritrea gained its independence from Ethiopia in May 1993.[*]

*There was general agreement among African leaders that however illogical the borders drawn by Europeans were, reopening border questions would lead to too many debilitating conflicts.*

---

[*] Over the objections of many Eritreans, the former Italian colony of Eritrea had been given to Ethiopia in 1952 by the United Nations with the idea that a federal state would be created, thus affording Eritreans some autonomy. When Ethiopia reneged in 1962 and made Eritrea a province instead, an independence movement was spawned that fought a 30-year war against Ethiopia.

## The Division of the World

By the end of the 20th century, as a result of this line-drawing, all states had a clearly de-marcated territory, and all territory was clearly occupied by a state. Except for a pie-shaped slice of Antarctica—the so-called "Pacific Sector" which runs from 90° longitude west to 150° longitude west—there is no longer any territory in the world considered to be *terra nullius* (no one's land). Ownership of every square metre of the Earth's land surface—and a goodly portion of the ocean surrounding the land—is claimed by states.

It is true that there exists a formally recognized "neutral zone" deemed to belong to no state: the uninhabited sandy isthmus between the British territory of Gibraltar and the Spanish town of La Línea.* However, this cannot be considered a true case of *terra nullius*, even though theoretically such territory lies outside the jurisdiction of the states on either side. If a third state actually tried to claim this zone, there can be little doubt that Spain and Britain would quickly abandon the present arrangement.

Although all territory is claimed, not all claims are settled. Some territory is subject to rival or overlapping claims. Most territorial disputes occur between two states, such as the Indian and Pakistani claims to Kashmir, the Spanish claim to Gibraltar, the Argentinean claim to the British territory of the Falkland Islands, or the Portuguese claim to East Timor. Occasionally, numerous states contend for the same territory. For example, many of the states claiming Antarctic territory do not recognize each others' claims. Both the Republic of China on Taiwan and the People's Republic of China dispute Japanese owner-ship of a small group of rocks in the East China Sea, called Diaoyutai by the Chinese and Senkaku-shotō by the Japanese. Ireland and Iceland have contested Britain's claim to Rockall, a rocky outcropping in the North Atlantic. And fully six states claim to own part or all of the variety of atolls, reefs, and rocky outcroppings, collectively known as the Spratly Islands, in the South China Sea.

## Population

A state's population consists of all those human beings who are physically located within the boundaries of the state's territory at any given time. For the purposes of the state, the population is divided into a number of identifiable groups of people.

### Citizens and Noncitizens

The bulk of the population consists of the state's **citizens**, those individuals who are deemed to be bona fide members of the state, endowed with the various rights, privileges, and obligations assumed to accompany such membership. For the most part, the grant of membership is nominal rather than actual: normally, people born within a particular territory are simply assumed to be citizens until or unless they seek formal state recognition or confirmation of their status, such as a passport. At that point, the state will bring to bear

---

* In 1981, Saudi Arabia and Iraq agreed to partition their "neutral zone"—a small diamond-shaped patch of un-inhabited desert between them that had been created in 1922 to allow nomads access to pastures and watering areas.

its own particular rules on determining citizenship. Being born in the state does not automatically give one the right of citizenship: it depends on the rules of the particular state. In some states, citizenship is conferred automatically on all those born in the state, a convention known in international law as *jus soli* (law of the soil); in other states, citizenship is derived from the citizenship of one's parents (*jus sanguinis*, or law of blood). In some states, one's ethnicity is the crucial determinant of citizenship. For example, under the Hong Kong Basic Law, critical distinctions are made between "Chinese citizens," those of "Chinese nationality," and all others, but no effort is made to define what constitutes "Chinese nationality." In other states, religion is the key. Under Israel's "Law of Return," all Jews have the right to immigrate to Israel, and indeed Israel has on occasion gone to great lengths to offer the protection of the Israeli state to Jews in other countries. In the mid-1980s and early 1990s, for example, the Israeli government airlifted some 14 000 Ethiopian Jews, or Falashas, to Israel after they suffered persecution in Ethiopia.

All other people are classified as noncitizens, and require special permission to enter, visit, reside, settle, or work in the state. There are several kinds of noncitizens. **Resident aliens** are those citizens of other states who have been given the right to live and work in the state. Most, but not all, resident aliens may want to settle permanently in the state as immigrants. States employ different methods of deciding who to admit as resident aliens. Virtually all states adhere to the principle of "family unification," and readily admit the spouses and children of their citizens; some states assign quotas and hold lotteries; some states use a "point system," in which a prospective immigrant is given points for each attribute considered desirable; some states readily sell resident alien status as a form of job creation to those who are willing to invest several hundred thousand dollars in a new business.

Immigrants and resident aliens bear two of the key responsibilities of citizenship—paying taxes and obeying laws—but do not enjoy all the rights of citizens. While in most communities they have access to public services on the same basis as citizens, they may face legal discrimination in public affairs, such as being banned from holding some positions in public institutions. Most importantly, noncitizens do not have the right to vote, a discriminatory practice almost universally embraced. Nor is their right of residency as absolute as a citizen's: it may be revoked by the state at any time, albeit for cause. Moreover, in many states, one automatically loses one's rights as a resident alien if one takes up residence in another country.

The nationality laws of most states permit some resident aliens to become citizens. Someone who has lived in a state as a resident alien, or who has married a citizen, may apply for citizenship, a process called **naturalization**. However, most states put considerable barriers in the way of attaining citizenship in this way. Only in so-called "immigrant countries"—notably Australia, Canada, and the United States—is naturalization a relatively easy process.

States may also revoke citizenship. For example, a number of immigrants to the United States who were later accused of war crimes committed during the Nazi period have had their citizenship revoked, and have been deported to the state of original citizenship. The law of some states demands exclusivity, stripping citizenship from those who take up the duties of citizenship in another state, such as swearing allegiance to another sovereign, serving in another state's armed forces, or even voting in another state's elections. However, in general, revocation of citizenship for native-born citizens contravenes established international rules, and most states have provisions for dual citizenship. On several occasions states have simply expelled large numbers of their citizens or pressed them into leaving. In 1935, for example, the Nazi party convention in Nürnberg stripped all German Jews of their citizenship (and much else besides). And while Jews were not expelled outright in the 1930s, there is little doubt that they were encouraged to leave. In 1972, the state of Uganda confiscated the property of all Asian citizens and threw them out of the country. Vietnam did the same thing to Vietnamese of Chinese extraction—the Hoa—in the late 1970s.

At any given time, a state's population also includes a number of other categories of people. *Visitors* have been given permission to enter the state on a temporary basis, for business, pleasure, or tourism, or to visit family, or study. Those who are in the country without permission are termed by different names—illegal aliens in the United States, illegal immigrants in Canada, overstayers in Australia. **Refugees** are those fleeing from persecution in their homeland: normally they are allowed to enter a state temporarily while their request for asylum is being considered; if their request is rejected, they are generally deported back to their homeland. There may be **stateless persons**—those who through some circumstance have been deprived of formal membership in a state—who exist in a kind of legal limbo until the state where they live can decide their fate. Finally, among those physically present at any time, but not counted as part of the population for purposes of governance, are the official representatives of other states or interstate organizations. These individuals enjoy a special exempt status called **diplomatic immunity**, which allows them to be free from prosecution by any government other than their own.[*]

## The Importance of State Classification

It should never be forgotten that how individuals are identified and classified by a state can have a huge impact on their lives, often making the difference between life and death. For

*How individuals are identified and classified by a state can have a huge impact on their lives, often making the differ-ence between life and death.*

example, consider the fate of Jews in central Europe—after 1933 in Germany, after 1938 in Austria, and after 1939 in Czechoslovakia. These people were twice classified by states in the 1930s. First, everyone in the Third Reich was given one of four classifications by the Nazi bureaucracy according to the religion of their grandparents: *Deutschblütig* ("German-blooded," in other words, no Jewish grandparents), two grades of *Mischlinge* (literally, hybrids or half-breeds), or *Juden*. It did not matter if one actually was a Jew; having four grandparents born Jewish made one Jewish in Nazi eyes. As noted above,

---

[*] While many diplomats use diplomatic immunity to avoid having to obey parking laws in other countries, this privilege does not mean that diplomats can break any law they wish to and then invoke immunity. In cases where a diplomat commits a serious crime—drunk driving, murder, or trafficking in drugs—the government of the state in which the offence occurred asks the diplomat's home government to waive immunity so the diplomat can be prosecuted. Only in exceptional circumstances is such a request denied.

Jews were not expelled outright, but were coerced by discriminatory laws or by pogroms. Such a pogrom occurred on the night of 9 November 1938, **Kristallnacht**—the "night of glass"—when across Germany and Austria, Jewish shop windows were smashed and nearly every synagogue was burned.

However, those who were wealthy enough to move faced a second classification by another set of states. In other words, Jewish refugees needed to be classified as welcome immigrants by other states, and few states were interested in taking Jews from Central Europe. The United States, for example, admitted approximately 150 000 between 1936 and 1941. After *Kristallnacht*, the Australian government announced it would admit 15 000, but the offer did not come until 1 December 1938, with the result that less than half that number made it to Australia before war broke out in September 1939. Canada, by contrast, kept the doors tightly closed: anti-Semitism and concerns about unemployment combined to keep European refugees out: 748 were allowed into Canada in 1938, 1763 in 1939. "None is too many" was the way this refugee problem was perceived in Canada.[11] In short, the closed doors that millions of Central European Jews found in the late 1930s, trapping them in the Third Reich where so many died in the Holocaust, underscores how important such classifications can be.

Because of the difference one's citizenship can often make in the world, the right to enter some states is highly sought after. For example, so many people in the world want to move to the United States that the U.S. Immigration and Naturalization Service (INS) instituted a lottery to determine who would be given a prized "green card," the common metonym for the right to enter the United States as a resident alien. Likewise, many Hong Kong people went to considerable lengths in the 1980s and early 1990s to establish the right of citizenship in Canada, the United States, or Australia so that they might have an "insurance policy" just in case the return of Hong Kong to the People's Republic of China in 1997 went sour. For this reason there is a thriving illegal market in counterfeit passports, but it is no coincidence that forged passports for some states are in higher demand than others.

We have surveyed these fine distinctions made about people to show that governments are as finicky about population as they are about territory. They know that citizenship matters, as we will see below when we look at the case of South Africa during the apartheid era. States therefore engage in considerable efforts to make and preserve these careful distinctions about people, both inside and outside their borders.

## Government

All states have a government, or a state apparatus designed for the governance of a population located within a particular territory. Here we run into some terminological confusion, for we tend to use "the state" in a number of different ways. We refer to "the state" as an entity in international politics, as a way of organizing political authority, and as the governing structure of a polity. (And, to add to the confusion, "the state" can also mean an administrative division of some federations, such as Australia, India, Mexico, or the United States.) While the multiplicity of meanings may appear confusing, context usually reveals whether one is referring to "the state" as a political entity in international politics, as the governing apparatus of a country, or as one of the constituent units of a federal system.

One of the reasons we have come to use "the state" to refer to both the political entity in international politics and the government of that entity is because of the intimate relationship between the two. "The state" *qua* government acts in the name of "the state" *qua* international entity. In that sense, "the state" as international entity is personified by the individuals who occupy the offices of "the state" as government. This is why we need to locate the "personality" of the state. And this leads us to the Head of State and the Head of Government.

## The "Personality" of the State: Head of State/Head of Government

The governing apparatuses of contemporary states show considerable homogeneity. The vast majority of governments (though not all) have essentially the same structures, even if they employ different names for their structures and the offices of state. These include an executive, a legislature, a judiciary, a bureaucracy, and armed forces. However, while these institutions of governance may look the same at a superficial level, they function very differently from state to state.

For all their differences, however, there are two commonalities: each government has a **head of state**, the individual who personally embodies the sovereignty of the state in its relations with other states in international affairs; and each government has a **head of government**, the individual who is (as the name suggests) the leader of the executive, or governing, group within the state apparatus.

In many states, these are separate offices, occupied by separate individuals. For example, in European states which retain constitutional monarchies inherited from an earlier era (Andorra, Belgium, Britain, Denmark, Liechtenstein, Luxembourg, Monaco, Norway, Netherlands, Spain, and Sweden), a king, queen, prince, or grand duke serves as head of state, while there is a separate head of government, usually a prime minister or a premier.

This same political form is also found in those states which modelled their institutions of government along these lines. In the 15 former colonies or territories in the British empire, shown in Table 9.1, the serving British monarch also serves as head of state. Elizabeth II is Queen of Antigua and Barbuda, Queen of Australia, and so on at the same time as she is Queen of the United Kingdom of Great Britain and Northern Ireland.

*Table 9.1* • **ONE MAJESTY, SIXTEEN SOVEREIGNS**

| Elizabeth II is Queen of the following countries, and is thus the head of state of each: | |
| --- | --- |
| Antigua and Barbuda | New Zealand |
| Australia | Papua New Guinea |
| Bahamas | Saint Kitts and Nevis |
| Barbados | St Lucia |
| Belize | St Vincent and the Grenadines |
| Canada | Solomon Islands |
| Grenada | Tuvalu |
| Jamaica | United Kingdom of Great Britain and Northern Ireland |

In other former British colonies—India, Malaysia, Tonga, and Western Samoa—the constitutional-monarchical form is retained, though the head of state is known by a different name and is selected by different methods. In India, the head of state is the president, selected for a five-year term by an electoral college of members of the federal and state legislatures; in Malaysia, a *Yang di-Pertuan Agong*, or supreme or paramount ruler, is elected for a five-year term by a Conference of Rulers consisting of the hereditary rulers that head nine of the 13 states in the federation.

By contrast, in some political systems, the head of state and head of government may be the same individual. For example, in the Sultanate of Oman, one of the few remaining absolute monarchies, the sultan reigns supreme as the head of state and the head of government (indeed, Sultan Qabus ibn Sa'id is head of *everything* political in Oman, for there is no constitution, no legislature, no political parties, and no civil judiciary). In the United States, the president is both the symbolic head of state and the head of government. In some political systems, such as France and China, there may be a prime minister or premier, but generally the president acts as head of government.

These three attributes—territory, people, and government—come together in the fourth attribute of the contemporary state, sovereignty. However, because sovereignty is so important for understanding the contemporary state, we need to explore sovereignty in practice in a separate chapter.

## CONCLUSION

This chapter has ranged widely, trying to provide in a few short pages a simple account of highly complex phenomena. The evolution of the contemporary state—with its precisely demarcated territory, its bureaucratized classifications of people, and its homogenous governmental structures—from the European experience of the period we call the Middle Ages was a process that spanned centuries, with interwoven fronds of causality that form deeply intricate patterns. For example, it is difficult to unravel the interrelationship between what was happening then in the world of world politics, the world of ideas, and the world of economics. Struggles over the conceptions of the divine were intertwined with more worldly struggles of kings and princes over control of people and territory. And these in turn were drawing their inspiration from the blood being shed in the palaces, towns, and battlefields of Europe. Likewise, these struggles were occurring in the wake of (and because of) changes in the way in which wealth was created, distributed, and regarded.

But for all the complexity of that process, the purpose of this chapter has been relatively simple: to describe the rise of a set of ideas about how to organize political authority that would have profound implications for the division of humankind. The rise of the territorial state with deeply rooted political and economic interests created the kind of hard geopolitical divisions between human beings that had simply been unknown to previous generations. Moreover, this source of division spread widely across the globe as the notion of the state, derived from intra-European politics of the mid-millennium, was universally embraced by the millennium's end. Finally, it should be noted that these divisions have in turn been entrenched by the immense power of the contemporary state, which squelches, often ruthlessly, those who have tried to put in place alternative ideas about how to exercise political power.

There are still, however, two pieces left in the puzzle. One is the issue of how sovereignty has been put into practice in the contemporary era—as distinct from the evolution of the sovereign idea surveyed in this chapter. Sovereignty in practice represents the legal entrenchment of the geopolitical divisions of the contemporary state, and we look at this in the next chapter. The second piece of the puzzle is the nation as a source of human division; that is discussed in Part V.

## Keyword File

| | |
|---|---|
| Feudal system | Monopoly trading corporation |
| Possessive individualism | Mercantilism |
| Commodification of land | Colonies |
| Divine right of kings | Glorious Revolution |
| Holy Roman Empire | Separation of powers |
| Interdict | Federalism |
| Indulgences | Sovereign state |
| Renaissance | Subsequent boundaries |
| Reformation | Antecedent boundaries |
| Huguenots | Superimposed boundaries |
| Schmalkaldic League | *Terra nullius* |
| Sovereignty | Citizens |
| *Majestas* | Resident aliens |
| Wars of religion | Naturalization |
| Defenestration of Prague | Refugees |
| Peace of Westphalia | Stateless person |
| Age of exploration | Diplomatic immunity |
| Empire | *Kristallnacht* |
| Bullion | Head of state |
| Slave trade | Head of government |

## For Further Exploration

### HARD COPY

Bartelson, Jens. *A Genealogy of Sovereignty*. Cambridge: Cambridge University Press, 1995.

Cox, Robert W. "Social forces, states and world orders," in Robert O. Keohane, ed. *Neorealism and its Critics*. New York: Columbia University Press, 1986.

Jackson, Robert H. *Quasi-States: Sovereignty, International Relations, and the Third World.* Cambridge: Cambridge University Press, 1990.

James, Allan. *Sovereign Statehood.* London: Allen and Unwin, 1986.

Keen, Maurice. *The Penguin History of Medieval Europe.* Harmondsworth, U.K.: Penguin, 1968.

Spruyt, Hendrik. *The Sovereign State and Its Competitors: An Analysis of Systems Change.* Princeton, NJ: Princeton University Press, 1994.

### WEBLINKS

**http://www.orb.rhodes.edu/default.html**

Site of Online Reference Book for Medieval Studies, providing resources on the feudal era

**http://www.ucr.edu/h-gig/horuslinks.html**

Horus' History Links provides resources on major historical topics

## Notes to Chapter 9

1. The phrase is C.B. Macpherson's: *The Political Theory of Possessive Individualism* (Oxford: Clarendon Press, 1962).

2. Hendrik Spruyt, *The Sovereign State and Its Competitors: An Analysis of Systems Change* (Princeton: Princeton University Press, 1994), 96–98.

3. See Jens Bartelson, *A Genealogy of Sovereignty* (Cambridge: Cambridge University Press, 1995), 100–102.

4. Harvey C. Mansfield, Jr., "On the impersonality of the modern state: a comment on Machiavelli's use of *stato*," *American Political Science Review* 77 (1983), 849–57.

5. Michael Walzer, "On the role of symbolism in political thought," *Political Science Quarterly* 82 (June 1967), 194.

6. Jean Bodin, *On Sovereignty: Four Chapters from The Six Books of the Commonwealth,* ed. and trans. Julian H. Franklin (Cambridge: Cambridge University Press, 1992), xiii.

7. Bartelson, *Genealogy of Sovereignty,* 154.

8. Quoted in J.M. Roberts, *The Penguin History of the World* (London: Penguin, 1992), 608.

9. Max Weber, *The Theory of Social and Economic Organization,* ed. Talcott Parsons (New York: Free Press, 1964), 155–56.

10. See Roy E.H. Mellor, *Nation, State, and Territory* (London: Routledge, 1989), 88.

11. Irving Abella and Harold Troper, *None Is Too Many: Canada and the Jews of Europe, 1933–1948* (Toronto: Lester and Orpen Dennys, 1982).

# Juridical Divisions:
# Sovereignty
# *in* Practice

**I N T R O D U C T I O N** The idea of sovereignty, as it evolved in the 16th and 17th centuries, brought the elements of territory, people, and government together. As noted in the previous chapter, the idea of sovereignty suggests that within a particular defined territory, one government should exercise supreme political authority over all the people physically present in that territory.

But as states began to put that idea into practice, several related corollaries of sovereignty emerged. First, sovereignty implies political supremacy that is both divisible and indivisible. Second, sovereignty implies supremacy *inside*, but equality *outside*. Third, sovereignty implies that no other government should attempt to exercise authority or control over these people or this territory: a sovereign state has the right to be free from interference in its internal affairs. Fourth, sovereignty implies that a government should not try to exercise authority over anyone who is outside the boundaries of that state. Fifth, sovereignty implies that a crucial part of maintaining supremacy lies in the ability of a government to maintain control over what and who comes into their space. Sixth, sovereignty implies that the state has been admitted to the "club" of sovereign states. To each of these implications of the sovereign idea in practice we now turn.

## DIVISIBILITY AND INDIVISIBILITY

Sovereignty is both divisible and indivisible. The American republican form of government, with its separation of powers between the executive, legislative, and judicial branches of government, or the Westminster form, with its construction of the Crown-in-Parliament, would both be impossible without the **divisibility of sovereignty**. Likewise, no federation could function unless the central government and the governments of the constituent units agreed to divide supreme political authority between them.

But sovereignty is deemed to be *indivisible* when the state turns to the outside world. Whatever the political divisions might be within the state, sovereignty assumes that the state becomes one singular sovereign for the purposes of dealing with the outside world. For those purposes the sovereign is indivisible: only one sovereign can exercise political authority over people in the same geographical space.

It is true that a **condominium**—two sovereign states working out a way to share the same territory or the same people—is theoretically possible; a number of states have tried to create condominiums, as the Focus on the opposite page reveals. But if one takes the idea of sovereignty seriously, condominiums are difficult to manage. Indeed, only one condominium

The Panama Canal is within the Panama Canal Zone, a condominium jointly administered by the United States and Panama. See the Focus on the opposite page.

has not posed political problems: Roosevelt Campobello International Park works because it is apolitical. This park, open only during the summer months, does not involve significant economic or symbolic interests for either country; moreover, it is administered by two governments which have long-established patterns of cooperative management of apolitical issues.[1]

## SOVEREIGNTY AND EQUALITY

In theory, sovereignty is about supremacy in the exercise of authority, but in practice a paradox is created. Sovereignty demands that the state must try to be supreme *within* its own territory, but sovereignty also demands that states must *not* try to assert supremacy *outside*—in other words, over other sovereign states. If sovereignty is to work, each state must be left to be supreme. The paradox is that an idea about supremacy must also create a system of equality.

Note here that the understanding of the **equality of states** follows the distinctions that liberal theorists make between "equality of condition" and "equality of right." The sovereign

---

# FOCUS

### *Condominiums in World Politics*

**ANDORRA**

Until 1993, when they voted to put an end to the arrangement, Andorra was ruled by two sovereigns—a French Co-Prince (whoever was the president of France) and a Spanish Episcopal Co-Prince (whoever happened to be the Bishop of Seo de Urgel in Spain)—an arrangement dating back in various forms to 1278.

**VANUATU**

The New Hebrides (which became Vanuatu in 1980) was ruled by a British-French naval commission from the 1880s until 1906, when a condominium was established. The islands were jointly administered by Britain and France, with each colonial power having jurisdiction over their own citizens.

**NAURU**

This island, seized from Germany during the First World War, was jointly administered by Australia, New Zealand, and Britain under United Nations trusteeship before it achieved independence in 1968.

**PANAMA CANAL ZONE**

Under the 1977 treaties returning the Panama Canal to Panama, the United States and the Panamanian government jointly administer Panama Canal Zone until Panama acquires full sovereignty on 1 January 2000.

**ABU MUSA**

This small island in the Persian Gulf is claimed by both Iran and United Arab Emirates. In 1971, Iran occupied the island but the two countries agreed to jointly administer the island and share offshore oil revenues. However, in early 1992, Iran expelled all UAE residents and seized complete control of the island, warning that UAE forces would have to cross a "sea of blood" to recover the island.

**ROOSEVELT CAMPOBELLO INTERNATIONAL PARK**

This park on Campobello Island, New Brunswick, is a memorial to Franklin Delano Roosevelt, president of the United States from 1933 to 1945. The park is built around the cottage where Roosevelt and his family summered before he contracted polio. Although it is located in Canada, the park is administered jointly by the governments of Canada and the United States.

idea does not assume that all states enjoy equality of *condition* (in size, power, population, or any other attribute); sovereignty assumes that states range from large communities such as the People's Republic of China, with 1.2 billion people, an area of 9.6 million km$^2$, and a diverse and burgeoning economy; to small states like Nauru, with a population of 10 000, an area of 21 km$^2$, and a narrow economy based on the mining of a single product, phosphate.

Rather, sovereignty assumes that all states, from China to Nauru, enjoy equality of *right*. In other words, all sovereign states, no matter how large or small, powerful or weak, populous or not, are assumed to enjoy the same rights. The most important of these rights is that they must be regarded as supreme within their territory.

## NONINTERFERENCE IN DOMESTIC AFFAIRS

Sovereignty in practice implies that no sovereign has the right to intervene or interfere in the internal, or domestic, affairs of another sovereign. In other words, each sovereign state has the right to organize the political, cultural, social, economic, and spiritual affairs for the community in the manner which it deems appropriate. This idea of **noninterference in domestic affairs** has been enshrined in a number of international declarations, ranging from the Peace of Westphalia to the Charter of the United Nations. The Peace of Westphalia, as we saw in Chapter 9, entrenched the agreement of the Peace of Augsburg of 1555 that gave princes the right to determine the religion of their land. The UN Charter, signed in 1945, was no less explicit: Article 2 commits states to "act in accordance with the following Principles," one of which (Article 2.7) is:

*"Nothing contained in the present Charter shall authorize the United Nations to intervene in matters which are essentially within the domestic jurisdiction of any state."*

> Nothing contained in the present Charter shall authorize the United Nations to intervene in matters which are essentially within the domestic jurisdiction of any state or shall require the Members to submit such matters to settlement under the present Charter...

To be sure, it has proven almost impossible to define what the phrase "essentially within the domestic jurisdiction" actually includes. As a result, it has become one of the sources of contemporary conflict between political communities, both governments and peoples. In general, however, the definition of what is within "domestic jurisdiction" (and thus outside the scope of intervention of outsiders) gets worked out in practice, as the following examples suggest.

### The Case of Structural Adjustment Programs

In general, sovereignty is supposed to give political communities the right to organize their political, social, economic, and cultural lives as they see fit. However, when they sign a bilateral or multilateral agreement, they limit these rights. Thus, for example, the Canada-United States Auto Products Trade Agreement (or Auto Pact) of 1965 created a **sectoral free trade** agreement—a set of rules for a single continental market in autos and auto products that precluded either government from pursuing its own policies in this sector. Likewise, the Australia New Zealand Closer Economic Relationship Trade Agreement

(ANZCERTA, or CER for short) of 1983 committed governments in both Canberra and Wellington to harmonize their business law, quarantine procedures, customs rules, and regulation in a variety of sectors, such as communications and aviation.

Multilaterally the same dynamic holds. By joining the General Agreement on Tariffs and Trade (GATT) or its successor, the World Trade Organization (WTO), a state places constraints on its economic decision-making. Multilateral agreements such as the Arrangement Regarding the International Trade in Textiles, usually known as the Multifibres Arrangement (MFA), the General Agreement on Trade in Services (GATS), or Multilateral Agreement on Investment (MAI) put limits on the sovereign ideal. Other regional trade and economic agreements that do the same include the Caribbean Community and Common Market (CARICOM), the Economic Community of West African States (ECOWAS), the Common Market of the Southern Cone (MERCOSUR), and the institutions of the European Union (discussed in Chapter 17).

These agreements are situations in which governments willingly agree to surrender some of their decision-making capacity in a particular area, in anticipation of gains to be derived from the agreement. But governments may also agree to limit their sovereign rights in more coercive circumstances. Consider those countries in financial difficulties which have sought assistance from international financial institutions (IFIs), such as the International Monetary Fund (IMF), the International Bank for Reconstruction and Development (IBRD, or World Bank) or a regional development bank. In return for IFI financing, countries agree to a package of measures, dictated by the IFI, designed to provide an economic "corrective." This *quid pro quo* was embraced in Mexico during both the debt crisis in the early 1980s and the "peso crisis" of December 1994 (both discussed in Chapter 16 below). The same agreement occurred during the "Asian meltdown" of 1997, when Asian currencies lost a great deal of their value; the governments of South Korea and Indonesia agreed, albeit reluctantly, to IMF correctives in return for IMF financing.

In countries with persistent economic problems, such as high debt and low export earnings, many governments agree to abide by a package of policy demands set out by the IMF called **Structural Adjustment Programs** (SAPs). The precise details vary from country to country, but the policy demands usually involve the devaluation of the country's currency, the deregulation and/or privatization of key economic sectors, and reductions in public spending and the state bureaucracy.

Such programs might offer some temporary relief from the debt burden, but they also tend to produce other effects: inflation, distortions in the distribution of wealth, the decline of the middle class, the massive expansion of the **informal economy**, a rise in crime, and a decreased sensitivity to environmental concerns. Moreover, such measures also tend to have effects that are not well counted by aggregate statistics collected by the state: SAPs also tend to affect women hard, since in most societies it is women who must deal with any dislocations caused in the day-to-day lives of individuals in the marketplace and on the street. When expenditures on social programs (such as health care, education, and other services) are drastically reduced, women and their dependents, as the primary users of these programs, are disproportionately affected by the decreases.[2] Nonetheless, because SAPs provide some immediate relief from the problems of indebtedness, many African governments feel that they have no choice: the conditionality that limits their sovereignty and allows officials from the IMF and the World Bank to dictate what policies they must pursue is the necessary price that they reluctantly pay.

### The Case of the United States and "Fair Trade"

The same exercise of power can take place in those areas of a country's domestic economy that are not covered by a bilateral or multilateral agreement. This can most clearly be seen by the efforts of the United States government to promote what Americans call "fair" trade.

In Chapters 15 and 17, we will look in more detail at the involvement of the United States in the creation and maintenance of the institutions that gave shape to the international economy after the Second World War. The Americans who participated in that effort were driven by the "lessons of the 1930s." Among them was the idea that closing one's borders to international trade in an effort to deal with financial crises was ultimately ruinous. Thus many Americans after 1945 became ardent devotees of the idea of **free trade** (examined in more detail in Chapter 12), seeking to make the movement of goods, services, and capital as free as possible. This has meant a consistent effort to eliminate barriers to trade such as tariffs placed on imports and **nontariff barriers** (NTBs) such as discriminatory purchasing policies or government subsidies to particular firms or industry sectors. As the United States Trade Representative (USTR) put it baldly in 1990, the goal of the United States "is to get governments out of business: out of the business of making steel, selling grain, growing beef, building ships, and the hundreds of other ways that governments distort trade and interfere with market access."[3]

In practice, this has meant that Americans have taken an active interest in how other countries organize themselves economically and politically. For example, over the last two decades, Americans objected to how China was organizing its laws regarding copyright and intellectual property rights (IPRs); how much British Columbians were charging loggers in stumpage fees; how the Europeans were organizing their agricultural sector; how Canada was arranging its taxation system to favour Canadian-produced magazines; how Australia was pricing its steel; and how Mexicans were catching tuna in drift nets.

But it was Japan, which had developed a massive trade surplus with the United States, that fixated Americans—and particularly the government in Washington. Both the White House and Congress placed numerous demands on Japan. American officials demanded that the Japanese change how they ran their construction and retail industries. They complained that Japanese were not buying American cars. They insisted that Japan open up the way bidding is done on public projects. They demanded that Japan reform its land pricing system. They demanded that the *keiretsu* **system**—the "families" or coalitions of businesses in different industrial sectors that supply one another with the factors of production—be reformed. The United States government even went so far as to suggest how the Japanese spend their "social wage"—insisting, for example, that the government spend ¥430 trillion on public facilities over a period of years.[4]

In the case of Japan and the other countries, the United States government was responding either to specific complaints from American producers being hurt by foreign competition,

*"When domestic policies have an important impact on international relations, they become a proper item for discussion and negotiation."*

or to generalized concerns about the growing size of the American trade deficit. But in each case, Americans were driven by the notion that how a country organized itself internally was a matter on which Americans should *not* remain quiet. On the contrary, as Edward Lincoln put it, "When domestic policies have an important impact on international relations, they become a proper item for discussion and

negotiation."[5] Of course, what Lincoln was really saying was "When how foreigners organize themselves has a negative impact on us Americans, we should tell them how we want them to behave"—for, in fact, it is concern over American well-being that has driven the United States to interfere in the internal affairs of other countries in the name of **fair trade**.

Not surprisingly, those targeted by such intrusions deeply resent the presumptuousness of Americans telling them how they should order their lives. But, as in the case of structural adjustment programs, power governed outcomes. The United States has powerful trade weapons that it can use against those in the international system who do not share Washington's definition of what constitutes "fair" trade. Countries accused of "unfair" trading practices have to face Section 301 of the United States trade code and its variant, **Super 301**, introduced by the Omnibus Trade and Competitiveness Act of 1988. Under "regular 301," the United States can appeal an unfair trading practice to a multilateral institution like GATT or the WTO; however, if the appeal is unsuccessful, United States trade law allows the government to impose "countervailing" measures—duties or quotas designed to offset the advantage enjoyed by the "unfair" trader. Super 301 allows the United States to by-pass multilateral institutions altogether. As John Gerard Ruggie notes, under Super 301, the United States "completely arrogates to itself the right to act as accuser, judge, and jury in assessing which trading practices by others are unfair and imposing punishment on those it deems guilty."[6]

While many countries thought that by the 1980s the United States had become "the bully of world trade,"[7] all those targeted by the United States proved to be more interested in continuing to do business with Americans than they were in bringing down the delights of Super 301—or worse—on their heads. So instead they mostly bowed to American wishes. For example, numerous countries agreed to impose **voluntary export restraints** (VERs) on shipments of goods to the United States, and to sign **voluntary restraint agreements** (VRAs). The word "voluntary" is prominently displayed as a slender and ironic figleaf to cover the reality that VRAs are the international trade equivalent of "the offer you can't refuse." The Japanese were increasingly resentful of *gaiatsu*—as "foreign pressure" is called in Japanese—but nonetheless imposed VERs against automobile exports to the United States and agreed to negotiate these disputes with the United States. These negotiations, called the **Strategic Impediments Initiative** (SII), resulted in Japan giving in to a number of American demands. Australia and Canada also imposed VERs on goods like steel and wheat. In the case of Canadian government efforts to promote the indigenous magazine industry by differential taxation rates, the United States got its way when a WTO panel considering the Canadian practice ruled in favour of the American objection.

In short, sovereignty gives a state the right to structure its domestic economy as it wishes, but only if it is prepared (or powerful enough) to accept the costs that come with alternative courses of action. Sheila Copps, the Canadian heritage minister, could, if she wished, ignore the WTO and the United States and simply do what she wants on magazine policy; the government in Tokyo could, if it wished, tell American negotiators precisely where they might put their helpful suggestions about how to organize Japanese society; President Daniel arap Moi of Kenya could, if he wished, send officials of the World Bank and the IMF packing on the next flight out of Nairobi. The fact that they do not is a reflection of the realities of power. The desire to keep engaged, to keep doing business, takes precedence over the desire to maintain the theory of sovereignty pristine. Having a USTR official decide what is acceptable industrial policy, or having a neoclassical economist from the World Bank in Washington dictate the terms of a structural adjustment program—such is the price to be paid for the economic benefits of continued engagement in the international political economy. And most states are willing to pay it.

## The Case of Human Rights

A similar exercise of power is evident in cases of human rights, which also provide good examples of how the idea of "domestic jurisdiction" gets shaped in practice. On the surface of it, Article 2.7 of the Charter of the United Nations (see p. 230) suggests that whatever happens within a state is essentially its own business, and no one else's. If one took a strict interpretation of this article, it would mean that a government could treat its people any way it wished. It could legislate away the rights of some people within its borders; it could discriminate against some groups. Article 2.7 could even be used to justify genocide.

### Genocide

The reality of Article 2.7, as it is worked out in international practice, is rather different. **Genocide** (from the Latin *gens*, people) is the systemic and deliberate putting to death of an entire people. But by universal agreement, genocide cannot be justified by invoking Article 2.7. We look in more detail at the systemic and deliberate efforts of the Nazi German state to exterminate Jews and others in Chapter 14; but it is because of the Holocaust that no one accepts the idea that what happened in Germany in the 1940s could be justified by the sovereign ideal.

That does not mean that genocide—or genocide-like killings*—no longer occur. On the contrary, we have numerous examples. In the late 1970s, the Pol Pot regime in Cambodia killed hundreds of thousands of Cambodians, more or less systematically and very deliberately, before it was overthrown. As part of its long campaign to suppress the Kurds, the Iraqi

---

* What the Nazis sought to do to Jews and others was clearly a case of genocide. Since the 1940s, however, the word genocide has been debased from overuse. The word is often used loosely to describe large-scale killings that, while horrific, are not in fact systematic efforts to exterminate an entire people.

government of Saddam Hussein dropped nerve gas and mustard gas on the village of Halabja on 16 March 1988, killing some 5000 people. As the former Yugoslavia disintegrated into civil war in 1991, groups of Serbs, Croats, and Muslims began to fight for control of different areas, either expelling or simply slaughtering members of the other groups in a process called **ethnic cleansing**. In Bosnia, for example, Bosnian Serbs opened concentration camps to hold Muslims and Croats expelled from their homes. In July 1995, they slaughtered some 7000 Bosnian Muslim men and teenage boys, dumping their bodies into mass graves. Beginning in April 1994, government-backed members of the Hutu tribe in Rwanda massacred some half-million members of the Tutsi tribe and anti-government Hutus. While such killings continue, the point is that no one tries to justify such genocidal actions by saying that sovereignty gives them the right to engage in such behaviour. Rather, perpetrators of genocide depend on the unwillingness of others in the international system to do anything about it.

Since the late 1940s, the act of genocide has been made a **crime against humanity**—in other words, it is not a crime against any *specific* country, but against humankind as a whole. This began with the decision of the victors of the Second World War to put both German and Japanese leaders on trial. The International Military Tribunals at Nürmberg and Tokyo found a number of German and Japanese officials guilty of crimes against humanity, including genocide. The idea that genocide was a crime against humanity was institutionalized under the Universal Declaration of Human Rights (1948) and the Convention on the Prevention and the Punishment of the Crime of Genocide (1949). In the wake of the civil wars in both the former Yugoslavia and Rwanda, the United Nations established war crimes tribunals to prosecute those accused of genocide. However, while indictments have been issued against a number of leaders, no one has done to them what the Israeli secret intelligence service Mossad did with Adolf Eichmann in 1960. Mossad agents sneaked into Argentina where Eichmann had secretly gone after the Second World War, kidnapped him, and spirited him back to Israel to stand trial for his role in organizing the deaths of millions of Jews in the Holocaust. As a result, in both Rwanda and Bosnia, only relatively minor officials have actually been brought to trial.

## Apartheid

The case of apartheid in South Africa demonstrates how a human rights practice can move from being protected under Article 2.7 to being put in a category not unlike genocide. In the 1950s, the National Party government of South Africa regularly declared that South Africa's policies of strictly separating the various races were "essentially within the domestic jurisdiction" of South Africa. Thus, anyone who commented on how the South African government treated blacks in South Africa was seen to be infringing on its sovereign right to decide its own policies for itself. Most other governments, even those which did not agree with apartheid, agreed that apartheid was an internal matter. However, as Audie Klotz has shown, over a period of years fewer and fewer people outside South Africa believed in the rightness of allowing the South African government to hide behind Article 2.7. By the 1980s, people all over the world were protesting against apartheid in a variety of ways, from refusing to buy South African produce to refusing to play cricket and rugby against South African teams. More importantly, governments of states had begun to openly criticize the South Africans and to impose their own measures and sanctions.[8]

Eventually, even the National Party, which had created apartheid in the 1940s, recognized that the separation of the races was no longer tenable. In 1990, it began to "negotiat[e] itself out of power," as Klotz put it, resulting in a multiracial government that took office in 1994 under the presidency of Nelson Mandela.

### Humanitarian Intervention: Iraq and Somalia

Following the end of the Cold War we have seen the willingness of many people to ignore the claims of the sovereignty of states for humanitarian and human rights reasons. In the early 1990s, the international community was moved to intervene in Iraq and Somalia for humanitarian reasons.[9]

**Iraq: Operation Provide Comfort**   On 24 February 1991, the coalition of states seeking to reverse the Iraqi invasion of Kuwait began their ground offensive against Iraq. They moved rapidly, retaking Kuwait City and driving Iraqi forces back across the border. In Iraq itself, groups opposed to Saddam Hussein organized uprisings in anticipation of an invasion of Iraq by the coalition forces. After all, President George Bush himself had compared Saddam Hussein to Adolf Hitler, and had reportedly authorized the Central Intelligence Agency to find ways of eliminating the Iraqi leader.

But on 28 February, when the Iraqi government sued for peace, Bush decided to suspend hostilities rather than continuing the march to Baghdad. However, opposition groups in both the southern and northern parts of the country were already in the process of launching uprisings. With hostilities suspended, Hussein ordered the army to suppress these uprisings, inflicting brutal casualties on both the Shi'ite "Marsh Arabs" in the south and the Kurds in the north. The massacres prompted over 1.5 million refugees to flee into neighbouring Iran and Turkey.

The American decision to halt the advance was driven by what is known as *realpolitik* (from the German, *real*, practical; hence "practical politics"), in which policy is driven by material or practical considerations, rather than ethical or moral concerns. For all its overblown rhetoric about Saddam Hussein being evil, the Bush administration was more worried about what would happen to Iraq if Hussein were overthrown. They feared that Iraq would disintegrate into civil war, with the possibility that the United States would be called on to provide an army of occupation. Moreover, there were concerns that a fragmented Iraq would leave Iran the dominant country in the region, also a prospect that did not appeal to either Bush or his successor. Thus Hussein was left in power.

But when the full magnitude of the refugee disaster became apparent in March, the Bush administration, prodded by both the French and British governments, embraced an innovative policy designed to protect both the Kurds in the north and the Shi'ites in the south. On 5 April 1991, the UN Security Council adopted Resolution 688, which called on the Iraqi government to cease its repression and allow international humanitarian aid organizations into the affected areas, which came to be known as **safe havens**. In June 1991, to further reduce the power of the Iraqi government, the United States and other members of the coalition declared a **no–fly zone** over the northern part of Iraq, threatening to shoot down any Iraqi aircraft flying in Iraqi airspace north of the 36th parallel. In August 1992, a no–fly zone was created in the south, forbidding Iraqi aircraft to fly south of the 32d parallel.

The measures taken in what was called **Operation Provide Comfort** had the desired impact: the attacks by the Iraqi army ceased and international relief organizations began delivering supplies. But Resolution 688 and the no–fly zones deeply infringed on Iraq's sovereign rights—even though, in an appropriately Orwellian twist, Resolution 688 solemnly reaffirmed "the commitment of all Member States to respect the sovereignty, territorial integrity and political independence of Iraq and of all States in the region."

**Somalia: Operation Restore Hope**    Over the course of the 1980s, the regime of Muhammad Siad Barre in Somalia faced growing opposition from other clans which Barre was systematically excluding from government positions. By the late 1980s, the other clans had joined forces and were rebelling against the Barre government. By the end of 1991, a full-scale civil war was underway, and the fighting had engulfed the capital of Mogadishu. In early 1992, the United Nations Security Council authorized the creation of UNOSOM, the UN Operation in Somalia, designed to bring humanitarian assistance to civilians caught in the fighting and to encourage an end to the civil war. By August, the fighting had caused such a famine that thousands of people were dying every day; international relief supplies were simply stolen by clan armies the moment they were delivered to the country.

By mid-November, the famine had worsened. Although George Bush had by this time been defeated in the 1992 presidential elections, he played an active part in proposing that 30 000 American troops be despatched as part of an international intervention force that would go to Somalia to protect relief supplies. Despite the objections of some of the clan warlords (notably Gen. Mohamed Farah Aidid, leader of one of the subclans which controlled parts of Mogadishu), on 9 December an international force landed in Somalia in what was known as **Operation Restore Hope**. This force was not authorized by the United Nations; it was an American-led operation. However, its name, United Task Force, which just happened to contract to UNITAF, handily sounded as though it were a UN operation. Operation Restore Hope eased the famine as troops from a number of different countries guarded and distributed food supplies. The forces of UNITAF were withdrawn in May 1993 and replaced with a UN operation, called UNOSOM II.

UNOSOM II was unlike other peacekeeping operations. As we will see in Chapter 15, **peacekeeping** had been a part of United Nations operations since the mid-1950s. But peacekeeping forces were only despatched to areas where the sovereign governments agreed to their deployment, and virtually never played an active part in local politics. Only on one occasion—in the Congo in the early 1960s—had the Security Council authorized a UN force to actively intervene in local politics with the use of force, to prevent the secession of Katanga province.

In Somalia, the UN forces were given wide latitude for local political and military action, mainly because there was no sovereign government, only clan lords claiming to control pieces of Somalia. The mandate of the UN forces in Somalia was extended beyond the original humanitarian goals; instead UNOSOM II was authorized to disarm the various armed factions in Somalia, by force if necessary.* This was known as **peacemaking** (to distinguish it from peacekeeping, which is keeping a peace which is already there).

UNOSOM was then to engage in **peacebuilding**, which involves creating the institutions of civil order. Peacebuilding had been successful in ending more than a decade of civil

*One American diplomat claimed that UNOSOM's purpose was to "re-creat[e] a country." Perhaps not surprisingly, some Somalis responded to efforts to "re-create" them by declaring war on the UN.*

war in Cambodia: since 1991, a UN Transitional Authority in Cambodia (UNTAC) had been in place, run by thousands of peacekeepers from the United Nations (commonly called "blue berets" because the headgear normally worn is the same colour as the UN flag). UNTAC in essence involved a massive administrative takeover of the country; the British foreign secretary, Douglas Hurd, called it "painting a country blue."[10] Clearly it was hoped that the same process would work in the Somali case. As Robert Oakley, the United States special envoy to Somalia, put it, the mission was "total pacification and nation-building"; one American diplomat claimed that UNOSOM's purpose was to "re-creat[e] a country."[11]

Perhaps not surprisingly, some Somalis responded to efforts to "re-create" them by declaring war on the UN. This led to the deaths of a number of international peacemakers, including 23 Pakistanis killed in an ambush in June 1993. This, in turn, led to an escalation of the fighting between Somalis and UNOSOM. For their part, American "snatch teams" were sent to find and capture Aidid. He managed to elude them, but helicopter gunship attacks killed a number of Somalis. In retaliation, Aidid's soldiers targeted blue berets. In one clash in early October 1993, 15 American servicemen were killed. The body of one of the Americans, bound and naked, was dragged by Somalis through the streets of Mogadishu. A press photographer happened to be on hand, and so the photograph of Somalis rejoicing over the body were splashed across front pages worldwide.** This image caused a crisis in the United States: Clinton announced an American withdrawal from Somalia. With the decline of American enthusiasm, the era of humanitarian activism came to an end.

As a result, when the slaughter began in Rwanda in April 1994, there was no armed humanitarianism. Instead, the UN peacekeeping forces there simply withdrew. It was left to the French to land an armed force of 2500 troops in June 1994 to create a small safe

* Thus UNOSOM II was turned into a combat operation. Most contributors to the force sent hardened combat units. Perhaps not surprisingly, some of these units were ill-suited to play the role of peacekeepers—Canadian, Italian, and Belgian soldiers were all accused of committing atrocities against Somalis during their tours of duty.

** Most of the stills of the incident, shot by Paul Watson, a *Toronto Star* photographer, were unusable because they showed the serviceman's full naked body. However, one photograph stopped at the navel: it showed the dead American's bruised and bloody torso; the foot of a Somali is planted on the serviceman's stomach. This was the shot that was widely published. See "Star man's photo etched in history," *Toronto Star* (17 October 1993), F8.

area. Likewise, the lessons of the Somalia case hung over efforts to end the civil war that had broken out in the former Yugoslavia in 1991. Although a UN force, UNPROFOR (UN Protection Force) was deployed in Bosnia-Herzegovina to create "safe areas," it could not use force to protect civilians targeted for ethnic cleansing.[12] In other words, both UNPROFOR and the two forces established by the Dayton Accords of December 1995 that brought the war to an end (IFOR, or Implementation Force and SFOR, or Stabilization Force), were traditional peacekeeping forces, working more or less within the limits of sovereignty.

Thus the experiments with intervention on behalf of human rights did not last long. Angry Somalis forced those who had enthusiastically embraced humanitarian intervention to confront what peacemaking in the cause of human rights actually entailed. To be sure, peacemaking was described as "conservatorship" of "failed states," as Gerald B. Helman and Steven R. Ratnor put it.[13] Peacemaking foreigners claimed that they were acting in the name of the international community, and there can be little doubt that their cause was good. But this did not change the essence of the operation: peacemaking, as it was practised in the early 1990s, involved a clear violation of sovereignty: it was the imposition of a foreign will on a people, and thus little different than the colonialism we will examine in Chapter 13 below.

## Capital Punishment

Likewise, a wide variety of human rights practices still remain well protected behind Article 2.7. Consider, for example, the use of capital punishment. A large number of states in the international community consider the execution of criminals to be a violation of Article 5 of the Universal Declaration of Human Rights that guarantees that no human should be subjected to cruel punishment. Those states which continue to shoot, hang, inject, poison, suffocate, behead, stone, or electrocute criminals would not take kindly if other states insisted that capital punishment was a barbaric practice that should be abolished everywhere. Instead they would insist that it was their 2.7 right to treat offenders as they wish. For this reason, many human rights practices remain highly contested, and protected by sovereignty.

> *Those states which continue to shoot, hang, inject, poison, suffocate, behead, stone, or electrocute criminals would not take kindly if other states insisted that capital punishment was a barbaric practice that should be abolished everywhere.*

## The Case of Secessionist Movements

Usually, governments reject attempts by others to interfere in their domestic politics, calling it a violation of the understanding of the sovereign ideal. But this sensitivity becomes particularly pronounced when domestic politics involves secessionist movements. Thus, for example, since the 1960s, the Canadian, Québec, and French governments have played a 30-year game with one another over the secessionist movement in Québec. A succession of French presidents, beginning with Charles de Gaulle, have been attracted to the possibility of a francophone country in the North American heartland. Thus, on a visit to Canada in

July 1967, de Gaulle decided to add one line to a series of "Vives!" that he used to end a speech on the balcony of Montréal's *Hôtel de Ville* (or city hall). In addition to "Vive le Canada!" and "Vive le Québec!" he shouted "Vive le Québec libre!" ("Long live free Québec").[14] The federal government in Ottawa took strong exception to what it regarded as an attempt to promote the separatist movement in Québec; the prime minister, Lester B. Pearson, effectively declared de Gaulle **persona non grata** (literally, "person not acceptable"—the diplomatic expression used for indicating that an individual is no longer welcome in a country), and brought his official visit to an end. Canada's relations with France were soured for a decade. But France has also been pushed by sovereigntist provincial governments in Québec City to declare its support for Québec's independence. Since the imbroglio of the late 1960s, French government officials have developed a standard response: France's position is one of "noninterference but nonindifference."

The People's Republic of China is equally sensitive to signs of external interference. As we will see in Chapter 11, the Chinese government in Beijing has an exceedingly low tolerance for other governments giving even the slightest symbolic expression of support for those who Beijing regards as a threat to Chinese unity—such as the Republic of China on Taiwan or the Dalai Lama of Tibet.

## APPLYING ONE'S LAWS OUTSIDE: EXTRATERRITORIALITY

Sovereignty in practice also means that states should not try to extend their control or political authority outside the tightly defined territorial boundaries of their state; they should ensure that their laws apply only to the people who are physically within the borders of the state. There are some states in the international system which adopt laws or practices that are explicitly **extraterritorial**—in other words, these laws try to reach beyond the borders of the state to control the behaviour of individuals in other countries.

### European Extraterritoriality in 19th Century China

In the 19th century, the main practitioners of extraterritoriality were Europeans and Americans in China. Imperial China was never colonized by European states or the United States; these governments formally regarded the Qing emperor as China's sovereign. But they did not *practise* the sovereign ideal. To these governments, the Qing emperor was not the supreme political authority over all Chinese territory, nor over all the people in China.

Instead, in a series of what the Chinese call "Unequal Treaties," Europeans and Americans forced the Qing to grant them rights to occupy sections of some Chinese cities, the so-called **foreign concessions**. More importantly, the Unequal Treaties provided extraterritorial legal protection for Europeans and Americans: those who committed crimes were not to be tried by Chinese courts; instead, they were to be tried under the laws of their own state.

### American Extraterritoriality Today

In the 20th century, the most persistent practitioner of extraterritoriality has been the United States. Beginning with the Trading with the Enemy Act of 1917, the government in Washington has passed a number of laws which make it illegal for Americans to have contacts with certain other countries. Over the years, amendments to the 1917 act and a variety of other specific laws have made it illegal for Americans to: trade with Vietnam, possess antiques purchased in the People's Republic of China, sell computer equipment to the Soviet Union, or do business with Cuba. Now there is nothing at all objectionable in that *per se*: the notion of sovereignty permits the United States government to make whatever laws that it wants to govern the behaviour of its citizens. If the government in Washington decides that it wants to use such techniques against countries it does not like, that is its sovereign right.

The difficulty is that the United States government has insisted that these laws apply to people *outside* the United States. In particular, these laws are applied to American citizens— and American companies—wherever they are in the world. Thus, under extraterritorial legislation, a subsidiary of an American corporation located in Madrid which started doing business in Havana may not be breaking Spanish law, but is deemed to be breaking American law. Therefore its head office in the United States is liable to punishment. Because of this, some foreign subsidiaries of American firms have been deterred from initiating trade with prohibited countries, for fear that by doing so, they will risk prosecution of the firm's executives back in the United States.

This extraterritoriality was taken one step further in the mid-1990s. The Cuban Liberty and Democratic Solidarity Act of 1996 (usually known as **Helms-Burton** after its Congressional sponsors, Senator Jesse Helms, Republican of North Carolina, and Representative Dan Burton, Republican of Illinois) provided punishments for anyone, American citizen or not, who invested in certain Cuban properties claimed by Americans to have been wrongfully expropriated by the Cuban government following the revolution. The Iran and Libya Sanctions Act of 1996, introduced by Senator Alfonse D'Amato, Republican of New York, likewise provided that anyone in the world who invested in the oil or gas sectors of Iran or Libya could be punished by the United States government. Even American states have decided to get into the act: for example, foreign companies doing business with Myanmar (Burma) may not bid on government contracts in Massachusetts.

The reaction of other governments to these American policies tends to be indignation. According to the principles of sovereignty, say Europeans, Canadians, and Mexicans, the law of their state should be the only standard of legality for individuals and firms on their territory. Let Americans make it illegal for those on American soil to do business with Cuba if they wish, but do not try to make those in other sovereign states obey American laws.

Indeed, many countries have enacted legislation of their own that makes it illegal for a firm to comply with American extraterritorial legislation. This creates the awkward catch-22 position: hapless firms have to choose which state's law to break. For example, in February 1997, a Wal-Mart Canada store in Winnipeg withdrew Cuban-made pyjamas for sale, apparently because it was concerned that its American parent, Wal-Mart of Bentonville, Arkansas, could be punished under United States laws governing Cuban assets control. However, pulling products in that way has been made illegal in Canada: under the provisions of the Foreign Extraterritorial Measures Act (FEMA) of 1985, fines of up to

$1 million can be imposed on those in Canada who obey such American laws. Reminded by Lloyd Axworthy, Canada's foreign minister, of the penalties, Wal-Mart Canada put the pyjamas back on the shelf—with its parent in Bentonville registering a formal objection (to cover themselves under American law).

## CREATING SOVEREIGNTY'S "HARD SHELL": BORDERS REVISITED

Sovereignty implies that governments try (with varying degrees of success) to create a "hard shell"[15] around their state; they try to control the territory they claim sovereignty over as well as all those things that flow across the borders of their states—goods, services, capital, technology, ideas, and people. Sovereignty thus brings together the three components of territory, people, and government, and explains why borders continue to be so important in world politics.

### Controlling Space: The Bounds of Territorial Integrity

Sovereignty implies that a state has effective control over a certain defined territory—the land, inland waters, the airspace above, and the sea immediately surrounding it. **Territorial integrity** implies that no one else can occupy, use, exploit, or even be in that geographical space without the approval of the sovereign state; those who do so are violating the territorial integrity of the sovereign state. States generally get quite testy over violations of their space, as the examples below suggest.

#### Temporary Violations: Raids and Snatches

There are several instances where one government purposely violates the territorial integrity of other states, albeit temporarily. In Chapter 7, we looked at the Israeli kidnapping of Adolf Eichmann from Argentina in 1960 and the American capture of Mir Aimal Kansi in Pakistan in 1997. These are examples of explicit, deliberate temporary violations of the sovereignty of another state. In May 1975, the president of the United States, Gerald Ford, ordered American forces to raid Cambodia after the Cambodian government seized an American merchant vessel, the *Mayaguez*, and imprisoned its crew. We will see in Chapter 15 that a similar rescue mission was ordered by President Jimmy Carter in April 1980 to try and rescue hostages from the American embassy seized by the Iranian government.

In July 1976, the Israeli government openly violated Uganda's sovereignty. Palestinian and West German guerrillas had hijacked an El Al plane and flew it to Entebbe airport near Kampala. Israeli passengers were held hostage; those of other nationalities were released. Commandos from Sayeret Matkal, an elite Israeli anti-terrorist unit, staged a raid on the airport on 3–4 July 1976. All the guerrillas and three of the hostages were killed, as were a number of Israeli commandos (including Yonatan Netanyahu, brother of Benjamin Netanyahu, who in 1996 was to become the Israeli prime minister). The Israelis acted without securing the Ugandan government's permission. In retaliation, the president of Uganda, Idi Amin Dada, ordered that the only Israeli passenger not evacuated by the commandos, Dora Bloch—who had been transferred to a hospital in Kampala after falling sick—be killed.

## Seizures and Invasions

The central assumption of sovereignty is the inviolability of a state's geographic space—the land on which its people live, and from which the state, *qua* government, draws its sustenance. Land, as we will see in Part V, is also intimately connected to the idea of nation. For reasons of state (as well as for reasons of nation), the occupation of the land of another state normally is a cause of war. Thus, for example, when Argentina seized the Falkland Islands in April 1982, the British government responded by sending an armada to the south Atlantic to reclaim them by force. Sometimes other states come to the aid of a small state seized by another country. President Ronald Reagan provided Stinger missiles to the *mujahideen*, the Afghanis fighting the Soviet occupation forces, radically altering the correlation of forces in Afghanistan. Indeed, sometimes larger states assist without even being asked. For example, when Iraq seized Kuwait in August 1990, the Kuwaitis did not even have to ask for the support of the United States; by all accounts, President George Bush simply took the decision to reverse the invasion without even talking to the Kuwaiti government.*

Sometimes the state whose land has been seized has neither the capacity nor the friends to use force to retrieve the lost territory. That does not lessen the anger at having been violated. When Indonesia seized East Timor from Portugal in 1975, the government in Lisbon strongly objected; its anger extended to those who accepted (and thereby legitimized) the Indonesian occupation, such as Australia. Portugal took Australia to the International Court of Justice for signing an agreement with Indonesia over the use of seas that it claims are still Portuguese. As late as 1996, Portugal was still getting its own back at Australia, working assiduously to ensure that Australia did not get enough votes for a seat on the Security Council.

## Controlling Airspace: Shootdowns in World Politics

Airspace is treated no differently: governments are prone to shoot down those who violate their airspace. Some have been military aircraft, such as an American C-130 shot down in September 1958 as it flew into the USSR on a spying mission. All on board were killed. Likewise, a U-2 spy plane flown by Francis Gary Powers over the USSR was shot down on 1 May 1960. Powers survived, was put on trial, and imprisoned. Some have been civilian aircraft, such as the two Cessnas shot down on 24 February 1996 by the Cuban air force, killing the two pilots and two passengers. Registered in the United States, the Cessnas were being flown by members of Brothers to the Rescue, a group of Cuban-American exiles based in Florida. The Cessnas had just completed a pass over Havana dropping protest leaflets.

---

* After Defense Intelligence Agency (DIA) satellite photographs revealed that Iraq had invaded Kuwait in the early hours of 2 August 1990, the Bush administration swung into high gear, ordering a freeze on Kuwaiti assets and arranging for a military response. Secretary of State James Baker negotiated with the Soviet Union; the president himself called other leaders: King Fahd ibn Abdul Aziz of Saudi Arabia, King Hussein of Jordan, Hosni Mubarak of Egypt, Turgut Ozal of Turkey, and Brian Mulroney of Canada. In all this flurry of activity, however, there is no indication that anyone high up in the administration actually talked to a Kuwaiti leader. Only on 4 August—when all the major decisions had already been taken—did Bush manage to talk to the emir of Kuwait, Sheikh Jabir al Ahmed al Sabah. See Bob Woodward, *The Commanders* (New York: Simon and Schuster, 1991), 222–55.

Commercial airliners have also been shot down. In 1954, a Cathay Pacific aircraft was shot down by fighters from the People's Republic of China near Hong Kong. In July 1955, an El Al Constellation that strayed over Bulgaria was shot down by Bulgarian fighters. In February 1973, a Libyan Airlines Boeing 727, which had accidentally passed Cairo airport, was shot down over the Sinai desert by Israeli fighter pilots who believed it was on a suicide raid against Tel Aviv. On 20 April 1978, Korean Air Lines flight 902, from Paris to Seoul, was shot at over the USSR, killing two passengers; however, the pilot managed to land the damaged Boeing 707 on a frozen lake. As a result, the other 108 people on board survived.

The worst case of a state shooting down a commercial airliner straying into its airspace was Korean Air Lines flight 007.* Bound from New York on the night of 31 August 1983, 007 was due to arrive in Seoul on the morning of 1 September. During a refuelling stop in Anchorage, the KAL pilots accidentally programmed the wrong numbers into the Boeing 747's navigational computers. Instead of flying along a route that would keep it out of the Soviet Union's airspace, the plane flew off course, directly into the USSR. Soviet jet fighters were sent up to tail KAL 007 as it headed toward Soviet military installations on Sakhalin Island. One of the fighters tried to raise the 747 by radio. When no response was received, the pilot was ordered by ground control to stop (*presech'*) the intruder. Two missiles hit the jumbo jet, which took 12 minutes to spiral into the sea just outside Soviet territorial waters, killing all 269 people aboard.[16]

### The Law of the Sea: Enclosing the Global Commons

Controlling the sea around a state has been more difficult than land or airspace. While the territorial aspect of sovereign control has become well established in international practice, as we saw in Chapter 9, defining territorial integrity as it relates to the sea offers a good illustration of how practice shapes theory.

Throughout history, the sea has never been able to be occupied, and thus controlled, as land has; as a consequence, the rules governing it have evolved haphazardly. It was not until the expansion of trade following the age of exploration that Europeans thought about extending the same ideas about control of land to the sea. Not surprisingly, given their dominant position as global traders, many of the ideas about controlling the sea came from the Dutch. In 1604, the Dutch East India Company was looking for a legal justification for capturing ships of its commercial rivals, the Portuguese. The company engaged the historiographer of the States of Holland, Hugo Grotius, who provided the company with a justification. Grotius argued that since Portugal had tried to deny the Dutch the right to trade in the Indian Ocean, Holland was justified in

*Arvid Pardo, Malta's ambassador to the United Nations, reflected that Grotian tradition when he proclaimed that the oceans were the common heritage of humankind.*

harming Portuguese ships. However, a part of his treatise, published in 1609 as *Mare Liberum* (The Free Seas), laid out an argument for the freedom of the seas. Grotius argued that since the sea was not like property, it could not be owned, and was thus subject to no state's sover-

---

* The worst case of an accidental shootdown of a commercial airliner involved an aircraft flying in international airspace. Crossing the Persian Gulf in July 1988, Iran Air 655 was mistaken for an attacking military fighter by an American naval vessel deployed in the Gulf, the *USS Vincennes*, and shot down. All 290 people on board were killed.

eignty. In 1967, Arvid Pardo, Malta's ambassador to the United Nations, reflected that Grotian tradition when he proclaimed that the oceans were the common heritage of humankind.[17]

In fact the seas were not entirely free. Waters along the coasts of nations could be controlled cost-effectively after the development of cannon at the end of the feudal era. In a modification of the Grotian notion published in 1702, another Dutch jurist, Cornelius van Bynkershoek, argued that since land-based artillery could extend the effective range of governmental control of the seas, **territorial waters** should be distinguished from the seas that were owned by no one, commonly called the **high seas**. From then until the early 1950s, long after the development of artillery with a range much longer than three miles, there was general agreement under the **law of the sea** that the jurisdiction of sovereign states extended three nautical miles beyond their shoreline—the **three-mile limit**.

On occasion, however, states have extended their territorial limits for particular purposes. For example, to enforce the 18th Amendment prohibiting the manufacture and sale of alcohol, the United States government unilaterally declared that its jurisdiction extended to 12 nautical miles for the purpose of enforcing Prohibition against smugglers. In 1952, Chile, Peru, and Ecuador claimed a limit of 200 nautical miles off their coasts to protect their fisheries; Iceland followed suit. In 1970, following the experimental sailing of an American supertanker (strengthened for ice) through the Northwest Passage, the Canadian government of Pierre Elliott Trudeau introduced legislation to protect the Arctic environment against the possibility of oil spills. The Arctic Waters Pollution Prevention Act extended Canada's jurisdiction to 100 miles in both the eastern and western Arctic for the purpose of pollution prevention (see Figure 10.1 below).[18]

*Figure 10.1* • **CANADA'S ARCTIC WATERS POLLUTION PREVENTION ZONE**

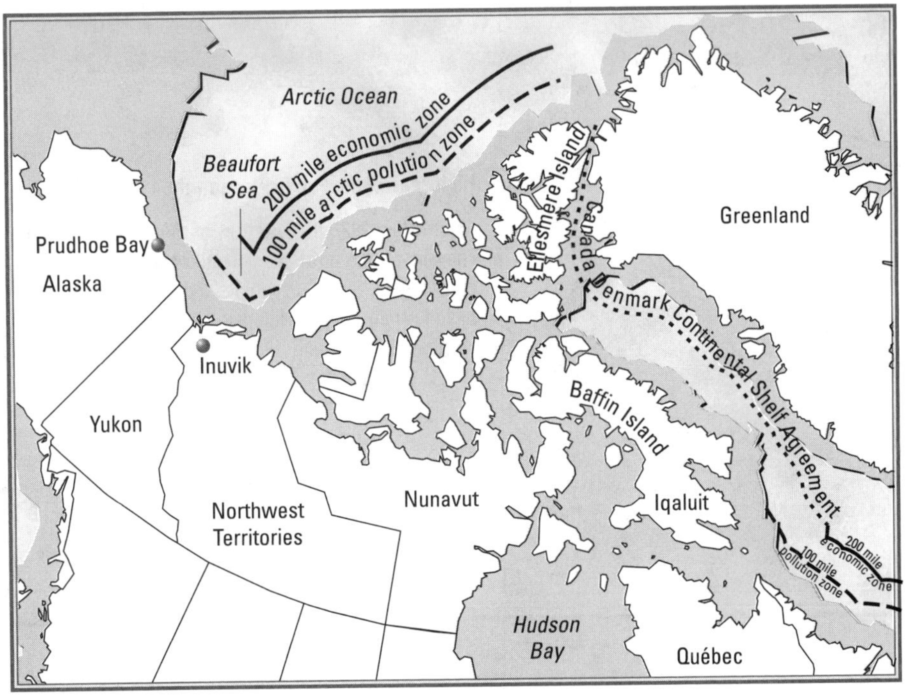

The idea of extending sea boundaries for specific purposes gave rise to yet another modification. At the Third United Nations Law of the Sea (UNCLOS III) conference that began in December 1973, it was proposed that the old three-mile limit be replaced with a 12-mile limit, over which states would have total sovereignty, plus a new 200-mile limit for certain economic activities, such as fishing and resource exploitation. This **Exclusive Economic Zone** (EEZ) was enshrined in the final Law of the Sea Convention accepted by the vast majority of states on 30 April 1982. Even the United States, which was one of only four countries to vote against the treaty, tacitly acknowledged the new limits until Washington eventually signed the Convention in 1994. UNCLOS III was a radical step: in a stroke, the free seas of Grotius, the high seas of van Bynkershoek, and the common heritage of Pardo shrank dramatically, as Figure 10.2 demonstrates.

*Figure 10.2* • **THE SHRINKING HIGH SEAS IN THE PACIFIC**

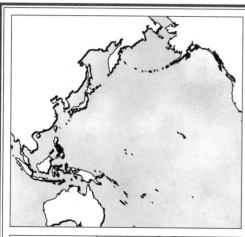

**High seas in the Pacific Ocean with a 3-mile limit**

In this projection of the Pacific Ocean, the traditional 3-mile limit is essentially indistinguishable from the coastal boundaries of states, maximizing the amount of ocean considered "high seas" and owned by no one.

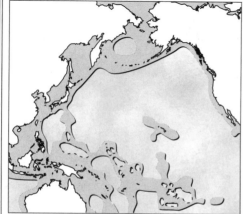

**High seas in the Pacific Ocean with a 200-mile EEZ**

As of 1 May 1982, when the Law of the Sea Convention came into force, all states were allowed to extend their control over certain economic activities to 200 miles beyond their coasts. This map of the Pacific demonstrates what a dramatic difference the EEZ made to the size of the "high seas."

The opposition of the administration of Ronald Reagan to UNCLOS III reflected a deeper conflict of interests between the so-called **maritime states** and **coastal states**. Maritime states are those countries with large navies or merchant marine fleets, such as the United States, Japan, Russia, Germany, and Britain.[19] These countries have an interest in an international legal regime that maintains as much of the world's oceans as high seas as possible. By contrast, coastal states are those countries with coastlines but no global maritime interests; these states have an interest in a law of the sea that allows them to extend their national jurisdiction out as far as possible. The coastal states found allies in a third group of states—land-locked countries like Niger which have no coastline, or countries like Cameroon, whose location at the "bend" in the Gulf of Guinea gives it a tiny EEZ, and thus "disadvantages" it. These **land-locked and geographically disadvantaged states** had an interest in seeing the international community gain control of the oceans and redistribute benefits to those states which did not have ready access to the resources of the sea.

The conflict between the maritime and coastal states was played out in different ways, depending on how friendly the protagonists were. For example, relations between the Libyan government of Mu'ammar al-Qadhafi and the United States had deteriorated badly in the late 1970s. In December 1979, protestors in Tripoli invaded and trashed the United States embassy in solidarity with the Iranian students who had seized the U.S. embassy in Teheran the previous month; in May 1981, the Reagan administration ordered the Libyans to close their embassy in Washington. Given this, it was perhaps not surprising that a quarrel between Libya and the United States over maritime claims in the Gulf of Sidra (Sirte) easily spilled into violence. In 1973, the Libyan government had declared its jurisdiction over the gulf by drawing a **straight baseline**[*] across the gulf from Misratah in the west to Benghazi in the east; in 1981, Qadhafi warned that Libyan forces would attack anyone crossing what he called the "line of death." The standing practice of the United States government is to respond forcefully and aggressively to measures that they regard an inappropriate enclosure of the high seas. So the Reagan administration sent the United States Navy into the Gulf of Sidra, but outside the internationally recognized 12-mile limit. When the Libyan air force jets challenged these ships, U.S. Navy fighters attacked them, shooting two of them down. Five years later, in March 1986, the United States Navy destroyed two Libyan ships in another encounter inside the "line of death."

A similar dispute arose with Canada over Canadian claims to sovereignty over the Northwest Passage, the route through the Arctic archipelago from the North Atlantic to the Beaufort Sea. The United States government regards the Northwest Passage as an **international strait** (and thus, under international law, open to what is termed "innocent passage" by ships of all nations). With an eye firmly on what other countries might do if Canada were allowed to assert its claim over the Northwest Passage, the United States government routinely denied the Canadian claim. Matters came to a head in the summer

---

[*] Under customary international law, a state is allowed to draw a line across the mouths of bays to turn what otherwise would be high seas (over which it has no jurisdiction) into internal waters (over which it has full sovereignty). Thus Hudson Bay in Canada is considered internal waters.

of 1985, when a U.S. Coast Guard icebreaker, the *Polar Sea*, sailed through the Northwest Passage. In this instance, there was no violence. The two governments worked out a face-saving deal: under the Arctic Cooperation agreement of January 1988, the United States agreed to ask Canada's consent to send U.S. government vessels on scientific missions into the Passage, but refused to recognize Canadian claims over the Northwest Passage. For its part, the Canadian government would be asked by the United States to enter the passage, which would give the *appearance* of Washington agreeing that the Passage was Canadian.[20]

## Controlling People: Border Crossings

It has become fashionable to dismiss borders as no longer having any relevance, as Kenichi Ohmae did in his 1990 book, *The Borderless World*. As we will see in Chapter 17, such a characterization might be appropriate to describe (and understand) how some factors of production move across borders in a "borderless" way in the contemporary global economy, but it bears little relationship to the world of borders encountered by at least one factor of production—people.

In one place in the world, borders between sovereign states have disappeared: there are no border posts, no customs checks, no passports examined, no visas required. In the European Union, frontiers between members of the Schengen group* have been transformed into the kind of borders that exist between Victoria and New South Wales, Alberta and Saskatchewan, Gauteng and Free State, Massachusetts and New Hampshire: to people travelling between them, they are just signs on a highway welcoming them to another jurisdiction.

But other than northern Europe, where else in the world can one find such borderlessness? In a word, nowhere. Even the European Union, for all of its borderless

*The world is dominated by borders that are very real, drawn around territory carefully defined, including and excluding people carefully classified.*

"inner core," insists on maintaining an "outer" frontier to control entry to the EU from "outside." "Inner" countries even refuse to admit some "outer" countries to the Schengen scheme because they regard their borders as too porous. For example, border checks still exist between Germany and Austria because the Germans are not satisfied with Austrian control of its eastern borders with Hungary, the Czech Republic, or Slovakia.

Instead, as in the case of the "outer" frontier of the EU, the world is dominated by borders that are very real, drawn around *territory* carefully defined, including and excluding *people* carefully classified. *Governments*—as protectors of the state, and, in the 20th century, providers of social welfare to the citizens of a state—invest considerable energy and resources in defining and maintaining these borders. State agencies exist to keep people out (and occasionally to try to keep people in), and at all times these agencies try to ensure that all those who do pass across borders are checked, controlled, and noted. In short, sovereignty helps explain this pervasive attachment to borders, for the hard shell created by borders defines the state.

---

* In March 1995, France, Germany, Belgium, Luxembourg, the Netherlands, Portugal, and Spain signed an agreement in Schengen, Luxembourg, to create passport-free frontiers.

The best indication of this attachment to borders is the contemporary bureaucratic system of requiring passports and visas, which were unnecessary for international travel in previous centuries. With the advent of coding, scanning, and computerization, tracking and controlling flows of people has become much easier, particularly if a state uses **passport control**, discussed in the Focus below.

The porousness of borders is highly variable; some are constructed to be almost impermeable. Perhaps the nastiest borders in the contemporary world have been those dividing countries partitioned by war. When Germany was partitioned after the Second World War, the East German authorities constructed a particularly impenetrable border, though it was designed to keep people in rather than to keep people out. This border extended back almost six kilometres from the West German frontier, and included three lines of electrified, booby-trapped, and barbed-wire fences, surrounded by mines and a 10-metre "death strip" where intruders would be shot on sight. Around the West German enclave of Berlin, which had also been partitioned, was the Berlin Wall, constructed in the summer of 1961.

# FOCUS

### Passing through the Membrane: Passport Control

A state using passport control permits only those who have passports to enter the country. This control can be loose or tight. Loose control involves checking each person's passport on arrival and stamping those of noncitizens with the conditions of entry. Tight control involves not only checking and stamping, but also swiping each person's coded passport information into a computer. In some cases of tight control, the state may require that visitors from some countries obtain prior permission to enter the country, usually in the form of a visa—often itself computer-coded. (Often, governments hold airlines financially responsible for ensuring that only those with a valid passport and visa are allowed to board flights.)

Some countries employ two-way passport control, requiring inspection of the passports of all who leave as well as those who arrive. This may be used as a means of political control. Because a passport is required to enter other countries, the most simple way to prohibit travel by a particular citizen or group is to refuse to issue them a passport.

Passport control at point of departure also allows a government to monitor its population more exactly. Thus, for example, the Australian government, which uses tight two-way control, can know which of its citizens are abroad at any time, or which visitors have not left at the expiry of their visa and have become "overstayers." By contrast, the Canadian government, which employs loose control only on airport arrivals and does not track departures at all, has no idea whether Canadian passport-holders are in or out of the country, or whether visitors have left or are overstaying.

Tight passport control is more feasible in some circumstances than others. For example, the Australian government can readily employ tight control because there are no roads in and out of the country. Almost all of those who arrive in Australia come by air, and thus can easily be lined up to have their passports swiped or their names keyed into computers. By contrast, there are 96 legal border-crossing points between Canada and the United States, and more than 28 million people cross the border each year. There, tight passport control would be more difficult. Moreover, passport control would be impossible unless both countries did away with the present rule that allows Canadian and American citizens to cross the border with any official photo-identification, such as a driver's licence.

Running through the middle of the city, the Wall consisted of a patchwork of bricked-up buildings and concrete barriers four metres high, opening only at Checkpoint Charlie; around the outskirts it consisted of fencing and another gate. It too had its own "death strip": 59 people were shot to death trying to cross the Wall before Berliners eventually began tearing it down on 9 November 1989. Likewise, the border between the Republic of Korea in the south and the Democratic People's Republic of Korea in the north runs roughly along the 38th parallel, the armistice line drawn at the end of the Korean War in 1953. A half-century on, the results of that war linger in a border that is heavily guarded, booby-trapped, and sown with land mines.

Other borders may not be as deadly as those between the two Germanies or the two Koreas, but may reflect a degree of enmity between two countries. The Indo-Pakistani border at Wagha, between Lahore and Amritsar, for example, reflects the lingering memories of the massacres of Hindus, Muslims, and Sikhs at the time of partition in 1947 and periodically entrenched in several wars in the three decades afterward. Barbed wire, a half-dozen checkpoints and a kilometre of no-man's land divide the two countries.

Other borders, by contrast, are relatively more pleasant, even those specifically designed to keep people out, such as the internal border between the Hong Kong Special Administration Region (HKSAR) and the rest of the People's Republic of China. This border retains much of the character it had as an international border when Hong Kong was a British territory. Another example is the international border between the United States and Mexico, designed to keep Mexicans from crossing illegally into the U.S. People have died trying to cross both of these borders. In Hong Kong, people drowned trying to swim across from China; in the United States, people died from suffocation and heat prostration after being locked in trucks or boxcars or been killed by running onto highways (indeed, the state of California goes so far as to post yellow warning signs on Interstate 805 and other highways running north from the border at San Ysidro, alerting motorists to the hazard of illegals darting across the highway). But only rarely does death come at the hands of government agents. There might be fences and floodlights along these borders, but there are no machine-gunners in watch-towers with orders to shoot to kill; there are no mines sown in death strips. Instead, the HKSAR police and the U.S. Border Patrol play a cat-and-mouse game with illegals, catching whom they can and driving them back across the border: approximately 30 000 a year in Hong Kong and 1.2 million a year on the Mexican-American frontier.

At the other end of the spectrum are the borders that are not only relatively easy to cross at legal crossings, but highly permeable for those who want to make the crossing without talking to a customs officer. For example, the Canadian-American border can be crossed informally at thousands of points along its entire stretch—from the Arctic Ocean in the north to the bottom of the Alaskan Panhandle, from Blaine, Washington in the west to Lubec, Maine in the east. A pleasure-boat ride or a stroll through the bush is all it takes.

# THE "CLUB" OF SOVEREIGN STATES

As the sovereign idea was put into practice in the 16th and 17th centuries, it became increasingly systematized, institutionalized, and bureaucratized. There is no magic moment when the interactions of sovereign states came into being as an institution, marked by a system or set of practices. Clearly, however, we can see most of the key elements by the time that leaders gathered at the Congress of Vienna, over the winter of 1814–15, to settle the Napoleonic Wars, the last of a series of intra-European wars precipitated by the French Revolution of 1789.

What had emerged by the 19th century was a *system* for the conduct of relations between sovereign entities. Its institutional elements consisted of endowing sovereign states with three formal rights and then working out a set of rules for the exercise of those rights. The three rights are: the right to engage in formal relations with other sovereigns by exchanging ambassadors (*jus legationis*); the right to sign treaties with other sovereigns (*jus tractatuum*); and the right to use force in defence of one's interests under certain conditions (*jus belli*, or the right of war).

Highly specific rules have been developed for the exercise of these rights, the language, practices, and rituals of contemporary interstate relations dating back to this emergent period. For example, rules, often written in fine detail, emerged about the conduct of war by sovereign states—when it was legal to wage war, what weapons could be used, and even what were the rights and duties of prisoners of war. A similar process occurred in the realm of relations between sovereigns, commonly called diplomatic relations, including rules about the ranks of diplomatic representatives and how they would interact with one another.

Such rules tended to emerge as they were needed. For example, the evolution of the British Empire into the Commonwealth of Nations posed a small definitional problem. Normally, diplomats were designed to be one sovereign state's representative to another sovereign state (both personified by their heads of state). But the symbolic rituals that were developed for this (such as the formal presentation by a new ambassador of a **letter of credence**, a letter from one sovereign to another stating formally that this individual really did represent him or her) did not anticipate the possibility that sovereign states could emerge with the same person as their head of state. This is of course precisely what happened in the case of the Commonwealth, as we noted in Table 9.1 on p. 222. But when states who share Elizabeth II as head of state want to engage in the formalities of sovereign-state relations, the existing rules were not very helpful; obviously the Queen cannot send diplomatic representatives from herself to herself. So a new rule had to be invented: states which share the Queen as head of state conduct their relations on a "government-to-government" basis rather than a "state-to-state" basis. The diplomatic representatives they exchange are thus called **high commissioners** rather than ambassadors—even though they have all the rights and privileges of ambassadors. (Eventually this style for diplomats was adopted by all states in the Commonwealth, even those who do not use the Queen as head of state.)

Sovereignty, in short, gives a state (through its government) admission to something quite similar to an exclusive club. One would not want to push the analogy too far, but there can be little doubt that sovereignty permits entry to a special network of intercourse between governments of states, carried on by state leaders and professional diplomats. A sovereign state's government is invited to have its leaders and diplomats join that network, participating in everything from summit meetings to the day-to-day rounds of the cocktail circuit. A sovereign state is invited to participate in a range of international projects; it is admitted to international and intergovernmental organizations; and it can sign treaties with other states to smooth commercial or other interactions between them. As importantly, "club" membership and access to the network are denied to all those who lack sovereign status. These include international actors of every kind: nonsovereign governments, organizations, firms, and individuals; everyone, in short, except the approximately 190 sovereign states which comprise the club.

But these 190 members of the sovereign club can admit who they want, and on whatever terms they desire; one does not have to be sovereign to join, and mere admission does not automatically confer sovereignty. For example, Hong Kong is not a sovereign state, but its government has been allowed to join the club on a special basis. Operating as "Hong Kong, China," the government of the Hong Kong Special Administrative Region (HKSAR) belongs to a large number of international organizations, including the World Trade Organization (WTO) and the Asian Pacific Economic Cooperation (APEC) forum. It maintains separate offices around the world that enjoy special diplomatic status in some countries, such as Canada. HKSAR officials are treated specially: the Chief Executive is invited on official visits to other countries and given head-of-government treatment, and HKSAR officials are part of the diplomatic circuit, often appearing at functions with their counterparts from the embassy or consulate of the People's Republic of China.[21]

## THE SPECIAL CASE OF IRAQ IN THE 1990S

We have argued to this point that sovereignty must be seen as a set of practices engaged in by governments. Practice inevitably breeds exceptions—anomalies or unusual cases that simply depart from the standard. A good example is Iraq after it was defeated by the U.S.-led international coalition in the Gulf War of 1991: it had its sovereignty and territorial integrity persistently violated by other members of the international community.

As noted in the section on humanitarian intervention above, the United States, Britain, and France imposed no-fly zones in different parts of the country and created safe havens for Kurds. In addition, under Resolution 687, adopted by the Security Council of the United Nations on 3 April 1991 after Iraq's defeat, a UN Special Commission (UNSCOM) was established to supervise the destruction of Iraq's long-range ballistic missiles and the nuclear-biological-chemical (or NBC) weapons of mass destruction accumulated by the regime.

Over the next seven years, under the terms of Resolution 687, teams of officials from both UNSCOM and the International Atomic Energy Agency (IAEA) toured Iraq on numerous occasions. The United States Air Force routinely conducted overflights of Iraqi territory with spy planes on behalf of UNSCOM. UNSCOM teams destroyed Iraqi stockpiles of VX nerve agent; mustard gas; and biological weapons such as botulinum, anthrax, aflatoxin, and Ricin. The teams removed as much nuclear fuel from Iraq as they could find. They destroyed 817 of the 819 SCUD missiles purchased from the Soviet Union in the 1980s. Plants and research institutions capable of producing NBC weapons were dismantled or destroyed.

All these activities were carried out with the nominal acquiesence of the regime in Baghdad. But the Iraqi government persistently objected to the infringements on its sovereignty. Moreover, the Hussein government kept trying to elude efforts to destroy Iraq's NBC capacity. Often the Iraqis were caught openly lying about their weapons systems, and forced to issue retractions or "explanations." On occasion, the United States resorted to threats or military attacks to secure grudging compliance.[22]

But the case of Iraq is an anomaly. No other state has had its formal claims to sovereignty challenged by the international community in quite this way. In part, this is because no other state in the international system has so enthusiastically pursued a NBC weapons acquisition program *and* shown a willingness to use weapons of mass destruction, as Saddam Hussein did against Iranian forces in the Iran-Iraq war or against his own citizens. And no other regime has proved as resistant to international pressure, military attacks, and crushing sanctions as the Hussein government. In part, the treatment of Iraq was the result of a unique conjuncture of forces. The period 1990–91 saw an extraordinary degree of cooperation between the United States and the Soviet Union. As well, Bush was more multilaterally minded than either Ronald Reagan before him or Bill Clinton after him, thus providing an opening for the use of the Security Council. But mostly the anomalous treatment of Iraq in the 1990s flowed from Bush's decision in February 1991 to stop the military advance once Kuwait had been recovered, discussed above.

*"There is no evidence from this one case to conclude that sovereign rights are losing their peremptory standing in international relations."*

For these reasons, it would be premature to draw conclusions about the evolution of the sovereign idea from the case of Iraq. As Robert H. Jackson has noted, while the international community has shown an unprecedented willingness to infringe on Iraq's sovereignty, "There is no evidence from this one case to conclude that sovereign rights are losing their peremptory standing in international relations."[23]

## CONCLUSION

This chapter has explored the assumptions of the sovereign idea in practice. We have looked at how the sovereign ideal assumes that states are indivisible, even though political authority is divided "inside." It assumes that all states are equal, even though it is an equality of right rather than an equality of condition. We explored the realities of sovereignty in practice—how states and governments put into practice the idea that they are the supreme political authorities over a particular geographic space and over an identified group of human beings. We have also looked at the idea that sovereignty assumes admission to a special "club" to which the vast majority of actors in world politics are not admitted. Finally, we examined the special case of Iraq in the 1990s to see if the unprecedented infringements on Iraqi sovereignty suggested that sovereignty as an idea was evolving in a different direction.

But we have not dealt how we know when a state is sovereign, when it enjoys the condition of sovereignty. To this issue we now turn.

## Keyword File

Divisibility of sovereignty

Condominium

Equality of states

Noninterference in domestic affairs

Sectoral free trade

Structural Adjustment Programs

Informal economy

Free trade

Nontariff barriers

*Keiretsu* system

"Fair trade"

Super 301

Voluntary export restraints

Voluntary restraint agreements

*Gaiatsu*

Strategic Impediments Initiative

Genocide

Ethnic cleansing

Crime against humanity

*Realpolitik*

Safe havens

No-fly zone

Operation Provide Comfort

Operation Restore Hope

Peacekeeping

Peacemaking

Peacebuilding

*Persona non grata*

Extraterritoriality

Foreign concessions

Helms–Burton

Territorial integrity

Territorial waters

High seas

Law of the sea

Three-mile limit

Exclusive Economic Zone

Maritime states

Coastal states

Land-locked and geographically disadvantaged states

Straight baseline

International strait

Passport control

*Jus legationis*

*Jus tractatuum*

*Jus belli*

Letter of credence

High commissioner

## For Further Exploration

### HARD COPY

Augustin, John V. "Use of weapons against civil aircraft," *ICAO Journal* 52 (October 1997), 11–13.

Dallin, Alexander. *Black Box: KAL 007 and the Superpowers*. Berkeley, CA: University of California Press, 1985.

Boutros-Ghali, Boutros. *An Agenda for Peace: Preventative Diplomacy, Peacemaking and Peacekeeping*. New York: United Nations, 1992.

Greenwood, Christopher. "Is there a right of humanitarian intervention?" *The World Today* 49 (February 1993).

Klotz, Audie. *Norms in International Relations: The Struggle against Apartheid*. Ithaca, NY: Cornell University Press, 1995.

Kuper, Leo. *Genocide: Its Political Use in the Twentieth Century*. New Haven, CT: Yale University Press, 1981.

Roberts, Adam. "Humanitarian war: military intervention and human rights," *International Affairs* 69 (July 1993), 429–49.

Ruggie, John Gerard. *Winning the Peace: America and World Order in the New Era*. New York: Columbia University Press, 1996.

Sanger, Clyde. *Ordering the Oceans: The Making of the Law of the Sea Treaty*. Toronto: University of Toronto Press, 1987.

Staub, Ervin. *The Roots of Evil: The Origins of Genocide and Other Group Violence*. New York: Cambridge University Press, 1989.

WEBLINKS

**http://www.icrc.org/icrcnews/247a.htm**

Site focusing on humanitarian law maintained by the International Committee of Red Cross

**http://www.ita.doc.gov/**

Site of the International Trade Administration of the U.S. Department of Commerce; information on trade statistics and U.S. trade policy

**http://www.spfo.unibo.it/spolfo/ILMAIN.htm**

University of Bologna's research guide to international law; jumping-off point for human rights, air and space law, law of the sea information

**http://www.un.urg/Depts/dpko/**

Site of the UN's Department of Peacekeeping Operations: full listing of all UN peacekeeping operations, including useful information on each

## Notes to Chapter 10

1. Kim Richard Nossal, "Institutionalization and the pacific settlement of interstate conflict: the case of Canada and the International Joint Commission," *Journal of Canadian Studies* 18 (Winter 1983–84), 75–87.

2. See Timothy M. Shaw and E. John Inegbedion, "The marginalization of Africa in the new world (dis)order," and Sandra Whitworth, "Theory as exclusion: gender and international political economy," both in Richard Stubbs and Geoffrey R.D. Underhill, *Political Economy and the Changing Global Order* (London, New York, Toronto: Macmillan, St Martin's, McClelland and Stewart, 1994), 121 and 397–98; also see Jeanne Vickers, *Women and War* (London: Zed Books, 1993), 41

3. Quoted in Pierre Martin, "The politics of international structural change: aggressive uni-lateralism in American trade policy," in Stubbs and Underhill, *Political Economy and the Changing Global Order*, 439.

4. See, for example, Leonard J. Schoppa, "Two-level games and bargaining outcomes: why *gaiatsu* succeeds in Japan in some cases but not others," *International Organization* 47 (Summer 1993), 353–86; Frank K. Upham, "Retail convergence: the Structural Impediments Initiative and the regulation of the Japanese retail industry," in Suzanne Berger and Ronald Dore, eds., *National Diversity and Global Capitalism* (Ithaca, NY: Cornell University Press, 1996), 263–97.

5. Quoted in Miles Kahler, "Trade and domestic differences," in Berger and Dore, eds., *National Diversity and Global Capitalism*, 316.

6. John Gerard Ruggie, *Winning the Peace: America and World Order in the New Era* (New York: Columbia University Press, 1996), 126.

7. William A. Niskanen, "The bully of world trade," *Orbis* 33 (Fall 1989), 531–38.

8. See Audie Klotz, *Norms in International Relations: The Struggle against Apartheid* (Ithaca: Cornell University Press, 1995).

9. For example, James Mayall, "Nonintervention, self-determination, and the 'new world order,'" *International Affairs* 67 (July 1991).

10. Quoted in Marrack Goulding, "The evolution of United Nations peacekeeping," *International Affairs* 69 (July 1993), 459.

11. Quoted in George F. Will, "America's inoculation by Somalia," *Newsweek*, (6 September 1993), 62.

12. Rosalyn Higgins, "The new United Nations and the former Yugoslavia," *International Affairs* 69 (July 1993).

13. Gerald B. Helman and Steven R. Ratnor, "Saving failed states," *Foreign Policy* 89 (Winter 1992–93), 3–20.

14. The speech is reprinted in Arthur E. Blanchette, *Canadian Foreign Policy, 1966–1976* (Toronto: Gage, 1980), 304.

15. The phrase is usually attributed to John Herz, "Rise and demise of the territorial state," *World Politics* 9 (July 1957).

16. For accounts of this incident, see Alexander Dallin, *Black Box: KAL 007 and the Superpowers* (Berkeley: University of California Press, 1985); Seymour M. Hersch, *"The Target Is Destroyed": What Really Happened to Flight 007 and What America Knew About It* (New York: Vintage, 1986).

17. United Nations, General Assembly, 22d session, A/6695, 18 August 1967: "Declaration and treaty concerning the reservation exclusively for peaceful purposes of the sea-bed and the ocean floor underlying the seas beyond the limits of present national jurisdiction, and the use of their resources in the interests of mankind."

18. See Franklyn Griffiths, ed., *Politics of the Northwest Passage* (Montreal and Kingston: McGill-Queen's University Press, 1987).

19. See Donald Cameron Watt, "To sign or not to sign: the debate in Britain on the Law of the Sea Convention," *International Journal* 38 (Summer 1983), 493–506.

20. Christopher Kirkey, "Smoothing troubled waters: the 1988 Canada-United States Arctic cooperation agreement," *International Journal* 50 (Spring 1995), 401–26.

21. See Kim Richard Nossal, "A high degree of ambiguity: Hong Kong as an international actor after 1997," *Pacific Review* 10:1 (1997), 84–103.

22. The best source for this episode is United Nations, *The United Nations and the Iraq-Kuwait Conflict, 1990–1996*, Blue Book Series, vol. 9 (New York: Department of Public Information, 1996).

23. Robert H. Jackson, "Armed humanitarianism," *International Journal* 48 (Autumn 1993), 594.

CHAPTER ⟨ 11 ⟩

# *The* Key

# *to the* Club:

# Determining Sovereignty

## INTRODUCTION

How do we know when a state is sovereign? In other words, how does this entity—this "government-ruling-people-within-a-defined-territory"—actually acquire the sovereignty that thereby transforms it into a sovereign state? How does a state get through what Öyvind Österud has evocatively called the "narrow gate" that blocks the way to sovereign statehood?[1] In other words, what is the "key" that gets a state admitted to the "club" of sovereign states?

### POSSESSING SOVEREIGNTY?

We can readily see all the other three attributes of the Westphalian state: people, territory, and government. They are tangible and objective, able to be seen, touched, and measured. Can sovereignty's existence be determined in a similar fashion? The short answer is no. Sovereignty may be something that one *has*, but it cannot be seen in such an objective fashion. For example, we talk of a state *having* supreme political power over citizens, in just the way suggested by Jean Bodin, whose views on sovereignty we explored in Chapter 9. However, merely having supreme political power over a people or a territory is neither a necessary nor a sufficient condition for sovereign statehood.

Consider the polity that calls itself the Republic of China on Taiwan (ROC). This polity clearly has all of the objective attributes of statehood: it has a defined territory, it has 21.3 million people who live on the island of Taiwan, and it has a government apparatus centred in the capital of Taipei that clearly exercises supreme political authority over these people.

Yet the Republic of China on Taiwan does not have sovereignty. The vast majority of countries do not allow the ROC to maintain diplomatic missions on their territory, for most countries do not maintain formal diplomatic relations with Taiwan. The ROC is not a member of the United Nations or of most other international organizations. It has been admitted to the Asian Development Bank, but only if its officials agree to use "Chinese Taipei" instead of its official name. The ROC attends the annual APEC summit, but is not represented by the head of government. Its officials are routinely excluded from the normal intercourse of other sovereign states: they do not receive invitations to summit meetings or diplomatic cocktail parties. Even ordinary overseas travel can be difficult for its officials. In 1996, for example, the president, Lee Teng-hui, wanted to visit the United States in order to receive an honourary degree. Even though he was travelling in a private capacity, rather than as president, the trip became highly political because of Taiwan's lack of sovereignty.

By the same token, consider the polity that calls itself Sierra Leone. It has the same three attributes that the ROC on Taiwan does: there is a defined territory, there are approximately 4.7 million people within that territory, and there is a government located in the capital of Freetown. That government, however, does not exercise supreme or exclusive political power over all 4.7 million people within the borders of Sierra Leone; indeed, the full control of the government has barely extended outside Freetown for many years. Certainly the government does not exercise a monopoly on the legitimate use of force over the territory that is defined as Sierra Leone. That monopoly has been challenged by rebels, both those spilling over into Sierra Leone from fighting in Liberia and home-grown guerrillas fighting the government in Freetown; peacekeepers from other West African countries; and soldiers employed by the South African transnational security corporation, Executive Outcomes.

Yet Sierra Leone enjoys that fourth attribute of contemporary statehood—sovereignty. It is a member of the United Nations and numerous other international organizations. Most other sovereign states maintain formal diplomatic relations with Sierra Leone, and numerous countries maintain diplomatic representatives in Freetown. Sierra Leone's diplomatic representatives overseas are part of the network in the "club" of sovereign states. This contradiction has led Robert H. Jackson to characterize such countries as **quasi-states**, because they have sovereignty and yet don't.[2]

The way to understand this apparent contradiction is to stop thinking of sovereignty as a *possession* that a state can *have*—like a "key" to the "club"—which implies that sovereignty has an objective quality. Rather, it is more useful to think of sovereignty as a *status* that a state *enjoys*. Status is always defined as what others perceive, and so it is with sovereignty, in this view. The sovereignty of a state lies in what *other states* perceive and do, rather

*Thus, the Republic of China on Taiwan is not sovereign because other states do not regard it as sovereign; Sierra Leone is sovereign because other states have said it is.*

than deriving from any particular attribute of the state (or lack thereof). Thus, the Republic of China on Taiwan is not sovereign because other states do not regard it as sovereign; Sierra Leone is sovereign because other states have said it is.

How does a state acquire sovereign status? First, a state, or more accurately the government of a state, *claims* to exist as a "government-ruling-people-within-a-defined-territory," and *claims* thereby to be a sovereign state—in other words, to be the supreme political authority over all those people within that defined territory. Then, if other states (or again, more accurately, other governments of sovereign states) agree with that claim, the state enjoys sovereign status. Simply put, what gives that entity the additional attribute of sovereignty is how other sovereign states respond to the claim. It all depends on *recognition*.

## CONFERRING SOVEREIGNTY: THE ACT OF RECOGNITION

**Recognition** (sometimes called diplomatic recognition) constitutes a formal action by governments that confers sovereignty on states. The Peace of Westphalia endowed Switzerland, the United Provinces of the Netherlands, and some 300 German princes with sovereignty by *recognizing* their existence as polities organized on sovereign lines (*majestas est summa in cives* and all that). Thereby, the signatories to the Peace promised to treat them as sovereigns. And what the Peace of Westphalia did for Switzerland has been done, either as a formal act or by practice, for every other sovereign state in the world.

Acts of recognition come in two distinct forms. One is the act of recognition of a *state*. When a new state proclaims its existence, governments of other sovereign states around the world have to make a decision: should they recognize this new entity, which calls itself a state, as sovereign? The other form is the recognition of a new *government* of a state. In other words, when governments change, other governments have to ask themselves, "Do we accept this government as the legitimate and sovereign ruler of this state?"

Having to respond to these two claims provides a range of possibilities. For example, it is possible to recognize the state but not the government of that state. However, if one does not recognize the state, then, *ipso facto*, one does not recognize the government of that state; likewise, it is not theoretically possible to recognize a government without also implicitly recognizing the state which it claims to govern, since the state presupposes the existence of a government. Indeed, as we will see below, this is why states pay such close attention to who talks to whom in international affairs.

The decisions that other states make on these two forms of recognition depend entirely on politics; there is nothing automatic or mechanistic about recognition. On the one hand, the creation of a new state or a change in government may not be a problem; recognition may flow readily. On the other hand, the issue of recognition may become more political and hence more problematic.

*Figure 11.1* • **THE RECOGNITION CONTINUUM**

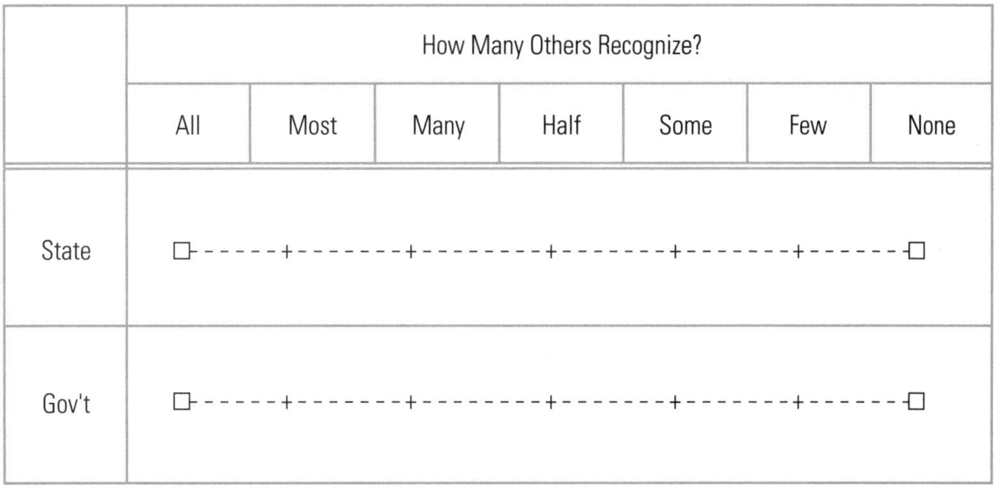

| | How Many Others Recognize? | | | | | | |
|---|---|---|---|---|---|---|---|
| | All | Most | Many | Half | Some | Few | None |
| State | □- - - - - +- - - - - - - +- - - - - - - +- - - - - - +- - - - - - +- - - - - -□ | | | | | | |
| Gov't | □- - - - - +- - - - - - - +- - - - - - - +- - - - - - +- - - - - - +- - - - - -□ | | | | | | |

It is therefore useful to think of the recognition of new states or new governments that have come to power as occurring on a continuum (see Figure 11.1). At one end are the states or governments that were widely accepted as sovereign by virtually all other states soon after they claimed sovereign independence or came to power. At the other end of the continuum are states that have declared themselves sovereign, or governments which have come to power, but neither are recognized by other states. At the extreme ends of the continuum, there is sufficient agreement among states that recognition and nonrecognition are virtually nonpolitical. In between these ends, however, is the messy, and highly political, middle.

## New States

When created, most states are readily welcomed to what is often called the "community of states" by the vast majority of other sovereign states. Thus, for example, when the British Raj ("rule") on the Indian subcontinent dissolved, with Britain formally granting independence to India and Pakistan on 15 August 1947, to Burma (now Myanmar) on 4 January 1948, and to Ceylon (now Sri Lanka) on 4 February 1948, recognition was immediate and virtually universal: the vast majority of other sovereign states accorded these new states recognition. This is done either *explicitly*, through a formal declaration, or simply by treating the new state as sovereign, such as exchanging ambassadors. This is an *implicit* recognition that a state regards the new state as a member of the "club" of sovereign states. Indeed, the vast majority of the other 190 states in the system began their "sovereign lives" in this uncomplicated way.

## Ignored States

At the other end of the continuum are those states which declare themselves sovereign but which virtually no one recognizes—**ignored states**, such as Manchukuo in the 1930s,

Buganda and Rhodesia in the 1960s, and the South African homelands in the late 1970s and early 1980s.

The state of Manchukuo (literally "country of the Manchus") was created by the Japanese after the "Mukden Incident" of September 1931. This incident provided the excuse for the conquest of all Manchuria (see the Focus on p. 263), which the Japanese then tried to legitimize by setting up a new state. They persuaded the last emperor of the Qing dynasty in China, Puyi, to become the "chief executive" of a new state that was declared on 18 February 1932. When he was forced to abdicate in 1912 following the republican revolution of 1911, Puyi was only six years old; at the age of 25, he became head of the new Manchu state.

Japan, of course, immediately recognized Manchukuo. And eventually, when Japan signed the Anti-Comintern Pact in 1936 with Nazi Germany and thus aligned itself with the so-called Axis powers (named for the Berlin-Rome "axis"), both Italy and Germany recognized the state. But El Salvador was the only other country in the world to extend recognition, which it did in 1934.*

Buganda and Rhodesia provide good examples of what can happen to unilateral declarations of independence. Buganda was a tribal kingdom within the British colony of Uganda, under the rulership of its own king or *kabaka*. In 1960, the British were preparing to give independence to Uganda. Not wanting to be submerged within a larger Uganda, the *kabaka*, Sir Edward Frederick Mutesa II, declared independence for the Kingdom of Buganda. Not a single state in the international system recognized the declaration, and Sir Edward had to content himself with a compromise under which Buganda was forced to enter a Ugandan federation, albeit with greater autonomy. Although Sir Edward was subsequently elected president of the new federation, he and Bugandan autonomy lasted merely three years. In 1966, he was overthrown in a coup and Bugandan autonomy was brought to an end.

It was a similar story in Rhodesia, which had been a self-governing British colony since 1923. Dominated by white settlers, its government pressed Britain for independence in the early 1960s, but the government in London refused on the grounds that no provisions were being made for political participation by the black majority. As a result, on 11 November 1965, the white-minority government of Ian Smith issued a **unilateral declaration of independence** (UDI)—in other words, without the consent of Britain. Once again, not a single government recognized the new Rhodesian state. Eventually, the white-minority regime capitulated, and on 17 April 1980, the state of Zimbabwe was declared. Unlike UDI, however, this declaration was met with virtually universal recognition.

---

* It is perhaps not surprising that El Salvador aligned itself with an outcast state, for Gen. Maximiliano Hernández Martínez, who had come to power in a *coup d'état* in 1931, was himself an outcast. Because of his ruthless killings of political opponents, his regime was not recognized by either the United States or his Central American neighbours. El Salvador also maintained close relations with both Germany and Italy because the citizens of those countries had considerable investments in the Salvadoran economy.

Japanese soldiers in China in the 1930s

# FOCUS

### The "Mukden Incident"

The "Mukden Incident" marked the beginning of the Japanese attempt to conquer China in the 1930s. It had its origins in the desire of some Japanese army officers and industrialists to extend Japanese control over Manchuria, a manifestation of nationalism discussed in more detail in Chapter 13. Japanese businesses owned key railways and the Japanese government controlled much of the Liaodong peninsula (which it called Kwantung), including the cities of Lüshun (formerly Port Arthur), a key Japanese naval base, and Dalian (or in Japanese, Dairen), a manufacturing centre and gateway to the mineral wealth of Manchuria.

A number of officers in the Japanese Kwantung army were itching for an excuse to conquer all of Manchuria; the Japanese government in Tokyo, by contrast, was more hesitant. In September 1931, the War Ministry was about to order the Kwantung army to cease its provocations. Commanders in Lüshun, however, were aware of these orders, and so decided to create the excuse themselves. On 18 September 1931, they blew up a stretch of railway at Mukden, blamed the blast on Chinese nationalists, and launched a full-scale attack on Mukden. The commander of Japanese forces in Korea decided on his own initiative to send forces into Manchuria. By the end of 1931, all of Manchuria was under Japanese control.

Transkei, Ciskei, Bophuthatswana, and Venda fared only marginally better than Buganda and Rhodesia: at least one state recognized them as sovereign. These were four former **bantustans** (homelands) of the Bantu, the dominant language group in South Africa. "Homelands" were the integral component of how the races were kept apart under apartheid in South Africa before 1994. All blacks, no matter where they lived or worked in South Africa, were classified by the state as belonging to one of 10 different ethnic groups. Each group was assigned to its own territory, usually consisting of unconnected patches of some of South Africa's poorest land. The members of each bantustan had dual citizenship, their group's and South African. Under the homelands scheme, each bantustan would eventually be given self-governing status, and then full independence. Importantly, when this happened, members of independent homelands would cease to be South African citizens. It should be noted that although they were classified as belonging to a particular homeland, the majority of blacks did not actually eke out their existence in the homelands; for example, three-quarters of the two million South Africans classified as citizens of Ciskei lived and worked outside that homeland. By the early 1980s, nine of the 10 homelands had been given self-governing status; and four of those nine had moved to full independence. Transkei had declared its independence in October 1976, Bophuthatswana in December 1977, Venda in September 1979, and Ciskei in December 1981.

The homelands policy was, in fact, an elaborate political sleight-of-hand designed to eliminate international criticism of the policies of apartheid that barred blacks from political participation. The policy was supposed to work like this: all blacks, no matter where they actually lived and worked in South Africa, were deemed to be members of one of the homelands. Once their homeland became independent, they would cease to be South African citizens but instead citizens of another sovereign state, and thus only resident aliens in South Africa. Since, as noted in Chapter 9, no country in the international system allows noncitizens to vote, no country could possibly criticize South Africa for excluding all resident aliens (as blacks would become) from voting. Thus, criticism would have to cease.

*Thus, when each of the four homelands declared their independence, the declarations were met with studied indifference by the rest of the international community.*

Needless to say, every state in the international system saw this scheme for what it was—they knew that if they recognized the independent homelands, they would be legitimizing apartheid. Thus, when each of the four homelands declared their independence, the declarations were met with studied indifference by the rest of the international community. The only state in the international system to recognize them as sovereign states was the Republic of South Africa.

At this end of the continuum we must also include failed secessions. Secession involves a group within an existing sovereign state which tries to create a new state over the objections of the existing sovereign.[3] A number of secessionist movements failed to secure recognition before being defeated by force. This was the fate of the Confederate States of America, the group of slave-holding states which seceded from the United States in February 1861. Following the outbreak of the civil war and the blockade of the south by the Union, the new Confederate government immediately despatched envoys to Britain, France, Belgium, and the pope in Rome to seek recognition and support for breaking the blockade. They believed that Europeans were sufficiently dependent on southern cotton that they would recognize the new republic. On their way to the continent, the British foreign minister received the envoys, albeit informally. In France, Napoleon III promised them that France would recognize the Confederacy if Britain did. But nowhere was there any support for recognition; indeed, back in London, the British government refused to talk to the emissaries. The Confederacy survived until its defeat by Union forces in April 1865 without a single country recognizing its existence.

The fate of the Bougainville rebellion provides a contemporary example of a secessionist state declaring itself without achieving sovereign recognition by any other state in the international system. A dispute over mining erupted on the island of Bougainville in Papua New Guinea (PNG) in May 1989, and subsequently blossomed into a full-scale rebellion. A former land surveyor, Francis Ona, organized a Bougainville Revolutionary Army. On 17 May 1990, he declared the independence of Meekamuii, with himself as president of the Bouganville Interim Government (BIG). The PNG government responded to the rebellion by a combination of tactics, including bilateral negotiation, political reforms, and military action (including an abortive scheme to hire foreign mercenaries to reestablish control). The rebellion caused a dispute between PNG and the Solomon Islands, which borders Bougainville (Bougainville is geologically the largest of the Solomon Islands group, even though it is part of PNG). PNG accused the Solomons of providing arms and safe havens to the rebels; the Solomon Islands accused PNG of launching raids into Solomons territory. Indeed, the Solomon Islands is the only government that came close to implicit recognition of the Bougainville rebels: in 1991, a Solomons minister declared his support for Bougainville independence or incorporation into the Solomon Islands, and the prime minister, Solomon Mamaloni, expressed support for the secession in a private letter that was leaked. But that was the extent of it; most countries regarded Meekamuii and BIG with indifference.

All of the above cases are the easy ones. It is not hard to conclude that India's sovereignty flows from the overwhelming recognition of the Indian state; it is not hard to conclude that Venda had no sovereignty during its few years as a polity claiming to be a sovereign state. The cases in the messy middle of the continuum are, by contrast, much more difficult. What happens, for example, when a new state is declared and some states decide to recognize its existence and others do not?

### Acquiring Sovereignty By Degrees: Successful Secessions

As noted above, the Confederate States of America lived its brief life without being recognized by a single state. At the end it even promised to free all the slaves in return for British recognition. But it sits at the polar end of our continuum because it failed on the battlefield; had the Confederacy fought the Union to a draw, recognition and sovereignty would likely have followed—eventually.

By contrast, the United States of America, itself originally a secessionist state, sits at the other end of our continuum precisely because it was successful against the British.

Recognition by other countries, particularly by the defeated sovereign, tended to come slowly. For example, the American colonists issued their declaration of independence from British sovereignty on 4 July 1776; the British did not formally recognize the new state for seven years—until it signed the Peace of Paris on 3 September 1783. But in the end, Britain and all other states in the system recognized the United States, and every state that has been created since has extended recognition.

The different experiences of the Union and the Confederacy point out how sovereignty tends to be acquired when a secessionist war is fought. All secessions pose an initial dilemma for other states in the system: they have to decide whether to recognize the new entity, and if so, when. They have to decide whether to sit on the sidelines, waiting to see whether the secessionists are successful, or to recognize sooner rather than later, knowing that recognition or its denial can occasionally tip the balance. Victory or defeat on the battlefield usually determines which way the flow of recognitions will go: if defeat looms, other states will sit on their hands; if victory seems assured, there is usually a **bandwagon effect** at the end, with recognition by several states precipitating a rush of recognitions.

At times, however, the acquisition of sovereign recognition can be exceedingly slow. Consider the states that emerged from the collapse of the Spanish empire in Latin America in the early 19th century. It took almost a century for the states that emerged from the viceroyalties of New Spain, New Granada, Peru, and La Plata to be recognized after the outbreak of revolt and their formal declarations of independence. Venezuela declared itself independent in 1811; Mexico in 1814;* the United Provinces of the Río de la Plata (from which Argentina, Uruguay and Paraguay eventually emerged) in 1816; Chile in 1818; and Gran Colombia, a union of New Granada, Venezuela, and Ecuador, in 1819 (it would eventually become Colombia, Panama, Ecuador, and Venezuela). In 1821, independence was declared by Peru (which included Alto Peru, later to become Bolivia in 1825) and the smaller states in the Captaincy-General of Guatemala (Guatemala, El Salvador, Honduras, Nicaragua, and Costa Rica).

But international recognition of all these declarations of new states was slow in coming. For example, after the Spanish were ousted in Venezuela in April 1810, one of the leaders of the independence movement, Simón Bolívar, was immediately sent to Britain to ask for recognition. The government in London chose to wait until the political situation had stabilized. Finally, fearing the possibility that the French might try to restore Spanish power in Latin America, the British foreign secretary, George Canning, informed the French that Britain would not tolerate any "foreign force" trying to subjugate the Spanish possessions. London recognized Gran Colombia (as Venezuela had become in 1819) in 1824. The United States recognized Gran Colombia in 1822. In his annual message to Congress on 2 December 1823, President James Monroe implicitly recognized the sovereignty of the new states in his declaration that the United States would regard the interference of European

---

* It should be noted that a rebellion started in Mexico on 16 September 1810, and that is the date celebrated as Independence Day in Mexico. However, that rebellion was quickly crushed, and it was not until the emergence of a second rebellion that a constitution was drawn up and an independent state declared.

powers in the affairs of the western hemisphere "as dangerous to our peace and security," a declaration that has become known as the **Monroe Doctrine**.

The Spanish, for their part, were less forgiving and less forthcoming. Spain did not recognize any of the new states until it recognized Mexico in 1839, and it was not until the recognition of Honduras in 1895 that the government in Madrid finally acknowledged the last of the states that had won their independence during the Wars of Independence.

### Most, But Not All: The Case of Israel

The state of Israel emerged from a unique combination of imperial lassitude, international involvement, and warfare. The origins of the contemporary state can be traced back to the Zionist movement, founded in 1897, that sought a Jewish homeland in Palestine, then part of the Ottoman Empire. Relatively few Jews lived there, about 85 000 in 1914. The British government, in an effort to gain Jewish support during the First World War, sent a letter on 2 November 1917 from the foreign secretary, Arthur Balfour, to a British Zionist leader, declaring support for the Zionist idea. However, London noted that "nothing shall be done which may prejudice the civil and religious rights of the existing non-Jewish communities in Palestine."

After the First World War, the Ottoman Empire was dismembered and its various parts given to the different victorious countries to administer as "mandates" by the League of Nations, discussed in more detail in Chapter 13. Palestine was given to Britain, and the Balfour Declaration of 1917, as it came to be known, was incorporated into the terms of the mandate. During the interwar period (1919–1939), Jewish emigration to Palestine increased, particularly after the rise of the Nazis to power in Germany in 1933. The indigenous Arab population became increasingly concerned, and a general Arab revolt in 1936 took the British authorities three years to suppress.

The pressure to create a Jewish homeland in Palestine dramatically increased in the wake of the Holocaust. The British, seemingly tiring of the effort to manage the contending forces, eventually turned the issue over to the United Nations. On 29 November 1947, the UN approved a resolution partitioning Palestine into a Jewish state and an Arab state, linked by an economic union, with the holy areas of Jerusalem and Bethlehem established as international enclaves. Arabs in both Palestine and the surrounding Arab states rejected the plan. For their part, the British declared that they would simply leave at the end of their mandate on 15 May 1948, and would not implement the UN decision by force. Palestine was plunged into virtual civil war, with both Arabs and Jews engaging in terrorist attacks on each other and on the British. On 14 May 1948, the British departed and the Jewish leadership proclaimed the state of Israel.

Recognition of the new state came unevenly. The United States recognized Israel immediately; the Soviet Union recognized it on 17 May. Canada's recognition came in an indirect form: by voting in favour of Israel's admission to the United Nations on 11 May 1949, Canada accorded the new state recognition. For many years, Arab states remained in a perpetual state of war with Israel, fighting four general wars (1948, 1956, 1967, and 1973), imposing a worldwide economic boycott against "Zionists," and some vowing to eradicate Israel and push the Jews into the sea. Throughout this period, Arab states consistently refused to recognize Israel's existence. Not even Israel's name could be mentioned; when Arab states wanted to refer to Israel, they called it "the Zionist entity."

The slow process of peacebuilding in the Middle East undid some of the nonrecognition. In November 1977, when Anwar al-Sadat, president of Egypt, made his surprise visit to Israel to pursue a peace accord, he implicitly recognized the state of Israel; in November 1988, the Palestine Liberation Organization (PLO) formally recognized Israel's sovereignty; in July 1994, Jordan extended recognition.

## Sovereignty Stalled: Failed Secessions

Sometimes, wars of independence produce some recognitions by other states, but nonetheless fail. This was the fate of Biafra and Timor. Biafra emerged from the collapse of political order in Nigeria and the outbreak of warfare between the Ibos of eastern Nigeria and other groups. The war was triggered by a series of coups in 1966 that resulted in the slaughter of thousands of members of the Ibo tribe in other parts of the country, and the flood of perhaps a million Ibos back to the Ibo-dominated eastern region of Nigeria. The failure of negotiations in 1967 to settle the intertribal and interregional differences led to a declaration of independence by the Republic of Biafra on 30 May 1967, with Lt. Col. Odumegwu Ojukwu as head of state. The Nigerian government immediately declared war on the break-away state. Biafra's declaration was greeted by silence from the international community. Just four states—Tanzania, Gabon, Côte d'Ivoire, and Zambia—recognized Biafra, and not until the spring of 1968. To be sure, a number of states supported the Biafran struggle. The People's Republic of China provided the regime with rhetorical support but little else. France also supported Biafra: unlike China, Paris actually arranged for arms to be shipped to the rebels, but like China, it never recognized the break-away regime. The white-minority regimes in southern Africa—South Africa and Rhodesia—and Portugal (which at this point still had two colonies in southern Africa, Angola and Mozambique) also supported Biafra, but for different reasons. They were happy to be able to try and undermine African unity and also to be able to reinforce for their own white minorities the message that black majority regimes were unstable and murderous.

The rest of the international community either supported the federal Nigerian government—often selling them arms—or ignored the Biafrans. Some went to considerable lengths to deny the secessionist government even the legitimacy of mentioning its name. When Canada's prime minister, Pierre Elliott Trudeau, was asked what Ottawa's policy toward Biafra was, he feigned ignorance. "Where's Biafra?" he asked. Trudeau, of course, was taking no chances: as the prime minister of a federal state where the *Front de Libération du Québec* (FLQ) was placing bombs in mailboxes in support of Québec secession from the Canadian federation, he understood full well that extending Canadian recognition to a secessionist regime ran the risk of having others extend recognition to secessionists in Canada. The same thinking underlay the support of the vast majority of African states for Nigeria. The total lack of support from the international community was too much for the Biafrans to sustain: the regime was forced to surrender in January 1970, but not before Biafrans had suffered an estimated 1.5 million casualties, many from starvation.

East Timor illustrates the problem of partial recognition. In 1974, a bloodless military coup in Portugal brought an end to four decades of civilian dictatorship. The new regime in Lisbon decided to allow the various Portuguese colonies around the world to decide their own futures. In East Timor, there were three main factions: one group favoured annexation to Indonesia; another favoured independence, but with a general pro-Indonesian and pro-American tilt; and the third, the *Frente Revolucionário do Timor Leste Independente*, or FRETILIN, was a left-wing group with ties to the Soviet Union. In 1975, after the pro-American group joined the pro-Indonesian faction, fighting broke out in East Timor; by September, FRETILIN controlled much of the territory, including the capital of Dili. As the civil war intensified, FRETILIN declared the Democratic Republic of East Timor an independent state on 28 November 1975. The new state was immediately recognized by the Soviet Union and a number of its allies. One week later, on 7 December 1975, the Indonesian government launched a large-scale invasion of Timor, capturing Dili, setting up a provisional government, and eventually annexing East Timor as a province of Indonesia. However, the annexation did not bring an end to the conflict: FRETILIN and the Indonesian armed forces continued to engage in a protracted civil war.

This survey of what can happen to new states which are recognized by some states at the outset but not by others leaves us no closer to a definitive answer on when precisely a state acquires sovereignty through the act of recognition. Unfortunately, there is no answer to that question. If a state does not have a core of supporters willing to help sustain it, it will find survival difficult, particularly if it faces military action, as both Biafra and East Timor did. By contrast, the case of Israel demonstrates that a state which has the backing of states willing to sustain it can overcome the opposition of those states wishing to deny it sovereign status.

## New Governments

A similar process obtains when governments of sovereign states change. With each change, all other governments must decide, at least nominally, whether they accept the new government as the legitimate sovereign of the state. In the vast majority of cases, the new government is immediately accepted; other governments do not even bother to express their acceptance formally. Rather, implicit acceptance is the norm: a congratulatory phone call from one leader to another following an election; a diplomatic note on some matter sent to the new government; a positive statement to the media about the new government—this generally is all that is necessary to "recognize" a change in government. As with new states, however, some changes can prove thorny, particularly those that occur as a result of violence, such as a foreign invasion, a *coup d'état*, or a civil war. In these cases, governments tend to be more cautious about recognizing the new regime.

Normally, other governments will wait to see whether a group that seizes power has actually been able to oust the old government. Such caution avoids the embarrassing fate of Barbara MacDougall, Canada's foreign minister, who greeted the *coup d'état* against Mikhail S. Gorbachev, president of the Soviet Union, on 19 August 1991 with a statement that amounted to a recognition of the coup's leaders. By 21 August, however, the new "government" was in a shambles. Some of its leaders remained in a drunken stupor; one committed suicide; and others were arrested by forces loyal to Boris Yeltsin, the president of Russia, who organized resistance to the coup.

Likewise, governments tend to refuse to recognize the new authorities until they have been able to organize a government. Thus, for example, the Taliban, the radical Islamic group that seized the Afghani capital of Kabul in September 1996, has had a difficult time securing international recognition. This was mainly because Taliban members have not organized themselves into a normal governing apparatus. Rather, after September 1996, governance in Taliban-controlled parts of Afghanistan was dominated by attempts to (re)create a "pure Islamic society." The Taliban mullahs issued decrees demanding, for example, that all men had to grow beards and wear turbans and that women could not go to work or school, could not go outside the house without an approved reason, and could not talk to any male who was not a blood relative. The General Department for the Preservation of Virtue and the Elimination of Vice sent young men armed with Kalashnikov submachine guns around the streets of Kabul to make sure all the decrees were being obeyed. They conducted "beard checks" on males and made sure that women were not wearing white socks, decreed by the Taliban to be sexually provocative. During the year after the takeover, revenue-generation for the new regime was largely limited to seizing men during beard checks and holding them in freight containers until they were ransomed by relatives. As one bureaucrat of the former government noted, the Taliban did not seem interested in establishing a government: "All the Taliban can offer is beards, turbans, and Kalashnikovs."[4] Few governments have recognized the Taliban as the legitimate government of Afghanistan.

*"All the Taliban can offer is beards, turbans, and Kalashnikovs."*

## Recognition in Practice: The Case of China

But the thorniness of recognition is not just because of the uncertainty that can accompany violent changes of government, as the case of China illustrates. By the late 1940s, a civil war had been raging off and on for 20 years between the Chinese Communists under Mao Zedong and the Nationalists (Kuomintang, or KMT) under Chiang Kai-shek. In 1949, the Communist armies launched a huge offensive which resulted in the seizure of Beijing and other major cities. On 1 October 1949, Mao declared that the People's Republic of China was henceforth the legitimate government of all China. Unfortunately for Mao and the PRC, the KMT had not been entirely defeated. The United States, which had provided military support to the KMT throughout the 1940s, had helped to evacuate Chiang and the Nationalist government to the Chinese province of Taiwan, which the communists, who had neither air power nor any naval capacity, had no way of seizing. The KMT set up shop in what they called the "temporary capital" of Taipei, still declaring that they were the rightful government of all China.

Thus by 1 October 1949, other governments were faced with two governments, both claiming to be the Chinese government. Neither government controlled all the territory that it claimed to be rightfully its own: the communists did not control Taiwan and the KMT did not control the mainland. Moreover, the new communist government, which was deeply anti-American because of the aid that had been provided to the KMT, proved not at all inclined to play by the rules of the diplomatic game. Soldiers of the People's Liberation Army (PLA) trashed a number of diplomatic establishments and roughed up foreign diplomats.

Notwithstanding these problems, some governments made the switch immediately, recognizing the new communist government and "**de-recognizing**" (i.e., officially withdrawing recognition from) the KMT: the Soviet Union on 2 October, and its East European allies, Bulgaria, Romania, Poland, Hungary, and Czechoslovakia on the 3d and 4th. Yugoslavia followed on 5 October, Burma on 9 December. Britain and other members of the Commonwealth discussed what to do at the Commonwealth Prime Minister's meetings in December 1949. A split emerged as some, such as Britain, India, and Pakistan, favoured immediate recognition and others, including Australia and Canada, favoured a delay. As a result of that meeting, India moved to recognize on 30 December, Pakistan on 4 January, and Ceylon and Britain on 6 January. By the end of January, four of the five Nordic states (Norway, Denmark, Finland, and Sweden) had recognized Beijing, as had both Israel and Afghanistan.

The role of the United States government in the case of China illustrates the essentially political nature of recognition. For many countries, recognition is assumed to have no normative content: by recognizing a government, one is not passing moral judgment on the goodness or badness of that government. One may not like the government, which may be controlled by a band of murderous thugs; one may even be at war with that government. One simply recognizes the government in power simply because it is in power.

For some countries, by contrast, the act of recognition is a deeply normative act. By admitting the government to the sovereign club, recognition confers the legitimacy of that club on the regime. Recognition thus implies approval of the regime; **nonrecognition** signals disapproval. The United States took this approach to the Chinese communist government. It refused to recognize the PRC government—not because it believed that the PRC did not control mainland China, but because it did not like the regime. Moreover, it put considerable pressure on its friends and allies to refuse to recognize. Most governments in Europe, the Americas, and the South Pacific either agreed with Washington's approach or bowed to American pressure, so that by the time North Korea attacked South Korea in June 1950, most states in the system continued to recognize the KMT.

The Korean War transformed the equation considerably. When the PRC entered that war against the United Nations forces that had been despatched to defend South Korea, it became doubly difficult to resist American demands that Beijing be denied the legitimacy of recognition. In addition, anti-communist voices in the United States were becoming more strident and hysterical. Professional diplomats in the United States Department of State were accused of "losing" China to the communists and were forced to resign from their jobs by an anti-communist movement, known as **McCarthyism** because it was spearheaded by Senator Joseph McCarthy, Republican of Wisconsin. In such a bitter atmosphere, many states simply chose not to risk their relations with the United States by recognizing China.

The government in Beijing thus remained unrecognized by large numbers of countries throughout the 1950s and 1960s. One of the problems was that Beijing put an important condition in the way of recognition: the PRC would refuse to recognize any government that did not acknowledge the PRC's claim to Taiwan. While many governments were interested in recognizing Beijing, they did not want to have to formally acknowledge that the government and people of Taiwan were part of the PRC. One government chose to ignore the PRC threat to refuse to recognize governments which did not acknowledge their sovereignty over Taiwan: Charles de Gaulle, the president of France, simply issued a unilateral declaration recognizing the PRC as the government of China.

In the late 1960s, a formula was discovered that proved to be acceptable to the PRC. In the formal exchange of recognitions, the PRC asserted that Taiwan was a province of China; the other government merely "took note" of this assertion.★

> *"The Chinese government reaffirms that Taiwan is an inalienable part of the territory of the People's Republic of China. The Canadian Government takes note of this position of the Chinese Government."*

The **Canadian formula**—for it was the Canadian foreign minister, Mitchell Sharp, who stumbled on this wording—was the basis for a raft of recognitions that eventually saw the PRC admitted to the United Nations in 1971. The KMT government was forced to give up its seat.

For its part, the United States clung to its policy of non-recognition, despite the initiatives of President Richard Nixon in 1972 to forge a new relationship with the PRC, taking an historic trip to China. But it was not until 1 January 1979, almost 30 years after the communists seized power on the mainland, that the United States officially recognized the People's Republic and de-recognized the Republic of China on Taiwan.

By the late 1990s, nearly 30 states, mostly poorer countries, continue to recognize Taiwan. In some of these cases, recognition is something that can be bought and sold. Both Beijing and Taipei conduct a fierce bidding war for recognition, using development assistance as an inducement. In 1997, Beijing was able to outbid Taiwan for St Lucia's affections, with the government in Castries making the switch in recognition; in September 1997, the five central American countries that recognize Taiwan—Costa Rica, El Salvador, Guatemala, Honduras, and Nicaragua—successfully manoeuvred Taiwan into doubling its development assistance contributions to them.

The China case also underscores one further distinction that must be made about recognition: the difference between *de facto* **recognition** (recognition in fact) and *de jure* **recognition** (recognition in law). While one may be forced to choose whether to recognize a new government, one can often have it both ways by recognizing one government *de jure* (officially or legally) and another government *de facto* (unofficially). Many countries may not have recognized the PRC officially, but they nonetheless dealt with Beijing unofficially, even though to do so was to *de facto* recognize its existence. For example, Canada did not

---

★ The exact wording of the formula in the final communiqué was: "The Chinese Government reaffirms that Taiwan is an inalienable part of the territory of the People's Republic of China. The Canadian Government takes note of this position of the Chinese Government." See B. Michael Frolic, "The Trudeau initiative," in Paul M. Evans and Frolic, eds., *Reluctant Adversaries: Canada and the People's Republic of China, 1949–1970* (Toronto: University of Toronto Press, 1991), 209.

recognize the PRC until October 1970, but it had been doing business with the PRC since the early 1960s. At that time, widespread famines, produced by the failure of an economic policy known as the Great Leap Forward, prompted the PRC government to buy Canadian wheat. Likewise, after Nixon's trip to China, the PRC and the government in Washington established "liaison offices" in each other's capitals that on 1 January 1979 became embassies once sovereign recognition was established.

The possibility of *de facto* recognition permits the conduct of *de facto* relations. And certainly the Republic of China on Taiwan provides an instructive example of how a government can be denied recognition but nonetheless remain relatively active internationally. Although the government in the capital city of Taipei has not been admitted to the "club" of sovereign states, a number of sovereign states nonetheless maintain relations with the ROC on a *de facto* basis. In Taipei, one finds only a handful of diplomatic missions from sovereign states: the apostolic nunciature (as diplomatic missions of the Vatican City State and its government, the *Santa Sede*, or Holy See, are called), plus a number of embassies from Central and Latin American countries.

But one also finds a number of other offices with names like American Institute in Taiwan, Brazil Business Center, Canadian Trade Office, Japan Interchange Association, Malaysian Friendship and Trade Center, and Spanish Chamber of Commerce. These are the **"unofficial" missions** of countries who want to do business and conduct relations with the ROC but recognize the PRC. So a careful fiction is maintained: these are not "official" missions; they are "private" links between Taiwan and foreign individuals, not governments. Often they are technically maintained by a private organization, like a chamber of commerce. But often these offices look just like diplomatic missions: they are laid out with the same security features as real diplomatic missions; they are staffed by professional diplomats technically "on loan" to the chamber of commerce; and these diplomats operate as they would in any other capital city. What is important, however, is that technically there is not a whiff of *de jure* recognition in any of this. As a result, honour is satisfied: the PRC in Beijing has proved willing to look the other way as some 33 countries which conduct sovereign relations with Beijing also conduct *de facto* relations with the ROC.

The same gamesmanship is evident in the annual APEC summit. All the members of APEC believe that it is useful for Taiwan and the PRC to participate in this summit. But how to keep the leaders of the two governments of China from actually confronting each other at the summit? The solution lies in everyone dancing a carefully choreographed minuet. Each year, the host government formally invites leaders of all APEC's member "economies" to attend the summit, including the president of the ROC, Lee Teng-hui, who is invited to attend under the name "Chinese Taipei." And every year, Lee regretfully declines the kind invitation, offering instead to send a trusted confidant in his place. Everyone else happily agrees: Koo Chen-fu of the ROC's Council for Economic Planning and Development will be most welcome as the representative of "Chinese Taipei." Again, honour is satisfied: under this formula, Jiang Zemin, the president of the PRC, is not threatened by the implicit recognition that Lee's presence would signal. Because the ROC is called an "economy" rather than a "state," and participates under a highly ambiguous name rather than its official name, PRC claims to sovereignty are preserved. But the choreography ensures that Taiwan and China can both participate in this important summit, despite their conflicting claims to sovereignty.

We have looked at the case of the recognition of China in some detail because it provides an excellent example of the dynamics of recognition at work. It points out the fundamental lack of agreement between the American view of recognition, which ties recognition to approval, and the view of recognition held by most other countries. It points out some of the difficulties arising from two governments both claiming to be the legitimate authority over the same space and the same people. And it also points out the degree to which sovereignty must be seen as a set of practices conferring a status—which can be an eminently flexible arrangement when governments wish it.

### Governments-in-Exile

In the Chinese case, two governments vie for recognition, each from a securely held territorial base. But governments, to be recognized as governments of states, do not have to actually control any territory. It is enough that they claim to be the rightful government of a piece of territory, and that other governments recognize that claim. To do this, governments can be anywhere. If they are outside the territory they claim to govern, they are called **governments-in-exile**.

Securing recognition for a government-in-exile is exceedingly difficult unless one has a core of backers who are willing to provide, at a very minimum, space to operate, plus crucial diplomatic support. A good example of this is the Cambodian government-in-exile during the 1980s. In April 1975, the Khmer Rouge under Pol Pot seized power in Cambodia and changed the country's name to Democratic Kampuchea. In an effort to "purify" Khmer society, the Khmer Rouge began a policy of genocide (a highly sanitized, but nonetheless chilling, account of the horror of Khmer Rouge rule can be found in the movie *The Killing Fields*). The widespread killings prompted large numbers of Cambodians to flee the country. Partly in response to the press of refugees coming down the Mekong River, partly in response to provocations by the Khmer Rouge, and partly because the Khmer Rouge were backed by China, the Soviet-backed Vietnamese government decided to overthrow the regime in Phnom Penh. In December 1978, Vietnamese forces invaded Democratic Kampuchea; within two weeks, the capital had been seized and a new government had been established. The remnants of the Pol Pot regime retreated to the country's northwest, establishing a government-in-exile in a camp just inside the borders of Thailand. In 1982 this government was broadened to include other Cambodian groups and called the Coalition Government of Democratic Kampuchea (CGDK). Aid was channelled to it from the United States and China through Thailand.

The existence of two rival Cambodian governments posed a rather thorny problem for other governments. Did one support the new government in Phnom Penh, which had been installed by force and moreover was backed by the Vietnamese, recently an enemy of the Americans, and very much an ally of the USSR? Or did one support the CGDK, which included the Pol Pot group that had committed genocide against its own people, but which was opposed to the USSR and Vietnam? The calculation was made more difficult because the governments of the Association of Southeast Asian Nations (ASEAN), worried about Vietnamese expansionism, were keen to oppose Vietnam, regardless of whom they had to ally themselves with to do so.

At least one government, Britain, neatly resolved the problem by withdrawing recognition from the ousted Pol Pot regime but refusing to recognize any other government—on the grounds that no other government deserved recognition. For others, however, the struggle in Cambodia played itself out as a microcosm of the Cold War tensions between the Soviet Union and its allies on the one hand, and their many opponents on the other. In the Asia Pacific in the 1980s, there was a broad anti-Soviet group that included the United States, China, Japan, the countries of ASEAN, and smaller allies of the United States like Australia, Canada, and New Zealand. Cold War alignments dictated which government was recognized: throughout the 1980s, numerous governments associated with the anti-Soviet alliance firmly continued to recognize the genocidal government of Pol Pot, regularly voting to deny the government in Phnom Penh the Cambodian seat at the United Nations and inflicting sanctions against the Vietnamese-backed regime.

Some governments tried to cover their embarrassment at their support of a genocidal government-in-exile by constantly denouncing Pol Pot. This was the Canadian approach, but the government in Ottawa never wavered from its anti-Soviet/anti-Vietnamese position despite its obvious discomfort. For at least one country, the hypocrisy became too much: in Australia, there was growing pressure from domestic opinion and the Australian Labor party opposition to de-recognize the Pol Pot government-in-exile. Within Prime Minister Malcolm Fraser's own Liberal party/Country (now National) party coalition government, the move for de-recognition was championed by Andrew Peacock, the minister for foreign affairs, and some Liberal backbenchers. In February 1981, the government in Canberra took the British course and de-recognized.

But the Australians and the British were almost alone in the anti-Soviet camp. With strong backing from China and the United States, the CGDK survived throughout the 1980s, outliving Soviet involvement in Southeast Asia. When the Soviets effectively withdrew from the region and a peace settlement was reached for Cambodia, the government-in-exile (though not Pol Pot himself) returned to Phnom Penh to rule with the Vietnamese-backed regime in an uneasy coalition that lasted until 1997.

The CGDK demonstrates the importance of international support for the successful functioning of a government-in-exile. Four other examples, outlined in the Focus on p. 276, also illustrate how important it was for these governments-in-exile that states like Britain, India, Jordan, Lebanon, Tunisia, and Algeria provided a base for their activities.

Sometimes efforts to create a government-in-exile founder on divisions within the opposition movement. For example, the Iraqi National Congress was formed in Vienna in June 1992 to overthrow the Iraqi regime of Saddam Hussein. The following year, 170 representatives from virtually every anti-regime group met in Kurdish-controlled cities inside Iraq itself to select a three-member presidential council. However, feuding broke out. Although united in opposition to the regime in power, the members of the coalition had few other commonalities. The INC's divisions became so pronounced that open civil war broke out in 1995. This made efforts to gain recognition even more difficult, for other sovereign governments are hesitant to accord a deeply divided coalition the legitimacy of formal diplomatic recognition.

# FOCUS

*Governments-in-Exile*

## SECOND WORLD WAR

When Europe was overrun by Nazi Germany in 1939 and 1940, the governments of Belgium, Czechoslovakia, Greece, the Netherlands, Norway, Poland, and Yugoslavia moved to London. France was in a special situation: although the Nazis occupied much of France, they allowed a government under Henri Pétain to operate out of Vichy in central France. A French National Committee (known as the Free French) was also established in London.

## TIBET

In October 1950, the Communist Chinese invaded Tibet, bringing to an end nearly 40 years of independent statehood. For the next nine years, an uneasy peace was maintained: Beijing left the traditional spiritual ruler, the Dalai Lama, in place while communist rule was imposed. But the contradictions grew too pronounced, and open rebellion broke out in 1959. Tenzin Gyatso, the 14th Dalai Lama, fled to exile in India where he waged a persistent campaign for the restoration of Tibetan independence; in 1988, he modified this demand to greater autonomy. While the Dalai Lama is not formally recognized as a government-in-exile, his legitimacy was enhanced in 1989 when he won the Nobel Peace Prize. In 1995 and 1996, he travelled extensively in North America and Europe, speaking before the German *Bundestag*, for example.

## PALESTINE LIBERATION ORGANIZATION

The PLO was widely recognized as the "sole legitimate representative of the Palestinian people," in the words of the 1974 summit of Arab states meeting in Rabat, Morocco, although it was not until 1988 that the PLO constituted itself formally as a government-in-exile. Between 1964 and 1988, the PLO with its leader, Yasir 'Arafat, operated as a political movement in a number of different states. In the 1960s, they were hosted by Jordan, but when they used Jordan for guerrilla attacks against Israel, prompting Israeli counter-attacks, King Hussein I expelled them in 1970. They then moved to Lebanon, which quickly disintegrated into civil war and eventually prompted a full-scale invasion by Israel in June 1982. 'Arafat then moved to Tunis, where some Palestinians continued to attract Israeli bombings and assassination teams. The movement became a government when a Palestinian state was declared on 15 November 1988; in April 1989, 'Arafat was selected the first president, which was quickly recognized by over 100 countries. After the PLO renounced terrorism and accepted Israel's right to exist, peace negotiations were held. On 13 September 1993, Israel and the PLO signed an agreement establishing a Palestinian "entity" consisting of the West Bank and Gaza Strip, which had been occupied by Israel after the Six Day War in 1967. On 1 July 1994, 'Arafat and the PLO moved to Gaza City, where the Palestinian Authority was established.

## SAHARAN ARAB DEMOCRATIC REPUBLIC

Polisario (*Frente Popular para la Liberación de Saguia el Hamra y Rio de Oro*) was established in 1973 to gain independence for Spanish Sahara. However, after Spain withdrew, Mauritania and Morocco partitioned the territory, excluding Polisario. It then declared itself the government of the Saharan Arab Democratic Republic, and from the safety of Algeria began to fight a guerrilla war. Some 70 countries recognized the Polisario as the government-in-exile of the SADR, often prompting quarrels at the Organization of African Unity.

Yasir 'Arafat, the PLO Leader. See "Palestine Liberation Organization" in the Focus.

It should be noted that not all opposition groups try to form a government-in-exile. Consider, for example, the opposition that formed against the Sudanese government in the 1990s. In June 1989, the democratically elected government of Sadiq al-Mahdi was overthrown by units of the Sudanese army with the backing of one of the opposition parties, the National Islamic Front (NIF). They installed Lt. Gen. 'Umar Hassan Ahmad al-Bashir as prime minister. The policies pursued by the al-Bashir regime generated considerable opposition. The regime introduced a new penal code based on a fundamentalist interpretation of the *Shari'a*, or Islamic law. It abandoned the efforts of the al-Mahdi government to end the civil war with non-Muslim groups in southern Sudan; it repudiated the ceasefire agreement negotiated with the Sudanese People's Liberation Army (SPLA) under John Garang and reopened hostilities against the south. It pursued a repressive campaign to squelch domestic opposition, periodically arresting al-Mahdi and outlawing any opposition. In February 1992, a loose coalition of a wide range of groups opposed to the regime met in London to form the National Democratic Alliance (NDA). The coalition consists of political parties, trade unions, and military officers opposed to the al-Bashir government. Working mainly in Eritrea, which has given the NDA leadership asylum, it seeks to overthrow of the regime in Khartoum. However, the NDA is not a government-in-exile, and thus does not seek formal diplomatic recognition from other states.

## The Sliding Scale of Sovereign Support

We can best conceive of sovereignty being conferred on states along a continuum, ranging from none at one end to all the other states at the other end. If we divide the continuum into recognition of new states and recognition of changes of government, Figure 11.2 shows how some of the examples we have looked at in this chapter might be displayed. Note that the United States is used as an exemplar of a state and government commanding virtually unanimous recognition.

It should be noted, however, that recognition is always a fluid affair, changing over time. Thus, for example, had we placed the PRC and ROC on the government continuum in 1950, we would have almost precisely the opposite picture that we had in 1990. But, as intimated in the discussion above, there is no magic point on this continuum where one can declare definitively that a state enjoys sovereign status or a government enjoys legitimacy as the government of a sovereign state. Instead, in those cases where the sovereignty of a state or the legitimacy of a government is not universally recognized, we have to use much

*Figure 11.2* • **THE RECOGNITION CONTINUUM APPLIED**

| | How Many Others Recognize? | | | | | | |
|---|---|---|---|---|---|---|---|
| | All | Most | Many | Half | Some | Few | None |
| State | USA | Israel | Palestine | | Timor | Biafra | CSA |
| | | | | | | Manchukuo | Venda |
| Gov't | USG | PRC | PA | SADR | CGDK | ROC | BIG |
| | | | AG-E | | | Taliban | GCSA |

AG-E: Allied governments-in-exile
BIG: Bougainville Interim Government
CGDK: Coalition Government of Democratic Kampuchea
CSA: Confederate States of America
GCSA: Government of the Confederate States of America

PA: Palestinian Authority
PRC: People's Republic of China
ROC: Republic of China on Taiwan
SADR: Saharan Arab Democratic Republic (Western Sahara)
USG: United States Government

more flexible benchmarks to determine sovereignty. For example, one could use membership in the United Nations, which is limited to sovereign states, as such a measure. Does the state in question have sufficient recognition to gain admission to the United Nations, and does a government have the support to retain its seat in the UN?

## SOVEREIGNTY, INDEPENDENCE, AND AUTONOMY

Many people use *sovereignty* and *independence*, which we looked at in Chapter 4, as though these words were interchangeable. But if one does not make careful distinctions between these terms, it is easy to draw the wrong conclusions. Many people appear to believe that sovereignty and independence both mean that a state is able to do precisely what it wants. Based on this view, they believe that when the state is *unable* to do what it wants, or is *prevented* from doing what it wants by another state, somehow that means that the state lacks sovereignty and independence.

As we will see in Chapter 17, this assumption is particularly prevalent in how people think about the impact of the global economy on the contemporary sovereign state. Many agree with Mark Zacher's evocative suggestion that the pillars of the Westphalian temple are decaying.[5] Governments the world over, they argue, try hard, and without much success, to fashion the world to their liking; they try hard to protect the interests of their citizens. Instead, these governments that are supposedly sovereign are forced to bend to the dictates of the global market; they are incapable of protecting their citizens against the vagaries of the international economy. Therefore, they conclude, state sovereignty must be "eroding," "less meaningful," or "in decline."[6]

But are sovereignty and independence synonymous? And does either mean the unfettered ability to do what one wants? As we noted in Chapter 4, independence can mean freedom from the control of others or the ability to make one's own decisions, not governed by others. But there is nothing in any of the meanings of independence that suggests that being free to make one's own decisions gives one the ability to do whatever one desires.

Sovereignty certainly implies independence (for a political community cannot be sovereign without, *ipso facto*, being independent), but sovereignty constitutes a special kind of independence. Sovereignty is not independence *per se*, but rather a juridical recognition of a set of conditions and rights: the freedom that a government enjoys from the control of others; the formal delineation of a specific set of rights that a government has supreme authority in one geographical space, unchallenged by others. But sovereignty is the set of rights and practices that is highly specific in terms of time and place. Independence, by contrast, does not carry the juridical baggage that sovereignty has: it just means the ability to be free from the control of others.

The distinction is crucial for understanding a dynamic that we will explore in more detail in the chapters ahead. The desire to be free of the control of others, I argued in Chapter 4, is one of the most pervasive goals of political communities. It is also one of the foremost causes of global disharmony. It appears in all parts of the world, and at all times in the human experience. The compulsion of contemporary Palestinians to gain independence, examined above, is little different from the desires of countless peoples through the ages to be free of the control of others, to command their own destinies. By contrast, sovereignty, as a particular kind of independence, is heavily determined by the last five hundred years of political struggles. Thus, unlike earlier peoples, today's Palestinians seek to frame their independence in the form and practices of the sovereign state. In short, they seek to be both independent *and* sovereign.

But independence can exist without sovereignty. Consider all those political communities which were independent before sovereignty was even invented. Likewise, consider that period in the histories of Australia, Canada, India, New Zealand, and South Africa when these states were independent, and even exercised some sovereign-like powers such as membership in the League of Nations or conducting diplomatic relations, but were not fully sovereign. Australia, Canada, New Zealand and South Africa were given full sovereignty by the Statute of Westminster in 1931; India's sovereignty came in 1947. Today, the ROC on Taiwan might wish that it was recognized a little more widely as being sovereign, but there can be little doubt that the 21 million people living on Taiwan enjoy independence (much to chagrin of the People's Republic of China).

*It is possible to be independent but not sovereign, and sovereign but not autonomous.*

When people talk about the ability to do what they want, they are referring to **autonomy**. Autonomy means the ability to have one's actions accord with one's preferences—to be able to do what one wants. All political communities (like individuals) appear to strive for autonomy; but very few communities—or individuals—are in the fortunate position of being able to do precisely what they want. Instead, they must content themselves with the bounds and limits that are inexorably placed on their desires by their own limitations, or by the demands, actions, and constraints of others.

Drawing careful distinctions in this way allows us to draw different combinations of independence, sovereignty, and autonomy—permutations that may appear almost paradoxical at first. It allows us to recognize that it is possible to be independent but not sovereign, and sovereign but not autonomous.* Some states, like Taiwan, are not sovereign, but they are independent; the vast majority of states are independent and sovereign, but not autonomous. Some political communities lack all three—independence, sovereignty, and autonomy: the Kurds who live at the nexus of the Turkish, Syrian, Iraqi, and Iranian borders would be one example of such a community. And at least one political community can arguably be said to possess all three: the United States is independent, sovereign, and relatively (though not fully) autonomous—in the sense that the United States government gets pretty much what it wants (when it wants it badly enough).

## CONCLUSION

In the last two chapters we have explored how the sovereign idea *works* as it has been put into practice over the years since the Peace of Westphalia. In Chapter 10 we looked at the core assumptions of sovereignty in operation, focusing in particular on the sovereign ideals of indivisibility, equality, and noninterference. We also dwelt on borders at some length because borders remain an essential construct for the sovereign state. The state must know the extent of its authority, and the way it does this is by defining a territory and then claiming supreme power over all those who are located within those territorial boundaries. But borders, and the wide variety of governmental practices that sustain and entrench them, help also to sustain and entrench divisions between people.

Apparently, so does sovereignty. Sovereignty, as the title of Chapter 10 suggests, is a *juridical* attribute, a legal status granted to a state and its government by the act of recognition. But that status is crucial for the legitimacy of the state, both in the eyes of its people and in the eyes of others. Sovereignty as a set of practices thus reinforces the geopolitical divisions of the state and adds legitimacy to them.

In this wide-ranging discussion of the sovereign nation-state, we have one part of the triplet yet to explore. The next part of the book looks at the idea of "nation," and in particular the ideology of nation, "nationalism," that has been grafted onto the twin ideas of state and sovereignty. As we will see, the deep attachment to nation complements the divisions of state and sovereignty.

---

* Other combinations would reveal that it is possible to be neither sovereign nor independent, but nonetheless autonomous. Consider those living in the British colony of Bermuda: they overwhelmingly reject independence and sovereignty; to the extent that these wishes are respected by Britain, Bermudians are autonomous in that very limited respect.

## Keyword File

Quasi-states

Recognition

Ignored states

Unilateral declaration of independence

Bantustan

Bandwagon effect

Monroe Doctrine

De-recognition

Nonrecognition

McCarthyism

Canadian formula

*De facto* recognition

*De jure* recognition

"Unofficial" missions

Governments-in-exile

Autonomy

## For Further Exploration

### HARD COPY

Hamilton, Keith and Richard Langhorne. *The Practice of Diplomacy: Its Evolution, Theory and Administration*. London: Routledge, 1995.

Jackson, Robert H. *Quasi-States: Sovereignty, International Relations and the Third World*. Cambridge: Cambridge University Press, 1990.

Newsom, David D., ed. *Diplomacy under a Foreign Flag: When Nations Break Relations*. New York: St Martin's, 1990.

Nicholson, Sir Harold. *Diplomacy*, 3d ed. New York: Oxford University Press, 1963.

Strange, Susan. "States, firms, and diplomacy," *International Affairs* 68 (January 1992).

Zacher, Mark W. "The decaying pillars of the Westphalian temple," in James N. Rosenau and Ernst Otto-Czempiel, eds. *Governance without Government*. Cambridge: Cambridge University Press, 1992, 58–101.

### WEBLINKS

**http://condor.depaul.edu/~traffens/determination/**

Links to WWW home pages of independence movements are available from this site

**http://www.embassy.org/**

Home page of the Electronic Embassy, providing links to different national embassies

**http://www.tufts.edu/fletcher/multilaterals.html**

Fletcher School of Law and Diplomacy at Tufts University has a range of resources on international law and diplomacy

## Notes to Chapter 11

1. Öyvind Österud, "The narrow gate: entry to the club of sovereign states," *Review of International Studies* 23 (April 1997), 167–84.

2. Robert H. Jackson, *Quasi-States: Sovereignty, International Relations and the Third World* (Cambridge: Cambridge University Press, 1990).

3. Some insist that the use of force is a crucial component of any definition of secession: see, for example, James Crawford, *The Creation of States in International Law* (Oxford: Clarendon Press, 1979). I would argue that the crucial element is consent.

4. John Burns, "Growing fear, frustration mar life in Afghan capital," *New York Times Service*, 25 September 1997.

5. Mark W. Zacher, "The decaying pillars of the Westphalian temple," in James N. Rosenau and Ernst Otto-Czempiel, eds., *Governance without Government* (Cambridge: Cambridge University Press, 1992), 58–101.

6. For a quintessential example, see James N. Rosenau, "Powerful tendencies, startling discrepancies, and elusive dynamics: the challenge of studying world politics in a turbulent era," *Australian Journal of International Affairs* 50 (April 1996), 26.

# PART 5

# Nation, Nationalism, *and the* Nation-State

# A Religion *of* Division: Nation *and* Nationalism

**I N T R O D U C T I O N** The rise of the territorial state and the evolution of sovereignty that hardened the shell of the state occurred as another idea emerged about how humans should divide themselves: the idea of "nation." In this chapter, we look at the nation, and the ideology of nation that has emerged to guide both thought and political action. That ideology has become, as the English essayist Aldous Huxley once put it, a kind of religion, endowing the nation with a spiritual existence. The sovereign state assumes a particular importance in nationalist ideology. Sovereignty, with its liberal assumption that each community should live and let live, ensures that each nation is given the opportunity to develop in its own particular way; the post-Westphalian state is seen as the political form best suited to protect the nation.

## THE "GIVENNESS" OF THE NATION

The idea of nation is so pervasive that we tend to take it for granted. The symbols of the nation are all around us, all the time, even if we are not consciously aware of them. **National symbols** include the nation's name, heard and uttered without a second thought; flags that flap from a hundred unnoticed flagpoles; the symbols that adorn the currency that we use; the national anthems that we sing; the names of national heroes that dot streets, monuments, statues, and buildings; and the holidays taken in the nation's name. Most of us also take our political attachment to the nation—usually conceived of in terms of "loyalty" and "love"—very much for granted: as we will see below, many of us simply do not conceive of ultimate political loyalty in terms other than nation.

We also tend to see the nation as *natural*, in other words, a form of political organization that spontaneously and naturally arose. Any other forms that might have preceded the nation tend to be seen as merely steps in the natural evolution to nationhood; any other forms that might be proposed to supplant the nation are, in this view, *unnatural*, and hence to be regarded as we regard all things unnatural, with aversion.

*The nation tends to be seen as eternal: the nation is here, has been here from the start, and will always be here.*

We also see the nation as *self-evident*, as something that exists without having to be explained or even thought about very much. Finally, we see the nation as *inevitable* in two senses: it was inevitable that the nation should have arisen, and it is inevitable that it will always be there. As we will see below, nations are not conceived of as things that can come to an end. Rather, the nation tends to be seen as eternal: the nation is here, has been here from the start, and will always be here.

The nation is indeed a powerful source of division between individuals and political communities. But it is neither natural nor self-evident. Nor is it inevitable that we should have developed the nation as a form of political loyalty, or that the nation must endure.

## "WHAT IS A NATION?"

That the definition of nation is not self-evident can be seen by posing the deceptively elementary question that was the title of a lecture given by the French historian Ernest Renan in March 1882: "Qu'est-ce qu'une nation?" Renan wanted to show that while everyone thinks that they know the answer to this simple question, in fact there are considerable misunderstandings about the notion of nation.[1]

At first blush, defining the nation seems simple enough: go to a dictionary and look up the word. A nation, says *Webster's Ninth*, is a "politically organized nationality." And what is a nationality? Nationality is defined, in circular fashion, as national character; national status; membership in a particular nation; "a people having a common origin, tradition, and language and capable of forming or actually constituting a nation-state; an ethnic group constituting one element of a larger unit (as a nation)."

The *Oxford English Dictionary* is more helpful and less circular: "an extensive aggregate of persons, so closely associated with each other by common descent, language or history as to form a distinct race or people, usually organized as a separate political state and occupying a definite territory." But the *OED*'s definition is no less problematic. For whether we tease apart this definition and look at the different components, or look at the definition as a whole, we are in fact no closer to understanding what a nation is.

## A First Cut: Trying to Define the Nation Objectively

The *OED* definition tries to define nation *objectively*: it looks for things we can see, and attributes that we can measure, so we can distinguish those things we might call nation from those things that are not nations. As we will see, however, trying to determine the nation objectively is a trap to be avoided. To understand why, we have to look at the objective attributes that supposedly define nations. Let us begin with the different parts of the definition.

### "Common Descent"

At one obvious level we all share a common descent. All six billion humans alive today are possibly descended from a single *Homo* mother, called by geneticists and paleontologists **"African Eve."** A woman who lived 100 000 to 200 000 years ago, probably in Africa, she was an evolutionary adaptation from earlier hominid and *Homo* ancestors; her children would be the forebears of all future members of the species *Homo sapiens sapiens*. One makes that obvious observation because it begs an equally obvious question: when does "descent" start and stop for the purpose of defining the nation? One thousand generations ago? One hundred generations ago? Ten generations ago? Five generations ago? One generation ago? Moreover, what does "common" mean in practice? There are large numbers of nations today whose members simply cannot trace a common descent: the United States is an excellent example of a nation whose people manifestly do not share a common descent even one or two generations ago.

### "Common Language"

This is no less problematic an attribute, for little coincidence between **language** and nation can be observed beyond a small number of cases, such as Japanese and Icelandic, where the fit between language and nation is almost perfect. But in the rest of the world, it is much messier. First, it is evident that language transcends nation. English, for example, is a **global language**. It is spoken in Britain, the United States, Australia, New Zealand, many countries in and around the Caribbean, and by many in Canada, Ireland, Malta, Namibia, and South Africa. It is an official language in a number of other nations, including many of the island nations of the South Pacific; Singapore and India in Asia; Mauritius in the Indian Ocean; and 15 other nations in Africa besides South Africa and Namibia (Botswana, Gambia, Ghana, Kenya, Liberia, Lesotho, Malawi, Nigeria, Sierra Leone, Swaziland, Tanzania, Uganda, Zambia, and Zimbabwe). And on 1 July 1997, English even became an official language of China (albeit limited to the Hong Kong Special Administrative Region). The same is also true for other languages, including Arabic, various dialects of Chinese, French, German, Hindi, Italian, Portuguese, Russian, Spanish, and Swahili: these are languages spoken by the peoples of more than one nation.

Likewise, people of the same nation can speak many languages, officially or unofficially, without affecting the sense of nation. The multilingualism of South Africa—where under the constitution there are 11 official languages—or Switzerland, or the bilingualism of Belgium or Canada, does not preclude the existence of nation in any of those countries. Many countries are officially **bilingual** or **multilingual**. And even in nations such as the

United States that pride themselves on being resolutely English in theory, one will find a polyglot nation in practice: in how many American homes is the language of mealtime and bedtime a language other than English?

### "Common History"

The notion that a nation is a group of people with a "common history" is also problematic. As we will explore in more detail below, all nations have indeed constructed a "common history" for themselves—the officially sanctioned "story" of where the nation came from. But this is a **constructed story**, not a reflection of how the members of a nation actually got to where they are today, either individually or collectively. And what of those nations where the members of the nation do not share a common historical experience, but come from other nations, with other stories (often conflicting with those of other groups)? For example, the world's prime immigrant nations—the United States, Canada, and Australia— comprise numerous peoples with highly diverse "stories." Moreover, what of those nations where the stories of different groups of people differ radically in the telling? Muslims and Hindus in India have markedly different histories, as do Muslims, Serbs, and Croats in Bosnia, Québécois and English-speaking Canadians in Canada, and English, Irish, Scots, and Welsh in the British Isles.

### "A Separate State and Territory"

Trying to identify nation in territorial or political terms—a people organized as a state and occupying a distinct territory—is likewise not helpful. There are too many states where there is more than one nation within the territorial bounds of the state (for example, Basques in Spain, Québécois and aboriginal nations in Canada, Scottish and Welsh in Britain, Sikhs in India); and too many examples of nations occupying more than one state (for example, Kurds in Turkey, Syria, Iraq, and Iran).

### Abandoning the Dictionary

Taken separately, the different parts of the *OED* definition prove unhelpful, for they do not identify a *distinctive* set of objective attributes that belong to a nation and not to other groups. The definition, taken as a whole, can readily be applied to a variety of groups. Were the people who occupied the *polis* of Athens not "an extensive aggregate of persons, so closely associated with each other by common descent, language or history as to form a distinct race or people, usually organized as a separate political state and occupying a definite territory"? Or the Welsh of the 11th century? Or the Maoris of 15th-century New Zealand? Or the Iroquois of the 17th century? Or the Chinese or Japanese during their imperial periods?

Now it is true that we can *call* those peoples "nations" if we want, but that would be to commit the same "presentist" error as calling the political formations of those peoples "states." Like the state, the "nation" as a form of political identity is a modern and essentially European invention. And like the state, the idea of nation has spread across the globe and been adopted by large numbers of peoples. But while Welsh, Iroquois, Maoris, Chinese, and Japanese call themselves nations today, it can be argued that they were manifestly *not* nations in the past. Indeed, one does not have to go back too far to get to a point where there were no nations at all.

To understand how this can be, we have to abandon the dictionary approach and try a second cut at defining nation.

## A Second Cut: Defining the Nation Intersubjectively

Many people, like dictionaries, try to define nations objectively. They ask: what is it about a nation that makes it a nation? They then think of a nation they know and try and figure out what characteristics they can observe that make it a "nation." This leads to a number of errors. As noted above, it leads to "presentist" thinking—applying a modern concept backward in history, turning every "extensive aggregate of people" into a "nation." It also leads some people to try and evaluate whether a particular nation exists or not, which leads all too easily to the *denial* of nation. For example, many Turks simply deny that there is more than one nation within Turkey; in their eyes, the Kurds do not constitute a "real" nation. One can find similar denials in Canada about Québécois and in Spain about Catalonians.

A better way to conceive of nation is to think of it as something fundamentally subjective, existing purely in the mind of the subject rather than existing in the objective world. A nation is a "state of mind," to use Hans Kohn's memorable phrase; it is, as Benedict Anderson has put it, an "imagined community," existing in the imagination of the member of the nation.[2] From such observations it could be argued that a nation is *any group of people who define themselves as a nation.*

This is only one part of a good definition of nation, however. If it is taken no further, such a subjective definition does not tell us a great deal about the notion of nation itself. It suggests that nation can be devoid of content: anyone wishing to call themselves a "nation" can do so without having to anchor their self-definition in any objective characteristics. If "nation" is to have meaning, we have to give it characteristics that are **intersubjective**—that is, neither wholly objective nor wholly subjective, but where the subjective is capable of being known objectively. I argue that the way to think about nation is to think about it as an *ideological* construct: a distinctive set of beliefs that members of a nation must have, and a distinctive political agenda that members of a nation must work toward. We call this ideology of nation **nationalism**; adherents of this ideology are **nationalists**. **Nation**, then, becomes *any group of people who define themselves as a nation and are committed to the ideology of nationalism.*

*Nation, then, becomes any group of people who define themselves as a nation and are committed to the ideology of nationalism.*

This definition enables us to make a distinction between **ethnicity**, **nationality** and nation. Groups identifiable by their nationality or ethnicity may have many nationlike qualities. For example, millions of Americans, Australians, and Canadians whose families immigrated from Italy retain their "Italianness": they continue to speak Italian at home; they have strong ties of family and friends in Italy; their cultural traditions are distinctly Italian; and they have a deep love of the "old country" and a national pride that reveals itself, for example, in the worldwide celebrations that greeted the victory of Italy in the 1982 World Cup (or the worldwide sadness at the narrow loss to Brazil in 1994).

Likewise, there can be no denying the ethnicity of any one of Joel Kotkin's **"global tribes"**—the millions of Anglo-Saxons, "overseas Chinese," Indians, Japanese, and Jews, who are able to live anywhere in the world without even shedding their ethnic identity.[3] Or consider the millions of Roma (sometimes called Gypsies) who live in Europe: they constitute a distinct ethnic group, recognized as such by the United Nations in 1979. But not one of these groups embraces the ideology of nationalism.

A definition of nation that hinges on ideology allows us to differentiate those who use nation to describe themselves but who are not committed to the ideology of nationalism. For example, gays and lesbians celebrate Queer Nation, but, as will be clear from our discussion below, they are not using the word in its strictly ideological sense. Aboriginal groups in Canada call themselves First Nations, but they are not committed to achieving the primary goals of nationalists. Many African Americans conceive of themselves as a "nation within a nation," but relatively few agree with the ideas of the Nation of Islam, a black Muslim group founded in the 1930s that has periodically advocated the establishment of a separate homeland for African Americans, and thus is properly nationalist.[*]

However, even defining nation as any group of people who see themselves as a nation and are committed to the ideology of nationalism, we are still left with having to answer Renan's question: "What is a nation?" What is this thing that people are defining themselves as? For even an intersubjective formulation still leaves us in the same circular and tautological conundrum as *Webster's Dictionary*: we are still defining nation by reference to nation. To get some sense of nation, we must define the nationalist ideology.

## THE IDEOLOGY OF NATIONALISM

An ideology is a systemic set of doctrines or beliefs, particularly about the social world. The ideology of nationalism creates an idea about a particular kind of political community, and provides a set of doctrines to believe in and a set of political objectives to be reached. We now explore each of these components of the nationalist ideology.

### The Growth and Spread of the Idea of Nation

Like the ideas of state and sovereignty, the idea of nation is the result of a slow historical evolution. It began when a group of people, dispersed across a territory, recognized that they constitute a *people*. This recognition is something that had to be entirely imagined, for there was no way that any individual could ever get to know all of his or her "people." It was a recognition that this "people" constituted something distinct from others: they spoke a common language of their own; they could be the source of their own civilization and

---

[*] An autonomous black state was advocated by Elijah Muhammad, leader of the Nation of Islam from 1934 until his death in 1975, and Malcolm X, a minister within the organization. He eventually broke with Muhammad and in 1964 formed his own organization before he was assassinated in February 1965. In 1978, Louis Farrakhan revived the Nation of Islam and its nationalist program.

culture; they could organize their economic lives separately from others. And most importantly, the recognition depended on the growth of the idea that an individual's political loyalties should be to an abstract political entity rather than to someone or something very concrete, like one's liege lord or to one's village where one's kin lived. Thus the consciousness that underlies the idea of nation is a mass consciousness, an idea that can unite different people in various parts of a political community in the belief that they belong to an abstract entity, and can love and be loyal to that abstraction.[4]

### Emerging National Consciousness: The Case of Britain

The growth of such a **national consciousness** occurred first in England and France, and depended on a number of developments. First, the consolidation of the "state" as a postfeudal political form occurred earlier in these countries than in other parts of Europe, providing a political and territorial base for an abstraction like "nation" to emerge. The decline of the feudal economy that had restricted movement beyond the village also meant the increased mobility of individuals in these postfeudal communities.

Second, war-fighting also contributed to the growth of such a consciousness: wars between France and England helped nourish the growth of the idea of nation. It was galvanized by legendary figures such as Jeanne d'Arc, who as a teenager led troops against the English in 1429, scoring an important victory and turning the Hundred Years' War in France's favour. The defeat of the Spanish Armada of 1588 by the English navy likewise gave rise to what we would readily recognize as nationalist sentiment.

*"This England never did,*
*nor never shall,*
*Lie at the proud foot of a*
*conqueror"*

Finally, communications between different parts of the territory improved. The printing press and increased literacy both served to increase people's awareness of the existence of community. For example, playwrights like William Shakespeare could both reflect and promote national consciousness with unabashedly nationalistic sentiments:

> This England never did, nor never shall,
> Lie at the proud foot of a conqueror,
> But when it first did help to wound itself.
> Now these her princes are come home again,
> Come the three corners of the world in arms,
> And we shall shock them. Nought shall make us rue,
> If England to itself do rest but true.

These lines, from *The Life and Death of King John*, (Act V, vii, 112–118), may appear unremarkable to people in the late 20th century. But that is only because we are so used to thinking in terms of love and loyalty to abstractions like "America" or "India." In the 1590s, Shakespeare was expressing sentiments that were unlikely to have been expressed in those terms in the 13th century, a good example of the growth of the idea of feeling pride in an abstraction known as "England."

Soon, "England" was to become "Great Britain," and one can see efforts to build a comparable sense of nationhood from the mergers and incorporations that saw the submerging of Scottish and Irish independence in an English-dominated Great Britain. By the 17th century, dynastic and religious manoeuvres had resulted in the independent kingdoms of England and Scotland being ruled by the same person: in March 1603, James VI of Scotland also became James I of England. This union of the crowns—James would style himself king of "Great Britain"—was followed a century later by a "union of the parliaments." On 1 May 1707, Scotland and England were united, prompted by a Scottish desire for the economic security that commercial union with England would provide, and an English desire to prevent France from trying to restore a Catholic to the throne in England.

The Act of Union between Great Britain and Ireland, proclaimed on 1 January 1801, must be traced back to the first invasions by the English in the 12th century. English control over Ireland consolidated progressively over the following centuries: the suppression of local chieftains; the use of English settlers to consolidate English ownership; the confiscation of Irish land; and, after the Reformation, the increasing infringements on the Irish, who had overwhelmingly remained Roman Catholics. The Act of Union that was passed by the all-Protestant Irish Parliament was the last step in that process. It was triggered by Irish Catholic rebellions of 1798 which, in turn, were inspired by the French Revolution of 1789.

By 1801, then, a new British state existed, and efforts were made to forge a national identity for the abstraction "Britain." One small but illustrative measure was the use of the flag to promote a sense of union. The **union flag** of Britain evolved from the red cross of St George, representing England, superimposed on the flag of St Andrew—a white saltire (or diagonal cross) on a blue field—representing Scotland. This was the flag used by King James (I of England and VI of Scotland) in the 17th century. After the Act of Union between Britain and Ireland in 1801, the red saltire of St Patrick was layered on. (The flag used by Wales today—a winged dragon on a green and white field—is not represented on the union flag. The Welsh were subjugated by the English in the 15th century,[*] well before flags were used to symbolize nation.)

### The Industrial Revolution and the Changing World Economy

The consolidation of the idea of nation in Britain occurred at the same time as the British economy was experiencing a profound change. For much of the 18th century, Britain was already enjoying the fruits of the mercantilist policies that had been pursued for the previous century. London had become the centre of an active international export trade fed by produce from overseas empires. The raw materials were processed in Britain and exported,

---

[*] English efforts to subjugate the Welsh began in the 11th century. Beheading Welsh leaders—the fate of David ap Gruffydd in 1283—and naming the heir to the English throne the Prince of Wales did little to dampen Welsh rebellion. The last major revolt ended in 1416 with the death of its leader, Owen Glendower; the Act of Union of 1536 incorporated Wales into England.

mainly to other European countries, but increasingly to the British settlements and colonies around the world. Some produce—sugar, tobacco, spices, and Indian textiles—were simply reexported directly.

By the end of the century, however, this export trade experienced a dramatic growth. This was the result of the complex of interrelated developments that we collectively term the **Industrial Revolution**. This term is applied specifically to Britain in the 18th century to describe the process that transformed a predominantly agricultural economy, serving local markets, to a predominantly industrial economy with international links. It is also applied more generically to those economies in which similar changes occurred.

In Britain, the Industrial Revolution occurred in a relatively brief period of time— from the middle of the 18th century to the mid-1800s. The developments that made the "revolution" were numerous. Many were the result of fortuitous discoveries: the discovery of the use of coal (which Britain possessed in abundance) in blast furnaces, rather than charcoal, which revolutionized the iron industry; the discovery of new methods of textile manufacturing, such as the spinning jenny, the mule, the flying shuttle, and the roller spinning frame; the invention of the cotton gin which propelled the United States into the position of Britain's foremost supplier of raw cotton; and the discovery of the application of steam power to rotary movement. As these discoveries and their applications were combined with other developments, faster methods of transportation evolved, including roads, railways, and steamships; labour was increasingly devoted to manufacturing; labour became more specialized within the manufacturing process that rapidly expanded the quantity and efficiency of production; and manufacturing was consolidated into limited locations, leading to increased urbanization.

One of the key consequences of the Industrial Revolution was its impact on the ability of Britain to sustain its long war against France following the French Revolution of 1789. The costs of waging almost 25 years of war were tremendous—for example, by 1815, when the Napoleonic Wars finally ended, over half the country's annual revenues went to servicing the sizeable public debt. But the size and power of the British economy allowed governments to resist the temptation to sue for peace, and instead to continue to wage the war. By 1815, the British emerged as a dominant economic and military power as a consequence of territories transferred by the peace accords of Paris and Vienna. Cyprus, Malta, Ceylon, Mauritius, the island of Heligoland in the North Sea, the Cape of Good Hope, and numerous islands in the Caribbean were transferred to Britain, giving it a worldwide naval capability, and affording the government in London an increasingly dominant position in European politics. Moreover, Britain's position as the leading European country in manufacturing, engineering, investment, and trade had been enhanced by war-time procurement and expansion. These developments had a direct impact on British conceptions of themselves in the world. A good example of this was the brashness of George Canning, who was made foreign secretary in 1822 and who pursued a foreign policy that set Britain distinctly apart from its European neighbours and European despotism. Instead, under Canning, Britain supported the newly independent states in South America, encouraged the independence movement in Greece, and supported Portugal against Spain.

## The American and French Revolutions

Most students of nationalism agree that national consciousness began to grow most rapidly under the impetus of the American and French revolutions of the latter part of the 18th century. Indeed, the United States of America can reasonably be seen as the first **nation-state**, a sovereign state marked by a widespread consciousness among those who lived in the 13 colonies that they constituted a separate people. To be sure, the "foundation documents" of the new republic—the Declaration of Independence that was issued by the 13 states on 4 July 1776 and the constitution approved by Congress on 17 September 1787—are both framed in terms of "the people" rather than "the nation." In fact, the word nation appears but once in the declaration and twice in the constitution, none referring to the United States. But we would have no difficulty describing the consciousness of those who embraced the American Revolution in the 1770s as "national."

Likewise, the French Revolution of 1789, challenging as it did the privileges of nobility and enshrining conceptions of equality and rights, did much to enhance the idea of "the people." The wars that followed were undertaken in the name of "the people." The Napoleonic Wars, Evan Luard reminds us, "both expressed the emergent national spirit of France and aroused the national spirit of those [France] conquered."[5] Certainly, as we have seen above, those wars had a profound impact on the national idea in Britain.

## The Consolidation of Nation

This "national spirit" manifested itself slowly over the course of the next century and a half. It was first consolidated in Europe, where the Napoleonic Wars inspired a generation of what has come to be known as the romantic nationalist movement. Poets, artists, and musicians were inspired by the notion of their nation, free and independent. For example, when the Greeks rose in rebellion against their Turkish rulers in 1821, the English poet Lord Byron was moved to join the struggle for national independence. He died there in 1824 of a fever at the age of 36. Three years later, the great powers decided to intervene in this lingering conflict and in 1827 fought a war that resulted in the creation of an independent Greece. Belgium was also created by the great powers: in October 1830, it won its national independence from the Netherlands, its existence and neutrality confirmed by the great powers. The national ideal inspired many of the revolutions that swept across Europe in 1848, beginning with uprisings in Italian towns and cities in January. While the immediate consequences of the "Year of Revolutions" were few, the goal of national independence became deeply entrenched in Italy, Germany, and the Balkans.

In the Balkans, indigenous nationalist sentiment combined with the rivalries of the great powers to produce what was known as the **Eastern Question**. The "question" was how to deal with the Ottoman Empire, which was under stress from both inside and outside. Outside stresses mainly came from the designs that European governments had on territory controlled by the Porte, as the Ottoman government was colloquially known.*

---

* The "Sublime Porte" was the high gate that led to the government offices in Constantinople. "The Porte" was used as a shorthand for the Ottoman empire; see the discussion of metonyms in Chapter 6.

This led to a series of wars with Russia during the 19th century, the most important of which was the Crimean war of 1853 to 1856.

Inside, the stresses came from periodic nationalist revolts by groups seeking independence. The Porte dealt with manifestations of nationalism by repressing them. For example, when the Bulgars rose in revolt in 1876, the Turks put down the rebellion, and then, in retaliation, systematically massacred some 30 000 Bulgarian men, women, and children. This prompted the Russians to intervene in yet another war against Turkey, out of which an autonomous Bulgaria emerged. But Balkan nationalist sentiment was not to be satisfied during this period.

By contrast, the "national spirit" forged the creation of two other important European nations. Under the leadership of Piedmont's premier, Camillo di Cavour, the unification of Italy was finally completed in January 1861, after a struggle of more than 30 years. The unification of the 38 German states and principalities was achieved more quickly under the deft diplomacy of the minister-president of Prussia, Otto von Bismarck. In rapid succession, Bismarck enlisted Austrian aid to seize Schleswig and Holstein from Denmark; he then turned on Vienna and fought a brief war with Austria that drove it from the German *Bund*, the loose confederation of German states; finally, he provoked a brief war with France in 1870 that resulted in the formation of the German Empire in January 1871.

By the end of the 19th century, the idea of nation was firmly planted in the European context. By the mid-1800s, independent states had emerged everywhere in the western hemisphere as well, except British North America. As we will see in the next chapter, the national idea was to spread further. Like the notion of the state, it eventually spread throughout the international system.

## The Nationalist "Credo"

The growth of the *idea* of nation was matched by the growth of an *ideology* of nationhood. This ideology can be best understood as comprising a set of beliefs that nationalists have to believe in. These beliefs are not unlike the creeds (from the Latin *credo*, I believe) formulated by the early Christian church. Creeds are statements of Christian beliefs and are still recited by several Christian denominations today. The **nationalist credo** might not be set out in a standard and agreed-upon text that mirrors the compact sentences of the Nicene Creed approved by the Church in 381, but a credo—a set of beliefs for nationalists, wherever they are—can nonetheless be determined from the writings and practices of nationalists over the years. In brief, that credo demands a belief in the essential rightness of the division of the world into nations, in the existence of one's own nation, and in the rightness of a love for that abstraction and its many parts.

### Self-Determination

The key item in the nationalist credo is a firm belief in the principle that every nation should have the right to determine its own destiny. As James Mayall has pointed out, the belief in **national self-determination** is the product of a specific historical consciousness that had its roots in the French Revolution and the emergence of notions of human rights.[6] Concepts of emancipation and liberty combined with the growth of the national idea to produce the notion that it was normatively good for the world to be divided into nations. It was normatively good for nations to rule themselves, most appropriately in a sovereign state; it was likewise normatively bad for foreigners to govern nations.

In the 19th century, this was a radical idea. Most of the world's population was governed by foreigners. As we saw above, national consciousness had emerged or was emerging in some countries, but empire was still the dominant form of political organization. However, empires could no longer stand against the principle of self-determination, for those who believed in national self-determination as a normative good had to regard empire, which was a denial of self-determination, as normatively bad. By the 20th century, however, the idea of self-determination had become a universal norm, and underwrote the explosive growth of the nation-state during that century.

### An Imagined Community

The nation is, as Benedict Anderson suggests, an **imagined community**, an imagined abstraction about very real and concrete things: land, people, institutions, practices, culture, and language. These all *exist* in objective reality; but the nationalist *imagines* them interacting in a way that forms the nation. Together, the combination of a special group of people occupying a particular patch of territory, with a special set of cultural practices and a special set of institutions and ways of doing things—that constitutes the nation. That imagined community likewise has numerous symbolic representations: a national flag, national anthem, national coinage and currency, national institutions, and a set of national understandings that are widely shared.

The nationalist believes that he or she *belongs* to the national community, which includes any number of other individuals who are identified as "fellow nationals." Fellow nationals not only identify themselves as believers in the existence of the same nation, but they also engage in a process of identification that may or may not include that individual. There is a necessary element of mutuality in membership identification here. It is not enough that I identify with nation; nation must also identify with me. Simply moving to San Sebastián, Trois Rivières, or Llandudno, learning the language, becoming steeped in local culture and history, and declaring myself to be Basque, Québécois, or Welsh, is not sufficient. Membership in the nation must include a mutual recognition by other nationals that I am part of the nation, a process of formal and informal acceptance that is deeply determined by many of the objective characteristics noted above—language, descent, ethnicity.

This process of acceptance varies by nation. For many nations, ethnicity is crucial for acceptance: Caucasians would have difficulty being accepted as "fellow nationals" in numerous countries around the world, no matter how well they spoke the language or knew the culture. For others, lineage is critical: most First Nations in Canada would not accept those not descended from aboriginal peoples as members of their nations. For others still, a mixture of language and lineage is important: for example, many Québécois regard only those who speak French with a Québec accent and are descended from many generations of French-speaking Quebeckers as *pure laine* (pure wool). Others who might *live* in Québec are often not regarded as members of the Québécois nation, sometimes dismissed simply as *les autres* (the others). Formal acceptance does not necessarily bring with it informal acceptance: it is relatively easy for most legal immigrants to Australia, Canada, and the United States to secure legal acceptance of their membership in those nations in the form of citizenship papers. However, it has been difficult for some to be accepted by everyone else in those countries as "real" Australians, Canadians, or Americans, regardless of their legal status.

In short, nationalism demands that nationals share an identity with each other. Importantly, it does not specify on what basis such an identity should be constructed. Nationalism does not demand that identity *must* be based on language, or skin colour, or lineage, or ethnicity, or religious belief, or cultural practices, or economic system. Rather, nationalism is hugely flexible: national identity can be built on one, some, all, or none of these criteria. All it demands is that fellow nationals share an identity.

## A Beloved Community

Nationalism implies that this imagined abstraction be *loved*, in the sense of arousing the passions and emotions of human experience. Such emotions can be aroused by the land and its distinctive features; by the sense of kinship with the people who occupy that land; or simply by the very idea of the nation itself.

We can see love of nation manifested in numerous ways. In particular we can see it in the celebration of nation that is deeply woven into the fabric of most political communities—in national day celebrations, in the celebration of the nation's contributions to humankind in the arts and sciences or in culture, or in the celebrations of sports victories by national teams or competitors.

Perhaps the best example of this is the Olympic Games. Although Pierre de Coubertin, a French educator, had proposed the idea of reviving the ancient Greek games as a way of promoting a more united world, in fact the "modern" games that began in 1896 have become a quadrennial opportunity for the unabashed celebration of national divisions. The nation which hosts the Games uses the opportunity to put on an opening extravaganza that seems to get more spectacular (or tacky, depending on one's taste) each time. And those who watch the Games are immersed in an unabashedly *national* affair: the "parade of nations"; the identification of the athletes by nation; and particularly the medal ceremonies, where the national flags of the gold, silver, and bronze medal winners are hoisted and the gold medallist's national anthem is played.

Moreover, the national element is reinforced by each country's media. The International Olympic Committee (IOC), which organizes the Games, contracts with a television network to provide a live feed for each event, but national networks are left to decide which events they want to cover live. While the "big" events, such as the marathon and the 100-metre dash, tend to be broadcast live by all the carrying networks to all countries, the remaining events tend to receive partial coverage at best, with national networks choosing to broadcast live only those events in which their nation's athletes are participating. The result is that one's picture of the Games varies widely depending on which country one is in.

National symbols are crucial for love of nation. Symbols do not *create* these sentiments, but rather constitute a kind of shorthand for kick-starting the emotions of nationalism: hearing the strains of the national anthem, seeing the national flag, or any number of other symbols that signify "my nation." Mass participation accelerates and amplifies such emotions; the singing of the national anthem by thousands of people is always stirring (even for nonnationals).

Nationalism also demands that one love one's fellow nationals as much as one loves the abstraction known as nation. The love that one is supposed to bear for fellow nationals is abstract and symbolic. It does not imply that one must even *like* one's fellow nationals; it does not even imply that one will *know* more than an infinitesimal percentage of the members of one's nation. But it is possible to conceive of "the people" as a singular abstraction, even in a community that is deeply divided. Consider the speech that Thabo Mbeki, at the time South Africa's executive deputy president, gave on 8 May 1996, after a constitutional assembly adopted a new South African constitution (see the Focus below).

Even as an abstraction, this sentiment has concrete implications: it means that one loves the *idea* of having fellow nationals, however anonymous. That love leads one to take an interest in their welfare, to be concerned for their well-being, to want to protect them, to be angered by their mistreatment by others. Most important, that love implies a willingness to struggle, suffer, fight, and die for fellow nationals.

# FOCUS

## *Thabo Mbeki, on Being South African, 8 May 1996*

I am an African.

I owe my being to the Khoi and the San, whose desolate souls haunt the great expanses of the beautiful Cape, they who fell victim to the most merciless genocide our native land has ever seen, they who were the first to lose their lives in the struggle to defend our freedom...

I am formed of the migrants who left Europe to find a new home on our native land. Whatever their own actions, they remain still part of me.

In my veins courses the blood of the Malay slaves who came here from the east...The stripes they bore on their bodies from the lash of the slave master are a reminder embossed on my consciousness of what should not be done.

I am the grandchild of the warrior men and women that Hinsta and Sekhukhune led, the patriots that Cetshwayo and Mphephu took to battle, the soldiers Moshoeshoe and Ngungunyane taught never to dishonour the cause of freedom...

I am the grandchild who lays fresh flowers on the Boer graves at St Helena and the Bahamas, who sees in the mind's eye and suf- fers the suffering of a simple peasant folk, death, concentration camps, destroyed homesteads, a dream in ruins.

I am the child of Nongqause. I am he who made it possible to trade in the world markets in diamonds, in gold, in the same food for which my stomach yearns.

I come of those who were transported from India and China, whose beings resided in the fact, solely, that they were able to provide physical labour, who taught me that we could both be at home and be foreign...

I have seen our country torn asunder as these, all of whom are my people, engaged one another in a titanic battle...But it seems to have happened that we looked at ourselves and said the time had come...to respond to the call to create for ourselves a glorious future...

Today it feels good to be an African.

Source: http://www.constitution.org.za/ speeches.html

## Other Beliefs about Nation

There are, in addition, a number of related beliefs and assumptions about the nation that are common to nationalists everywhere.[7]

### Indifference or Hostility toward Others

A logical corollary to the love one bears for fellow nationals is that one cannot feel the same sentiments for those who are not defined as part of the nation. The nationalist credo does not rule out gradations of feelings about those who are organized in other nations. On the contrary, members of nations can have warmer regard for some nations than others. Feelings of closeness are evident between nations where there are ties of language, religion, culture, or history: such a warmth is evident among members of many Arab nations, for example, or among a number of English-speaking countries.* Those in immigrant nations typically retain strong feelings of attachment to their homeland.

But on the whole, the nationalist ideology tends to promote indifference toward others. Thus, we might feel sympathy, pity, or anguish at the suffering, misfortune, or deprivation of others, but nationalism implies that these are not "our own," with the result that one does not have to do very much about trying to alleviate such suffering (a marked contrast to the demand that one love one's fellow nationals enough to do something concrete about their suffering).

The nationalist credo does not necessarily imply hostility toward others. While this may be true *generally*, there can be little doubt that nationalism often involves the creation of hostility *specifically*. Most nations, like groups more generally, define themselves in terms of opposition to others around them. Sometimes those others are defined as being deeply hostile to the nation or its good works or its rightful place in the world, a hostility that can then be legitimately reciprocated. Mostly the hostility takes essentially nonviolent forms: the anti-Americanism that is deeply rooted in many national cultures is this kind of hostility. Sometimes a residue of an historical enmity remains, often below the surface of contemporary good relations: the memory of Japanese predations against China from 1931 to 1945, for example, still lingers in Chinese memory. But sometimes there is deep and open antagonism, as the Baltic peoples of Estonia, Latvia, and Lithuania feel toward the Russians; or between Vietnamese and Chinese; Israelis and Palestinians; Greeks and Turks; Iraqis and Iranians; Indians and Pakistanis. Such antagonism may easily lead to warfare, which in circular fashion inexorably feeds and reoxygenates the hostility.

Sometimes nationalist hostility can take gruesome forms. The efforts of Germans under the leadership of Adolf Hitler to "purify" the German nation in the 1930s and 1940s by removing "contaminating" elements remains the best example of such hostility (though, as we will see in Chapter 14, Hitler's own personal project was not at all nationalist). A contemporary example, less widespread but no less gruesome, occurred during the civil war

---

* Samuel P. Huntington, *The Clash of Civilizations and the Remaking of World Order* (New York: Simon and Schuster, 1996), argues that such feelings of international "kinship" derive from membership in the same "civilization." Such views will be discussed in Chapter 17.

in the former Yugoslavia in the mid-1990s. Bosnian Serb soldiers under the command of Gen. Ratko Mladic routinely and systematically used the rape of Bosnian Muslim women as a tool of war; through "ethnic cleansing," they removed Bosnian Muslim residents from villages either by forcing them out or simply killing them; they established and maintained concentration camps where people were routinely tortured and put to death; and over a period of a few days in July 1995, they slaughtered some 7000 Bosnian Muslim men and boys in Srebrenica, and then buried the bodies unceremoniously in mass graves. In Nazi Germany and in Bosnia, all of this killing, done proudly in the name and cause of nation, reflected the deep loathing that nationalist ideology may not *create*, but does *permit* and *legitimate*. We will return to this issue in Chapter 14.

**Paramount Loyalty to the Nation**    Nationalism implies that an individual should feel ultimate political loyalty to the nation and its people. Subnational political loyalties are permissible—loyalty to city, region, or state—as long as they do not conflict with or interfere with national loyalties. Thus nationalism does not preclude someone in Houston from being a good Texan—having a sense of pride in Texas, displaying a "Don't Mess with Texas" bumper sticker, having a sense of fellowship with other Texans (and a shared sense of antipathy toward Americans from other parts of the Union such as the Yankee northeast)—provided that the loyalty to Texas is subordinate to loyalty to the United States of America.

**A Shared Vision of the Nation's Past**    Nationalism implies that the nation must have a history—its own story about where it came from, a tracing of the particular genius of national growth. The remembering, and retelling, of that story is considered critical for the maintenance of the sense of nation. That is why, for example, the Québec government provides a daily and pervasive exhortation to Québécois to keep remembering their past: every Québec licence plate carries the tag *Je me souviens*, I remember. Likewise, Afrikaaner nationalists in South Africa continue each year to reenact the Great Trek of the 1830s and 1840s, when the *Voortrekkers*, or pioneers, engaged in a mass migration into the interior of South Africa to escape British rule.

The history must portray the nation's emergence as essentially *natural* and *inevitable*, if not preordained. It must paint larger-than-life pictures of national heroes and national villains. It must triumphantly celebrate the victories of the nation over its enemies or opponents, particularly those from whom independence was won. One example of many serves to illustrate how ancient stories of valiant struggle against foreign oppressors can become deeply woven into the national history. Vietnamese still celebrate revolts against Chinese rule that occurred two thousand years ago. In 39 AD, Trung Trac, a Vietnamese aristocrat, sought to avenge the killing of her dissident husband by a Chinese commander by organizing a rebellion with her younger sister, Trung Nhi, and another woman, Phung Thi Chinh. They gathered enough support to rout the Chinese, and Trung Trac was established as queen of an independent Vietnamese polity that stretched from Hué to southern China. The independence was brief: in 43 AD, imperial Chinese forces returned and crushed the new state; the Trung sisters satisfied honour by committing suicide. Another revolt was led by Trieu

Au in 248 AD. Legend has it that at the age of 23 she led a thousand soldiers into battle against the Chinese, wearing a suit of golden armour and riding an elephant. Neither helped: the Chinese defeated her army and she too chose an honourable suicide.

The Vietnamese celebration of its women rebels points out the importance of defeat in the telling of the national story. A good national history must wallow in the nation's defeats, mourning the disasters that have befallen the nation at the hands of others. Thus Serbs remember the disastrous Battle of Kosovo Polje on 15 June 1389, when they were defeated by the Turks and subjected to centuries of Muslim rule. Québécois nationalists remember *la Conquête* (the Conquest)—the battle of the Plains of Abraham at Québec City on 13 September 1759 that led to the incorporation of Québec into British North America. Poles remember the defeat of the national hero Tadeus

*The shared history of the nation need bear no relationship to reality ... for the purpose of national history is to provide a national mythology.*

Kościuszko, who had fought in the American Revolution; after returning to Poland, he was appointed to head the small Polish army and later assumed dictatorial powers. But he could not prevail against the predations of Austria, Prussia, and Russia: Russian forces defeated the Polish armies in September 1794 and captured and imprisoned Kościuszko himself. In 1795 and 1796, the three powers partitioned Poland; as Polish nationalists like to put it, Poland was wiped from the map of Europe for more than a century.

As we will see in later chapters, French nationalism thrived on the defeat at the hands of the Germans in 1871, and in turn German nationalism thrived on the humiliation that the nation suffered at the hands of the Allies in 1918 and 1919.

The shared history of the nation need bear no relationship to reality. For example, deeply embedded in Mexican national history is the story of *los niños héroes*—the boy heroes. Six cadets at the national military academy defended their school against invading American troops storming the hill at Chapultepec where the academy was located. On 13 September 1847, with defeat imminent, the boys wrapped themselves in Mexican flags and leaped to their deaths rather than surrender. Their heroism is celebrated by a national monument and an annual celebration, and remembered in numerous street names and a subway stop on the Mexico City Metro. However, as Ernesto Fitsche Aceves reminds us, in real life *los niños héroes* were neither so young nor so heroic, and the account of their deaths was much embellished to provide a focal point for Mexican nationalism.[8] But to dwell on the gap between story and reality is to miss the point: the purpose of national history is to provide a **national mythology**, a common focus for the nation—in this case a celebration of how seriously Mexicans take their independence from the United States—rather than to provide an *accurate* account of history. After all, to strive for accuracy would be to have to tell the story warts and all, and that might not be too pleasant or too inspiring. As a consequence, it may be necessary to conveniently forget or downplay some of the unpleasantness that marks any human story; some creative rewriting may be necessary to "set the record straight."

**A Shared Hope for the Nation's Future**     Nationalism demands that all nationals have a shared hope that the nation will enjoy a happy future. That is why nationalists become so concerned about developments that they believe will weaken the nation in the future. As nationalists, they *must* be concerned about the future, for, importantly, nationalist ideology does not permit the nation to have an ending. To suggest that perhaps it is time to put an end to one's nation—that it has lived a long and full and useful life but now it is ready to pass from this world—is disloyalty of the first order. There is simply no place for it in the dogma of the nationalist.

## The Nationalist Agenda

Nationalism suggests more than merely "articles of faith" to believe in about the nation. It also lays out a highly specific political and economic agenda for the nation. The **nationalist agenda** has two key components: land and statehood. Nationalism also demands a strong "national economy"; that issue is discussed in the following section.

### "This Blessed Plot": A Homeland for the Nation

As intimated above, territory is crucial for a definition of nation. The nationalist *idea* is that each nation has its own proper territory; the national political *objective* is that the nation occupy that proper territory.

The nationalist ideal is that the nation has a "natural" *home*, and the **national home-land** is conceived of in just those terms. The land is *la patrie* (from the Latin *patria*, land of one's father), "our home and native land/*terre de nos aïeux*." The land is often conceived of in parental terms; it is the "motherland" or the "fatherland." It is spoken of as home: the homeland, *Heimat*. It inspires emotion and waxing poetic: Shakespeare has the dying Gaunt in *The Tragedy of King Richard the Second* (II.i.40–50) describe England as "this blessed plot":

This blessed plot, this sceptred isle,
This earth of majesty, this seat of Mars,
This other Eden, demi-paradise,
This fortress built by Nature for herself,
Against infection and the hand of war,
This happy breed of men, this little world,
This precious stone set in the silver sea...

The land itself often acquires a mystical or transcendental quality; it is the "true north strong and free."[9] Nations frequently celebrate the features of their lands in their national anthems: the "golden soil" and "boundless plains" of *Advance Australia Fair*, Iraq is the "land of the two rivers," Austria the "land of mountains, land of rivers," and Uganda the "Pearl of Africa."

It is important to recognize that not any old "plot" of land will do. Each nation has its own conception of where it *properly* should be located. For example, the modern Zionist movement, founded at the end of the 19th century by Theodor Herzl, sought a homeland for the Jewish diaspora in Palestine. When Herzl could not secure Ottoman approval for a charter for a Jewish homeland in Palestine, he approached the British, who offered the

Jews more than 15 000 square kilometres of uninhabited land in the Ugandan highlands for Jewish colonization. This would have given Jews a national homeland (not to mention a safe haven in the 1930s), but the offer split the Zionist movement at the time. The reason was simple: Uganda was not the proper homeland of the people of Israel; that proper homeland was the Holy Land, Palestine.

A similar conception of the "proper home" of the nation could be seen in the debates over Canadian national unity in the mid-1990s. Some Canadians suggested that if Québec wanted to leave the federation, it should be allowed to take with it only the territory that Québec had when the country was created in 1867 (a small strip of territory on either side of the St Lawrence River, which would not include the mineral or hydroelectric wealth of the Ungava peninsula). Québécois nationalists reject this and all other proposals for creative revisions of existing borders. They have little doubt where the proper boundaries of their nation is—the present boundaries of the province of Québec.

Because nations tend to have very precise ideas about what their "natural" territory should be, quarrels frequently arise when territory seen as national land is held by other nations. In these cases, the nation claims that a portion of its homeland has been unjustly taken or kept from it. We call this **irredentism**, from the Italian, *irredenta*, "unredeemed," the colloquial name Italian nationalists gave to those Italian-speaking territories that remained under Austrian or Swiss rule after unification in 1861. Examples of irredentist claims include the Nazi German claim on Sudetenland, a frontier region of the Czech Republic, which before 1945 was home to some three million German speakers whom Adolf Hitler claimed should be reunited with the fatherland. On 29 September 1938, Britain, France, Germany, and Italy signed the Munich Pact which returned Sudetenland to Germany. This arrangement lasted until 1945, when Sudeten Germans were reunited with the fatherland in another way: Sudetenland was returned to Czechoslovakia, but the Germans living there were unceremoniously shipped to Germany.

A more persistent case of irredentism has been the claim that the government of Argentina continues to make on the Falkland Islands, which Argentineans call the Islas Malvinas. Argentina claims that Britain unjustly seized the islands from it in 1833. The islands are populated by approximately 2300 people who want the islands to remain a British dependency—not a surprising outcome since the British government, always mindful of the principle of national self-determination, refused to allow Argentinean settlement on the islands. In April 1982, Argentina invaded the islands and ousted the British governor. Joyful demonstrations erupted in the streets of Argentina's major cities at the recovery of this bit of the national homeland, followed by just as much sorrow when the British armed forces seized the islands back after a short war that was exceedingly costly for the Argentineans.

The importance of territory for national consciousness can be seen when divided national territory is reunified. For 45 years, Germans, for example, were separated into eastern and western zones by a very concrete border. During this period, two sovereign states each governed a part of Germany—the *Bundesrepublik Deutschland*, or Federal Republic of Germany (FRG) in the west, and the *Deutsche Demokratische Republik*, or German Democratic Republic (GDR) in the east. But few Germans on either side lost their desire to have

Germany reunited. After the symbolic breaching of the Berlin Wall on 9 November 1989, the East German government collapsed. A new government began negotiations for a merger with West Germany. *Die Wende* (the change) came on 3 October 1990, when the GDR was dissolved and all East Germans became citizens of the FRG.

Likewise, one could see the importance attached to the return of Hong Kong to China on 1 July 1997. When Prince Charles formally passed sovereignty over Hong Kong to President Jiang Zemin, it marked the end of what Chinese nationalism has always celebrated (if that is the right word for it): the shameful humiliation of the Chinese nation by European and American imperialists in the 19th century. Extraterritoriality—examined in Chapter 11—was one manifestation of that humiliation. The seizure of Hong Kong in 1841, and the territories around it later in the century by forcing the Chinese emperor to sign what Chinese call **Unequal Treaties**, was another humiliation, one that was formally erased in a large national celebration organized by the government in Beijing.

## A State for the Nation

The other key political objective in the nationalist program is that the nation be self-governing, with the state endowed with the formal rights of sovereignty. This is a logical outgrowth of the belief in national self-determination. If the nation is to thrive, it must be protected. In this view, the nation needs constant nurturing: its national symbols need to be preserved; its language needs to be guarded against corruption from the outside; its children need to be educated properly in the nation's history and the national language; the national culture in its many forms needs to be fostered; and the precious land of the nation needs to be guarded against the predations of others, whether from physical attack or environmental damage. Moreover, as we will see in the next section, the nation's economy needs to be carefully protected, so that foreigners do not end up controlling the economic wealth of the nation, and thereby the nation itself. And there is only one agency powerful enough to take on this multitude of crucial tasks: the sovereign state, with its governmental apparatus.

*"India will awake to life and freedom. A moment comes which comes but rarely in history, when...the soul of a nation, long suppressed, finds utterance."*

The committed nationalist simply cannot permit something as critical as the protection of the nation's well-being to be left to nonnationals. Thus, solutions that involve less than full autonomy, like federalism; the autonomous regions created in China; or the semisovereign arrangements enjoyed by aboriginal peoples in Australia, Canada, and the United States, should not satisfy the committed nationalist. As long as the nation does not govern itself, others will *never* protect the nation as well as nationals, no matter how well meaning they might be. As Jawaharlal Nehru said on the evening of 14 August 1947, just before the creation of a new Indian state, "At the stroke of the midnight hour, when the world sleeps, India will awake to life and freedom. A moment comes which comes but rarely in history, when...the soul of a nation, long suppressed, finds utterance."

It is precisely because of this idea—a nation without a state is a nation asleep—that secessionist nationalism thrives throughout the world.[10] In Canada, Québécois say they want to be *maîtres chez nous*—masters of our own house, controllers of our own destiny. Kurds in Turkey want an independent Kurdistan, Sikhs in India want an independent Khalistan. It is for this reason that Tamils are fighting a civil war in Sri Lanka and the Karen are fighting government forces in Myanmar. Palestinian nationalists will struggle to turn the semisovereign Palestinian Authority into a fully sovereign state. Québécois, Basques, Kurds, Sikhs, Tamils, the Karen, and Palestinians—if they are good members of their own nations—simply cannot trust the state in Canada, Spain, Turkey, India, Sri Lanka, Myanmar, or Israel to take care of their nation properly. And history suggests that the fears of nationalists are not misplaced: too often, not having an independent and sovereign state to safeguard the nation leads to its decimation, as shown by the case of the Kurds discussed in the Focus.

Kurdish Democratic Party fighters in northern Iraq. See the Focus on p. 305.

# FOCUS

## The Kurds: A Nation in Many States, None Their Own

About 26 million people in the world call themselves Kurds. Pastoral and seminomadic, they speak their own language, Kurdish, a branch of Iranian. They live in the Zagros and Taurus mountains that extend in an arc from western Iran in the east to Turkey in the west, and are thus spread across a number of different jurisdictions. Over half live in Turkey; the remainder live in the area around the nexus of the Turkish, Syrian, Iraqi, Armenian, and Iranian borders that is colloquially known as Kurdistan.

Historically, Kurdish tribes were able to maintain an independent existence despite the invaders who periodically swept through this area, often occupying Kurdish territory. The area was brought into the Ottoman Empire in the 14th century, but semiautonomous Kurdish kingdoms continued to flourish. Indeed, in the 19th century, these kingdoms were in fact encouraged along the empire's borders with Persia (Iran). With the end of the Ottoman Empire after the First World War, the Kurds were promised their own national homeland, Kurdistan, by the Treaty of Sèvres, signed in August 1920. This treaty was never ratified, and the Treaty of Lausanne of 1923 which replaced it made no mention of Kurdistan. As a consequence, the Kurds found themselves citizens of five different states.

The consequences of having to live in other people's states have been dire. Since the end of the First World War, considerable efforts have been devoted to denying Kurdish nationhood. In 1925, the Turks put down a Kurdish rebellion, executed 48 nationalist leaders, and relocated others. The Turkish government also passed strict laws banning any manifestation of Kurdish nationalism: for example, the use of the Kurdish language was forbidden. In the late 1970s and early 1980s, extremist Kurdish groups began a guerrilla war against the Turkish government; thousands have been killed on both sides, many more made homeless.

The situation was little better in other countries. For example, toward the end of the Second World War, a Kurdish Republic was established with Soviet assistance in Iran, but when Soviet forces were withdrawn, the president of the short-lived republic, Qazi Muhammad, was executed. Both Iran and Iraq have used Kurdish homelessness in their conflicts with one another. For example, Iran encouraged the Kurds to rebel in 1974 during a border dispute with Iraq; the rebellion collapsed when Iran withdrew its support after the dispute had been settled. The Kurds in Iraq were left to face the hostility of the regime in Baghdad. Undeterred, the Kurds again sided with Iran during the 1980–1988 Iran-Iraq war. This time, the Iraqi government of Saddam Hussein declared open war on Iraqi Kurds, including the use of chemical weapons against Kurdish civilians in 1988, leaving thousands dead. The Kurds were yet again encouraged to rise up during the Gulf War of 1991, believing the United States-led international coalition that was at war with Iraq would bring down the government of Saddam Hussein. Once again they were mistaken. The coalition did not try to unseat Saddam Hussein, who took the opportunity to attack the Kurds with such ferocity that the international community was moved to intervene.

# THE POLITICAL ECONOMY OF NATIONALISM: THE RISE OF THE PROTECTIVE STATE

The political agenda of the nationalist ideology demands a homeland for the nation and a state for the nation. Nationalism also demands that the nation must have a strong and independent **national economy** to sustain it. Just as nationalists look to the state to protect and nurture the nation, so too do nationalists look to the state to develop, nurture, maintain, and protect the national economy.

As noted in Chapter 9, the mercantile system evolved along with the sovereign state; the mercantile objective was to enhance the economic strength of the state by developing indigenous industry, accumulating bullion and territories overseas, and encouraging trade surpluses. In this, the role of the sovereign state was critical. The state regulated flows in and out by levying taxes and duties on both imported and exported goods. The state encouraged overseas development by granting monopolistic company charters. The state provided the infrastructure for the accumulation of overseas wealth: armies and bureaucracies to seize and administer colonies, and navies to ward off privateers and pirates and provide for the safe passage of goods and bullion. The state, when necessary, sought to blunt the competition of merchants or traders from other countries. And the state provided the environment in which the huge transformations of the Industrial Revolution occurred.

## From Mercantilism to Free Trade

As the notion of nation took root in Europe, a concern to maximize *state* wealth naturally flowed into a concern to maximize *national* wealth. However, the mechanisms by which this was to be done differed considerably, for the methods of mercantilism were challenged and roundly discredited by the liberal economists of the late 18th century. But the means these liberal economists advocated as the most effective way to ensure the wealth of nations were also widely rejected; only Britain fully embraced their teachings. Others had rather different views about how the nation's economy should be protected.

### The Liberal Critique of Mercantilism

The mercantilism that had been dominant for so long was finally challenged in the latter part of the 18th century. The clearest critique of the ideas of mercantilists is to be found in the views of Adam Smith (1723–90), a Scottish philosopher whose 1776 book *An Inquiry into the Nature and Causes of the Wealth of Nations* analyzed how wealth is produced and distributed. Smith fixed his attention on the wealth derived from the division of labour, and in particular from the results of the pursuit of self-interest by individuals in the market-place, captured best in the classic sentence: "It is not from the benevolence of the butcher, the brewer, or the baker that we expect our dinner, but from their regard to their own interest."[11]

In part, Smith's thought was inspired by his exposure to François Quesnay, the founder of a group at the French court in Versailles that called themselves *les Économistes* (much later, in the 19th century, they came to be known as the Physiocrats, from the title of a collection of Quesnay's works). Although the economics of *les Économistes* proved rather less sophisticated than Smith's economic analysis (the Physiocrats yearned for a France dominated by an agricultural economy), they did share a critical view of mercantilism. The Physiocrats believed that the economy should be allowed to work without government interference or artificial supports for manufacturing. Their exhortatory slogan was simple: *laissez faire*—let it be.

In a similar vein (but with a very different vision), Smith's economic analysis led him to the same view—a critique of all parts of the mercantile project. First, in different parts of *The Wealth of Nations*, he analyzed why no good comes of the state's intrusive regulation of domestic trade, encouraged by mercantilist policy. In Book IV, he outlined why regulation by the state upsets the "natural balance of industry" that would be achieved if every individual were left to pursue his or her own advantage. To be sure, Smith was no enemy of the state. But his analysis led him to the view that "how honourable, how useful, or how necessary soever" the state may be,[12] the restrictive practices it sanctioned and maintained placed needless obstacles in the way of individual effort and the "invisible hand" that turned individual self-interest into a common good. Rather, in Book V he outlines his belief that the proper role of the state should be limited purely to ensuring that individual security and liberty were provided for, and to building only the necessary public works that would not be produced by private entrepreneurs, such as roads.

*"If a foreign country can supply us with a commodity cheaper than we ourselves can make it, better buy it of them with some part of the produce of our industry, employed in a way in which we have some advantage."*

Second, Smith was critical of the barriers that mercantilist policies put in the way of international trade. As in the case of domestic trade, Smith's analysis led him to the view that people would be better off if the benefits of an international division of labour were allowed to prevail, unrestrained by state intervention through taxes, duties, artificial encouragements to particular industries, or support for monopolistic companies via royal charters. He stated succinctly the notion that would later be developed as the economic theory of **comparative advantage**: "If a foreign country can supply us with a commodity cheaper than we ourselves can make it, better buy it of them with some part of the produce of our industry, employed in a way in which we have some advantage."[13]

Third, Smith's analysis of money, the "great wheel of circulation," revealed the flaws of the mercantilist preoccupation with bullion and the notion that wealth consists of money. What drives people to want money is not for its own sake, but for the goods it purchases and the wealth its investment can bring.

Finally, Smith devoted a chapter of Book IV to colonies, arguing that in fact a country like Britain actually was worse off with colonies than it would be if it granted its overseas possessions independence. Moreover, in his view the existing restraints on trade between the metropole and the colony did little more than privilege a few. The nation as a whole would reap far more benefits, he argued, if trade between the imperial centre and the periphery were freed and the market allowed to work its magic.

### Britain and the Embrace of Free Trade

Such views had radical implications for state policy as it was widely practised at the time, and for the way in which states and markets interacted. Smith's theories suggested that if people really wanted to maximize their wealth, they would demand that their governments abandon charter companies, monopolies, the nurturing of manufacturers, tariffs, duties, and taxes that "artificially" shifted the market; they would even abandon colonies. Instead, they would allow goods to move across national borders unimpeded by government interference, a policy that slowly came to be known as **free trade** (a phrase that up to that point had had a number of other meanings, including as a euphemism for smuggling). Consumers would buy the best goods at the lowest price; sellers would specialize in those goods where they had a comparative advantage. To use the example favoured by David Ricardo (1772–1823), a British free trade advocate, it made no sense for both Portugal and Britain to try and produce wine and wool. Portugal's climate and soil were well suited to wine-making but not at all suited to wool-growing; Britain was in exactly the opposite situation. Therefore, it was more efficient for Portugal to produce wine and Britain to produce wool, and for the two nations to trade with one another to satisfy the demands for those commodities which were inefficient to produce.

The radical views of academics like Smith, and his successors like Ricardo and John Stuart Mill (1806–73), were eventually embraced by those in the political realm. Within ten years of the publication of *The Wealth of Nations*, William Pitt the Younger, the prime minister of Britain from 1783 to 1801 (and again in 1804–06), negotiated a commercial treaty with France that removed a number of barriers to trade in both countries. The Napoleonic Wars—and the huge state interference in the marketplace necessitated by that struggle—put a temporary stop to the attempts to institute freer trade. Following those wars, the idea of free trade was again pressed on a number of different fronts. Two sets of regulations were seized on as symbols of mercantilism by the burgeoning manufacturing classes in England: the Navigation Acts of 1651 and 1660 and the Corn Law of 1815.

Under the Navigation Acts of 1651 and 1660 and subsequent amendments, all trade between Britain and its colonies and all foreign countries had to be carried out in ships that were owned by British subjects, registered with the British government, and operated mainly by British sailors. These restrictive laws ensured that the British merchant marine fleet would grow to dominate world trade in the 18th century.

The **Corn Laws** dated back to 1437 and 1463, when English growers of wheat and other grains (called "corn" in England) were given a monopoly that involved price supports and restrictions on both exports and imports of grain. The Corn Laws were frequently amended in the centuries thereafter to take account of shifting patterns of harvests, but the essential purpose—to benefit landowners by keeping grain prices high—never varied. Following the Napoleonic Wars, the government passed another Corn Law in 1815 that excluded foreign grains, leading to yet another rise in the price of bread.

However, the changing face of the British economy in the early 19th century was radically altering the political landscape. The growing urban working class was increasingly upset at the high price of bread caused by these restrictions; widespread protests greeted the 1815 law. At least one protest caused the authorities to panic: when 60 000 men, women, and children gathered in St Peter's fields in Manchester on 16 August 1819 to protest the high price of bread, the local magistrates called out members of the militia, who charged the crowd. Over 600 people were killed in the ensuing Peterloo Massacre. But it was not only the urban workers who were opposed to the Corn Laws; the industrial capitalists likewise bridled at the artificial protections the landed gentry were receiving.

Moreover, government policy was slow to change. The system of representation in the House of Commons at this time undisguisedly favoured the agricultural land-owning classes, and underrepresented or even completely excluded large portions of the population.

The franchise was limited to those with property, and the "borough" system of representation had remained unchanged for centuries despite huge shifts in population. As a result, the country was overrepresented and cities underrepresented. Indeed, some large cities which had come into existence since 1600, such as Birmingham and Manchester, were not represented in the House of Commons at all. On the other hand, constituencies like Old Sarum, with seven voters, or Dunwich, which by the 19th century lay partially under the sea and had 14 voters, each sent a member to the House of Commons.

Thus, the struggle for free trade in the early 19th century must be examined in the context of the wider class conflicts of British politics of this era. By slow degrees, these pressures resulted in change. William Huskisson, appointed president of the Board of Trade in 1823, consolidated and simplified some 1500 pieces of protective legislation, lowered tariffs on a number of items, and reformed the Navigation Acts. The Reform Act of 1832 radically altered the system of representation.

But the Corn Laws remained basically untouched. Because they symbolized the privilege of the landed class, much of the free trade movement was centred on this legislation and its repeal. In the 1820s, the laws were tinkered with, but no substantive changes were made. In the wake of a depression in 1837, an Anti–Corn Law League was formed in London. In 1838, a similar league was formed in Manchester by Richard Cobden and John Bright, two cotton manufacturers, who began a campaign to press for the repeal of the Corn Laws. Cobden was elected to the House of Commons in 1841, where he also argued the free trade case. These efforts changed the mind of Sir Robert Peel, prime minister of the rural-dominated Conservative government. In 1842 Peel introduced some reforms, and in January 1846, in the wake of a blight that ruined the potato crop in Ireland and caused a massive famine, he introduced an act that would lower duties as of 1849. This measure was only passed with the votes of the opposition members in the House of Commons, for the Conservatives were deeply split on repealing the Corn Laws. (Indeed, in June 1846, Conservative backbenchers and the opposition combined to vote down a measure, prompting Peel to resign.)

With the Corn Laws repealed and the balance of power in the House of Commons shifting, the pace of British embrace of free trade accelerated. In 1849, the Navigation Acts were completely abolished. William Gladstone's government reduced tariffs further, and in 1860, a commercial treaty with France was signed reducing tariffs. By 1874, Britain had fully embraced free trade. All export duties had been abolished; shipping was free of all restraints; and the only tariffs on imports were revenue-generating duties on tobacco and spirits, all of which were countervailed by excise taxes on British tobacco and spirits (and hence not protectionist).

## The Economic Nationalist Challenge

The embrace of free trade by Britain in the 19th century was not widely copied. In large measure this was because the idea of free trade sits uneasily with nationalists. Arguments for free trade rest on the assumption that unfettering trade will lead to the expansion of economic activity and increased economic benefits for everyone. For the nationalist, however, free trade poses a problem. The economic component of the national idea—or economic nationalism—emerged in response to the liberal economic theories of Smith, Ricardo, and Mill, as did the idea, and practice, of the protective state.

## What is "Economic" Nationalism?

All good nationalists must be concerned about how unfettered economic exchange might affect the ability of the nation to protect itself. As international trade increases, the welfare of *individual consumers* may increase as the factors of production, responding to the demands of the market, are allocated more efficiently. But as is clear from the discussion earlier in this chapter, the nationalist is moved not so much by concern for the welfare of the *individual* per se as of the *individual-within-the-nation*. Thus the nationalist is concerned about what impact the workings of the "invisible hand" of the market and the magic of comparative advantage will have on the nation as a whole.

*Having a nation of rich consumers may not provide the nation with the strength it needs to resist the importunities of others, and to be independent and autonomous.*

In particular, the nationalist worries that while the market may allocate "efficiently" from the perspective of an individual consumer, it may not allocate in a way that allows the nation to be strong. The nationalist tends to make a distinction between a *rich nation* and a *strong economy,* not necessarily assuming a linkage between the two. In the nationalist view, the nation needs a strong economy to remain free and separate, and a strong economy is not something that can simply be purchased on the open market. Having a nation of rich consumers may not provide the *nation* with the strength it needs to resist the importunities of others, and to be independent and autonomous.

The logical and obvious end implied by the ideal of national independence is the creation of an **autarky**, a totally self-sufficient economy that is not connected to, dependent on, or vulnerable to anyone else.[14] This was the vision of Johann Gottlieb Fichte (1762–1814), a philosopher of the Romantic school who is remembered for his work on Immanuel Kant. But he was also an ardent German nationalist, his nationalism rooted in the Kantian ethic of the achievement of autonomy. In 1800, he took what Carlton Hayes terms an "excursion into economics,"[15] and wrote what can be regarded as the germinal work of **economic nationalism**. *Der geschlossene Handelstaat* (The Closed Commercial State) was a prescription for a particular kind of national economy. It argued for an abandonment of both mercantilism—which Fichte argued caused wars between competing dynastic states—and *laissez-faire* free trade—which Fichte argued caused the kind of exploitation of the individual seen in the mills and mines of England. Rather, he argued that if each national state strove for self-sufficiency—in other words, closed itself off from economic intercourse with other states—these evils would be eliminated.

The key means to this autarkic end was the steady and relentless reduction of external trade by the pursuit of what would later be known as a policy of **import substitution**, in which the needs of the nation were to be met by indigenous production that was fostered by the state, and **protectionism**, in which barriers were erected against foreign competition by high tariff walls. What little interstate trade remained in Fichte's ideal system would be strictly regulated, conducted by the state itself.

## The Protective State

Fichte's ideas had little immediate impact on the policies of the European states in the early 19th century. Moreover, his place as the foremost economic nationalist has been eclipsed by others such as his fellow-German Friedrich List (1789–1846) and the American publisher who also wrote books on economics and sociology, Henry Carey (1793–1879). But by 1900, the essence of his advocacy was well rooted in the national policies of the vast majority of states except Britain. The Fichtean ideal of numerous economic autarkies coexisting in peace and harmony was never achieved. But Fichte's notion that nation-building depended on an economy that was in essence closed to the forces of truly free economic exchange between states was widely embraced. Likewise, the free trade ideas being pressed by the British were as widely rejected. Many simply did not believe that their nations would benefit from free trade. Others pointed to the fact that Britain's industrialization had been achieved because of the protectionist benefits of mercantilism, and that from a position of industrial, economic, and financial strength, it was easy for the British to open their markets completely. Instead, the **protective state**, embracing protectionism for the purpose of building the nation, expanded everywhere.

Throughout the 19th century, for example, the policies of the United States government were driven by economic nationalism. From the outset, American politicians worried that the United States would never catch up to Britain. Albert Gallatin, the secretary of the treasury in 1810, bemoaned the obstacles to the growth of American industry posed by "the vastly superior capital of Great Britain which enables her merchants to give very long-term credit, to sell on small profits, and to make occasional sacrifices."[16] A succession of administrations were considerably attracted to protectionism: governments consistently targeted defence expenditures to encourage American production. Likewise, a national tariff on imports remained consistently above 30 per cent throughout the 19th century; on some products, such as rolled bar iron, the tariff was set as high as 95 per cent. In some sectors, the tariff worked to produce a huge expansion. For example, in the 1870s, the tariff on steel rails was almost 100 per cent, with the result that those few American firms which owned the patents to use the Bessemer process of making steel made vast profits while meeting the massive demand for steel rails.

The idea of embracing the protective state proved no less attractive to newer nations which emerged in the 1800s. Otto von Bismarck, the minister-president of Prussia and the first chancellor of a united imperial Germany in the 1870s, embraced a range of protectionist measures to discourage foreign competition and encourage German industry. The Meiji restoration in Japan—which we will look at in more detail in the next chapter—embraced the protective state as a means of encouraging indigenous industrial growth.

In Canada, Sir John A. Macdonald won the 1878 election on a promise of a "National Policy" that was designed to make the new Dominion economically self-sufficient. Under the National Policy of 1879, the government in Ottawa erected high tariff barriers on imports to promote indigenous industry and completed a transcontinental railway, in part to encourage the growth of east-west trade within the country. The National Policy was also designed to encourage American firms to establish branch plants in Canada, which they did in large numbers. But there was another, more paradoxical, purpose, as J.L. Granatstein has reminded us: to get the United States to open its markets to Canadian products. As Macdonald said, "It is only by closing our doors and by cutting them out of our markets that they will open theirs to us."[17]

In Australia, following federation in 1901, the high tariffs that had fostered the growth of a manufacturing sector in Victoria were embraced, and indeed enhanced, by the Commonwealth, or federal, government, much to the chagrin of many in New South Wales, where pastoralists remained firmly committed to the benefits of free trade. Between 1905 and 1908, the Liberal Protectionist prime minister, Alfred Deakin, with support from the Australian Labor party, passed a series of acts known as the "New Protection," which sought to pass along the benefits of tariff protection to workers via enhanced wages, better working conditions, and a range of social welfare programs. Although some of the New Protection legislation was struck down, the essence of the protectionist deal remained intact. Industrialists and manufacturers received state protection, and in return, workers were provided with better wages and working conditions from employers and social welfare benefits from the state.[18]

## Protectionism and the "National Economy"

Many scholars use "mercantilism" as a synonym for the protectionism favoured by economic nationalists. But sloppily equating mercantilism and the kind of protections that emerged in the 19th century (and, as we shall see in later chapters, the 20th century as well) is to commit a double error. First, it fails to recognize the important differences between the mercantile system of the 16th, 17th, and 18th centuries and the protectionism of the 19th, not least the radical shift in how bullion was regarded.

Far more importantly, however, equating the two terms entirely misses the fact that the kind of protectionism advocated by Fichte and embraced by so many states around the international system was first and foremost an outgrowth of the national idea and the nationalist's political agenda. For "economic nationalism" is not a thing unto itself—it is merely nationalism whose attention is turned to the economic aspects of the nation's existence.

As Fichte and all other writers in the economic nationalist school understand, nationalists tend to place great importance on the development of a "national" economy. *Inter alia*, that means rejecting the assumptions of comparative advantage, because a proper national economy, in the nationalist view, must be "well rounded." Frequently a "well-rounded" economy means that sectors are nurtured not necessarily for their pure economic benefit, but for their value as symbols of national competence. Thus, for example, in the 19th and early 20th centuries, a steel industry was often seen as the *sine qua non* of a mature nation; in the middle of the 20th century, an automobile industry was regarded in the same way. At the 20th century's end, as we will see in Chapter 17, economic nationalists are no less concerned about the national economy, though it is more difficult to create "national" industries in a globalized economy.

Moreover, nationalist conceptions of a national economy focus on the importance of economic factors to the existence, strength, and durability of the nation. This means that the culture of the nation—its language, arts, letters, sport, and entertainment—is as much a part of the "economic" equation as the production of widgets. For the nationalist, protecting the "economy" also means protecting the economic basis of the national culture. In other words, the protective state refuses to try to separate human activity into discrete economic, cultural, or political spheres.

## CONCLUSION

In this chapter we have looked at the national idea and how it is manifested in an ideology of nationalism. We have also looked at the nationalist agenda, and in particular at the emergence of the protective state as a successor to the mercantilist state.

As the title of this chapter suggests, it is useful to think of attachment to the nation, and the ideological and economic constructs of that attachment, in religious terms. The nation is something that people believe in; like beliefs about the divine, belief in nation is an act of faith. And as such, it is pointless to deny nation or try to show rationally why nation does not, should not, or cannot exist. Trying to deny the existence of nation to a committed nationalist is like trying to deny the existence of God to someone who believes in a supreme being.

I have argued in this chapter that the embrace of the national idea and the nationalist credo has been worldwide and pervasive. To be sure, the identification with nation is not unanimous. Not everyone defines their political identity in national terms. For example, those who occupy marginal locations in the community may be utterly indifferent about their political identity. Ask a squeegee kid in Toronto, a crack addict in the South Bronx, a shanty-town dweller in Rio de Janeiro, a child construction worker in Yangon, a teenage prostitute in Bangkok, or an illiterate and landless grandmother in Biharipur about their feelings about their nation. One is unlikely to get the same kind of reaction as if you asked well-off bourgeois members of those communities about their feelings about Canada, the United States, Brazil, Myanmar, Thailand, or India.

*The nationalist sentiment works equally well in centrally planned totalitarian dictatorships, fascist authoritarian regimes, revolutionary peasant movements, fundamentalist theocracies, or capitalist liberal democracies.*

But there can be little doubt that nationalism is both dominant and pervasive among the political elites and the broad mass of societies throughout the world. In part, the global reach of nationalism is a function of the ease with which the national idea travels. Its flexible tenets allow the nationalist ideal to be embraced in a wide variety of cultural, economic, and political settings, for nationalism does not require a certain soil to flourish. The nationalist sentiment works equally well in centrally planned totalitarian dictatorships, fascist authoritarian regimes, revolutionary peasant movements, fundamentalist theocracies, or capitalist liberal democracies. Nationalism as an ideology can be layered onto any culture, religion, economic system, or political form. It can be embraced by a tiny number of people—the 10 000 people on Nauru, for example—or a number in the hundreds of millions. It can be easily "taught," since its precepts are few, easily understood, and readily adaptable to universal human emotions. For nationalism systematizes and plays on (and to) the desire to belong to community, and the tendency to have the emotions aroused by community.

But the national idea, once grasped and believed in by billions of people, has a profound impact on world politics and the international political economy. To a discussion of nationalism's different impacts we now turn.

## Keyword File

| | |
|---|---|
| National symbols | Eastern Question |
| "African Eve" | Nationalist credo |
| Language | National self-determination |
| Global language | National mythology |
| Bilingual | Nationalist agenda |
| Multilingual | National homeland |
| Constructed story | Irredentism |
| "Imagined community" | Unequal Treaties |
| Intersubjectivity | *Maîtres chez nous* |
| Nationalism | Comparative advantage |
| Nationalist | Free trade |
| Nation | Corn Laws |
| Ethnicity | Autarky |
| Nationality | Import substitution |
| "Global tribes" | Protectionism |
| National consciousness | Protective state |
| Union flag | Economic nationalism |
| Industrial Revolution | National economy |
| Nation-state | |

## For Further Exploration

HARD COPY

Anderson, Benedict. *Imagined Communities: Reflections on the Origin and Spread of Nationalism,* 2d ed. London: Verso, 1991.

Eddy, J. and D. Shreuder, eds. *The Rising of Colonial Nationalism.* Sydney: Allen and Unwin, 1988.

Fallows, James. "How the world works," *The Atlantic Monthly* (December 1993), 61–87.

Hayes, Carlton J.H. *The Historical Evolution of Modern Nationalism.* New York: Russell and Russell, 1931.

Ignatieff, Michael. *Blood and Belonging: Journeys into the New Nationalism.* Toronto: Penguin, 1994.

James, Paul. "Reconstituting the nation-state: a postmodern republic takes shape," *ARENA Journal* 4 (1994–95), 69–89.

Mayall, James. *Nationalism in International Society.* Cambridge: Cambridge University Press, 1990.

WEBLINKS

**http://condor.depaul.edu/~traffens/determination/**

Site maintained by DePaul University; resources on self-determination and nationalism, including hotlinks to independence movements

**http://www.aber.ac.uk/~inpwww/res/nateth.htm**

Site maintained by the Department of International Relations at the University of Wales, Aberystwyth, focusing on ethnicity and nationalism

## *Notes to Chapter 12*

1. Originally, Ernest Renan, "What is a nation?" in *Poetry of the Celtic Races and Other Essays* (New York: Kennikut Press, 1896), 61–83. This essay has been reprinted in numerous anthologies: for example, Mark O. Dickerson, Thomas Flanagan, and Neil Nevitte, eds., *Introductory Readings in Government and Politics* (Toronto: Methuen, 1983).

2. Hans Kohn, *The Idea of Nationalism* (New York: Macmillan, 1961); Benedict Anderson, *Imagined Communities: Reflections on the Origin and Spread of Nationalism*, 2d ed. (London: Verso, 1991).

3. Joel Kotkin, *Tribes: How Race, Religion, and Family Determine Success in the New Global Economy* (New York: Random House, 1992).

4. E.J. Hobsbawm, *Nations and Nationalism Since 1780: Programme, Myth, Reality* (Cambridge: Cambridge University Press, 1990).

5. Evan Luard, *War in International Society: A Study in International Sociology* (New Haven, CT: Yale University Press, 1986), 57.

6. James Mayall, *Nationalism in International Society* (Cambridge: Cambridge University Press, 1990), 38–40.

7. The following list is adapted from Boyd C. Shafer, *Nationalism: Its Nature and Interpreters* (Washington: American Historical Association, 1976); see also Shafer, *Nationalism and Internationalism: Belonging in the Human Experience* (Malabar, FL: Robert E. Krieger, 1982).

8. Ernesto Fritsche Aceves, "La representación épica de la guerra: el discurso oficial en torno de los héroes," International Colloquium on the Mexican-American War, Mexico City, 23 September 1997 (http://sunsite.unam.mx/revistas/1847).

9. See, for example, the discussion of Canada's "northern-ness" in Carl Berger, "The true north strong and free," in Peter Russell, ed., *Nationalism in Canada* (Toronto: McGraw-Hill Ryerson, 1966), 3–26.

10. For a detailed post–Cold War survey listing the struggles for self-determination around the world, see Morton H. Halperin, David J. Scheffer and Patricia L. Small, *Self-Determination in the New World Order* (Washington: Carnegie Endowment for International Peace, 1992), Appendix.

11. Adam Smith, *The Wealth of Nations*, ed. Andrew Skinner (Harmondsworth, U.K.: Penguin, 1970 [1776]), 119 [14].

12. Smith, *Wealth of Nations*, 430–31.

13. Smith, *Wealth of Nations*, 401.

14. For a further exploration, see Kim Richard Nossal, "Economic nationalism and continental integration: assumptions, arguments and advocacies," in *The Collected Research Studies/The Royal Commission on the Economic Union and Development Prospects for Canada* (Macdonald Commission), vol 29: *The Politics of Canada's Economic Relationship with the United States*, Denis Stairs and Gilbert R. Winham, eds., (Ottawa: Supply and Services Canada, 1985), 55–94.

15. Carlton J.H. Hayes, *The Historical Evolution of Modern Nationalism* (New York: Russell and Russell, 1931), 263.

16. Quoted in James Fallows, "How the world works," *The Atlantic Monthly*, December 1993, 86.

17. J.L. Granatstein, "Free trade between Canada and the United States: the issue that will not go away," in Stairs and Winham, eds., *Canada's Economic Relationship with the United States*, 17.

18. Ann Capling and Brian Galligan, *Beyond the Protective State: The Political Economy of Australia's Manufacturing Industry Policy* (Cambridge: Cambridge University Press, 1992).

# *The* Homogenizing Impact *of* Nationalism: Empire *and the* Nation-State

**I N T R O D U C T I O N**

The nationalist ideology that seized Europe and the Americas in the 19th century eventually spread all over the globe, changing how people perceived their communities. It had a powerful impact on the dominant forms of political organization in the international system, solidifying the hegemonic position of the sovereign state. It has had an equally deep impact on ideas about the role of economy in the life of the nation, leading to the growth of the protective state. The national idea has also had an impact on war and how it is fought.

The purpose of this chapter and the one that follows is to explore the various impacts on world politics of the idea of nation. We begin in this chapter with an examination of how the national idea shaped, and then was transformed by, the dominant form of political organization in the 19th century—imperialism. Chapter 14 looks at the effects of nationalism on war.

## NATIONALISM'S IMPERIAL FACE

European empires expanded dramatically in the 16th and 17th centuries; in the late 18th and early 19th centuries, they declined equally dramatically as the European powers lost their empires in the western hemisphere. By the middle of the 19th century, European imperial holdings in the Americas had been reduced to Belize in Central America, the coast of Guiana on the northern littoral of South America, and the Caribbean islands. However, that loss revealed that the logic of the mercantilist argument was seriously flawed: although European flags no longer flew over much of the Americas, these former colonies continued to trade with the metropolitan powers of Europe. Actually holding them as colonial territories did not seem to be necessary to derive economic benefits from them.

This is one of the key reasons for the indifference to overseas colonies that European powers demonstrated for much of the 19th century. It was not that Europeans lacked interest in overseas trade during this period. On the contrary: they demonstrated considerable interest in expanding trade, particularly in Asia, where Britain, France, and other countries such as the United States sought to open the closed markets in China and Japan to foreign trade.

Nor is this to suggest that territorial acquisitions came to an end during this period. Russians pushed eastward and southward to gain an overland empire. Americans pushed south and west against Mexico, north and west against British North America, and everywhere against the native peoples in their quest for **Manifest Destiny**.[*] And the countries with established overseas empires such as Britain and France also expanded. France extended its control in Algeria; Britain did the same in India, and acquired new possessions during this period that would be important for both trade and the projection of its already formidable naval power. In 1833 the British occupied the Falkland Islands over Argentinean objections, providing the British navy with a future coaling station in the South Atlantic. In 1841, British forces occupied a small Chinese fishing port at the mouth of the Pearl River (now the Zhu Jiang), downstream from the major trading centre of Canton (now Guangzhou). A year later, the Chinese emperor was forced to sign a treaty ceding the island of Hong Kong to Britain in perpetuity. A private French company, with strong backing from the French government (and equally strong initial opposition from Britain), secured a concession from the Egyptian government to build a canal across the 120-km-wide Isthmus of Suez; the Suez Canal Company opened the canal for business on 17 November 1869.

### Imperial Expansion, 1870-1914

In the latter part of the 19th century, however, Europeans experienced a fresh burst of enthusiasm for imperialism. Between 1870 and the outbreak of the Great War in 1914,

---

[*] In 1845, John Louis O'Sullivan, an American editor, wrote that it was America's "manifest destiny" to populate the entire continent. The Philadelphia *Public Ledger* put it more bluntly in 1853: the United States, it wrote, was bounded on the "East by sunrise, West by sunset, North by Arctic Expeditions and South as Far as we darn please." Quoted in Charles W. Kegley and Eugene R. Wittkopf, *American Foreign Policy: Pattern and Process* (New York: St Martin's, 1979), 32.

European powers scrambled to establish empires in those places of the world not yet claimed, mainly Africa, the South Pacific, and parts of Asia.

## European Imperialism: The Scramble for Africa

In the 1870s, European settlement in Africa was limited to coastal enclaves dotted along its littoral; Europeans found the interior of the continent quite impenetrable. By the outbreak of the First World War in 1914, however, Africa had been fully carved up among Belgian, British, French, German, Italian, Portuguese, and Spanish possessions. Only a few European states—Austria, the Netherlands, the Nordics, and Switzerland—were not immersed in the scramble. And only two African communities remained independent and sovereign states: Ethiopia and Liberia. Ethiopia managed to stay independent by beating Egyptian and then Italian efforts at military conquest, along with some skilful diplomacy by the emperor, Menelik II. Ruling from 1889 to 1913, he managed to play the European imperial powers off against each other. Liberia was deemed "untouchable": it had been founded as a result of efforts of the American Colonization Society to resettle freed American slaves. Independent since 1847, Liberia enjoyed recognition and support from both Britain and the United States.

The process of carving up an entire continent in the space of a generation was triggered by a relatively unremarkable incident. At the Congress of Berlin, which was held in 1878 to deal with the consequences of the most recent Russo-Turkish war, Otto von Bismarck, the chancellor of Germany, decided to try to soothe French anger over the loss of Alsace-Lorraine in the Franco-Prussian war of 1870–71 by encouraging the French to seize Tunis. French forces did so, and set off a chain reaction of interstate rivalry that was to reverberate across the continent.

The French occupation of Tunis annoyed the Italian government, for 20 000 Italians lived in Tunis, and the Italians had been considering establishing a north African colony like French Algeria; now they had to look elsewhere. A rebellion in Egypt in 1882 prompted a British intervention, but after putting down the rebellion, they simply stayed and occupied the country, much to the chagrin of the French. On the west coast of Africa, Leopold II of Belgium tried to establish a personal kingdom along the Congo river. France immediately responded by sending an explorer to lay claim to the area. Britain tried to thwart both by supporting Portugal's claim to the Congo mouth, prompting Bismarck to move to isolate Britain with French support. Bismarck, who was skeptical of the value of colonies for Germany, even secured the beginnings of an African empire for Germany in what is now Namibia. In November 1884, Bismarck invited Britain and France to a conference in Berlin where the lands around the Congo and the Niger Rivers were divided up.

The Berlin conference did not bring the gamesmanship and rivalries between the European powers in Africa to an end, however. Germany and Britain continued to quarrel over land in east Africa; Britain, Italy, and France quarrelled over Somaliland; Britain and France maintained an on-going rivalry over Niger and Guinea; an "incident" at Fashoda in May 1894 was triggered by British attempts to block French access to the upper Nile. Bit by bit those African territories unclaimed by a European power were taken over. The last to go was Morocco: in March 1912, the sultan was compelled to sign a treaty turning his country into a French protectorate.

*The partition of Africa was played by European leaders exactly like a giant game of Risk. Armies were moved around the game board; territories were traded between the players; secret deals were struck.*

It should be noted that the **scramble for Africa** in the late 1800s tends to be told as a European story rather than an African one. This is not at all coincidental: the partition of Africa was played by European leaders exactly like a giant game of *Risk*. Armies were moved around the game board; territories were traded between the players; secret deals were struck; merchants and traders were bought off at key moments; lines were drawn on maps in conference halls in Berlin. Often the territory that was the object of these games lacked obvious economic value to the new European "owner" except as something that could be traded in the next round of negotiations.

Needless to say, all of this was done without reference to the wants, desires, or interests of the indigenous inhabitants. If Africans appeared in the consciousness of European diplomats during this period, they tended to be as problems that had to be solved: How to cope with a rebellious khedive (ruler) of Egypt? What to do about Muhammad Ahmad, who claimed he was the Mahdi (messiah) and whose followers were laying seige to Khartoum, defended by Gen. Charles "Chinese" Gordon? How to get the Sultan of Zanzibar to cease objecting to German claims on his land?*

### Japanese Imperialism: The Meiji Restoration and After

The expansion of empire in this era was no longer a purely European affair. Both Japan and the United States also actively engaged in the imperialist rush.

By this time Japan had also joined the ranks of the industrializing world. In the 1840s and 1850s, the United States had tried to do in Japan what Americans and Europeans had done in China—open the country to trade beyond the lone Dutch trading station at Deshima. In the summer of 1853, a naval mission headed by Commodore Matthew Perry sailed into Edo harbour and presented the U.S. demands that Japan open its cities to foreign traders. Unable to match the firepower of the United States naval vessels, the Japanese signed a treaty in March 1854 agreeing to open their ports.

However, the arrival of Americans and Europeans provoked an antiforeign backlash, which had a powerful effect on domestic Japanese politics. At that time, the structures of governance during the Tokugawa era were essentially feudal-like: the emperor was a symbolic figure who reigned but did not rule from the imperial city of Kyōto. Real political power was exercised over a network of clans from the city of Edo, where the shōgun, or ruler, resided. But every shōgun after 1854 proved incapable of stemming the growing antiforeign violence. Moreover, every antiforeign act provoked the European powers to punish

---

* The "solutions" chosen were, respectively: plot with the Ottoman Empire to have him overthrown; procrastinate for eight months so that the relief column eventually sent arrives two days after the fall of the city and the death of Gordon; threaten him with naval bombardment.

the Japanese by shelling their cities or demanding indemnities. This merely fuelled more resentment against the foreigners and against the governors in Edo incapable of protecting Japan against the predations of the Europeans and Americans. In 1867, Prince Mutsuhito became emperor, and took as his reign name Meiji, or "enlightened rule," which galvanized opposition to the shōgunate. Eventually, the shōgunate collapsed: Tokugawa Yoshinobu resigned in 1868, and control over the government was reasserted by the emperor (from whom we derive the term commonly used to describe this period, the **Meiji restoration**).

During the Meiji reign, important aspects of the Japanese political economy were transformed, primarily by the simple expedient of copying the practices in Europe and the United States. Thus, for example, Europeans were engaged to create a European-style army and navy; the *samurai* class of professional warriors was abolished and universal male conscription was introduced. A new system of universal education was introduced on the American model. The feudal-like structures of governance were changed. The great clans were abolished, and their lords, or *daimyō,* were given a pension. In their place, a European-style system of government was established. Symbolically, the emperor moved from Kyōto to Edo, which he renamed Tokyo (or "eastern capital"). Most importantly, rapid industrialization, driven by the ideas of economic nationalism, was also a mark of the Meiji restoration.

Thus outfitted with the trappings of the modern state, the Japanese government also sought to copy other European behaviour, notably the acquisition of empire. It began modestly enough. Liuqiu, on what is now the Ryukyu archipelago, was an independent kingdom but a suzerain of both China and Japan. In 1879, the Japanese government pensioned off the Liuqiu prince like the other clan lords and turned Liuqiu into Okinawa prefecture, much to the Chinese emperor's chagrin.

Conflict between Japan and China escalated in the 1880s as a consequence of Japanese designs on Korea, which was China's most important suzerain (see the discussion of imperial China in Chapter 2). In 1894, an antiforeign rebellion in Korea prompted the government in Seoul to ask the Chinese for assistance in putting it down. But Japan, without having been invited, despatched a sizeable army to Korea which did not depart when the rebellion was suppressed. When China protested, Japan simply declared war. The modernized Japanese forces quickly defeated the Chinese, who were forced to recognize Korean independence; give Taiwan, the Pescadores Islands, and the Liaodong peninsula to Japan; pay 200 million *taels* (a *tael* is roughly equivalent to 25 g) of gold as an indemnity toward the costs of the war; and give Japanese the same extraterritorial privileges as Europeans and Americans in China enjoyed.

The European powers were not quite ready to accept Japan as a bona fide imperialist, however. They forced the government in Tokyo to give the Liaodong peninsula back to the Chinese. It did not remain long in Chinese hands. The Russian government was eager to get the ice-free naval base at Port Arthur (present-day Lüshun) that the Chinese had established with British help during the 1880s, and hoped to extend a branch of the Trans-Siberian railway down to Dalian. In 1898, the Russians forced China to cede the peninsula to them (much to the chagrin of both the Chinese and Japanese).

Russia's obvious designs on Manchuria and the Liaodong caused a serious deterioration in Russo-Japanese relations as both countries vied for control of the same territory. For example, the Russians angered the Japanese government by taking advantage of the confusion of the **Boxer Rebellion**\* in China to seize southern Manchuria, thus blocking even more firmly Japanese desires to secure a colony on the mainland. The Japanese, however, bided their time. In 1902, they signed an alliance with Britain that committed the government in London to staying out of any war involving Japan and only one other power. In 1903, the Japanese army had grown enough that the Japanese were ready to use force if negotiations with Russia over the future of Manchuria broke down—which they did on 5 February 1904. On 8 February, without bothering with the formalities of a declaration of war, the Japanese fleet attacked the Russian navy at Port Arthur, launching an 18-month war which saw the Russian fleet devastated by a superior Japanese navy and Russian armies ground down in Korea and Manchuria. The Treaty of Portsmouth of September 1905 gave Japan what it had long sought: the Liaodong lease, control of Port Arthur, a Russian evacuation from Manchuria, formal recognition of a Japanese sphere of influence in Korea, and even half of Sakhalin Island.

### United States Imperialism: America's Pacific Vision

For much of the 19th century, American attention was directed inward, at the continent, marked by either indifference to the outside world or the kind of xenophobia (fear of strangers) evident in the Know-Nothings, a secret antiforeign party. However, the growth of imperialism by other powers in the international system during this period also had an impact on the United States.[1] Some Americans began arguing that the United States had an oceanic version of Manifest Destiny. Capt. Alfred Thayer Mahan, a naval officer, lecturer, and in 1886, president of the Naval War College in Newport, Rhode Island, argued that national greatness and wealth flowed from seapower, and American national greatness depended on developing a strong navy, acquiring overseas colonies, developing America's trade abroad, and building a canal across the isthmus of Panama. His ideas were widely circulated and had considerable influence on both public attitudes and government policy. By the 1890s, the United States Navy had powerful new battleships and a burgeoning merchant marine engaged in a growing Pacific trade.

Moreover, in a brief two-year period, American leaders also acquired overseas territories—all the while insisting loudly that the United States was not an imperial power and that it had no imperial designs. Americans might not have been able to bring themselves to call what they seized an empire, but, as Juliet might say, "What's in a name? that which we call a rose/By any other name would smell as sweet." So too with imperial possessions: between

---

\* In China, a key antiforeign movement was the Righteous and Harmonious Boxing Order, which emerged in Shandong province in 1898. Named after a form of martial arts calisthenics, the Boxers, as they were called by Europeans, sought to expel foreigners from China. In June 1900, when Boxers began murdering Europeans in Beijing, the Empress Cixi expressed her approval, prompting Britain, France, Japan, Russia, and the United States to send in 20 000 troops to protect their nationals in the Chinese capital and put down the rebellion.

1898 and 1900, the Philippines, Guam, Puerto Rico, Hawai'i, Wake, and Samoa were all ceded to, claimed, or annexed by the United States.

**The Philippines, Guam, and Puerto Rico**    The United States came by these territories indirectly: all three of these Spanish colonies were ceded to the United States by the treaty of Paris of 10 December 1898 that brought the Spanish-American war of that year to an end. It was ironic that the peace resulted in the acquisition of colonial possessions by the United States, for they had fought that war in support of an independence movement in Cuba. A rebellion against Spanish rule in Cuba had started in 1895, bringing trade and commerce to a halt, threatening American investments in the island, and prompting a humanitarian outcry in the United States at the methods used by Spanish forces to repress the revolt. There was support for American intervention on the side of the rebels from both the media and Congress, but the only action taken was the dispatch of the battleship *USS Maine* to Havana in December 1897 to protect American lives and property.

On 15 February 1898, a huge explosion sunk the *Maine* and took the lives of 266 Americans, triggering accusations that the Spanish had planted a mine under the ship. As a result, the United States demanded that Spain withdraw from Cuba, and in response, the Spanish declared war on 24 April. The conflict was short, with American forces prevailing in the Philippines, Puerto Rico, and Cuba. After the fall of Santiago de Cuba on 17 July, the Spanish government sued for peace. (The cause of the explosion remains a mystery. A U.S. Navy investigation in 1911 concluded that a mine was indeed responsible; in 1976, another Navy study, based on photographs collected in the 1911 investigation, argued that an accidental fire in a coal bunker had set off munitions stored nearby. In 1998, however, a National Geographic Society investigation, using computer models, suggested that the available evidence supports both theories.[2])

**Hawai'i**    If the United States came to own the Philippines, Puerto Rico, and Guam by an indirect route, the acquisition of Hawai'i was a result of expatriate American owners and traders trying to subvert local authority for their own commercial ends. They called on the government in Washington to protect their interests by taking over the territory as an American protectorate.

After Capt. James Cook came across the islands in 1788, Hawai'i became an important port of call for ships engaged in the trans-Pacific fur trade and, later, those engaged in whaling. Hawai'ian sandalwood was shipped to southeast Asia, and commercial crops were developed to feed fleets and for export to California. Although Hawai'i remained an independent kingdom, the settlement by foreign (mostly American) traders and the arrival of American missionaries transformed political, religious, and social life. In the 1840s, Kamehameha III was persuaded to introduce a Euro-American political system, including Euro-American notions of land ownership. Land which had belonged to the king was divided and distributed and made available for sale. Foreigners were allowed to buy land, which quickly resulted in the accumulation of large European and American land holdings in the islands.

The development of the sugar industry brought the end of Hawai'ian independence. In 1875, the Hawai'ian government managed to negotiate an exemption to the high tariffs on sugar maintained by the United States. This boosted sugar production and attracted American investors, concentrating ownership of the sugar plantations in foreign (mainly American) hands.

The profound changes in the Hawai'ian political economy over the course of the 19th century produced a backlash. King Kalakaua, who reigned from 1874 to 1891, tried to revive indigenous customs, and was thus regarded as anti-American. In 1887, a group of business leaders organized an armed militia and imposed a new constitution that introduced property and racial qualifications for voting. The new rules disenfranchised most Hawai'ians, and all Chinese and Japanese who had been brought to work the plantations, but foreigners were given the vote. These new rules shifted the balance of voters in favour of a growing movement to have Hawai'i annexed by the United States.

*"The Hawai'ian pear is now fully ripe, and this is the golden hour for the United States to pluck it."*

When Kalakaua's sister Liliokalani took the throne in 1891, she opposed the annexation movement, but in so doing brought down the monarchy. In January 1893, American plantation owners overthrew her and established a committee of public safety. The United States minister in Honolulu ordered American troops to land to protect American lives and property, reporting to his superiors in Washington that "The Hawai'ian pear is now fully ripe, and this is the golden hour for the United States to pluck it."[3] A treaty of annexation was drafted and introduced into the United States Senate. There was a short reprieve: President Grover Cleveland's opposition to imperialism blocked the annexation. But his successor, William McKinley, who came to office in 1897, had no such qualms. He approved a resolution by Congress to annex Hawai'i on 12 August 1898.

**Pacific Islands**   By 1900, the United States had acquired four more colonial possessions in the Pacific Ocean: Johnston Atoll, Midway Islands, Wake Island, and Samoa, plus a number of islets identified by the so-called "Guano Act" of 1856 that codified United States claims to guano-rich South Pacific islands deemed to have been discovered by Americans. Johnston, a coral atoll 1100 km southwest of Hawai'i, was annexed in 1858; Midway, a coral atoll 2100 km northwest of Hawai'i, was claimed by the United States in August 1867. In January 1899, the United States also claimed Wake Island, a tiny atoll that lies approximately halfway between Hawai'i and Guam. Midway and Wake provided crucial stations for the laying of the trans-Pacific cable in the early 1900s (and as commercial airline refuelling points in the 1930s).

Three foreign countries developed interests in the Samoan islands in the South Pacific in the 19th century: Britain, the United States, and Germany, each of which established trading stations in the islands. In addition, in January 1878, the United States signed an agreement with the king of Samoa for rights to establish a coaling station at Pago Pago, the best harbour in the islands. Similar privileges were given to the British and Germans, but the three powers frequently clashed. The issue came to a head in 1899 as the result of a civil war among Samoans: American and British naval vessels shelled the German trading station at Apia. Subsequent negotiations divided the islands, with the Germans getting the islands west of 171° longitude west, and the United States were given the islands east of that meridian. Britain withdrew from Samoa entirely in return for an American and German agreement to recognize British supremacy in Tonga and the Solomon Islands. All that remained was the formality of getting the high chiefs on Tutuila and Aunuu to cede their islands to the United States, which they dutifully did on 17 July 1900.

We should also note here the realization of the other element of Capt. Mahan's Pacific vision—an isthmian canal. Following the Spanish-American War, Theodore Roosevelt, who had become president after McKinley's assassination in September 1901, moved to build a canal across the Colombian province of Panama. He secured British approval, opened negotiations with Colombia, and approved an agreement within two years. When the Colombian Senate balked at the terms of the agreement, the Panamanians rose in revolt. Protected by some strategically placed American ships, they declared their independence and signed the agreement that allowed work on the canal to proceed; it was opened on 15 August 1914. For $10 million down and $250 000 a year, the United States got a six-mile wide Canal Zone in perpetuity to add to its other roses.

It is of course no small irony that the country that had led the way in opposing European empire in the 1770s should itself turn into a colonial and imperial power. However, when they were offered to the Philippines, Puerto Rico, and Guam, the temptations of imperialism were considerable. And, as the case of Hawai'i demonstrates, the same dynamic that prompted European states to dot their flags around the globe during the era of imperialism knew few boundaries.

### Explanations of Imperialism

Over the course of the 19th century, much of the map of the world was repainted in the different colours of the imperial nations whose armies and navies ventured out to claim colonies, settlements, and protectorates. By 1914, Africa had almost completely been carved up and the Indian subcontinent was fully controlled by Europeans. In southeast Asia, Siam (Thailand) was the only independent kingdom remaining after the French colonization of Indochina in the 1880s; China had not been colonized, but it might well have been since it was deeply penetrated by Europeans, Americans, and Japanese; Australia and New Zealand were fully established as self-governing Dominions within the British Empire; and virtually all the South Pacific islands had been claimed by European powers and the United States.

A number of broad explanations have been offered for this concentrated feeding frenzy. The **economic theory of imperialism** argues that overseas colonies were vital to the economic well-being of those in the imperial centre, or the **metropole**. J.A. Hobson, for example, argued that colonies offered captive markets for the sale of the metropole's surplus goods that could not be consumed in the home market because the unequal distribution of wealth left relatively few consumers. In addition, colonies provided a crucial outlet for the capital that had been accumulating as a consequence of the rapid industrialization and economic growth. Using a Marxist analysis, V.I. Lenin went one step further, arguing that the very nature of the capitalist system itself had *forced* Europeans to seek overseas colonies. Falling rates of profit, overproduction, underconsumption, a surplus of capital, and a decline in investment opportunities within Europe all would have produced an economic crisis and political revolt. But because imperialism provided an outlet for both overproduced goods and surplus capital, such a crisis was averted. The **Leninist theory of imperialism** portrays the scramble as a *necessary* phase of capitalist development: "The Empire...is a bread and butter question. If you want to avoid civil war, you must become imperialists."[4]

The difficulty with the economic arguments is that the numbers do not bear them out. There was indeed a huge capital outflow from Europe during the latter half of the 19th century as capital accumulated. But, as numerous scholars have pointed out, Lenin's own figures show that overwhelmingly, this capital was invested not in the territories which Europeans were scrambling for in Africa or Asia, but in economies that were either independent, such as the United States or Argentina, or well-established colonies, such as Australia, Canada, India, and South Africa.[5] Finance capitalists in London were investing precious little capital in the territories that European diplomats were trading so cavalierly over conference tables in Berlin. If anything, finance capital was what Robert Gilpin has termed the "servant of foreign policy" during this period.[6]

These contending views reflect the **flag/trade debate**. This debate poses a deceptively simple question: did "trade" (all those owners, planters, traders, and firms who established business interests in an overseas territory) follow governments (or "the flag"), or did the flag follow trade? There can be no single answer to this question. In some cases, traders established themselves overseas and then asked to be protected; the imperial state complied by wrapping the territory in its flag as a colonial possession. We explored the case of American imperialism in Hawai'i in some detail above because it offers an almost perfect illustration of the flag-follows-trade argument. But in many cases, trade followed the flag. For their own political, diplomatic, strategic, or military reasons, governments claimed a territory (or were traded a territory) where its nationals could subsequently develop commercial interests. Some of the scramble for Africa and the "opening" of China provide good examples of governments laying the ground for later commercial activity. Certainly, Japanese imperialism was motivated by economic interests—securing access to the raw materials of Manchuria—but the efforts to establish control over Korea and Manchuria were spearheaded by the Japanese state, not by Japanese firms or owners of capital.

The economic argument, by seeking to focus on a single cause, also overlooks a number of other reasons why European states, Japan, and the United States were prompted to gain overseas possessions during this period. As the scramble for Africa suggests, an intricate dynamic of "me-too" rivalry overtook these states. Once one power gained a colony, that created a ripple effect, prompting others to join in. The sequence of colonial acquisitions in Africa and the South Pacific during this period suggests a domino effect, where acquisition took on almost a life of its own. Europeans sought colonies for the sake of seeking colonies—and for the sake of denying them to rivals—rather than for any concrete benefits to be gained.

Not that the possession of colonies did not bring benefits. On the contrary, as we noted above, colonization usually brought in its wake economic activity. Moreover, colonies provided an opportunity for those wishing to escape the metropole to pursue lives overseas in the army, the colonial bureaucracy, or commerce. (This, it should be stressed, might have been an *ex post facto* benefit, but it was not a *cause* of imperialist expansion. There is little indication that governments actively went about acquiring colonies in order to provide their citizens with overseas employment opportunities.)

*"Take up the White Man's burden—*
*And reap his old reward:*
*The blame of those ye better,*
*The hate of those ye guard."*

It should also be noted that in most cases, Europeans and Americans were driven by civilizational convictions that they, as colonizers, were bringing the benefits of a Christian civilization to people who were commonly seen as savages, heathen, backward, childlike, and incapable of governing themselves. For the French, it was the **mission civilisatrice**; for the English, it was Rudyard Kipling's *White Man's Burden*—to "guard" and "better" the "new-caught, sullen peoples/Half devil and half child."

Frequently, imperialists expressed the conviction that the dominance of the Europeans over other "lesser peoples" was "natural." This was the era of Charles Darwin's *On the Origin of Species*, published in 1859, and, as is often the case with popularized science, widely misunderstood. While Darwin's theory of natural selection did challenge existing ideas about human evolution, it had nothing to do with how some members of the species *Homo sapiens sapiens* might consciously choose to treat other members of the species at a brief moment in history. However, **Darwinian theory** and "survival of the fittest" soon became a mantra that was used as a scientific-sounding justification for patterns of domination and dependence. (Eventually, as we will see in the next chapter, this was taken to an extreme by Adolf Hitler and the Nazis in Germany in the 1930s and 1940s).

Often, however, imperialism was driven by a mix of all of these motives. Consider President McKinley's explanation of how he puzzled through his decision to support the annexation of the Philippines:

> And one night it came to me this way...(1) that we could not give [the Philippines] back to Spain—that would be cowardly and dishonorable; (2) that we could not turn them over to France or Germany—our commercial rivals in the Orient—that would be bad business and discreditable; (3) that we could not leave them to themselves—they were unfit for self-government—and they would soon have anarchy and misrule over there worse than Spain's was; and (4) that there was nothing left for us to do but to take them all, and to educate the Filipinos, and uplift and civilize and Christianize them, and by God's grace do the very best we could by them, as our fellowmen for whom Christ also died. And then I went to bed, and...slept soundly.[7]

## THE COLLAPSE OF EMPIRE

As will be evident from the account above, imperialism as it was practised by Europeans, Japanese, and Americans was deeply connected to the "national idea" in the 19th century. Possession of overseas colonies became part of the fulfilment of the nation's "destiny." Any self-respecting nation *had* to have colonies: for the national economic development they were assumed to produce, for the national strategic advantages they afforded, and for the national prestige they were assumed to bring. Even those who were not initially inclined toward colonialism, such as Bismarck and McKinley, proved unable to resist the lure.

## The Contradictions of the Imperial Idea

However, there were deep contradictions embedded in the interrelationship between empire and nation. To fulfil the nation, one had to have colonies; but to have colonies, *ipso facto* one had to deny the nationhood of those one was colonizing. Moreover, the nationalism embraced by imperial powers came in an ideological form, as we argued in the previous chapter, that could be readily absorbed by colonial peoples. How could one explain to a colonized individual, who had read and absorbed the ideology of nationalism (often while attending university in the metropole), why some nations could enjoy the luxury of an independent existence in their own sovereign nation-state, while other nations had to be governed by imperial overlords and were denied sovereignty?

And here the *idea* of imperialism was deeply deficient, for the answers it provided to this elementary question only worked for some people in the empire. "Empire" made most sense to those with a direct and personal connection to the imperial centre: those who had been born there, or whose families had come from the metropole, or who still had family there. In their eyes, *empire* was seen as a natural extension of *nation*. All the symbols of the British Empire—the union flag on the fly of their local territory's flag, the monarch's bust on the postage stamps or on the reverse of their local currency, the ubiquitous schoolroom map coloured in the crimson that signified a British Empire possession—were not only warm reminders of the unity of a global empire on which the sun never set. More importantly, they were reminders that that global empire had an unmistakable *national* home.

As a result, "empire" managed to generate considerable loyalty and love as a political entity, often coexisting with notions of nation. At the turn of the century, many Australians, Canadians, Indians, New Zealanders, South Africans, and others defined themselves not only as members of their particular country, but also as members of the British Empire. They could "love" both equally. Indeed, as we will see below, that love prompted several million people throughout the British Empire to volunteer to fight in the First World War and to die for the cause of empire.

But the idea of empire had little appeal for those millions of others who could not identify nation and empire in such a fashion; or, as importantly, those who were excluded from such an identification in those colonies where there was a colour bar. For example, in the British Empire, Indians, Africans, Caribbeans, and Hong Kong Chinese were never recognized as "real" fellow nationals by other British colonials, much less by those at "home" in Britain. And it was here that the imperial idea simply could not transcend the deep contradiction inherent in nationalist imperialism.

Nor could imperialism deal with the ideas of nationalism that were spreading throughout the imperial world. Those from the European or American imperial centres, when asked by colonial nationalists to grant them the same fulfilment of the national ideal that

Europeans and Americans enjoyed, had no shortage of reasons for why it was right and proper that they should be denied independent nationhood. Their reasons were either grounded in some notion of racial superiority ("It is natural that the white races should govern the nonwhite races") or pragmatic concerns about the effects of independence ("You're not ready/mature enough/developed enough to govern yourselves; chaos would result if we left. We can only grant you independence when you're good and ready. In the meantime, you'll have to learn from us how to govern yourselves properly").

But such reasoning simply never convinced indigenous colonials. First, such reasoning ignored the fact that these peoples had already proven quite capable of governing themselves before the imperialists arrived. Second, such reasoning patronized colonized peoples as children, and was thus deeply insulting. Finally, when the actual foundations of Euro-American imperial control were peeled away, one discovered that the basis for empire in the late 19th century lay not in some notion of "natural" white supremacy, but in the oldest reason for empire—raw power. Far from being preordained to dominate, Europeans and Americans were able to establish their empires simply because they had hugely superior military capability to defeat or intimidate anyone in their way. Had the indigenous peoples of Australasia, the South Pacific, China, southeast Asia, India, and Africa had the machine guns invented by Americans— Gatling, Maxim, Browning, and Lewis—or the rifled artillery, the fleets of modern battleships, and the industrialized economies to feed these war machines, the outcome would have been different. (This is why Meiji Japan—and particularly the thrashing of "white" Russia by "nonwhite" Japan in 1904–1905—was such a powerful inspiration to colonial nationalists all over the world.) In short, imperialism offered ideas about political organization that, to the colonized at least, were either manifestly shonky, or deeply offensive, or both. Nationalism, by contrast, simply made much more sense—which is why so many of those who lived in the colonies became ardent nationalists rather than committed imperialists.

*Europeans and Americans were able to establish their empires simply because they had hugely superior military capability to defeat or intimidate anyone in their way.*

(It might be noted that although Japan served as a model for colonized peoples, the Japanese themselves tended to have an exceedingly raw view of nationalist imperialism, and thus were not as disingenuous as their European or American counterparts. Japan never pretended that its colonial possessions existed for anything but the pure benefit of the Japanese nation; nor did the government in Tokyo claim that Japan was "preparing" its colonies for independence. Rather, Japanese imperialists understood that empire depended mainly on the capacity to prevail over others. As a result, they rarely bothered to respond to local manifestations of nationalism with condescending arguments, but simply with unabashed brutality.)

## The Expansion of the Nation-State, 1918-1997

For these ideological reasons, imperialism, as it was practised in an age of nationalist beliefs, carried with it the seeds of its own collapse. As it spread beyond the imperial centres of Europe, Japan, and the United States, the national idea exposed the contradictions of empire. Over the course of the 20th century, empires contracted, surely but steadily, replaced everywhere with nation-states. The expansion of the nation-state system came in three distinct waves: following the First World War, after the Second World War, and after the end of the Cold War.

## The First World War and After

In the next chapter we will look in more detail at the impact of nationalism on the First World War; here I want to explore the impact of the First World War on nationalism. In the previous chapter, we saw that the Napoleonic Wars had a powerful effect on the growth of nationalism in the early 19th century. Therefore, it should come as little surprise that the First World War had an equally powerful effect on the development of the national idea in those that the war touched. Three areas can be briefly noted: the dismantling of the European empires, the reshaping of the British empire, and the growth of nationalism in China.

### The Fourteen Points and European Empires

By the start of the First World War, there were three empires in Europe: the Austro-Hungarian, the Ottoman, and the Russian. A further step in the process of the consolidation of the nation-state in Europe was taken in the aftermath of the First World War, when the Austro-Hungarian and Ottoman empires were dismantled. This idea was legitimated by the ardent advocacy of the president of the United States, Woodrow Wilson. In his address to Congress on 18 January 1918, he laid out 14 proposals for a lasting peace in Europe. Eight of what eventually became known as the **Fourteen Points** dealt with issues of nationhood, particularly the right of people to have their own separate nation, or self-determination, discussed in Chapter 12. The terms of the peace in 1919 thus led to the creation of new nation-states in Central Europe and the Balkans: Austria, Poland, Hungary, Czechoslovakia, and Yugoslavia.

The Treaty of Versailles also gave the non-European possessions of the German and Ottoman empires to the victors. But Wilson's advocacy of self-determination did not sit well with the imperialist notion that some peoples outside Europe were so "backward" that they were incapable of governing themselves. So an interesting variant of colonialism was invented. Drawing on the Roman law tradition of *mandatum*, in which a person undertook to do something for free at the request of another, the victors created the **mandate system**. Under this system, all the territories seized from the conquered powers were taken over by the new international organization that was established by the peace conference, the League of Nations. These territories were then assigned to a **mandatory power**, a country which would govern the territory on behalf of the international community. Three classes of mandates were established. "Class A" mandates were those territories judged to be almost capable of self-governance; it was not expected that the mandatory powers would govern them for long. Class B mandates were not expected to gain early independence; they were to be administered like other colonies. Class C mandates permitted the mandatory power to incorporate the territories directly into their colonial systems. Following the Second World War, the League of Nations mandate system was replaced by a United Nations trusteeship system. As Table 13.1 shows, the mandate (and trusteeship) arrangement took fully 75 years to work: with Palau's independence in 1994, the system established in 1919 came to an end.

*Table 13.1* • **THE MANDATE SYSTEM**

| Mandated Territory (1919) | Mandatory Power | Independence Gained | Name at Independence (if different) |
|---|---|---|---|
| *Class A* | | | |
| Iraq | Britain | 1932 | |
| Syria | France | 1941 | Syria |
| | | 1941 | Lebanon |
| Palestine | Britain | 1946 | Jordan |
| | | 1948 | Israel |
| *Class B* | | | |
| Togoland | Britain | 1957 | (joined Ghana) |
| | France | 1958 | Togo |
| Cameroons | Britain | 1960 | (joined Nigeria) |
| | France | 1960 | Cameroon |
| Ruanda-Urundi | Belgium | 1961 | Rwanda |
| | | 1962 | Burundi |
| Tanganyika | Britain | 1964 | Tanzania |
| *Class C* | | | |
| Samoa | New Zealand | 1962 | Western Samoa |
| Nauru | Australia | 1968 | |
| New Guinea | Australia | 1975 | Papua New Guinea |
| Marshall Islands | Japan* | 1986 | |
| Caroline Islands | Japan* | 1986 | Micronesia |
| | | 1994 | Palau |
| South-West Africa | South Africa | 1990 | Namibia |
| Northern Marianas | Japan* | – | |

* Following Japan's defeat in World War II, Japanese mandates were passed to the United States under the United Nations trusteeship system. In a referendum, the Northern Mariana Islands voted to remain part of the United States as a Commonwealth.

**The Transformation of the British Empire**    In August 1914, Britain's declaration of war on Germany put the entire British Empire at war; the various governments of the self-governing Dominions (Australia, Canada, New Zealand, and South Africa) were not consulted. It was simply assumed that all parts of the empire would contribute to the war. As Henri Bourassa, a leading anti-imperialist in Canada, said, the seven million Canadians of that era had less say in imperial matters "than one single sweeper in the streets of Liverpool...[H]e at least has one vote to give for or against the administration of that Empire."[8]

But the question of which level of government got to declare war was quite irrelevant for many in the Empire. The result would have been the same—willing participation on the side of the "Mother Country in her time of need." Hundreds of thousands of people from across the Empire volunteered to fight. The number that each of the self-governing Dominions and India put in uniform was considerable: 330 000 Australians, 619 000 Canadians, 1.3 million Indians, 124 000 New Zealanders, and 250 000 South Africans. There were even 200 000 volunteers from Ireland, despite the government in London's refusal to grant Irish nationalist demands for home rule.[*]

As we will see in the next chapter, the First World War was unlike any other in human experience. Two opposing armies were entrenched in a vast front that stretched from Switzerland to the English Channel, lobbing artillery shells as fast as they could be produced and engaging in numerous bloody attempts to break through the opposing lines. The human and material costs of this kind of warfare were massive, as the large numbers of those who died over the four years of the conflict suggest: 60 000 Australians, 60 600 Canadians, 36 600 Indians, 16 000 New Zealanders, and 12 500 South Africans.

The huge casualties suffered created political stresses for the self-governing Dominions. They were expected by the imperial government in London to provide men for the trenches and money for the war effort, but had no say in the actual running of the war. Indeed, in some instances, soldiers from the Dominions were put under the command of British officers. As David Lloyd George, the British prime minister, admitted in December 1916, the Dominions "have made enormous sacrifices, but we have held no conference with them as to either the objects of the war, or the methods of carrying it out. They hardly feel that they have been consulted."[9]

One consequence of this was to radically alter how Britain was seen in the Dominions. For example, the abject failure of the Gallipoli campaign, in which thousands of ANZAC (Australian and New Zealand Army Corps) soldiers died, was commonly blamed on the campaign's British organizers and commanders. The unchanging routines of trench warfare, in which British officers kept ordering Dominion soldiers "over the top" into enemy machine-gun fire despite the mounting casualty rates, fostered anti-British sentiment among the troops of the Empire, and a sense of nationalism and a desire to decide questions of war policy for themselves. Moreover, the First World War revealed anti-imperial cleavages in the Dominions themselves: Irish immigrants in Australia, French-speaking Quebeckers in Canada, Afrikaaners in South Africa, and nationalist dissidents in India. It also created po-litical difficulties for some Dominion governments. In South Africa, Afrikaaner republicans, including some former generals, rose in armed rebellion when Parliament voted to send men and money to fight what was seen as an "English" war. In India, there were armed rebellions in Punjab and Bengal. On two different occasions, Australians rejected conscription. Likewise, a Canadian election was held on conscription in 1917. However, the government

---

[*] This number is even more surprising given that the British minister of war, Lord Kitchener, was so distrustful of Irish Catholics that he refused to allow Irish volunteers from the south to serve together or to fly their own regimental flag; no such bans were placed on Protestant volunteers from Ulster.

of the Conservative Sir Robert Borden, which won that election, paid dearly for its advocacy of conscripting French-Canadians during what was also seen in Québec as an "English" war: not until 1957 would Conservative candidates again receive significant numbers of votes in that province.

The war accelerated the growth of nationalism in all the Dominions, albeit at different rates. In Ireland, agitation for independence accelerated as a consequence of the failure of the Easter Rebellion of 1916 and the British overreaction that included the execution of 15 Irish nationalists. In January 1919 a national assembly declared independence. Following a period of civil war, an agreement was reached forming a new self-governing entity, the Irish Free State, with the same rights as Australia and the other Dominions.

The nationalism in other parts of the Empire took different forms. Among the governments of the self-governing Dominions, a desire to control all elements of their policy, domestic and external, had already emerged during the war. This was a logical outgrowth of the autonomy in domestic policy that they had achieved with Dominion status. The desire was reflected in the demands of the Australians, Canadians, and South Africans that there be more effective consultation in the conduct of the war; separate representation for the Dominions at the peace conference; and separate membership for each of the Dominions in the League of Nations.

> The Dominions were "autonomous communities within the British Empire, equal in status, and in no way subordinate one to another in any aspect of their domestic or external affairs, though united by a common allegiance to the Crown, and freely associated as members of the British Commonwealth of Nations."

The fulfilment of these demands led to the transformation of the Empire into the Commonwealth. At a succession of conferences in the 1920s, the Empire was negotiated out of existence. In 1926, the Imperial Conference agreed with the report of the interimperial relations committee, chaired by the Earl of Balfour, that the Dominions were "autonomous communities within the British Empire, equal in status, and in no way subordinate one to another in any aspect of their domestic or external affairs, though united by a common allegiance to the Crown, and freely associated as members of the British Commonwealth of Nations."[10] The essence of the Balfour committee's statement of 1926 was enshrined in the **Statute of Westminster**, 1931, which put a formal end to the British Empire, replacing it with the Commonwealth of Nations. It also brought into formal *de jure* existence the sovereign nation-states that had enjoyed *de facto* sovereignty since 1926: Australia, Canada, Irish Free State, Newfoundland, New Zealand, and South Africa.

India, however, still did not have self-governing Dominion status. Nationalist agitation, which had had its start in the 1880s and had spread across India, was also catalyzed by the First World War. The refusal of the British to yield to nationalist demands had begun to provoke sporadic violence. This occasionally took a gruesome turn, as it did at Amritsar, where between April 10 and 12, 1919, Indian nationalists murdered 11 Europeans and destroyed churches, banks, and the telegraph office. In retaliation, British troops opened fire on a crowd on 13 April, killing 379 and wounding 1200. But the nationalist movement also had a peaceful side. Under the leadership of Mohandas Gandhi, a concerted effort was made to persuade the British by peaceful means to grant India self rule. Although the British kept promising home rule, it was not until 1935 that the Government of India Act was introduced that brought in limited autonomy, and full independence would not be granted for another 12 years.

**China**    China did not enter the First World War until the closing months of the conflict. However, many Chinese served on the Western Front between 1914 and 1918, mostly as labourers recruited by France and Britain. In return for their labour, they received all their food and clothing and their families in China received ten dollars a month. Although some 2000 Chinese died during the First World War, tens of thousands returned to China after the armistice, many of them literate and relatively rich.[11]

The Chinese republican government, which had emerged in January 1912 from the anti-Qing revolts of 1911, finally declared war on Germany in August 1917. It did so in response to pressure from the United States, which had entered the war in April of that year, and from Japan, who offered the republican government sizeable loans. The Chinese government also hoped that by participating in the defeat of Germany, it would regain Germany's concession areas in Shandong province.

Unfortunately for the Chinese government, however, this participation was for nought: Britain, France, Italy, and Japan came to a secret agreement in 1917 giving all of Germany's holdings in China to Japan. Moreover, the premier of China, Duan Qirui, had done some secret deals of his own: in return for massive personal loans from the Japanese, he had signed away income from some new railways and had agreed to allow Japanese to station military garrisons on Chinese soil. When news of these deals reached China in May 1919, huge demonstrations swept across Chinese cities on 4 May, protesting the sell-out by Duan and the secret deals of the other powers. Chinese protestors at the peace negotiations at Versailles surrounded the Chinese delegates, forcibly preventing them from signing the Treaty of Versailles. The date—4 May 1919—is still marked as an important date in Chinese history, for it helped galvanize its nationalist movement.

Although the May Fourth movement, centred in universities in Beijing, was multifaceted, it was united in its desire that China be free of foreign—European, American, and Japanese—domination. The anti-Versailles protests of 1919 gave rise to the two parties which were to dominate Chinese politics for the next 80 years: the more revolutionary and radical nationalists in the Chinese Communist Party (CCP), eventually headed by Mao Zedong; and the National People's Party (Kuomintang (KMT), pronounced *Gwo-min-dang*), eventually headed by Chiang Kai-shek. China disintegrated into anarchy. This was the **warlord period**, when the forces of the Communists and the Nationalists battled with one another and with many of the regional warlords whose military power had grown following the collapse of the imperial dynasty. And, as we saw in Chapter 11, the internal Chinese quarrels were being played out against a broader background—the desire of Japan to expand its power and influence in Manchuria and central China. Following the Japanese occupation of Manchuria in 1931 and the full-scale Japanese war against the whole country that began in 1937, there was a significant spread of the nationalist idea. Both the CCP and the KMT worked hard to exploit the growing sense of the national community among Chinese, not only in the city but in the countryside. The CCP was most successful in spreading nationalism among the Chinese peasantry; the KMT found most success in the cities. In short, the process of actually fighting or struggling against the Japanese for some 50 years—from the war of 1895 through the more figurative struggles in the 1920s to full-scale war from 1931 to 1945—consolidated the idea of nation in China.

## The Era of Decolonization, 1945-1989

The nation-state system underwent a massive expansion in the era after the Second World War, as Table 13.2 indicates. The territorial possessions of the European powers, the United States, and Japan were given their independence or decolonized. **Decolonization** came in distinct waves. It began with those Asian countries that had been invaded by the Japanese or touched by the war. In China, the CCP and KMT began to war openly with each other once Japan was defeated; on 1 October 1949, Mao Zedong declared the People's Republic of China in Beijing, bringing to an end the era of empire on the Chinese mainland.

Likewise, nationalist sentiment grew dramatically in other countries touched by the war with Japan. Thus, within days of the Japanese surrender, Indonesia's nationalist leaders, Sukarno and Muhammad Hatta, who had enjoyed a measure of local autonomy under Japanese occupation, declared Indonesia's independence. (Japanese troops who had surrendered were even used for police duties in the new state.) The Dutch, however, tried to reestablish their colonial control over Indonesia, and fought a three-year guerrilla war against Indonesian nationalists before being compelled to the negotiating table in 1949. In Indochina, the nationalist sentiment was also resisted by the French, whose attempts to reestablish colonial control also sparked a fierce war that delayed Vietnamese, Cambodian, and Laotian independence for eight years.

Some Asian states emerged peacefully: the Philippines were granted independence by the United States on 4 July 1946, and the Korean peninsula was divided by the victorious powers, a division that was solidified in August and September of 1948. The Indian nationalist movement finally achieved their aims when Britain decolonized the entire subcontinent in 1947 and 1948. The initial post–Second World War period also marked the independence of a number of states in north Africa and the Middle East: Israel and Jordan became independent in 1948.

The independence of these states created a bandwagon effect as nationalist movements developed everywhere, seeking to gain the independence that their neighbours had been given. The resulting pattern of decolonization very much reflected the response of the European powers to nationalism. Britain, for example, chose not to try to retain its empire by any means. Instead, it adopted a policy of negotiated divestment of its colonial possessions, often using a timetable for independence determined by local colonial elites. For that reason, British decolonization in Africa, the Caribbean, and the South Pacific tends to have been spread evenly across all four decades and was relatively peaceful.

*Table 13.2* • **THE ERA OF DECOLONIZATION, 1945-1989: NATION-STATES GAINING INDEPENDENCE (DIVISIONS OR FORMER NAMES IN PARENTHESES)**

| Nation-State | Former Sovereign* | Date of Independence |
|---|---|---|
| *1940–1949* | | |
| Indonesia | Netherlands | 17 August 1945 |
| Syria | France | 17 April 1946 |
| Philippines | United States | 4 July 1946 |
| Israel | Britain | 14 May 1948 |
| Jordan | Britain | 25 May 1946 |
| India | Britain | 15 August 1947 |
| Pakistan | Britain | 15 August 1947 |
| Myanmar (Burma) | Britain | 4 January 1948 |
| Sri Lanka (Ceylon) | Britain | 4 February 1948 |
| Korea (South) | Japan | 15 August 1948 |
| Korea (North) | Japan | 9 September 1948 |
| *1950–1959* | | |
| Oman | Britain | 20 December 1951 |
| Libya | Italy | 24 December 1951 |
| Laos | France | 23 October 1953 |
| Cambodia | France | 9 November 1953 |
| Vietnam (North) | France | 21 July 1954 |
| Vietnam (South) | France | 26 October 1955 |
| Sudan | Britain | 1 January 1956 |
| Morocco | France | 2 March 1956 |
| Tunisia | France | 20 March 1956 |
| Ghana | Britain | 6 March 1957 |
| Malaysia | Britain | 31 August 1957 |
| Guinea | France | 2 October 1958 |
| *1960* | | |
| Cameroon | France | 1 January 1960 |
| Togo | France | 27 April 1960 |
| Madagascar | France | 30 June 1960 |
| Congo-Kinshasa (Zaire) | Belgium | 30 June 1960 |
| Somalia | Italy/Britain | 1 July 1960 |
| Benin (Dahomey) | France | 1 August 1960 |
| Niger | France | 3 August 1960 |
| Burkina Faso (Upper Volta) | France | 5 August 1960 |
| Côte d'Ivoire | France | 7 August 1960 |

| Nation-State | Former Sovereign* | Date of Independence |
|---|---|---|
| Chad | France | 11 August 1960 |
| Central African Republic | France | 13 August 1960 |
| Congo-Brazzaville | France | 15 August 1960 |
| Cyprus | Britain | 16 August 1960 |
| Gabon | France | 17 August 1960 |
| Senegal | France | 20 August 1960 |
| Mali | France | 22 September 1960 |
| Nigeria | Britain | 1 October 1960 |
| Mauritania | France | 28 November 1960 |
| *1961–1969* | | |
| Rwanda | Belgium | 28 January 1961 |
| Sierra Leone | Britain | 27 April 1961 |
| Kuwait | Britain | 19 June 1961 |
| Western Samoa | New Zealand | 1 January 1962 |
| Jamaica | Britain | 6 August 1962 |
| Trinidad and Tobago | Britain | 31 August 1962 |
| Burundi | Belgium | 1 July 1962 |
| Algeria | France | 3 July 1962 |
| Uganda | Britain | 9 October 1962 |
| Kenya | Britain | 12 December 1963 |
| Tanzania | Britain | 26 April 1964 |
| Malawi | Britain | 6 July 1964 |
| Malta | Britain | 21 September 1964 |
| Zambia | Britain | 24 October 1964 |
| Gambia | Britain | 18 February 1965 |
| Maldives | Britain | 25 July 1965 |
| Singapore | Britain | 9 August 1965 |
| Guyana | Britain | 26 May 1966 |
| Botswana | Britain | 30 September 1966 |
| Lesotho | Britain | 4 October 1966 |
| Barbados | Britain | 30 November 1966 |
| Yemen | Britain | 30 November 1967 |
| Nauru | Australia | 31 January 1968 |
| Mauritius | Britain | 12 March 1968 |
| Swaziland | Britain | 6 September 1968 |
| Equatorial Guinea | Spain | 12 October 1968 |
| *1970–1979* | | |
| Tonga | Britain | 4 June 1970 |
| Fiji | Britain | 10 October 1970 |

*Table 13.2 • continued*

| Nation-State | Former Sovereign* | Date of Independence |
|---|---|---|
| Bangladesh | Pakistan | 26 March 1971 |
| Qatar | Britain | 1 September 1971 |
| Bahamas | Britain | 10 July 1973 |
| Bahrain | Britain | 15 August 1973 |
| Guinea-Bissau | Portugal | 10 September 1974 |
| Mozambique | Portugal | 25 June 1975 |
| Cape Verde Islands | Portugal | 5 July 1975 |
| Comoro Islands | France | 6 July 1975 |
| São Tomé and Príncipe | Portugal | 12 July 1975 |
| Papua New Guinea | Australia | 16 September 1975 |
| Angola | Portugal | 10 November 1975 |
| Suriname | Netherlands | 25 November 1975 |
| Seychelles | Britain | 29 June 1976 |
| Djibouti | France | 27 June 1977 |
| Solomon Islands | Britain | 7 July 1978 |
| Tuvalu | Britain | 1 October 1978 |
| Dominica | Britain | 3 November 1978 |
| Kiribati | Britain | 12 July 1979 |
| St Lucia | Britain | 22 February 1979 |
| St Vincent & the Grenadines | Britain | 27 October 1979 |
| *1980–1989* | | |
| Zimbabwe | Britain | 18 April 1980 |
| Vanuatu | Britain/France | 30 July 1980 |
| Belize | Britain | 21 September 1981 |
| Antigua and Barbuda | Britain | 1 November 1981 |
| St Kitts and Nevis | Britain | 19 September 1983 |
| Brunei | Britain | 1 January 1984 |
| Marshall Islands | United States | 21 October 1986 |
| Micronesia | United States | 21 October 1986 |

*Includes all forms of formally dependent relationships (imperial possessions, colonies, mandates, trusteeships, and protectorates).

By contrast, some other powers struggled mightily to retain their empires, often fighting long and bloody wars against irregular armies or guerrillas, usually known as **national liberation movements**. We have already noted the attempts of the Dutch in Indonesia and the French in Indochina. The French government of the Fourth Republic seemed to have learned little from its symbolic defeat by nationalist forces of the Viet Minh at the colonial stronghold of Dien Bien Phu in May 1954. That defeat had led to the independence of the Indochinese states. On 1 November 1954, merely months after Dien Bien Phu, Algerian nationalists under Ahmed Ben Bella launched a drive for independence. A bloody war, marked by massacre and terrorism, broke out between the *Front de Libération nationale* (FLN) on the one side and the French government and the local French *colons* on the other. Eventually, more than 500 000 French troops were engaged. On 13 May 1958, the *colons* in Algeria, backed up by French generals, demanded that General Charles de Gaulle be brought out of retirement to form a government. The premier, Pierre Pflimlin, resigned; de Gaulle was invested with emergency powers; and the Fourth Republic was replaced by the Fifth Republic. In 1960, the constitution of France was revised to allow French colonial possessions to seek their independence, which, as Table 13.2 shows, they did in large numbers. Fully 18 countries gained their independence in 1960, the vast majority of them French colonies. However, Algeria was not to become independent until 1962.

Portugal also tried to use force to keep its colonies. Rebellion broke out in Angola in early 1961, with three nationalist groups—the FNLA, MPLA, and UNITA—fighting Portuguese forces. Armed uprisings began in Portuguese Guinea in 1962 and in Mozambique in the autumn of 1964. Throughout the 1960s, the government in Lisbon devoted increasing amounts of soldiers and money to the prosecution of these wars, which grew increasingly unpopular in Portugal itself. Finally, on 25 April 1974, a group of army officers overthrew the government of Marcello Caetano and immediately pledged to give Portuguese colonies their independence. As Table 13.2 indicates, the Portuguese empire rapidly disintegrated in the year and a half after the revolution: Guinea-Bissau, Mozambique, Cape Verde Islands, São Tomé and Príncipe, and Angola received their independence. Table 13.2 does not show the fate of another Portuguese possession, East Timor: Timor was invaded by Indonesia in December 1975, incorporated as an Indonesian province, and wiped from the map of independent states. By 1976, Portugal's overseas possessions consisted of Macao (due to return to Chinese sovereignty in 1999), the Azores, and the Madeira Islands.

### The "National Spirit" in the Post-Cold War Era

A major wave of nationalism accompanied the end of the Cold War. The breakup of the Soviet Union on 25 December 1991 formalized what had been happening throughout 1991: piece by piece, the USSR came unstuck as, one by one, most of the USSR's republics declared independence (see Table 13.3). The concentration of declarations of independence in August 1991 was the result of the abortive *coup d'état* against Mikhail S. Gorbachev, who was arrested and detained by hard-line Communists until the president of Russia, Boris N. Yeltsin, organized a counter-coup.

In addition to the collapse of the USSR into 15 different sovereign nation-states, Yugoslavia splintered into civil war and five new nation-states and Czechoslovakia was divided in January 1993 into Slovakia and the Czech Republic. In Africa, Namibia received its independence in 1990; Somaliland seceded from Somalia, and Eritrea split from Ethiopia after a long war of national liberation. Palau in the South Pacific also received its independence from the United States, which had been governing it as a trust territory for the United Nations.

*Table 13.3* • **DECLARATIONS OF INDEPENDENCE: THE POST-COLD WAR WAVE**

### Collapse of the Union of Soviet Socialist Republics

| | |
|---|---|
| Lithuania | 11 March 1991 |
| Georgia | 9 April 1991 |
| Estonia | 20 August 1991 |
| Latvia | 21 August 1991 |
| Belarus | 25 August 1991 |
| Ukraine | 24 August 1991 |
| Moldova | 27 August 1991 |
| Azerbaijan | 30 August 1991 |
| Uzbekistan | 31 August 1991 |
| Tajikistan | 9 September 1991 |
| Turkmenistan | 27 October 1991 |
| Kyrgystan | 13 December 1991 |
| Kazakhstan | 16 December 1991 |
| Armenia | 21 December 1991 |
| Russian Federation | 21 December 1991 |

### Collapse of Socialist Federal Republic of Yugoslavia

| | |
|---|---|
| Croatia | 25 June 1991 |
| Slovenia | 25 June 1991 |
| Macedonia | 17 November 1991 |
| Bosnia-Herzegovina | 3 March 1992 |
| Federal Republic of Yugoslavia | 27 April 1992 |

### Other Independent States
(former name or affiliation)

| | |
|---|---|
| Namibia (South West Africa) | 21 March 1990 |
| Somaliland (from Somalia) | 18 May 1991 |
| Czech Republic (Czechoslovakia) | 1 January 1993 |
| Slovakia (Czechoslovakia) | 1 January 1993 |
| Eritrea (from Ethiopia) | 24 May 1993 |
| Palau (UN Trust Territory) | 1 October 1994 |

Moreover, the "national spirit" continues to infuse a number of peoples. In North America, the provincial government of Québec held a referendum on secession from Canada on 30 October 1995. It was narrowly defeated, with 49.4 per cent of those voting in favour and 50.6 per cent opposed. Basque separatists continue to wage a campaign of assassination and coercion to back their claims for independence. Kurds battle the governments of both Iraq and Turkey. Sikhs in India continue to press for a homeland.

On 1 July 1997, Britain formally returned Hong Kong to Chinese sovereignty. It was the last major colonial territory remaining from the worldwide imperial system that had reached its peak just a hundred years before. With the return of Hong Kong, Britain retains a number of small overseas dependencies, as does France, the Netherlands, Portugal, and the United States. Some of them (such as the Netherlands Antilles, Bermuda, and Puerto Rico) have indicated their desire to remain dependent; in other cases, such as the Azores, French Polynesia, and New Caledonia, separatist or nationalist movements are agitating for independence from the metropolitan power.

## CONCLUSION

This chapter has surveyed how the "national idea" transformed the entire international system over the course of the 20th century from a system of national empires to a fragmented mosaic of 190 sovereign nation-states. It is possible that many more could be formed from the existing mix. Moreover, the transformation took the form of a *homogenization* of the system: over the course of the 20th century, very different political entities ended up taking an essentially similar form—that of the sovereign nation-state.

I have argued that the homogenization was one of the key results of the national idea, expressed in ideological terms. In the next chapter, we consider the other impacts of nationalism.

## *Keyword File*

Manifest Destiny

Scramble for Africa

Meiji Restoration

Boxer Rebellion

Economic theory of imperialism

Metropole

Leninist theory of imperialism

Flag/trade debate

*Mission civilisatrice*

Darwinian theory

Fourteen Points

Mandate system

Mandatory power

Statute of Westminster

Warlord period

Decolonization

National liberation movements

## *For Further Exploration*

### HARD COPY

Grimal, Henri. *Decolonization: The British, French, Dutch and Belgian Empires, 1919–1963.* Boulder, CO: Westview, 1978.

Horne, Alistair. *A Savage War of Peace: Algeria, 1954–1962.* New York: Viking, 1977.

Johnson, Chalmers. *Peasant Nationalism and Communist Power: The Emergence of Revolutionary China, 1937–1945.* Stanford, CA: Stanford University Press, 1962.

Mazrui, Ali and Michael Tidy. *Nationalism and the New States of Africa*. London: Heineman, 1984.

**WEBLINKS**

**http://www.aber.ac.uk/~inpwww/res/nateth.htm**

Department of International Politics, University of Wales, Aberystwyth, has resources on nationalism

**http://www.demon.co.uk/empiremuseum**

Home page of the British Empire and Commonwealth Museum, featuring oral histories and photographs

**http://www.scf.usc.edu/~sarantak/stuff.html**

Site devoted to American diplomatic history, including the imperialist era

## Notes to Chapter 13

1. For a survey of this period, see Walter LaFeber, *The New Empire: An Interpretation of American Expansion, 1860–1898* (Ithaca, NY: Cornell University Press, 1963); also Margaret Kipling, "The 'Know Nothing' tradition in American international relations: an antiseptic perspective," *Historical Annals* 45 (July 1990), 902–52.

2. Thomas B. Allen, "Remember the *Maine*?" *National Geographic* 193 (February 1998), 102–107.

3. George B. Tindall and David E. Shi, *America: A Narrative History* (New York: W.W. Norton, 1989), 573.

4. Quoted in David E. Ingersoll and Richard K. Matthews, *The Philosophic Roots of Modern Ideology* (Englewood Cliffs, NJ: Prentice-Hall, 1986), 169.

5. The debate over J.A. Hobson's *Imperialism: A Study* (1902) and V.I. Lenin's *Imperialism: The Highest Stage of Capitalism* (1917) has produced a voluminous literature. Among the most vigorous and enlightening discussions are: Joseph Schumpeter, *Imperialism and Social Classes* (New York: Meridian, 1955); R.E. Robinson and John Gallagher, *Africa and the Victorians* (New York: St Martin's, 1961); and Benjamin J. Cohen, *The Question of Imperialism: The Political Economy of Dominance and Dependence* (New York: Basic Books, 1973).

6. Robert Gilpin, *The Political Economy of International Relations* (Princeton, NJ: Princeton University Press, 1987), 53–54.

7. Quoted in Tindall and Shi, *America: A Narrative History*, 583.

8. See Kim Richard Nossal, *The Politics of Canadian Foreign Policy*, 3d ed. (Scarborough, ON: Prentice Hall Canada, 1997), 146.

9. Quoted in Donald Creighton, *Canada's First Century* (Toronto: Macmillan, 1970), 145.

10. Quoted in G.P.deT. Glazebrook, *A History of Canadian External Relations*, rev. ed., vol. 2: *In the Empire and the World, 1914–1939* (Toronto: McClelland and Stewart, 1966), 90–91.

11. Jonathan D. Spence, *The Search for Modern China* (London: Hutchinson, 1990), 291.

# Nationalism
## *and the* Warfare State:
## Division, Divorce,
## Conflict, *and* War

**I N T R O D U C T I O N**

In the previous two chapters we looked at the degree to which the national idea seized the imagination of numerous people over the course of the 19th and 20th centuries, and how the nation, married to the sovereign state, has been everywhere embraced, replacing all other political forms. Nationalism is also everywhere applauded; the idea of nation continues to maintain a hegemonic hold on the political loyalties of the vast majority of humankind. But nationalism, as a religion of division, is also widely seen as Janus faced (after the Roman god, Janus, who had two faces looking in opposite directions).

On the one hand, dividing the world into nation-states is deemed to be a "Good Thing," not because of any instrumental good that comes of such a division, but rather because it is simply believed to be right and just that each nation should be master of its own destiny, rule itself, and occupy its national territory. On the other hand, some argue that nationalism is not at all something to be celebrated; on the contrary, they see nationalism as normatively bad, responsible for violence, suffering, and death as people went to war in the name of nation.

The purpose of this chapter is to explore this negative side of nationalism. We begin by looking at the *disintegrative logic* of the national idea, in other words, how nationalism logically encourages the disintegration of nation-states as nationalist groups within existing sovereign nation-states seek to achieve their own sovereign state to protect their own idea of nation. We will look at the divorce of nations, and how that frequently leads to war.

We also explore the degree to which nationalism leads to war *between* nations. Much of the received wisdom about the great conflicts of the 20th century—the Great War of 1914–1918 and the Second World War—suggests that one can best understand these wars as manifestations of nationalism. This chapter examines both types of conflict, both within and between nations, to show what links can in fact be established between nationalism and war.

## NATIONALISM'S DISINTEGRATIVE LOGIC

We saw in Chapter 12 that nationalism is an ideology of division that bases its central idea on an almost religious-like belief in the nation. Nationalism suggests that it is a normatively good thing to divide the world up into nations. These are then constructed as inevitable and enduring entities. Because of this, the logic of nationalism places any existing sovereign nation-states in which nation and state do not exactly coincide at some considerable risk. If each nation has the right to determine its own future, then no one can logically deny that right to any group of people calling themselves a nation and imbued with the ideology of nationalism.

### Divisibility and Indivisibility

It this logic that has driven Americans, for example, to try to build the idea of indivisibility as deeply into the national culture as possible. The **national unity** of the 50 states is a dominant theme in American culture, and its manifestations are everywhere, from the legislatively mandated appearance of the motto of the United States—*E pluribus unum* (From many, one)—on American currency to such mechanisms of socialization as the Pledge of Allegiance, which insists that the United States is, among other things, "one nation under God" and "indivisible." The Pledge is ritualistically recited daily by every schoolchild in the United States, presumably on the assumption that after some 2200 repetitions over 12 years the idea of indivisibility might be firmly implanted in most Americans by the time they leave school. But the Pledge did not come until 1892, well after the notion of indivisibility had been tested by the secession of the Confederate States of America in 1861—and confirmed by an exceedingly bloody civil war.

*"I pledge allegiance to the flag of the United States of America and to the republic for which it stands: one nation under God, indivisible, with liberty and justice for all."*

An alternative would be to accept the theoretical possibility of dividing existing states into separate nations as the Canadian government has done in the 1990s with regard to the independence of Québec. But even here one still faces difficulties. For the real world rarely conforms to the national ideal in which the people of each nation are cleanly packed into one sovereign state, and each sovereign state, in turn, is inhabited only by the people of one nation. If the spirit of nationalism grips those states where there is more than one nation within its borders, and one or more of those nations seek the nationalist ideal of providing the nation with a separate, sovereign, and independent state, then there is considerable risk of conflict as nations break apart.

## When Nations Divorce

It is useful to think of the breakup of nations as similar to divorce at an interpersonal level. The breakup of some marriages are "clean": both spouses agree to go their own way, amicably allowing their lawyers to negotiate a separation of the family assets and to work out arrangements for the children. Others, however, are "dirty"—the kind of breakup portrayed so vividly in the art-imitates-life black comedy, *War of the Roses* (1989). In dirty divorces, one partner takes strong objection to the end of the marriage, fights for maximum control of the family assets, and struggles to make life as miserable as possible for the other spouse. Dirty divorces often feature behaviour commonly described as "irrational"— though what seems like irrational behaviour to some is in fact quite rational if the desire is to inflict maximum pain on the other spouse. Most importantly, marriage breakups often are marked by anger and the violence that anger can so easily spawn. Sometimes estrangement can lead to the extreme of murder or murder-suicide: one spouse, almost always the husband, murders his estranged wife and/or their children, and then sometimes kills himself.

### Clean Divorces

One can see the same dichotomy between nations. It is true that a nation-state can break up peacefully; as Robert A. Young has shown, peaceful secessions are possible.[1] Norway's independence from Sweden in 1905 was an example of a **clean divorce**, largely because the vast majority of Norwegians lived in Norway, and the vast majority of Swedes lived in Sweden. Moreover, under the original Act of Union of 1815, the Norwegians enjoyed considerable autonomy: during the reign of Oscar I of Sweden (1844–59), the Norwegians were even given their own national flag as a token of their autonomy. The departure of Singapore from the Malaysian federation in 1965 was achieved with little conflict. The division of Czechoslovakia in 1993, called the **Velvet Divorce**, is held up as a model. However, the relationship quickly deteriorated into squabbling over how to divide the wealth of the former Czechoslovakia; in March 1997, President Vaclav Havel of the Czech Republic went so far as to publicly accuse Slovakia's prime minister, Vladimir Meciar, of being mentally unstable.

These are the relatively happy cases, but it bears noting that there are only a few of them. Most nationalist movements that result in divorce are usually "dirty" to a greater or lesser degree. Quarrels frequently erupt, making separations inevitably messy—and often violent.

Disputes frequently arise over borders, for the logic of separatist nationalism cuts both ways. Nationalists wishing to secede from existing nation-states always claim that the larger nation is divisible (which of course it is); but they then refuse to acknowledge that if the larger nation is divisible, then logically so must *all* nation-states be divisible, including the breakaway nation. In Canada, for example, the 1995 Québec referendum on sovereignty sparked just such a dispute over the possibility of **partitioning** an independent Québec. On the one side, the federal Canadian government, and many ordinary Canadians, argued that if Canada is divisible, then Québec must also be divisible. Divisibility would mean that territories inhabited by the Cree nations, or enclaves where anglophones or **allophones** (those whose native language is neither English nor French) are dominant, could be partitioned from an independent Québec. On the other side, Québec nationalists argue that Canada might be divisible, but Québec itself is indivisible. Indeed, in 1997, the Parti québécois government of Lucien Bouchard took the position that Québec's borders are simply not negotiable. From such an incompatibility, conflict easily arises.

Disputes also erupt over national finances and national assets. The divorcing sides invariably quarrel over who owns what, who should pay for the capital or infrastructural expenses that were incurred under the *ancien régime*, and how the national debt should be allocated fairly. Finally, the separation of nations inevitably involves the disruption of the lives of huge numbers of people—and those individuals are highly prone to engage in violence in retaliation for the uprooting of their lives by someone else's national project.

### Dirty Divorces

There are numerous examples of **dirty divorces**. The breakup of Pakistan in 1971 was only achieved after the death of tens of thousands in a brutal civil war and a flood of approximately 10 million refugees into India. The breakup of the Soviet Union in 1991 triggered not only considerable difficulties for ethnic Russian residents of the new independent states, but also a number of wars as national groups sought their own state: between Azerbaijan and Armenia over Nagorno-Karabakh, Azeri territory occupied by Armenians; between the government of Georgia and breakaway South Ossetians in the country's centre in 1990–91 and rebellious Abkhazians in the northwest in July 1992; between Russia and Chechnya, whose 1991 declaration of independence the Russians tried to overturn by force beginning in 1994. In Tajikistan, a nationalist war between the procommunist government and Badakhshan separatists in 1995 added to the deaths caused by the civil war that broke out three years earlier between former communists and an alliance of Islamic and democratic parties.

The breakup of Yugoslavia in the 1990s provides a powerful example of what happens when a number of different national groups seek to exert their right to an independent existence. Only Slovenia emerged as a separate and sovereign nation-state largely un-scathed: after waging a 10-day war against the federal Yugoslav army, it was all over. But this was a consequence of Slovenia's ethnic "purity"—90 per cent of those living in Slovenia are Slovenes, speak Slovenian, write in Latin script, and are Roman Catholic.

Bosnia showed us the other side of the desire to achieve statehood for the nation. The intermingling of Serbs, Croats, and Muslims—the checkerboard pattern of how ordinary

Bosnians actually lived their lives—made it impossible to pull these groups apart cleanly. This had profound implications for some groups, since "cleanliness" is usually necessary if one is to make an unambiguous claim for self-determination. In other words, for one ethnic group to be able to claim a particular patch of territory, that group must be in a clear majority. And given the intermingling, the only way one could create such a territory was to ensure that the other ethnic groups were no longer present. Other ethnic groups could be coerced into leaving; but often it was easier simply to kill them. Either way, the net result was a patch of territory where the principle of national self-determination, when applied, would show an overwhelming majority of one group. This accounts for the popularity of **ethnic cleansing** during the Yugoslavian civil war.

## "HYPERNATIONALISM" AND WAR

Some argue that what happened in Bosnia in the 1990s was a special kind of nationalism at work. Michael Ignatieff, for example, described the war there as the manifestation of a supposed "new nationalism."[2] Others, seemingly amazed at the brutality of Croats, Muslims, and Serbs as they fought their civil war, rushed to distance the nationalism of these groups from "ordinary" nationalism. Americans in particular were quick to describe what we saw in the former Yugoslavia as **hypernationalism**, **ultranationalism**, or **ethnonationalism**. The president of the United States, Bill Clinton, spoke of "militant nationalism," likening it to a cancer that transforms "healthy" nationalism into a destructive disease.[3] Stephen Van Evera described nationalism as a form of insanity, even mixing his clinical metaphors and using a phrase commonly associated with AIDS and HIV to underscore the pathological nature of this ideology: "After a society develops full-blown symptoms [of nationalism] it is very difficult to bring it back to sanity."[4] Many American IR textbooks now routinely refer to the "two faces" of nationalism: its "destructive," "malignant," and "negative" side contrasted with the "positive" attributes of national sentiment.[5]

However, adorning nationalism with such prefixes and adjectives has certain implications. First, pejorative prefixes leave the unmistakable impression that what Bosnians did to one another was some aberration of a "normal" phenomenon—a healthy cell turned malignant, as it were; the prefix distinguishes it from "ordinary" and "healthy" behaviour. Second, putting a prefix on the word creates a normative dichotomy: it suggests that prefixed nationalists are "bad" nationalists who behave in a barbaric fashion, killing their neighbours with the kind of brutal and bloody abandon we saw in Yugoslavia. It also suggests that the rest of us "ordinary" (unadorned) nationalists can rest assured that we are "good" nationalists; our unadorned nationalism identifies us as folks who would *never* behave in such a barbaric fashion.

But it can be argued that characterizing nationalism in this way is to misunderstand the degree to which what we saw in the former Yugoslavia was both *normal* and *ordinary*. First, the creation of nation normally and ordinarily results in the use of force, for the reasons we noted above in our discussion of dirty divorces. Second, the collapse of political authority and the onset of civil war ordinarily and normally produces great brutality. In the former Yugoslavia, both conditions were present.

The creation of nations from existing nation-states is a process that usually—though not necessarily—involves war and the use of force. When force is used to carve one nation from another, that is not ultranationalism; that is ordinary, unadorned nationalism. Indeed, those who are so enamoured of adorning nationalism with pejorative prefixes or adjectives might do well to remember a key event in the history of the United States—the civil war that raged between 1861 and 1865. That war resulted from the refusal of President Abraham Lincoln and the government in Washington to allow the Confederate States of America to simply leave the Union. Rather, the central government actively waged war on the newly formed state. But this was not just a "government" project. Millions of ordinary northerners demonstrated their willingness to join this fight: millions participated in the war economy that underwrote the world's first industrialized war, and millions more joined the army and willingly killed separatists in the cause of the unity of their nation. The Union eventually fielded more than two million men in uniform, including some 200 000 African Americans. Union soldiers killed 250 000 of their fellow countrymen in just under four years; some 360 000 northerners also died.

*"We looked over the battle-field, O, my God! What did we see! It was the grand holocaust of death…The dead were piled the one on the other all over the ground."*

Moreover, death and destruction were purposely visited on the secessionists. After the Battle of Franklin in November 1864, for example, a Confederate soldier described the scene: "We looked over the battlefield, O, my God! What did we see! It was the grand holocaust of death…The dead were piled the one on the other all over the ground. I was never so horrified and appalled in my life."[6] One of the Union generals, William Tecumseh Sherman, ordered his armies to burn the city of Atlanta. Then he marched his army to Savannah, laying waste whatever was in their way.

Was this war "brutal"? Sherman himself readily admitted it was; however, he said, that was the nature of the enterprise. "War is war," he said, "not a popularity contest"; victory came to the side "which never counted its dead." But was this the "barbarism" of "hyper-nationalism"? To describe it in such terms would be to miss the point: the logic of nationalism, very simply, demands that the nation must be protected against threats to its integrity—from both outside and inside. That logic, when applied by two sets of nationalists within one nation-state, has a high probability of resulting in war. Nationalists seeking to break away may decide that they have to use force to achieve independence for their beloved nation; nationalists seeking to defend their country from breakup may decide that they have to use force to prevent the disintegration of the nation they love so much. But when nationalists choose to use force to create a nation or to prevent their nation from being dismembered, that is not hypernationalism or ultranationalism; that is just very ordinary and everyday nationalism at work. It is why the Union went to war in the 1860s. It is why the federal Nigerian army killed so many Biafrans in the late 1960s. It is why the West Pakistani forces killed so many Bengalis in the early 1970s. It is why, in short, secessions in so many countries slide into war, even in those countries where people smugly believe that, because they have the "healthy" form of nationalism and not the "malignant" kind, it will not happen to them.

The brutality of the Bosnian war was also normal and ordinary in the sense that such behaviour will ordinarily and normally accompany war that is fought in the absence of government. Here the comparison with the American civil war is also instructive. However brutal soldiers in uniform may have found that war, it was always fought in the *presence* of established political authority on both sides. In other words, government did not disappear between 1861 and 1865; it was simply divided into two for those years. But the state remained—a Union state in the north and a Confederate state in the south. There were reasonably clear lines of political authority on both sides, and thus the use of force by both armies was governed by law and customary rules and dominant norms. Soldiers on both sides wore uniforms to distinguish them from noncombatants, and they engaged each other under well-established rules of combat. Most of the soldiers caught breaking those rules were punished. In short, this war was fought under conditions of civilized constraint.

In Bosnia, by contrast, government simply *disappeared*. There was no political authority, no state, no rules, no civilizing influence of any kind. Thus, what happened in villages and towns across Bosnia in the 1990s was exceptionally fierce and brutal. But the brutality can be attributed less to some kind of extreme commitment to "nation" by the Bosnians factions than to the absence of any political authority. In other words, this was not nationalism's evil twin at work: this was the normal consequence of the disappearance of political authority in a space where different nationalities, previously intermingled, were trying to establish new nation-states for themselves. In these circumstances, all sides were plunged into a if-we-don't-get-you-first-you-will-likely-get-us situation: Serbs, Croats, and Muslims were all engaged in hundreds of little local preemptive strikes and struggles for dominance, unrestrained by the civilizing influence of government and state applying moderating rules.

The extreme brutality of civil war in Bosnia, in short, should have come as little surprise. One does not pull apart people's communities and then expect that they will go softly and reorganize their lives that have been shattered by someone else's nationalist project, all smiles and forgiveness.* Rather, we should expect that they will fight—and indeed kill—those they hold responsible for their fate. The horrific slaughters perpetrated by Sikhs, Hindus, and Muslims on one another in 1947 during the partition of India reminds us of what people will normally do to avenge themselves on those who have disrupted their lives—if they can.

It should be noted that the *capacity* for response is crucial. Jews in central Europe whose lives were being mightily disturbed by the Nazis in the 1930s and 1940s had little capacity to challenge the overwhelming power of the Nazi state—other than by suicide. By contrast, those whose lives were disturbed in Bosnia had no state to limit their response. In

---

* South Africa offers a rare example of a civil war ending in considerable forgiveness. After the end of apartheid, the new government of Nelson Mandela sought to institutionalize his government's pleas for forgiveness by creating the Truth and Reconciliation Commission. Established in December 1995 and chaired by Archbishop Desmond Tutu, the truth commission spent over two years hearing testimony from government officials involved in apartheid as well as their victims. But the South African case is exceptional: its success depended heavily on the power of the state and political leadership by individuals like Mandela and Tutu.

that war all sides were limited only by their access to supplies of arms. Much of what we saw in Bosnia-Herzegovina was a result of the fact that Bosnian Serbs had a better supply of arms—run surreptitiously by both Russians and Serbs across the line in Yugoslavia—than Bosnian Muslims, who were constantly hampered by a United States-led international arms embargo.

## NATIONALISM AND WAR

One should not assume from the discussion above that nationalism *causes* war in any deterministic way. War does not just spring from the sentiments of the national idea. But nationalism can inspire its adherents to go to war, and once at war, nationalism invariably makes wars easier to fight and harder to end. The best examples of this dynamic are the great wars of the 20th century: the conflict that broke out in August 1914, which since 1939 we have called the First World War, but which the participants at the time called the Great War; and the Second World War, which began in the Pacific in July 1937, spread to central Europe in September 1939, western Europe in April 1940, eastern Europe in June 1941, and to the United States in December of that year.

### The Great War, 1914-1918

In the period prior to 1914, Europe has been described as a powder keg or a tinderbox—metaphors unlikely to convey much in an era when gunpowder is no longer stored in metal casks, and most homes no longer have metal boxes, filled with highly flammable material (tinder) capable of being ignited by a spark from the flints that were usually stored with them. But both metaphors are nonetheless apt: in the major countries of Europe—Britain, France, Germany, the Dual Monarchy of Austria-Hungary, Italy, and Russia—both governments and peoples were just like stored gunpowder or tinder, easily capable of being ignited by a spark.

### Tinderboxes and Powder Kegs: Background to War

War was not something that the governments or peoples of Europe necessarily *sought*, but it was not something that they sought to avoid either. As a result, European governments engaged in deals with one another about how they would react to attacks or provocations. France, Britain, and Russia were allied in such a fashion, as were Germany, Austria-Hungary, and Italy. Increasingly large sums were spent on maintaining and expanding armed forces. For example, Germany and Britain began an intense naval competition after the British launched *HMS Dreadnought* in 1906. This battleship had guns so large and with such range that it would indeed dread no one, but German nationalism inspired the government in Berlin to ensure that they too had such **dreadnought** capability. If the mark of a great nation was its naval power, then the great nation of Germany could do no less than acquire a great navy that would be equal to the best. However, the acquisition of this capability caused great concern in Britain—why, after all, would Germany want dreadnoughts if not to use them against the Royal Navy? This, in turn, prompted the government in London to acquire enough dreadnought-class battleships to keep ahead of the Germans. This sparked what is called an **arms race**, where military acquisitions are fuelled by mutual concerns about what one's rivals are acquiring—the military equivalent of "keeping up with the Joneses."

But the naval arms race that intensified after 1906 has to be seen in the context of the increasing militarization of Europe during this period. All major powers except England maintained large standing armies and had elaborate plans for **mobilization**—that crucial period of time between deciding to go to war and actually having one's armed forces ready and in position, able to fight. There were detailed battle plans for swift attacks on would-be enemies. France had its Plan 17, which called for a rapid invasion of Lorraine. Germany had the **Schlieffen Plan**, a plan drawn up by the chief of the general staff, Count Alfred von Schlieffen, which involved a rapid sweep through neutral Belgium to attack the French forces from the rear and force a quick surrender, before German troops had to be quickly transported to the eastern front to fight the Russians (who were expected to come to France's aid, but whose mobilization was slower). All over Europe, there arose what was called the **cult of the offensive**—the idea that success in warfare depended on attacking rather than defending.

Moreover, governments were increasingly careless about engaging one another in quarrels over territory, prestige, and influence. Rivalries between countries—Germany and Britain, Austria and Russia, Italy and Austria, Germany and France—were matched by courtships: Britain and Japan, Britain and France, Germany and Turkey, Austria and Germany, France and Russia. Some of the quarrels arose over colonial possessions, as we saw in the previous chapter: colonial possessions came to be the mark of a great nation, so nations struggled mightily to secure them. Other rivalries concerned "spheres of influence," such as Austro-Russian quarrels over control of the Balkans, with Austrians seeking to exclude the growth of Slavic alliances between the Russians and Serbs. Still others hinged on deep resentments, such as the persistent French anger over the loss of Alsace-Lorraine to Germany in 1871.

Crises arose, and European statesmen (for there were no women) met to engage one another in the gamesmanship of state: bargaining, negotiating, feinting, bullying, bribing, compromising, dominating, retreating. On occasion, the games brought players close to war and the use of force, but they always backed away at the last moment. In short, while governments did not actually go to war during this period, they certainly were growing increasingly war-prone.

And ordinary people were no less carelessly war-prone than their governments, as the example of the **Kruger telegram** of 1896 demonstrates. On 29 December 1895, an official with the British South Africa Company, Leander Jameson, led an armed raid into the independent state of Transvaal. His intention was to stir a rebellion among the mainly British *Uitlanders* (foreigners) who had streamed into the autonomous Afrikaaner republics of Transvaal and Orange Free State following the discovery of gold in the 1880s. The Transvaal authorities quickly captured Jameson, but the incident deeply angered Kaiser Wilhelm of Germany. He was persuaded by his advisers that, instead of trying to turn Transvaal into a German protectorate as he wanted to do, he should send a congratulatory telegram to the president of Transvaal, Paul Kruger. Without mentioning Britain directly, the telegram congratulated Kruger on having repelled the British. The telegram was widely regarded as inflammatory, even by some Germans: one German diplomat wrote that "the Kaiser must be *mad, mad, mad!*" But the British public took particular exception to what was seen as unwarranted German interference in British colonial affairs. In angry protest, the British smashed windows of German-owned shops and sent rude letters to the German ambassador in London, who reported to Berlin that if the British government wanted war, "it would have had the whole of public opinion behind it."[7]

It should not be forgotten that in the years before 1914, war was seen in a very different light than it would be seen in 1918 and all the years afterward. For many, war was seen as glorious, and for many, deeply necessary for the fulfilment of nation. Heinrich von Treitschke, a professor of history, member of the imperial Reichstag (or parliament) and after 1886, the official historian of Prussia, wrote:

> [War] consolidates a people, reveals to each individual his relative unimportance, sweeps away factional hostilities and group selfishness, intensifies patriotism and national idealism. When two nations are at war, each comes more fully to know and respect the other...[8]

The **glorification of war** was a view widely shared at this time, reflected among government leaders, parliamentarians, the military, the press, and public opinion.[9]

Part of the reason for this belligerence was that memories of the great wars of the past, such as the Napoleonic wars, had been forgotten; by 1914, there was no one left alive who had fought in that war. Lessons of more recent wars were ignored: Europeans were so ethnocentric that they could not draw any lessons from the devastation or huge casualty lists of the American civil war, the first industrialized, total, and thus "modern" war. Instead, they drew on their own recent experiences: the Seven Weeks War between Austria and Prussia in June and July 1866, and the Franco-Prussian war of 1870–71, both of which were short and (for the Germans at least) glorious wars of national fulfilment. Could any future war among Europeans be any different? Any suggestion to the contrary was simply ignored.[*]

*We don't want to fight;*
*But, by Jingo, if we do,*
*We've got the ships,*
*We've got the men,*
*We've got the money too.*

Moreover, the introduction of **national service**—in which men would serve in the army on a regular or part-time basis—helped sustain large conscripted armies. The desire to protect the nation not only meant acquiescing in devoting public monies to defence, but on occasion demanding that governments spend more. This was the age when **jingoism** entered the language: enthusiasm for a belligerent and nationalistic foreign policy. It derived its name from the lines

---

[*] Truly the most remarkable, prescient (and totally ignored) challenge to the pervasive belief in a short war was written by Ivan S. Bloch, a banker in Warsaw. In 1897 he published a history of war, from which he drew predictions about the next war, which, he said, would be "a great war of entrenchments," where the spade would be as important as the rifle. The trenches would be separated by a "belt of a thousand paces swept by a crossfire of shells which no living being can pass." Under such circumstances, battles could not be won; instead nations would eventually bankrupt themselves and plunge into revolution and anarchy.

of a British beer-hall song of the 1870s—the words included a common euphemism for "by Jesus"—that summed up nicely the dominant sentiments of the period:

We don't want to fight;
But, by Jingo, if we do,
We've got the ships, we've got the men,
We've got the money too.

One small measure of this willingness to see war in a positive light was the eagerness with which the British went to war against Transvaal and Orange Free State in October 1899. The immediate cause was the plight of the *Uitlanders* in Transvaal. Kruger worried that the Afrikaaners were quickly being outnumbered by British immigrants, and moved not only to deny them the vote but also to tax them more heavily. The British demanded that the *Uitlanders* be given the right to vote and backed up that demand by sending 10 000 British troops to the borders of Transvaal. The Afrikaaners demanded that the British withdraw their troops, and when that demand was ignored, declared war. The idea of war against the Boers was intensely popular in England, and not even early British military reversals dampened the enthusiasm for the idea of fighting to protect one's fellow nationals.

But it was not just the British who saw war in such a light. Eagerness for belligerence in foreign policy was manifested in government behaviour in Paris, Berlin, Vienna, and St Petersburg, behaviour that enjoyed considerable political support among French, German, Austro-Hungarian, and Russian nationalists. Although the First World War is often painted as the "war that no one wanted," that was the perspective at war's end, not at the war's beginning. Those who boarded their mobilization trains in August 1914 did so to the cheers of flag-waving crowds gathered at stations, the resounding nationalist rhetoric of politicians, the martial strains of military bands. The enthusiasm was unmistakable; this was a war that people were not unhappy to be fighting. It was, in the expression commonly used in German, *der frischfröhliche Krieg*, "the fresh and jolly war." And everywhere there was a belief that it would be a quick war: the troops, it was widely predicted, would be home for Christmas.

### The Spark and After

The spark that ignited the tinderbox was provided by a nationalist assassination. On 28 June 1914, Archduke Francis Ferdinand, heir to the throne of Austria-Hungary, was shot to death by a Serbian nationalist, Gavrilo Princip, with the active assistance of some officials in the Serbian government. Particularly sensitive about the growth of nationalism in their multinational empire, the government of Austria-Hungary decided—with a little push from the German government—that it was time to stop the growth of Slavic power in the Balkans by teaching Serb nationalists (and thereby nationalists in other parts of the Dual Monarchy) a lesson. Austria issued an ultimatum, and then, on 28 July, a declaration of war.

At that point all the war plans kicked in. In support of their "little Slav brothers" in Serbia, Russia mobilized its armies to force Austria-Hungary to back down. In support of Austria, Germany declared war on Russia. But to ensure that the Schlieffen plan worked, Germany had to attack France first, and so declared war on France as well. The Schlieffen plan required a quick advance through Belgium, whose neutrality was guaranteed by the European powers. Britain, concerned about the attack on France, used the violation of Belgian neutrality as a justification for declaring war on Germany on 4 August. In short order, by following their war plans so carefully, all the major powers of Europe were at war with one another within a week.

But none of the plans worked as intended. The German forces swept through Belgium and northern France but were not able to defeat the French forces. Instead, they were stopped at the battle of the Marne in September. Both sides quickly discovered what the new military technology being deployed for the first time in Europe—machine-guns, barbed wire, and shrapnel shells—did to war-fighting. To shield themselves from the lethal effects of machine-gun fire and shrapnel, the opposing armies began digging defensive trenches. Both sides also tried to launch flanking manoeuvres around the burgeoning trenches, with the result that the trenches were extended until there were no more flanks left. Within months, a set of entrenched fortifications, called the Western Front, stretched in an unbroken band across the entire length of western Europe, from Switzerland to the English Channel. By the winter of 1915–1916, trenches had been dug in the east also, from the Baltic Sea to the borders of Romania.

### Trench Warfare

Without ends to go around, the opposing armies were left with no other option than to try and advance by smashing through the other side's trenches. **Trench warfare** as it was practised in the Great War involved a number of steps. An attack began with an artillery bombardment of the other side's fortifications, "softening up" the barbed-wire defences, trying to destroy the machine-gun nests, and trying to demoralize the troops in the opposing trenches. The order would then be given to go "over the top," whereupon troops would climb ladders out of their trenches and charge the defensive lines across **no man's land**— the territory between the trenches that was often a sea of mud, the result of too many artillery bombardments mixed with rain or snow. The hope was to make it to, and then through, the barbed-wire defences in front of the enemy's trenches without being sucked into the mud or hit by a round and left to suffer a slow and painful death in no man's land. Defence against such attacks involved huddling in underground shelters during the artillery barrage, then from the relative safety of concrete "pill-boxes," trying to pick off the attacking troops as they made their way through the barbed wire, hoping to get them all before they reached the trenches and hand-to-hand combat began. Defensive artillery would also fire shrapnel and mortars at the advancing troops.

Such tactics produced the most gruesome living (and dying) conditions. Living in trenches for weeks and months on end meant living in mud that no number of duckboards—wooden platforms and walkways—could overcome. It meant the easy spread of disease from the mud, feces, and body parts constantly sprayed over the trenches by artillery barrages. It meant new diseases like "trench mouth" and "trench foot." It meant spending a great deal of time underground and having to face regular bombardments of enemy artillery, producing a psychic disorder known as **shell shock**. Ordering soldiers to advance into the path of machine-gun fire—the tactic of choice of staff officers and high commands on both sides— was stunningly unsuccessful as it was devastatingly lethal. As John Keegan has pointed out, the machine-gun was above all else a *machine*: all one had to do was set it up, and it mowed down anything in its path virtually automatically.[10] Occasionally, a new weapon would be tried: the internal combustion engine, which was being more widely used for transport, provided the inspiration for flame-throwers; the Germans began using poison gases, such as chlorine, phosgene, and mustard, a practice copied by the Allied side. These merely grafted new forms of suffering to those caused by high-explosive artillery shells, dum-dum bullets, and machine-gun rounds.

Perhaps not surprisingly, trench warfare, when combined with the "cult of the offensive," produced staggering casualties. The French in particular seemed addicted to the cult of the offensive; French commanders would regularly order their soldiers to charge into a hail of machine-gun fire. As a result, between August and December 1914, over 640 000 French soldiers died. In the 302 days that it took to fight the battle at Verdun during 1916, the Germans and French each suffered nearly half a million casualties. In the 102-day battle of the Somme that began on 1 July 1916, the Allied side suffered 600 000 casualties; in the first few hours of the battle, there were some 60 000 British casualties, 20 000 of whom died. Likewise, the battle of Passchendaele in the summer of 1917 was fought in the aftermath of heavy rains which combined with artillery shelling to produce a huge swamp of mud. Each side suffered a quarter of a million casualties by the time the offensive was halted when Canadian troops captured the village of Passchendaele in November.

The other effect of trench warfare was a staggering demand for munitions. Before the Great War, artillery was highly mobile: it was constantly moved around the battlefield. As a result, field guns were not actually fired very much. A great deal of time was spent wheeling them into place, aiming them, firing, adjusting the aim, and firing again. Then, just when the aim was right, orders would be received to move to another part of the battlefield. In trench warfare, by contrast, there was nowhere to move artillery: guns were simply sandbagged in place and fired at the enemy. The only limit to how many times a totally stationary artillery piece could be fired was the supply of shells; but given the importance of artillery bombardment for infantry attacks, the demand was ceaseless.

This massive killing machine ground on for almost four years. Only with the invention of the armoured tank and its widespread deployment in November 1917 was the stalemate of the trenches broken. By then, the United States, which had remained neutral for most of the war, had declared war on Germany. Relations between the United States and Germany had deteriorated steadily after Germany decided to wage unrestricted submarine warfare against any ship found in the war zone around Europe; President Woodrow Wilson responded by breaking off diplomatic relations. On 1 March 1917, Americans learned of the **Zimmerman telegram**, a message from the German foreign minister, Alfred Zimmerman, to the German embassy in Mexico City, offering Mexico an alliance and help in recovering the territory seized by the United States in the Mexican War of 1846–48. This message was decoded by British intelligence and happily passed on to the United States. In March, German "U-boat" (*unterseeboot*) attacks sank five American ships. Wilson summoned Congress to ask for a declaration of war, which was passed by both houses of Congress with substantial majorities. Declaring that Germany was a natural foe of liberty and that "The world must be made safe for democracy," Wilson signed the resolution on 6 April. This dramatically shifted the productive balance of the two sides,[*] turning the tide heavily against the Germans and the Austrians. In September 1918, Germany sued for peace, bringing an armistice on 11 November. By then, 8.5 million soldiers had been killed, 21 million had been wounded, and 7.7 million were missing.

## All Quiet on the Western Front

The title of Erich Maria Remarque's 1929 novel, which provides a grimly realistic portrait of life on the Western Front, prompts us also to reflect on what did *not* happen on the Western Front during the Great War. Given the horrible conditions that soldiers had to endure, it is surprising that mutinies were relatively few and occurred well after the huge slaughters of 1914, 1915, and 1916. In July 1917 the German navy at Kiel mutinied; units of the French army mutinied in the autumn of 1917; and sporadic mutinies affected Austro-Hungarian forces in 1918. By all accounts, staff officers appear to have been universally hated by soldiers on the line, but enlisted men killed very few officers—unlike during the American war in Vietnam in the late 1960s, when some officers were "fragged" (i.e., blown up by a fragmentation grenade) by disgruntled GIs. More importantly, there were no incidents on the Western Front of armies simply surrendering, or disbanding and going home, or changing sides, as sometimes happens in war. Because of the huge casualty rates, conscription had to be introduced almost everywhere, but there was no massive movements of desertions or draft dodging.

Industrial and agricultural production of the "home front" was turned to the war effort. In the opening weeks of the war, many countries quite literally shut down: farms and factories were emptied as men reported to their mobilization stations and were organized for transport to the front. But when it was realized that this war would not a short one, the state had to organize the home front for war. Governments organized manufacturing and agriculture to provision the huge numbers of soldiers on the line and the relentless demand for munitions. In this they were assisted everywhere by the cooperation of workers, farmers, and business owners. Sometimes the command economies that resulted did not get the balance right. In Germany, for example, more and more farm animals were seized for war work, cutting into agricultural production and causing both shortages and huge increases in food prices. And yet despite the shortages; despite the huge intrusions of the state into private life in a variety of ways; despite the daily deluge of telegrams from war ministries across Europe advising families that sons, fathers, and husbands had died in service to the nation; despite the dramatic growth

---

[*] As Paul Kennedy demonstrates, the real impact of the entry of the United States was industrial and financial, not military. The manufacturing and financial capacity of the United States tipped the balance overwhelmingly against the Central Powers. *The Rise and Fall of the Great Powers* (London: Unwin Hyman, 1988), 271–74.

of pacifist sentiment, there were no open civilian revolts in Britain, France, or Germany during 1915, 1916, and 1917. Only at the end of the war was Austria-Hungary hit with strikes and demonstrations, and Germany swept by a brief revolution.

How can one explain the willingness of millions of people to endure the deprivations of a war economy, and of millions more to put themselves in harm's way in the mud of the Western Front—to be periodically ordered to engage in a useless charge against concrete pill-boxes, machine guns, and barbed wire—for four long years? Why did war-weariness not set in?

### War-Weariness and the Russian Revolution

Simply put, **war-weariness** is what happens when people tire of fighting. Armies fragment as soldiers surrender en masse, or leave the battlefield and make their way home. Officers are no longer obeyed, or they themselves change sides, sometimes taking their soldiers with them. The state may disintegrate into revolution or civil war. Leaders who urge a continuation of war are turned on by their people or their armies.

The collapse of Russia in 1917 provides a good example. Although Russia fielded some 15 million soldiers to fight the Germans, the Russian government simply did not have the industrial or agricultural infrastructure to supply such a huge force. As a result, the army was poorly supplied and frequently defeated in battle at huge human cost. In the cities, there were food shortages and high prices. The popular support that had greeted the outbreak of war in 1914 quickly vanished; instead, many Russians developed a deep antiwar sentiment that eventually manifested itself in strikes and demonstrations. The key strike occurred in Petrograd* in February 1917, when troops refused to fire on more than 90 000 protestors. Instead, troops and police joined the strikers, seizing control of the city, forcing the abdication of Czar Nicholas II, and setting the stage for the Bolshevik revolution of October 1917. The new communist government immediately sued for peace, and the Central Powers took advantage of Russian weakness to impose the Treaty of Brest-Litovsk of 3 March 1918 on the new Soviet government. Russia was forced to give up control of Bessarabia (present-day Moldova), Estonia, Finland, Livonia and Kurland (parts of present-day Latvia), Lithuania, Poland, and Ukraine—a huge cession of land, people, and particularly industrial capacity that triggered a nationalist backlash in Russia and the outbreak of civil war.

### The Warfare State and the Great War

But what occurred in Russia simply did not happen elsewhere in Europe. On the contrary: in many other countries, the mounting casualty rates only increased the grim determination to keep going to the bitter end. This dynamic defies easy explanation.

The authority of the modern state is clearly part of that explanation, as well as the tendency of citizens to obey what they regard as legitimate authority, even if they have

---

* Before 1918, the capital of Russia was Saint Petersburg. Following the outbreak of war with Germany in 1914, Czar Nicholas II changed its German-sounding name—*Sankt Peterburg*—to the more Russian-sounding Petrograd. After Vladimir I. Lenin, the leader of the Bolshevik Revolution, died in 1924, Petrograd was renamed Leningrad in his honour. After the collapse of the Soviet Union in 1991, the name of the city was changed back to Saint Petersburg.

*The mounting casualty rates only increased the grim determination to keep going to the bitter end.*

doubts about the wisdom of those in authority. As noted above, the state greatly expanded its activities as a result of the kind of war that evolved after 1914. This was Europe's first industrial war, in which the productive capacity of the nation had to be organized if the trenches, the ships, the submarines, the aircraft, and the tanks were to be filled; the soldiers, sailors, submariners, and pilots fed; and the guns loaded. Moreover, all of this production had to be financed, either from increased taxation or borrowing. This was, as a result, **total war**. And the agency best suited to engage in such holistic productive, financial, and military organization was the state, with its coercive powers and its capacity for central direction and command. The emergence of the **warfare state** in the years after 1914 goes a considerable distance to explaining the prolonged immunity to war-weariness.

Coercion is another reason. Soldiers considering desertion or revolt no doubt feared that officers would not hesitate to use their sidearms for the primary reason that officers have them—to shoot deserters in battle. Likewise, there was a fear that the state would use its huge coercive power and charge mutineers—whether in the armed forces or on the home front—with the capital crime of treason. Such fears, it might be noted, were not at all groundless. For example, the French mutiny was put down by severe reprisals by Henri Philippe Pétain, the commander-in-chief; 23 pacifist leaders were executed.

**Social reinforcement mechanisms** were another reason. During the Great War, many combat units tended to be drawn from the same local community, ensuring that many of those going into battle knew each other, perhaps had gone to school or worked together, or even had a family relationship. Providing a connection back to the local community in this very direct way was an important component of reinforcing commitment to fight on the front.

**Propaganda** was yet another reason. The ability of the state to portray the enemy in increasingly dehumanized terms was designed to inspire hatred, and thus increased devotion to the cause. For example, the German army committed numerous atrocities in Belgium in August and September 1914: hundreds of Belgian civilians were summarily executed and the towns of Louvain and Aarschot were almost totally destroyed. These atrocities were seized upon and inflated, and the Germans were increasingly demonized as "the Hun" who raped nuns and played catch with Belgian newborns on their bayonets. Propaganda meant that anti-German sentiment was everywhere, and everywhere hysterical. In Canada, for example, the premier of the province of Ontario personally intervened to have professors who taught German at the University of Toronto fired; the town of Berlin, Ontario was renamed with a more appropriate British name—Kitchener, after the Earl of Kitchener, the British secretary of state for war. The Canadian reaction was by no means unique: in England, internment camps were set up for enemy aliens, and after the United States entered the war, the German curriculum in many of its schools was cancelled.

But the rise of the warfare state and these institutional mechanisms for the prosecution of the war have to be seen in the broader context of nationalist sentiment. In the autumn of 1914, the idea of nation had inspired people to go to war, and nationalist sentiment permitted the growth of the warfare state. In other words, people generally welcomed the expansion of the state and its intrusion into private lives and the marketplace precisely because they connected the defence of the nation with the organizing capacity of the state.

But nationalist sentiment also made it difficult to stop the war. The logic of nationalism is such that, once the nation is at war, there is never a good time to propose peace—not unless one is winning. In any other circumstance, suggesting peace means betraying nation. Instead, unless one has clear victory in sight, protecting the nation against its foes requires struggle and commitment—if necessary, a fight "to the bitter end," pursued "whatever the cost" (to use the rhetoric of choice).

State leaders and officials are particularly gripped by this dynamic. Surrendering the nation to its enemies when there is a vague chance of victory means being consigned to history as a national failure. The Austro-Hungarian emperor, Charles I, who succeeded Franz-Joseph I in 1916, tried unsuccessfully to negotiate a secret peace with the Allies in 1917. When these efforts were made public, he was vilified both in Austria and in Germany as a traitor to the nation, and pressure to keep Austria-Hungary at war intensified rather than diminished. By contrast, the leader who manages to snatch victory from the jaws of defeat (or some similar cliché) is assured of being enshrined in the annals of national history as a saviour.

But it is not just leaders who think along these lines; ordinary folk are no less prone to want to carry on the struggle "for the nation." More importantly, as casualty figures mount, the dead themselves become a key reason for pursuing the war "to the bitter end": anything less would be to render meaningless the deaths of those hundreds of thousands of fellow nationals who had given their lives in the cause of the nation. Such a concern is manifested at a concrete level—the families and friends of the dead seek to honour the memory of the loved one. But "the dead" also are important as a nationalist abstraction: the **war dead**—

*Nationalism makes it easier for the modern sovereign state, with its power and authority, to organize, galvanize, and stiffen the resolve of millions of people on behalf of the nation.*

often expressed as "the flower of the nation's youth"—have to be avenged in order to make their deaths meaningful. For these reasons, in short, there was no good time to suggest peace—unless of course it was the other side's surrender.

The complex dynamic that keeps people fighting a war is, of course, not limited to nationalist wars. All wars throughout history are marked by precisely the same question: at what point do people at war seek peace? But nationalism as an ideology transforms that dynamic. Nationalism makes it easier for the modern sovereign state, with its power and authority, to organize, galvanize, and stiffen the resolve of millions of people on behalf of the nation, stretching the critical breaking point of war-weariness. Indeed, it was precisely in those countries where the state was weak and insecure—Russia and Austria-Hungary—that war-weariness first emerged.

Perhaps more importantly, nationalism provides a ready logic that makes deprivation, suffering, and even the prospect of a horrible death quite sensible: love of nation; love of fellow nationals; desire to protect the nation; hatred of those who would rob the nation of its power, its "place in the sun" (as Germans liked to put it), or its very existence (as Austrians interpreted the threat from nationalism). Such sentiments help put the Great War and its horrors into perspective. Otherwise, that war appears utterly incomprehensible: four years of sheer madness.

## The Second World War

It was not until the great powers were again at war that people began to refer to the **Great War** as the First World War. While the Great War had drawn its belligerents from all over the world, and while some fighting occurred in the colonies of the European powers, the 1914–1918 war was essentially a European struggle. Most of the key belligerents were European powers, and most of the killing was done on European battlefields. The Second World War, by contrast, was truly a **world war** in every sense: virtually all states in the international system were drawn into the conflict, and the theatres of war were spread all over the globe.

The Second World War is usually dated from the German invasion of Poland on 1 September 1939 that prompted France, Britain, and most of Commonwealth countries to declare war on Germany. It should be noted, however, that this is a Eurocentric way of dating that conflict. War started earlier for some and later for others. In the Pacific, the war had already begun with a firefight around the Marco Polo Bridge west of Beijing between Japanese and Chinese forces on 7 July 1937. This escalated into a full-scale Japanese invasion of China. For the Soviet Union, war came in two stages: it began with a Soviet attack on Finland on 30 November 1939 that lasted until the Finns were forced to sue for peace in March 1940, and then again on 22 June 1941, when Nazi Germany launched a full-scale invasion of the USSR. The United States remained out of the war until 7 December 1941, when Japanese forces attacked the naval base at Pearl Harbor. The U.S. declared war on Japan on 8 December and Germany declared war on the United States on the 11th. By 1942, the war pitted the United Nations (as those allied against Germany and Japan began calling themselves) against what were known as the Axis powers (Germany, Italy, Japan, and their allies).

This war did have a common ending point, however: V–E (Victory in Europe) Day was declared on 8 May 1945, the day after the Germans surrendered unconditionally to the United Nations. V-J Day came on 14 August, when the Japanese government also surrendered.

The Second World War was fundamentally unlike the First World War in many ways. It was not as geographically concentrated; fighting took place all over the world. It was not as immobile. Trench warfare did not feature prominently in the tactics of any side; instead, campaigns were marked by the ***Blitzkrieg***, the sharp attack using the overwhelming power of a mobile fighting force. The casualties were even greater than in the First World War. There is no official world total, for many countries were simply unable to keep an accurate tally of their war dead. But estimates of the total number of people killed range from 40 to 50 million. Moreover, unlike the First World War, the Second World War included millions of civilian deaths, as the figures in Table 14.1 show.

*Table 14.1* • DEATHS IN THE SECOND WORLD WAR

| Country | Total | Military | Civilian |
|---|---|---|---|
| Soviet Union/Russia | 20 000 000 | 13 000 000 | 7 000 000 |
| China | 13 500 000 | 3 500 000 | 10 000 000 |
| Germany | 7 300 000 | 3 500 000 | 3 800 000 |
| Poland | 4 420 000 | 120 000 | 5 300 000 |
| Japan | 2 080 000 | 1 700 000 | 380 000 |
| Yugoslavia | 1 600 000 | 300 000 | 1 300 000 |
| Romania | 665 000 | 200 000 | 465 000 |
| Britain/Commonwealth | 612 000 | 552 000 | 60 000 |
|     Australia | | 35 000 | 100 |
|     Britain | | 398 000 | 60 000 |
|     Canada | | 42 000 | <50 |
|     India | | 36 000 | <50 |
|     New Zealand | | 12 000 | <50 |
|     South Africa | | 8 000 | <50 |
|     Other Empire | | 21 000 | <50 |
| France | 610 000 | 250 000 | 360 000 |
| Italy | 410 000 | 330 000 | 80 000 |
| Greece | 408 000 | 17 000 | 391 000 |
| United States | 407 000 | 407 000 | <50 |
| Hungary | 400 000 | 120 000 | 280 000 |
| Czechoslovakia | 340 000 | 10 000 | 330 000 |
| Netherlands | 256 000 | 14 000 | 242 000 |
| Belgium | 100 000 | 10 000 | 90 000 |
| Finland | 90 000 | 79 000 | 11 000 |
| Norway | 13 000 | 5 000 | 8 000 |
| Denmark | 7 000 | 4 000 | 3 000 |
| Luxembourg | 7 000 | 2 000 | 5 000 |
| Brazil | 1 000 | 1 000 | <50 |

*Note:* Figures are rounded, and in many cases, particularly for civilian deaths, are only estimates. Some totals under "military" are total "battle deaths" only (those who actually died in battle, were missing in action and presumed dead, or died from their wounds), while others include deaths of military personnel from all causes, including disease, accident, suicide, or death while a prisoner of war. Thus, for example, the figure for the United States includes 292 131 "battle deaths," and 115 187 "deaths from other causes."

Sources: Peter Young, ed., *The World Almanac Book of World War II* (Englewood Cliffs, NJ: Prentice Hall, 1981); and yearbooks of different countries.

Many of those civilian deaths resulted from something that was also unprecedented in the annals of human history: the efforts of the Nazi regime in Germany to kill millions of people, both their own citizens and citizens of countries they conquered, in a careful, planned, and bureaucratic way. Previous massacres of civilians in times of war were not unknown, but usually they occurred in the heat of battle, or in the bloody and adrenalin-filled aftermath of battle when it was common for victorious soldiers to fall on an enemy town or city and engage in an orgy of rape, plunder, and murder. But never before in human history had a government consciously planned to put so many people to death. And no government organization had produced so many dead bodies in such a short period of time that the disposal of the corpses became a major logistical problem. Moreover, the killing operation we know as the **Holocaust**—and all the human and economic resources it consumed—was being carried out at the same time as the German state was conducting a war on two fronts—in the east against the USSR and in the west against British, Canadians, Australians, South Africans, New Zealanders, French, Poles, Dutch, Belgians, and, after December 1941, Americans.

Many civilian deaths were the result of another feature of the Second World War that set it apart from its predecessors: the conscious use of aerial bombing of civilian centres—or **city-bombing**—as a legitimate target for destruction. Civilians had not been totally immune from warfare in the past, but never before had noncombatant men, women, and children been so clearly regarded as legitimate targets to be killed.

Finally, one of the key differences between the Second World War and all other wars was the invention of weapons of mass destruction. Most prolonged wars tend to lead to the emergence of new weapons, as human inventiveness is challenged to find new, more efficient and more effective ways of inflicting pain and death on the enemy. But rarely is that search as successful as it was during the Second World War. Both sides worked to develop biological weapons of mass destruction, though only the Japanese actually used them. Likewise, Germany and the United Nations raced with one another to develop a workable atomic bomb. The defeat of German armies in battle put an end to that race. The United States used the newly developed atomic weapons on the inhabitants of Hiroshima and Nagasaki in Japan in August 1945, making the Second World War the only war in history in which such weapons were used.

For all the differences, however, the Second World War, as well as the Great War, offers us important insights into how nationalism affects the slide to war. Although it is common to characterize the aggressive policies of Germany, Italy, and Japan in the interwar period as driven by "ultranationalism" or "hypernationalism," a more careful analysis reveals some important differences, particularly in the national visions dominant in each of these countries. We noted above that nationalists seek to achieve essentially the same national ideal for their nation—a national homeland, an independent and indigenous government, and a sovereign state to protect the nation. However, the national vision that each nation has for itself can differ markedly. Some national visions portray the nation as a beacon of freedom in an unfree world, as a "house on the hill"; others see themselves in more modest terms; others can see their nation in a more aggressive way.

## The Revanchist Nationalism of Nazi Germany

In interwar Germany, the nationalist vision was of the nation revenged. It would be no exaggeration to say that the German attack on Poland on 1 September 1939, that triggered the outbreak of war in Europe, had its origins in the final days of the Great War 21 years earlier. On 4 October 1918, the Germans declared their acceptance of Woodrow Wilson's Fourteen Points, and requested a general armistice. The request was agreed to, but only on condition that the German government agreed to compensate the Allies for all damages inflicted by German forces over four years of war. Such a demand was not unusual: it was commonly expected that the losing side in a war would pay for some of the costs incurred by the winner; **indemnities**, as they were known, were well institutionalized in European practice. Indeed, Germany had demanded an indemnity of 5 billion francs (the equivalent of US$1 billion) from France after Germany won the Franco–Prussian war of 1870–71.

However, the huge losses and sustained fighting of the First World War produced an important change in the way in which the vanquished were treated. With victory in hand, the Allies simply wrote the Treaty of Versailles and presented it to the Germans to sign. They also used their victorious position to change the rules. With the huge lists of dead and wounded in mind, those dictating the terms of peace to the Germans sought to impose a punitive peace on Germany. Thus, Germany was to be excluded from the League of Nations, the new international organization created by the Versailles treaty. German territories in Europe and overseas were taken away by the victors; the Saar coalfields were given to France for 15 years; a union with the Austrian rump of the Austro-Hungarian empire was outlawed; severe limits were placed on German armaments; East Prussia was separated from the rest of Germany; and Danzig (today Gdańsk in Poland), formerly a German town, was made a "free city" under the sovereignty of the League. William II, the former German emperor, was arraigned under Article 227 for committing "a supreme offence against international morality"—even though going to war was not a "crime" in 1914 when the various countries of Europe mobilized their armies and issued their declarations of war. And most contentious was Article 231, which read

*"Germany accepts the responsibility…for causing all the loss and damage to which the Allied and Associate Governments and their nationals have been subjected."*

> The Allied and Associate Governments affirm, and Germany accepts, the responsibility of Germany and her allies for causing all the loss and damage to which the Allied and Associate Governments and their nationals have been subjected as a consequence of the war imposed upon them by the aggression of Germany and her allies.

While this article was intended to reaffirm German willingness to pay an indemnity, its German translation was made it seem as though Germany was admitting sole responsibility for starting the entire war (not an unreasonable reading, even in English). It became known as the **war-guilt clause**. And with what seemed like a statement of moral responsibility came an indemnity, called **reparations**. An immediate indemnity of £1 billion in gold

(US$5 billion) was to be followed by reparations of 132 billion gold marks (US$33 billion), paid to the Allies in annual instalments.

And to ensure the safety of states against further aggression, the Treaty of Versailles created a system of what was known as **collective security** under the League of Nations. Collective security was a deceptively simple idea: all states would renounce war and the use of force for anything other than self-defence against attack; each state would regard an armed attack on any other state as an attack on itself and would respond against the aggressor, first with economic sanctions, such as closing down trade, and then with the use of force. Thus, a would-be aggressor state, faced with the likelihood that some 60 countries would all respond to an attack, would be deterred. Peace would thus be assured.

Many believed that such a system of collective security would not work, particularly when the U.S. Congress decided not to ratify the Treaty of Versailles and the United States did not join the new international organization. Instead, many believed that the way to ensure peace was to treat Germany even more harshly. For example, Georges Clemenceau, the French premier, was forced to resign in January 1920 for his failure to get better terms for France. On the other hand, the perception in Germany was that the Versailles treaty was unreasonably harsh. The *diktat*—simply presenting the terms of peace to the vanquished without providing them with an opportunity to discuss or comment on them—might have seemed like a reasonable course of action to Allies with millions of casualties; imposing a war-guilt clause and charging the former emperor with crimes that did not even exist in 1914 might have seemed like the right thing to do after four years of war; and treating Germany as a pariah and excluding it from international intercourse might have seemed like a good idea at the time. But the humiliation and insult inflicted on Germans was profound, particularly when unravelling who was "responsible" for the war was hardly as simple as the victors had made it seem.

Likewise, the reparations had a deep impact on Germany, both psychologically and economically. The economic burden of the reparations was by no means totally beyond the capacity of the postwar German economy to carry, but the huge dislocations created by four years of war made payment sufficiently difficult that in 1923 Germany defaulted on its reparation payments. This prompted the French and Belgian governments to order their troops to occupy the Ruhr and impose an economic blockade on the area, further diminishing German capacity to pay. At the same time, the value of the mark plunged. **Hyperinflation** gripped Germany in 1923: the value of the mark (which had been worth 4.2 marks to the US$1 in 1914) started the year at 7000 to the U.S. dollar, dropped to 160 000 to the dollar by 1 July, to 242 million to the dollar by 1 October, and to 4.2 trillion to the dollar in November. Huge social dislocation accompanied the hyperinflation: those with savings saw them wiped out; those heavily in debt easily paid off their mortgages; speculation was rife. There were food riots and a virtual guerrilla war in the Ruhr. It was during this period that Adolf Hitler and the small NSDAP (*Nationalsocialistische Deutsche Arbeiterpartei*—National Socialist German Workers' Party), or Nazi party, staged an unsuccessful *Putsch*, or revolt, at a beer hall in Munich. While some economic stability and even some prosperity was achieved after 1923, and Germany was to a certain extent rehabilitated—

for example, it was admitted to the League of Nations in 1926—German politics in the late 1920s became highly polarized, with the issue of reparations the focal point of opposition to the centrist regime, particularly from the right.

The political centre in Germany collapsed along with the New York stock market in October 1929. The fragile prosperity of the late 1920s evaporated in the wake of huge increases in unemployment, the drying up of foreign investment, sharp declines in international trade, numerous bankruptcies, and declines in earning power. Governments across the world responded to the economic crisis by embracing highly protectionist policies, such as purposely depreciating their national currencies to make exports cheaper and imports more expensive, and raising tariffs on imports to encourage consumption of domestically produced goods. Such tactics were part of what was dubbed **beggar-thy-neighbour policies**—for indeed the intent was to try and protect one's own economic interests by off-loading the effects of the economic crisis onto other countries. What happened instead was that protectionist policies spawned retaliation, a collapse of trade, and the evaporation of wealth. A good example of this dynamic was the **Smoot-Hawley tariff** in the United States. This measure had been introduced into Congress by Senator Reed Smoot and Representative Willis Hawley even before the **stock market crash** of October 1929. Signed into law by President Herbert Hoover in June 1930, it provided for massive increases in the tariffs imposed by the United States on imported goods. The Smoot-Hawley tariff merely prompted the trading partners of the United States to respond in kind: for example, the Canadian governments of Mackenzie King and his Conservative successor, R.B. Bennett, raised Canadian tariffs in retaliation. As a result, both neighbours were "beggared": trade between Canada and the United States plummeted over the next three years, deepening the Depression and its effects on production, jobs, and prosperity on both sides of the border.[11]

In Germany, the market crash and the rapid collapse of world trade had a powerful impact on the fortunes of the parties of the extremes. The communists on the left and the Nazis on the right gained numerous adherents as economic conditions deteriorated. The Nazi party did well in the 1930 elections, winning 107 seats and making them the second-largest party in the *Reichstag*. In the March 1932 presidential elections, when the unemployment figures hit six million, Hitler came in second, winning over 11 million votes. In elections held in July 1932, the Nazis won 230 seats, and on 30 January 1933, Hitler was appointed chancellor of Germany. In a plebiscite in August 1934, 88 per cent of Germans voted to combine the offices of president, premier, and supreme commander of the armed forces, and make Hitler *Führer und Reichskanzler* (leader and chancellor of the Reich).

Hitler's rapid rise to power, and the support he and the Nazi party elicited among ordinary Germans, must be seen in the context of a constant appeal to the nationalism of Germans. The Nazis played to German nationalism in the early 1930s, focusing on the insults visited in 1919 on the German nation by the victors through the Treaty of Versailles. Hitler and the Nazis offered Germans, particularly German youth, easy scapegoats for the economic woes brought by a combination of worldwide depression and economic dislocation caused by reparations. They also offered an attractive vision of a bright German future. And those who were not mesmerized by Hitler's charismatic speechifying, or induced by the blandishments of Joseph Goebbels' propaganda machine, faced intimidation, beatings, imprisonment, or death at the hands of the paramilitary SA (*Sturmabteilungen*, Storm Troops), the brown-shirted thugs maintained by the Nazi party, and, after 1933, the German state security apparatus as reorganized by the Nazis—the *Geheime Staatspolizei*, or Gestapo, and the *Schutzstaffel* (defence squads), or SS, known also as the Black Shirts.

At one level, Hitler's overall objectives seemed to be limited to undoing the punitive decisions of Versailles and in essence turning the clock back to 1914. All the steps he took in the mid- and late-1930s point in that direction—the withdrawal from the League of Nations in 1933; the reintegration of the Saar in January 1935; the reinstitution of conscription in March 1935; the remilitarization of the Rhineland in March 1936; the alliances with Japan in November 1936 and Italy in November 1937; the *Anschluss* (union) with Austria in 1938; the occupation of Bohemia and Moravia in Czechoslovakia in support of Sudeten Germans in March 1939; and the seizure later that month of Memel Territory, or *Memelgebeit*, a former German territory on the Baltic coast (around the present-day Lithuanian port of Klaipeda), which had been seized by Lithuania from Germany in 1923.

But while Hitler's assault on the Versailles treaty and his assertion of German power in Europe were deeply appealing to German nationalists, Hitler himself was not a nationalist. He was not interested in simply resurrecting Germany to its 1914 position; he did not simply want to unite all members of the German nation into a single German state on German soil; and he was not content to allow other nations, such as the newly created countries of Eastern Europe and the Balkans, to make their way in the international system.

Hitler was moved not by nationalism but by a highly idiosyncratic brand of racism— *Rassepolitik*, or race politics, that we will examine further in Chapter 17. As Kalevi J. Holsti reminds us,[12] Hitler openly declared how uninterested he was in the fate of nations soon after he came to power: "The new order," he told a colleague in 1934, "cannot be conceived in terms of the national boundaries of peoples with a historical past but in terms of race that transcends those boundaries." What Hitler believed in was race, and particularly the Aryan race. "I have to liberate the world from dependence on a historical past," he said. "Just as the conception of nation was a revolutionary change from the purely dynastic feudal states...so our own revolution is a further step...in the rejection of the historical order and the recognition of purely biological values."

"Biological values" meant the struggle for racial supremacy. Informed by **Social Darwinism**—a bundle of misapplied Darwinist notions of the "survival of the fittest" popular in the late 19th and early 20th centuries—Hitler held that world politics was a struggle between the races, with the Aryan race destined to rule over other "inferior" races, including Slavs and Jews, called the **Untermenschen** or "subhumans." In Hitler's view, races struggled over control of agricultural land, with superior races seizing land, exterminating those who owned that land, and fighting for even more land. *Lebensraum*, or "living space," was crucial for a dominant race.[13] Thus in Hitler's view, "Germany" was not a nation but rather a crucible for the Aryan race. The crucible had to be cleansed of those who polluted its racial purity, and then its need for land had to be fed. That meant removing inferior races from Germany and then seizing the land of lesser races, particularly land to the east in Eastern Europe and the Soviet Union occupied by Slavs. It meant exterminating these lesser races so that the Aryan race could live dominant and fulfilled.

It might be noted that these ideas were all outlined in his book, *Mein Kampf* (My Struggle), dictated from prison where he was doing time for his role in the 1923 beer hall *Putsch*. Hitler held steadfastly to these ideas from his early days in Munich to his last will and testament written shortly before he committed suicide on 30 April 1945 as Soviet troops were on the outskirts of Berlin.

But in the 1930s Hitler was interpreted in purely nationalist terms, particularly by leaders in Britain and the United States. And because there was a general recognition that the Versailles treaty had treated the German nation punitively, there was a widespread belief that Hitler's plans, which could be interpreted as nationalistic, were justified. Such sentiments underwrote the Munich Pact that divided Czechoslovakia. On 29–30 September, the leaders of Britain, France, Germany, and Italy (but not Czechoslovakia, or the Soviet Union which had offered to provide military assistance to the Czechs) met in Munich. The ensuing agreement gave all the German-dominated areas of Czechoslovakia to Germany. The British prime minister, Neville Chamberlain, returned home, brandishing the agreement and saying that he had achieved **"peace in our time,"** a phrase that became emblematic of the policy of **appeasement**—trying to buy off the Nazis by making concessions. It was not until March 1939, when Germany took over non-German parts of Czechoslovakia and then presented Poland with demands that it yield its rights to the "corridor" between Germany and East Prussia, that Chamberlain began to recognize the nature of Hitler's ambitions and that a policy of trying to appease those ambitions would not keep the peace in Europe. As a result, Poland was encouraged to reject the German demands by a British and French promise to protect Poland against German aggression.

But it was too late. Hitler believed that Britain and France were not interested in fighting on behalf of central European countries. As we will see below, first Japan and then Italy had committed acts of aggression, and the collective security system of the League had not worked in either case. Likewise, neither France nor Britain had responded forcefully to any of Germany's assaults on the Versailles treaty. So on 23 August 1939, Hitler signed a nonaggression pact with Joseph Stalin of the Soviet Union and secretly agreed to allow the USSR to take eastern Poland. On 1 September 1939, German troops invaded Poland, prompting Britain and France to declare war. The United States remained neutral. While President Franklin Delano Roosevelt was sympathetic to Britain and France, many Americans believed that a victory by Hitler in Europe, while distasteful, would not have hugely negative consequences for the United States.

*Many Americans believed that a victory by Hitler in Europe, while distasteful, would not have hugely negative consequences for the United States.*

Hitler's long-held plans unfolded over the next several years. In the spring of 1940, German troops attacked France, Belgium, the Netherlands, Denmark, and Norway. In short order, Denmark, Norway, and the Benelux countries (Belgium, Netherlands, and Luxembourg) were occupied, with Luxembourg absorbed into the Third Reich in 1942.

France was dismembered: Alsace-Lorraine became part of the Reich, the northern areas of France were occupied by Germans, and the southern half of France was allowed to organize a pro-German government at Vichy under the presidency of Henri Pétain. Hitler believed that, faced with such military reversals, Britain would sue for peace. When the British government showed no sign of wanting to negotiate, preparations were made for an invasion of Britain, beginning with a bombing campaign against British cities during 1940. The Battle of Britain—the air battle between British fighters and German bombers—was won by the Royal Air Force (RAF), and put an end to German plans for an invasion.

By the summer of 1941, however, Hitler felt prepared enough to launch his push to the east, or Operation Barbarossa. On 22 June 1941, almost three million troops from Germany and its allies—including Finns, Romanians, Hungarians, Italians, and Slovaks—launched a massive attack on the USSR. The *Führer* was seemingly unconcerned about engaging the huge war-making capacity of the Soviet Union, or about trying to fight during a continental winter.

Hitler seemed no more worried in December, following the Japanese attack on Pearl Harbor, which brought a declaration of war on Japan by the United States. Without a provocation, and given the isolationist sentiment in the United States, an American declaration of war against Germany would have been difficult for Roosevelt. But Hitler made it easy for the president: he immediately declared war on Washington, bringing the power of the United States to bear against Germany. This ensured that German forces would have to fight on two fronts against continental-sized powers with vastly superior economies and populations.

At the same time as Hitler was provoking both the United States and the Soviet Union, he was also putting into practice his ideas about what should happen to the "inferior races." In the USSR, special units called *Einsatzgruppen* (action squads) accompanied the invading troops, rounded up local residents, and machine-gunned them to death, dumping the bodies in ditches and mass graves. The bureaucratic apparatus for the "Final Solution" to the "Jewish problem" was also put in place. German Jews and the millions of other Jews from countries that had been added to the Nazi regime through conquest were rounded up. Along with other "undesirables"—Roma (Gypsies), gays and lesbians, and political opponents of the Nazi regime such as communists and some Catholic priests—were "deported" to the different kinds of camps established throughout Germany and eastern Europe. In the concentration camps, people died of disease, malnutrition, or random executions, or as the result of medical experiments. In the slave camps, they were worked to death. In the death camps, they were systematically exterminated, usually by gassing.

But in the end, Hitler's attempts to put his plans into action caused his undoing. Simply put, 80 million Germans did not have the resources to sustain such wide-ranging goals. Vital materials and troops that could have been used for war-fighting were diverted to the Final Solution. On the eastern front, German troops were utterly unprepared for the weather— or for the ferocity of the national spirit of those whom Nazi propagandists had dismissed as *Untermenschen*. While their Soviet opponents were dressed in quilted coats and padded boots, German troops had to stuff their boots and uniforms with newspapers and burn precious supplies of gasoline to try to keep warm. Nor was the German war machine capable of operating in an environment where temperatures plunged to −40°C, congealing oil and stopping tanks and other vehicles. By the early months of 1943, the Germans were being pushed back by Soviet troops, who eventually pushed south into the Balkans and north into Finland, defeating Germany's allies there.

To the south, the Allies invaded Italy in July 1943. And on the western front, the huge resources of the United States were combined with the armed forces of the other allies to launch a seaborne invasion of France on 6 June 1944, or D-Day. By late April 1945, the Soviets had reached Berlin and the allies in the west were pushing eastward, linking up with the Soviets. On 30 April, Hitler committed suicide in his bunker in Berlin, and Germany surrendered on 7 May; 8 May was declared V-E ("Victory in Europe") Day.

### The Atavistic Nationalism of Fascist Italy

In Italy, by contrast, racism played little part in the road to war. The vision for the Italian nation that was widespread during the interwar years was that of a nation dominant in its own region. In Italy, that nationalist vision was shaped by Benito Mussolini, the editor of a political newspaper. In 1919, he founded a political movement, the *Fasci di Combattimento*, after the *fasces*, the bundle of sticks that symbolically represented the unbreakable bond of the many-in-one and which was ritualistically carried by lictors before the chief magistrates during the Roman empire. Although Mussolini had at one time been a socialist, after the Great War his political success came from organizing attacks on the Italian Socialists. Funded by industrialists fearful of socialism and communism, supported by former servicemen dislocated in the postwar economy, and with the implicit approval of the government and the army, Mussolini's *Squadre d'Azione* (action squads) attacked the Socialists, killing hundreds in the process. Following a Fascist convention in Naples in October 1922, Mussolini led the assembled *Squadre* on a "march on Rome," whereupon the Italian king asked Mussolini to form a government.

Domestically, the Fascist period in Italy saw the progressive elimination of the principles and institutions of liberal democracy and the consolidation of absolute rule. Political activity was banned; the independent judiciary was abolished; parliament was abolished; and all appointments were made by *Il Duce* (the leader) himself. Mussolini's fascism was also marked by a glorification of the state, and the notion that "all is in the state; nothing exists outside the state." Thus much of the economic life of Italy during the fascist period was organized by the state itself, in particular the *Corporazioni*—the 22 "corporations" of different economic activities, each headed by Mussolini himself.

In foreign policy, Mussolini's dream for the Italian nation was atavistic—in other words, it represented a throwback to the days of the Roman empire. Mussolini dreamed of an Italian nation that would be as glorious and as great as the Roman empire had been two thousand years before. He dreamed of dominating the Mediterranean Sea, making it into, as he called it, "an Italian lake." He also wanted Italy to play a dominant role in the Balkans and the countries of the Danube. And he wanted Italy to own northeastern Africa. To these ends, Mussolini strengthened the Italian navy and tried to undermine British and

French dominance in the Mediterranean. He allied himself closely to revisionist groups in Hungary, Bulgaria, and Croatia. And in October 1935, he launched a massive attack against Ethiopia, then called Abyssinia, eventually occupying the capital. Although the League of Nations imposed sanctions on Italy, Mussolini correctly judged that neither Britain nor France wanted to go to war over Ethiopia; the collective security system put in place in 1919 proved to be no deterrent to Mussolini.

With the rise of the Nazis in Germany, Mussolini tied Italy closely to Germany, helping Hitler secure parts of Czechoslovakia in 1938 and signing a formal military alliance in March 1939. When war in Europe broke out in September 1939, Mussolini did not immediately commit Italian forces to the struggle. Only when he believed that the Nazis had won the war—following the fall of France in 1940—did he declare war on Britain and France. Mussolini's visions of a new period of Italian greatness lasted no longer than the Allied invasion of 1943 that led to Mussolini's removal as Fascist leader. He was later installed by the Nazis as leader of those parts of Italy still controlled by the Germans, but eventually he was captured by Italian partisans in April 1945. He was given a quick trial, executed, and his body hung in public in ignominy.

### The Expansionist Nationalism of Imperial Japan

As noted in Chapter 13, by the end of the First World War, imperialism was in decline, collapsing under the pressure of its own deep contradictions. True, most Europeans were skeptical of applying to non-Europeans the idea that people had a right to national self-determination, but the idea of empire had lost a great deal of legitimacy.

In Japan, however, the idea that the nation was to be fulfilled by empire was kept alive and nourished over the interwar period. The dream of a regional empire of the sort that the British and French enjoyed was particularly catalyzed by the collapse of the global economy in 1929. The onset of the Great Depression had profound effects on Japan, causing massive increases in unemployment and the collapse of trade. This had an effect on Japanese politics, which became highly radicalized during this period. Political violence by some groups, particularly assassination, dramatically increased. Most importantly, there was a growing split in civil-military relations. The Japanese armed forces chafed at civilian control and become increasingly radicalized and politicized. Moreover, as we saw in the case of their role in the creation of the state of Manchukuo, discussed in Chapter 11, the military was more than ready to ignore civilian orders.

The collapse of the Japanese economy also gave rise to a nationalism that put a premium on self-sufficiency, a celebration of "Japaneseness," and a concomitant rejection of European and American ways and values, particularly notions of liberalism, individualism, and democracy. Self-sufficiency for the nation, however, meant secure access to the raw materials that Japan lacked—coal, oil, ores, and minerals. Empire was a logical solution. Thus the nationalist vision for Japan, encouraged in the 1930s, was that of a **"co-prosperity sphere,"** in which Japanese interests would be advanced by control of the Chinese mainland. As we have seen, by 1931, the armed forces had conspired to take Manchuria. When the League of Nations protested, Japan simply withdrew from the organization.

Following the 1937 general elections, in which civilian-dominated parties did well, the armed forces again conspired to weaken civilian control by arranging for another "incident." Japanese troops opened fire on Chinese forces at the Marco Polo bridge outside Beijing on 7 July 1937, expanding the war, and bringing Japan into conflict with other imperial powers, notably France and Britain, both of which sought to aid the Chinese.

The outbreak of war in Europe in 1939 emboldened the Japanese military. They saw an opportunity to use the weakness of the European imperial powers with holdings in Asia—Britain, France, and the Netherlands—to increase Japanese hegemony. The national vision was of a new order in Asia with Japan at the centre of an industrial bloc that would include Korea and northern China, supplied by a ring of resource-rich Southeast Asian countries under Japanese suzerainty. Indeed, the invasion of western European countries by the Nazis in the spring of 1940 prompted the Japanese to seize all of Indochina, precipitating a conflict with the United States, which protested the expansion of Japanese control. The government in Washington imposed oil sanctions against Japan, trying to deny it access to the one resource necessary for the maintenance of Japan's military capacity.

The **oil sanctions** imposed by the United States brought matters to a head in Japan. In October 1941, the civilian government was pressured into resigning by the military, and the war minister, General Tojo Hideki, became premier and decided to go to war. But it was not the nationalism of the Japanese military that precipitated the war in the Pacific. Rather, what led to war were some exceedingly faulty assumptions about liberalism held by nationalists in the Japanese military. Many officers believed that liberal democracy was essentially "un-Japanese." Japanese were "hard" and not afraid to fight; democracies were "soft" and afraid of war. The idea dominant among nationalists in the Japanese military was that if one struck hard at the democratic countries, destroying their military, they would be demoralized and immediately sue for peace. The idea for a Pacific-wide strike at the democracies was formed around this assumption. The coordinated strike was set for 8 December 1941 in the western Pacific and 7 December across the international date line. Japanese forces struck simultaneously at the United States naval base at Pearl Harbor; the American-held Philippines; the British colonies of Hong Kong, Singapore, and Burma; and Dutch-held Indonesia.

The assumptions of the nationalists were deeply faulty. Americans responded to the attack on their nation not with a request for peace but with an enthusiasm for war that rapidly brought the massive resources of the United States to the global conflict. After the battle of Midway in June 1942, the Japanese high command concluded that the prospects of a Japanese victory were slight. A string of military defeats led to the ouster of Tojo in 1944 and a determination to keep fighting. However, the atomic bombs dropped by the United States on Hiroshima on 6 August 1945 and Nagasaki on 9 August brought the war to an end, with V-J Day on 14 August. Tojo was tried as a war criminal, found guilty, and executed in December 1948.

## The Warfare State and the Second World War

Different sentiments of nationalism led people all over the world to take up arms in the cause of nation between 1931, when the Japanese first invaded Manchuria, and 1945, when the war came to an end. In Germany, nationalism contributed to the outbreak of war in Europe in 1939 in an indirect way. Germans were attracted to Hitler because his message was deeply appealing to nationalists; likewise, much of the Nazi program in the 1930s was consistent with the nationalist project of reuniting members of the German nation. But the Nazi project itself was not nationalist: as the Final Solution, the invasion of the USSR in 1941, and the impetuous declaration of war against the United States all demonstrated, Hitler himself was moved by ideas that had little to do with nationalism. Nonetheless, the seizure of the German state by the Nazi party and the willingness of numerous Germans to see in the Nazis what they wanted to see—a saviour for the nation—meant that the state was able to carry Germans into a war that could be interpreted as nationalist. However, it was quickly transformed into a struggle to transform Hitler's ideas about racial superiority into reality. In Italy and Japan, conquest was a logical outgrowth of the nationalist visions of Mussolini and militarists like Tojo. Because both East Asia and the Mediterranean were already dominated by existing imperial powers, the only way for Italy or Japan to expand their control was to use force.

Nationalism also underwrote the responses to Germany's, Italy's, and Japan's efforts to use force to revise the status quo. Each time an Axis power used force, national sentiment was transformed. In China, as we saw in the previous chapter, the military campaigns of the Japanese gave rise to a galvanizing nationalism that sustained Chinese opposition to Japanese overlordship for 14 years. In Britain, the pacifism that was widespread in the 1930s—driven by memories of the Great War—literally evaporated when war finally came. When France was overrun in 1940 and England itself was actually attacked later that year, those who had embraced the view that anything, even a victory by the Nazis, was preferable to war now evinced a national willingness to fight. While some considered the idea of negotiating a peace with Hitler early in 1940, the air raids on British cities that began in September galvanized opinion against negotiation. The attacks on Britain also had an effect on opinion in other parts of the Commonwealth, where defence of the "mother country" galvanized support for war against Germany, Italy, and Japan.

The attack by Germany on the USSR in 1941 provoked a similar display of nationalism among Russians, who rallied around the flag and engaged in a fierce war against the German invaders. The **Great Patriotic War**, as the Soviet involvement in the Second World War is known in Russia, was marked by grim displays of determination such as the 900-day seige of Leningrad (now St Petersburg), in which over a million residents died and 10 000 buildings were destroyed, and the battle of Stalingrad (now Volgograd), which lasted from August 1942 to February 1943 and resulted in the eventual surrender of 200 000 German soldiers.

Finally, the effects of nationalism can perhaps best be seen in the United States, where, as in Britain, the use of force by Japan on 7 December and the declaration of war by Germany on 11 December had a remarkable effect on the attitude of Americans, transforming it to one of war-fighting. There was no thought of surrender or suing for peace, as the Japanese had expected. The deep reservations about entering a European war—reservations that had so constrained the sympathetic Roosevelt—also evaporated.

*There was little of the enthusi-
asm that had been evident in
August 1914; this was no
"fresh and jolly war."*

It should be noted that the nationalism evident in Britain, the Soviet Union, the United States, and others who fought the Germans, Italians, and Japanese differed in tone from the nationalist spirit that had infused Europe in 1914. There was little of the enthusiasm that had been evident in August 1914; this was no "fresh and jolly war." Yet the *purpose*—the defence of the nation—was exactly the same.

To be sure, in each case the state played an important role in galvanizing and focusing the national ideal and the national war effort. The warfare state that had emerged during the Great War re-emerged between 1939 and 1945. In Germany, Italy, and Japan, the state was particularly important in framing a nationalist vision that inspired support, and using propaganda to consolidate that support. In Germany, the efforts of the state apparatus to construct a nationalist veneer for the racist vision of the Nazis was aided by the personality of Hitler himself. A dramatic and powerful orator, Hitler inspired deep and emotional support from ordinary Germans. Moreover, in these countries, the state was also important in silencing those voices whose vision for the nation differed from the aggressive and expansionist policies being embraced by the leadership. In all three countries, the state security apparatus was vigilant in hunting down enemies of the regime. And in all three states, non-governmental or quasi-governmental groups assisted the state in these efforts: in Italy the *Squadre*, in Germany the SA and the SS, and in Japan the assassination campaigns of the Blood Pledge Corps.

Among the Allies, the state was no less important in rallying opposition to the expansionism of the Axis powers. In the Soviet Union, patriotism was to be "encouraged," albeit in typical Stalinist fashion: Order Number 270 of 1941 decreed that all the members of the families of deserters from the military were liable to be executed. Other allied governments were more deft at governance: while they moved against those suspected of hampering the war effort, they mainly used propaganda to encourage national sentiment.

Finally, the state was crucially important in all countries in organizing the economy for war. The economies of most belligerents became command economies, where the state took what it needed in labour and economic capacity to fight. Some measure of the degree of state control needed to prosecute the Second World War can be seen from state expenditures on the war—more than US$1 000 000 000 000. Of this $1 trillion, the United States spent US$341 billion, Germany $272 billion, the Soviet Union $192 billion, Britain $120 billion, Italy $94 billion, and Japan $56 billion. (Note that these figures do not represent the full cost of the war: for example, while the Japanese government spent the least of the major powers, the true cost of the war to Japan has been estimated at over US$550 billion.)

## Nationalism and the Causes of War

We have looked at the major conflicts of the 20th century in some detail in order to reveal the relationship between nationalism and war. The account in this chapter suggests two, somewhat paradoxical, conclusions. First, the national idea was intimately *connected* with both major wars. Secondly, we nonetheless cannot conclude that nationalism, as a way of conceiving of political community, directly *caused* either of the world wars.

## War and Nationalism: Connections

The nationalistic belligerence of Europeans in 1914 is crucial to understanding why everywhere the outbreak of war was greeted with such enthusiasm. But nationalism was also at the root of what kept Europeans fighting each other for so long and under such horrific conditions. Likewise, nationalism was intimately connected to the expansionism of Germany, Italy, and Japan in the interwar years. The national humiliation of Germany by Versailles created fertile soil for the nationalistic-sounding promises of Adolf Hitler and the Nazis; the appeals to a long-dead imperial Roman glory drove Italian nationalism; and the celebration of a Japan free of dependence on Euro-American liberal dominance lay behind ideas of Japanese national expansion.

Nationalism also drove the responses to the rise of the Axis powers. Collective security, for example, was always doomed as an idea because it was utterly incompatible with the national ideal. Nationalism commands nationalists to put their nation, its interests, and its well-being first. Thus, nationalists are not inclined to spill the precious blood of the nation's young (as it is usually, but not inappropriately, phrased) on causes that are not seen to be connected to the well-being of the nation. The arrangements created by the League of Nations violated this fundamental understanding in two ways. First, collective security ignored the fact that nationalists were unlikely to go to war in every case of aggression: some wars simply did not have any impact on the well-being of the nation. As Senator Raoul Dandurand, representing Canada at the League in 1924, put it, Canadians "live in a fire-proof house, far from inflammable materials."[14] Dandurand was complaining about the fundamental inequity in the collective security system—although Canada might be asked to contribute troops to stop aggression by others, it would never have any need of the collective security system, since the only threat to Canada, the United States, would never attack. But Dandurand's view about Canada's distance from "inflammable materials" illustrates how the nationalist vision destroys universal collective security.

*According to Dandurand, Canadians "live in a fire-proof house, far from inflammable materials."*

Second, collective security ignored the reality that nationalists, as we noted in Chapter 12, inevitably have sentiments of friendship about some other nations. War against "friends" of the nation, even in pursuit of a noble community-oriented goal like "collective security," simply lay outside the realm of the possible. Would Australians go to war against Britain? Would Belgians declare war on France? Would Austria use force against Germany? Would Canadians go to war against the United States, Britain, France, Australia, New Zealand, or South Africa? These were utterly unthinkable scenarios back in the 1920s and 1930s (as indeed they remain some 70 years later). But because such behaviour was unthinkable, the collective security project was doomed: responses to aggression lacked the automaticity and universality demanded by the idea of collective security.

Nationalist sentiment in the United States kept Americans not only out of the League, but out of the war in Europe for over two years. (Moreover, we can only speculate on what would have happened had Hitler not impetuously declared war on the United States, fortuitously providing Roosevelt with the provocation for an American declaration of war on Germany.) But the American response to aggression demonstrated the broader dynamic of nationalism at work: as in the First World War, the ideology of nationalism provided the basis for defence of nation against the predations of the aggressor.

### War and Nationalism: Causation?

The second broad conclusion is that nationalism and those two wars may have been *connected*; but we cannot conclude that nationalism, as an ideological way of conceiving of community, *caused* either of them in any direct way. There is nothing inherent in the national idea that leads those who believe in that idea—nationalists—to go to war (or, for that matter, to stay at peace). On the contrary: a nationalist is inherently no more peaceable or war-prone than an individual moved by any other conception of attachment to political community. Rather, a nationalist will make the same kind of calculation about war and peace that all those who lived before the era of nation made: do I wish to use force to advance or protect my interests and the interests of my community?

In the first half of the 20th century, nationalists of all sorts answered that question in different ways. In the case of the Great War, Europeans slid into war through carelessness and a belief that war was a glorious tool that could enhance their nation's prestige and power. In the Second World War, there were no such delusions about the gloriousness of war, but large numbers of Germans, Italians, and Japanese still believed that their nations would be better off being at war than at peace. Such beliefs were doubtless driven by other factors, such as a sense of humiliation, or the deprivation resulting from global depression and unemployment, suggesting that the Great Depression was a more potent "cause" of the Second World War than nationalism.

By the same token, throughout the 1930s, numerous people—Americans, Belgians, Britons, Canadians, Dutch, French—believed that their nations would be better off being at peace than at war. However, by the end of 1941 the vast majority had changed their mind, and dramatically so. In Britain and throughout the Commonwealth, the vast majority came to believe that the very existence of Britain depended on using force against Germany. In the United States, the existence of the nation was never at issue; rather, the overwhelming American sentiment for war was driven mostly by a desire for national revenge against the Japanese aggressor and partly by a more inchoate vision of the United States inherited from the founding of the republic as the standard-bearer of liberty. John Quincy Adams, president of the United States between 1825 and 1829, had asserted a century and a half earlier that America was "a grand scheme and design in Providence for the illumination and the emancipation of the slavish part of mankind all over the Earth." Much of that vision was evident in the response of Americans to Nazi Germany, and in their self-proclaimed role as the "arsenal of democracy."

## CONCLUSION

This chapter has explored the negative side that many associate with nationalism: the dis-integrative logic of the nationalist ideology that encourages nations to seek fulfilment of the national idea by the creation of a sovereign state, and the pursuit of national goals that can lead to war between nations. This chapter has argued that the nationalist ideology is not of necessity violent, belligerent, or war-prone; this can readily be seen by the hundreds of millions of people who have pursued the nationalist vision since 1945 without resorting to force. But I have argued that nationalism, as an ideology of identity, commits its members to a prescribed path of protecting and advancing the nation and its well-being. And that *can* lead to conflict and violence.

## *Keyword File*

National unity

Clean divorce

Velvet Divorce

Partition

Allophones

Dirty divorce

Ethnic cleansing

Hypernationalism

Ultranationalism

Ethnonationalism

Dreadnought

Arms race

Mobilization

Schlieffen Plan

Cult of the offensive

Kruger telegram

Glorification of war

National service

Jingoism

Trench warfare

No man's land

Shell shock

Zimmerman telegram

War-weariness

Total war

Warfare state

Social reinforcement mechanism

Propaganda

War dead

Great War

World war

*Blitzkrieg*

Holocaust

City-bombing

Indemnity

War-guilt clause

Reparations

Collective security

Hyperinflation

Beggar-thy-neighbour policies

Smoot-Hawley tariff

Stock market crash

*Rassepolitik*

Social Darwinism

*Untermenschen*

"Peace in our time"

Appeasement

"Co-prosperity sphere"

Oil sanctions

Great Patriotic War

## *For Further Exploration*

HARD COPY

Albertini, Luigi. *The Origins of the War of 1914*, 3 vols. Oxford: Oxford University Press, 1952–1957.

Carr, Edward Hallett. *The 20 Years' Crisis, 1919–1939*, 2d ed. London: Macmillan, 1946.

Kagan, Donald. *On the Origins of War and the Preservation of Peace.* New York: Doubleday, 1995, chaps. 2, 4.

Liddell Hart, B.H. *History of the Second World War.* New York: Putnam, 1971.

Toland, John. *The Rising Sun.* New York: Random House, 1971.

WEBLINKS

**http://www.historyplace.com/worldwar2**

Site for historical materials about the Second World War, including a well-documented section on the Holocaust

**http://www.lib.muohio.ed/~skimmel/wwii/**

Site maintained by Miami University, Ohio: multimedia resources about all aspects of the Second World War

**http://www.lib.byu.edu/~rdh/wwi/**

The World War I Documents Archive features multimedia items, personal memoirs, commentaries, and other resources

**http://www.pbs.org/greatwar**

Site of PBS series "The Great War and the Shaping of the Twentieth Century" (November 1996); photographs, oral histories, other resources

## *Notes to Chapter 14*

1.  Robert A. Young, "How do peaceful secessions happen?" *Canadian Journal of Political Science* 27 (December 1994), 773–92.

2.  For example, Michael Ignatieff, *Blood and Belonging: Journeys into the New Nationalism* (Toronto: Penguin, 1994).

3.  John T. Rourke, *International Politics on the World Stage*, 6th ed. (Guilford, CT: Dushkin/McGraw-Hill, 1997), 147.

4.  Stephen Van Evera, "Primed for peace: Europe after the Cold War," in Sean M. Lynn-Jones, ed., *The Cold War and After: Prospects for Peace* (Cambridge, MA: MIT Press, 1992), 239.

5.  See, for example, Dean A. Minx and Sandra M. Hawley, *Global Politics* (Belmont: West/Wadsworth, 1998), 88; Rourke, *International Politics on the World Stage*, 144–55; Daniel S. Papp, *Contemporary International Relations*, 5th ed (Boston: Allyn and Bacon, 1997), 31–32.

6. Quoted in George B. Tindall and David E. Shi, *America: A Narrative History* (New York: W.W. Norton, 1989), 436. The six-volume collection of photographs edited by William C. Davis, *The Image of War, 1861–1865* (New York: Doubleday, 1981–1988) provides a grim visual history of the bloodiness of this war.

7. Quoted in Donald Kagan, *On the Origins of War and the Preservation of Peace* (New York: Doubleday, 1995), 132.

8. Quoted in Evan Luard, *War in International Society: A Study in International Sociology* (New Haven, CT: Yale University Press, 1986), 355.

9. For an excellent survey of representative views that leave in little doubt the common view of war, see ibid., 354–61.

10. John Keegan, *The Face of Battle* (Harmondsworth, U.K.: Penguin, 1978), 229–30.

11. C.P. Stacey, *Canada and the Age of Conflict*, vol. 2: *1921–1948: The Mackenzie King Era* (Toronto: University of Toronto Press, 1981), 126–29; also Peter Kasurak, "American foreign policy officials and Canada, 1927–1941: a look through bureaucratic glasses," *International Journal* 32 (Summer 1977), 544–58.

12. Kalevi J. Holsti, *Peace and War: Armed Conflicts and International Order, 1648–1989* (Cambridge: Cambridge University Press, 1991), 222.

13. See the discussion in Kagan, *On the Origins of War*, 336–37.

14. Kim Richard Nossal, *The Politics of Canadian Foreign Policy*, 3d ed. (Scarborough, ON: Prentice Hall Canada, 1997), 153.

# Beyond *the* State Divide

# Division *by* Compass Point: East *and* West

We saw in Chapter 13 that the sovereign nation-state, girded by a belief in the ideology of nationalism, had grown to dominate the way in which human beings divided themselves from one another. The argument advanced so far is not that the sovereign nation-state *replaced* other bases of division evident in the many centuries before state, sovereignty, and nation were invented, but rather grew alongside those other forms of division, dominating them.

In a similar fashion, other forms of division can be layered on the divisions we have discussed to this point. For the 45 years after the defeat of Germany, Italy, and Japan, world politics was dominated by another set of divisions that appeared alongside the national division. For much of this period, the various sovereign nation-states of the world were divided into camps, or blocs, identified colloquially by the four points of the compass: North, South, East and West. We look at these divisions in this chapter and the next. We look first at the ideological divide that created a group of states known as the "East" and another group known as the "West," and defined the period we know as the Cold War. In Chapter 16 we look at another divide along an economic fault line between rich and poor, called respectively "North" and "South." These divisions, it should be noted at the outset, did not supplant the deep state divide; rather, compass-point divisions emerged very much within the framework of the system of sovereign nation-states.

## MAKING SENSE OF COMPASS-POINT DIVISIONS

Before we begin our exploration of the "East/West" and "North/South" dimensions of world politics, we should examine the terminology that is so commonly used to talk about world politics in the 20th century. Most people talk about "North," "South," and "West" (the "East" having disappeared with the collapse of the Soviet Union in 1991). But those who divide the world by compass point in this fashion rarely give much thought to who is actually included in these characterizations. In other words, on what basis are we dividing up the 190 countries of the world in this manner? Who actually is in the "North," and who comprises the "South"? What is the "West" west of and how does it differ from the "North"? What is the "East" east of, and where did it actually *go* when it disappeared at the end of the Cold War?

At one level, these are mischievous questions. Like all shorthand, the compass-point divisions were invented to represent quickly and easily a conception of groups of countries. Thus, as we will see below, the "East" came generally to mean those countries which had communist governments and were tied by ideological affinity, economic interconnections, and military alliance or agreement to the Soviet Union. The "West" referred to those countries with liberal, democratic, and capitalist systems that were highly industrialized relative to the rest of the world. The "North," in common parlance, comprised all the nations of the "West" plus those nations of the "East" that were relatively highly industrialized and rich. The "South" was simply defined by a process of exclusion: all those countries not in the "North" were in the "South."

As will be evident from this brief sketch, the attributes by which countries were assigned to different compass points tended to be based on type of political system, level of industrial/economic development, and wealth. But while the terminology is deeply embedded in the way we talk—and think—about world politics, there are good reasons to question the appropriateness of these terms to describe the divisions that we will explore below. This is one of the reasons why I have used the admittedly annoying technique of tagging these descriptors with quotation marks. (And although the quotation marks disappear after this mention, my concern about using these terms to describe groups of countries remains.)

Consider the West, a term that people all over the world tend to use without thinking. Sometimes it is used to describe a group of countries in which a particular set of socio-economic and political assumptions, practices, and institutions are embedded; the kind of liberal, democratic, and capitalist countries which are members of the Organisation for Economic Cooperation and Development (OECD). Sometimes West is used as shorthand to describe one of the sides in the Cold War—countries that were members of a group of military alliances headed by the United States. Sometimes, as we will see when we discuss Samuel P. Huntington's civilizational perspective in Chapter 17, it is used to describe a civilization. But which countries are included in the West thus depends on who is doing the defining, as Table 15.1 shows.

*Table 15.1* • WHAT IS WEST? THREE WAYS OF DEFINING A COMPASS POINT

| | OECD Membership | Formal U.S. Ally | According to Huntington[a] |
|---|:---:|:---:|:---:|
| United States | • | — | • |
| Australia | • | • | • |
| Austria | • | | • |
| Belgium | • | • | • |
| Britain | • | • | • |
| Canada | • | • | • |
| Czech Republic | | b | • |
| Denmark | • | • | • |
| Estonia | | | • |
| Finland | • | | • |
| France | • | • | • |
| Germany | • | • | • |
| Greece | • | • | |
| Hong Kong, China | | | • |
| Hungary | | b | • |
| Iceland | • | • | • |
| Ireland | • | | • |
| Italy | • | • | • |
| Japan | • | • | |
| Latvia | | | • |
| Lithuania | | | • |
| Luxembourg | • | • | • |
| Mexico | • | c | |
| Netherlands | • | • | • |
| New Zealand | • | • | • |
| Norway | • | • | • |
| Papua New Guinea | | | • |
| Poland | | b | • |
| Portugal | • | • | • |
| Slovakia | | | • |
| Slovenia | | | • |

| | OECD Membership | Formal U.S. Ally | According to Huntington[a] |
|---|:---:|:---:|:---:|
| Spain | • | • | • |
| Sweden | • | | • |
| Switzerland | • | | • |
| Turkey | • | • | |

[a] Samuel P. Huntington, *The Clash of Civilizations and the Remaking of World Order* (New York: Simon and Schuster, 1996), map 1.3.

[b] Recommended for admission to North Atlantic Treaty Organization, July 1997

[c] Signatory to the Rio Pact, 1947

The lists in Table 15.1 reveal the difficulties of trying to define countries by compass point. For example, Huntington's list of Western countries includes Hong Kong but excludes Japan. Hong Kong is part of China; does that not make it South? But it has numerous commonalities with other Western countries: a very high level of wealth, economic development, and education; a deeply embedded capitalist system; and a political system with liberal democratic elements. Likewise, the exclusion of Japan from membership in the West might seem strange, given Japan's attributes as a liberal democratic country with one of the highest levels of economic development in the world.

Likewise, do we count as members of the West all those countries which were allied, aligned, or otherwise connected with the United States during the Cold War? This would expand the list greatly, to include countries in the Asia Pacific such as Indonesia, Malaysia, the Philippines, Singapore, South Korea, South Vietnam, and Taiwan; Pakistan in South Asia; and South Africa in Africa.

The difficulties we have in clearly defining what is West can be seen at other compass points. Defining the East, for example, is made difficult by the general assumption that "Easternness" was always connected to the degree of closeness to the Soviet Union, but not necessarily having a communist government. Thus countries slip in and out of the East: in 1955, the East included China but not Cuba; by 1965, China was no longer included but Cuba had been added.

*Many people in the North in fact live in worse conditions than many people in the South.*

In short, the difficulties of compass-point definition mean that some of the countries of the North are located in the south, and some of the countries of the South are well north of the equator. Not all countries of the West are always Western—it depends on context and who is doing the defining. Some countries of the South are richer than some countries of the North. Moreover, these categorizations are arrived at using the steamroller method analyzed in Chapter 6; when one begins to disaggregate these countries and look at individuals, we find that many people in the North in fact live in worse conditions than many people in the South; likewise, some Southerners live in luxury.

Despite all of the problems we encounter with division by compass point, there were divisional lines between East and West and between North and South during the Cold War era, and to these divisions we now turn—keeping in mind the definitional problems examined above.

## THE IDEOLOGICAL DIVIDE

Ideology divided the world into those political communities which embraced the tenets of Marxism-Leninism, generally referred to as the East, and those which were organized on liberal, democratic, and capitalist lines, and referred to as the West. The incompatibilities between these two systems were sharp and marked. The role of the communist party as the vanguard of the proletariat, or working class, simply could not be reconciled with liberal democratic notions of the consent of the governed. Leninists can find no theoretical or practical way of tolerating the idea of political opposition that is so central to liberal theory and practice. The Marxist notion of the abolition of private property, and the concomitant requirement of a state-directed command economy, is incompatible with the bundle of liberal/democratic ideas that makes a capitalist economy function.

There have always been differing ideas about how to organize the political, economic, and social structures of political communities, as we have noted in previous chapters. But when fundamentally incompatible ideological approaches are embraced by the most powerful members of the international community, it is likely that the ideological clash is overlaid with other differences and divisions. This is certainly what happened in the case of the Soviet Union and the United States during the Cold War.

## ORIGINS OF THE COLD WAR

In 1944, as the armies of the United Nations began to push the Axis armies back, the wartime alliance between the Soviet Union and other powers began to fracture. The "hot war" of the fight against the Axis turned into what is called a "cold war"—a deep conflict between two camps that is marked by a lack of fighting. When capitalized, the **Cold War** refers to the conflict between East and West. However, it should be noted that cold war describes many international relationships, such as the relationship between India and Pakistan or the People's Republic of China and the Republic of China on Taiwan; these cold wars continue long after the Cold War ended.

### The Anti-Bolshevik Legacy

The fracture that appeared in the mid-1940s was the reopening of a division that went back to the aftermath of the Bolshevik revolution in 1917. Then, Britain, France, the United States, Japan, and Canada were fearful of the radical ideology of the communists, and intervened in the civil war that broke out after the revolution by sending troops with the intention of ousting the Bolsheviks. From Vladivostok in the east to Archangel in the north, foreign troops overthrew local "Red" Soviet authorities and aided anti-Soviet forces, known as "the Whites." While these interventions were ultimately unsuccessful, they confirmed for the new Soviets what communist ideology predicted: that the forces of communism and the forces of capitalism were locked in a deadly struggle.

Moreover, the highly negative views that Soviets and capitalists had of one another did not change much over the interwar years. Although the rise of Hitler in Germany prompted the leader of the USSR, Joseph Stalin, to moderate his anticapitalist policies, no effort was made to forge an anti-Nazi alliance. Instead, the USSR was pushed into making an accommodation with Hitler: during the Munich crisis in 1938, Moscow was excluded by Britain and France. As a result, Stalin radically changed his approach, signing the August 1939 nonaggression pact that gave Hitler a free hand in Poland.

The differences between the USSR and the West were papered over after 1941 as an anti-Nazi coalition, known as the United Nations, was formed. The three leaders of the largest powers—the British prime minister, Winston Churchill; the American president, Franklin D. Roosevelt; and Stalin—met to coordinate policy on a number of occasions: at Teheran in November 1943, at Yalta in Ukraine in February 1945, and at Potsdam, Germany, from 17 July to 2 August 1945. Their representatives also met at Bretton Woods and Dumbarton Oaks.

### Bretton Woods and Dumbarton Oaks

All three powers cooperated in the creation of the various international organizations that were designed to manage political and economic relations after the war. The United States government hosted a conference at a vacation resort in New Hampshire to discuss postwar economic arrangements. The **Bretton Woods** conference, as the United Nations Monetary and Financial Conference was known colloquially, was attended by 44 countries, including the United States, the USSR, and Britain. The negotiations at Bretton Woods ran from 1 to 22 July 1944, and three key international financial institutions (IFIs) emerged. The International Monetary Fund (IMF) was to supervise the operation of a new system of fixed exchange rates and convertibility on current account transactions, which was designed to avoid the debilitating economic policies, pursued by governments in the 1930s, that had exacerbated the Great Depression. The International Bank for Reconstruction and Development (IBRD, or, more colloquially, the World Bank) was set up to assist in the reconstruction of the European industrial plant destroyed by war. In particular, the Bank was designed to facilitate the investment of capital, either by private investors, or, when private was not available, through its own capital that would be raised by subscriptions. The third institution was the International Trade Organization (ITO), which was designed to encourage the reduction of tariffs and to establish rules for international trade in the postwar era. (This third institution was eventually rejected by the United States Congress as being too intrusive on American domestic policy; as a result, international trade was regulated by the General Agreement on Tariffs and Trade, or GATT.)

These three institutions were organized in such a way as to give member countries considerable latitude in the organization of their own domestic economic policies; they were designed to facilitate exchange *between* national economies. These institutions are frequently described in American textbooks as having been designed, established, run, and led by the

United States—which is usually characterized as a "hegemonic leader" providing the "international public good" of "stability" to other smaller "free riding" capitalist countries.* However, what gets lost in the usual American telling is that the Soviet Union actively participated in the Bretton Woods discussions. Indeed considerable arrangements were made to accommodate centrally planned, state-managed communist economies. It is true that the IMF and the World Bank *eventually* evolved into international institutions for an international capitalist economy dominated by the United States, but they certainly did not begin life this way. They began as a cooperative venture between the great powers, including the USSR.

Likewise, the Soviet Union actively cooperated in the formulation of security arrangements for the postwar order. Representatives of the USSR, the United States, Britain, and China held a series of negotiations at **Dumbarton Oaks**, a private estate in Washington, D.C., from August to October 1944. Out of these discussions came the original blueprint for a United Nations organization that would form the basis for postwar security. Once again, the Soviet Union was an active partner in these efforts.

### Yalta and Potsdam

But the cooperation among the great powers was not to outlast the defeat of Germany. By the end of the war in Europe, serious differences of opinion were emerging between the USSR and its other allies. The rawest bone of contention was over how postwar Europe was to be organized. On one point, there was widespread agreement: in the words of the **Yalta** declaration, Germany should never again "be able to disturb the peace of the world." But on how this might actually be achieved, there was little common ground beyond the agreement reached at the conference held in **Potsdam** from 17 July to 2 August 1945. The powers agreed that Germany would be divided between the victorious powers, occupied militarily, demilitarized, and reorganized economically with an emphasis on agriculture. From the outset, Stalin demanded that any postwar settlement include Russian control over large parts of eastern Europe, particularly Poland. In other words, the Soviet Union wanted to create a **sphere of influence**—an area where a great power is widely recognized as having a dominant interest, and over which it exercises considerable influence. A sphere of influence

---

* According to **hegemonic stability theory**, the peace and prosperity of the Cold War era can be attributed to the willingness of the United States to create and maintain an international economic order. American economic capacity relative to the rest of the world gave the United States the power to order the economic system. According to enthusiasts of this line of argument, "a hegemon basically has the same interests as the common good of all states," as Joshua S. Goldstein put it (*International Relations*, 2d ed [New York: HarperCollins, 1996], 103). Likewise, hegemons "selflessly" provide global stability as a "public good" or "collective good" to all states. Because public goods, by their very nature, can be enjoyed by all, other states are characterized as "free riders," enjoying what the United States is "producing" without having to contribute. While the power of the United States to shape the international order cannot be denied, the presumption that its exercise of power in its own self-interest is in the "common good of all states" is fanciful, to say the least. For an outline of hegemonic stability theory, see Robert Gilpin, *The Political Economy of International Relations* (Princeton, NJ: Princeton University Press, 1987), 72–92. For an excellent critique of the theory, see Isabelle Grunberg, "Exploring the 'myth' of hegemonic stability," *International Organization* 44 (Autumn 1990), 341–78.

in Eastern Europe would not only create a **buffer zone** against a repeat of Operation Barbarossa, but it would also allow the USSR to extract reparations from eastern European countries as a means of rebuilding Soviet economic capacity destroyed by war and invasion.

By contrast, Roosevelt wanted to avoid the creation of great-power spheres of influence. He had two major reasons for this. First, Roosevelt was sensitive to American opinion, particularly in Congress, that was firmly opposed to such practices as spheres of influence, believing them to be a manifestation of "European power politics" that had plunged the world into two world wars within 25 years. (Of course, those Americans objecting to others having spheres of influence never bothered to extend their objections to the Monroe Doctrine of 1823, discussed in Chapter 11. That doctrine created nothing less than a sphere of influence.)

An equally important reason for objecting to a Soviet sphere of influence in eastern Europe was the idea being pushed by the Roosevelt administration that in order to ensure prosperity after the war, national economies should be kept as open as possible. Closely tied to American ideas for a postwar international economic order, discussed in more detail below, this ideal would not work well if great powers such as the Soviet Union, Britain, or France were able to close countries in their spheres of influence off to trade. For both these reasons, Roosevelt preferred to delay a firm decision on the disposition of eastern Europe.

For his part, Churchill was not opposed to spheres of influence for each great power. Indeed, in October 1944, he suggested to Stalin that they divide up influence over Romania, Greece, Hungary, and Yugoslavia between them. But Churchill was not entirely comfortable with how easily spheres of influence were created. He asked Stalin: "Might it not be thought rather cynical if it seemed we had disposed of these issues, so fateful to millions of people, in such an offhand manner?"[1] But if Churchill had qualms, he knew that Roosevelt would not like it. Churchill suggested to Stalin that they describe their deal "in diplomatic terms and not...use the phrase 'dividing into spheres,' because the Americans might be shocked."[2]

As it turned out, Stalin interpreted the notion of sphere of influence rather differently than either Churchill or Roosevelt. Used in Western parlance, this term had a relatively benign connotation: generally a country in a great power's sphere of influence would be allowed generous freedom in its "domestic" affairs; only if an external power was interfering would the great power be moved to intervene. Thus it was hoped that with the liberation of eastern Europe from the Nazis, there would be free elections in each country. But Stalin was no liberal. On the contrary, his Leninist and totalitarian principles of governance suggested a radically different interpretation. In his view, "influence" meant control, and thus Stalin ensured that the Soviet Union would directly control all the countries that the Red Army liberated on its way to Berlin in 1944 and 1945, putting in place communist-dominated governments and eliminating potential rivals to pro-Soviet forces.*

---

\* In Poland, for example, the Soviet Union refused to recognize the Polish government-in-exile in London, and instead established a pro-Soviet government in Lublin. As Soviet troops approached Warsaw in July 1944, the Polish underground, which supported the London government-in-exile, rose up against the Nazi occupation forces. When Stalin learned of the **Warsaw uprising**, he ordered Soviet forces to cease fighting and wait outside Warsaw while the Nazis put down the revolt and executed thousands of Poles who supported a rival to the pro-Soviet Lublin government.

*"From Stettin in the Baltic to Trieste in the Adriatic, an iron curtain has descended across the Continent."*

As Churchill put it in a famous speech delivered in Fulton, Missouri in March 1946, "From Stettin in the Baltic to Trieste in the Adriatic, an iron curtain has descended across the Continent." And indeed the Soviet Union did directly control a broad swath of countries from the Baltic to the Balkans: Poland, Czechoslovakia, Hungary, Romania, and Bulgaria, as well as the Soviet-occupied zone of Germany. Churchill's evocative metaphor was widely embraced; the **iron curtain** was the dividing line between East and West.

In addition, there were communist governments in Yugoslavia and Albania that had come to power independently of Soviet assistance. In October 1947, the Soviet government created the Communist Information Bureau, or Cominform. Its purpose was to coordinate the policies and programs of communist parties everywhere. However, Josip Broz Tito, the Yugoslav leader, broke with Stalin over Moscow's criticism of his policies. As a result, Yugoslavia was expelled from the Cominform in June 1948.

The fate of eastern Europe was the most obvious manifestation of the split between the former wartime allies. On it hinged a succession of disputes between the United States and the USSR after Roosevelt died in April 1945 and was succeeded by Harry S Truman. In their actions and their speeches, the leaders of both the United States and the Soviet Union gave the other side cause for suspicion and annoyance. The Americans, for example, often tried to use the monopoly in atomic weaponry that they enjoyed to exercise power over Moscow until the USSR exploded its own device in 1949. Stalin, for his part, complained of the "**capitalist encirclement**" of the USSR, and repeated his view that as long as capitalism existed, another war was inevitable. The Soviet Union gave political support to revolutionary movements in China, Iran, Indochina, and Indonesia; Moscow backed the communist faction in a civil war in Greece and sought to expand Soviet influence in Turkey. There was concern about the USSR's support for communist parties in western Europe. In short, to Americans and western Europeans alike, it seemed as though the Soviets were picking up where Hitler had left off.

In this growing dispute between the USSR and the other western allies, the USSR had an important advantage: it knew a great deal about what both the British and Americans were doing and thinking. The network of spies put in place in the 1930s (discussed in Chapter 7) was paying off, as those who had been recruited to the communist cause were appointed to important positions within the British government that allowed them to pass information back to Moscow. Thus the Soviet leadership was never worried about the threats Americans occasionally made about the use of atomic weapons—because Stalin knew precisely how few weapons the United States actually had, and how tenuous American delivery systems were. Moscow also received important insights into Anglo-American thinking on a variety of issues. At least one student of Soviet foreign policy has argued that had Stalin not had this intelligence, he may have been more cautious in pushing the Americans and the British.[3] But while the British and Americans did not know of this spy ring until later, they did know that the USSR was spying because of the revelations of a defecting Soviet cipher clerk, Igor Gouzenko, in 1945—revelations that only served to deepen suspicions about Soviet intentions.[4]

# EAST AND WEST INSTITUTIONALIZED, 1945-1955

As tensions between the Soviets and the countries of the West mounted, the international institutions that had been forged in the cooperation during the war against Germany started to become highly polarized. In both military and economic affairs, the UN was cleaved by East/West dissension.

In military affairs, the West responded to what they saw as Soviet expansionism by doing what the Soviets accused them of doing—encircling them. The smaller countries of western Europe were deeply concerned that the isolationism that had gripped the United States after the Great War, and kept it from joining the League of Nations, would reassert itself. They wanted to obtain an American military guarantee for their security, and began to push hard for the creation of a formal military alliance. If Washington committed its forces to the defence of western Europe through such an alliance, they believed, this would deter any designs the Soviets may have on western Europe. The Canadian government, which also believed that the security of Western Europe rested on an explicit American promise of military aid, added its voice to those of the Europeans.[5]

## The Truman Doctrine and Containment

The European and Canadian desire for a formal alliance fitted well with the view of the Truman administration and some in Congress that Soviet expansion had to be stopped. By early 1947, urged on by his undersecretary of state, Dean Acheson, Truman decided to respond to what they saw as Soviet expansionism by embracing the **Truman Doctrine**. Truman introduced this Doctrine in a speech to Congress on 12 March 1947 that requested $400 million in military aid for Greece and Turkey. The Truman Doctrine has been likened to a "declaration of Cold War,"[6] since it asked Congress for authorization to undertake a commitment to defend "free peoples" and oppose "totalitarian regimes" everywhere. With the support of the chairman of the Senate Foreign Relations Committee, Arthur Vandenberg, Republican of Michigan, Truman's proposals were embraced by Congress.

This policy came to be known as **containment**. Shortly after the Truman Doctrine was enunciated, a Soviet specialist in the United States Department of State, George Kennan, contributed a lengthy analysis of Soviet behaviour—and his suggestions for an appropriate American response—to the journal *Foreign Affairs*. Because he was a civil servant, his article appeared under a pseudonym, "X." In his view, the Soviet Union was aggressive and expansionist and thus had to be "contained by the adroit and vigilant application of counterforce at a series of constantly shifting geographical and political points." In other words: whenever and wherever in the world the Soviets pushed, the United States had to push back.[7]

Military alliances were used to "contain" the USSR. The first alliance was the Inter-American Treaty of Reciprocal Assistance, signed by the United States and 19 Latin American countries in Rio de Janeiro on 2 September 1947. The Rio pact, as it was colloquially known, used the language of universal collective security but applied it regionally (as Articles 51 and 52 of the Charter of the United Nations allowed countries to do). The treaty stated that an attack "against an American state shall be an attack against all American states," and drew a "hemispheric defense zone" that included the entire western hemisphere. The zone even included some areas which were not formal signatories to the Rio treaty, such as Canada, Bermuda, and Greenland. It was, as we will see below, the first of many such alliances featuring the United States as alliance leader.

## The Marshall Plan and Its Consequences

Another part of containment involved economic aid. In June 1947, the U.S. secretary of state, George Marshall, announced the European Recovery Program, a $13-billion package of American economic aid to devastated European nations. The Soviet Union was invited, with some hesitation, to the planning meeting for the distribution of **Marshall Plan** aid in Paris, and Moscow was indeed inclined to take advantage of this act of American generosity. However, because Soviet spies had penetrated the British government, Molotov, the Soviet foreign minister, learned that the United States secretary of the treasury, William Clayton, was discussing with the British foreign minister, Ernest Bevan, how to use Marshall Plan aid to extract political concessions from the Soviet Union.[8] When Stalin heard of this, he decided to pull out of the Marshall Plan discussions. Consequently, the USSR was not part of the Committee of European Economic Cooperation which was formed in July 1947 to administer Marshall Plan funds. Moreover, Stalin pressured the communist governments of Eastern Europe to withdraw, and created his own "Molotov Plan" that eventually was institutionalized as the Council for Mutual Economic Assistance (COMECON) in 1949.

## The Evolving Western Alliance System

The Marshall Plan also contributed to the institutionalization of East and West on the security side. Under the moderate leadership of Eduard Beneš, the president, and Jan Masaryk, the foreign minister, Czechoslovakia was within the Soviet sphere, but had resisted communist control. Stalin, believing that Beneš was being lured toward the West by Marshall Plan money, decided to stage a *coup d'état* in Prague. By 25 February 1948, Beneš had been ousted and the communists were in complete control; on 10 March, Masaryk's body was found on the ground outside the foreign ministry. Though the new communist-dominated government claimed he had jumped to his death, most people, then as now, believe that he was thrown out of his office window by communist agents.

The Czech coup, followed as it was by a similar move in Hungary, had a galvanizing effect on the West. The Truman administration moved to strengthen the parts of Germany still being occupied by the West. The Yalta agreements had provided for the partitioning of Germany into four zones of occupation—the American, British, French, and Soviet. Berlin, which was located in the Soviet zone, was also split four ways by the victors, with two million Germans in the Western sectors. Abandoning the spirit of the Yalta agreement that sought to keep Germany poor and squashed for the foreseeable future, the Truman administration proposed merging the American, British, and French zones of occupation into a separate state with a distinct currency. The Soviet Union saw this as the first step in an attempt by the West to rebuild Germany. They responded by blockading the Western sectors of Berlin on 24 June 1948, refusing to allow surface access to the city, hoping to force the three Western powers out of the city. Britain, France, and the United States responded to the **Berlin blockade** by organizing a massive airlift of food to West Berlin. Planes from the United States, Britain, France, and the smaller countries of Western Europe, together with the Commonwealth countries of Australia, New Zealand, and South Africa (but not Canada⋆) flew more than 13 000 tonnes of supplies each day into Berlin. The Soviet Union eventually backed down; after 324 days, the blockade was lifted.

The coup in Czechoslovakia also triggered discussions about an alliance that would commit the United States to the defence of western Europe. The Europeans themselves had been moved to create their own defence treaty: in March, Belgium, Britain, France, Luxembourg, and the Netherlands signed the Brussels Treaty, pledging to support one another if any of them were attacked. In Washington, the Truman administration persuaded Vandenberg to introduce a formal resolution to smooth Congressional opinion. The **Vandenberg Resolution**, approving the formation of "mutual aid" associations (in other words, alliances), was passed on 11 June 1948. On 4 April 1949, the North Atlantic Treaty was signed in Washington by 12 North Atlantic states.⋆⋆

> *"the Parties agree that an armed attack against one or more of them in Europe or North America shall be considered an attack against them all."*

Like the Rio pact, the North Atlantic Treaty was structured as a regional collective security agreement: an attack on one was an attack on all. In the language of **Article 5** of the North Atlantic Treaty, "the Parties agree that an armed attack against one or more of them in Europe or North America shall be considered an attack against them all," and that they would respond with force if necessary. This was the so-called **trigger clause** which created the formal obligation—deemed crucial by West Europeans and Canadians—that tied the United States to West European defence.

## China, Korea, and the Cold War in the Asia-Pacific

Further polarization occurred in what was then known as the Far East. In China, the growing East/West rivalry also manifested itself in the Chinese civil war being fought between the Chinese communists under Mao Zedong, supported by the Soviet Union, on the one side, and the Kuomintang (KMT, or Nationalist) regime of Chiang Kai-shek,

---

⋆ Canada's prime minister, Mackenzie King, refused to join in the Berlin airlift because he was annoyed that the British government's request for Canadian assistance had been leaked to the press before the government in Ottawa could come to a decision. This was a replay of the "Chanak crisis" of September 1922, when Britain had leaked a request for Canadian troops to help in an operation against the Turks in the Dardanelles. The prime minister in 1922—much embarrassed domestically by the British action—had been none other than Mackenzie King. For the Berlin airlift, see James Eayrs, *In Defence of Canada*, vol. 4, *Growing Up Allied* (Toronto: University of Toronto Press, 1980) 39–51; for the Chanak crisis, see C.P. Stacey, *Canada and the Age of Conflict*, vol. 2: *1921–1948: The Mackenzie King Era* (Toronto: University of Toronto Press, 1981), 17–31.

⋆⋆ The original signatories were Belgium, Britain, Canada, Denmark, France, Iceland, Italy, Luxembourg, the Netherlands, Norway, Portugal, and the United States. Greece and Turkey were admitted in 1952, West Germany in 1955, and Spain in 1982. In July 1997, Poland, the Czech Republic, and Hungary were invited to join.

supported by the United States, on the other. In the spring of 1949, the communists launched an offensive that defeated the KMT; on 1 October 1949, Mao proclaimed the establishment of the People's Republic of China (PRC).

The victory of the communists in China added considerable fuel to the East/West division. The defeat of the Nationalists sparked a bitter dispute in the United States over who was responsible for what was called the **loss of China**. Blithely oblivious to the arrogance in the assumption that China was theirs to "win" or "lose," Americans became embroiled in hysterical politics over communism. The phenomenon has been called **McCarthyism** because the charge was led by Senator Joseph McCarthy, Republican of Wisconsin, who alleged in a speech on 9 February 1950 that the government had been infiltrated by communist sympathizers. This prompted a series of what were called witch-hunts: China experts in the Department of State and American diplomats serving in China were subjected to loyalty investigations and accused of being communist sympathizers. Many were hounded from their positions.[9]

The belief that China had been "lost" by Truman just as Eastern Europe had been "lost" by Roosevelt prompted yet another shift in American policy. In April 1950, the United States National Security Council (NSC), the president's advisory council on defence matters, presented Truman with a set of recommendations intended to be a compass for American foreign policy. Known after its publication number as **NSC–68**, the paper argued that the world was marked by a "polarization of power which inescapably confronts the slave societies with the free." It argued that the Soviet Union was bent on world conquest, and that the United States had to stop it. Moreover, because "the absence of order among nations is becoming less and less tolerable," the United States had to impose order on the world so that "our free society can flourish." Among its recommendations were a rapid expansion in American military forces and a system of alliances around the world dominated by the United States.[10]

The proposals in NSC-68 were given a particular push by the outbreak of the Korean War on 25 June 1950. The roots of that conflict lay in the division of the Korean peninsula following the defeat of Japan. North of the 38th parallel, Soviet occupation forces suppressed moderate nationalists and supported Kim Il Sung, who had been an anti-Japanese guerrilla fighter in Manchuria. South of the 38th parallel, the United States suppressed leftists and supported Syngman Rhee, who had spent the war in exile in the United States. Efforts to negotiate a reunification of Korea in 1946 and 1947 failed because of the same Cold War distrust evident elsewhere. The result was the emergence of two different governments: in the south, the Republic of Korea was declared in August 1948; in September the Democratic People's Republic of Korea was created in the north.

From the outset Kim Il Sung championed the cause of reunification, and actively worked to undermine the Rhee government. Eventually, Kim secured general approval from Stalin for an armed attack on the south. In the West, where the East was seen as a monolith whose every move was dictated by Moscow, it was assumed that Stalin had ordered the invasion. Indeed, there was a widespread fear that the attack in Korea was merely a feint, providing a diversion for a Soviet attack on Western Europe.

The attack on South Korea has to be seen in the context of the broad anticommunist hysteria in the United States and the concern about the motives of what was seen as a monolithic communist bloc. Taking the view that the attack represented a replay of the expansionism of Nazi Germany in the 1930s, the Truman administration decided that there should be no appeasement of the aggression. As a consequence, the United States government organized a multilateral response to the invasion using the United Nations: 19 countries contributed combat troops or medical units to the UN force;[*] an American, General Douglas MacArthur, was appointed commander.

By the time the UN responded, the South Korean capital of Seoul had fallen to North Korean forces, and almost all of South Korea had been overrun. UN forces landed at Pusan, and launched a successful counterattack, forcing a North Korean retreat. However, the U.S. government decided that the UN forces would not stop at the 38th parallel, but would continue into the North, following the well-established military principle of **hot pursuit** (when the enemy is "on the run," it makes sense to continue pursuing and attacking them rather than stopping, which would give the enemy time to regroup and possibly launch a counter-offensive). But what may have been wise military tactics made little political sense. For as the North Koreans were driven back up the peninsula and Seoul was retaken by the UN, the aims of the war shifted. No longer was it a matter of restoring the South Korean government; rather, now there was a possibility of eliminating the North Korean regime.

As the U.S./UN armies began to approach North Korea, the Chinese communists became more concerned. The revolution was barely a year old; control over all China had not been consolidated. The leadership under Mao was convinced that the capitalist countries were dedicated to overthrowing the revolution. Their belief was driven not only by their own Marxist-Leninist beliefs about the inevitability of struggles between communism and capitalism, but also by their reading of the anticommunist hysteria in the United States. The PRC privately tried to alter U.S./UN policy. Through the Indian government, it signalled that Chinese troops would intervene in the war if the advance were not halted.

The warnings were ignored. UN forces crossed the border into North Korea on 7 October 1950; on 19 October they captured the northern capital of Pyongyang and continued to drive north toward the Yalu River, the Chinese border. MacArthur issued an ultimatum for North Korea's unconditional surrender. Just as they had promised, the Chinese intervened militarily: beginning in late October, Chinese "volunteers" crossed the border to assist North Korean units. On 26 November, Chinese forces launched a massive offensive against the UN forces, pushing them back down the peninsula, well across the 38th parallel; on 4 January 1951, Seoul fell to the communists a second time. The war seesawed one more time: the UN forces counterattacked in February, recapturing Seoul on 14 March, and pushing the Chinese and North Koreans back to the 38th parallel, where the positions of both sides more or less solidified. In June 1951, truce talks were proposed, but it was not until July 1953 that an armistice was signed at Panmunjom.

---

[*] Combat units were contributed by Australia, Belgium, Britain, Canada, Colombia, Ethiopia, France, Greece, Luxembourg, the Netherlands, New Zealand, the Philippines, South Africa, Thailand, Turkey, and the United States. Denmark, India, and Sweden contributed medical units.

The **Korean War** radically altered the relationship between East and West, deepening the hostilities and making reconciliation impossible. The United States lost more than 33 000 soldiers in the war, more than four-fifths of them killed after the Chinese had been provoked into intervening. Nearly 3100 troops from other countries died. It is estimated that there were over two million casualties on the North Korean and Chinese side; among the Chinese killed was one of Mao Zedong's own sons.

The war also accelerated the institutionalization of the West's defence systems called for in NSC-68. First, the North Atlantic alliance was transformed from a pact into a fully fledged institution for military cooperation. American and Canadian troops were stationed in Europe; a joint command structure was created; and an American, Gen. Dwight D. Eisenhower, was appointed as the first Supreme Allied Commander in Europe (SACEUR). These measures put the "Organization" into the North Atlantic Treaty, transforming it into NATO.

In the Asia Pacific, the United States created several alliances. Washington moved to normalize relations with Japan, which was still being occupied by American forces when the Korean War broke out. A peace treaty was negotiated in 1950 and 1951, restoring full sovereignty to Japan. Tied to the peace agreement that was signed on 8 September 1951 was a Mutual Security Treaty that guaranteed American protection of Japan in return for the use of bases by the United States. The week before, the United States had signed a defence pact with Australia and New Zealand. Like the other alliances, the Security Treaty between Australia, New Zealand, and the United States (the ANZUS treaty) committed the signatories to defend one another in the event of an armed attack.[11] Defence agreements were also signed with South Korea and the Republic of China on Taiwan.

Thus by the end of the Korean War, a ring of American-led alliances encircled the USSR and its allies. Within the next several years, both superpowers would put the finishing touches on the two alliance systems. After the French defeat at the battle of Dien Bien Phu on 7 May 1954, Vietnam was added to the negotiations at Geneva being held to end the Korean war. Under the Geneva Accords of July 1954, Vietnam was divided into North and South. The United States government moved to shore up the West's position in Southeast Asia. On 8 September 1954, Australia, Britain, France, New Zealand, Pakistan, the Philippines, Thailand, and the United States created a new regional alliance modelled on NATO, the Southeast Asia Treaty Organization (SEATO). An American-backed alliance was thus created on the USSR's southern flank.* In May 1958, the United States signed an agreement with Canada that "continentalized" air defence by treating the entire North American continent as a single land mass for the purposes of defending against an attack by Soviet bombers. The North American Air Defence (NORAD) agreement established a joint command system with an American commander and a Canadian deputy commander.[12] As Figure 15.1 shows, the allianceman-ship of the United States—some at the time called it American **"pactomania"**—meant that by the late 1950s, the USSR was indeed "contained" by a ring of alliances.

---

* The Baghdad Pact between Turkey and Iraq was signed in February 1955; this was transformed in November 1955 into the Middle Eastern Treaty Organization (METO) when Britain, Iraq, and Pakistan joined. In 1959, Iraq withdrew from METO, which renamed itself the Central Treaty Organization, CENTO.

*Figure 15.1* • **THE WEST'S ALLIANCE SYSTEM, LATE 1950S**

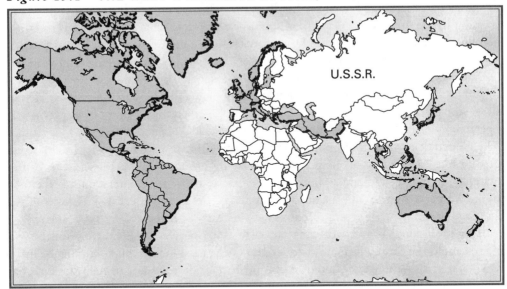

The Western alliance system in the late 1950s consisted of the following pacts:

**Nato:** Belgium, Britain, Canada, Denmark, France, West Germany, Greece, Iceland, Italy, Luxembourg, Netherlands, Norway, Portugal, Turkey, United States

**Cento:** Britain, Iraq, Iran, Pakistan, Turkey, (observer: United States)

**Seato:** Australia, Britain, France, Thailand, Philippines, New Zealand, United States

**Rio Pact:** Argentina, Bolivia, Brazil, Cuba, Chile, Colombia, Costa Rica, Ecuador, El Salvador, Guatemala, Haiti, Honduras, Mexico, Nicaragua,

Panama, Paraguay, Peru, United States, Uruguay, Venezuela

**Anzus:** Australia, New Zealand, United States

**Defence Pacts:** US-Japan, US-Taiwan, US-South Korea

In the East, the People's Republic of China aligned itself with Moscow, as did North Korea and North Vietnam. In Eastern Europe, the USSR did not decide to formalize its relationships with the Eastern European countries it had dominated until 1955, just after United States and its allies decided to admit West Germany to NATO on 9 May 1955. On 14 May, the Soviet Union gathered its allies—Albania, Bulgaria, Czechoslovakia, East Germany, Hungary, Poland, and Romania—in Warsaw to sign the Warsaw Treaty of Friendship, Cooperation, and Mutual Assistance (the Warsaw Treaty Organization, or simply the Warsaw Pact).

## THE EVOLUTION OF EAST/WEST RIVALRY, 1955-1991

The division of many of the world's states into two rival camps in the years between 1945 and 1955 was to have an impact on global politics for the next 35 years. The ideological division touched virtually every country; it coloured numerous decisions of global actors; it absorbed trillions of dollars in military spending, diverting funds from other purposes, and leaving its imprint on countless national budgets each year; it served to sustain some of the most repressive regimes in power in the name of "national security"; and it drove many of the wars of this period, not only between sovereign nation-states, but also the many civil wars fought during this era. It also produced some unintended side-effects: the Interstate highway system in the United States and the St Lawrence Seaway—both projects funded in the name of national security—helped to transform the North American economy over the course of the Cold War. Likewise, massive spending on military projects had some identifiable "spin-offs" in civilian life: miniaturization, computers, aircraft avionics.

The rivalry evident in the first decade after 1945 persisted. For the next 30 years, the leading power on each side sought to gain the advantage over the other in numerous ways, including the search for superior military technology and the search for allies, friendly states which could serve as sources of raw materials, markets for products, bases for military operations, or simply places that would be friendly to one side and unfriendly to the other. The United States tried to keep the USSR contained; for its part, the Soviet Union struggled to break through this encirclement, partly by trying to compete with the United States in military technology, and partly by seeking to befriend countries outside the orbit of the West and even to shift the allegiance of countries from West to East. The result was a seesawing shift of actions and reactions between the superpowers.

Few local conflicts avoided being tarred with a Cold War brush during this period. For example, the **Suez crisis** of October 1956 began as a local conflict but turned into a Cold War crisis. When the United States and Britain decided not to help the Egyptian government of Gamal Abdul Nasser finance a dam across the Nile near the city of Aswan, Nasser decided to nationalize the Suez Canal and use proceeds from the canal tolls to finance the Aswan High Dam. This move threatened not only the interests of the primary owners of the Canal, the British and French governments, but also the primary route for moving goods and people between Britain and its colonies and markets east of Suez. Consequently, it threatened the interests of countries like Australia. The British and French decided to use force. They negotiated a secret agreement with the Israeli government, which had its own reasons for using force against Egypt. Israel wanted to wipe out the bases of the *fedayeen* commandos (literally, "those who sacrifice themselves") who were attacking Israel from Egyptian soil. On 29 October 1956, Israeli forces invaded the Sinai desert; two days later British and French forces seized the Canal. The invasion caused a crisis in East-West relations: the Soviet government of Nikita S. Khrushchev threatened to use force against Paris and London if British and French forces were not withdrawn.

The issue seriously split the Western bloc. The Eisenhower administration was furious with the governments in London, Paris, and Tel Aviv for having used force to resolve the issue. This split so concerned some of the smaller Western governments that they tried hard to patch up the split between the allies. Canada's foreign minister, Lester B. Pearson, came up with the idea of using a force under the UN flag to replace British and French forces. The idea won favour with the protagonists, and the crisis was temporarily resolved when the United Nations Emergency Force (UNEF) was deployed. One consequence was the birth of UN peacekeeping missions; another was that Pearson won the 1957 Nobel Peace Prize; a third was that Nasser turned to the Soviet Union for financial assistance for the Aswan High Dam, which was completed with Soviet assistance (the last turbines being installed in 1970, the same year that Nasser died).

The Hungarian revolt of 1956 also became a Cold War issue. The rebellion against Soviet domination—which had been marked by the collectivization of Hungarian agriculture; the imprisonment of the head of the Catholic church in Hungary, József Cardinal Mindszenty; and the requirement that Hungarians learn Russian in school—bubbled over in protests that brought Imré Nagy to power. Nagy freed Mindszenty, promised an end to one-party rule and demanded the withdrawal of Soviet forces from Hungarian soil. On 1 November 1956, Nagy withdrew from the Warsaw Pact, and declared Hungary a neutral state. Khrushchev's response was quick, blunt, and brutal: Soviet troops moved against the protestors, killing hundreds. By 4 November, a new regime under János Kádár was installed; hundreds of Hungarian protestors were summarily executed; and Nagy was arrested, given a secret trial, and executed in 1958. While the governments of the West did not do anything concrete to assist the Hungarian rebels (other than open their doors to a flood of Hungarian refugees after the crisis), the use of force to keep Hungary in the Eastern bloc became a symbol in the East-West struggle.

## Fragmentation of the East: The Sino-Soviet Dispute

The Hungarian crisis demonstrated the essential fragility of the Eastern "alliance." This was an alliance forged under duress. The Hungarians had no option but to remain in the Soviet orbit as long as Moscow believed that its security and economic interests were best served by retaining control over all of Eastern Europe. Moreover, the Hungarians were not as lucky as the Yugoslavs: Tito had been able to defy Stalin in 1948 because the rugged mountainous territory of Yugoslavia, and the strong army inherited from the partisan fights against the Nazis, effectively deterred the Soviets from trying to impose communist orthodoxy on Yugoslavia at the point of a gun.

The same dynamic obtained in the case of China when, in the mid-1950s, the Chinese Communist Party (CCP) challenged the ideological dominance of the Communist Party of the Soviet Union (CPSU). The dispute between China and the Soviet Union arose over the ideological line being pursued by Khrushchev. At the 20th CPSU Party Congress in January and February 1956, Khrushchev gave a "**secret speech**" in which he openly criticized Stalin, and promised to undo many of Stalin's policies (a policy called **de-Stalinization**). Mao Zedong, no great admirer of Stalin himself but a Stalinist by inclination, was mightily upset by the secret speech. Khrushchev had not bothered to consult other communist leaders, all of whom were in the habit of venerating Stalin as a great leader—and who now looked rather stupid. Moreover, by openly criticizing Stalin, Khrushchev was admitting that communist party leaders could be criticized, something quite unfamiliar to Stalinists like Mao (even though, as we saw in Chapter 2, he briefly experimented with such criticism in the Hundred Flowers campaign in 1957 before critics of the CCP were consigned to prison or the firing squad).

Mao and Khrushchev also differed over how to achieve a communist society, with the Soviets insisting that heavy industrialization was a necessary step in the path to "building communism." Mao, faced with China's vast agricultural society, had a different view. Beginning in 1958, the CCP inaugurated a massive experiment in social reorganization. Agriculture was collectivized; all private plots were abolished; all household activities—cooking, cleaning, childcare—was communized in order to free women for labour; and industrialization was brought down to the village level by creating more than a million backyard steel furnaces. This was the **Great Leap Forward**, and it was Mao's answer to Soviet orthodoxy about the necessity of heavy industrialization. The Great Leap Forward was, however, a huge and disastrous failure. Because leaders of communes that did not produce their required quotas were punished, they simply lied about their commune's agricultural production to the central government. While leaders in Beijing were crowing about huge increases in production, in reality Chinese harvests were crashing, leading to famine and millions of deaths. The backyard steel furnaces were a total failure, since they simply could not produce steel of useable quality.

While de-Stalinization and different paths to communism opened small fissures in the CPSU–CCP relationship, differences of opinion over the strategic implications of nuclear weapons provided the grounds for an open break. In 1957, the USSR started to provide active support for a Chinese nuclear-weapons program—and then immediately wished

> *"The East wind was prevailing over the West wind."*

they hadn't. It turned out that Mao Zedong had a radically different view of nuclear weapons than the one dominant in Moscow. At the 20th CPSU Congress, Khrushchev had publicly declared that he no longer believed that war between the capitalist and socialist worlds was inevitable, as Marxist-Leninist theory asserted. This was an entirely sensible statement given the enormous destructive capacity of nuclear weapons.

Mao, by contrast, believed that the Marxist-Leninist theory about the inevitability of war was not affected by nuclear weapons. On the contrary, nuclear weapons provided the socialist world with a means to vigorously challenge the West. Mao argued that "the atomic bomb is a paper tiger"—in other words, no threat at all. Moreover, his analysis led him to the view that if the West unleashed a nuclear war, the East would readily survive. "The East wind," he said to a gathering of students while on a trip to Moscow in November 1957, "was prevailing over the West wind...If the worst came to the worst and half of mankind died, the other half would remain while imperialism would be razed to the ground and the whole world would become socialist."[13] Given such views, Khrushchev hastily reneged on his promise to give the Chinese a prototype atomic bomb. The government in Moscow left in no doubt that it believed the Chinese view of nuclear weapons to be both stupid and dangerous. In the summer of 1960, the USSR summoned home all 1390 Soviet nuclear experts and advisers working in China—with their plans and blueprints.* The Sino-Soviet alliance was at an end.

## The Nuclear Arms Race

The competition between the United States and the Soviet Union over atomic weapons seesawed throughout the 1940s and 1950s. The West's **nuclear monopoly** lasted until

---

* Almost all the blueprints made it: two Russian scientists simply tore up their documents (rather than shredding them). Retrieved from the garbage by the Chinese and painstakingly put back together, these documents provided vital information for the development of the Chinese nuclear weapons program. See Jonathan D. Spence, *The Search for Modern China* (London: Hutchinson, 1990), 589.

August 1949, when the USSR exploded its first bomb, prompting the United States to accelerate its own research program into thermonuclear (or hydrogen) devices. Shortly after the United States tested a thermonuclear weapon in November 1952, the Soviet Union followed with its own thermonuclear device in August 1953.

The United States and the USSR also engaged in a race for more efficient ways of delivering these weapons of increasing destructive capability to their targets. Both countries quickly developed long-range bombers such as the Boeing B-52 "Stratofortress" in 1952.[14] But increasingly the focus was on rocket technology. The competition to develop a rocket capable of leaving the Earth's atmosphere was nominally "won" by the USSR. Eisenhower had declared 1957 to be a year of technological cooperation with the USSR, and had purposely postponed the launch of an American satellite in order not to appear to be engaged in a game of one-upmanship with the USSR. However, when the Soviet Union launched its *Sputnik* satellite on 4 October 1957, the reaction in the United States was one of great alarm. For many Americans, *Sputnik* meant that the USSR was now capable of attacking the United States from space. Eisenhower was prompted to create the National Aeronautics and Space Administration (NASA) and to begin a massive military buildup.

*Appealing to the insecurities of American voters no doubt contributed to Kennedy's victory over Richard M. Nixon in 1960, but in fact the "missile gap" was the other way around.*

Ironically, John F. Kennedy, the Democratic candidate for the presidency in the 1960 elections, accused Eisenhower of allowing what he called a **missile gap** to appear between East and West. Appealing to the insecurities of American voters no doubt contributed to Kennedy's victory over Richard M. Nixon in 1960, but in fact the "missile gap" was the other way around. In January 1961, when Kennedy was sworn in, the United States had some 200 intercontinental ballistic missiles (ICBMs) or intermediate range ballistic missiles (IRBMs) and some 1700 strategic bombers with intercontinental range, in addition to hundreds of fighters armed with nuclear weapons. By contrast, the Soviet Union had but 50 ICBMs and 150 intercontinental bombers. It did have 400 IRBMs, but they were not capable of reaching the United States.[15]

The Soviets were deeply concerned about the implications of this American power. Khrushchev decided to try and correct it by taking advantage of the departure of Cuba from the West, the result of a revolution led by Fidel Castro Ruz. Castro had spent time in jail in the early 1950s for protesting against the government of Fulgencio Batista y Zalvídar. Following his release, Castro organized a guerrilla movement that seized power from Batista on 1 January 1959. While his brother Raoul was a Marxist-Leninist, Fidel was not a communist when he came to power. However, he soon became one as a result of a bitter struggle with the United States over the nationalization of American property in Cuba. When Castro refused to pay compensation at the levels demanded by American owners, they appealed to the government in Washington to protect their interests. The Eisenhower administration imposed sanctions, barring the importation of Cuban sugar. With the main market of Cuba's primary staple closed, Castro turned to the USSR, which was only too happy to buy Cuban sugar at well-above world prices and provide Havana with other assistance.

As his ties to the USSR increased, Castro began pursuing an overtly Marxist-Leninist line. What had started as a nationalist revolution turned Leninist, featuring repression of opponents, uncompensated expropriation of property, and a wave of executions of those deemed to be "enemies of the revolution." This prompted thousands of Cubans to flee to the United States. In March 1960 the Eisenhower administration authorized the Central Intelligence Agency to organize, train, finance, and equip an army of exiles. It was to land in Cuba, spark a popular uprising, and overthrow the Castro regime.

The CIA plan was given the go-ahead by Kennedy shortly after his inauguration. It went disastrously wrong: on 17 April 1961, approximately 1300 Cuban exiles were landed on the south coast at Bahía de Cochinos, the **Bay of Pigs**. But there was no uprising; the soldiers never got off the beach. A series of errors allowed the Cuban army to pin the invasion force down. Within two days, 90 had been killed and the remainder taken prisoner.[16]

### The Cuban Missile Crisis and Its Aftermath

The U.S.-organized invasion of Cuba in 1961 provided Khrushchev with an opportunity to try to shift the strategic nuclear imbalance. While the USSR did not have many ICBMs, the Soviet Strategic Rocket Forces had a large number of IRBMs. If some of these were positioned in Cuba, they would shift the balance of power somewhat. So Khrushchev proposed to Castro that IRBMs be placed in Cuba; construction on the installations began in 1962.

When routine American spy flights over Cuba revealed the construction of missile sites in the autumn of 1962, the Kennedy administration responded by insisting that the installations be dismantled. Kennedy resisted the urgings of some of his military advisers to launch what is known as a **surgical strike** (in other words, a limited air attack) against the installations in Cuba. Instead, on 22 October 1962, an American naval blockade was imposed around Cuba, with a threat that if the USSR tried to run the blockade, force would be used. Khrushchev eventually backed down, securing a public agreement from Kennedy that the United States would not invade Cuba, and a private agreement to dismantle American IRBMs in Turkey. However, these concessions were not enough to save Khrushchev from being deposed on 14 October 1964 by a troika of party officials led by Leonid Brezhnev, a secretary of the Communist Party of the Soviet Union. There is no coincidence that among the "political errors" that were cited as grounds for removing Khrushchev from power and turning him into a **"nonperson"*** was the humiliation he caused the USSR in 1962.[17]

Some IR scholars say that the Cuban missile crisis is important because it was a key turning point in the Cold War; it was the point when, in the words of Donald M. Snow and Eugene Brown, "the two superpowers took a sobering look into the abyss and backed away."[18] In this view, the world came perilously close to a nuclear war in October 1962,

---

* Making someone a "nonperson" was a form of political punishment peculiar to the USSR. A nonperson was no longer formally acknowledged to exist by the Soviet state. In some instances, all evidence that the individual had even existed was eradicated. Khrushchev remained a nonperson until his (officially unacknowledged) death in 1971.

and was avoided only because Kennedy, in the words of Ernest May, "handled [the crisis] superbly."[19] In other words, Kennedy's brinkmanship prompted both superpowers to come to their senses and realize that nuclear war would be mutually devastating. That is why a treaty banning the testing of nuclear weapons in the atmosphere was signed in 1963, and a **"hot line"**—a direct and secure teletype/telephone line between the American president and the Soviet premier—was established.

The Cuban missile crisis was indeed a turning point, but it can also be argued that if one focuses (as Americans are inclined to do) on the American president's performance, one misses the real significance of this crisis: it pointed out to the USSR how weak it was. Khrushchev knew that he had few options once the Americans decided to object to the missiles: either war with the United States, which would have been suicidal given the slim arsenals of the USSR, or a humiliating capitulation.

When the Cuban missile crisis is seen as a crushing humiliation for the Soviet Union and its leader, rather than as a deft act of statesmanship by the American president, its true historical significance as a turning point in East/West relations is revealed. The crisis should be seen as the point when the Soviet leaders who followed Khrushchev decided that never again would their country have to bow to the United States. After the ouster of Khrushchev in 1964, there was a dramatic shift in Soviet global policy. Beginning in the mid-1960s, the Soviet Union began a massive drive for parity with the United States. One measure of this commitment can be seen in the steady—and often dramatic—increases in the Soviet defence budget. As Table 15.2 shows, Soviet expenditures on defence rose from US$36.9 billion per year at the beginning of the decade to nearly US$90 billion by the end of the decade. This drive had three interrelated dimensions.

First, the acquisition of nuclear weapons was accelerated so that Soviet leaders would never again be confronted by a situation in which the dominance of strategic forces dictated

*Table 15.2* • **SOVIET DEFENCE EXPENDITURES, 1960–1969**

|  | Expenditure (US$ billion) | % change |
|---|---|---|
| 1960 | 36.9 | |
| 1961 | 43.6 | +18 |
| 1962 | 49.9 | +14 |
| 1963 | 54.7 | +10 |
| 1964 | 48.7 | −10 |
| 1965 | 62.3 | +27 |
| 1966 | 69.7 | +11 |
| 1967 | 80.9 | +16 |
| 1968 | 85.4 | +5 |
| 1969 | 89.8 | +5 |

Source: Adapted from Paul Kennedy, *The Rise and Fall of the Great Powers: Economic Change and Military Conflict from 1500 to 2000* (London: Unwin Hyman, 1988), 384.

the outcome in so dramatic a fashion as in 1962. No longer would an American president be able to dictate terms to a Soviet premier; no longer would the USSR have to back down in humiliation. Soviet leaders were exceedingly fortunate that their drive for parity coincided with the invention of a new nuclear delivery system that exponentially increased military capability. In the early 1960s, each ICBM could carry only one nuclear warhead. By the end of the decade, it was possible to pack a number of warheads into a "bus" that could be fired into orbit atop a single ICBM. At the end of its orbit, the "bus" would release its warheads—numbering anywhere from three to ten—which would then descend ballistically onto preprogrammed targets. These were known as **MIRV**s—multiple independently targetable reentry vehicles. "MIRVing" ICBMs dramatically increased their destructive capability. By the mid-1970s, both the USSR and the United States had mammoth firepower aimed at each other. Figure 15.2 shows the speed and intensity of the Soviet effort to achieve parity with the United States during the 1960s. Moreover, atop these delivery vehicles sat weapons of awesome destructive capability. The average American nuclear warhead was 200 times as powerful as the atomic bomb that destroyed Hiroshima in August 1945; the average Soviet warhead was even more powerful.

Second, in the mid-1960s the Soviet Union embarked on a plan to build a **blue water navy**—in other words, a navy capable of operating around the world, just as the United States Navy did. After 1965, the number of keels laid rose dramatically, with increased Soviet capacity in aircraft carriers, cruisers, destroyers, and submarines. Moreover, the expanding Red Navy was sent to "show the flag" in the oceans of the world. It regularly patrolled in the Mediterranean beginning in 1964, in the Indian Ocean from 1968, in the Caribbean from 1969, and up and down the Atlantic beginning in 1970.[20]

Finally, the USSR began a concerted effort to expand its influence throughout the world. Soviet leaders, diplomats, intelligence agents, aid officials, and military personnel all intensified their efforts to gain allies. The search for global influence involved the USSR in politics in Southeast Asia, South Asia, Africa, and the Caribbean.

*If one country was taken over by communists, they would spread revolution to neighbouring states, and one by one, countries would "fall" like a row of dominoes.*

Moscow backed North Vietnam in its continuing struggle against foreign intervention in the Indochinese peninsula. Although the French had departed following their defeat at Dien Bien Phu in May 1954, the plans of the communist government in Hanoi to seize control of the entire country were foiled by the willingness of the United States to continue where the French had left off. The U.S. backed the anticommunist regime in Saigon (as Ho Chi Minh City was then known). Partly, the U.S. decision was based on a calculation that came to be known as the **domino theory**: if one country was taken over by communists, they would spread revolution to neighbouring states, and one by one, countries would "fall" like a row of dominoes.

The Americans became involved in propping up the South Vietnamese domino slowly. It began with supplying military assistance to the government of Ngo Dinh Diem, the South Vietnamese president. Then American advisers were sent to train the Army of the

*Figure 15.2* • "NEVER AGAIN": THE STRATEGIC CONSEQUENCES OF THE CUBAN MISSILE CRISIS. NUCLEAR STRATEGIC DELIVERY VEHICLES, 1955-1975

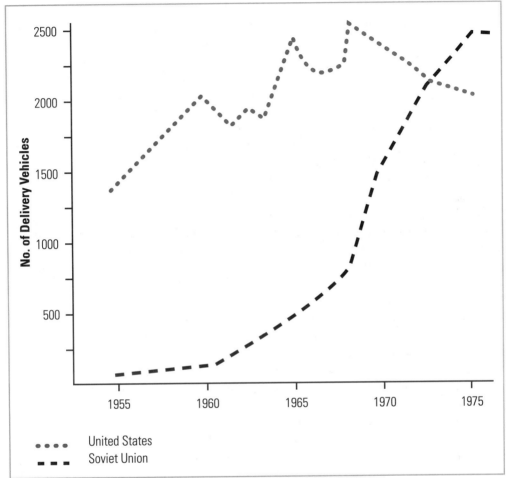

Delivery vehicles includes all ICBMs, submarine-launched ballistic missiles, and "strategic" bombers (i.e., those with intercontinental range).
Source: Harvard University Nuclear Study Group, *Living with Nuclear Weapons* (Cambridge, MA: Harvard University Press, 1983), 75.

Republic of Vietnam (ARVN). On 8 July 1959, two American advisers, Maj. Dale Buis and Serg. Chester Ovnand, were killed by communist forces, the first of over 58 000 Americans to die serving in Vietnam. In 1962, John F. Kennedy increased the number of advisers from 700 to 12 000. Indeed, his administration began to become more deeply immersed in South Vietnamese politics. As the Diem regime became increasingly unpopular, Kennedy himself became active in plots against Diem and his brother, Ngo Dinh Nhu, both of whom were eventually assassinated by their own generals in a *coup d'état* on 1 November.

By the time that Kennedy was himself assassinated three weeks later, the number of advisers had grown to 15 000, and the United States had devoted US$500 million in military assistance to the anticommunist regime. This was followed in 1964 by the start of American bombing of North Vietnam. After a North Vietnamese gunboat attacked the *USS Maddox* in the Gulf of Tonkin, the United States Congress passed the **Gulf of Tonkin Resolution** on 7 August, giving President Lyndon B. Johnson wide authority to prosecute the war in Vietnam. In early 1965, Johnson authorized Operation Rolling Thunder, a bombing campaign against North Vietnam, and two battalions of United States Marines were sent to defend Danang airfield on 8 March. More troops followed: by December 1965, there were over 200 000 troops in Vietnam. By the end of 1967, that number had climbed to over 500 000—without an appreciable change in the military situation.[21]

The Soviet Union played a crucial role in this conflict, primarily in supplying the government of North Vietnam with military equipment. This was then moved south by regular North Vietnamese soldiers, using what the Americans colloquially called the **"Ho Chi Minh trail"**—a system of jungle tracks through Laos and Cambodia to South Vietnam. The USSR also provided high-technology surface-to-air missiles (SAMs) that dented American air superiority and cost numerous American fliers their lives or freedom. In this way, Moscow helped to keep the Americans bogged down in Vietnam. Washington was prompted to spend increasing sums of money on military assistance, with the result that the war sparked protests and division in the United States itself.

Eventually the Soviet "investment" in the 1960s paid off. The United States gave up the fight in 1973, leaving the way open for the North Vietnamese and the South Vietnamese guerrillas to complete their military conquest of South Vietnam in April 1975, which was then incorporated into a unified Socialist Republic of Vietnam in 1976.

The communist victory in Vietnam provided the USSR with an important set of military bases: Danang airfield and Cam Ranh Bay. Later in 1975, as we saw in Chapter 11, the USSR also tried to capitalize on the conflict between the Timorese and Indonesia: Moscow and its allies quickly recognized the Democratic Republic of East Timor declared by the *Frente Revolucionário do Timor Leste Independente* (FRETILIN) on 28 November 1975.

Although its efforts to secure a base in the Timorese capital of Dili came to nought, the USSR did manage to expand its influence throughout Indochina through the efforts of the Vietnamese government in Hanoi. In 1978, Vietnam moved against Pol Pot's Khmer Rouge regime in Cambodia, following border skirmishes and a massive refugee flow into Vietnam as a result of the genocidal policies of the Khmer Rouge. In December, Vietnamese troops invaded Cambodia and established a government more to Hanoi's liking in January 1979. Vietnam also maintained strong and friendly relations with the communist government of Laos, which supported both Hanoi and the USSR.

In South Asia, the Soviet Union decided to back India in its quarrels with Pakistan, signing a treaty of friendship and supplying India with military matériel. The clearest support came over the civil war that broke out in East Pakistan in March 1971. As the West Pakistani-dominated army began to attack East Pakistani civilians, millions of refugees fled across the border into India, prompting the Indian government to intervene in December 1971.

Quickly routing the Pakistani army, the Indians helped establish an independent Bangladesh. In this local dispute, the United States backed its military ally Pakistan in the war; the USSR—which in August 1971 had signed a 20-year peace treaty with New Delhi—backed India.

In Southwest Asia, the Soviet government was actively involved in Afghani politics. Soviet military advisers participated in the overthrow of the government of Mohammad Daoud on 27 April 1978. The new regime was communist, and the USSR quickly increased both its military aid and the number of advisers it had in Kabul. The new Afghani president, Nur Mohammed Taraki, signed a treaty of friendship and cooperation with the USSR. However, the Soviet-backed government quickly alienated a great many Afghanis, partly because of the brutality with which it governed, partly because its land reforms angered so many villagers, and partly because the communist rulers demonstrated little concern for the religious sensitivities of Afghani Muslims. The USSR became embroiled in the factional disputes that broke out in Kabul, backing Taraki even after he had been deposed by Hafizullah Amin. But under Amin's rule, the political situation deterioriated, and the Brezhnev government decided to relieve Amin of the presidency by force. On 24 December 1979, Soviet troops arrived at Kabul airport; by 27 December, there were 5000 troops in Afghanistan. These forces seized control of the capital. Amin was discovered at a palace compound outside the city and killed. A new leader, Babrak Karmal, was installed, setting in train an intervention the results of which we will explore in the next section.[22]

In the Middle East, the USSR tried to fashion allies among the governments and groups contending in that area. It supported South Yemen, with Cuban troops providing training, and the port at Aden becoming the key operating facility for Soviet naval operations in the Indian Ocean. Moscow sold military equipment to a range of governments, including those of Libya, Syria, and Iraq. In addition, there were repeated reports of active Soviet support for Middle Eastern groups which engaged in terrorism.[23]

In Africa, the USSR became actively involved when the Portuguese government abandoned its war against nationalist guerrillas in the colonies of Angola and Mozambique, following the revolution in Lisbon in April 1974. This development provided the USSR with an opportunity to develop its influence in southern Africa, and indeed to press South Africa itself. In Mozambique, Soviet military assistance was provided to the nationalist *Frente de Libertação de Moçambique* (or FRELIMO), which gained independence in June 1975 under Samora Machel. The USSR also supported Mozambique in its bitter war with South Africa, which was providing military aid to the *Resistência Nacional Moçambicana* (RENAMO), an anticommunist guerrilla movement noted for its use of terror and torture.

On the other side of the continent, the USSR also became involved in the civil war in Angola that had been underway since 1961. The Angolan nationalist movement was divided into three groups: the FNLA led by Holden Roberto; UNITA under Jonas Savimbi; and the MPLA under Agostinho Neto. With the departure of the Portuguese in 1975, the Angolan civil war became a Cold War conflict. The United States backed the FNLA, which was based in Zaire (as Congo-Kinshasa was called during the rule of Mobutu Sese Seko), and UNITA was supported by both South Africa and the United States. The USSR supported the MPLA and arranged to have the Cuban government "volunteer" some 18 000 troops for service in Angola. The USSR then transported these troops to Africa, where they fought with the MPLA. While the Cubans helped turn the tide of the war and establish the MPLA in power, they did not defeat either UNITA, which was supported by 20 000 troops from South Africa, or the FNLA, which was given money by the Central Intelligence Agency to recruit mercenaries to assist its military operations. Both groups continued a low-intensity war in Angola: the FNLA fought until it was defeated militarily in the late 1970s, and UNITA engaged in a war that continues to this day, long after the Cubans went home.

The relatively successful Cuban adventure in Angola prompted the USSR to try the same model elsewhere in Africa. After Emperor Haile Selassie of Ethiopia was deposed in a *coup d'état* in September 1974, a military government under Col. Mengistu Haile-Mariam emerged. Mengistu invited the USSR to assist it in establishing order within Ethiopia, which was in a state of civil war. Eritrean guerrillas were fighting for independence in the north, and ethnic Somalis in the Ogaden were fighting for incorporation into Somalia, which claimed the Ogaden region as its own. The Soviet Union obliged, providing training, East German military equipment, and 11 000 Cuban soldiers to fight the Ogaden war in 1977–78.

The Soviet Union was also active in the Caribbean, not only supporting its long-standing ally, Fidel Castro, but also assisting the Cubans in providing aid to other groups in the region. Cuban assistance was funnelled to the *Frente Sandinista de Liberación Nacional* (FSLN), a group established in Nicaragua in 1961 as a Castro-like guerrilla group. The FSLN survived numerous government "eradication" campaigns, and tried to organize a nation-wide uprising in October 1977. In response, the Nicaraguan government of Anastasio Somoza Debayle grew even more repressive. Somoza's U.S.-trained National Guard was involved in numerous human rights violations, including the assassination in January 1978 of Pedro Joaquín Chamorro Cardenal, a political leader and newspaper editor. Chamorro's assassination galvanized the opposition, and open civil war broke out. In June 1979, members of the National Guard arrested an American news reporter, Bill Stewart of ABC; he was forced to kneel on the street and was executed with a shot to the head. However, Stewart's camera crew managed to record the murder and smuggle the tape out of Nicaragua. When the tape was replayed on U.S. networks, Washington's support for the Somoza regime evaporated. On 17 July 1979, Somoza fled into exile (eventually settling in Asunción, Paraguay, where he was assassinated on 17 September 1980 in a bazooka attack). The Sandinistas under Daniel Ortega Saavedra took power.

The Sandinistas encouraged groups in neighbouring countries to rise up against U.S.-backed repressive regimes. In El Salvador, leftist and rightist forces were locked in a struggle that was marked by street assassinations and human rights violations by the armed forces and police. On 24 March 1980, the archbishop of San Salvador, Msgr. Oscar Arnulfo Romero y Galdames, was assassinated by rightists while saying Mass. As in Nicaragua, the assassination prompted the formation of an antigovernment organization, the *Frente Farabundo Martí para la Liberación Nacional* (FMLN), to fight the government of José Napoleón Duarte Fuentes.

Cuban assistance was provided to the government of Grenada. On 13 March 1979, the leader of the opposition New Jewel Movement in the Grenadan parliament, Maurice Bishop, overthrew the prime minister, Eric Gairy, and declared a People's Revolutionary Government. He immediately negotiated a two-year technical assistance agreement with Cuba.

Thus, by the 1970s, the USSR had radically altered the global correlation of forces. Although the government in Moscow pursued a policy of **détente**—a relaxation of tensions— with the West in the late 1960s and early 1970s, Soviet leaders never lost sight of the broader strategic goal of parity with the United States. Thus, the government in Moscow pursued friendlier relations with the West, and participated, for example, in the two-year Conference on Security and Cooperation in Europe (CSCE) in Helsinki that resulted in lowered tensions in Europe. But all the while, the government in Moscow continued to expand its military production, its military projection on a global basis, and its efforts to find friendly countries around the world which would provide air and naval bases. As Figure 15.3 shows, by 1980 the amount of "friendly" territory had expanded considerably from the 1950s, when, as we saw in Figure 15.1 (p. 397), the USSR was tightly encircled by unfriendly alliances.

### The American Reaction

The expansion of the sphere of Soviet influence over the decade and a half after the Cuban missile crisis spawned a political reaction in the United States. Although President Jimmy

*Figure 15.3* • **FRIENDLY SPACES: THE USSR AND ITS FRIENDS AND ALLIES, 1980**

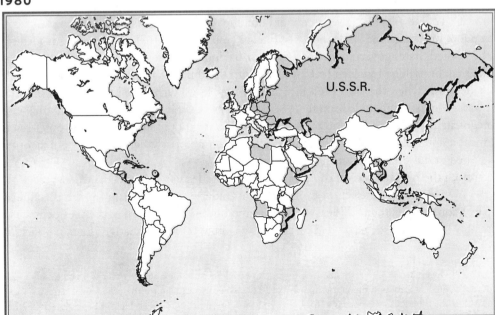

Carter, elected in 1976, had a number of foreign policy "successes"—notably the Middle East peace agreement of March 1979, known as the **Camp David Accords**[*]—he came under increasingly sharp domestic criticism for his handling of American foreign policy. Two events in particular galvanized opinion in the United States: the revolution in Iran and the Soviet invasion of Afghanistan.

The Soviet invasion of Afghanistan occurred at the same time as the Carter administration was grappling with the consequences of a revolution in Iran that deprived the U.S. of a key ally in southwest Asia. The revolution was fuelled in part by the rapid and large-scale increases in wealth in Iran. As we will see in Chapter 16, the oil embargo imposed by the Organization of Petroleum Exporting Countries (OPEC) during the Yom Kippur war between Israel and its neighbours produced sharp increases in oil prices. The secularization and westernization that tended to come with that wealth was welcomed by the regime of Muhammad Reza Shah Pahlavi, who had aligned his government with the United States. But these trends were bitterly criticized by Islamic leaders in Iran. In turn, Islamic opposition was suppressed with increasing brutality by the shah's secret police, Savak. The political crisis came to a head in 1978. Teheran was overwhelmed with demonstrations, directed by the ayatollah (or revered leader) of the Iranian Islamic movement, Ruhollah Khomeini, from Paris, where had been exiled by the shah in 1963. By January 1979, the shah, who was terminally ill, was forced into exile and an Islamic republic was established. The new regime left its alignment in no doubt. It executed large numbers of Savak agents and members of the shah's regime, and began pursuing a stridently anti-American policy, perhaps best captured in the new regime's common characterization of the United States as the **"Great Satan."**

When the shah was admitted to the United States for medical treatment in November 1979, Iranian militants stormed the United States embassy in Tehran and took 66 Americans hostage. The new Islamic government did nothing to stop this violation of international conventions that guaranteed the sanctity of foreign embassies. On the contrary, it demanded that the United States government apologize for having supported the shah's regime and that the shah himself be returned to Iran to stand trial. While the latter demand was eventually made moot when the shah died in Cairo in July 1980, what was known as the **Iranian hostage crisis** lingered through 1980. When the Carter administration was unable to negotiate the release of the hostages, the U.S. military mounted a daring helicopter rescue mission, intending to pluck the hostages from Tehran. But when one of the helicopters crashed in the desert, the mission was aborted.

Both the Soviet invasion of Afghanistan and the Iranian hostage crisis occurred as the 1980 U.S. presidential election campaigns got underway. A candidate for the Republican party nomination, Ronald Reagan, secured the nomination and then the presidency itself mainly because he attacked what he argued was the weakness of Carter's foreign policy. He

---

[*] On 19 November 1977, the president of Egypt, Anwar al-Sadat, made a surprise visit to Israel to seek peace. Carter invited al-Sadat and the prime minister of Israel, Menachem Begin, to the presidential retreat at Camp David, in the Blue Ridge mountains in Maryland, to negotiate a peace agreement. Held in September 1978, these negotiations resulted in the Camp David Accords, signed by the three leaders in Washington on 26 March 1979, bringing a 30-year state of war between the two countries to an end.

argued that under Carter, American power had been allowed to slip; everywhere the Soviet Union was beating the United States. The seeming powerlessness of the United States was

*Reagan's promise to the electorate was simple: he would "make America No. 1 again."*

nowhere better seen than in Washington's inability to secure the release of the hostages in Iran. Reagan's promise to the electorate was simple: he would "make America No. 1 again." It was a patriotic line that appealed to a majority of American voters in 1980.

"Making America No. 1 again" involved a multifaceted strategy of pushing back in as many places as possible over the next six years.* As we saw in Chapter 10, American forces shot Libyan jet fighters out of the sky in a territorial dispute in 1981. Military aid was channelled to the *contras*, as rebels opposing the Sandinista government in Nicaragua were known. Indeed, even after the U.S. Congress expressly forbade it, the National Security Council authorized one of Reagan's aides, Col. Oliver North, to secretly move money to the *contras*. That money was gained by the illegal sale of weapons to Iran (activities for which North was eventually tried and convicted in May 1989, although the conviction was subsequently overturned). Aid was also given to the Coalition Government of Democratic Kampuchea (CGDK), which was fighting the Vietnamese-backed regime in Cambodia, even though that coalition included Pol Pot, whose Khmer Rouge had engaged in the worst case of genocide since the Holocaust. In October 1983, the Reagan administration authorized an American invasion of Grenada after a *coup d'état* offered an opportunity to eliminate the island's pro-Cuban government.

But much of the Reagan administration's efforts were aimed directly at the USSR. He took particular pleasure in vilifying the Soviet Union: in one of his first news conferences, the American president accused the USSR of being prepared to "commit any crime, to lie, to cheat"—to do anything to promote world communism. Borrowing from a popular movie series—*Star Wars* (1977) and *The Empire Strikes Back* (1980)—Reagan branded the USSR the **"Evil Empire."** He took the lead in criticizing the USSR for its threats of a Czechoslovakia-like invasion unless the Polish government imposed martial law in December 1981, and for shooting Korean Air Lines flight 007 out of the sky, as we saw in Chapter 10.

The Reagan administration also tried to "spend the USSR into the ground." Working on the assumption that the Soviet government would try to maintain the gains achieved in the 1970s, and thus try to match American spending, the administration embarked on a program of massive and rapid increases in military spending. Potentially the most expensive program was the Strategic Defense Initiative (SDI), the space-based defence scheme we looked at in Chapter 4.

Huge quantities of military assistance were funnelled through Pakistan to the **mujahideen**, the fighters opposing the Soviet occupation army in Afghanistan. Included in this aid were

---

* Indeed, the pressure began shortly after the election. With the Algerian government acting as a go-between, an agreement was reached between Iran and the U.S. on 19 January 1981, the day before Reagan's inauguration. The hostages would be released in exchange for unfreezing several billion dollars of seized Iranian assets in the United States. But another factor prompted Iran to come to an agreement: Reagan's transition team had left no doubt that the new administration would launch a military attack against Teheran if the hostages were not returned.

advanced Stinger surface-to-air missiles, which effectively eliminated Soviet air superiority in Afghanistan and dramatically increased Soviet casualties. Indeed, many American officials spoke openly of the SAMs sent to Afghanistan as "pay-back time" for the Soviet support of Vietnam in the 1960s that had cost so many American lives.

## The End of the Cold War

The Soviet Union did not react as the Reagan administration had anticipated: the Kremlin did not try to match American spending. But the result was nonetheless the same. The USSR bent to the assertion of American power, and eventually collapsed as a consequence of its own internal contradictions and weaknesses.

As the pressure was tightened by the Reagan administration in the early 1980s, internal quarrels within the USSR were already leading some in the Soviet leadership to question the wisdom of the expansionist policies of the Brezhnev era. The various friends and allies of the USSR proved to be a serious drain on the Soviet treasury. These "ruble-suckers" (as they were rather rudely called) remained on the margins of the international economy. Countries like Vietnam, Cambodia, Afghanistan, Yemen, Cuba, and Nicaragua were forcefully excluded from the capitalist economy, and thus offered the USSR few tangible benefits other than "friendly space." Moreover, economic growth in the USSR itself had come to a virtual standstill, in large part because of the massive spending on the military. The demand for consumer goods, however, increased dramatically, far exceeding the capacity of the centrally planned Soviet economy to meet. Finally, the increasing casualties in Afghanistan were having the same impact in the USSR that the Vietnam casualties had had in the United States 20 years earlier. As the bodies of their children began coming home, Soviet citizens began to question what they were dying for, and the Soviet leadership had no better answer than the American leadership had had in the 1960s.

When Brezhnev finally died in November 1982, he was succeeded by Yuri Andropov, who had headed the KGB. Although Andropov was mortally ill when he took power, his short time in office marked a decisive break with the Brezhnev era.

Likewise, on the American side, there was a change as well. Reagan began to soften his anti-Soviet rhetoric after the shootdown of KAL 007 in September 1983. Beth A. Fischer has argued convincingly that Reagan became increasingly concerned about the possibility that nuclear war could result from East-West rivalry. His fears of nuclear war were heightened by two other events during the autumn of 1983: in October, he watched a preview of the made-for-TV movie *The Day After*, a realistic portrayal of the effects of a nuclear war on a Kansas town; and in November, there was a nuclear scare involving a massive NATO exercise called "Able Archer 83."* According to Fischer, Reagan was deeply

---

* Able Archer 83 was a huge NATO exercise involving a scenario in which there was a nuclear exchange with the USSR. Because the Soviet Union's own military plans called for a strike against the West during military exercises, some KGB agents became convinced that the United States was planning a strike against the USSR using the cover of Able Archer. Serious war preparations were undertaken on the Soviet side before it became apparent that NATO was not intending to launch a strike against the USSR.

affected by both events and changed his attitude toward the Soviet Union, embracing a more conciliatory approach.[24]

But the full effect of the new era in Soviet-American relations would not be seen until March 1985 when the official Andropov had named as his second-in-command, Mikhail S. Gorbachev, came to power.[*] Gorbachev sought to transform the domestic condition of the USSR through the twin policies of *perestroika* (restructuring of the economy), and *glasnost* (greater openness in politics). In foreign affairs, Gorbachev embraced what was called **"new thinking,"** in effect a rejection of the Cold War divisions between East and West. "New thinking" involved seeking arms control agreements with the United States; withdrawing Soviet troops and/or financial support from countries like Afghanistan, Vietnam, and Cuba; and normalizing relations with China. Most radically, new thinking included letting go of the countries of Eastern Europe in 1989 when the Berlin Wall, that symbol of East-West division, was breached and one by one the communist regimes in those countries were swept away by reformers.

By this time, there had also been a change of regime in Washington, as Reagan was succeeded by his vice-president, George Bush, in the 1988 presidential elections. A former CIA director, Bush proved both cooperative and receptive to Gorbachev's desires to change the USSR. By August 1990, Cold War enmity had given way to cooperation: the Soviet foreign minister, Eduard Shevardnadze, and the American secretary of state, James Baker, actively collaborated on international measures to be taken in response to the Iraqi invasion of Kuwait. The final acts in the end of East-West division were played out in the early 1990s: the dissolution of the USSR in December 1991, and the decisions, taken by both Russia and the United States in 1994, to "de-target" each other by officially reprogramming their nuclear warheads to fall into the ocean.

## EAST/WEST DIVISION: AN ASSESSMENT

For much of the second half of the 20th century, world politics was dominated by the East/West division. The struggle for power and dominance by the United States and the Soviet Union seesawed back and forth for nearly half a century. Each superpower's efforts to gain the upper hand produced a reaction on the other side.

In the end, the country with the strongest economy prevailed. Despite the rough equivalence of their populations, the USSR was incapable of matching, much less surpassing, the United States on any measurable criterion. In size and diversity of economy, technological prowess, access to capital, and exploitation of natural resources, the United States was able to spend massively on both "guns" and "butter"—and weather a succession of financial and domestic political crises while doing so. By contrast, massive Soviet military spending in the 1970s resulted in huge shortages in both consumer goods and agricultural produce, causing the USSR to succumb to what Paul Kennedy calls **imperial overstretch**—the tendency of great powers to bite off, as it were, more than their power resources permit them to chew.[25]

---

[*] Andropov died in office in February 1984 at the age of 70, and was succeeded by Konstantin Chernenko, a 70-year old member of the Politburo. Chernenko himself lasted but 13 months in office before dying.

Nor could the USSR match American political unity. Throughout the Cold War period, a succession of U.S. administrations pursued policies that were deeply divisive, and indeed contributed to the dramatic growth of a huge underclass in the United States. But as a political formation, the United States remained impressively united, despite deep cleavages of class and race. By contrast, the USSR demonstrated its essential fragility: once reformers took over and resolved not to use the coercive agencies of the state inherited from the Stalinist era, the unity of the Union of Soviet Socialist Republics and its alliance crumbled. Not only did the long-time "allies" of the USSR engage in an unseemly rush to the West, eagerly pleading to join the European Union and the North Atlantic Treaty Organization; but in December 1991 the USSR itself split up into 15 different republics. The only link remaining between them was a loose intergovernmental organization known as the Commonwealth of Independent States (CIS). Moreover, in most of the **successor states**, the strong governments of the communist era have been replaced by quintessentially weak state apparatuses, often deeply penetrated by criminals and speculators.

## CONCLUSION

The rivalry between the U.S. and the USSR during this period quite literally dominated the politics of the rest of the world. Few states were able to avoid the impact of this rivalry. Many who actively threw their lot in with one side or the other found their own domestic politics and economy deeply affected by the rivalry—and its eventual outcome. Not even those who actively tried to avoid the rivalry were able to do so, as both great powers insisted on drawing as many small states as possible into the vortex. Moreover, as we shall see in the next chapter, the East/West division had a deep and powerful impact on another division that developed at the same time—the North/South divide.

## *Keyword File*

| | |
|---|---|
| Cold War | Truman Doctrine |
| Bretton Woods | Containment |
| Hegemonic stability theory | Marshall Plan |
| Dumbarton Oaks | Berlin blockade |
| Yalta | Vandenberg Resolution |
| Potsdam | Article 5 |
| Sphere of influence | Trigger clause |
| Buffer zone | "Loss" of China |
| Warsaw uprising | McCarthyism |
| Iron curtain | NSC-68 |
| Capitalist encirclement | Hot pursuit |

| | |
|---|---|
| Korean War | Domino theory |
| "Pactomania" | Gulf of Tonkin resolution |
| Suez crisis | "Ho Chi Minh trail" |
| Khrushchev's "secret speech" | Détente |
| De-Stalinization | Camp David Accords |
| Great Leap Forward | "Great Satan" |
| Nuclear monopoly | Iranian hostage crisis |
| Missile gap | "Evil Empire" |
| Bay of Pigs | *Mujahideen* |
| Surgical strike | *Perestroika* |
| "Nonperson" | *Glasnost* |
| "Hot line" | "New thinking" |
| MIRV | Imperial overstretch |
| Blue water navy | Successor states |

## For Further Exploration

### HARD COPY

Bradsher, Henry S. *Afghanistan and the Soviet Union* (expanded ed.). Durham, NC: Duke University Press, 1985.

Gaddis, John Lewis. *The United States and the Origins of the Cold War, 1941–1947.* New York: Columbia University Press, 1972.

Hobsbawm, Eric. *Age of Extremes: The Short Twentieth Century, 1914–1991.* London: Little, Brown, 1994.

Karnow, Stanley. *Vietnam: A History.* New York: Viking, 1983.

Kennedy, Paul. *The Rise and Fall of the Great Powers: Economic Change and Military Conflict from 1500 to 2000.* London: Unwin Hyman, 1988.

Shawcross, William. *Sideshow: Kissinger, Nixon and the Destruction of Cambodia.* New York: Simon and Schuster, 1979.

Tuchman, Barbara. *Stilwell and the American Experience in China, 1911–1945.* New York: Macmillan, 1970.

Whiting, Alan S. *China Crosses the Yalu: The Decision to Enter the Korean War.* New York: Macmillan, 1960.

WEBLINKS

**http://cwihp.si.edu**

Home page of the Cold War International History Project at the Woodrow Wilson Center; excellent resources for Cold War history

**http://www.saclant.nato.int/nato.html**

Home page for the North Atlantic Treaty Organization, plus useful links to each of the member countries

## *Notes to Chapter 15*

1. Winston S. Churchill, *The Second World War*, vol. 6: *Triumph and Tragedy* (London, 1954), 197–98.

2. Quoted in Walter LaFeber, *America, Russia, and the Cold War, 1945–1990*, 6th ed. (New York: McGraw-Hill, 1991), 14.

3. Jonathan Haslam, "Stalin's war or peace," in Niall Ferguson, ed., *Virtual History: Alternatives and Counterfactuals* (London: Picador, 1997), 360–61.

4. Denis Smith, *Diplomacy of Fear: Canada and the Cold War, 1941–1948* (Toronto: University of Toronto Press, 1988).

5. James Eayrs, *In Defence of Canada*, vol. 4: *Growing Up Allied* (Toronto: University of Toronto Press, 1980).

6. LaFeber, *America, Russia, and the Cold War*, 49.

7. See X [George Kennan], "The sources of Soviet conduct," *Foreign Affairs* 25 (July 1947), 566–82.

8. According to evidence released from the Foreign Ministry archives of the former Soviet Union: cited in Haslam, "Stalin's war or peace," 359.

9. See Lewis Purifoy, *Harry Truman's China Policy: McCarthyism and the Diplomacy of Hysteria, 1947–1951* (New York, 1976).

10. Quoted in LaFeber, *America, Russia, and the Cold War*, 96–97.

11. Norman Harper, *A Great and Powerful Friend: A Study of Australian-American Relations between 1900 and 1975* (St Lucia, QLD: University of Queensland Press, 1987); the text of the ANZUS treaty is reproduced in Coral Bell, *Australia's Alliance Options*, Australian Foreign Policy Papers 1 (Canberra: Australian National University, 1991), Appendix 1.

12. See Joseph T. Jockel, *No Boundaries Upstairs: Canada, the United States and the Origins of North American Air Defence, 1945–1958* (Vancouver, BC: UBC Press, 1987).

13. Quoted in Jonathan D. Spence, *The Search for Modern China* (London: Hutchinson, 1990), 576.

14. See Fen Hampson, *Unguided Missiles: How America Buys Its Weapons* (New York: W.W. Norton, 1989).

15. Edgar M. Bottome, *The Balance of Terror: A Guide to the Arms Race* (Boston: Beacon Press, 1971), 120, 158.

16. Irving L. Janis, *Victims of Groupthink: A Psychological Study of Foreign-Policy Decisions and Fiascoes* (Boston: Houghton Mifflin, 1972), 14–49. For the CIA's own secret assessment, see http://www.seas.gwu.edu/nsarchive

17. Graham T. Allison, *Essence of Decision: Explaining the Cuban Missile Crisis* (Boston: Little, Brown, 1971); James A. Nathan, ed., *The Cuban Missile Crisis Revisited* (New York: St Martin's, 1992).

18. Donald M. Snow and Eugene Brown, *The Contours of Power* (New York: St Martin's Press, 1996), 218.

19. Interview, *Globe and Mail* (Toronto), 20 October 1997; see Ernest May and Philip Zelikow, eds., *The Kennedy Tapes: Inside the White House during the Cuban Missile Crisis* (Cambridge, MA: Harvard University Press, 1997).

20. For naval force comparisons, see North Atlantic Treaty Organization, *NATO and Warsaw Pact: Force Comparisons* (Brussels: NATO, 1982).

21. The most readable history of the Vietnam war is Stanley Karnow, *Vietnam: A History* (New York: Viking, 1983).

22. For an account of the Soviet intervention in Afghanistan, see Henry S. Bradsher, *Afghanistan and the Soviet Union*, exp. ed. (Durham, NC: Duke University Press, 1985).

23. For example, Ray Cline and Yonah Alexander, *Terrorism: The Soviet Connection* (New York: Crane, Russak, 1984).

24. Beth A. Fischer, *The Reagan Reversal: Foreign Policy and the End of the Cold War* (Columbia, MO: University of Missouri Press, 1997), 102–43.

25. Paul Kennedy, *The Rise and Fall of the Great Powers: Economic Change and Military Conflict from 1500 to 2000* (London: Unwin Hyman, 1988), 513–14.

# Division *by* Compass Point: North *and* South

If the East/West division disappeared with the end of the Cold War, the other fault line that marked global politics in the second half of the 20th century continues to divide the world. If the East/West divide was primarily ideological, the North/South divide was, and remains, primarily economic. It is a division between rich and poor, between those who have and those who do not, between those whose access to good things provides them with a comfortable life and those whose lives are marked by deprivation.

## THE ECONOMIC DIVIDE: DEFINING NORTH AND SOUTH

The usual way of defining this fault line is to divide the states of the world into "rich" and "poor." Although defining "poverty" and "richness" is difficult because these terms are so relative, we can come closer to an understanding of this dichotomy by reflecting on what some people have in abundance and what others lack. The rich states in contemporary world politics are endowed with diversified economies that feature a relatively small agricultural sector, considerable manufacturing production, and large service and "knowledge" sectors. They are the sources of technological developments, the result of wealth spent by both the public and private sectors on research and development (R&D). These countries are the centres for international banking and finance; they serve as transportation hubs for air travel and sea-borne goods. These activities add high value to raw materials, thus creating considerable wealth.

Because of the low birth rates and low population growth rates of these countries, they are well able to ensure that the people who live there enjoy lives marked by access to the *necessities*, the *conveniences*, and the *luxuries* of life. Among the necessities we include predictable and plentiful supplies of food, whether by subsistence farming or in a money economy where food must be purchased; supplies of potable water; appropriate systems for disposing of waste and garbage; appropriate shelter from the elements; and basic security against physical harm. Conveniences of life include universal education from kindergarten through to postsecondary education; relatively stable employment; a reasonably harmonious natural environment free from pollutants and other threats to health; basic medical care; access to social services provided by the community; predictable supplies of power; and well-established systems of transportation and communications. The luxuries include single-family dwellings, multiple automobiles, electronic gadgets of all sorts, highly developed social welfare systems; and huge amounts of leisure time and leisure "toys" such as boats, campers/caravans, snowmobiles, or even personal aircraft.

The poor countries, by contrast, tend to be agricultural and not developed or industrialized. They tend to have little manufacturing capacity and virtually no "knowledge" sector. There is little indigenous R&D. These countries tend to be spokes rather than hubs; transportation, financial, and knowledge peripheries rather than centres. What economic surpluses these countries generate tend to come from providing unprocessed food or raw materials from forests or mines to other countries. In short, the economic activity in these countries tends to add little value. The problems of small surplus are compounded, however, by the tendency to have very high birthrates, with a correspondingly high percentage of young people. As a result, the governments of such countries often cannot provide for the needs and wants of their growing populations. In some poor countries, even the necessities of life are often simply not available. Food supplies are unpredictable, occasionally resulting in famine and large-scale deaths from starvation, as occurred in China in the early 1960s, Ethiopia in the mid-1980s, and Somalia in the early 1990s. Water supplies are often polluted, sometimes because of a lack of rudimentary waste disposal techniques. Shelter is often rude—corrugated metal or cardboard—and useless against typhoons, monsoons, or hurricanes. Personal insecurity is high. In many places, the conveniences taken for granted in the North—electrification, telephone service, paved roads, tapped water, underground sewage systems—are often only partially provided: television, for example, may only be available on a communal basis. In urban areas, the quality of life tends to be degraded by overcrowding, persistent noise and pollution, and limited social services. Sprawling cities that lack well-developed transit systems may require daily commutes of many hours in length. In such communities, the luxury of owning a family car or a house is unknown.

Over the years, we have called this dichotomy by different names. During the Cold War era, when the colonial possessions of the European and American powers began receiving their independence, it was common to speak of the different "worlds" of development, a usage popularized by Frantz Fanon. In this usage, the **First World** comprised the rich countries of the West (usually characterized as the "industrialized" or "developed" countries); the **Second World** included the rich countries of the East. All the rest were the *tiers monde*, or **Third World**—a deliberate echo of the *Tiers-État*, the group (or "estate") in the Estates-General of prerevolutionary France which represented the majority of the people. These countries were often called "underdeveloped," "developing," or "LDCs" ("less developed countries"). (And when the poverty gap *within* the Third World deepened in the 1960s, people started talking of the LLDCs—the least developed countries; these countries, it was said, occupied a **Fourth World**.)

*But the term "Third World" was eventually rejected because of its intimations of inferiority: to be third is to be ranked "last and lowest behind the 'First' and 'Second World' countries"*

But the term "Third World" was eventually rejected because of its intimations of inferiority: to be third is to be ranked "last and lowest *behind* the 'First' and 'Second World' countries" as Marianne H. Marchand reminds us.[1] The terms North and South increasingly began to be employed instead, even though the geographic division is not entirely perfect. As will be evident, some of the states of the North are south of the equator (such as Australia and New Zealand), and some of the poorest states of the South are well north of that dividing line (such as Afghanistan). And some economies, such as Hong Kong and Singapore, simply do not fit cleanly at either point of the compass.

As with all code, these categories provide us with a useful way to paint politics in broad brushstrokes and reduce complexities to convenient shorthand. But like other code, we also have to recognize that these compass-point terms either obscure or mask entirely distinctions that are important for an understanding of the patterns of world politics.

In particular, it means recognizing that a geographic compass point is only useful as a predictor of poverty and deprivation at an aggregate and abstract level. In other words, what kind of life would one likely have if one were an *average* Vietnamese or Nigerian, an *average* Mexican or Indonesian, or an *average* American or Australian? One can answer such a question using such aggregate statistics as Gross National Product (GNP) or **purchasing power parity** (PPP).* Ranked by GNP per capita, the United States and Australia are ranked as high-income economies (over US$9300 a year per capita); Mexico and Indonesia as middle-income economies ($766–$9300); and Vietnam and Nigeria as low-income economies (less than $766). But while aggregate statistics give us a reasonable picture of the

---

* GNP per capita is the total of all goods and services produced in a country, divided by that country's population. While it has some utility as an aggregate statistic, GNP per capita tends to distort economic reality. For example, it does not measure well the "invisible" economic output of women, and it can only guess at the output of the informal economies of many countries. Moreover, it inflates the income individuals actually have at their disposal. PPP, by contrast, tries to come closer to providing a comparative measure of international standards of living by comparing the purchasing power of a country's currency in that country.

average condition of a political community, we have to remember that averages often hide those at the upper and lower ends. It is important to remember that there are individuals in the South who live in greater luxury than many in the North; and there are those in the North whose lives are marked by deprivation and insecurity that is often worse than one would find in many places in the South.

## THE "WORLDS" OF THE SOUTH

In Chapter 15, we noted that the South is somewhat of a default category in contemporary world politics: it comprises all those countries which are not part of the North. However, although we speak of "the South" in the singular, in fact the South is a conglomeration of hugely disparate communities, divided along numerous lines. One cleavage is wealth itself: the South includes what the World Bank describes as upper middle income countries like Argentina, Brazil, Chile, Malaysia, Mexico, South Africa, and South Korea, along with lower middle income countries like Angola, Ecuador, and Indonesia, and low-income countries like Congo, Mozambique, and India. It also includes countries that are technically high income on account of their huge oil revenues, but are nonetheless considered to be part of the South: Brunei, Kuwait, Qatar, and the United Arab Emirates.

Other cleavages include religion, language, culture, and historical experience. Consider the degree to which the communities of the South have had very different histories—beyond the single commonality of being colonized or dominated by European peoples. For example, the communities of Central and Latin America shrugged off European empire at the outset of the 19th century, but did not develop like other **settler societies** such as Australia, Canada, and New Zealand. The countries of Asia, which became independent in the immediate aftermath of the Second World War, were immediately immersed in the Cold War. This had a profound impact on the development of their economies, as we will see below. The countries of Africa, as we saw in Chapter 13, were generally colonized in a rush, and decolonized in no less a rush. This has meant that the patterns of economic development have differed markedly across the international community, as the following brief sketches suggest.

### Tigers and Dragons: The "Asian Miracle"

We begin with the economies of the Asia-Pacific, since of all the economies of the South, these have shown the most persistent growth over the long term. Between 1960 and 1980, Hong Kong, Singapore, South Korea, and Taiwan all showed an annual average growth rate in their Gross Domestic Product (GDP) of well over 9 per cent. Because of the rapid rate of industrialization, these countries came to be known as the **newly industrializing countries** (NICs), or **dynamic Asian economies** (DAEs) if one wanted to include Taiwan without offending the sensibilities of the People's Republic of China by calling Taiwan a "country." More colloquially, they are called the Asian "tigers" or "dragons" because of their aggressive economic growth. Since 1980, other countries in the region—particularly Brunei, Indonesia, Malaysia, the Philippines, and Thailand—have also showed similar patterns of economic expansion.

What explains the growth of these countries? Part of the reason lies in the active pursuit of the kind of economic nationalist policies we surveyed in Chapter 12—where the protective state takes an active hand in the management of the national economy. Many protective states encourage a strategy of **import-substitution**, in which either local producers or subsidiaries of multinational corporations are encouraged by high tariff walls to satisfy domestic demand by establishing manufacturing plants within the country. On the other hand, the governments in South Korea and Taiwan embraced an **export-oriented strategy**, in which the government nurtures and protects selected industries and industrial sectors, not to meet domestic demand but to compete on world markets. This is the major difference in the case of South Korea and Taiwan. A second reason was the high rate of domestic savings achieved in each of these economies. In 1990, for example, the rate of gross domestic savings in Hong Kong, South Korea, and Taiwan was around 35 per cent of GDP; in Singapore, it was 40 per cent. Tight fiscal policies and a deep aversion to budget deficits encouraged these high levels of savings.[2]

Finally, as Richard Stubbs has argued, a crucial ingredient for the growth of Asian economies in the 1980s and 1990s was the long-term impact of the Korean and Vietnam wars in the 1950s and 1960s. In each case, the United States was prompted to channel huge quantities of aid to the various regimes around the Asia–Pacific that it regarded as important for its global defence against what was seen as Soviet expansionism. Stubbs argues that the benefits were both direct—upward of US$8.3 billion in direct economic and military assistance was pumped into the South Korean economy by the United States between 1953 and 1969—and indirect—the economies of both Malaysia and Singapore benefitted from American strategic concerns, even though these two countries were not directly involved. The Vietnam war also created a huge market for Taiwanese and Korean goods, most purchased with the funds that were being provided by the United States. Finally, Stubbs points out the degree to which the demands of the Cold War strengthened the governmental apparatus in each of these countries, creating "strong states" both willing and able to take a key role in shaping the domestic economy in the name of national security.[3]

## Opening the Door: China and the Global Economy

China constitutes a special member of this group of "tigers" and "dragons." In the 1950s and 1960s, the Chinese government made few efforts to engage the international capitalist economy. Some interaction was made necessary by the giant famines created by the dramatic failure of the Great Leap Forward; China purchased wheat from both Canada and Australia. Some foreign exchange was earned by selling water and fresh produce to Hong Kong, then still a British colony. Some trade was carried on within the communist bloc. The government in Beijing ran a modest development assistance program in Africa. But essentially, the Chinese economy was closed to the world.

China's economic isolation was also a result of another Maoist initiative, the Great Proletarian Cultural Revolution, or more colloquially, the **Cultural Revolution**. This was an effort by Mao to maintain the revolutionary spirit that was quickly fading as communism in China became routinized and bureaucratized. Launched in 1966, the

Cultural Revolution did indeed bring back the revolutionary spirit: numerous libraries, religious shrines, and other cultural centres were destroyed; universities were closed down for being "antirevolutionary" and university presidents were dressed in dunce caps and sent to clean the toilets. Students in the youth wing of the party, the "Red Guards," took the lead in helping to purge antirevolutionary elements and in preaching the wisdom of "Mao Zedong Thought" (as the collected political wisdom of Chairman Mao was officially called). The Cultural Revolution was marked by purges, forced "self-criticism" sessions, and a major shake-up of every established institution in China. The luckier victims of these purges merely got "sent down" to the countryside to work in the rice paddies— "to get some dirt under their fingernails" was the way it was often put. Others less fortunate were hounded from their jobs; tens of thousands were sent to prison; many more thousands were simply killed outright, or frequently prompted to commit suicide (among them one of the sons of Deng Xiaoping, who would rise to prominence as China's leader in the 1980s).

Like another of Mao's ideas, the Great Leap Forward, the Cultural Revolution ended up producing nothing but social and economic dislocation. By 1969, the disruption to the economy had produced a severe reaction within the Chinese leadership. Moderate voices reasserted themselves, prompting Mao's heir apparent, Lin Biao, to try and stage a *coup d'état* in September 1971 (when it failed, Lin tried to flee to the Soviet Union; he was killed when his plane crashed en route).

The leadership that eventually emerged after Mao's death in September 1976 was committed to a very different economic course. Beginning in 1978, the Chinese government under Deng Xiaoping pursued an **"Open Door" policy** that was marked by increasing connections with the capitalist economy. **Special economic zones** were created, and foreign investment, even from Taiwan, was welcomed. Hong Kong played a central role in this strategy, providing a gateway for a burgeoning export trade to the West. In short order, the economy was transformed from the command economy of the 1950s and 1960s to a more mixed economy. The consequences of this were two decades of considerable economic growth, a developing interconnectedness with the global economy, and a growing importance as a trader, particularly with the United States. This spurt of growth created considerable domestic problems, which erupted most visibly in the student protests during the spring of 1989, when the central square in Beijing was clogged for several weeks with protestors. When Tiananmen Square was eventually cleared by the army on the night of 4 June 1989— killing hundreds in the process—the Beijing government was widely criticized, and a number of countries imposed sanctions on China in response. But the **Tiananmen massacre** did not affect the continuing economic integration of China into the Asia-Pacific economy.

## Oil Shocks: The OPEC Countries

In previous chapters we have seen how particular commodities can play a crucial role in world politics at different times. Perhaps the single most important commodity in global politics throughout the 20th century has been crude oil or petroleum. Petroleum has been critical in the mechanization of warfare and for manufacturing, transportation, and electricity generation. Petroleum derivatives are used to make plastics, fertilizers, medicines, and a range of other products crucial to an industrialized economy. It is therefore little wonder that world politics has been deeply affected by the production and supply of this commodity. In particular, production has been highly concentrated: the world's two largest producers of crude oil happen to be the two superpowers which emerged after the Second World War. Russia produces approximately 12 million barrels a day, the United States about 9 million barrels, and Saudi Arabia some 3.5 million barrels. These three countries account for almost half of the world's daily production of approximately 50 million barrels of crude oil each day.

Because both superpowers have never been dependent on foreign sources of oil in the way that an earlier generation of great powers were, global oil politics have tended to focus on foreign supplies to the lesser powers of the contemporary period—Britain, France, Germany, Italy, and Japan. Certainly the European powers, in collaboration with American oil companies, managed to ensure that their supplies from the Middle East were as cheap as possible.* Indeed, until the early 1970s, one of the unique features of the petroleum industry was that it was totally controlled by seven "oil majors," often called the **Seven Sisters**—five American multinational corporations (Chevron, Exxon, Gulf, Mobil, and Texaco), one British firm (British Petroleum), and one Anglo-Dutch MNC (Shell). These firms paid a per-barrel tax to host governments but otherwise controlled production, refining, delivery, and marketing. In 1960 the oil-producing countries organized themselves into a cartel, the Organization of Petroleum Exporting Countries (OPEC),** to try and coordinate production. However, the oligopolistic control of the oil majors meant that the per-barrel price was kept depressed throughout the 1960s.

The first challenge to the very comfortable status quo enjoyed by the oil majors (and, of course, Western consumers) came after Mu'ammar al-Qadhafi came to power in a *coup d'état* in Libya in September 1969. Qadhafi's revolutionary regime nationalized a range of businesses, including banks. The government extracted a new deal from the majors that dramatically increased Libya's oil revenues. Likewise, Qadhafi encouraged other oil exporters to begin to negotiate higher prices and more control over production; modest gains were made in 1971 and 1972. More importantly, however, Qadhafi urged other Arab oil producers to consider using the dependence on oil of parts of the North—Europe and Japan—as a weapon in the Arab struggle with Israel.

The opportunity to do just that came when Egypt and Syria launched a surprise attack on Israel on the Jewish sacred holiday of Yom Kippur. The **Yom Kippur war** (also known as the Ramadan war, after the month in the Muslim calendar) provided the impetus for the

---

* For example, when Anglo-Iranian Oil Company was nationalized by the Iranian government of Muhammad Mossadegh in April 1951, Anglo-Iranian closed down the refinery and made an effort to pressure Iran by organizing a worldwide boycott of Iranian oil. Eventually Iran negotiated a compromise agreement with an international consortium of oil companies, including Anglo-Iranian.

** By 1973, membership included Algeria, Ecuador, Gabon, Indonesia, Iran, Iraq, Kuwait, Libya, Nigeria, Qatar, Saudi Arabia, United Arab Emirates, and Venezuela. Ecuador withdrew in 1993.

Arab producers (which had their own organization, the Organization of Arab Petroleum Exporting Countries (OAPEC)), to declare an **oil embargo** to all nations friendly to Israel. The embargo revealed the degree of Western European and Japanese dependence on Middle Eastern oil, with the result that in the autumn of 1973, OPEC raised the price of crude from US$3 to US$12 a barrel.

The result was a huge increase in wealth for oil producers. In 1973, OPEC revenues were US$27 billion; in 1974, they were US$125 billion. All major oil exporting countries benefited from the rise in the world price, not only OPEC members, but also other oil-exporting countries of the South that were not members of the cartel (Angola, Bahrain, Congo, Mexico, Oman, Syria, and Trinidad and Tobago).

The windfall increases in revenues during the 1970s (augmented even more by a second **oil shock** in 1979, when the price per barrel jumped to US$40) in effect set oil exporters in a class by themselves in the South. But the effect of the huge cash surpluses did not change the overall condition very much. In the sparsely populated states of the Arabian peninsula, oil revenues allowed governments to rapidly develop an urban and developed infrastructure. But there has been no transformation in the structure of the Gulf economies comparable to the structural changes seen in the Asia-Pacific. In both Iraq and Iran, oil revenues radically transformed the political economy. In Iran, as we noted in Chapter 15, oil revenues enabled the shah to spend on development, which in turn created the seeds of his own ouster as increasing Westernization spurred religious opposition. In Iraq, the regime of Saddam Hussein encouraged increasing dependence on oil wealth, with the result that the traditional strength of the Iraqi economy—its agriculture—was allowed to decline. In more populous countries, notably Nigeria and Indonesia, the results of massive increases in oil wealth were more mixed.

Nassau A. Adams has argued that the huge new-found wealth had little longer-term impact on the economic development of these states because their governments, suddenly

*Much of the wealth simply ended up back in the North— in the pockets of megaproject contractors, arms manufacturers, and commercial bankers.*

awash in **petrodollars**, made little effort to spend in ways that would create sustainable economic growth.[4] Instead, the tendency was to spend massive amounts on capital projects, often wasting millions of dollars. Governments also purchased massive quantities of arms; indeed, Iran and Iraq spent much of the 1980s fighting each other. After eight years, hundreds of thousands of lives, and the expenditure of hundreds of millions of dollars, this ruinous war was essentially fought to a draw.* Other oil-exporting countries which were not in a capital-surplus position decided to borrow heavily, with the result that by the early 1980s, Algeria, Ecuador, Indonesia, Nigeria, and Venezuela had accumulated a massive debt of US$80 billion, much of it owed to private banks in the North. Paradoxically, then, much of the wealth simply ended up back in the North— in the pockets of megaproject contractors, arms manufacturers, and commercial bankers.

---

* War between Iran and Iraq broke out on 22 September 1980; a ceasefire was finally declared on 20 August 1988. For a good survey of the numerous causes of this war, see Tareq Y. Ismael, "The Iraq-Iran conflict," *Behind the Headlines* 39:3 (1981–82).

## The Debt Crisis and After: The Caribbean Basin and Latin America

The countries of the Caribbean Basin, Central America, and Latin America generally have economies that are less industrialized than the Asian tigers, but are nonetheless in the range of middle-income economies. The largest economy of the Caribbean Basin, Mexico, is diversified and rapidly industrializing, and has a burgeoning trade with the United States and Canada as a consequence of the 1993 North American Free Trade Agreement (NAFTA). Mexican acceptance of that pact marked a dramatic reversal in traditional attitudes toward economic integration with the United States. Mexican policy-makers had traditionally sought to insulate Mexico from the United States both politically and economically. This was partly a function of history: the United States seized a great deal of Mexican territory in the 1840s, and Americans played an active and often interventionist part in Mexican politics, particularly in the decade after the revolution of 1910. As a result, a succession of presidents from the party that has governed Mexico since 1928—the *Partido Revolucionario Institucional* (Institutional Revolutionary Party) or PRI (pronounced "pree")—erected nationalist barriers to economic intercourse with the United States. In 1938, for example, Lázaro Cárdenas expropriated the oil industry and created *Petróleos Mexicanos* (PEMEX). The closed nature of the Mexican economy continued unabated throughout the post-1945 period: import licences were imposed on virtually every product, and duties of 100 per cent were common. Indeed, Mexico's attitude toward the international economy was perhaps best indicated by the explicit decision of José López Portillo in 1980 to keep Mexico out of the General Agreement on Tariffs and Trade (GATT), and his decision to nationalize Mexico's banks in 1982.

However, the political and economic elites were prompted to rethink their commitment to economic nationalism and statist intervention by a number of developments. The most important of these was the debt crisis of 1982. Throughout the 1970s, private banks, primarily in the United States, had loaned large sums to Latin American countries on the dubious (and quite ahistorical) assumption that countries do not go bankrupt. In general their lending exposure had far exceeded their capital: for example, American banks with a combined capital of $29 billion had together lent Argentina, Brazil, and Mexico a total of US$31 billion. In the case of some banks—BankAmerica, Chase Manhattan, Chemical Bank, Citicorp, and Crocker National—loans exceeded 150 per cent of capital. The Latin American countries had little difficulty servicing these debts until American monetary policy shifted after the second oil shock in 1979. Paul Volcker, the new chair of the board of governors of the central bank of the United States, the Federal Reserve System (or simply "the Fed"), decided to combat high inflation rates by sharply decreasing the money supply and sharply driving up interest rates. All of a sudden, the debt became unserviceable. In August 1982, the Mexican minister of finance announced that Mexico could no longer make payments on its debt. This posed a considerable threat to the overexposed American banks. Moreover, if other countries in the South followed the Mexican lead, these banks would face bankruptcy, which would throw the entire international financial system into a crisis.

A rescue package was quickly put together by the United States and the other members of the **Group of Ten**. The G–10 agreed that additional liquidity should be provided to the indebted states, mainly by increasing the IMF's line of credit from 6.4 billion in **Special Drawing Rights** (SDRs) to SDR 17 billion.[*] Debts were rescheduled and the IMF was assigned the task of making sure that debtor countries restructured their domestic expenditures so that they could pay as much as possible to their creditors. The rescue package sought to avoid a collapse of the system, even though, as Matthew Shepherd has pointed out, the price paid for the reckless lending of the American banks was exceedingly high. American taxpayers ended up paying massively for the bailout, and the harsh terms of repayment imposed by the IMF forced Latin American countries to slash their imports from the U.S. This had considerable unemployment effects in the United States.[5] But in Mexico, the debt crisis had the effect of radically altering how the elites conceived of the relationship between the Mexican economy and the international system.

In addition, other factors were changing Mexican attitudes. The shift in the centre of economic gravity in the United States from the "Rust Belt" in the northeast to the "Sun Belt" in the south had ripple effects in Mexico's northern regions; the development of petroleum reserves turned Mexico into an oil exporter; and in the 1980s a broader ideological movement emerged toward neoconservative policy options such as deregulation and privatization. Small steps were made during the presidency of Miguel de la Madrid Hurtado: in 1986, Mexico joined GATT, and in 1987, Mexico and the United States signed a "framework agreement" to hold discussions on trade. But it was not until Carlos Salinas de Gortari became president in December 1988 that policy took a pronounced turn.

Salinas renegotiated Mexico's debt, cut public expenditures, privatized or eliminated over 800 state enterprises, denationalized 18 large banks, and reduced trade barriers. Inflation fell from 160 per cent in 1987 to 10 per cent in 1992. Foreign investment doubled. Manufacturing exports increased dramatically. But the wealth created by this industrialization was not well distributed, with the result that many Mexicans continue to live in poverty despite the aggregate indicators. Moreover, the economy has been shaken by crisis and political instability. The 1994 elections were marked by the assassination of the PRI candidate, Luis Donaldo Colosio Murrieta; he was replaced by his campaign manager, Ernesto Zedillo Ponce de Léon. After Zedillo assumed the presidency in December 1994, foreign investors responded to a government decision to devalue the peso by taking their capital

---

[*] The G–10 actually consists of 11 states—the original ten (Belgium, Britain, Canada, France, Germany, Italy, Japan, Netherlands, Sweden, and the United States) plus Switzerland, which joined in 1984. There are also four "non-state participants": the IMF, the Organisation for Economic Cooperation and Development (OECD), the Bank for International Settlements (BIS), and the Commission of the European Union. The G–10 oversees the International Monetary Fund's General Arrangements to Borrow (GAB), a supplementary loan agreement designed to increase the lending resources of the IMF.

The unit of account used by the IMF, the SDR has value a based on the weighted average value of five major currencies; today it is worth approximately US$1.45. Each member of the IMF is assigned an SDR subscription according to the size of its economy; a country's subscription determines its vote in IMF proceedings and how much foreign exchange it may withdraw from the fund.

out of Mexico, forcing the government to seek a US$50 billion loan from the United States and international financial institutions.

According to aggregate indicators, the smaller countries of Central America—Belize, Guatemala, Honduras, El Salvador, Nicaragua, Costa Rica, and Panama—are worse off than Mexico (although Costa Rica has a large middle class and enjoys a relatively high standard of living by Central and Latin American standards). In Nicaragua, Guatemala, and El Salvador, economic development in the 1980s was severely hampered by civil war. Even after a modicum of peace was achieved in the early 1990s following the end of the Cold War, the economies of these three countries continued to be marked by a dependence on agriculture and a concentration of land ownership in a tiny elite.

The islands of the Caribbean show a broad economic diversity. Some islands—Bahamas, Barbados, and Trinidad and Tobago—have generally high living standards, even if their economies are narrowly based. At the other end of the spectrum, the countries that divide the island of Hispaniola—Haiti and the Dominican Republic—are the poorest states in the region; indeed, Haiti is the poorest country in the hemisphere. Its economy has steadily shrunk over the 1990s; its unemployment rate is estimated to be approximately 40 to 50 per cent. Moreover, the already underdeveloped economy was further devastated as a result of the economic sanctions imposed by the Organization of American States (OAS) after Lieut.-Gen. Raoul Cédras seized power from the duly elected president, Jean-Bertrand Aristide, in September 1991.

Another economy severely affected by international sanctions is that of Cuba. Since the revolution that brought Fidel Castro to power in 1959, Cuba has been sanctioned by the United States government. While other countries in the hemisphere maintain relations with Cuba, and the Cuban president is routinely invited to the regular *Cumbre iberoamericana* (Latin American summit), the United States government takes care to exclude Cuba from anything that it organizes. Thus, for example, Cuba was the only country in the entire hemisphere that President Bill Clinton purposely did not invite to the Summit of the Americas, held in Miami in December 1994 to discuss hemispheric free trade.

The Guiana coast of northern South America is the only part of South America that was colonized by powers other than Spain and Portugal: the Netherlands, Britain, and France established colonies along the coast in the 17th century. Today, Suriname and Guyana are independent, but France still maintains its colony as the overseas *département* of *Guyane* (French Guiana). These countries are, however, much less developed than other former British, Dutch, and French colonies in the Caribbean basin; they rely primarily on forestry and mining.

The largest economies in South America—Brazil and Argentina—are relatively diversified, with considerable industrialization. However, in each of these countries, development coexists with poverty, in both rural and urban areas. Although much smaller in size, Chile's economy is one of the region's most robust: the traditional dependence on copper mining and production has been replaced by an economic base that is diversified between mining, industry, fishing, and agriculture. The smaller economies of Latin America range widely, from the predominantly agricultural economies of Paraguay, Uruguay, and Peru to the commodity-based economies of Bolivia, Colombia, Ecuador, and Venezuela.

The aggregate economic statistics do not include the economic impact of illegal drugs, even though the drug trade is an important aspect of the economies of the countries that

*The social, political, and economic distortions of the drug trade are far worse in the cultivating and transporting countries of the South than they are in the consuming countries of the North.*

grow coca (Peru, Bolivia, and Colombia) as well as those countries that lie between the coca fields and the consumers in the North. Drugs not only provide cash revenue to those involved in the cultivation, refinement, and transportation of these products, but their illegality creates huge distortions in the political economy of drug-producing countries. Indeed, it can be argued that the social, political, and economic distortions of the drug trade are far worse in the cultivating and transporting countries of the South than they

are in the consuming countries of the North. As we have noted elsewhere, the demand for these drugs in the North is so intense that profits are vast—thus bribery and corruption are the inevitable results.

## Islands Apart: The South Pacific

Most discussions of the South simply overlook the small island communities of the South Pacific. But the 13 states and nine territories differ considerably from other states of the South. The main difference is size. These countries are small in population and land area. For example, some 6 million Melanesians, Micronesians, and Polynesians occupy some 500 000 square kilometres. But these states control huge geographic areas—approximately 24 million square kilometres of ocean.

On the other hand, the economic conditions of these countries present in microcosm some of the structural difficulties facing all nations of the South. While the population is small, there are nonetheless shortages of land. There is still considerable subsistence farming and fishing. Social problems arise from the drift from rural areas to urban centres. Moreover, the island economies tend to depend on very narrow bases, though few are like Nauru, which has one of the narrowest based economies in the world. Nauru's economy rests on a single product, the phosphate found in the central plateau. While returns from phosphate mining make the 10 000 Nauruans among the richest people on Earth (on a per capita basis, at least), the deposits are expected to be exhausted within a decade. Moreover, the mining has made much of the island uninhabitable.

Other communities in the region have a slightly larger economic base. Most South Pacific countries depend on revenues from fishing (or licences granted to foreign fishing fleets operating in the huge exclusive economic zones); a limited range of agricultural produce, such as sugar, coconuts, or vanilla; revenues from the tourist trade from Australia, New Zealand, and North America; remittances from fellow nationals working in other countries; and development assistance funds from donors in the North (primarily Australia and New Zealand). While light manufacturing exists on some islands, and some countries such as Fiji have tried to woo foreign investment and manufacturing by creating tax-free zones, the capacity for industrialization and development over the longer term is limited. Part of the problem is simply distance: the population is too thinly spread, over too great a distance, on islands too far away from the main global shipping routes, making transportation costs for anything but the highest-value manufactured goods prohibitively expensive.

## The Diverse Subcontinent: South Asia

The region of South Asia extends from Afghanistan in the west to Myanmar (formerly Burma) in the east. It includes India, Pakistan, Bangladesh, Sri Lanka, Maldives, Bhutan, and Nepal. Two are among the world's most populous countries: India is the second-largest country in the world by population—nearly one billion people, 200 million fewer than China—and Bangladesh has over 128 million people, making it the eighth most populous country in the world. With about 900 people per km$^2$, Bangladesh is one of the most densely populated countries in the world.

This region is marked by extreme diversity. On the one hand, there is considerable poverty in each of the states of the region. Nepal, for example, is among the world's least developed economies: over 90 per cent of the workforce is engaged in agriculture, much of it subsistence; its principal foreign exchange earnings are derived from carpets, leather goods, tourism, and remittances from Gurkha soldiers working abroad.

Warfare has deeply affected development in the region. India and Pakistan came to independence in 1947 amid horrific interethnic massacres. In the decades since, the two countries have been in a state of cold hostility that has on occasion turned into hot war. Afghanistan's economy, not well developed to begin with, has been almost completely destroyed by nearly two decades of warfare, first against the Soviet Union and then civil war. Bangladesh, which was attached to Pakistan in 1947, suffered two decades of neglect at the hands of West Pakistanis before a brutal civil war was fought in the early 1970s. Civil war has also raged in parts of Sri Lanka, Myanmar, and India. In Pakistan, a low-intensity but bloody civil war has been fought between Sunni and Shi'ite Muslims. In addition, Myanmar's economy has been distorted by sanctions imposed on it by the North, by both governments and individuals engaging in consumer boycotts. The economy has also been affected by the drug trade that originates in the fields of the Golden Triangle.

On the other hand, there are pockets of prosperity and development. Maldives, for example, is relatively well off, even if it does not have a developed economy. The Pakistani economy has been growing at a persistent rate of around five per cent, and has become increasingly diversified.

The Indian economy presents perhaps the fullest range of contrasts of any economy in the world. When the indicators are aggregated at the national level, India ranks as a "poor" country. Indeed, in India, one can find tens of millions of people who live in abject poverty, scratching out a subsistence existence from often inhospitable soil. Hundreds of millions work in commercial agriculture raising a range of crops from rice and jute to tea and sugar-cane, a function of the increased productivity that came with the so-called **Green Revolution** of the 1960s that saw large increases in agricultural output as a result of crop diversification and selective breeding to create high-yield hybrids. Millions live and work on city streets, running small businesses such as bicycle repair, barbering, and leather-working. Millions more are employed in a range of industrial sectors, marked by large-scale assembly plants. But one also finds economic activity comparable to the "knowledge" economies of Northern states: a burgeoning computer software programming industry, a large music industry, 180 universities and 8000 other postsecondary colleges, and the world's largest film industry. As a consequence, there is a huge Indian middle class, slightly larger in size than the entire population of the United States.

## The Marginalized Continent: Africa

Subsaharan African countries, with the exception of South Africa, are the only group of nations of the South which have shown little economic growth in the decades since independence. Indeed, during the 1980s in some countries, the economy actually contracted (or, in the euphemistic expression favoured by economists, demonstrated "negative growth"). The band of countries on the southern edge of the Sahara—Mauritania, Mali, Burkina Faso, Niger, and Chad—are among the poorest countries in the world. They are predominantly pastoral, and have tiny manufacturing sectors and only limited foreign trade, usually heavily dependent on a single commodity and usually a single market. As a result, these countries are extraordinarily sensitive to changes in the world prices of commodities, for fluctuations have a pronounced effect on revenues and expenditures. For example, after the oil shocks of the 1970s, many African countries which are dependent on imported oil (and petroleum derivatives such as fertilizers) were so devastated by the rapid rise in the price of oil that the World Bank decided to create a separate category for them. They became known as the MSAs, the "most seriously affected," and the oil-producers themselves were moved to establish a special fund to assist them. The limited economic capacities of these countries mean that they have a tiny social wage compared to most Western countries. For example, Mauritania's annual budget in the early 1990s was approximately US$260 million, or roughly US$111 per capita; by contrast, Australian government expenditures during the same period amounted to some US$83 billion a year, or approximately US$4600 per capita.

In some African countries, structural economic problems have been compounded by civil war. In Somalia, Liberia, Sierra Leone, Rwanda, and Congo-Kinshasa (formerly Zaire), the national economy simply collapsed when civil war broke out. In Somalia, the annual GNP per capita fell from an already-low US$290 to an almost unbelievable US$36. In 1991, before the civil war, Somalia's external trade amounted to some US$240 million: US$80 million in exports and US$160 million in imports. To get some idea of the magnitude of Somalia's poverty, contrast this annual figure with the trade between Canada and the United States: each day, US$1 billion in goods crosses the Canadian-American border, four times more in one day than Somalia traded in an entire year. The outbreak of civil war also brought starvation, as the food distribution system collapsed. Some 300 000 Somalis probably died before the international community, through the United Nations, moved in to establish a food-distribution system, as we saw in Chapter 10.

In Liberia, the story was the same: the civil war that raged in the early 1990s destroyed much of the infrastructure that had been built in the 1980s around Monrovia. Government revenues tumbled to the minuscule amounts it collected for registering merchant shipping.

In Sierra Leone, rebels seized so much of the country (and its mineral resources) that the government hired Executive Outcomes, a transnational security corporation based in South Africa, to form an army, wage war against the rebels, and retake the diamond and rutile mines seized by the rebels.

South Africa is an exception to the general impoverished and marginal conditions of subsaharan African countries. South Africa has both Northern and Southern features. On the one hand, it has highly urbanized areas which are industrialized, developed, and wealthy; the service sector dominates employment, with only 13 per cent engaged in agriculture, forestry, and fisheries. It has a powerful mining sector, producing diamonds, gold, titanium, platinum, and other minerals. On the other hand, there are deep pockets of rural and urban poverty, and a marked maldistribution in income, inherited from the apartheid period when separate economic development patterns for the different racial groups in South Africa was state policy. But the results of decades of apartheid policy are not easily undone. In the postapartheid period, per capita government expenditures reflect South Africa's in-between position. In the mid 1990s, government spending was approximately US$800 per capita, well above most of South Africa's neighbours, but well below Northern states like Australia (US$4600) and even below middle-income countries like Argentina (US$1400).

## The Worlds Contrasted: The Human Development Index

This brief survey reveals that the South is quite heterogenous. Yet when one contrasts North and South, we find that in some important respects, the South demonstrates considerable homogeneity. If one took all six billion people in the world and divided them according to their access to wealth and their quality of life, one would undoubtedly find that only a minority enjoys a quality of life that is marked by plenty, privilege, security; such a life eludes the majority of humankind. There are numerous aggregate indicators of this—child mortality rates, life expectancy rates, literacy rates, education rates, unemployment rates, death rates. One evocative indicator is the "champagne glass" that one gets when one divides global GNP by quintiles of world population on a global basis. As Figure 16.1 suggests, a tiny minority (20%) of humankind has the most wealth (82.7%), and the bulk of those at the "champagne" end live in the North.

Another, equally illustrative indicator can be gained by ranking the political communities in the international system on the **Human Development Index** (HDI) developed by the United Nations Development Program (UNDP). Three aggregate statistics were selected: life expectancy, adult literacy and average years of schooling, and purchasing power. The UNDP's HDI rankings for 1997 are reproduced in Table 16.1 on p. 434.

One can level a number of criticisms at exercises such as this. It could be argued, for example, that the three measures chosen do not fully reflect what it means to be "developed." It could be argued that since the aggregate data used to calculate the rankings are based on statistics supplied by governments, they are subject to considerable error. Likewise, definitions of measures like "adult literacy" are notoriously elastic and hence quite slippery. But, even if the methodology employed in the HDI exercise is problematic, the index is useful

*Figure 16.1* • **THE CHAMPAGNE GLASS: WORLD INCOME DISTRIBUTION**

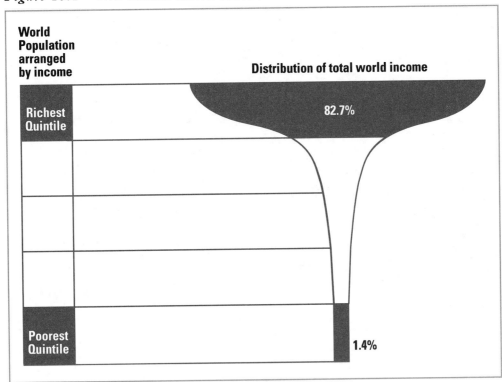

Source: UN Development Program, *Human Development Report 1992* (New York: UNDP, 1992).

*The index is useful because it demonstrates so clearly the divide that appears when humankind is separated into 194 separate economies and then ranked.*

because it demonstrates so clearly the divide that appears when humankind is separated into 194 separate economies and then ranked on roughly comparable data that bear on quality of life, even if inexactly.

The index highlights the geographic concentrations of wealth and poverty in contemporary world politics. Of the 20 highest-ranked states, all but Japan are in Europe, North America, or Australasia; all but one of the 20 lowest-ranked states are in Africa. Countries from different parts of the globe are found in the "low" category: Yemen in the Middle East; Bangladesh, Bhutan, India, Nepal, and Pakistan in South Asia; Cambodia, Laos, and Myanmar in Southeast Asia. In Southwest Asia, Afghanistan has been in this category in the past, though it was not included in the 1997 rankings because of the civil war raging in that country. But no country in Europe, North America, or the South Pacific has a "low" level of human development, and Haiti is the only country in the entire western hemisphere to be ranked in that category. By contrast, it is notable that the bottom category is dominated by African countries.

*Table 16.1* • **HUMAN DEVELOPMENT INDEX RANKINGS, 1997**

*High Human Development*
1. Canada
2. France
3. Norway
4. United States
5. Iceland
6. Netherlands
7. Japan
8. Finland
9. New Zealand
10. Sweden
11. Spain
12. Austria
13. Belgium
14. Australia
15. Britain
16. Switzerland
17. Ireland
18. Denmark
19. Germany
20. Greece
21. Italy
22. Hong Kong
23. Israel
24. Cyprus
25. Barbados
26. Singapore
27. Luxembourg
28. Bahamas
29. Antigua & Barbuda
30. Chile
31. Portugal
32. South Korea
33. Costa Rica
34. Malta
35. Slovenia
36. Argentina
37. Uruguay

38. Brunei
39. Czech Republic
40. Trinidad & Tobago
41. Dominca
42. Slovakia
43. Bahrein
44. United Arab Emirates
45. Panama
46. Fiji
47. Venezuela
48. Hungary
49. St Kitts & Nevis
50. Mexico
51. Colombia
52. Seychelles
53. Kuwait
54. Grenada
55. Qatar
56. Saint Lucia
57. Saint Vincent
58. Poland
59. Thailand
60. Malaysia
61. Mauritius
62. Belarus
63. Belize
64. Libya

*Medium Human Development*
65. Lebanon
66. Suriname
67. Russia
68. Brazil
69. Bulgaria
70. Iran
71. Estonia
72. Ecuador
73. Saudi Arabia

74. Turkey
75. North Korea
76. Lithuania
77. Croatia
78. Syria
79. Romania
80. Macedonia
81. Tunisia
82. Algeria
83. Jamaica
84. Jordan
85. Turkmenistan
86. Cuba
87. Dominican Rep.
88. Oman
89. Peru
90. South Africa
91. Sri Lanka
92. Latvia
93. Kazakstan
94. Paraguay
95. Ukraine
96. Samoa
97. Botswana
98. Philippines
99. Indonesia
100. Uzbekistan
101. Mongolia
102. Albania
103. Armenia
104. Guyana
105. Georgia
106. Azerbaijan
107. Kyrgyzstan
108. China
109. Egypt
110. Moldova
111. Maldives

| | | |
|---|---|---|
| 112. El Salvador | 139. Pakistan | 167. Guinea |
| 113. Bolivia | 140. Comoros | 168. Eritrea |
| 114. Swaziland | 141. Nigeria | 169. Burundi |
| 115. Tajikistan | 142. Congo-Kinshasa (Zaire) | 170. Ethiopia |
| 116. Honduras | 143. Zambia | 171. Mali |
| 117. Guatemala | 144. Bangladesh | 172. Burkina Faso |
| 118. Namibia | 145. Côte d'Ivoire | 173. Niger |
| 119. Morocco | 146. Benin | 174. Rwanda |
| 120. Gabon | 147. Togo | 175. Sierra Leone |
| 121. Viet Nam | 148. Yemen | |
| 122. Solomon Is | 149. Tanzania | *Not Ranked* |
| 123. Cape Verde | 150. Mauritania | Afghanistan |
| 124. Vanuatu | 151. Central African Rep. | Andorra |
| 125. São Tomé and Príncipe' | 152. Madagascar | Bosnia |
| 126. Iraq | 153. Cambodia | Kiribati |
| 127. Nicaragua | 154. Nepal | Liberia |
| 128. Papua New Guinea | 155. Bhutan | Liechtenstein |
| 129. Zimbabwe | 156. Haiti | Marshall Islands |
| 130. Congo-Brazzaville | 157. Angola | Micronesia |
| | 158. Sudan | Monaco |
| *Low Human Development* | 159. Uganda | Nauru |
| 131. Myanmar | 160. Senegal | Palau |
| 132. Ghana | 161. Malawi | ROC on Taiwan |
| 133. Cameroon | 162. Djibouti | San Marino |
| 134. Kenya | 163. Guinea-Bissau | Somalia |
| 135. Equatorial Guinea | 164. Chad | Somaliland |
| 136. Laos | 165. Gambia | Tonga |
| 137. Lesotho | 166. Mozambique | Tuvalu |
| 138. India | | Vatican City |
| | | Yugoslavia |

Source: UNDP, *Human Development Report, 1997*: http://www.undp.org/undp/hdro/table2.htm

## EXPLAINING UNDERDEVELOPMENT

Why is there such a pronounced divide between North and South? As we noted in Chapter 8, at one point in human history, the economic condition of all human beings was precisely the same. Since the Neolithic, however, unequal economic development between different groups has been the norm, as we have seen. But only in the past century has the gap between levels of development among the world's various communities grown so marked. There are several theories that try to explain this gap. It should be noted that these theories not only claim to explain the gap; they contain highly normative prescriptions about how to resolve it.

## Modernization Theories

In the immediate post-1945 period, it was common to see economic development as a series of steps that an economy went through on its way to becoming "developed" and "modernized." Modernization theorists looked back at European and American history since the Industrial Revolution, and extrapolated from those experiences. By implication, therefore, the reason for the gap observed in the 1950s and 1960s was simple: these countries were just like European societies had been in a preindustrial incarnation. Just as wealth had been created and widely distributed throughout European and American society by the processes of industrialization, so too could the same process occur in the countries of the South. The American economist most closely associated with the **modernization thesis**, Walt W. Rostow, gave various stages in the process names like "take-off" and "drive to maturity."[6]

Rostow and other development economists stressed the importance of the accumulation of capital by domestic savings and investments in manufacturing, and the progressive abandonment of agriculture in favour of manufacturing and industrialization. Once these stages had been passed through, the countries of the South would look just like those of the North: industrialized, modernized, mass-consumption societies.

## Dependency Theories

Dependency theory rejects the optimistic view that capital accumulation will, like a rising tide, lift all boats, and that the underdeveloped countries will become "developed" in due course. Scholars like Andre Gunder Frank argued that the key error made by modernization theorists was to regard the countries of the South as comparable to the countries of the North hundreds of years ago. In Frank's view, the countries of the North moved from a state of being *un*developed to being developed; they were never *under*developed as were the countries of the South.[7]

This is not just a cute play on words; rather, it points to an essential difference in the way in which North and South "developed." Countries of the North developed while they were dominating the peoples of the South through imperialism and colonialism; empire and the wealth it generated was a crucial component of the industrialization of Europe, as we saw in previous chapters. The peoples of the South, organized into political units that were an integral part of what in essence was a European world economy, thus experienced something that the European countries of the North never experienced: political subjugation by others and incorporation into an imperial economy.

For scholars like Frank, the evolution of the disparities between North and South in the mid-20th century was a function of power in the international division of labour. The capitalist world system was divided into a **core** (or **metropole**) and a **periphery** (or satellite), corresponding to the colonial powers and their former colonial possessions, now gaining independence. In this view, the periphery was dependent on the core, and unable to develop as long as they were connected to the core by economic ties.

Moreover, the dependency was deeply structural: in all countries, North and South, there was the same dichotomy between core and periphery. This led to the observation that in the countries of the periphery, there was also a core (the local political and economic elites) and a periphery (the workers and peasants). The core in the periphery was sustained in power through its relationship with the core in the core; thus local elites in the South had a shared interest with those in the North in order to perpetuate the status quo. Such conclusions led inexorably to the policy prescription that in order to develop, countries of the South should seek to develop outside the clutches of the capitalist system.

## Neoclassical Economic Theories

Neoclassical economists argue that if dependency theory were entirely right, then South Korea would still be a predominantly agricultural economy with an exceedingly low income; Taiwan would not have the huge foreign exchange reserves it has; Malaysia would still be a giant rubber plantation; and people in Singapore and Hong Kong would still be in the kind of poverty their parents knew under the British colonial regime in the 1950s. In other words, if dependency theory were correct, the "Asian miracle" could not have happened. Nor should there have been such patterns of industrialization in countries like Chile, Argentina, Brazil (the countries, it might be noted, that Frank was primarily writing about).

Rather, neoclassical/neoconservative economists argue that all of those countries which sought to encourage development by closing their economies to the international capitalist economy in fact did not enhance their wealth over the long term. By contrast, the lessons of the 1980s and early 1990s seem, on the surface at least, to be unambiguous: open the national economy to the forces of the global market; embrace deregulation and privatization; abandon nationalization; encourage foreign investment; embrace an export-oriented strategy; and abandon import substitution.

## An Assessment

Certainly when one looks at the impressive growth rates of the countries of East Asia, and the radical shifts in countries like Argentina, Brazil, Chile, Mexico, and India, the structural perspective of the dependency school seems overly static. In other words, it does not allow for the possibility of change.

On the other hand, the brief sketch of the "worlds" of development above suggests that the neoclassical/neoconservative route might provide an option for some governments in the South. But neoclassical theory does not provide an explanation for the deep poverty and deprivation we continue to see dividing the international system.

Part of the answer lies in the politics of the Cold War. Above, we looked at the role that United States military spending played in the economic development of South Korea, Taiwan, Hong Kong, Singapore, and other states in Southeast Asia. But Cold War politics had equally destructive effects. Consider how the games of the great powers during the Cold War simply destroyed the economies of Cambodia, Afghanistan, and Mozambique. In Cambodia, the Chinese, Soviets, and Americans all encouraged their proxies to fight one another for control. Substantial resources were expended, and much of the productive capacity of the community was destroyed in the process. Consider, for example, the development consequences of the vast number of antipersonnel land mines still sown in the

Cambodian countryside. The story is the same in Afghanistan, where the superpower struggle simply overtook the local community.

Part of the explanation for the unequal distribution of wealth lies in the attitudes and
behaviour of local elites in many countries. In how many countries did local elites, in
order to preserve their privileged position, engage in civil war against their own people? In
how many countries were local elites willing to define development priorities for the
community according to tribal loyalty? How many were driven by simple venal greed and
a penchant for high living copied from generations of European colonials? In how many
countries did the armed forces become the dominant group, repeatedly leaving their
barracks for the attractions of the presidential palace? Again, colonialism and imperialism
played an important part: all too often the imperial powers did not leave a well-functioning,
peaceful, and *civil* society behind when they lowered their flags in the 1950s and 1960s
and went back to Europe.

Finally, in understanding the evolution of the deep division between North and South,
we have to look at the attitudes of the North toward the plight of the South. And here we
see an interesting paradox. On the one hand, most Northerners express deep concern
about the economic gulf that separates them from the other four-fifths of humankind.
On the other hand, most Northerners have generally done as little as possible to change what
is fundamentally a conflict of interests. To a discussion of that paradox we now turn.

## THE NORTH/SOUTH CONFLICT

It may seem odd to call the relationship between North and South a *conflict*, since there is
no open fighting or quarrelling between the two sides of the economic divide. Indeed, an
observer might be led to the conclusion that there is a great deal of cooperation between
North and South: numerous aid programs are in place to encourage development, and
numerous international forums have evolved for the discussion and coordination of efforts
to correct the imbalances of wealth between the rich and the poor.

### Development Assistance

Part of the effort to close the gap between levels of development comes in the form of
development assistance, or what used to be called "foreign aid." Development assistance
comes in a variety of forms. Numerous nongovernmental organizations provide a great
deal of assistance in a variety of forms. Northern optometrists volunteer their time to visit
Southern countries to conduct eye examinations and distribute glasses discarded by their
patients in the North; *Médicins sans frontières* (MSF—Doctors without Borders) deliver
emergency medical aid; Christian churches in the North run mission services; surplus
tools are sent to artisans in the South; scholarship schemes bring students from the South
to the North; and educational programs of all types are developed.

When governments provide aid, it is known as **Official Development Assistance**
(ODA). Aid to the South was modelled on the European Recovery Plan (or Marshall
Plan), examined in Chapter 15. Aid planners hoped that, just as American aid provided to
Europe after the Second World War helped rebuild Europe's economies, so too would

governmental aid to Southern governments assist in building industrial capacity. ODA includes all forms of transfers between donor and recipient governments. Bilateral assistance involves transfers between two governments. Multilateral assistance is aid channelled by donor governments to an intergovernmental organization, such as a regional development bank, and is then distributed to countries in the South.

Bilateral assistance includes grants, lines of credit, or loans made on a concessional, or "soft," basis. **Soft loans** come with interest rates well below market rates—usually a nominal 1 or 2 per cent. They usually feature an initial period of forgiveness when no interest is charged, along with long repayment schedules.

Normally, assistance is tied to the purchase of goods and services in the donor country: the recipient government in the South is not simply given several million dollars in foreign exchange and allowed to spend the funds as it wishes. Rather, several million dollars in credit is arranged, which can be spent on purchasing goods and services from the donor. Because assistance comes with these conditions, it is known as **tied aid**. Even multilateral flows are tied, although more implicitly: donations to an IGO carry with them an implicit understanding that the assistance delivered to Southern recipients will be purchased from the various donors.

Included in ODA flows are any measures taken to reduce the indebtedness of Southern countries. Debt forgiveness, as a form of development assistance, was made necessary by what is known as the **debt trap**, which describes what happens to countries of the South when soft loans are used as a form of development assistance over the long term. The original idea behind soft loans was that by the time the nominal interest kicked in after the ten-year forgiveness period, the recipient country would be wealthy enough to repay the loan without a problem. What happened, however, was that countries of the South accumulated soft loans year after year, eventually becoming dependent on these loans to meet their annual operating expenses. But after 20 years, recipients of soft loans found themselves trapped by this debt. Even soft rates of interest produce severe debt servicing problems if one has accumulated a large number of loans over a long period. This situation is often made worse if loans were taken from private lenders at market interest rates. Thus, by the early 1980s, **debt forgiveness** had become a form of development assistance.

Official development assistance has become a deeply institutionalized feature of contemporary world politics. It began modestly enough in the early 1950s, when the leaders of the Commonwealth met in January 1950 at Colombo in Ceylon (now Sri Lanka). The communists had just triumphed in China, and there was considerable concern that communism would prove as attractive an ideology to the poor of the Indian subcontinent as it obviously had to the Chinese peasantry. As noted above, policy makers were using the model of the Marshall Plan, so the Commonwealth leaders put in place the **Colombo Plan**. Unlike the Marshall Plan, however, the package of assistance created at Colombo in 1950 was exceedingly modest.

Eventually, the Colombo Plan grew to include other donors and recipients; its programs developed and were copied by others. Eventually donor governments decided they needed specialized bureaucracies for the administration of development assistance.

Throughout the North bureaucracies were created, such as the United States Agency for International Development (USAID), the Overseas Development Administration (ODA) in Britain, the Ministry for Development Cooperation in the Netherlands, the Canadian International Development Agency (CIDA), and the Australian International Development Assistance Bureau (AIDAB). And in turn, an intergovernmental agency was established to oversee and coordinate the efforts of various national agencies: the Development Assistance Committee (DAC), a subsidiary organ of the Organisation for Economic Cooperation and Development (OECD). DAC includes the governments of most of the world's economically advanced states, together with the European Commission.

Multilateral agencies for the delivery of development assistance loans also proliferated. There are 11 "development banks" for various regions of the South, including banks for Asia (ADB), Africa (AfDB), Caribbean (CDB), and the western hemisphere, the Inter-American Development Bank (IADB). In addition, there are specialized subregional banks such as the West African Development Bank (BOAD) or the Central American Bank for Economic Integration (BCIE). There are also such specialist banks as the Islamic Development Bank (IDB), a lending facility for members of the Organization of the Islamic Conference.

As the discussion above suggests, development assistance was embraced in the post-1945 period—and sustained in the decades since—for a number of different motives. In the mixed-motives approach to ODA, one can identify at least four factors why ODA is given. Partly the motivation was (and is) *humanitarian*, driven either by a discomfort that many in the rich North had when confronted with the grinding poverty in the South, or by a sense of obligation.[8] Humanitarianism is a key motivation for the vast majority of individuals who persistently express their support for development assistance; it is the driving force behind the NGOs and the individuals who work for and with them.

For governments, by contrast, the motivations have tended to be political and economic. The *economic* motivation has always been extremely important for donor governments.

> *Tying aid makes it a great way to recycle tax revenues back into the donor economy, in places and to individuals of the government's choosing.*

Tying aid makes it a great way to recycle tax revenues back into the donor economy, in places and to individuals of the government's choosing. Thus in Canada, for example, CIDA contracts have persistently been used by the federal government as a form of regional development to the provinces, frequently guided by electoral considerations. The *political* motivation for ODA is also uppermost for governments, for ODA has been judged useful at the level of world politics. Much ODA during the Cold War was driven by the same kind of fears evident at Colombo: efforts to encourage development would ward off the attractions of communism. But ODA also has been seen as a useful tool of statecraft, to woo, threaten, or bludgeon other governments.

And finally one must include the motivation of *prestige*. Prestige works both ways in this case. On the one hand, governments like the prestige that comes with assistance; by the same token, however, a government that ceased to give development assistance would become an international pariah, criticized by both recipients and other donors alike.[9]

## Attempts at Correction

The second reason why the North-South conflict may not *look* like a conflict is the degree of institutionalization of the divisions of North and South. Since the early 1950s, the international community has been grappling with the gap in wealth, but it has done so within the bounds of international organizations, primarily the United Nations. As early as 1951, the secretary-general was circulating reports with titles like "Measures for the Economic Development of Under-Developed Countries"; these were proposals for special development funds to promote economic growth and ideas for channelling private investment to the South.

The response of the countries of the North to these early efforts was, broadly speaking, one of resistance. Because of opposition from the United States, it took a number of years to secure a development fund and a finance facility. In 1956, the International Finance Corporation (IFC) was established to help with investment flows to the South; in September 1959, the International Development Association (IDA) was created to provide soft loans. But both the IFC and IDA were associated with the World Bank, in which the countries of the North had controlling votes based on weighted voting, rather than the United Nations, where the countries of the South had a majority under the one-state, one-vote arrangement.

The attitude of the countries of the North in the 1950s fuelled a growing assertiveness among countries of the South in the 1960s. A common consciousness among these nations emerged and became institutionalized. It began with the institutionalization of non-alignment, a political idea that grew directly out of the East/West division. First embraced by Jawaharlal Nehru, prime minister of India, **nonalignment** rejected the idea of having to belong to one of the blocs that were developing. Nonalignment involved rejecting membership in a military alliance and refusing to allow foreign troops to be stationed on one's soil. Other leaders who embraced nonalignment in the 1950s were Sukarno, president of Indonesia, Gamal Abdul Nasser of Egypt, and Kwame Nkrumah of Ghana. The only European leader to embrace nonalignment was Josef Broz Tito, after his split with the USSR. The nonaligned countries began to institutionalize their movement with a conference held in Belgrade in September 1961 with 25 countries from the South. By 1964, when the nonaligned heads of state met in Cairo, there were 47 members and the beginnings of the Nonaligned Movement (NAM).

The concerns of nonalignment were essentially strategic—a desire to steer a middle course between East and West. But common concerns about the effects of the Cold War had an impact on the consciousness about common concerns about development. In July 1962, a conference of Southern countries, held at Cairo, attempted for the first time to coordinate their development concerns. From this conference, the idea emerged that the international community should address the issue of trade between the North and South, and in particular trade in commodities—so important to the economies of Southern countries.

## UNCTAD

As a result, a major international conference was held under UN auspices in Geneva from March to June 1964. The 119 governments which attended the United Nations Conference on Trade and Development (UNCTAD) focused on what was seen as the dominant problem of the South: their dependence on commodity trade for export earnings and the dominance of manufactured goods from the North in their imports. This **trade gap** was seen as a key impediment to Southern development.

At the conference, Southern governments demonstrated considerable solidarity, often choosing to take positions against their own interests in favour of maintaining a united front. They eventually came to be known as the **Group of 77**, or G-77 (a designation that stuck even when the number of South countries climbed well beyond 77). The industrialized countries of the North were, by contrast, not united in how to respond to the demands of this new bloc with its almost automatic voting majority at the UN. While many Northern countries accepted, with varying degrees of reluctance, the UNCTAD conference's decisions, the United States ended up voting against most of the clauses in the final declaration.

Another consequence of UNCTAD in 1964 was that it established an institutionalized mechanism for the expression of Southern concerns. It was envisaged that similar meetings would be held on a regular basis, and that a new international bureaucracy would be created to oversee trade and development concerns. In particular, the bureaucracy would reorient the international economic system so that more benefits from the international economy flowed to the countries and peoples of the South.

## The NIEO

But it was not until the oil shock of October 1973 that a new tone in the attitudes of the South emerged. The rapid rise in the price of oil, and the willingness of OPEC to withhold this important commodity, provided the impetus for renewed demands for a reorientation of the international economy. In early 1974, Houari Boumedienne, the president of Algeria, who was also the head of the NAM, pressed for a special UN General Assembly meeting on development. As Boumedienne put it, the existing world order "continually impoverishes the poor and enriches the rich," and was "the major obstacle standing in the way of any hope of development and progress for all the countries of the Third World."[10] This would later be seen as the first call for what was termed the **New International Economic Order** (NIEO)—a program that was designed to readjust the workings of the entire international economy. Included in the NIEO were such recommendations as linking the price of manufactured goods to prices of commodities; increasing accessibility of the South to development financing; and lowering tariffs and expanding the preferential access of manufacturing goods from the South, known as the **generalized system of preferences** (GSP).\*

The response of the North to these Southern demands was as divided in the 1970s as it had been in the 1960s. The United States government, reflecting the relative independence

---

\* The GSP was designed to help "infant industries" in the South overcome the difficulties of trying to compete with Northern manufacturers. It would provide Southern manufactured goods with preferential access to Northern markets, thus allowing industries located in the South to become more competitive over time. An initial GSP scheme was put into place in the early 1970s.

of the American economy, was less disposed to respond positively than the European countries, which were less self-sufficient. Thus, one concrete result of the NIEO was the **Lomé Convention** of 1975, an agreement that provided greater access to the markets of the members of the European Economic Community (as it was then) for the products of Southern countries. However, the products in which the South had a comparative advantage, textiles, faced persistent protectionism from most Northern governments, which put their own textile sectors first.

Otherwise, there was a great deal of talk about international development during this period. The Conference on International Economic Cooperation (CIEC) was called by the French government and met periodically between 1975 and 1977. NIEO demands were also pursued through UNCTAD conferences. There were a number of pledges undertaken but never fulfilled by the states of the North. For example, the CIEC resulted in a

*Most other Northern countries simply changed the target date at their convenience, moving it back every couple of years even while they ritualistically promised to meet it—eventually.*

pledge to create a **Common Fund**—a scheme designed to provide a fund that would allow commodity-dependent Southern countries some protection against commodity price swings on the international market. Likewise, the CIEC formally embraced a recommendation made by the Pearson Commission* in 1969 that the developed countries allocate 0.7 per cent of their GNP in Official Development Assistance. Neither goal was met. Although some international commodity agreements (ICAs) were negotiated, the Common Fund itself died for lack of ratifications. And only a few European countries actually met the **0.7-per-cent target**; most other Northern countries simply changed the target date at their convenience, moving it back every couple of years even while they ritualistically promised to meet it—eventually.

The beginning of the end of the NIEO came at one of the conferences held to discuss the North/South issue. A report by the Independent Commission on International Development Issues, a body chaired by a former chancellor of Germany, Willy Brandt, recommended the convening of a summit of the major Northern and Southern countries to discuss economic relations between North and South. In October 1981, just such a meeting was scheduled for Cancún, Mexico. But the discussions came to nothing; no agreement on any substantive issue was reached. The sense of impasse deepened at UNCTAD a year later, when North and South lined up in opposition to one another over the issue of the seating of Israel, and led the United States to intimate that it would no longer take an active part in UNCTAD proceedings (thus, in effect, rendering the organization moribund). Indeed, resistance from the government in Washington would transform UNCTAD over the course of the 1980s, so that by the end of the decade Southern states were no longer using it as a forum for pressing the issue of global economic reform.

---

* Following his retirement as prime minister of Canada in 1967, Lester B. Pearson was appointed head of an international commission to investigate the North-South relationship: see Pearson et al., *Partners in Development: Report of the Commission on International Development* (New York: Praeger, 1969).

The transformation of the North/South debate in the 1980s can be attributed to three main factors. First, the rise in commodity prices in the 1970s proved to be a temporary phenomenon. By the early 1980s, the supply of important commodities was high and prices fell, thus undercutting numerous national budgets. Second, shifts in American monetary policy had forced interest rates up, creating a debt crisis for many more countries besides the Latin American countries examined above. Third, there was a pronounced ideological shift occurring. As we have noted in the context of other discussions, the coming to power of Margaret Thatcher in Britain and Ronald Reagan in the United States was both a reflection and a reinforcement of a general shift to neoconservativism in the North. Numerous other Northern governments were also taking their fiscal and policy cues from a line of thought that decried *dirigisme* (i.e., state direction of the economy), state ownership, and protection against the forces of the market. But the neoconservative challenge was also reflected in North/South relations, as Northern states—particularly the United States, Britain, Germany, and Japan—pressed Southern states to abandon *dirigisme* and state ownership and to embrace the market along with denationalization, deregulation, and marketization. In such an ideological climate, many of the solutions for a "new order" put forward in the 1970s—which inexorably featured a prominent role for the state—would simply not fly.

One can get some sense of the degree to which the North/South debate was transformed by looking at the role of the Southern countries in the Uruguay Round of GATT negotiations that began in 1986. In previous rounds—the Kennedy Round in the 1960s and the Tokyo Round of the 1970s—countries of the South had played a minimal role, preferring to press their trade-related concerns through other forums like UNCTAD. By the late 1980s, however, there was an increasing recognition that the countries of the South could gain more by participating actively in the international trading system.

Moreover, on many issues, the South abandoned its earlier negotiating strategies of subordinating particular national concerns so as to be able to present a united front to the North. In the Uruguay Round, issues did not split on strictly North/South divisions. The best example of this was the so-called **Cairns Group** of Fair Trading Nations. In August 1986 in Cairns, Queensland, the Australian Labor party government of Bob Hawke called together a group of 14 governments with an interest in liberalizing global agricultural trade. Argentina, Brazil, Canada, Chile, Colombia, Fiji, Hungary, Indonesia, Malaysia, New Zealand, the Philippines, Thailand, and Uruguay represented countries from all four compass points. They worked to pressure the major protagonists in the battles over protectionism in agricultural trade—Japan, the United States, and the European Communities—to lower barriers to agricultural trade such as the EC's Common Agricultural Policy (CAP). While the Cairns Group was not entirely successful in moving the great powers, the assortment of Northern and Southern countries in the group was an important indicator of the shift that was taking place in the North/South nexus.[11]

The end of the Cold War further changed these dynamics. No longer were states of the South sites of a larger struggle for dominance between Northern countries. The willingness of the North to assist them decreased accordingly. One measure of this is the degree to which official development assistance has diminished over the course of the 1990s, with the result that the North is further away from the 0.7-per-cent goal than ever. By the middle of the decade the United States was giving less than 0.3 per cent; Britain, Canada, and Japan less than 0.4 per cent.

## The North's New North/South Agenda

The changing dynamics can also be seen in the vigour with which those in the North are willing to push their own agenda in the South. Rather than simply resisting Southern demands, which was the policy of choice for Northern countries during the Cold War, Northern countries have been active in pressing some Southern countries on a variety of issues. Such concerns as "fair trade" in a range of products, the protection of intellectual property rights, nondiscriminatory treatment of foreign investment, and environmental protection have been pressed.

One example of this dynamic at work is the eagerness with which the United States government has renewed its **"war on drugs"** in the post–Cold War period. The disappearance of the Soviet threat has allowed the government in Washington to turn on people who were formerly in its pay, and to whose illegal activities a blind eye was turned. In the 1990s, the war has increasingly been prosecuted offshore, carried to countries where narcotics are grown, refined, or transported to the United States.

But this "war" also has development effects that are not often recognized. Regular trade, investment, and development assistance is now linked to antidrug performance by these countries. If a foreign country fails to wage war on its own narcotics industry to American satisfaction, that country can be "decertified" by the United States Congress, and made ineligible for a range of American assistance. (It might be noted, however, that no comparable "certification" program exists for assessing the vigour with which the United States government has been stopping the huge flow of illegal guns to the *narcotraficantes* in the South, the result of lax gun control laws in the United States. Nor do drug-cultivating states get to "certify" American performance in dealing with the other side to supply—the huge and insistent demand for narcotics by Americans.)

## The Case of Sustainable Development

Another good example of a willingness to press a specifically Northern agenda is the case of the environment. Northerners, both ordinary people and governments alike, have had few qualms about insisting that Southern countries structure their environmental policies to Northern satisfaction and to meet Northern concerns. The clearest example of this was the eager embrace by the North of the notion of **sustainable development**, a phrase that is rarely defined with any exactitude. Nonetheless, it has achieved the status of sacrosanctity in the North. Generally, sustainable development is the idea that economic growth should only be undertaken in a way that does not threaten the environment in the long term or deplete resources at a nonrenewable rate. Such an idea has immediate and wide-ranging implications for the countries of the South: it suggests that they must limit their development and economic growth in a way that is "environmentally friendly."

Many Northern environmental groups have argued that the equatorial rainforests are the "lungs of the planet," and thus what happens to the rainforests affects all humans. Therefore, they argue, these resources should only be developed in a way that benefits all humankind. According to this logic, it was quite appropriate to tell the countries of the South how far they should be allowed to exploit the rainforests, that happen to lie within their jurisdiction, for logging or grazing. Indeed, "Save the Rainforest" campaigns sprouted throughout the North, and deforestation made it to the agenda of a number of international conferences, including the United Nations Conference on the Environment and Development (UNCED), informally known as the "Earth Summit," in Rio de Janeiro in June 1992.

There was a certain irony in these campaigns. Here were environmental groups in rich countries, where long before, the natural forests had been completely stripped in the process of development, presuming to tell impoverished countries what they were not allowed to do with their forests. There was also a certain contradiction in this position, for no reciprocity was acknowledged by Northern environmentalists. Peoples of the South were not permitted to claim that the good things found in the territories of the North should only be exploited for the benefit of all humankind. But such ironies and contradictions were lost on environmental groups, their supporters, and the Northern governments which were also pressing the "sustainable development" agenda. They were, however, not at all lost on Southerners, many of whom saw the "sustainable development" campaign as simply another way in which the North was evading dealing with the North/South divide.[12] Not surprisingly, Southern governments with rainforests tend to reject completely the rights of Northern environmentalists or governments to dictate environmental policy to them. Some of the poorer or debt-laden states have been willing to be induced: **debt-for-nature swaps** involves Northerners arranging to cancel a Southern country's debt in return for agreeing to preserve a specified area of forest.

## POWER AND THE ENDURING DOMINANCE OF THE NORTH

Even when the North was brushing off attempts by the South to reform the system, we saw little overt *conflict* in the North-South relationship. However, this should not blind us to the deep conflicts of interest in the North/South division, between those who have—the rich—and those who do not—the poor or dispossessed. To get some sense of the depth of this conflict, ask the traditional political scientist's question about the present global system and how "good things" are distributed among six billion people, *"Cui bono?"*—who benefits? There is little doubt that the answer has not changed very much since Boumedienne spoke to the General Assembly in 1974. The system still operates to the advantage of those who have and to the disadvantage of those who do not. It certainly does not operate in the interests of the dispossessed.

Now ask the next obvious question, "how are these inequities sustained?" The answer must be: by power—the successful attempts of the rich to ensure that their interests prevail over the poor. The rich, not surprisingly, have sought to retain what they have. They tend to be happy when the poor or dispossessed make gains,* but they resist mightily when the dispossessed seek to make gains by redistribution of wealth or by dispossessing the rich. Thus we have to see the various forms of development assistance, the resistance to preferences, and the failure to address the demands for an NIEO, as efforts to retain privilege in the face of Southern efforts to make gains by redistribution.

In this exercise of power, the peoples of the North—and the governments who represent their interests in sustaining their privileged position—have been able to rely on important power resources. First, and most importantly, Northerners rely on the divisions within the South itself. The global condition of privilege and dispossession is recreated at a local level, with local elites in Southern countries as keen to retain their own local privilege as Northerners as a whole are to retain their global privilege. As a consequence, in virtually every country, there is an elite committed to the existing system and committed to working within the existing rules. Even the NIEO, which saw the achievement of impressive unity among Southern countries, was a political campaign organized by government elites with a pronounced interest in maintaining the system.

Northerners count on the tendency of local elites to resist local pressures for change if it involves redistribution or dispossession. Sometimes the struggle to retain privilege can become brutal: in some countries, union organizers, community activists, or reform-minded journalists are simply "disappeared" by paramilitary death squads, sometimes operating with the complicity of the state, sometimes operating at the behest of dominant groups.

Second, if Southern governments come to power that are not inclined to bend to the dictates of the system, the North has other tools of power. In the broadest sense, there is the "discipline of the market." Global capital tends to shun those localities where risks—such as appropriation, nationalization, or simply destruction in a civil war—are high relative to returns. The power of the multinational corporations to shape local conditions is considerable, but we tend to forget that this power works not only to the benefit of the MNC owners, but of the rich more broadly.

And when market "discipline" does not work, there is the power of the state. Northern governments tend to paint those governments and their leaders who challenge the dominant consensus as "rogues" or "pariahs," and with general approval, they move to isolate revolutionary movements, states, and leaders.

---

* It is true that people tend to be more concerned how they fare *relative* to others, rather than being content with what they have in absolute terms. Thus if A makes $10 000 a year and B makes $1000, but then in the next year A makes $15 000 but B makes $20 000, both A and B have made what are called **absolute gains**. However, B has gained more than A in relative terms. Instead of being content with the $5000 in absolute gains, A becomes concerned or resentful about B's **relative gains**. One can see this dynamic most clearly in the annoyance of many Americans at the growing wealth of the Japanese. The United States has not become poorer, but many Americans resent the fact that Japan has become relatively richer. Because there is little prospect that this dynamic will bedevil North/South relations any time soon, one can generally conclude that the North welcomes gains made by the South.

## CONCLUSION

This chapter and the previous one have surveyed two further sources of division in world politics that have been layered onto the divisions engendered by the sovereign nation-state. It is evident from the discussion that compass-point divisions in no way transcend the state divide. On the contrary, we saw in the East/West division that national conceptions of interest consistently confounded compass-point unity. The East was cleaved early and often. Yugoslavs, Albanians, Chinese, Hungarians, Czechoslovaks, Poles, Cubans—all had local and distinct conceptions of interest that frequently did not accord with Soviet interests. The West was no less divided by divergent national conceptions of interest. The Cold War period is rife with national annoyances among Western countries: allies annoyed at the propensity of Americans to be arrogant and unilateral; Americans annoyed at the cheapness or cautiousness of their allies.

We have also seen the importance of national cleavages in the North/South divide. Not all governments of the North have taken precisely the same approach to Southern issues, even if the North as a whole depends deeply on the continuing national divisions in the South as a key mechanism for the maintenance of Northern dominance.

But the end of the Cold War demonstrated how these compass-point divisions tend to be artifacts of particular conjunctures in world politics. While the North/South divide is still a prominent feature of world politics, the East/West division simply evaporated. The East simply disappeared as a compass point in world politics; the term no longer has any meaning politically. And in the absence of an "East," notions of what constitutes the "West" in the post–Cold War period has become highly contested, as is evident in the case of the expansion of NATO to include former allies of the former USSR.

In short, these compass-point divisions may have had a powerful impact on world politics in the latter half of the 20th century, and the North/South division promises to continue to play a prominent role in world politics in the next 50 years. But bloc formation has not altered in any sense the dominant commitment to the sovereign nation-state as the preferred political form. Part of the reason for this is the perpetuative logic built into the sovereign nation-state; and to that issue we now turn.

## *Keyword File*

| | |
|---|---|
| First World | Export-oriented strategy |
| Second World | Cultural Revolution |
| Third World | "Open Door" policy |
| Fourth World | Special economic zones |
| Purchasing power parity | Tiananmen massacre |
| Settler societies | Seven Sisters |
| Newly industrializing countries | Yom Kippur war |
| Dynamic Asian economies | Oil embargo |
| Import-substitution strategy | Oil shock |

Petrodollars
Group of Ten
Special Drawing Rights
Green Revolution
Human Development Index
Modernization thesis
Core
Metropole
Periphery
Official Development Assistance
Soft loans
Tied aid
Debt trap
Debt forgiveness
Colombo Plan

Nonalignment
Trade gap
Group of 77
New International Economic Order
Generalized system of preferences
Lomé Convention
Common Fund
0.7-per cent-target
*Dirigisme*
Cairns Group
"War on drugs"
Sustainable development
Debt-for-nature swaps
Absolute gains
Relative gains

## *For Further Exploration*

### HARD COPY

Adams, Nassau A. *Worlds Apart: The North-South Divide and the International System.* London: Zed Books, 1993.

Devlin, Robert. *Debt and Crisis in Latin America.* Princeton, NJ: Princeton University Press, 1989.

Hoffmann, Stanley. *Duties Beyond Borders: On the Limits and Possibilities of Ethical International Politics.* Syracuse, NY: Syracuse University Press, 1981.

Riddell, Roger C. *Foreign Aid Reconsidered.* London and Baltimore: James Currey and Johns Hopkins University Press, 1987.

Spence, Jonathan D. *The Search for Modern China.* London: Hutchinson, 1990.

Wong, Jan. *Red China Blues.* Toronto: Doubleday Anchor Books, 1996.

### WEBLINKS

**http://www.envirolink.org/**

Home page of EnviroLink, maintained by an environmental NGO and providing jumping-off points for all international environmental issues

**http://www.imf.org/external/pubs/ft/survey/sup0996/10sdr.htm**

International Monetary Fund site that provides the updated value of the SDR

**http://www.undp.org/undp/hdro/97.htm**

The UNDP site for updated listings of the annual Human Development Index rankings

**http://www.wfp.org/**

Home page of the UN World Food Program, with links to other sites relating to development

## Notes to Chapter 16

1. Marianne H. Marchand, "The political economy of North-South relations," in Richard Stubbs and Geoffrey R.D. Underhill, eds., *Political Economy and the Changing Global Order* (London/New York/Toronto: Macmillan/St Martin's/McClelland and Stewart, 1994), 296.

2. Gary Rodan, *The Political Economy of Singapore's Industrialisation: National, State, and International Capital* (London: Macmillan, 1989); James Fallows, *Looking at the Sun* (New York: Pantheon, 1994).

3. Richard Stubbs, "The political economy of the Asia-Pacific region," in Stubbs and Underhill, eds., *Political Economy and the Changing Global Order*, 366–77.

4. Nassau A. Adams, *Worlds Apart: The North-South Divide and the International System* (London: Zed Books, 1993), 138–39.

5. See Matthew Shepherd, "U.S. domestic interests and the Latin American debt crisis," in Stubbs and Underhill, ed., *Political Economy and the Changing Global Order*, 302–12.

6. Walt W. Rostow, *The Stages of Economic Growth* (New York/Cambridge: Cambridge University Press, 1960); although Rostow's thesis has been widely discredited, it keeps on going: the book went into a third edition in 1990.

7. Andre Gunder Frank, "The development of underdevelopment," *Monthly Review* (September 1966); widely republished, including in Robert I. Rhodes, ed., *Imperialism and Underdevelopment: A Reader* (New York: Monthly Review Press, 1970), 4–17.

8. For a thought-provoking exploration, see Stanley Hoffmann, *Duties Beyond Borders: On the Limits and Possibilities of Ethical International Politics* (Syracuse, NY: Syracuse University Press, 1981), especially Chapters 1 and 4.

9. For an elaboration of this argument, see Kim Richard Nossal, "Mixed motives revisited: Canada's interest in development assistance," *Canadian Journal of Political Science* 21 (March 1988), 35–56.

10. Cited in Adams, *Worlds Apart*, 123.

11. Richard A. Higgott and Andrew Fenton Cooper, "Middle power leadership and coalition building: the Cairns Group and the Uruguay Round of trade negotiations," *International Organization* 44 (Autumn 1990): 589–632.

12. See, for example, the acerbic remarks of scholars like Alvaro Soto, "The global environment: a Southern perspective," *International Journal* 47 (Autumn 1992), 679–705, and Nassau A. Adams, *Worlds Apart*, 200–207.

# Challenging
## *the* Nation-State:
## Alternative Visions

**I N T R O D U C T I O N**

In Chapters 15 and 16, we looked at the way in which ideological and economic cleavages created the compass-point divisions of North/South and East/West. But while the divisions between East and West were exceedingly deep during the Cold War, and while there is a seemingly unbridgeable gulf between North and South today, these cleavages did not *supplant* national divisions, but rather were (and are) layered onto them.

In this chapter, we explore a number of challenges to the primacy of the sovereign nation-state as the key source of division in world politics today. First, we examine the thesis that the forces of globalization are making the sovereign nation-state obsolete, superseding national identification. We then look at the argument, put forward most forcefully by Samuel P. Huntington, that civilizations, not nations, will be the most important source of conflict in world politics in the future. Finally, we explore a number of alternative ways of "imagining" political community.

## A BORDERLESS WORLD? THE IMPACT OF GLOBALIZATION

There are those who argue that the sovereign nation-state, as we have known it for the last century, is dying, rendered increasingly moribund by the forces of globalization. A world of sovereign states is being replaced by a "borderless world," to use the phrase made popular by Kenichi Ohmae.[1] The globalization argument, in brief, is that since the early 1970s the international political economy has been experiencing a profound transformation that has rendered the idea of national economies, enclosed by national borders and controlled by national governments, increasingly meaningless. The international (*qua* inter + national) economy, it is argued, has been replaced by a globalized economy.

### The Transformation of the International Economy

In the immediate aftermath of the Second World War, the international economy was just that—an economy of various national economies. Economic exchange was dominated by governments. The exchange of goods and services was tightly monitored and regulated, with governments maintaining numerous barriers to the free movement of goods and services across borders. The financial markets, such as they were, were tightly state controlled: most governments had in place stringent laws about the movement of funds across borders, even by tourists (in the 1950s, for example, British tourists going out of the country could take no more than £30 with them). Most governments tightly controlled their financial and banking sectors, making it impossible for foreigners, foreign firms, or foreign banks to conduct business without going through a domestic bank. Fifty years later, the economy at a global level looks very different.

### From Bretton Woods to Nixon Shocks

The international economy that emerged in 1945 from the six years of global war was shaped by a conscious effort on the part of the victorious governments to avoid what they regarded as the lessons of the Great Depression of the 1930s. Then, as we saw in Chapter 14, governments sought to offload the economic problems that followed the crash of the New York stock market in October 1929. That crash, which wiped out billions of dollars in investment, triggered a collapse in the banking sector, a drop in commodity prices, the closing of factories, and a rise in unemployment. As we saw, the depression deepened and spread throughout the international system, in large part because of the collapse of international trade. Governments of countries in economic distress tried to offload their problems to neighbouring economies by what have become known as **beggar-thy-neighbour** policies: raising tariffs, restricting imports, and subsidizing exports. Many governments tried to correct their balance of payments deficits by abandoning the **gold standard**,* which most countries had used to settle their international accounts up until

---

* Under the classical gold standard that operated between 1870 and 1914, governments agreed to exchange their national currencies for gold at fixed rates, thus providing a predictable mechanism for settling international accounts and also providing some discipline against simply printing money. Liquidity for this system was provided by the central bank of the most powerful economy of the period, the Bank of England, which covered short-term balance-of-payment deficits.

the start of the Great War in 1914, when it had collapsed. Efforts had been made to re-introduce it 1925 without success. By allowing their currencies to float, no longer tied to gold, governments could engage in currency devaluations, making imports more expensive and exports more attractive to foreigners. However, this merely triggered competitive devaluations by other governments, deepening the cycle of depression.

As we saw in Chapter 15, those who met at Bretton Woods in July 1944 sought to avoid these various problems. The United States government in particular sought to put in place a system for the conduct of international trade and the management of international finance that would provide the stability and growth that had been so lacking in the 1930s, while at the same time not forfeiting national independence (which would prove unacceptable politically in virtually all countries).

The result was what John Gerard Ruggie has called the compromise of **embedded liberalism**. It involved a trade-off: countries would agree to forego some of the benefits of pursuing their own economic policies without regard for others, by cooperating with one another in liberalizing the system; on the other hand, countries would be free to pursue their own economic and social policies at home.[2]

The key institutions to provide coordination and liberalization were the World Bank, the International Monetary Fund (IMF), and the International Trade Organization (ITO). The World Bank and IMF would regulate the international monetary system with fixed interest rates linked to gold and a limited pool of capital to ensure international liquidity; the ITO would seek to lower tariff barriers to trade. In the event, the ITO was never created: the United States Senate decided not to ratify it, and it was replaced with the General Agreement on Tariffs and Trade (GATT).

By 1947 it was clear that the Bretton Woods system was not working. The European economy, which had been largely built on trade, was in ruins, and the IMF pool was not sufficient to meet European (and Japanese) needs for economic reconstruction. As we saw above, the United States government decided to mount a massive recovery program, the Marshall Plan, to encourage the outflow of dollars. Even more dollars were spent by the United States government in maintaining forces abroad in support of the various alliances surveyed in Chapter 15. As part of what in essence was the self-appointed role as the system's central banker, the United States government also agreed to the use of the dollar as the primary currency and committed itself to exchange dollars for gold at the fixed rate of US$35 to the ounce.

Thus, after 1947, what we know as the **Bretton Woods system** was not working precisely as those who met in 1944 had envisaged. But the effect was precisely what the framers of the system had in mind. The European countries and Japan recovered, their economies increasingly robust and diversified. World trade grew. Confidence in the dollar remained strong.

Over time, however, the modified Bretton Woods system grew unstable. Ironically, this was in large part because of the success of the efforts to encourage recovery and reconstruction. By the end of the 1950s, dollars had flowed out of the United States in such quantities that overwhelmed the capacity of the U.S. government to meet its commitment to convert dollars into gold. By 1960, the number of dollars held by foreigners exceeded American gold reserves.

Through the 1960s, efforts by the United States and its major trading partners to correct this system created new organizations for multilateral management such as the Group of Ten, and new sources of international liquidity, Special Drawing Rights (SDRs), both discussed in Chapter 16. But a number of deep underlying problems were not resolved. These included an increase in the gap between foreign dollar holdings and U.S. reserves of gold; a massive increase in financial transactions involving Japan and Europe; the rise of multinational corporations moving money around the international system; and the rise of a market in **Eurodollars**—U.S. dollars deposited in, and traded by, foreign banks (mostly but not necessarily in Europe, the name notwithstanding) without being converted to local currency, thus not subject to domestic controls. By the early 1970s, these related elements of financial integration were creating monetary problems for the United States government, notably an continuing outflow of capital and a worsening trade balance.

*By 1971 a huge gap existed between foreign dollar holdings (US$80 billion) and U.S. reserves of gold (US$10 billion).*

The desire of a succession of administrations in Washington to spend increasing sums on domestic social welfare programs while at the same time pursuing a costly war in Vietnam only exacerbated these economic problems. In the spring of 1971, there was a run on the dollar, causing a sharp decline in American gold reserves. By 1971 a huge gap existed between foreign dollar holdings (US$80 billion) and U.S. reserves of gold (US$10 billion). This coincided with the announcement that the United States had experienced its first trade deficit. The response of the administration of Richard Nixon was to abandon the modified Bretton Woods system. On 15 August 1971, the United States government unilaterally announced that it would no longer convert dollars into gold. In addition, the United States would impose a 10-per-cent surcharge on all dutiable items in an attempt to bring American trade back into balance. These measures were known as the "Nixon shocks."

### The Emergence of Global Financial Markets

The Nixon shocks eventually led to a transformation of the world economy. First, by 1973, exchange rates between national currencies were generally established by market forces of supply and demand, giving rise to a huge expansion in global currency markets. Second, the move to deregulate financial flows by the United States government left other countries with little choice but to follow suit, leading to the emergence of a global financial market that demonstrated explosive growth: according to Joan E. Spero and Jeffrey A. Hart, by the early 1990s, transborder financial flows exceed trade flows by a factor of 30 to 1.[3] Two areas are particularly noteworthy: lending and innovation.

Borrowing on international capital markets has grown phenomenally. In part, this borrowing was fuelled by the price increases imposed by members of the Organization of Petroleum Exporting Countries (OPEC), discussed in Chapter 16. OPEC members could not absorb the resulting revenues, with the result that vast quantities of petrodollars washed into the global marketplace just as the other developments discussed above were occurring. The results were dramatic: in the late 1970s, the average annual borrowing on international markets was US$96.6 billion; by the late 1980s, it was US$427.4 billion; by 1993, it was US$818.6 billion, approximately 10 times what it was 15 years earlier.

Financial markets have also shown considerable diversification and innovation. No longer are flows primarily in the form of loans as they were in the late 1970s; now borrowers show a marked move to **securitization**—tradeable bonds and other securities, including such instruments as **dragon bonds**, traded only in the markets of the Asia Pacific, and **Eurobonds**, the name given to bonds denominated in U.S. dollars and issued outside the U.S. (but not necessarily in Europe, despite the name). Moreover, there has been considerable innovation in the form of instruments available on international capital markets that provide some hedge against changes in interest and exchange rates. These instruments include currency futures, options on stock market indices, interest rate futures, currency options, interest rate swaps, and such esoteric instruments as options on the terms of corporate takeovers (caps, collars, and floors). Collectively these are known as **derivatives** (because they are derived from another financial instrument).

### The Liberalization of Trade

Figure 4.2 on p. 64 provides a visual reminder of the explosive growth of world trade over the last 20 years. Much of that growth can be explained by the progressive liberalization of trade that has been a mark of international trading relations since the end of the Second World War. As noted in Chapter 12, **trade liberalization** refers to efforts to remove barriers to the transborder movement of goods and services. It begins with an attempt to lower, and then eliminate altogether, tariffs and duties. It seeks to replace discriminatory practices such as **preferences** with nondiscriminatory approaches like **Most-Favoured-Nation** (MFN), in which all states are treated as though they were indeed the "most favoured." It seeks to eliminate **dumping**—the selling of goods in a foreign market at a price below that charged in a home market. It also seeks to eliminate **nontariff barriers** (NTBs), the various policies that governments put in place besides tariffs and duties to favour their goods and services over those of foreigners.

The liberalization has occurred in a number of forums, both bilateral and multilateral. The key multilateral forum for the negotiated dismantling of barriers to trade has been at the GATT, in a series of multilateral negotiations called **GATT Rounds**. The earlier rounds were unnamed and relatively short.* Beginning in 1961, GATT rounds started to be given names: the Dillon Round (1961–62) was named after the U.S. secretary of the treasury who initiated it, C. Douglas Dillon. The Kennedy Round, named after John F. Kennedy, ran for four years (1963–1967); the Tokyo Round lasted for six years (1973–79); and the Uruguay Round began in August 1986 and was not completed until December 1993. The increasing length of the Rounds can easily be explained: each Round involved more and more actors, and each tried to dismantle barriers to trade in more and more sectors and categories. With each Round, the number of barriers to trade was reduced, but each Round grappled with thornier issues. Thus, for example, the Uruguay Round was supposed

---

* These were held at Geneva in 1947 and 1955–56; Annecy, France, in 1949; and Torquay, England, in 1951–52.

to conclude in 1990, but was delayed because of the magnitude of the Round's scope and the quarrels over the highly contentious issue of agricultural trade.[4]

Freer trade has also been pursued regionally or bilaterally. Canada and the United States established **sectoral free trade**—in which goods in one industrial or economic sector can pass duty-free—in defence products in 1958 and in automobiles and automobile parts (the "Auto Pact") in 1965. In 1989, an across-the-board free trade agreement came into force. Subsequently, the United States began negotiations with Mexico for a similar agreement; the Canadian government, concerned about the implications of the United States taking a **hub-and-spoke approach**[*] to North American free trade, pressed to be included. The North American Free Trade Agreement was approved in 1993. Other bilateral free trade agreements include the Australia New Zealand Closer Economic Relationship Trade Agreement (ANZCERTA, or usually CER for short), signed in 1983; Israel has signed free trade agreements with both the United States and Canada; and Canada and Chile signed a free trade agreement when the United States Congress balked at admitting Chile to NAFTA. In addition, there are a number of multilateral free trade areas or customs unions—the best known is the European Union, discussed in more detail below.

### The Transformation of Production

At the same time as we have seen changes in the financial and trade components of the international economy, we have also seen a shift in the nature of production. A useful way to describe this change is to borrow the terminology used by the political philosopher Antonio Gramsci to analyze the political implications of the way in which the Ford Motor Company organized capitalist production—**Fordism**.[5] While Henry Ford was by no means the first to use such techniques, his plants—and their products—quickly came to be icons of a particular way of organizing manufacturing. Fordism features mass production of products from standard interchangeable parts put together on an assembly line; Fordist production thus typically requires large aggregations of semiskilled workers in large plants and considerable inventories of component parts. Because of the high fixed costs of tooling and machining, production runs tended to be long and not marked by much variation.

In the last two decades, we have seen a partial eclipse of Fordist production, particularly in the countries of the North. For some, the rise of the fast-food industry is a case of neo-Fordist production: they see the minimum-wage teenagers and early retirees who are the staple labourers for the "McJobs" on the "assembly lines" at McDonald's, Hungry Jack's, or Harvey's as the "new" equivalent of the workers on automotive assembly lines. **Post-Fordist** production, by contrast, is completely different. It features smaller and more cohesive production units with shorter production runs, aimed at niche rather than mass markets.

---

[*] The "hub-and-spoke" approach refers to the preference of the United States (the hub) for dealing with each of its trading partners (the spokes) separately, rather than taking a multilateral approach. Some argue that a hub-and-spoke arrangement allows the United States government to divide and rule; however, many diplomats of smaller countries say they prefer to deal with the United States government one-on-one, where they have the undivided attention of American officials, rather than in large multilateral forums, where their views tend to be overlooked by American diplomats more interested in the views of larger powers.

The need for large inventories is eliminated by precisely timed (or just-in-time [JIT]) delivery of components for assembly. Computerization has been crucial: with the spread of electronic point of sale (EPOS) technology, information from each sale at the retail level can be constantly fed from the cash register back to the factory floor, allowing for almost instantaneous shifts in production and delivery.

Production is *delocalized*, placed instead in different sites, often in different countries, with the needs of production fitted more closely to the different labour markets and regulatory environments in the international system. Thus some tasks, such as straight assembly, can be done in low-wage or nonunionized labour markets; other tasks may be more suited for higher-wage labour markets. Some production that produces considerable pollution may be located in jurisdictions with lax environmental protection. Even knowledge-intensive sectors, such as research and development, which used to be performed almost entirely in MNC home countries, is now also delocalized.[6]

The changing nature of production, when combined with a massive increase in the amount of international capital available for investment, has considerable implications for firms in the contemporary political economy. Capital that is not tied down by large-scale plants is more mobile, with the result that production—and the jobs that go with it—can be moved from jurisdiction to jurisdiction far more readily than was ever possible under Fordist production.

## The Political Consequences of Economic Change

Some have suggested that these multifaceted changes in the international *economic* system have fundamentally altered the nature of the contemporary *political* system. In particular, it is argued that the arrival of a globalized economy has made the idea of a national economy obsolete. And this, in turn, has changed the nature and functions of contemporary sovereign national governments. In particular, the **globalization thesis** argues that governments have lost control over those very things that gave the sovereign nation-state its meaning and its legitimacy: the ability to protect the nation and its unique characteristics. Instead, governments everywhere find themselves bending to the dictates of others in the global marketplace.[7]

First, governments must bend to what is called—with no sense of irony—the **discipline of the market**: the tendency of capital to move out of a particular "national space" that does not provide investors and would-be investors with a high degree of comfort. **Capital flight** occurs for a number of different reasons. Sometimes it is because of a radical change in the politics of a country that transforms a space once deemed to be "friendly" to capital into a space highly risky for capital. Thus, for example, the outbreak of antiapartheid protests in the townships in South Africa in the southern spring of 1984 set in train a crisis for foreign capital, which to that point had happily moved to South Africa. Television images of South African security forces shooting at blacks from distinctively-styled South African armoured cars, or attacking blacks with dogs and whips, did little to reassure foreign investors that their capital in South Africa was safe. Those images galvanized a burgeoning **divestment** movement in North America, Western Europe, and Australia. Large-scale investment funds, such as pension funds or endowments, were pressured to sell shares in companies doing business in South Africa. As the nervousness of foreign investors grew, capital flight increased. For example 11 billion Rand were wiped off the value of shares on the Johannesburg stock market in just one week of trading in July 1985. And when Chase Manhattan, an American bank with US$600 million in loans to South Africa, decided that it would refuse to roll over short-term credits, other banks joined in. They were moved by what is known as the **herd instinct** on the international markets (the tendency of investors to move with the crowd for fear of being left holding a stack of investments made worthless by frenzied efforts to sell).[8] The consequences for the apartheid regime were considerable; indeed, it can be argued that the process of what Audie Klotz calls "the National Party's negotiating itself out of power"[9] between 1990 and 1993 began with the financial crisis of 1985.

Sometimes the herd instinct is sparked by something as evanescent as the comment of a political leader. For example, when Mahathir bin Muhammad, prime minister of Malaysia, mused at the Asia Pacific Economic Cooperation (APEC) summit in November 1997 that it would be desirable for APEC to regulate foreign exchange transactions to curb currency speculation, traders responded like a herd of grazing gazelles spooked into flight by the snap of a twig: they rushed to their phones to initiate a selling spree of Malaysian ringgits. (This prompted Mahathir to acknowledge that "I have been told not to shoot my mouth [off] too much, because every time I do, the ringgit falls."[10])

The global integration of financial markets means that withdrawal of capital from a locality can occur with amazing speed. Brokers and traders who operate the round-the-clock/round-the-world money markets monitor each other's movements; even ordinary "little" investors are able to monitor global markets in real time on the Internet. All these market players will on occasion engage in a rush to sell holdings of foreign exchange, stocks, futures, and other derivatives. This is what happened in December 1994, when a rapid sell-off sparked the "peso crisis" that we looked at in the last chapter. Alternatively, the consequence can be what is called a **meltdown**—currencies collapse, portfolios lose their value, stock market indices tumble. For example, it was estimated that by the end of the Asian meltdown of the autumn of 1997, fully US$300 billion had been wiped off the value of the markets.

The logical corollary for governments wishing to avoid such negative scenarios is the need to embrace measures that will keep—and indeed attract—foreign direct investment (FDI). Philip G. Cerny suggested that this has led to the rise of the **competition state**.[11] These are governments prompted to compete with other governments to make their jurisdiction as attractive as possible for what Robert Reich calls **footloose capital**—international capital that seeks solid returns from any market, anywhere.[12] But the rise of the competition state has deep consequences.

In particular, national distinctiveness gives way to **harmonization**—the process by which governments shape their policies to match as closely as possible the policies being pursued in other jurisdictions so as to attract (or so as not to lose) capital investment.[13] But harmonization means that governments often end up having to pursue lowest common denominator policies. In particular, distinctive national social welfare policies not widely pursued by others—national childcare, long-service leave provisions, universal health care—are logical targets for harmonization, since it can so easily be argued that such locally distinctive policies are expensive frills from which FDI shies away.

The process of globalization also gives rise to **cultural homogeneity**—as the consumer preferences of individuals are more and more shaped by global corporations marketing goods and services on a global basis. This, it has been argued, creates a "McWorld" of "fast music, fast computers, and fast food—with MTV, Macintosh, and McDonald's pressing nations into one commercially homogenous global network..."[14] In such a process, nations are assumed to lose their distinctiveness.

Finally, the globalization thesis assigns multinational corporations a central place in the new global economy. Whereas in the past, MNCs tended to be seen as working hand-in-hand with Northern governments; today they are commonly described as "stateless"—in the sense that they supposedly know no allegiance to particular nation-states, but will locate wherever an appropriate opportunity for high return/low risk investment presents itself. Wherever MNCs locate, they produce tangible political and economic effects, some deemed beneficial, others seen as negative. Whether their impact on the localities in which they locate are positive or negative, many observers seem to agree: it is troubling that the MNC is accountable to no one.

For these reasons, the processes of globalization provoke considerable concern for economic nationalists, who, as we noted in Chapter 12, place great value on the state being able to make independent decisions about the nation's economy. Thus, the special status that MNCs are likely to be given under the new rules being negotiated to guide international investment arouses concern for economic nationalists such as Maude Barlow, chair of the Council of Canadians, a nationalist group which has worked since the mid-1980s to oppose such initiatives as the Canada-U.S. Free Trade Agreement and NAFTA. Barlow notes that under the Multilateral Agreement on Investment (MAI), corporations are to be accorded standing comparable to states, able to participate in dispute settlement mechanisms as separate entities. According to her, this will "place unacceptable restrictions on the ability of democratically elected governments to act on behalf of citizens."[15]

Such concerns are not uncommon. Pauline Hanson, elected to the Australian House of Representatives as an independent in the 1996 elections, has also expressed fears about the costs of globalization. While Hanson is better known for her views on the perils of Asian immigration to Australia,* her maiden speech to Parliament also focused on the degree to which Australian independence was being undermined by the global economy, and called on the government in Canberra to "stop kowtowing to financial markets, international organisations, world bankers, investment companies and big business people." Similar sentiments have been expressed by Patrick Buchanan, who sought the

---

* In her maiden speech to Parliament, Hanson complained that Australia was being "swamped by Asians." In a subsequent interview, she told *The Bulletin* that "My mother has said for many years, the yellow race will rule the world... It's very frightening." See *The Bulletin* (22 October 1996), 22; for Hanson's maiden speech, see Australia, *Commonwealth Parliamentary Debates*, House of Representatives (10 September 1996), 3860–63.

*"America's Rust Belt testifies to the triumph of free trade ideology over national interests."*

Republican nomination for the United States presidency in both 1992 and 1996: "Since America's tariff walls have been torn down to propitiate the insatiable gods of 'free trade,'" he said in 1993, "vast swatches of our industry—radios, TVs, VCRs, steel, autos, textiles, shipping, mining, cameras, robotics—have been sacrificed. America's Rust Belt testifies to the triumph of free trade ideology over national interests."[16]

## The Impact of Globalization: An Assessment

Does globalization represent a challenge to the sovereign nation-state, as those who embrace the globalization thesis assert? Certainly the rhetoric of globalization has become a pervasive feature of contemporary discourse. Elites—corporate leaders, university presidents, newspaper editors, television producers, school board chairs, management gurus, and politicians—all chatter happily about "meeting the challenges of a globalized world." Advertising images are overlaid with the globalization idea, whether it be IBM showing us people everywhere going "on-line" or airlines touting their new global alliances.

Likewise, there can be no doubt that globalization has had an impact on the national state and national politics. The sovereign state's capacity to protect the nation and to preserve its distinctiveness vis-à-vis other nations has indeed been challenged by the forces of integration, internationalization, and globalization. National policies or orientations that diverge from the global norm quickly attract the "discipline of the market." As a result, the national state today pays less attention to some social issues than in the past: unemployment is one example. However, as Ann Capling notes, it is not because unemployment is either an insoluble or intractable public policy problem; rather, it is because efforts to use public spending to generate employment would quickly be punished by international financial markets.[17]

It is also true that we have seen the spread of elements of what might be called a global "culture." A number of scholars have pointed to the rise of a **globalized elite**, or class.[18] Certainly the pervasive spread of English as a global second language is a cultural phenomenon deeply associated with the rise of a global economy. One small but illustrative measure of homogenization is how many sites of human activity across the world today are virtually indistinguishable from one another: airports, city centres, stock exchanges, presidential offices, universities, shopping malls. One could even point to the growing homogenization in dress, or the ubiquitousness of sneakers as global footwear.

But if the homogenizing influence of globalization has had an impact on the *practices* of different nations, can we therefore conclude that it has had an impact on the *idea* of nation? Some, like Lewis H. Lapham, editor of *Harper's*, believe it has. Lapham has argued that for many in the globalized economy, "national identity becomes a sentimental novelty, comparable to a picturesque background for a trendy movie"—in other words, decorative form without substance.[19]

Others are equally sceptical about the relevance of the nation-state. **Postnationalists** like Yasemin Soysal and Mary Kaldor suggest that we are "beyond nationalism," and that the idea of nation has been supplanted by other concepts of identity. Soysal, for example, argues that the widespread embrace of universal human rights has had an important impact on the nation. In her view, the idea of *universal personhood* has superseded *national citizenship*, with the result that "the link between the individual and the state becomes more instrumental and routine rather than charismatic and sentimental."[20] The state, in other words, no longer exists to serve and protect a nation of individuals, but merely the individuals who happen to be located in that geopolitical space still called a nation. In this conception, the national state is reduced, in Margaret Canovan's evocative phrase, to the **"service-station state,"** in which people see the modern nation-state in a highly instrumental way as little more than a means of "servicing" their particular needs and desires.[21]

The postnationalist perspective may describe the attitudes of some, particularly those whose class, occupation, income, or personal wealth afford them a more internationalized, globalized, or cosmopolitan existence. But it is not at all clear that postnationalism comes close to describing the attitudes of large numbers of humankind today. On the contrary: it could be argued that the evidence strongly points in precisely the other direction. In other words, there is considerable evidence that, despite the unmistakable impact of the globalized economy on the national state, one can see nonetheless see evidence that the national idea continues to grip the imagination of the vast majority of people. The nation, and the sovereign nation-state that is designed to protect and nourish it, remain the focus of paramount political loyalty—in spite of the homogenizing influences of the global economy. We can perhaps see this best by looking at alternative ways of organizing political authority and political loyalty. To a consideration of these we now turn.

## ALTERNATIVE IMAGINED COMMUNITIES: HISTORICAL AND NOTIONAL

The degree to which nationalism has solidified the sovereign nation-state as the object of political loyalty is reflected in the failure of alternative ways of thinking about political community and organizing political authority to gain currency. In this section, we look at attempts to organize politics differently and to focus people's loyalties on a different level than the nation-state. We also look at an historical effort to rethink the basis of human division—Hitler's race politics. We then turn to a very different experiment, the "European idea," and explore supranational politics. Another kind of politics above the nation has been suggested by Samuel P. Huntington, who argues we should look at humankind as being cleaved not by nation-states, but by civilizations. Finally, we explore ideas about communities that remain totally notional, or imaginary, at this juncture.

### *Rassepolitik*: The Nazi Vision of Politics

I argued in Chapter 14 that the ideas of Adolf Hitler and the Nazis can be seen as a clear alternative to the nation-state: ***Rassepolitik*** ("race politics"). In this vision of politics, humankind was to be divided by race, and politics was to revolve around one's place in the racial hierarchy. The world would be governed by a master race, its governing apparatus centred in a Reich of German Aryans. The Reich's goal was the racial "purification" of as much of the world as it could control, with the *Untermenschen* (or subhumans) to be exterminated as little more than contaminating vermin, or used as expendable slave labour to serve the master race. In this scheme, nations were to be swept aside; what mattered was one's race.

However, the *Rassepolitik* of the Nazis was itself swept aside by those committed to the idea of nation. The "United Nations"—as they unambiguously described themselves—fought to uphold not only the independence of their political communities against domination, absorption, or destruction by the armies of Germany, Japan, and Italy. In the case of the war against Germany, the effect (if not the cause) was to sustain the notion of nation against the Nazi alternative. Moreover, as the extent of Nazi genocide was fully revealed after the war, conscious efforts were made to eliminate the ideas of *Rassepolitik*. These efforts included memorialization, such as the United States Holocaust Memorial Museum in Washington; legislation such as **race-hatred laws**, which makes it a criminal offence to advocate hatred against an identifiable group; and social marginalization of those who espouse racist ideas.

It is true that Hitler's vision of the necessary supremacy of one race over another did not die with him or with the other German Nazis who committed suicide or were put on trial after the war and executed. But today, Hitler's idea of dividing humanity into a racial hierarchy and organizing global governance through a master race is a fringe idea, pushed by a small number of neo-Nazi "skinhead" groups, Holocaust-deniers, or members of far-right militias in the United States. Given the ease with which one can create sites on the World Wide Web, it is not surprising that these ideas appear most frequently on the Internet. The Simon Wiesenthal Center, a nongovernmental organization that tracks Nazis, estimates that there are over 600 racist sites on the Web. Some governments routinely move against these sites: for example, a site known as "Virtual Auschwitz"—featuring a hotlink that despatched "subhumans" to a virtual replica of the Auschwitz death camp—was chased out of France, then appeared in Québec, and was closed down in that province. But racist sites readily migrate to the United States, where the Supreme Court decided in June 1997 that racist speech on the Web was protected by the First Amendment. One simply moves to an Internet service provider located in the United States, as one Canadian Holocaust-denier did when threatened with prosecution under those sections of the Criminal Code of Canada outlawing the public advocacy of race hatred. Likewise, banned sites are often "mirrored" (copied) by American Internet enthusiasts who are more interested in promoting free speech on the Web than the message on the sites themselves.

*But racist sites readily migrate to the United States, where the Supreme Court decided in June 1997 that racist speech on the Web was protected by the First Amendment.*

But a survey of racist sites on the Web suggests that those who advocate racial purification today—such as some neo-Nazi groups—are fundamentally *nationalist* before they are *racist*: they want their *nation* racially pure rather than wanting, as Hitler did, to do away with nations and organize political community around race.

## Transcending the Nation-State: Two Experiments

In this section, we look at efforts that have been made in the past half-century to transcend the nation-state. In one case, we look at the attempt to rise above the *nation* to create new supranational structures in Europe. In the other, we look at efforts among Arabs to rise above the *state* to create new structures for the nation.

### Supranationalism: The Case of the European Union

**Supranationalism** is an attempt to create political community *above* (supra) the nation, in essence to combine existing independent (and sovereign) political entities and fashion a new form of political authority over the existing sovereign nation-states. In other words, supranationalism is not traditional **federalism** of the kind practised in Australia, Canada, or the United States, which is the conscious merging of different (and usually self-governing) units into one state which shows a single "sovereign" face to the world, while sharing various sovereign powers between the central government and the governments of each of the constituent units. Rather, supranationalism involves the creation of new forms of political authority.

In Europe, the national idea has been complemented—one cannot say superseded—by another idea, the **"European idea."** In brief, the European idea begins with a general *economic* goal rather than a political goal: to create a single economic market. This has meant embracing the idea of eliminating national barriers to the movement of all the factors of wealth creation—finance capital, technology, goods, services, and labour; eliminating national differences in standards and regulations for a variety of economic activities; and trying to standardize transportation infrastructure that is deeply national in nature (British, French, and German railways all have different loading gauges, for example). It has meant trying to forge common policies and regulations on nationally contentious issues, such as agriculture; it has meant seeking to coordinate a huge range of government services. Most importantly, it has meant trying to create a single European currency and a single central bank for all European countries.

To govern this huge panoply of activities, the European idea was that the various sovereign nation-states of western Europe could form a political organization that would be more than an association of national governments, like the United Nations, the North Atlantic Treaty Organization, or the Commonwealth. At the same time, it would be less than a single, sovereign, federated "United States of Europe," in which all national governments would surrender their sovereignty over certain issue areas to a central government. Rather, the European "idea" is that national governments would continue to retain their sovereignty, but a supranational layer of governmental structures would be created to govern the economic coordination of the European area.

The institutions that govern what is commonly known as the "European area" today emerged out of the initial steps taken in the 1950s to integrate the economies of western European countries. Then, the European idea was articulated by the French foreign minister, Robert Schuman, who envisaged the deep intertwining of the German and French economies as a means of ensuring that the two countries would never again engage in the kinds of wars that had consumed them in 1870–1871, 1914–1918, and 1939–1945. Schuman began with the most important industries for both, coal and steel.

An agreement establishing the European Coal and Steel Community (ECSC) was signed in April 1951 and came into force in July 1952. From the outset, the governments of France, West Germany, Italy, and the "Benelux" countries (Belgium, Luxembourg, and the Netherlands) sought to make the "Community" much more than merely a common market in coal, steel, iron ore, and scrap. A headquarters in Luxembourg was established that featured all three branches of government: an executive branch consisting of a Council of Ministers and a High Authority; a legislative branch, or Assembly; and a Court of Justice.

The ECSC was expanded on 25 March 1957, when the **Treaty of Rome** was signed. This treaty created two new European communities: the European Economic Community (EEC) and the Atomic Energy Community (Euratom). New executive institutions were created for each community, but the legislature and court were shared by all three communities. In the mid-1960s, it was agreed to create a single executive authority for all three communities: as of 1967, they were served by the Common Institutions of the European Communities, more colloquially known in the singular as the European Community (EC). By what is colloquially known as the **Maastricht Treaty**★ that came into force on 1 November 1993, the EC's name was changed to the European Union (EU), even though the three Communities continue to exist.

The membership in the Communities has expanded since the early 1970s. On 1 January 1973, Britain, Denmark, and Ireland joined; on 1 January 1981, Greece was admitted, followed by Portugal and Spain five years later. Austria, Finland, and Sweden were admitted on 1 January 1995.

In the 36 years between the signing of the Treaty of Rome on 25 March 1957 that brought the European Economic Community into being, and the Maastrich Treaty that brought the European Union into force on 1 November 1993, European governments have created a cobweb of linkages between the various member states, linking not only the economies of the EU's members, but also establishing linkages between national capitals and the European centre in Brussels. A great deal of economic activity and policy is coordinated and controlled from that centre. Moreover, through its redistributive policies, citizens of richer EU members see their taxes indirectly reallocated to poorer EU members—the so-called "poor four" (Greece, Spain, Ireland, and Portugal). An additional layer of political identity has also been created: citizens of all member states are also citizens of the EU, and have voting rights throughout the Union at both the municipal and European levels (but not the national level, where voting is still limited to nationals). While the EU does not tax the citizen directly, it does have its own sources of revenues in addition to annual assessments provided by national governments.

During those 36 years, Europeans have seen the growth of another layer of government beyond the municipal, state, and national levels. This fourth level of government has an executive branch, a separate legislature to which members are directly elected, a court of justice, a bureaucracy, and even a police force. As the Focus on p. 466 suggests, these institutions constitute another level of governance above the sovereign nation-state.

The institutions discussed in the Focus make the EU a unique actor in contemporary international affairs. The EU is neither a federation nor an intergovernmental organization (IGO). Because it does not fit well into existing categories, some scholars have difficulty with the idea of characterizing it as a supranational actor. For example, Robert O. Keohane and Stanley Hoffmann prefer to use the expression "pooled sovereignty" to try to describe the

---

★ The Treaty on European Union was initialled by the heads of state and government of the European Communities at Maastricht, Netherlands, on 11 December 1991; it was signed on 7 February 1992 and ratified by the various members over the course of 1992 and 1993.

*For the EU itself is in fact a fully sovereign actor in global politics: as an entity, it and its officials enjoy the same privileges as other sovereign states.*

EU's essence. They argue that in the EU, sovereignty is shared, or pooled, but states still remain paramount, with no sovereign authority transferred to a central body.[22] But this does not quite capture the anomalousness of the EU's situation. For the EU itself is in fact a fully sovereign actor in global politics: as an entity, it and its officials enjoy the same privileges as other sovereign states. Likewise, the institutions of governance in Brussels, Strasbourg, Luxembourg, and other European cities do not resemble the sovereign apparatus of other states, either unitary (such as China) or federal (like the United States). But at the same time, the EU's governing apparatus has most of the characteristics of a state apparatus: it collects revenues; it makes, adjudicates, and enforces laws; it *governs*. And sometimes the EU apparatus takes actions against the wishes of a member state, and in that sense it also exercises power. Member states can be outvoted, overruled, fined, or sanctioned. In short, there is more than a pooling of sovereignty occurring in Europe.

But for all the changes to the practice of sovereignty that Europeans have introduced over the last 45 years, is there any evidence that the "European idea," as an idea to rival the national idea, has taken root in Europe or elsewhere in the world?

There is little doubt that the supranational institutions of the European Union have been embraced by Europeans, and that governance by Brussels is a deeply embedded part of European politics. To be sure, there are numerous "Euroskeptics," as they are called, but they tend to take issue with the pace of integration rather than the idea of the EU itself. For example, in no EU member can one find strong support for withdrawal. And only three European nations—Iceland, Norway, and Switzerland[*]—have chosen to remain outside the EU's embrace. Many more countries want to join, including Malta, Cyprus, Turkey, and a number of states in Central Europe.

For all of this, however, the "European idea" has not really supplanted the "national idea" in Europe. Europeans may demonstrate an enduring attachment to the evolution of pan-European institutions, but at the same time existing national identities remain much stronger than notions of "Europeanness." There is perhaps no better indication of this than the difficulties that the 15 members have had in effecting monetary union to complement, and strengthen, economic union.

Efforts to create a European monetary regime go back to the collapse of the Bretton Woods system, when EC members tried to create an exchange rate mechanism (ERM). They agreed to fix their exchange rates by agreeing to hold their currencies within a 2.25-per-cent band against one another, and holding that band to a 4.5-per-cent band against the U.S. dollar—an arrangement known as the **snake in the tunnel**. However, the Europeans were no more successful in keeping rates fixed than the rest of the international community was, and a number of members left the snake. In 1978, the EC tried to solve the problem by creating the European Monetary System (EMS), with a unit of currency like the Special

---

[*] After Greenland was given self-governing autonomy from Denmark in 1979, the Greenland government sought, and was given, permission to withdraw from the EU.

# FOCUS

## *Supranational Governance: The Institutions of the EU*

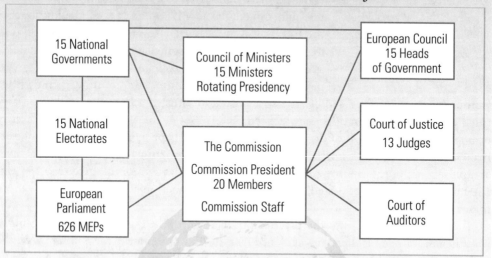

THE COUNCIL OF MINISTERS

This body is the executive decision-making body, deciding on policy and directing the Commission. (In addition, there is a body called the European Council, a regular meeting between all 15 heads of government and the president of the Commission.) Each member state sends one minister to the Council. The presidency of this body is rotated every six months, with a roster established alphabetically (though by how the nations are called in their national languages rather than their English names—hence Deutschland, Ellas, España, France, etc., not France, Germany, Greece, Spain). Each state has one vote for decisions requiring a simple majority or unanimity. For the budget, a **qualified majority** is needed. This is based on the weighted vote assigned to each state, as follows:

| | |
|---|---|
| 10 | Germany, France, Italy, Britain |
| 8 | Spain |
| 5 | Belgium, Greece, Netherlands, Portugal |
| 4 | Austria, Sweden |
| 3 | Denmark, Ireland, Finland |
| 2 | Luxembourg |

For a qualified majority, 62 of these 87 votes must be cast in favour (an abstention is a negative vote), and these votes must be from at least 10 of the 15 Members. This system ensures that it is difficult for any large country to get an item rejected, but comparably easier for two large countries to object. Likewise, it is difficult for the larger countries to pass items objected to by a number of smaller states, even though the smaller states may not have enough votes to stop it.

THE COMMISSION

This body is an *executive* body in the sense that its role is to execute decisions taken by the Council; however, it formulates proposals for decision by the Council and the Parliament. This body consists of 20 Commissioners serving five-year terms: each large state nominates two, and the smaller countries one. The Commission is supported by a bureaucracy of some 15 000 employees. It was also intended to be a properly supranational body: the Commissioners are supposed to be independent of their state. Decision is by consensus rather than voting. The Commission issues three kinds of instructions: *regulations*, which carry the force of law throughout the EU and supersede national law; *directives*, which are binding, but member states get to decide how to implement them; and *decisions*, which are binding on specific named parties (rather than being applied throughout the EU).

### THE EUROPEAN PARLIAMENT

There are 626 members of the European Parliament (MEPs), distributed among the member states in rough proportion to population. Different national electoral systems are used to elect them for five-year terms. The Parliament can order the Commission to resign, and has the right to approve the Commission. It can reject and amend the budget, and, under certain circumstances, reject Council positions. Under the Maastricht Treaty, Parliament's role was expanded to provide it with "codecision" powers.

### THE COURT OF JUSTICE

There are 13 judges on the Court of Justice, appointed for staggered six-year terms. The Court is designed to be the ultimate judge on the application of EU law. Member governments, individuals, and corporations can all bring actions against EU institutions; and the Commission itself can bring actions against member states. (Member states can only take actions against other member states after the dispute has first been brought to the Commission.) The decisions

of the Court, including fines imposed for behaviour judged wrongful, are binding.

The Court of Justice should not be confused with the European Court of Human Rights in Strasbourg, with whose decisions on human-rights violations European governments normally comply. Despite its name, the Strasbourg court is not an EU body.

### THE COURT OF AUDITORS

The EU created an agency to perform audits of the EU as well as national institutions. The auditors are also responsible for reviewing all EU expenditures and revenues. These revenues are derived from four sources: the common external tariff imposed on goods imported from other countries (a source that has largely dried up as a result of successive GATT Rounds of tariff-cutting); levies imposed under the Common Agricultural Program; a levy of 1.4 per cent of each member's revenues from the VAT (value-added tax, comparable to North American sales taxes); and a contribution from each member government, based on a GNP-derived formula. It should be noted that unlike a federation, in which both levels of government are able to tax citizens directly, the EU does not act directly on its citizens.

Drawing Right (SDR) used by the World Bank and International Monetary Fund. The European Currency Unit (**ECU**) was a basket of currencies on which an internal exchange rate could be fixed, but that would float against the rest of the world. Although Greece, Portugal, and Britain remained outside the EMS, this ERM worked relatively well until 1986, when the EC embraced the Single European Act (SEA). This was an agreement to deepen the processes of integration. Among its measures was the removal of controls on capital movements, which opened all the ECU currencies to the forces of the currency market, making the EMS system impossible to maintain.

As a result, the EC decided to try to take the next step, the creation of a **monetary union**. The Maastricht Treaty thus embraced a timetable for an Economic and Monetary Union (EMU). A central bank was proposed to replace the Council of Central Bank Governors, and to be phased in. A European Monetary Institute (EMI) was established in January 1994 in Frankfurt am Main to deepen the cooperation between the EU governments on financial matters, particularly the central banks of each of the countries, in preparation for the creation of a European Central Bank (ECB). By 1999, the ECB will be in place to make monetary policy for the EU, and a single currency, the euro, will replace francs, deutschemarks, pounds, lira, and the other national currencies.

But the road to a single currency was difficult. In particular, members were beset by the difficulties of having to lower their national deficits to below three per cent of gross domestic product to meet a target set at Maastricht in 1991 for the introduction of the new currency. This process of harmonization revealed not only how different national economies remained, but also how many governments and publics were attached to those national differences. As a result, the path to 1999 was marked by some foot-dragging, particularly by Britain, where Euroskepticism runs deepest.

The debate over a single currency was also marked by a debate over symbols, which also demonstrated some of the limits to the European "idea." A number of nationlike symbols have been adopted for the EU—a 12-starred flag, a common red passport—but symbolic issues have proven to be as deeply contentious as substantive ones. For example, as the EU tried to move toward the embrace of a single European currency in 1999, it discovered that there was considerable popular opposition to seeing the disappearance of a national currency. Likewise, the name of the new currency proved problematic. At first, the euro was going to be called an ecu, after the ECU, until it was pointed out that an *écu* was an old French unit of currency—and it wouldn't do to give the new currency a French name. Even the new banknotes—carefully designed to avoid national symbols—caused grumbles when they were released in December 1996.

This is not to suggest that the European idea will not, in the fullness of time, come to fully supplant the national idea. Rather, the quarrels over the single currency issue reveal the degree to which the national idea is still alive in a European context, and how difficult it is to supplant deeply entrenched ideas about identity.

The kind of supranational integration we have seen in Europe has become so deeply entrenched that we often take it for granted. Yet it is important to recognize that the patterns of cooperation and power sharing that mark the European idea took a long time to develop. Moreover, the success of the experiment always depended on deep levels of commitment to the process of integration by both political leaders and ordinary folk alike. In particular, it was always necessary to ensure that conflicts of interest between the different nations never derailed a commitment to the supranational objective. Just how difficult it is to rise above the restrictive divisions of the sovereign nation-state can be seen by comparing another, and less successful, experiment in transcendence: the pan-Arab experiment.

### Nation Transcending State: The Case of Pan-Arabism

During the colonial period, a strand of Arab nationalism focused on the possibility of a united North Africa. Throughout the Cold War era, a number of postcolonial Arab leaders were seized with this idea of **pan-Arabism** inherited from colonial-era nationalists—the creation of a political entity that would incorporate the different Arab states that were emerging from colonialism. Two leaders in particular were at the forefront of this idea: Gamal Abdel Nasser, who was the leader of Egypt from 1954 (he was officially elected president in 1956) until his death in 1970, and Mu'ammar al-Qadhafi of Libya, who came to power in 1969.

The first initiative to form a broader Arab union was an attempt to unite Egypt and Syria. Close military ties between the two countries and a common dislike for the West prompted Nasser and Shukri al-Kuwatli, the Syrian president, to form a union, known as the United

Arab Republic (UAR), on 1 February 1958. A plebiscite and presidential election held three weeks later in both countries confirmed the union and Nasser as president. The UAR did not last long. Nasser's policies ended up alienating a number of Syrians. He dissolved all Syrian political parties; sacked a number of army officers; abolished the Syrian bureaucracy; concentrated administrative power in Cairo; confiscated land in Syria for a program of land reform; and nationalized banks and insurance companies. The experiment ended with a *coup d'état* by Syrian troops on 28 September 1961.

After Gadhafi came to power in Libya in a coup in September 1968, he floated a proposal for a merger between Libya, Egypt, Sudan, and Syria which did not get beyond the negotiating stage in 1969. Undeterred, Gadhafi pursued the idea with Nasser's successor, Anwar al-Sadat. In 1972, they resurrected the idea of a federation, this time involving Egypt, Syria, and Libya. The Federation of Arab Republics was approved by referenda and a common legislature was established, but it never developed beyond this, and became moribund. On four subsequent occasions Gadhafi sought to merge Libya with other states as a first step in creating a broader Arab community: with Tunisia in 1974, with Syria in 1980, with Chad in 1981, and with Morocco in 1984.

While these unilateral efforts did not bear fruit, a later initiative by Algeria and Morocco gave rise to the Arab Maghreb Union (AMU), a conscious effort to copy the integrationist pattern established by the European Community (discussed in the previous section). On 17 February 1989, the leaders of Algeria, Libya, Mauritania, Morocco, and Tunisia signed the Arab Maghreb Treaty, designed to foster the same freedom of movement for goods, services, capital, and labour as in Europe. The treaty created a number of executive councils, a judicial body, and a secretariat. But the AMU was not able to surmount the deep political divisions among its members, which included territorial squabbles and quarrels over the admission of new members. Much of the integrationist process was effectively put on hold when the United Nations imposed mandatory sanctions against Libya in 1992 for refusing to extradite two suspects in the bombing of Pan Am flight 103 over Lockerbie, Scotland in December 1988—and other AMU members upheld the UN sanctions.

## Civilizational Divisions Revisited

These efforts to transcend the nation-state represent the forging of a new political identity from the existing division of the real world of sovereign nation-states. A very different kind of division has been suggested by some scholars in the wake of the end of the Cold War. No longer are the divisions between compass points; North and South, East and West are made irrelevant by the disappearance of the central rivalry between the two superpowers. Instead, it is argued that the post–Cold War world is cleaved by a **civilizational divide**.

### "The West and the Rest": The Clash Thesis

"Civilizations" (as opposed to civilization in the singular, which as noted in Chapter 8, refers to the movement out of the Neolithic Period) are usually defined in cultural terms—usually as an amalgam of ethnicity, language, religion, customs, self-identification, and "way of life." These civilizations, which can and do easily cut across the borders of nation-states, provide a focus for political and cultural identity that, it is argued, rival and indeed surpass the identity with nation.

Most importantly, it is argued that the ties that people feel for "their" civilization will provide the "fault lines" over which future world conflict will occur. Conflicts of interest will arise not so much between nations or states, but rather between civilizations, and the states and peoples which belong to these civilizations. In this view, states do not fade away. Rather, they rally to the civilizational cause, helping out when what Samuel P. Huntington calls a **kin-country** runs into trouble. For Huntington, the future is clear: "The clash of civilizations will dominate global politics. The fault lines between civilizations will be the battle lines of the future."[23]

> *"The clash of civilizations will dominate global politics. The fault lines between civilizations will be the battle lines of the future."*

Just as dividing the world by compass point requires identification of who is located where, so too does the civilizational thesis require that one begin by categorizing the civilizations themselves and identifying the kin-countries, usually using self-explanatory tags. Huntington divides the world into eight civilizations: Sinic (i.e., Chinese), Japanese, Hindu, Islamic, Western, Latin American, and African.[24] By contrast, Charles W. Kegley and Eugene R. Wittkopf divide the world into nine "cultural domains": European, Chinese, Russian, Islamic, black African, Hindu, Latin American, South African, and "other" (basically a category into which to put Papua New Guinea and Madagascar).[25]

Much of the civilizational argument concerns power. Of all the civilization fault lines Huntington sees, the one of prime concern is the fault line between the West and what Kishore Mahbubani called "the Rest."[26] In Huntington's view, the West is at the peak of its power and wealth, and there are significant conflicts of interest between the West and "the Rest" that cannot easily be overcome. But these are not just "descriptive hypotheses as to what the future may be like," as Huntington says; there are significant policy implications, as he admits on the next page: "This will require the West to maintain the economic and military power necessary to protect its interests in relation to these [other] civilizations."[27]

**The Civilizational Argument: An Assessment**

In response to critics, Huntington argued that he was proposing a new paradigm for thinking about world politics after the Cold War, and thus he had to use "simplified pictures of reality," as he put it.[28] In fact, when one looks at efforts, such as those of Huntington or Kegley and Wittkopf, to carve the world into civilizational divisions, the pictures are not just simplified; they are also of questionable accuracy.

Indeed, the efforts of these American scholars to divide the countries of the world into civilizations or cultural domains make for some interesting reading for folks abroad. Consider the Philippines. Both Huntington and Kegley and Wittkopf divide this country between civilizations: Kegley and Wittkopf paint some Filipino islands in the European domain, while others are classified as Hindu. Huntington paints the northern part of the Philippines as Sinic, and the southern half as Muslim. These are surely odd ways to categorize a country in which 84 per cent of the population are Roman Catholics, 10 per cent are

Protestants, four per cent are Muslims, and Hindus are such a minuscule minority that they do not even register on most data sets. Moreover, the last Sinic connections were in the 15th century, before the Spanish conquest.

Even odder is that Kegley and Wittkopf categorize all of Indochina, Indonesia, Thailand, Malaysia, Myanmar, and Bangladesh as part of the "Hindu" cultural domain, which would be news to the overwhelming number of Buddhists, Muslims, Christians, Taoists, and animists who make up the populations of this region (there are small Hindu minorities in Bangladesh and Malaysia). Their knowledge of Africa is not much better: Niger, Chad, Mali, Ethiopia are not classified as being part of the Islamic domain, but are listed as Black African.

Antipodeans are no doubt amused at how they are described in the civilization thesis. Huntington's map colours Papua New Guinea as a Western country; perhaps he and the cartographers at Simon and Schuster thought that this island was like Tasmania and belonged to Australia. Australia itself is described by Huntington as trying to "defect" from the West in the 1980s and early 1990s, an extreme reading of the policies of the Australian Labor Party (ALP) governments of Bob Hawke and Paul Keating, shared only by a right-wing fringe.[29] Kegley and Wittkopf at least know that PNG is not part of Australia, but they appear not to know what kind of civilization exists there, for PNG is categorized as "other"—which is one better, at least, than colouring it Hindu, as they did for PNG's non-Hindu neighbours.

Some categorizations are highly idiosyncratic. Kegley and Wittkopf give South Africa its own (mixed) cultural domain, the only country to be so honoured; likewise, Huntington assigns Japan its own civilization. Israel, which appears as a "Free World" country in Huntington's Cold War map, disappears into Islamic cross-hatching in his civilizational division, a shift of religious/cultural orientation which no doubt comes as a surprise to Israeli Jews. But this is no cartographic slip: Huntington makes quite clear in his various references to Israel that he does not regard it as a country of the West.

How important are such idiosyncratic, bizarre, or outright erroneous categorizations? Do they take away from the civilizational thesis? It can be argued that errors like this do have important implications for how we think about the argument that world politics in the future will be dominated by civilizational divisions.

For these idiosyncrasies and errors clearly demonstrate the foundation on which the civilizational argument rests: it depends above all else for its plausibility on being able to paint a portrait not unlike the "Civilized Self/Barbarian Other" dichotomy we examined in Chapter 8. This version still creates a dichotomy, but with a twist: instead of being confronted with a barbarian Other, the "Civilized We" is now surrounded by an "Other-Civilized Other." Note that for the dichotomy to work, one doesn't have to get the other civilizations right; indeed, it would appear that one really doesn't need to know much about the world beyond one's own civilization. Rather, it is enough simply to colour the map in a way that conveys the threat. But beyond the categorizations, there is little hard evidence offered either that people are beginning to define political identity in civilizational terms, or, more importantly, that the Rest is actually posing a threat to the West.

## Notional Forms of Political Identity

Of all the alternatives to the sovereign nation-state we have explored to this point, the "European idea" remains the only actual sustained experiment in alternative ways of organizing political authority and focusing people's political loyalty in the world. But it has not taken root anywhere else. Would it work anywhere else? To get some sense of the answer to that question, one must hypothesize how people would respond to proposals to alternatives to the nation. Imagine gathering roomfuls of people in Québec City, Winnipeg, Moose Jaw, Seattle, Boston, Houston, Monterrey, and Veracruz, and suggesting to them that the nation-state is passé, an outmoded political form that should be replaced. Pose the following alternatives to the present situation in North America, and imagine their reactions:

### Cosmopolitanism

The form of political authority and loyalty most commonly proposed as an alternative to the nation-state is nothing more than the nation-state writ large—a state-like apparatus for the entire globe, with all the coercive, regulatory, and taxing powers of the contemporary national state. In this vision of the future, all contemporary states, or even jurisdictions, would participate in a second, third, fourth, or fifth level of government (depending on what type of political system one lived in at present).

### Continentalism

Another possibility might be a North American superstate in which all existing internal political divisions—nations, states, and provinces—would be completely redrawn to reflect more accurately the north-south patterns of economic interaction and production and the increasingly integrated nature of the North American economy. Suggest that all existing symbols of *nation* be replaced by symbols of *continent*: a new continental name easily derived from north, norte, and nord (Normerica?); a continental flag; a continental currency stripped of the present national wording and artwork; even a new continental capital district constructed in the continental geographic centre around Topeka, Kansas. Suggest that the official languages of the new polity would be the official languages in place now; citizens of the new continent could of course expect to be served by their government in their choice of language. In short, suggest that people's political loyalty would be to the idea of *continent* rather than *nation*.

### Megapolitanism

Another possibility would be to downsize, to use Thomas Naylor's notion. An economist at Duke University, Naylor argued in 1994 of the United States that "Our nation is no longer manageable. The time has come...to begin planning the rational downsizing of America. We need to begin thinking about a new confederation of American states to replace the old Union."[30] Take Naylor's suggestion one step further: propose that the three nations of North America be dissolved and downsized, with supreme political authority vested in urban areas and their immediate hinterlands. In this vision of political organization, the *megapolis* would replace the nation as the source of ultimate political loyalty, not unlike the way in which hockey, baseball, and football fans see their city's teams now.

### A "New Medievalism"

In 1977, Hedley Bull, reflecting on the future of the international system, imagined the possibility of a return to the medieval period, when patterns of authority were blurred, when territoriality was not fully defined, and when allegiance and loyalty were marked by over-lapping obligations and responsibilities to different authority figures.[31] While it is unlikely that one would see the reemergence of the politico-religious institutions that underwrote the politics of medieval Europe, one could consider the forms of political authority favoured by the imaginations of Hollywood writers when they turn their minds to thinking about what the future will hold: the *corporation* as organizer of political authority and focus of political loyalty. Such a vision of dystopia is best portrayed in cult film classics like *Soylent Green* (1973), *Rollerball* (1975), and *Bladerunner* (1982), or TV's *Max Headroom*. In each, the symbols of nation would be replaced by symbols of corporation.

Indeed, Lewis Lapham might argue that life has already begun to imitate art. His tongue not entirely in his cheek, he suggests that the world has already splintered into an oligarchy of transnational corporate wealth: "Just as the Catholic church was the predominant institution in medieval Europe...so also the transnational corporation arranges the affairs of the late 20th century. The American congress and the American president serve at the pleasure of their commercial overlords."[32] In this view, the jump from loyalty to corporate brands and corporate-owned professional sports teams, to political loyalty, to the "corporation-as-liege-lord" is not altogether far-fetched.

## THE PERPETUATIVE LOGIC OF THE SOVEREIGN NATION-STATE

Each of the visions examined above proposes that instead of loving *nation*, people should love another political form—the *world*, or the *continent*, or a *megapolis*, or a *corporation*, or a combination of the above. Now imagine how our hypothetical panels would react to these suggestions for alternative political forms. It is likely that people in each of these cities would be willing to buy books and go to movies that sketch out such fantasies, but in the end they remain just that—fantasies, concoctions that amuse or intrigue, but which people simply will not wear in real life.

It is unlikely that our panels would accept the idea of world government. While some have argued that a global Leviathan is the only way to deal with political problems that are global in scope (for example, the environment or the redistribution of wealth), few enthusiasts of global government have thought through the implications of a world state. Most people who like the idea of global government tend to think that such a government would look like the governments they know, pursuing policies in their interests. But if a global government were created, reflecting the electoral preferences of all six billion humans, in whose interests would such a government likely operate? It is likely that a global government "of the people" would hold that the privileges of the wealthy few in the North could no longer be justified in the face of inequities in the south? Moreover, would a global state necessarily be a liberal democratic regime? Enthusiasts always assume that it would; they never reflect on the possibility that a global state may take a rather different form. On reflection, the members of our panels would likely have little enthusiasm for a world-state.

Would North Americans embrace the European idea? Americans might consider packing more stars into the fly of the Stars and Stripes if Canadians or Mexicans wanted to join the United States, but would they accept a scheme that would dismantle all of the symbols of nationhood that are so entrenched in their political culture? Mexicans and Canadians would be equally unlikely to accept such revisions of political loyalty. Deep antipathy toward the United States forms an important part of how many Canadians and Mexicans define their communities. It is one thing for Canada and Mexico to embrace free trade with the United States, as was done with the North American Free Trade Agreement (NAFTA) of 1993; it is another thing entirely to fashion a new political community with Americans.

Moreover, other elements of such a scheme would raise hackles of all sorts: Americans, for example, generally bristle at the idea of an "official" language if it is not English; what French-speaking member of our Québec City panel would agree to the dismantling of Québec's language laws in a way that would not only restore English as an official language in the territory formerly known as Québec, but would add Spanish too? Likewise, imagine trying to reconcile deeply entrenched differences between the three countries on such symbolic but contentious matters as gun control, the rights of women, capital punishment, and national health services.

A similar scepticism is likely to greet suggestions that political identity and authority be downsized to the level of city, or be transferred to corporations. It is not that our panellists

*Human notions of identity and community tend to change in the wake of large-scale disruptions and disasters.*

would not be capable of loving such entities as they love their nation; it is, rather, that they—or many other comparable panels in other places to whom these alternatives were put— would see no particular reason to do so under present conditions.

It is thus in the presumed reactions of our panellists that we can see the durability of the national idea—*under present conditions*. That qualifier is important. The survey of world politics in this book suggests that human notions of identity and community tend to change in the wake of large-scale disruptions and disasters. Great wars, revolutions, famines, plagues, epidemics, and depressions tend to produce shifts in world politics. It is by no means coincidental that the modern state took the shape it did after the disruption of the Great Depression; or that the "European idea" should have flourished so uniquely in an area that had known ten years of ruinous war, tens of millions of war dead, and a Holocaust; or that Chinese should have responded as pragmatically as they did after the violent disruptions of the Cultural Revolution.

That is the paradox of the end of the Cold War. The Soviet Union and the rivalry with the United States evaporated, profoundly altering the pattern of world politics. Life changed for hundreds of millions of people as defence industries everywhere downsized and as the

**peace dividend**—the "savings" from reduced defence spending—kicked in; as the Soviet Union and its allies fashioned a postcommunist existence; and as the South discovered both positive and negative consequences of the end of the Cold War. But the deep transformation was neither cataclysmic nor catastrophic; it did not catalyze profound changes in the way in which individuals *thought* about world politics.

The absence of cataclysmic change has particular implications for the dominance of the sovereign nation-state as the focus of individual loyalties—and hence for world politics. In Part 5, I argued that nationalism contains a logic that legitimates and enshrines political divisions based on nation; that logic also legitimates the use of force to create, sustain, or defend the nation. This is the *perpetuative logic* of nationalism. For nationalism holds up the Westphalian state as the political form most appropriate for the protection of the nation. As a result, because nationalism does not permit the end of nation (nationalists, by definition, cannot consciously seek to wind their nations down or declare them at an end), the sovereign nation-state becomes cast in stone, an unchanging necessity for the realization of the national ideal. As long as one believes in the nation, *no other political form, no other political loyalty, is permissible*. It is this perpetuative logic that shapes responses to notional alternatives.

## CONCLUSION

The survey of sources of human division in the last nine chapters has been essentially secular. Chapter 8 began by exploring the basis on which humans divided themselves as they emerged from the Neolithic. Much of its discussion focused on the political communities of antiquity, looking at tribes, empires, and *poleis*, and examining the tendency of humans to divide themselves along civilizational and religious lines. Essentially, the discussion focused on developments before the end of the Middle Ages. Chapter 9 picked up that story, tracing the evolution of a contemporary phenomenon that grew out of feudal times: the state. Chapters 10 and 11 looked at the juridical face of the geopolitical divisions of the world: the notion of sovereignty as it is practised in the contemporary era. In Chapter 12 we looked at another contemporary phenomenon, the nation, that, when layered onto the sovereign state, provides a tight basis for division. In Chapter 13, we examined how the idea of nation manifested itself in imperialism in the 19th century, but then was eclipsed by the spread of nationalism throughout the international system. Chapter 14 explored the divisive logic of the national idea in different areas, in particular its impact on warfare in the 20th century. In Chapters 15 and 16, we looked at two sets of divisions that were layered on top of the national divisions.

By dividing the discussion in this way, however, I do not mean to imply that one might think about the discussion of human division in Chapter 8 as purely historical phenomena that can be safely forgotten about—"Oh, that was way back *then*"—and the discussion of the sovereign nation-state as the contemporary phenomenon that is the only source of human division. On the contrary: it is necessary to indicate that one cannot apply the ideas of state, sovereignty, and nation *backward* in history to phenomena and events that occurred before these ideas were even thought of. To call the Athenian *polis* a sovereign state, or the Hellenes a nation, would be presentist and anachronistic, even if the *polis* may have had some state-like and sovereign-like features, and even if the ancient Greeks had some nation-like attributes.

By contrast, one not only can, but indeed must, analyze the sources of division from antiquity discussed in Chapter 8 down to the present day. That simplistic duality between the familiar "We" and the strange and alien "They"; ties of kinship and tribe; the religious division between true believer and nonbeliever; even some of the civilizational divisions between the civilized Self and the barbarian (or Other-civilized) Other—all of these remain important sources of how humans divide themselves. And they remain as potent for many people today as they were in antiquity.

If nothing else, those many human beings—in Algeria, Afghanistan, Bosnia, Cambodia, India, Liberia, Northern Ireland, Pakistan, Rwanda, Sierra Leone, Somalia and many other places besides—who have been killed in the contemporary period because they backed the "wrong" leader, or belonged to the "wrong" clan or tribe, or belonged to the "wrong" religious sect, or embraced the "wrong" civilization, bear mute witness to the enduring relevance of these sources of division.

## *Keyword File*

| | |
|---|---|
| Beggar-thy-neighbour | Discipline of the market |
| Gold standard | Capital flight |
| Embedded liberalism | Divestment |
| Bretton Woods system | Herd instinct |
| Eurodollars | Meltdown |
| Securitization | Competition state |
| Dragon bonds | Footloose capital |
| Eurobonds | Harmonization |
| Derivatives | Cultural homogeneity |
| Trade liberalization | Globalized elite |
| Preferences | Postnationalism |
| Most-Favoured-Nation | "Service-station state" |
| Dumping | *Rassepolitik* |
| Nontariff barriers | Race-hatred laws |
| GATT Rounds | Supranationalism |
| Sectoral free trade | Federalism |
| Hub-and-spoke approach | "European idea" |
| Fordism | Treaty of Rome |
| Post-Fordism | Maastricht Treaty |
| Globalization thesis | Qualified majority |

Snake in the tunnel                    Civilizational divide

ECU                                    Kin-country

Monetary union                         Peace dividend

Pan–Arabism

## For Further Exploration

### HARD COPY

Barber, Benjamin R. *Jihad vs. McWorld*. New York: Random House, 1995.

Cerny, Philip G. "Globalization and other stories: the search for a new paradigm for international relations," *International Journal* 51 (Autumn 1996), 617–37.

Hirst, Paul and Grahame Thompson. *Globalization in Question: The International Economy and the Possibilities of Governance*. London: Polity Press, 1996.

Huntington, Samuel P. *The Clash of Civilizations and the Remaking of World Order*. New York: Simon and Schuster, 1996.

Wallace, William. *The Transformation of Western Europe*. London: Royal Institute of International Affairs, 1990.

### WEBLINKS

**http://www.civilrights.org**

Home page of the U.S. Anti-Defamation League

**http://www.euro.net/innovation/Finance_Base/Fin_encyc.html**

Site provides a comprehensive encyclopedia of financial terms

**http://www.eurunion.org**

Home page of the European Union; jumping-off point for a variety of European sites

**http://www.oecd.org/**

Home page of the Organisation for Economic Cooperation and Development

**http://www.wiesenthal.com**

Home page of the Simon Wiesenthal Center

## Notes to Chapter 17

1. Kenichi Ohmae, *The Borderless World: Power and Strategy in the Interlinked Economy* (New York: HarperCollins, 1990).

2. John Gerard Ruggie, "International regimes, transactions, and change: embedded liberalism in the postwar economic order," *International Organization* 36 (Spring 1982).

3. Joan E. Spero and Jeffrey A. Hart, *The Politics of International Economic Relations*, 5th ed. (New York: St Martin's, 1997), 27.

4. For surveys, see Gilbert R. Winham, *The Evolution of International Trade Agreements* (Toronto: University of Toronto Press, 1992); and Robert Wolfe, *Farm Wars: The Political Economy of Agriculture and the International Trade Regime* (London: Macmillan, 1998).

5. See Robert W. Cox, *Production, Power, and World Order: Social Forces in the Making of History* (New York: Columbia University Press, 1987), 309–314.

6. See Lynn Krieger Mytelka, "Knowledge-intensive production and the changing internationalization strategies of multinational firms," in James A. Caporaso, ed., *A Changing International Division of Labour* (Boulder, CO: Lynne Rienner, 1987).

7. For an excellent discussion of globalization, see Claire Turenne Sjolander, "The rhetoric of globalization: what's in a wor(l)d?" *International Journal* 51 (Autumn 1996), 603–16.

8. Keith Ovenden and Tony Cole, *Apartheid and International Finance* (Ringwood, Vic: Penguin Australia, 1989), 75–98.

9. Audie Klotz, *Norms in International Relations: The Struggle against Apartheid* (Ithaca, NY: Cornell University Press, 1995), 159.

10. *Globe and Mail* (Toronto), 25 November 1997; for a discussion of the difficulty of "taming" capital markets, see Tony Porter, "Capital mobility and currency markets: can they be tamed?" *International Journal* 51 (Autumn 1996), 669–89.

11. See Philip G. Cerny, *The Changing Architecture of Politics: Structure, Agency, and the Future of the State* (London: Sage, 1990), 220–29.

12. Robert Reich, *The Work of Nations* (New York: Alfred A. Knopf, 1991).

13. For a survey of this process, see Michael C. Webb, *The Political Economy of Policy Coordination: International Adjustment since 1945* (Ithaca, NY: Cornell University Press, 1994).

14. Benjamin R. Barber, "Jihad vs. McWorld," *Atlantic Monthly* 269 (March 1992), 53.

15. *Globe and Mail* (Toronto), 29 November 1997.

16. Quoted in Charles W. Kegley and Eugene R. Wittkopf, *World Politics: Trend and Transformation*, 6th ed. (New York: St Martin's Press, 1997), 210.

17. Ann Capling, "Economic nationalism in the 1990s," *Australian Quarterly* 69:2 (1997), 7.

18. See, for example, Stephen Gill, *American Hegemony and the Trilateral Commission* (Cambridge: Cambridge University Press, 1990); Richard A. Higgott, "Economic cooperation: theoretical opportunities and practical constraints," *Pacific Review* 6 (Spring 1993).

19. Lewis H. Lapham, "Pax economica," *Behind the Headlines* 54 (Winter 1996–97), 6.

20. Yasemin Soysal, *Limits of Citizenship: Migrants and Postnational Membership in Europe* (Chicago: University of Chicago Press, 1994), 165; also Mary Kaldor, "Cosmopolitanism versus nationalism: the new divide?" in Richard Caplan and John Feffer, eds., *Europe's New Nationalism: States and Minorities in Conflict* (Oxford: Oxford University Press, 1996).

21. Margaret Canovan, *Nationhood and Political Theory* (Cheltenham, U.K.: Edward Elgar, 1996), 86. As Triadafilos Triadafilopoulos notes, the contemporary debate over the nature of the relationship between state and citizen continues a discussion that goes back at least as far as the early 19th century and G.W.F. Hegel's critique in of the liberal notion of *Notstaat* (literally, *need-state*, or state based on need): see "War and the national interest: on the relationship between nationalism and Hegel's conception of the state as an ethical community," Proceedings of the Canadian Political Science Association, St John's, Nfld., 8–10 June 1997.

22. Robert O. Keohane and Stanley Hoffmann, "Institutional change in Europe in the 1980s," in Keohane and Hoffmann, eds., *The New European Community: Decision-making and Institutional Change* (Boulder, CO: Westview, 1991), 1–39.

23. Samuel P. Huntington, "The clash of civilizations?" *Foreign Affairs* 72 (Summer 1993), 22.

24. Samuel P. Huntington, *The Clash of Civilizations and the Remaking of World Order* (New York: Simon and Schuster, 1996), 45–46; also see map, 26–27.

25. Kegley and Wittkopf, *World Politics*, 178.

26. Kishore Mahbubani, "The West and the rest," *The National Interest* (Summer 1992), 3–13.

27. Huntington, "Clash of civilizations?" 48, 49.

28. Samuel P. Huntington, "If not civilizations, what?" *Foreign Affairs* 72 (November/December 1993), 186.

29. For an examination of these policies, see Richard A. Higgott and Kim Richard Nossal, "The international politics of liminality: relocating Australia in the Asia Pacific," *Australian Journal of Political Science* 32 (July 1997), 169–85.

30. Quoted in Richard Gwyn, *Nationalism Without Walls: The Unbearable Lightness of Being Canadian* (Toronto: McClelland and Stewart, 1995), 15–16.

31. Hedley Bull, *The Anarchical Society: A Study in World Order* (New York: Columbia University Press, 1977), 254–55.

32. Lapham, "Pax economica," 8.

# The Patterns
# of World Politics

# Conclusion:
## *The* Patterns
## *of* World Politics

### INTRODUCTION

In the introductory chapter, I suggested that one of the purposes of this book was to provide a guide for understanding world politics over the longer term, when those few short years at university are long behind. The purpose of this concluding chapter is to summarize the patterns of world politics as observed in this book, and to lay out a path for the international politics that we are likely to encounter in the years ahead.

### DIVISION AND ITS CONSEQUENCES

Much of this book has dwelt on the boundaries that human beings erect to divide themselves from one another, boundaries that intensify the physical distances created by geography and the cultural distances created by language. We have looked at the numerous ways that humankind has divided itself, from the earliest civilizations to the contemporary nation-state. It is evident from the discussion in this book that the sources of this division are numerous and multifaceted, and heavily dependent on context. Language, race, class, tribe, religion, gender, culture, nationality, ideology, wealth—these are some of the facets of the human condition that may be the hinge on which division is hung. Or division may come simply from the heavy hand of history—that which has gone before but which is remembered and passed down, reinforcing patterns of difference and perhaps even enmity and hatred.

We have also looked at how hard it is for humans to overcome the conflicts of interest that come with these divisions, to get beyond the clichés about a global village and Spaceship Earth and the homogenizing impact of globalization so beloved by the chattering classes. This, after all, is the rhetoric of folks who, when one looks carefully, are able to live lives of security, comfort, and privilege precisely because of human division. The slum-dweller in the *barrios* of Lima, the destitute peasant in Bihar state, or the terrified villager in Algeria knows the emptiness of such phrases.

In his 1971 song *Imagine*, John Lennon asked us to imagine a world without countries, suggesting that it was easy to do so. The account of world politics in this book suggests that while it might be easy to *imagine* a world without divisions, it is exceedingly hard to actually get beyond the boundaries that have such a deep, and often fatal, impact on the lives of human beings. The one experiment in overcoming boundaries—the European Union—has been a slow and patient series of baby steps taken over four decades. Also, this experiment was driven by the violent death, ruinous destruction, and economic disruption of two world wars, a great depression, and a Holocaust. If it has been difficult for Europeans, it should not be surprising that nowhere else in the world have people managed to overcome their deeply entrenched barriers.

But from the existence of division and the difficulty of overcoming it flow the patterns of world politics, as we have seen. Seven distinct patterns can be discerned from the past; and from the past it can be surmised that we will see these patterns recur in the future. These patterns include: the search for independence and autonomy in an increasingly globalized world; the struggle for dominance by some political communities; the periodic resort to force that has always been a part of world politics; the challenge posed by the dispossessed to those who enjoy luxury and privilege; the conflict over what constitutes goodness and righteousness; the on-going challenge to the environment posed by the tragedy of the commons; and the persistent search for community at the global level.

## SEEKING INDEPENDENCE AND AUTONOMY IN A GLOBALIZED WORLD

A dominant theme in world politics is the persistence of the desire for an independent existence. This is manifested everywhere at a personal level, and usually gives rise to deeply seated social structures of dominance and control: parents over children, men over women, landowners over peasants, capital over labour, elites over masses, governments over peoples. But it is also manifest at the level of political community. As a consequence, world politics is very much about the different political communities that people create—under a huge array of different names and forms—from the huge empires of antiquity to the compact *poleis* of Hellas, to the vassal relations of the feudal period, to the contemporary sovereign nation-state. The ideal of an independent political community has inspired uprisings, revolts, and wars—across the world and across the centuries, from the periodic revolts of Iberian tribes against their Roman overlords to the struggles of the Eritreans against Ethiopian domination (the most recent war of national liberation to result in a sovereign nation-state). It continues to manifest itself in the number of peoples who think of themselves as a national community, and want to give their nation expression in a separate and sovereign state.

And once independence is achieved, it is often a struggle to maintain it. World politics is about the efforts of people to ensure that their communities are free from elimination, butchery, enslavement, absorption, exploitation, or domination by others. That desire to remain free drove the Melians and the Trung sisters no less than it did the Japanese on Okinawa.

Less dramatically, but no less importantly, there is the on-going struggle for autonomy and freedom from the impositions and importunities of the more powerful, a struggle that continues to inspire much of the politics of the contemporary era. The frustrations of Mexicans over American intrusions on their sovereignty in the hunt for narco-traffickers, or of Canadians over American extraterritoriality in the efforts to punish Cuba; the grumbling of the British over the disappearance of their pound or Austrian complaints about the effects of a single currency on the already-high unemployment rate; the concern of Ukrainians over pressures from Moscow on the issue of the Russian minority in Crimea.

The impact of globalization, and in particular the emergence of global financial markets, poses an even greater challenge to autonomy. Governments and peoples find their room to manoeuvre limited by the impact of the global economy and by the necessity of pursuing a course that will not attract the discipline of the market. The seemingly impersonal forces of the market produce a chorus of concerns—voices of protest that range from the prime minister of Malaysia complaining about currency trading to Swedish groups struggling against the integrationist forces of the EU.

To be sure, it remains within any community's power to take the path trodden by the Albanian government during the Cold War era—in other words, the steadfast pursuit of autarky, cut off from international intercourse. But most people recognize that disengaging from the world, and particularly from the world economy, would carry huge costs in terms of their standard of living. They have little difficulty making the trade-off, even if they grumble about it: limits on one's autonomy in return for the benefits that come from engagement in the world economy.

## IN THE POSTURE OF GLADIATORS: THE STRUGGLE FOR DOMINANCE

Division and independence also produces a struggle for dominance. Thomas Hobbes's description is still the most evocative of this dynamic:

> [I]n all times, Kings, and Persons of Soveraigne authority, because of their Independency, are in continuall jealousies, and in the state and posture of Gladiators; having their weapons pointing, and their eyes fixed on one another; that is, their Forts, Garrisons, and Guns upon the Frontiers of their Kingdomes; and continuall Spyes upon their neighbours...[1]

*"In all times, Kings, and Persons of Soveraigne authority, because of their Independency, are in continuall jealousies, and in the state and posture of Gladiators..."*

To be sure, this does not describe the condition of every political community toward every other polity. But even when neighbours do not have "weapons pointing" at each other, they invariably have them pointing at someone else. And even when there is no one to pose a threat worthy of a pointed weapon—as in the post–Cold War era—the tendency is to remain in the posture of a gladiator and keep them pointing in the abstract, just in case. That prudential argument—"one had better be prepared because an enemy could arise quickly"—inspires the expenditure of trillions of dollars around the world every year on arms and the maintenance of military forces, even while every major government in the world asserts that its neighbours do not pose a threat.

The rest of Hobbes's description remains accurate, however. There are continual jealousies—conflicts, tiffs, annoyances—between governments and between peoples; that is the day-to-day stuff of international politics. Frontiers are everywhere "fortified": even if the front lines consist of agents who swipe passports through their computers, interrogate foreigners, and check luggage, the coercive power of those "Persons of Soveraigne authority" are there to ensure that the frontiers are as impermeable as possible. And there are indeed spies everywhere—though their working lives are a good deal less glamorous than their silver-screen counterparts.

More importantly, the account in this book suggests that over the long stretch of history, those jealousies, on occasion, erupt into a struggle for dominance, an attempt to widen control, to achieve the security that can (but need not always) come with control. Those struggles for dominance tend to be periodic rather than omnipresent. Efforts to achieve dominance (or undermine the dominance of others) are more pronounced at some times than others. In other words, not all communities are consumed by such struggles all the time.

Indeed, the end of the Cold War between 1989 and 1991 ushered in one of those periods. With the end of the rivalry between the USSR and the United States, there has been no comparable struggle for dominance. For many communities, threats are unfocused; it is unclear whether any identifiable "enemies" exist. And, in the case of the United States, there is no one seeking to upset the dominance of Americans; and, by the same token, no one to dominate. Instead, the United States government has occupied itself seeking to control the government of Saddam Hussein, which has been able to defy the United States (but not vie with it for dominance).

It is true that there are those who see new enmities lurking in the shadows. Indeed, the "clash of civilizations" argument examined in the last chapter encourages this tendency. A good example of this dynamic at work is the demonization of Islam, particularly in the United States. Many American IR textbooks now feature sections on Islam and "Islamic fundamentalism"[2] which inevitably construct the Muslim world as an enraged Other, eager to fulfil the instructions of the Prophet and wage a *jihād*, or holy war, against nonbelievers. In such discussions, the Otherness of Islam is always stressed: the amputations specified in the *shari'a* (or Islamic law); the 1989 *fatwa* issued by the Ayatollah Ruhollah Khomeini against British author Salman Rushdie for offending Islam with his book *The Satanic Verses*—a decision that offered a US$5 million bounty for anyone who killed Rushdie; or incongruous photos, such as the one of the women of Iran's Olympic kayaking team practising in veils. One author even uses the term "green peril" (after the colour usually associated with Islam),[3] introducing a new "peril" to replace the "red peril" (used by Americans to describe communists) and the "yellow peril" (used to describe China). Indeed, Samuel P. Huntington even feels comfortable writing that "Islam has bloody borders,"[4] as though the interethnic conflict between Muslims and others in different countries can somehow be attributed to the religion.

But sometimes the enemy is identified more explicitly. China has been a favourite possibility for a new "enemy" for the United States. Huntington actually sketches out a scenario of a war between the West and China.[5] A similar scenario is painted by Richard Bernstein and Ross H. Munro, two journalists with experience in Asia, in their book, *The Coming Conflict with China*.[6] Both books claim to be just engaged in scenario-building, but both do a fine job of constructing China as an enemy against whom the United States might adopt the posture of a gladiator.

## WAR AND THE USE OF FORCE

The third general pattern is the persistence of the use of force in world politics. Much of the story of world politics is about wars of different types: civil wars, wars of secession, wars of independence, wars of national liberation, wars of absorption, wars of attrition, wars of elimination; colonial wars, hot wars, cold wars, dirty wars, limited wars, general wars. Wars have been driven by desire for land, or for resources, or for dominance. Some were fought between political communities of various sizes, some affected a large number of people—indeed, a war 60 years ago engulfed the majority of humankind. And much of the story of world politics is about the consequences of war, for every war that is fought, whether large or small, leaves long-lived traces, affecting all those who lived through its horror, terror, pain, and deprivation.

Once again, it is important to stress that war is not an omnipresent feature of global politics. Relatively few general wars have engulfed large numbers of communities, and in numerous periods in history, many (but not all) communities have not experienced war. It can be argued that we are in just such a period today. For hundreds of millions in the contemporary post–Cold War period, war is something that they themselves have never experienced; for hundreds of millions more, war is a memory from the past. The tens of millions of those who continue to be directly engulfed by war is a huge number in absolute terms, but small relative to the total global population.

But if war is *episodic*, there can be little doubt that war is *endemic* to politics generally, and to politics at a global level in particular. The central problem for political scientists continues to be trying to understand the causes of war and the conditions of peace both within political communities and between them. Whether at the "domestic" level or the level of world politics, we want to understand how and why people use force against one another in pursuit of their goals; we want to know what conditions must be met for people to eschew violence.

While war is endemic, it is by no means inevitable or deterministic. For using force—the *ultima ratio* in human affairs—involves conscious decisions by large numbers of people who come to believe that using force to achieve their goals is preferable to other instruments of power. By the same token, it is possible for certain kinds of war to become "unthinkable," with the result that the confrontation can end without violence erupting. Consider how a general nuclear war between the two blocs became unthinkable during the Cold War; consider how a general race war became unthinkable in South Africa. But it is when war becomes "thinkable" that it becomes possible. As the discussion of the Great War in Chapter 14 revealed, war was thinkable in the summer of 1914. Indeed, war has been thinkable on numerous other occasions since then and it is thinkable in many parts of the world today.

## THE DISPOSSESSED AND ECONOMIC DISPARITY

Among the persistent patterns that can be seen in politics at a world level is one that mirrors a pattern that is evident in other domains of politics—a basic division between those who have and those who do not. I have argued throughout this book that, when thinking about wealth and dispossession, we should keep in mind that wealth coexists with poverty all over the world. Also, the disparities are multifaceted, existing not only *between* North and South, but *within* North and South, and *within* each of the countries of both North and South.

It is important to keep in mind that neither economic disparity nor the lack of possessions per se necessarily has political consequences. There is a huge disparity between the world's super-rich and the rest of humankind, yet these folks are left in peace to enjoy their wealth rather than being carted off in tumbrels. Likewise, vast numbers of humans have lived contented, and even happy, lives without the trappings of contemporary consumer culture. What does make a political difference is when humans are *poor*—in other words they lack the necessities of life—or when they consider themselves as *dispossessed*—unfairly deprived of the conveniences and luxuries that others around them are enjoying.

While world politics has always been marked by an uneven distribution of wealth, contemporary world politics is marked by inequality, poverty, and large numbers of dispossessed in proportions not seen in the past. Huge numbers of people are destitute, lacking the necessities of life or even basic needs. Also, large numbers are dispossessed, able to see the wealth and comfort around them, both directly and indirectly through the medium of television.

As we noted above, the present distribution of good things is not at all in the interests of the dispossessed; by contrast, the present system is very much in the interests of the rich in both North and South. Moreover, the power of the rich lies in their capacity to ensure that the system does not change to their disadvantage.

That fundamental conflict of interests, however, is *latent*, in the sense that it is not observable: there is no generalized war being waged between rich and poor countries or between rich and poor within countries. But to the extent that this conflict of interests is not resolved, it will remain with us as an important issue in politics at the world level; the North/South dynamics we explored in Chapter 16 will not disappear.

## THE STANDARD OF JUSTICE: COMPETING NOTIONS OF THE GOOD

One of the most profound consequences of the kind of divisions we have explored in this book is the incapacity at the broadest level of politics to agree on a standard of justice that can be widely enforced.

The international community has been able to forge agreement on a wide variety of norms, laws, and rules to govern the behaviour of peoples, organizations, and governments. As we have seen in the chapters above, a huge body of international law guides a wide variety of human interactions. Likewise, a huge number of agreements between individuals, firms, organizations, and governments make it possible for the international system to function in a predictable way. Moreover, there are well-established institutions for the application of this law. There are "courts"—forums for the adjudication of the rules—at all levels: the international, the supranational, and the binational levels. Indeed, international law can even be made at the national level—in the sense that one court's decision will inevitably affect the decisions of other courts hearing other cases.

At the same time, however, we are faced with a paradox. In the midst of this highly developed and detailed body of law and these deeply entrenched institutional practices, there is a certain primitiveness to many aspects of international law. About the most important matters to human existence—life, death, and survival—there is nothing like the body of law that has grown up around, for example, the movement of container ships. Instead, law at this level tends to focus on grand and general principles. Thus, for example, the Universal Declaration of Human Rights sets out a number of rights that individuals are said to be able to claim, ranging from the right to life, liberty, and security of the person (Article 3) to the right "to a social and international order in which the rights and freedoms set forth in this Declaration can be fully realized" (Article 28). But as such they remain general guiding principles. Indeed, the Universal Declaration is not even a treaty, which governments usually commit themselves to obeying. Rather, it is a declaration that tries to establish a moral standard for people and governments to follow.

A measure of the immaturity of the law at this level can be seen in the enforcement of rules. One of the consequences of fragmented political authority at the level of world politics is that states which do not want to obey certain rules can break those rules with impunity, for there are few mechanisms for enforcing compliance.

Consider the use of poison gas weapons by the Iraqi government of Saddam Hussein. These weapons were used against Iran, and once against Iraq's own civilian population. There is widespread agreement that the use of such weapons contravenes international treaty law (such as the banning of such weapons by the First Hague Conference in 1899).

Indeed, the depth of agreement can be seen by the fact that not a single country other than Iraq has used these agents since Japan used nerve gas in its war against China in the 1930s and 1940s. Adolf Hitler (who had been gassed in the First World War) chose not to use these weapons against the United Nations, not even when the tide of the war had moved against Germany. Yet Iraq's violations were not punished, because they could not be punished. There were—and are—no mechanisms to enforce a common standard of justice. The same is true for other violations. As we noted above, there is widespread agreement that genocide is illegal, yet the capacity to pursue violations is limited.

This pattern is unlikely to change. We are likely to see a progressive thickening of rules and case law over economic matters as the processes of globalization prompt greater levels of harmonization. But it is unlikely that we will see the rapid development of law on questions that touch on the morality of the international political economy. For example, do individuals or political communities have economic rights? Article 28 of the Universal Declaration, cited above, suggests that they might. Yet international law on such matters is at its most primitive; only in the European context has supranational law on social issues been seriously developed.

But at the same time, some people are propelled to try and impose their standard of justice on others. This is likely to be a source of tension between communities, and in particular their governments, in the years ahead. For on those issues, there is little agreement. Hence "the standard of justice will depend on the equality of power to compel," just as Thucydides said it would some 2500 years ago.

## THE TRAGEDY OF THE COMMONS

In Chapter 4, we looked at the "tragedy of the commons," and the challenges that this poses for global governance. Everywhere we continue to see this dynamic at work in a divided world. Each political community seeks to advance its own interests, exploiting the resources that are available to it under the "property rules" of the contemporary system. In other words, states have freedom to exploit land and ocean resources considered its sovereign territory, and freedom to exploit whatever resources it can extract on the high seas, subject only to treaties limiting such access that it might have voluntarily signed. But, as Garrett Hardin pointed out, it makes sense for each individual political community to add as much "loading" to the commons as it can get away with (for if it doesn't, someone else surely will). That, of course, is the tragedy.

Overcoming the tragedy has been, and will no doubt continue to be, almost impossible. Some argue that the solution is a global agreement on keeping "loadings" down to sustainable levels to ensure the "carrying capacity" of the global ecosystem. But, as we have seen in the case of the quarrels over global warming, there is no particular incentive to agree to forego one's sovereign rights to exploit and develop (and pollute). Moreover, it is galling to some Southerners to be told that they must tailor their development plans to please rich Northerners, who produce more greenhouse gases per capita

*It is galling to some Southerners to be told that they must tailor their development plans to please rich Northerners.*

than countries of the South, and in whose interests the global system is structured in the first place. The logical and self-interested response of Southern nations will continue to be what it has been: to reject efforts by Northern states to negotiate a way out of the tragedy.

## CONCLUSION: THE SEARCH FOR COMMUNITY

Finally, I have suggested throughout this book that one of the key patterns of politics at a world level has been the search for community by peoples and their governments. Particularly since 1945 and the end of the Second World War, that search has been pronounced, spurred on by the disasters of the early 20th century. Between 1914 and 1945, the massive "die-off," to use William H. McNeill's evocative term, saw 10 million die in the Great War, 20 million die from the Spanish flu epidemic in 1918, and perhaps as many as 50 million die between 1937 and 1945.[7] At different times between 1919 and 1939, millions more experienced the disruptions of massive hyperinflation, deep depression, and huge unemployment.

But I have tried to show that the search for community is by no means a recent phenomenon, as some suggest. The historical record suggests that people have had a persistent compulsion to community—despite the obvious and clear divisions that have marked humankind. Such a compulsion has manifested itself in numerous ways: the efforts of people, from the ancient Greeks to the present, to create the rudiments of community, even as they were engaged in brutal wars with one another; the spread of commerce over virtually every part of the Earth, with merchants, traders, and producers always seeking security and predictability in order to lower risk and raise profit; and the persistent propensity to establish "rules of the game," and an equal willingness to abide by those rules a significant part of the time. In short, there has always been a willingness to conceive of politics as extending beyond the confines of the political communities into which humans have always divided themselves.

Such a search for community, it must be recognized, has always gone hand-in-hand with the other face of politics at a global level: a politics marked by often unimaginable brutality, cruelty, lack of compassion, and death. For evidence of this, one has to look no further than the killings during the Rwandan civil war between Hutu-dominated government forces and a rebel army of members of the Tutsi tribe. On 6 April 1994, the plane carrying Juvénal Habyarimana, a Hutu who was president of Rwanda, was shot down in mysterious circumstances outside the capital of Kigali. Habyarimana's Presidential Guard, together with other Hutu militants, began an orgy of killing in revenge. Within hours of the president's death, Hutus had slaughtered the prime minister, Agathe Uwilingiyamana, and all of her family. When 10 Belgian troops from the UN Assistance Mission to Rwanda (UNAMIR) tried to protect her, Hutu soldiers slit their throats. Following this initial bloodbath, the Tutsi rebels stepped up their offensive, widening the civil war and prompting the United Nations Security Council to vote to reduce UNAMIR personnel in Rwanda from 2500 to 270. With the UN effectively withdrawn, the Hutu militia began a systematic slaughter of Tutsis and moderate Hutus. Each day thereafter, thousands of Tutsis and Hutus were hacked to death by the militants, their bodies left to bloat in rivers or to rot in ditches, homes, and churches. Within a month, more than 500 000 Rwandans had died, and more than 1.5 million had fled to Burundi and Zaire (as Congo-Kinshasa was then called).

*With the UN effectively withdrawn, the Hutu militia began a systematic slaughter of Tutsis and moderate Hutus.*

All this time the United Nations and the wider international community was standing by and watching the slaughter happen. Unlike Cambodia in the mid-1970s, from which news of the genocide that was being committed by the Khmer Rouge did not slip out immediately, the international media had pictures of the results of the Hutu massacres immediately after they occurred. But after the Somalia mission in 1993, there was little will on the part of the sovereign states in the international community to intervene in this civil war. The NGO community, without effective military protection, could do little. It was not until the middle of June that the French government took the initiative and, with Security Council approval, landed 2500 troops, assisted by a military contingent from Senegal, to establish a "safe area" around Lake Kivu in the western part of the country. The French intervention spurred the Tutsi rebels to press their attack against the Hutu government; Kigali was captured on 4 July. By the middle of July, a Tutsi-backed transitional government, with Hutus as president and prime minister, was appointed.[8]

The brutality of the genocide in Rwanda—captured most vividly in the photo seen here—is an appropriate case with which to end this book. For Rwanda shows us the two faces of world politics: on the one hand, the wholesale destruction of community, in which hundreds of thousands met a gruesome death and millions more were terrorized, occurring at the same time as hundreds of thousands of others were busily going about their business, building community at a global level, and hundreds of millions more were engaged in the routines of international relations. Moreover, this case also demonstrates so well the enduring challenge of world politics for the student and the citizen: trying to understand the causes of war and the conditions of peace.

## Notes to Chapter 18

1. Thomas Hobbes, *Leviathan, or the Matter, Forme, & Power of a Common-Wealth Ecclesiasticall and Civill* (1651), ed. C.B. Macpherson (Harmondsworth: Penguin, 1968), 187–88 (chap. 13, p. 63 in original).

2. For a good argument on the fallacy of using this term indiscriminately, see Yahya M. Sadowski, "Bosnia's Muslims: a fundamentalist threat?" *Brookings Review* (Winter 1995).

3. John T. Rourke, *International Politics on the World Stage*, 6th ed. (Guilford, CT: Dushkin/McGraw Hill, 1997), 189.

4. Samuel P. Huntington, "The clash of civilizations?" *Foreign Affairs* 72 (Summer 1993), 35.

5. Samuel P. Huntington, *The Clash of Civilizations and the Remaking of World Order* (New York: Simon and Schuster, 1996), 312–16.

6. Richard Bernstein and Ross H. Munro, *The Coming Conflict with China* (New York: Alfred A. Knopf, 1997).

7. William H. McNeill, *The Pursuit of Power: Technology, Armed Force, and Society since A.D. 1000* (Chicago: University of Chicago Press, 1982), 314.

8. For a full account, see Gérard Prunier, *The Rwanda Crisis: History of a Genocide* (New York: Columbia University Press, 1997).

# Glossary of Names, Events, and Terms

A selected list of people, events, and vocabulary terms that appear in this book. Numbers in parentheses indicate the chapters where glossed vocabulary terms are mainly discussed. Cross-references are italicized.

**0.7-per-cent target**: promise by industrialized countries that their annual official development assistance (ODA) flows would be 0.7 per cent of GNP (16)

**Absolute gains**: a real increase in wealth over time, experienced by a political community, without reference to the wealth of others; see also *relative gains* (16)

**Acheson, Dean** (1893–1971): American diplomat and principal architect of postwar American foreign policy; assistant undersecretary of state, 1941–45; undersecretary, 1945–47; secretary of state, 1949–53

**Acid rain**: The acidic effect produced when emissions of sulphur dioxide ($SO_2$) and nitrous oxide ($NO_x$) combine with moisture in the atmosphere (7)

**"African Eve"**: name given to the *Homo* woman who lived, probably in Africa, between 100 000 and 200 000 years ago, from whom, it is thought, all members of the species *Homo sapiens sapiens* are descended (12)

**Age of enlightenment**: a term used to describe intellectual trends in Europe and North America in the eighteenth century, most notably the idea that science, logic, and reason could reveal objective truths about human nature and society.

**Age of exploration**: the term given to the period of outward expansion by Europeans. It began in the fifteenth century with Portuguese explorations of the African littoral in the 1440s and led to the "discovery" and settlement by Europeans of the western hemisphere and the antipodes in the 350 years thereafter. (9)

**Allophones**: in Québec, those whose mother tongue is neither English or French (14)

**Anarchical society**: in the context of IR, the idea that the world constitutes a community that exists in a condition of *anarchy* (4)

**Anarchism**: a political philosophy that posits the possibility of an anarchical political community (3)

**Anarchy**: (from Greek, *an* + *archos*) literally, without a ruler; a society without a formal government; often misdefined as chaos or civil war (3)

**Androcentrism**: the tendency of political phenomena to be male-centred, male-dominated, or structured in the interests of males rather than females (2, 3)

**Antecedent boundaries**: political borders that are established before any significant patterns of human settlement have occurred (9)

**Appeasement**: policy of trying to assuage aggressive behaviour by offering concessions; normally used to describe English and French policy toward Nazi Germany in the late 1930s (14)

**Armed forces**: the agents of the state charged with using force to advance the political community's interests as defined by the political leadership. This includes defending it against attacks by others, attacking other communities, and contributing to domestic order (known as aid to the civil power). Armed forces also play a variety of peace-time roles, such as *peacekeeping* and disaster relief. (7)

**Arms race**: a self-propelling dynamic in which two or more political communities acquire weapons systems to keep pace with the acquisitions of their neighbours (14)

**Article 5**: the so-called *trigger clause* in the North Atlantic Treaty of 1949 that commits its members to aid one another in the event of attack by another state (15)

**Autarky**: a totally self-sufficient economy, neither reliant on, nor connected with, the economy outside (12)

**Authority**: the complex human relationship in which actors are able to secure compliance with their wishes by simply ordering other actors to obey their commands, without actually having to engage in persuasion, inducement, coercion, or the use of sanctions or force. Authority may be an exercise in influence or power, depending on whether a conflict of interests exists. (5)

**Autonomy**: the capacity to have one's actions accord with one's preferences—being able to do what one wants (11)

**Balance of terror**: the Cold War condition in which the U.S. and the USSR threatened to attack each other's cities with nuclear weapons, creating a mutual terror (4, 7)

**Bandwagon effect**: the dynamic by which a cause gathers adherents or momentum by creating a desire to "climb on the bandwagon"; of particular importance in how states secure recognition (11)

**Bantustan**: "homelands" created under apartheid in South Africa for each of the tribal divisions of Bantu-speakers (11)

**Barbarian**: in most civilizations, those people either outside *the* civilization or, more generally, outside *a* civilization (8)

**Bay of Pigs**: term given to the invasion of Cuba by an army of Cuban exiles trained and financed by the CIA. The army was landed at Bahía de Cochinos (Bay of Pigs) on 17 April 1961, but virtually every aspect of the invasion was poorly planned; 90 exiles were killed and the remaining 1200 were taken prisoner. (15)

**Beggar-thy-neighbour policies**: efforts by governments in the 1930s to shift the effects of the Great Depression to neighbouring countries by raising tariffs and applying other protectionist measures (14, 17)

**Behaviouralism**: an approach to IR, popular in the United States in the 1960s and 1970s, that sought to apply scientific principles to politics at a global level, including the collection, quantification, and analysis of hard data (2)

**Berlin blockade**: the Soviet blockade of the road and rail links between West Berlin and West Germany that began on 24 June 1948 and lasted almost a year. During that time, the United States and its allies supplied West Berlin by air. (15)

**Bilingual**: speaking two languages; in a political context, those polities where two languages enjoy formal and/or informal political standing (12)

*Blitzkrieg*: (German) literally, lightning war; a form of warfare made famous by the *Nazis* in the late 1930s featuring a rapid and sudden attack by massed armour and infantry with air support (14)

**Blue water navy**: a navy that is capable of operating in all oceans around the globe (15)

**Bodin, Jean** (1530–1596): French political philosopher, law teacher, and jurist, who is best remembered for his theoretical works on sovereignty

**Bolshevik revolution**: also known as the October Revolution (according to the Russian calendar; 7 November 1917 according to the calendar used in other European countries); seizure of state power that led to the establishment of the Union of Soviet Socialist Republics. The October revolution was organized by V.I. Lenin, leader of the Bolshevik Party (Russian for "majority," this party having grown out of the majority wing of the Russian Social Democratic Labour Party in the early 1900s). (7)

**Botha, Pieter Willem** (1916– ): prime minister of South Africa, 1978–1984; president, 1984–1989

**Boutros-Ghali, Boutros** (1922– ): United Nations secretary general, 1992–1997; Egyptian minister of state, 1977–1991, deputy prime minister, 1991–1992; activist secretary general who oversaw the expansion of UN activities in the post–Cold War period

**Boxer Rebellion**: an antiforeign revolt in June 1900 spearheaded by members of the Righteous and Harmonious Boxing Order, called Boxers by Europeans (13)

**Bretton Woods**: resort in New Hampshire; site of international conference in July 1944 at which the postwar economic order was negotiated; also a *metonym* for that order (15, 16)

**Brezhnev, Leonid I.** (1906–1982): general secretary of the Communist Party of the Soviet Union, 1964–1982; oversaw the expansion of Soviet influence and military power in the 1970s

**Buffer zone**: generally, a space separating a country from a would-be invader; in Cold War politics, the zone of Eastern European countries separating the USSR from a putatively aggressive West (15)

**Bullion**: usually uncoined silver or gold in bars or ingots; for centuries the underpinning of the European-oriented international economy; see also *mercantilism* (9)

**Bush, George** (1924– ): president of the United States, 1989–1993; Republican Party; president during the end of the Cold War; pursued multilateralist and cooperative foreign policy, most notably during the Persian Gulf crisis, 1990–1991

**Cairns Group**: the fourteen governments which met in August 1986 at Cairns, Queensland to press for liberalizing trade in agriculture during the Uruguay Round of GATT negotiations (16)

**Camp David Accords**: the Middle East peace agreement signed in Washington on 26 March 1979 following negotiations held at the presidential retreat at Camp David, Maryland the previous autumn (15)

**Canadian formula**: in the context of the recognition of China, the wording proposed by Canada deemed acceptable to the PRC that Canada would "take note of" the PRC's claim to be the legitimate government of Taiwan (11)

**Capital flight**: the willingness of capital, particularly financial capital, to flee a market that owners and traders believe to be less than conducive to profitable returns (7, 17)

**Capitalist encirclement**: the complaint by Stalin that the USSR was being encircled by the capitalist countries of the West; also see *containment* (15)

**Carter, Jimmy** (1924– ): president of the United States, 1977–1981; Democratic Party; presidency was marked by the collapse of *détente* with the USSR, the Iranian hostage crisis, and the Soviet invasion of Afghanistan

**"Casino capitalism"**: Susan Strange's description of the financial markets, where changes in the value of the instruments being traded (stocks, foreign exchange, derivatives, etc.) largely depend on the same kind of luck one needs in a casino (7)

**Chamberlain, Neville** (1869–1940): Conservative politician; prime minister of Britain, 1937–1940; sought to avoid war with Nazi Germany through a policy of *appeasement*

**Chaos theory**: in physics, a theoretical perspective that denies the possibility of infinite predictability because seemingly predictable systems (such as a dripping tap) show considerable variations depending on initial conditions. Applied to the social sciences, chaos theory denies the possibility of developing if-then hypotheses; see also *path dependency* and *counterfactual*. (2)

**Chiang Kai-shek** (1887–1975): pronounced *jiang kai shek*; leader of China, 1927 until the establishment of the People's Republic of China; moved to Taiwan in 1950 and led the Republic of China on Taiwan until his death

**Child labour**: the employment of children, usually but not only pre-teenagers, in the labour market (6)

**Chrétien, Jean** (1934– ): prime minister of Canada, 1993–present; Liberal Party; member of Parliament, 1963–1986 and 1990–present

**Churchill, Winston S.** (1874–1965): Conservative politician; prime minister of Britain during the Second World War, 1940–1945; opponent of *appeasement* during the late 1930s

**Citizens**: individuals deemed by a sovereign state to be bona fide members of the political community, normally endowed with a range of rights relating to that community (9)

**City-bombing**: the use of cities (and hence concentrations of civilian populations) as legitimate targets of aerial attack in warfare (14)

**Civilizational divide**: the idea, embraced most enthusiastically by Samuel P. Huntington, that the contemporary international community is divided primarily by different civilizations (17)

**Civilizations**: societies that have developed complex cultural, economic, and social institutions, most notably marked by the invention of a written language (8)

**Clean divorce**: in international politics, the separation of a nation-state that is negotiated and does not feature violence or overt hostility (14)

**Clinton, Bill** (1946– ): president of the United States, 1993– ; Democratic Party; first U.S. president to be born after the Second World War

**"CNN factor"**: the impact that global television programming has on politics at all levels, including the world level (7)

**Coastal states**: countries with a coastline but no global oceanic interests. These states generally seek to maximize the amount of ocean they control, seeking to minimize the amount of ocean considered *high seas*. (10)

**Coercion**: a technique of power in which the use of the threat of harms against an actor are used as a method to bend that actor to one's will (5)

**Cold War**: uncapitalized, any deeply antagonistic relationship between two countries but which is not marked by open fighting; capitalized, that period between 1944–45 and 1989–91 when the relationship between the USSR and the United States was extremely hostile (15)

**Collective security**: a theoretical method for ensuring international peace in which each state renounces the use of force and commits itself to regard the use of force by any state as an attack on itself. It was believed that the threat of sanctions by every other state in the system would deter the use of force. (14)

**Colombo Plan**: first major development assistance plan for Southern countries, created by Commonwealth leaders at Colombo, Sri Lanka, January 1950 (16)

**Colonies**: the Latin root of the word (*colonus*, farmer) suggests that colonies are a group of people from one country who go and settle a new territory, retaining links with the "parent" community (9)

**Commodification of land**: the idea that land could be treated as a commodity—owned, bought, and sold—rather than ruled over by a king and assigned to feudal lords for their use (9)

**Common Fund**: a fund that would provide protection to countries of the South, which were dependent on commodity exports, against rapid swings in the price of commodities (16)

**Communism**: an ideology that fixes on the creation of class divisions based on the relationship to the means of production. As a normative political movement, it advocates state ownership of industrial capital, the abolition of private ownership of capital, and the collectivization of agriculture, in order to create a classless society. (7)

**Community**: a group of people who have a number of commonalities, consider themselves a community or a society separate from others, and share a common form of governance (3, 4)

**Comparative advantage**: the idea that a nation is better off buying what it needs from another nation which can produce it more cheaply and specializing, rather than trying to meet all its needs by domestic production (12)

**Compellent coercion**: threats of harm from actor A, designed to compel actor B to do something that is not in B's interests (5)

**Competition state**: Philip G. Cerny's characterization of the contemporary state's concern to pursue social and economic policies that will compete successfully for international capital (17)

**Complementary interests**: interests that either overlap or do not have any significant incompatibilities (4)

**Condominium**: in international politics, a territory and people whose governance is shared by more than one sovereign state (10)

**Conflict**: an antagonistic condition in which one's interests are not in harmony with those of other actors. Conflict may be overt, where one can see the antagonism, or it may be latent and thus not observable. (3)

**Conflicting interests**: interests that are incompatible or not in harmony; also see *conflict* (4)

**Containment**: the conscious effort by the United States to limit Soviet efforts to expand its influence in the 1940s and 1950s, notably by constructing a ring of military alliances around the USSR; see also *capitalist encirclement* (15)

**Convergent interests**: interests that demonstrate varying degrees of similarity (4)

**"Co-prosperity sphere"**: the zone of control in Asia that Japan sought to create in the 1930s and early 1940s that would assure it access to the natural resources of Asian countries (14)

**Core**: in the context of IR, those countries at the centre of the global capitalist economy which dominate the *periphery* and keep it dependent and underdeveloped (2, 16)

**Corn Laws**: a series of English measures dating back to the fifteenth century designed to protect English grain (corn) growers by keeping prices high (12)

**Cosmopolitan**: (from Greek, *cosmos* + *polis*) literally, "world *polis*"; in world politics, a worldwide political identity or view (8)

**Counterfactual**: a hypothesis about what might have been had certain initial historical conditions been changed; see also *path dependency* and *chaos theory* (2)

**Crime against humanity**: a wrongful act that is deemed to be not a violation of any particular nation's laws, but rather a violation against humankind as a whole (10)

**Crusades**: the military expeditions undertaken by European Christians from 1099 to the 1270s to seize the area around Jerusalem—considered the Holy Land—from Muslims (8)

**Cuban missile crisis**: confrontation between the United States and the USSR over the placement of Soviet nuclear missiles in Cuba, 22–28 October 1962, resulting in a humiliating defeat for the Soviet Union and the eventual ouster of Nikita Khrushchev (15)

**Cult of the offensive**: the belief, prevalent in military circles in Europe prior to 1914, that the advantage in battle always went to the army which took the offensive (14)

**Cultural homogeneity**: the process by which the preferences of individual consumers in different national markets converge, often as a result of marketing by multinational corporations (17)

**Cultural Revolution**: the Great Proletarian Cultural Revolution was an attempt by Mao Zedong to keep revolutionary zeal alive in China; in the three years between 1966 and 1969, hundreds of thousands of "rightists," "reactionaries," and "bourgeois-roaders" were purged, imprisoned, or killed (16)

**Darwin, Charles** (1809–1882): British scientist whose work on the Galapagos Islands in the 1830s led him to develop a theory of evolution in *On the Origin of the Species* (1859)

**Darwinism**: see *Social Darwinism*

***De facto* recognition**: (Latin) literally, in fact; recognition that is unofficial, rather than *de jure*, in law, or official (11)

***De jure* recognition**: (Latin) literally, in law; recognition that is official, rather than *de facto*, in fact or unofficial (11)

**De Klerk, Frederik Willem** (1936– ): president of South Africa, 1989–1994; leader of the National Party, 1989–present; oversaw the dismantling of the apartheid regime in the early 1990s

**De-recognition**: the formal process by which one government indicates that it no longer recognizes the existence of another government or state (11)

**De-Stalinization**: the policy introduced by Nikita Khrushchev in 1956 that sought to abandon some of Stalin's policies (15)

**Deakin, Alfred** (1856–1919): Liberal Protectionist prime minister of Australia, 1903–1904, 1905–1908, and 1909–1910

**Debt forgiveness**: a form of *ODA* that emerged in the 1970s and 1980s, made necessary because of the effects of the *debt trap* (16)

**Debt trap**: the accumulated long-term effects of taking numerous *soft loans* year after year that do not result in sufficient economic growth to pay off the concessional loans, resulting in a huge debt service load from loans at nominal interest rates (16)

**Debt-for-nature swaps**: a trade in which a Northern government arranges to forgive a portion of a Southern country's debt in return for agreement by the Southern country that it will not exploit a specified geographic area but will preserve it in its natural state (16)

**Decolonization**: the process by which the United States and European countries divested themselves (or were divested) of imperial possessions in the four decades after the Second World War (13)

**Defenestration of Prague**: (from French, *fenêtre*, window) literally, out the window. When Bohemian Protestants stormed the royal palace in Prague in May 1618, they threw two of the king's ministers out the window, sparking a rebellion that grew into the *Thirty Years' War*. (9)

**Defensive intelligence agency**: an intelligence agency that is allowed to post officials abroad for liaison purposes, but is not allowed to conduct active operations outside the country (7)

**Deng Xiaoping** (1904–1997): also rendered Teng Hsiao-p'ing, pronounced *dung shao ping*; vice-premier of China, 1952; general secretary of the Chinese Communist Party, 1962–66; purged in 1966 and 1976, emerged as paramount leader in 1980; responsible for *Open Door policy*

**Dependency theory**: a theory of relations between the rich countries of the capitalist economy (the *core*) and the poorer countries (the *periphery*) that focuses on the degree to which the poor are necessarily made dependent by the rich (2)

**Derivatives**: trading instruments that are "derived" from other market instruments, e.g., options that are bets on what the future value of a stock will be (17)

**Designer sanctions**: Margaret Doxey's term for international sanctions designed to target the "designer set" (i.e., the elite) in a country (5)

**Détente**: (French) literally, relaxation; the relaxation in tensions between East and West that began in the late 1960s and continued until the Soviet invasion of Afghanistan in December 1979 (15)

**Deterrence**: or deterrent coercion, threats of harm issued by actor A against actor B, designed to discourage B from acting in a way that would be in B's interests but not A's (5)

**Diplomat**: an agent of a state charged with conducting and maintaining relations with another government (7)

**Diplomatic immunity**: a set of rights that evolved to allow *diplomats* to engage in interstate relations without being constrained by local laws; those with diplomatic immunity are subject to no other authority than their own government's, regardless of where they are in the world (9)

***Dirigisme***: (French) literally, "control-ism"; in other words, state control or management, particularly of the economy (16)

**Dirty divorce**: in international politics, the fragmentation of a nation-state into two or more states that is marked by violence or hostility (14)

**Dirty War**: in Argentinean politics, the conflict that erupted between the armed forces which seized power in a *coup d'état* in March 1976 and left-wing groups, and lasted until 1983 (7)

**Discipline of the market**: the tendency of investors to punish jurisdictions that make decisions deemed unfriendly to investment capital by simply moving out of that market, normally triggering negative local effects such as a fall in the value of the local currency (17)

**Discrete interests**: interests that do not intersect with one another (4)

**Disinformation**: the purposeful spreading of false information in order to bolster one's own cause or discredit an opponent (5)

**Divestment**: decisions to withdraw investment capital from a particular market (17)

**Divine right of kings**: an idea dominant in Europe that kings and queens were representatives of God, and derived their right to rule from God, not dissimilar to the Chinese idea of the *Mandate of Heaven* (9)

**Divisibility of sovereignty**: the idea that sovereignty can in fact be divided—as it is in systems like that of the United States where there is the *separation of powers*, or in *federal* states such as Australia, Canada, and the United States (10)

**Domestic politics**: the political processes, institutions, and culture that occur within a political community (6)

**Domestic sources of foreign policy**: the impact of a country's political culture, ideas, electoral system, economic structure, political parties, interest groups, nongovernmental organizations, and unorganized interests on its foreign policy (7)

**Domestication of foreign policy**: the process by which a country's foreign policy is increasingly influenced and affected by domestic politics (7)

**Domino theory**: the notion that if one country embraces a revolutionary idea, that idea will be spread by policy contagion or other means to the neighbouring country; usually used in the context of the American struggle against communism (15)

**Dragon bonds**: securities tradeable only in Asian markets (17)

**Dreadnought**: a class of heavy battleship, first launched by Britain in the pre-First World War era (14)

**Drug trade**: the movement of illegal narcotics, primarily heroin, hashish, marijuana, cocaine, and crack, from Southeast Asia, Southwest Asia, Latin America and the Caribbean to the major consumer markets of the industrialized world (7)

**Dumbarton Oaks**: private estate in Washington, DC; site of discussions from August to October 1944 between the governments of Britain, China, the Soviet Union, and the United States on the nature of the postwar political order (15)

**Dumping**: the practice of selling a product in a foreign market at a price below its cost of production, usually to drive competitors out of business (17)

**Dunant, Jean Henri** (1828–1910): Swiss philanthropist whose exposure to the battlefield at Solferino in 1859 prompted him to work to create the Red Cross

**Dynamic Asian economies**: another term for the newly industrializing countries of Asia. Using the term "economies" allows Taiwan to be included without offending the People's Republic of China. (16)

**Dynastic identity**: a form of political identity in which the focus of loyalty is on a royal house and its members (8)

**Eastern Question**: the colloquial term used in Europe in the 19th century for the problems arising out of European relations with the Ottoman empire (12)

**Economic nationalism**: the economic program embraced by many nationalists that puts a premium on creating, maintaining, and protecting a *national economy* (12)

**Economic theory of imperialism**: the theory that the colonies acquired by Europeans and Americans in the 19th century were vital for the health of their economies (13)

**Economy**: any system of regular exchange involving goods, labour, services, and/or capital (3)

**ECU**: European Currency Unit, comparable to *Special Drawing Rights*, the unit of account for the EU whose value was based on the value of a basket of European currencies (17)

**Eisenhower, Dwight D.** (1890–1969): president of the United States, 1953–1961; Republican Party; built up American nuclear arsenals, actively pursued policies of *containment*

**Embedded liberalism**: John Gerard Ruggie's characterization of the understanding that underwrote the post-1945 economic order—a compromise under which countries could pursue their own economic and social policies domestically while seeking to liberalize international economic interactions (17)

**Empire**: a political formation with considerable territorial reach, usually involving political authority extended over different countries and peoples, sometimes but not always including *colonies*; when capitalized in English, usually refers to the British Empire (9)

**Engels, Friedrich** (1820–1895): German writer, revolutionary, and political theorist, who founded modern communism with Karl Marx, and after Marx's death edited the second and third editions of Marx's *Das Kapital*

**English School**: an approach to international relations—commonly associated with English scholars such as John Burton, Hedley Bull, and Martin Wight—that stresses the essentially social nature of relations among sovereign states (2)

**Environmental movement**: a social movement concerned with environmental issues such as sustainable development, minimal pollution, minimal interruption to the ecology, maximum conservation of energy, and zero population growth (7)

**Environmental NGO**: an NGO whose central mission is to enhance environmental protection, either generally or specifically (7)

**Epistemology**: the branch of philosophy dealing with the problems of knowledge: the definition of knowledge, the sources of what we know and how we come to know it, and the relationship between the one who knows and what is known (2)

**Equality of states**: the idea that each sovereign state should enjoy the same juridical rights as any other state, regardless of size, power, or importance (10)

**Ethnic cleansing**: term applied to the efforts by different ethnic groups during the civil war in Yugoslavia in the 1990s to remove members of rival ethnic groups from their territory, by either expelling or killing them (10, 14)

**Ethnicity**: (from Greek, *ethnos*, people); the particular racial, religious, cultural, and linguistic commonalities of a group (12)

**Ethnonationalism**: term applied to a nationalism that is based mainly on ethnicity (14)

**Eurobonds**: bonds denominated in U.S. dollars and traded outside the United States, primarily, but not necessarily, in Europe (17)

**Eurodollars**: U.S. dollars deposited, traded, or borrowed in financial institutions outside the United States, primarily, but not necessarily, in Europe (17)

**"European idea"**: the notion that the various countries of Europe can be united in a single market and a single polity without losing their particular national identities (17)

**European Union**: supranational organization of 15 European nation-states that had its origins in common markets created in the 1950s (3, 17)

**Evans, Gareth** (1944– ): Australian minister for foreign affairs, 1988–96; Australian Labor Party; proponent of the notion of "good international citizenship"

**"Evil Empire"**: the term, from the *Star Wars* movie series, applied to the Soviet Union by Ronald Reagan (15)

**Exclusive Economic Zone (EEZ)**: the waters that extend 200 nautical miles from a country's shores over which it has jurisdiction for such economic activities as fishing (10)

**Exclusive IGO**: an intergovernmental organization that restricts membership to particular governments depending on the purpose of the IGO (7)

**Export-oriented strategy**: an industrial strategy under which a government nurtures and protects selected industries and industrial sectors, not to meet domestic demand, but to compete on world markets (16)

**External sources of foreign policy**: those influences on government behaviour that come from the international system, such as geographic and strategic location, power, the impact of the international economy, and trade and investment (7)

**Extradition**: the process by which a suspected criminal is moved from one jurisdiction to another; usually requires agreement between the jurisdictions (4)

**Extraterritoriality**: the attempts by a government to apply its laws beyond its own territorial space, in other words, in the territory of another sovereign (10)

**"Fair trade"**: an idea, predominantly American, that other governments or peoples should place no barriers in the way of American trade or commerce; an idea, however, that does not extend to barriers placed by the U.S. in the way of foreign trade (10)

**Federalism**: a political formation in which two levels of government—a central or national government and several local or regional governments—share sovereign authority over a single territory and one group of people, the division based on territory and functional jurisdiction (9, 17)

**Female genital alteration**: also called "female circumcision" (or "female genital mutilation" by some opponents of the practice); the practice in some African and Islamic countries of altering young girls' genitalia by removing part or all of the clitoris and/or the labia, and sometimes sewing up the vaginal opening; intended to promote premarital chastity and/or to remove the capacity for sexual pleasure (6)

**Feminism**: in IR, an approach that stresses the importance of examining the degree to which the practice and the theory of world politics are gendered (2)

**Feudal domain**: the territorial extent of a feudal lord, most commonly the feudal estate, that eventually was transformed into the contemporary state (8)

**Feudalism**: the patterns of political, economic, and military relationships dominant in Europe from the ninth and tenth centuries, marked by a complex arrangement of personal lines of authority between vassals and lords that were not necessarily bounded by territory (8, 9)

**Fichte, Johann Gottlieb** (1762–1814): a philosopher who studied the thought of Immanuel Kant. He was also a German nationalist who wrote key works on economic nationalism.

**First World**: the industrialized countries of the West (16)

**Flag/trade debate**: the debate over whether colonialism was a function of commercial expansion—flag following trade—or of government expansion—trade following flag (13)

**Footloose capital**: Robert Reich's term for capital that is not bound by sentiment to any national market but will seek the best return it can, anywhere in the international system (17)

**Force**: a technique of power that uses violence against opponents, either to eliminate them altogether or to do them such harm that they bend to one's will (5)

**Fordism**: the term used by Antonio Gramsci to describe a system of production that came from the use of mass production techniques using assembly lines and large factories; see also *post-Fordism* (17)

**Foreign concessions**: the name given to those areas of China during the 19th century where non-Chinese—Europeans and Americans—were given special privileges and exemptions from Chinese law and taxation (10)

**Foreign ministry**: the agency of the contemporary state responsible for maintaining official diplomatic relations with other sovereign states (7)

**Foreign policy analysis**: the subdiscipline in IR that concerns itself with understanding the foreign policies of particular nation-states (7)

**Foreign policy**: all of the actions that a government takes in its dealings with the world outside its borders (3, 7)

**Formal economy**: those market exchanges in an economy that are monitored, tabulated, and measured; see also *informal economy* (6)

**Foucault, Michel** (1926–1984): French philosopher who wrote on the nature of power in the contemporary era

**Fourteen Points**: the name given to the 14-point program for world peace outlined by Woodrow Wilson, president of the United States, to Congress on 8 January 1918, including the right of self-determination and an association of nations (13)

**Fourth World**: a category that emerged in the 1970s to describe the poorest members of the Third World; also called "least developed countries" (LLDCs) (16)

**Frankfurt School**: those students of IR whose theoretical reflections were shaped by the thinking of the German sociologist Jurgen Habermas, who stressed the importance of a sociological and critical-theoretical understanding of the political world (2)

**Free trade**: the unimpeded movement of some or all of the factors of production across the borders of political communities (10, 12)

*Gaiatsu*: (Japanese) foreign pressure; in particular the pressure of the United States to open the Japanese economy (10)

**Gandhi, Indira** (1917–1984): prime minister of India, 1966–1977 and 1980–1984; daughter of Jawaharlal Nehru; assassinated by Sikhs in October 1984

**Gandhi, Mohandas** (1869–1948): Indian nationalist leader, advocate of nonviolence, passive resistance, and civil disobedience as political tools; assassinated by a Hindu extremist, January 1948

**Gandhi, Rajiv** (1944–1991): prime minister of India, 1984–1989; son of Indira Gandhi; assassinated by Sri Lankan separatists May 1991

**GATT Rounds**: the periodic multilateral negotiations held under the auspices of GATT from 1947 onward. The last, the Uruguay Round (1986–1993), transformed GATT into the WTO. (17)

*Gemeinschaft*: (German) literally, community; an understanding of society that suggests that political communities evolve rather than being created; see also *Gesellshaft* (4)

**Gender inequality**: the general inequalities between men and women that can be observed in a variety of contexts, from unequal pay for equal work to lesser access to food, education, and freedom for women as compared to men (6)

**Generalized system of preferences**: a program of giving exports from the South preferential access to Northern markets as a means of encouraging the growth of infant industries in the developing world (16)

**Genocide**: the systemic and deliberate elimination of an entire people (10)

*Gesellshaft*: (German) literally, society; an understanding of society that suggests that political communities are the result of a contractual understanding between individuals; see also *Gemeinschaft* (4)

*Glasnost*: (Russian) literally, openness; policy introduced by Mikhail Gorbachev in the 1980s that fostered greater openness in Soviet politics (15)

**Global governance**: the process by which the different actors—governments, organizations, and individuals—try to make common decisions for the global community (4)

**Global language**: sometimes called a universal language or *lingua franca* (literally, Frankish language); any language that is used between peoples of different languages for the purpose of conducting business or other relations (12)

**Global occasions**: those events that are watched on television by individuals around the world, thus creating a sense of global community (7)

**"Global tribes"**: Joel Kotkin's characterization of certain ethnic and national groups that have moved throughout the world without shedding their ethnic identity, such as Anglo-Saxons, Chinese, Indians, Japanese, and Jews (12)

**Globalization thesis**: the argument that sovereign nation-states are losing their relevance because they have lost the capacity to protect the nation against influences from "outside" because of the increasingly *globalized economy* (17)

**Globalized economy**: an economy in which all of the elements of wealth creation—finance, investment, production, distribution, marketing—are organized on a global scale (4)

**Glorious Revolution**: the name given to the events of 1688–89 in England, in particular the ouster of the Roman Catholic king, James II, by the Protestant William of Orange in November, and the passage by Parliament of a Bill of Rights that severely limited the power of the monarch and established the supremacy of Parliament. It was called glorious because, unlike the revolutions earlier in the century, it was bloodless. (9)

**Gold standard**: a monetary arrangement under which legal tender can be redeemed in a fixed amount of gold on demand, used primarily as a means of settling international commercial transactions (17)

**Gorbachev, Mikhail S.** (1931– ): general secretary of the CPSU, 1984; introduced revolutionary changes to domestic and foreign policies of the USSR (*glasnost, perestroika,* "new thinking"); dismantled the USSR, December 1991

**Governance**: the process by which decisions are made for and about the community (3)

**Government-in-exile**: a group that physically establishes itself outside a political community and declares that it is the rightful government of that community (11)

**Governmental sources of foreign policy**: the sources of a country's foreign policy that stem from its political form (republican, Westminster, federal, unitary) or its governmental structure (7)

**Gramsci, Antonio** (1891–1937): Italian political philosopher and activist who served time in prison for his opposition to Fascism, and who wrote on production and class

**Great Leap Forward**: a movement in China in the late 1950s that communized village life, collectivized agriculture, and introduced limited industrialization at the commune level across China. By 1960, the Great Leap Forward had resulted in famine that killed millions of peasants. (15)

**Great Patriotic War**: the name Soviets and Russians give to the war they fought against Nazi Germany and others between 1941 and 1945 (14)

**"Great Satan"**: the common characterization of the United States by the government of Iran after the ouster of the Shah in January 1979 (15)

**Great Terror**: the name given by Russians to the widespread political purge by Joseph Stalin during the 1930s in which millions of Soviets suspected of disloyalty were executed, imprisoned, or exiled (7)

**Great War**: the name given to the war fought between 1914 and 1918. After 1939 and the outbreak of the Second World War, the Great War was usually called the First World War. (14)

**Green parties**: political parties that are organized around environmental issues. Many parties now use the name Green, the colour adopted by environmentalists to symbolize a commitment to environmental protection. (7)

**Green Revolution**: the rapid increases in agricultural output as a result of crop diversification and selective breeding of strains to create high-yield hybrids in the 1960s (16)

**Group of 77**: the original 77 developing countries of the South which formed a solid front at the 1964 UNCTAD meeting. The G-77 designation has been used even though the Southern countries who are members of the group now number more than 130. (16)

**Group of Ten**: the ten industrialized countries which oversee the IMF's General Agreement to Borrow, a facility designed to maximize international liquidity (16)

**Guest Ritual**: the formal rituals in imperial China for receiving foreign visitors and giving them an audience with the emperor (2)

**Gulf of Tonkin resolution**: resolution passed by the U.S. Congress on 7 August 1964, following a North Vietnamese attack on an American naval vessel, that gave the president wide discretion to prosecute the war in Vietnam (15)

**Hanseatic League**: association of 200 *Hansa* towns in northern Germany in the 13th and 14th centuries that controlled the Baltic and North Sea trade (4)

**Harmonization**: the process by which governments shape their social and economic policies to closely match the policies being pursued in other jurisdictions so as to attract (or so as not to lose) capital investment (17)

**Hawke, Bob** (1929– ): prime minister of Australia, 1983–1991; Australian Labor Party

**Head of government**: the individual who is the head of the governmental apparatus of a state. Depending on the constitutional arrangements, the head of government may or may not be the same individual as the *head of state*. (9)

**Head of state**: the individual who is regarded as the personal embodiment of the state, and in whom the state's sovereignty is nominally located. Depending on the constitutional arrangements, the head of state may or may not be the same individual as the *head of government*. (9)

**Hegemonic stability theory**: a theory, popular with American scholars of international politics, that claims that the stability and prosperity of the post-1945 period was due to the leadership of a single dominant power (the United States), acting in the global interest (15)

**Helms, Jesse** (1921– ): Republican member of the United States Senate, 1973– present; chairman of the Senate Foreign Relations Committee, 1995–present

**Helms–Burton**: colloquial name for the Cuban Liberty and Democratic Solidarity Act of 1996, named after its Congressional sponsors, Senator Jesse Helms, Republican of North Carolina, and Representative Dan Burton, Republican of Illinois. The act seeks to punish anyone, American or not, doing certain kinds of business with Cuba. (10)

**Herd instinct**: in international trading, the tendency of individual investors to make decisions based on what they believe the majority of others are doing, producing trends of buying or selling (17)

**Hermeneutics**: the study of the methodological principles of interpreting texts. The term emerged in the 18th century to apply to the study of the Bible, but is now used more widely to apply to the interpretation of any written work. (2)

**Hidalgo y Costilla, Miguel** (1753–1811): Mexican priest and nationalist. On 16 September 1810, he led an unsuccessful revolt against the Spanish colonial regime, and was executed January 1811.

**High commissioner**: the name used for diplomatic representatives at the level of ambassador between countries belonging to the Commonwealth (10)

**High seas**: that portion of the world's oceans that lies beyond the territorial waters or *EEZ* of any state (10)

**Hitler, Adolf** (1889–1945): Nazi leader and German *Reichskanzler*, 1933–1945; sought supremacy for the Aryan race through world domination and systematic extermination of "lesser peoples"; committed suicide April 1945

**"Ho Chi Minh trail"**: a system of jungle tracks and roads stretching from North Vietnam through Laos and Cambodia to South Vietnam on which communist troops and military equipment were transported (15)

**Hobbes, Thomas** (1588–1679): English political philosopher whose works, such as *Leviathan* (1651), provide an exposition on sovereignty and a secular justification for political authority

**Holocaust**: name given to the organized effort of the *Nazis* to eradicate all the Jews, Roma (Gypsies), Slavs, and other so-called *Untermenschen* by transporting them to concentration camps and killing them (14)

**Holy Roman Empire**: a political formation in Western Europe that existed from 800 to 1806 under different names (Empire in the West, Roman Empire, Holy Empire, and, after the 13th century, Holy Roman Empire); throughout that period the centre of the Empire was in the German states (9)

**"Hot line"**: a secure teletype/telephone line linking the leaders of the United States and the USSR, established after the Cuban missile crisis of 1962 (15)

**Hot pursuit**: the assumption in military strategy that it is prudent to continue to attack an enemy even after it is in retreat, to prevent it from regrouping and perhaps launching a counterattack (15)

**Howard, John** (1939– ): prime minister of Australia, 1996–present; leader of the Liberal Party, 1985–1989 and 1995–present

**Hub-and-spoke approach**: a characterization for the preference of the United States (the "hub") to deal with each of its trading partners (the "spokes") separately rather than in multilateral forums (17)

**Huguenots**: name given to Protestants in France during the civil wars fought over religion during the 16th century; between 400 000 and one million Huguenots were forced out of France during the 17th century (9)

**Human Development Index**: the UN Development Program's annual ranking of countries by life expectancy, adult literacy and average years of schooling, and purchasing power (16)

**Human rights NGO**: an NGO whose central mission is to encourage the observance of human rights, either generally or more specifically by region or category of abused person (7)

**Humanitarian NGO**: an NGO whose central mission is to alleviate human suffering (7)

**Hussein, Saddam** (1937– ): president of Iraq, 1979–present; initiated the 1980–88 Iran-Iraq war and the 1990 invasion of Kuwait

**Hyperinflation**: a period of wild and severe inflation during which paper money loses nearly all its value (14)

**Hypernationalism**: see *Ultranationalism*

**Idealism**: an approach to international politics that assumes the essential goodness and peaceableness of individuals and the communities they form. In its dominant variant in the interwar years (1919–1939), idealism argued that international institutions such as the League of Nations would ensure peace.

**Identity**: the propensity of both individuals and groups to develop a sense of who they are, often by constructing a sense of who they are not; see *Otherness* (8)

**Ideology**: a comprehensive and integrated set of beliefs about the political world that provide not only the basis for understanding the world, but also a normative blueprint for a creating a better world (7)

**Ignored states**: states which declare their existence but which are then not recognized by the governments of other states (11)

**"Imagined community"**: Benedict Anderson's characterization of nation that stresses its subjective nature (12)

**Imperial overstretch**: what happens to a country when it seeks to expand its global influence but does not have the power resources to sustain that new reach (15)

**Imperialism**: see *Empire*

**Import substitution**: attempts to meet the needs of a national economy by producing locally rather than importing, even though importing might be cheaper (12, 16)

**In-group**: one part of a dualism that defines individuals as being within a particular group or inside that group; see *out-group* (8)

**Indemnity**: in international politics, the sum of money that the loser of a war was normally required to pay the winner to compensate for the losses incurred in war-fighting; see also *reparations* (14)

**Independence**: (from Latin *pendere*, to hang); being free from the control of others, the ability to make one's own decisions, not having to rely on anyone else, and not being guided or influenced by the opinions of others (i.e., not having to "hang" on others). In the context of world politics, independence usually refers to the ability of a political community to govern itself rather than to be governed by others. (4)

**Inducement**: a technique of influence in which actor B is offered a reward to do something that B would not otherwise have done, thus changing B's definition of interests so it is compatible with the interests of actor A who offers the inducement (5)

**Indulgences**: the practice of selling remission of one's sins for a cash contribution to the Church (9)

**Industrial Revolution**: the process of the transformation of a predominantly agricultural economy serving local markets to a predominantly industrial economy with international reach (12)

**Informal economy**: all economic intercourse that occurs that is not formally monitored or counted, whether illegal (such as trade in drugs or prohibited goods) or legal, such as barter or under-the-counter work (6)

**Inside/outside dualism**: in IR, the analytical distinction that portrays life and politics *inside* the political commu-

nity, or the "domestic sphere," in very different terms from politics *outside*, or in the "international sphere" (6)

**Interdict**: a ban, issued by the pope, on administering any of the sacraments of the Church to the faithful (7, 9)

**Interests**: the calculation by individuals or communities of the goals, objectives, values that they want (3, 4)

**Intergovernmental organizations**: institutions organized by governments of states that normally only sovereign governments can join (7)

**Internal waters**: any waterway or part of the ocean that is enclosed by *straight baselines*. These are not considered *territorial waters*, and states have full jurisdiction over these waters. (10)

**International law**: formal body of rules that have been agreed to by governments of states to govern numerous aspects of their relations. Unlike *municipal law*, which is enforced by an agency with coercive powers, international law depends on voluntary compliance. (4)

**International negotiations**: normally the formal or informal discussions that governments engage in, either bilaterally or multilaterally (5)

**International political economy**: a perspective on politics at a global level that explores the interaction between politics, society, culture, modes of production, class, and the market (2)

**International relations theory**: the philosophical, *ontological*, and *epistemological* assumptions that guide understanding of the field of study known as IR (2)

**International sanctions**: the use by governments of any nonviolent harm, usually directed at other governments or states (5)

**International strait**: term given to those narrow channels joining two larger bodies of water that are habitually and traditionally used for navigation. Although an international strait might technically lie within a state's 12-mile limit, it is not considered *territorial waters* and other nations have well-defined rights of passage. (10)

**Internationalized economy**: a single economy linking the local economies of different regions and countries of the world (4)

**Intersubjectivity**: something that is neither wholly objective nor wholly subjective, but where the subjective is capable of being known objectively (12)

**Iranian hostage crisis**: the seizure of the U.S. Embassy in Teheran, Iran, in November 1979 by radical students, and the holding of 52 Americans as hostages for 444 days (15)

**Iron curtain**: Winston Churchill's 1946 characterization of the divide between East and West (15)

**Irredentism**: (from Italian, *irredenta*, unredeemed); those Italian-speaking territories that remained under Austrian or Swiss rule after unification in 1861; applied to any part of a national homeland under foreign control (12)

**Jiang Zemin** (1926– ): general secretary of the Chinese Communist Party, 1989– present; president of the PRC, 1993–present; former mayor of Shanghai

**Jihād**: (Arabic) literally, striving; although commonly translated by non-Muslims as "holy war," more accurately *jihād*

refers to the permanent obligation of every Muslim to ensure the spread of Muslim rule over all the Earth (8)

**Jingoism**: an enthusiasm for a belligerent foreign policy (14)

**John Paul II** (1920– ): pope, 1978–present; born Karol Wojtyla; former archbishop of Kraków; highly active in world politics on such issues as communism and population matters

**Johnson, Lyndon B.** (1908–1973): president of the United States, 1963–1969; Democratic Party; deepened American involvement in Vietnam, chose not to run for a second term in 1968 after *Tĕt offensive*

**Jus belli**: (Latin) literally, the right of war; the right that a sovereign state is deemed to have to use force in defence of its interests. This right has become more and more limited over the course of the 20th century. (10)

**Jus legationis**: (Latin) literally, the right of legation; the right of a sovereign state to exchange diplomatic representatives with other sovereign states (10)

**Jus tractatuum**: (Latin) literally, the right of treaty; the right of a sovereign state to sign treaties with other states (10)

**Kant, Immanuel** (1724–1804): German philosopher who also published reflections on international politics, notably *Perpetual Peace* (1795), a treatise advocating a world federation of liberal republics

**Keating, Paul** (1944– ): prime minister of Australia, 1991–96; Australian Labor Party

**Keiretsu system**: in Japan, the groups or coalitions of firms in related sectors which supply each other with the factors of production (10)

**Kennedy, John F.** (1917–1963): president of the United States, 1961 until his assassination on 22 November 1963; Democratic Party; deepened American involvement in Vietnam, pursued anti-Cuban policies, and humiliated the USSR during the Cuban missile crisis

**Khrushchev, Nikita S.** (1894–1971): first secretary of the Communist Party of the Soviet Union, 1953–1964; premier of the USSR, 1958–1964; ousted after humiliation resulting from the Cuban missile crisis

**Khrushchev's "secret speech"**: a not-so-secret speech given by Nikita Khrushchev at the 20th CPSU Congress in January and February 1956 in which he criticized Stalin (15)

**Kin-country**: Samuel P. Huntington's term for the national equivalent of interpersonal *kinship ties* (17)

**Kinship ties**: the links of family that normally provide the closest bonds between individuals (8)

**Korean War**: war that began with the invasion of South Korea by North Korea on 25 June 1950, and widened to involve troops from the United Nations and China; concluded with the Geneva Accords, 1954 (15)

**Kristallnacht**: (German) literally, night of glass; the night of 9 November 1938, when *Nazis* across Germany set fire to virtually every synagogue, randomly killed more than 90 Jews, and broke the storefront of virtually every shop owned by Jews—hence the name (9)

**Kruger telegram**: telegram sent in 1896 from Kaiser Wilhelm of Germany to the president of Transvaal, Paul Kruger, congratulating him on repelling the Jamieson raid. The telegram inflamed the British, revealing the depth of anti-German sentiment in Britain. (14)

**Land-locked and geographically disadvantaged states**: those countries which either lack a coastline or whose coastlines are shaped in such a way as to deprive them of a large *Exclusive Economic Zone* (10)

**Law of the sea**: the body of international law that deals with the ownership, use, and exploitation of the world's oceans and the seabed (10)

**Lebensraum**: (German) literally, living room; the term used by the *Nazis* to describe the need of Aryan race for additional territory (4)

**Lee Teng-hui** (1923– ): former mayor of Taipei, first selected president by the electoral college in 1988; reformed Taiwanese political system; first popularly elected president of the Republic of China on Taiwan, 23 March 1996

**Legislators**: members of a country's legislature or parliament, many of whom play an important role in their country's international relations (7)

**Lenin, Vladimir Ilich** (1870–1924): the leader of the *Bolshevik revolution* in 1917 and first leader of the new USSR. Lenin consolidated the communists in power before being incapacitated by strokes in 1922 and 1923.

**Leninist theory of imperialism**: the idea that imperialism is a necessary stage of capitalism that occurs when a surplus of capital and overproduction in the metropole forces capitalist countries to seek markets for goods and capital elsewhere (13)

**Letter of credence**: (from Latin, *credere*, to trust); as part of the stylized rituals of diplomatic relations, new ambassadors to a country present a formal letter from their head of state indicating that they are entrusted to act as ambassador (10)

**Liberal institutionalism**: sometimes known as neoliberalism, this perspective rejects realist assumptions and instead examines the degree to which states cooperate in international relations, focusing in particular on their economic relations (2)

**Liberalism**: approaches to IR that focus on the individual and the possibilities of improvement in the human condition that come with cooperative behaviour (2)

**"Living-room war"**: Michael Arlen's phrase for the Vietnam War, since the war's course was so affected by the huge coverage of the war-fighting that was beamed by television into American living rooms (7)

**Localized economy**: systems of exchange, either barter or monetarized, that are limited in geographic scope, usually embracing the economies of several political communities (4)

**Locke, John** (1632–1704): English philosopher and political theorist noted for his contributions to liberal theory and in particular the idea that sovereignty lay in the people, not the ruler

**Lomé Convention**: an agreement, signed in 1975 between the European Community and a number of countries of the South, that gave a number of goods from Southern countries preferential access to the European market (16)

**"Loss" of China**: argument common in the United States in the early 1950s that pro-communist American officials in the U.S. State Department were responsible for "losing" China to communism (15)

**Maastricht Treaty**: the Treaty on European Union, creating the EU, initialled by the heads of state and government of the European Communities at Maastricht, Netherlands, on 11 December 1991; came into force 1 November 1993 (17)

**Macdonald, John A.** (1815–1891): first prime minister of Canada, 1867–1873 and 1878–1891; Conservative Party

**Machiavelli, Niccolò** (1469–1527): Italian political philosopher, historian, and official of the Florentine Republic after 1498. When the republic was dissolved in 1512, Machiavelli was imprisoned and tortured. On his release he retired to his farm, where he wrote his most influential works, *The Prince* and *Discourse on the First Ten Books of Titus Livius.*

**Mahathir bin Muhammad** (1925– ): prime minister of Malaysia, 1981–present; active proponent for Southern interests and outspoken critic of aspects of globalized financial markets

***Maîtres chez nous***: (French) literally, masters of our own house; the phrase that captures the *québécois* desire for sovereignty (12)

***Majestas***: (Latin) literally, majesty or greatness; because the Romans had no word for sovereignty, this word was used by Europeans in the 16th century when they wanted a "backward" translation of sovereignty into Latin (9)

**Mandate of Heaven**: (in Chinese, *Tianming*) the idea that Heaven gave the emperor of China, the Son of Heaven, the right to rule over all the Earth, and could revoke that mandate if the Son of Heaven was not ordering the world in a harmonious way; see also *divine right of kings* (8)

**Mandate system**: from the legal doctrine of *mandatum*, in which an individual's interests are looked after by another; a system created after the First World War under which the colonies of the defeated powers were given to the victorious powers to govern on behalf of the international community (13)

**Mandatory power**: one of the states which were given mandates under the *mandate system* (13)

**Mandela, Nelson** (1918– ): South African political leader; under the apartheid regime, he led the African National Congress; in 1964, sentenced to life imprisonment for treason; released 1990; and elected first president of postapartheid South Africa, 1994

**Manifest Destiny**: the idea, popular in the United States in the 19th century, that Americans were predestined to take over all of North America (13)

**Manipulation**: a technique of power in which actor A structures the situation in such a manner that actor B thinks a certain course of action is in B's interests (5)

**Mao Zedong** (1893–1976): also rendered Mao Tse-tung, pronounced *mao dze dung*; leader of the Chinese Communist Party, founder of the People's Republic of China, and paramount leader, 1949–1976

**Maquiladora** (Spanish) literally, the place where the miller is paid for milling one's grain; a twin-plant assembly system in which components made in the United States are assembled in Mexico and shipped back across the border duty-free (8)

**Maritime states**: those countries with global oceanic interests—those with large merchant marine fleets or a *blue water navy*; these states have an interest in maximizing the amount of the oceans considered *high seas* (10)

**Marshall Plan**: colloquial name for the European Recovery Program, a US$13-billion package of American economic aid to devastated European nations announced by the secretary of state, George Marshall, in June 1947 (15)

**Marx, Karl** (1818–1883): German editor, political philosopher, political organizer, who with Freidrich Engels founded modern communism

**Marxism**: in IR, those theoretical perspectives informed by the work of *Karl Marx*, focusing particularly on the role of modes of production on class, both within nations and between communities; sometimes referred to as "radicalism" (2)

**McCarthyism**: the name given to the anticommunist movement in the United States in the early 1950s spearheaded by Senator Joseph McCarthy, Republican of Wisconsin (11, 15)

**Media pool**: a technique used when it is physically impossible to have a large number of photographers and journalists cover an event; one or two journalists are chosen who then report back to their colleagues before filing their own stories (7)

**Meiji Restoration**: the term used to describe the process of westernization and modernization that occurred after Prince Mutsuhito became emperor of Japan in 1867, taking the reign name Meiji, "enlightened rule" (13)

**Melian dialogue**: debate between Athenians and Melians in 416 BC, reported by Thucydides, in which the Athenians threatened Melos with destruction if the *polis* did not surrender to Athens (4)

**Meltdown**: the rapid collapse in the relative value of a national currency as large numbers of investors, worried about their capital, try to sell their holdings all at once (17)

**Mercantilism**: the dominant approach of European governments to economic policy for much of the 16th, 17th, and 18th centuries that stressed the accumulation of *bullion*, the protection of domestic industry, and the accumulation of overseas *colonies* (9)

**Mercenaries**: soldiers who are hired to fight someone else's war and whose motive is usually (but not necessarily) economic gain. In other words, it excludes professional soldiers who work for their own community's armed forces for economic gain. (7)

**Mestizo** (Spanish) literally, mixed; in Mexico, those of mixed European and Native American ancestry (8)

**Metonym**: a figure of speech that uses the name of one thing to mean another with which it is associated, e.g., "the White House" to mean the president of the United States (6)

**Metropole**: the centres from which empires were ruled or the economic centre of the international capitalist economy; see also *core* (13, 16)

**Middle powers**: countries of middle size which tend to pursue a particular brand of community-oriented foreign policy (4)

**MIRV**: (multiple independently targetable re-entry vehicle) technology that allows from three to ten warheads (re-entry vehicles), each with their own target, to be placed atop a single ICBM (15)

**Missile gap**: the false allegation made by John F. Kennedy that the Eisenhower administration had allowed the U.S. to fall behind the USSR in the number of missiles; this issue played a part in the 1960 presidential elections (15)

*Mission civilisatrice*: (French) literally, civilizing mission; the idea that part of the European mission was to seize colonies so that "civilization" could be brought to the newly subjugated (13)

**Missionary religion**: a religion whose members try to convince others to embrace their conception of the divine (7)

**Mobilization**: the period of time between a declaration of war and the actual outbreak of fighting, usually several days, that was necessary to call up members of citizen armies (14)

**Modernization thesis**: the argument, popular in the 1950s and 1960s, that modernization and development occurs in stages, and that the South had to go through the same stages as the North in order to develop (16)

**Monetary union**: the creation of a single currency and monetary area by two or more sovereign nation-states (17)

**Monopoly trading corporation**: companies chartered by 17th century European governments to expand trade in specified regions of the world, protected against other domestic (but not foreign) competition (7, 9)

**Monroe Doctrine**: the doctrine promulgated by James Monroe, president of the United States, on 2 December 1823, that the United States would regard any intervention in the western hemisphere by European states which did not already have colonial possessions in the hemisphere "as dangerous to our peace and security" (11)

**Most-Favoured-Nation**: in international trade, an agreement by a country that it will give the imports of a country the same kind of access it grants to those of the "most favoured" country—in other words, nondiscriminatory access (17)

*Mujahideen* (Arabic and Persian) literally, those who fight in a *jihād*, holy warriors; in Afghanistan, guerrillas who fought against Soviet occupation forces. Also spelled *mujahidden*, *mujahidin*. (15)

**Mulroney, Brian** (1939– ): prime minister of Canada, 1984–1993; Progressive Conservative Party

**Multilingual**: speaking several languages; in a political context, those polities where a number of languages enjoy formal or informal political standing (12)

**Multinational corporation**: a company that has its head office in one country, but aspects of its production, marketing, and/or distribution are located in other countries; see also *transnational corporation* (7)

**Municipal law**: the formal body of rules operating within a sovereign nation-state, enforced by a state apparatus with coercive powers (3)

**Mussolini, Benito** (1883–1945): Italian premier, 1922–1943, leader of the Fascists; sought to expand Italian influence in the Mediterranean through an alliance with Germany; executed by Italian partisans, April 1945

**Mutual assured destruction/deterrence**: a situation in which two sides have sufficient *overkill* capability that both are mutually deterred from acting in a way that will provoke war because both are assured of destruction should such a nuclear war break out (5)

**Nation**: any group of people who define themselves as a nation and are committed to the ideology of nationalism (12)

**Nation-state**: a sovereign state populated by nationalists (12)

**National consciousness**: the development of the idea within a group of people that they constitute a separate *nation* (12)

**National economy**: the idea that the nation comprises an economic unit that must be kept strong and vibrant in order to sustain the nation (12)

**National homeland**: the territory deemed by a nation to be rightfully its own (12)

**National liberation movements**: the name given to any movement seeking to establish an independent state, usually in the context of colonial rule (13)

**National mythology**: the history of the nation that is told in such a way as to maximize adherence to nation rather than to reflect historical accuracy (12)

**National self-determination**: the idea that each nation has the right to decide its own future and establish its own government (12)

**National service**: requirement that individuals serve in their country's armed forces for a period of time to maintain large standing armies (14)

**National symbols**: the various symbolic representations of a nation, instantly identifiable to nationals, including flags, currency, and logos (12)

**Nationalism**: an ideology that sees nation as the centre of political identity, including a set of ideas about nation and a political agenda for the nation (12)

**Nationalist agenda**: at its most basic, the agenda consists of two goals: the nation must have a sovereign state to defend it, and the nation must occupy its proper homeland (12)

**Nationalist credo**: a set of beliefs that a nationalist has about nation (12)

**Nationalist**: an individual who has embraced the ideology of nationalism (12)

**Nationality**: an identification of national origin or membership that carries no presumption about nationalist sentiment (12)

**Naturalization**: the process by which a sovereign state grants the rights of citizenship to noncitizens such as immigrants or resident aliens (9)

**Nazi**: colloquial term derived from the first two syllables of the *Nationalsocialistische Deutsche Arbeiterpartei*—National

Socialist German Workers' Party (NSDAP)—led by Adolf Hitler (14, 17)

**Nehru, Jawaharlal** (1889–1964): first prime minister of an independent India, 1947–1964; advocate of *nonalignment* in world politics

**Neoliberalism**: see *Liberal institutionalism*

**Neolithic Era**: literally new stones, commonly used to describe the period when societies embraced agriculture and the domestication of animals, seen as the necessary conditions for the evolution of civilization (8)

**Neorealism**: see *Structural realism*

**New International Economic Order**: program embraced by the South in the 1970s that called for a readjustment in how the entire international economy worked, including adjusting the prices of manufactured goods, increasing accessibility to development financing, and lowering tariffs (16)

**"New thinking"**: term used to describe the "new" way of Soviet thinking about East/West relations that emerged in the 1980s under Mikhail Gorbachev (15)

**Newly industrializing countries**: those Third World countries which in the 1970s and 1980s showed strong economic growth and the spread of industrialization (16)

**Night-watchman state**: a conception of the role of the state, dominant in the 19th century, that believed that the proper role of the state was limited to the creation of domestic order and security against external threats (4)

**Nixon, Richard** (1913–1994): president of the United States, 1969–1974; Republican Party; withdrew United States from Vietnam; pursued *détente* with USSR; opened relations with the People's Republic of China; resigned August 1974 as a result of the Watergate scandal

**No man's land**: the area between trenches in trench warfare (14)

**No-fly zone**: an area over which one or more governments declare that flights may only be made with their permission; in the 1990s, most commonly used with prohibitions dictated by the United Nations against Iraqi aircraft flying over their own airspace (10)

**Nobel, Alfred** (1833–1896): Swedish chemist and the inventor of dynamite; bequeathed his fortune to a series of prizes bearing his name, including a prize for peace

**Nobel Peace Prize**: the annual prize, endowed by Alfred Nobel, awarded to the individual or organization that has done most to ensure "fraternity between nations, for the abolition or reduction of standing armies" (7)

**Nongovernmental organization**: any organization that is institutionally separate from government and is organized on a not-for-profit basis (7)

**Nongovernmental terrorism**: the use of terror as a political tool by nonstate actors, as opposed to the use of terror by states and governments (7)

**Nonalignment**: a policy first embraced by the governments of India, Yugoslavia, Egypt, and Ghana in the 1950s that sought to avoid having to align with either the United States or the Soviet Union (16)

**Noncentral governments**: all governments in a political community except the sovereign government, including governments of municipalities and constituent units of federations such as states, provinces, *länder*, and cantons (7)

**Noninterference in domestic affairs**: the idea that a sovereign state alone should have the right to make decisions about its territory and people (10)

**"Nonperson"**: the unique political punishment in Soviet politics in which the regime refused to acknowledge a public person's existence and tried to erase all evidence that he or she had lived, such as rewriting history books, taking down monuments, or renaming streets and buildings (15)

**Nonrecognition**: a conscious policy decision to refuse to recognize a regime, usually with the intention of denying it legitimacy (11)

**Nonstate actors**: any actor in international politics which is not the government of a sovereign state (7)

**Nontariff barriers**: any measure or way of doing things that is construed as placing a barrier in the way of "free" commerce, ranging from obvious measures, such as procurement policies that favour one's nationals, to not-so-obvious ways of doing things, such as having stricter health and safety standards (10, 17)

**NSC–68**: recommendations of the National Security Council, published in April 1950, that warned that the USSR was bent on conquering the world and that the U.S. should build up its military and create alliances to stop it (15)

**Nuclear deterrence**: the use of threats of nuclear war as a means of deterring unwanted action by an opponent (5)

**Nuclear monopoly**: that period of time between 1945 and August 1949, when the USSR exploded its first atomic weapon, during which the U.S. was the only state which had atomic weapons (15)

**October revolution**: See *Bolshevik revolution*

**Offensive intelligence agencies**: an intelligence agency that is allowed to carry out operations outside the country (7)

**Official Development Assistance (ODA)**: all governmental transfers between North and South, including bilateral assistance, multilateral flows, and such measures as debt forgiveness (16)

**Oil sanctions**: embargoes or boycotts involving oil; the term usually given to the measures imposed against Japan in 1941 that precipitated the collapse of its civilian government in October (14)

**Oil shock**: the large increase in oil prices in 1973 and again in 1979 (16)

**Ontology**: a branch of metaphysics concerned with describing the general nature of reality. Ontology deals with how many distinct kinds of entities comprise the universe and how we categorize what we understand to be reality; see also *epistemology*. (2)

**"Open Door" policy**: effort by the Chinese government under Deng Xiaoping to open China to the international capitalist economy after 1978 (16)

**Operation Provide Comfort**: the operation code name given to the joint effort of the United States, Britain, and France to provide aid to the Kurds who fled into the barren mountainous region of northwestern Iraq to escape persecution in 1991 (10)

**Operation Restore Hope**: the operation code name given to the efforts of the United States and others to secure supplies of food to famine-stricken Somalis during the famine of 1992 (10)

**Otherness**: the condition of being defined as an "Other" (with a capital O), in other words, a member of the *out-group* (8)

**Out-group**: one part of a dualism that defines individuals as not being part of a particular group; see *in-group* (8)

**Overkill**: applied exclusively to nuclear weapons; the accumulation of sufficient destructive capability that one is able to destroy a target many times over (4)

***Pacta sunt servanda***: (Latin) literally, agreements are to be kept; the understanding in world politics that treaties signed should be honoured (4)

**"Pactomania"**: the colloquial term given to the enthusiasm for military alliances shown by the United States government in the late 1940s and early 1950s (15)

**Paleolithic Era**: literally old stones, sometimes known as the Old Stone Age; an era spanning about two million years to the end of the last Ice Age, approximately 11 000 years ago (8)

**Pan-Arabism**: a political movement that seeks to create a single political community for all Arabs (17)

**Pariahs**: outcasts; the term is applied to any actor in world politics, but is most often applied to states, such as South Africa during the apartheid era (4)

**Partition**: the process of dividing a political community into different parts to create new communities (14)

**Path dependency**: the argument that events are shaped by (hence dependent on) a particular sequence, or path, of prior events and occurrences; see also *chaos theory* and *counterfactual* (2)

**Peace dividend**: the increased "savings" that came from reductions in military spending made possible by the end of the Cold War (17)

**"Peace in our time"**: the phrase used by Neville Chamberlain after signing the Munich Pact of September 1938 allowing Nazi Germany to seize portions of Czechoslovakia (14)

**Peace of Westphalia**: the name given to the two treaties signed by the Holy Roman Empire on 24 October 1648, one with France at Münster, the other with the Swedes and the German Protestant states at Osnabrück; brought the *Thirty Years' War* to an end and institutionalized the idea of state sovereignty (4)

**Peace research**: an approach to IR that focuses in particular on war and violence in their many forms, and explanations for war and the use of force (2)

**Peacebuilding**: the name given to the efforts of IGO operations in a country to "build" the institutions of civil society in order to promote peace (10)

**Peacemaking**: a euphemism employed in the post–Cold War period for inserting armed forces supplied by the international community into a civil war situation for some political purpose; usually the consent of all sides is not sought (10)

**Peacekeeping**: inserting military forces, supplied by different members of the international community, between warring armies that have agreed to some form of peace, usually under the authority of an international body, and always with the consent of the belligerents (10)

**Pearson, Lester B.** (1897–1972): Canadian; Liberal politician; secretary of state for external affairs, 1948–1957; prime minister 1963–1968; winner of the 1957 Nobel Peace Prize for diplomacy during the Suez crisis

***Perestroika***: (Russian) literally, restructuring; the policy introduced by Mikhail Gorbachev that sought to change the Soviet economy (15)

**Periphery**: in IR, those countries in the international political economy dominated by the *core*, and kept dependent and underdeveloped by unequal patterns of relations (2, 16)

***Persona non grata***: (Latin) literally, person not welcome; in diplomacy, a formal method for expelling a diplomat or foreign official (10)

**Persuasion**: a technique of influence in which actor A uses nothing more than argument to change actor B's conception of B's interests so that they are compatible or convergent with A's interests (5)

**Piracy**: the seizure by private (nonstate) actors of a ship on the *high seas* or an aircraft in international airspace, for private ends, and without the approval of any government. Seizure undertaken for political objectives or by states are violations of laws of particular countries, but not considered piracy under international law; seizure by private actors with the approval of a government is regarded under international law as *privateering*. (7)

**Policy convergence**: the process by which policy ideas from one jurisdiction are picked up and copied by other jurisdictions (7)

***Polis***: (Greek, plural *poleis*) the political formation dominant in the Greek peninsula 2500 years ago; sometimes translated as "city-state" (3)

**Political cleavages**: divisions within political communities that create conflict; cleavages can be based on numerous factors: language, region, ethnicity, race, religion, class, caste, gender, urban/rural, occupation, ideology, and/or beliefs (6)

**Political leadership**: the individuals who, either singly or as a group, have the authority or the power to make decisions in the name of the political community (7)

**Possessive individualism**: C.B. Macpherson's characterization of the nature of the liberal philosophy dominant after the 17th century, incorporating the notion that each person was an individual capable of owning property (9)

**Post-Fordism**: a system of production that features smaller and more cohesive production units with shorter production runs, no large assembly plants, low inventories, and products aimed at niche rather than mass markets (17)

**Postmodernism**: an approach to the social sciences in general and IR in particular that casts doubt on the *Enlightenment* project of seeking an absolute Truth. Postmodernism denies that the truth exists in objective reality, but is in fact "constructed" by social scientists and others. (2)

**Postnationalism**: the argument that nationalism has been supplanted with other notions of political identity (17)

**Potsdam**: conference of victorious powers at Potsdam, Germany, 17 July–2 August 1945, on how Germany would be treated (15)

**Power analysis**: an analytical perspective that seeks to define power and to analyze its exercise and its possession (5)

**Power resources**: any of those things necessary for the exercise of influence, power, and authority (5)

**Power**: the capacity to prevail in a conflict of interests; the ability of one actor to act in a manner contrary to the interests of another actor (3, 5)

**Preferences**: any system that gives the goods or services of one country privileged access in the markets of other countries; see also *Generalized System of Preferences* (17)

**Prestige**: the standing or reputation that actors have in the eyes of others, and a desire to have such standing (4)

**Private**: in political science, that sphere of human activity in which the community, state, or government is assumed to have no business (3)

**Privateering**: see *piracy*

**Propaganda**: spreading information or ideas in a way that will benefit one's cause, often suppressing or distorting information in a way to discredit an opposing viewpoint (5, 14)

**Protectionism**: efforts by states to protect the position of national firms and industries in the marketplace, usually by restricting trade (12)

**Protective state**: the idea that the state should take the lead in protecting the nation's economic structures and "way of life" against influences from outside (12)

**Public**: in political science, that sphere of human activity deemed to be appropriate for community or the state to involve itself in (3)

**Purchasing power parity**: an alternative measure of wealth (to GNP per capita) that provides a comparative measure of international standards of living by comparing the purchasing power of a country's currency in that country (16)

**Pure laine**: (French) literally, pure wool; in Québec politics, a French-speaking Québecker whose ancestry can be traced back to the original *habitants* (settlers) (8)

**Quadruple Alliance**: treaty signed at Paris on 20 November 1815 by Austria, Britain, Prussia, and Russia that, *inter alia*, provided for a regular "reunion" of governments for the management of international problems (7)

**Qualified majority**: the system of weighted voting in the EU Commission that provides protections both to small states against the power of large states and to large states against ganging up by smaller states (17)

**Quasi-states**: Robert H. Jackson's characterization of states which are deemed sovereign yet do not manifest many of the attributes of a theoretically sovereign state (11)

**Race-hatred laws**: the laws in many jurisdictions making it a criminal offence to advocate hatred toward an identifiable group (17)

**"Radicalism"**: see *Marxism*

**Rassepolitik**: (German) literally, race politics; the idea that political community should be defined on the basis of race, most fully expressed by the *Nazis* (14, 17)

**Rational choice**: an approach to IR popular mainly in the United States, hypothesizing that political outcomes are the consequences of aggregations of individual preferences that are assumed to be heavily materialistic in nature (2)

**Reagan, Ronald** (1911– ): president of the United States, 1981–1989; Republican Party; introduced neoconservative policies domestically and pursued a strong anti-Soviet and anticommunist program externally

**Realism**: an approach to IR that seeks to portray world politics as realistically as possible. It focuses on *Realpolitik* calculations of state leaders, arguing that their primary goal is the accumulation of power. (2)

**Realpolitik**: (German) literally, practical politics; stresses the importance of materialist rather than ethical or symbolic explanations of politics; important for *realist* approaches to IR (10)

**Recognition**: in international politics, a formal or informal act by one government that officially acknowledges the existence of another state or government; crucial for endowing the recognized state with *sovereignty* (11)

**Reformation**: the revolution within the Christian church during the 1500s that ended the supremacy of the pope in Rome and resulted in the establishment of Protestant churches (9)

**Refugees**: those who have fled from their country of citizenship because of any form of political persecution, or because of war or economic or natural disaster (9)

**Relative gains**: an increase in a community's wealth and well-being that is measured against the change in the wealth and well-being of others rather than absolutely; see *absolute gains* (16)

**Renaissance**: (French) literally, rebirth; the name commonly given to that period in European history, beginning in Italy in the 14th century and spreading elsewhere in Europe, when there was a renewed interest in the classical civilizations of Greece and Rome and a flourishing of culture and the arts (9)

**Reparations**: the name given the *indemnities* imposed on Germany after the First World War (14)

**Resident aliens**: those citizens of other states who have highly qualified rights of residence in a state. While resident aliens may be given access to some social services, normally aliens are denied rights of political participation, such as the vote. (9)

**Ricardo, David** (1772–1823): English economist, broker, member of Parliament, whose work on comparative advantage and international division of labour led him to advocacy for free trade

**Rolodex diplomacy**: the tendency of state leaders to engage in diplomacy with one another directly over the telephone (5)

**Roosevelt, Franklin Delano** (1882–1945): president of the United States, 1933–1945; Democratic Party; pursued anti-Axis policies in the early 1940s; led the United States during its participation in the Second World War after December 1941; died 12 April 1945, just before the Nazi surrender

**Rule of anticipated reaction**: a dynamic of power in which actors shape their behaviour to anticipate what they believe will be the reaction of other actors (7)

**Rules**: the mixture of formal and informal laws, understandings, taboos, and "rules of the game" that guide social action (3)

**Safe havens**: areas guarded or guaranteed by the international community where individuals will be safe from military action; in the 1990s, used in the civil wars in Iraq, Yugoslavia, and Rwanda (10)

**Safety**: see *Security*

**Sanctions**: a technique of power that involves harming in a nonviolent way those things that an actor values, such as freedom, reputation, or economic wealth, in order to bend the actor to one's will (5)

**Schlieffen Plan**: a military plan drawn up in 1906 by the chief of the German general staff, Count Alfred von Schlieffen, involving an attack on French forces from the rear through neutral Belgium (14)

**Schmalkaldic League**: a defensive alliance organized by German Protestant princes at Schmalkalden in February 1531 that helped organize opposition to the *Holy Roman Empire* (9)

**Scramble for Africa**: that period between 1880 and 1914, when European imperial powers carved up all of the African continent into colonies except Liberia and Ethiopia (13)

**Second World**: during the Cold War, term commonly applied to the developed and industrialized communist countries of Europe (16)

**Sectoral free trade**: the establishment of a free trade area in one economic sector only, for example, defence products or automobiles (10, 17)

**Securitization**: the movement of investment capital into tradeable securities such as bonds (17)

**Security**: a sense of well-being against threats of harm to things one values; security can be physical, economic, environmental, or cultural (4)

**Self-help**: the condition in a stateless community that requires that those in a conflict depend on themselves rather than on the government or the state to defend their interests (3)

**Semiotics**: a philosophical theory of signs and symbols in language that pays particular attention to how language is constructed and used in a social context (2)

**Semiperiphery**: in IR, those countries like Australia, Canada, New Zealand which are not at the centre of the global economy, and thus are not part of the *core*, but are wealthier and more developed than the *periphery* (2)

**Separation of powers**: the idea, bruited by Charles Louis de Secondat, Baron de Montesquieu, in 1748, that to maximize political freedom, governmental powers should be separated and balanced. The quintessential separation of powers was embraced by those who formulated the Constitution of the United States. (9)

**"Service-station state"**: Margaret Canovan's phrase to describe how the contemporary state is often seen: as little more than an agency that will "service" individual needs (17)

**Seven Sisters**: the seven oil companies—British Petroleum, Chevron, Exxon, Gulf, Mobil, Shell, and Texaco—which dominate the international petroleum market (16)

**Sex tourism**: tours arranged to other jurisdictions for the primary purpose of engaging prostitutes, in particular to jurisdictions where laws regarding pedophilia are not well enforced (6)

**Sex trade**: in international politics, any aspect of prostitution that crosses borders, such as *sex tourism* or international trade in prostitutes (6)

**Shell shock**: numerous psychological conditions that result from exposure to constant artillery bombardments, often marked by hysteria (14)

**Six, the**: the original six signatories of the *Treaty of Rome*: Belgium, France, West Germany, Italy, Luxembourg, and Netherlands

**Slave trade**: name generally given to the international market in slaves that developed after the 15th century. Arabs and Africans supplied West African slaves to Portuguese (and later other European) slave-ship owners who transported the majority to plantations in Brazil, the Caribbean, and North America. (7, 9)

**Smith, Adam** (1723–1790): Scottish philosopher whose 1776 book *An Inquiry into the Nature and Causes of the Wealth of Nations* was an analysis of how wealth is produced and distributed

**Smoot-Hawley tariff**: measure introduced into Congress in 1929 by Senator Reed Smoot and Representative Willis Hawley increasing duties on imports; signed into law by Herbert Hoover in 1930 after the stock market crash of October 1929, prompting a severe decline in American trade (14)

**Smuggling**: goods moved across borders that have not been declared to the authorities, either to avoid payment of duties, or because the goods are illegal in one or both jurisdictions (7)

**Snake in the tunnel**: efforts by European states to fix their exchange rates by agreeing to hold their currencies within a 2.25-per-cent band against one another, and holding that band to a 4.5-per-cent band against the U.S. dollar (17)

**Snatch operations**: kidnappings and abductions that are carried out by government agencies, often involving the violation of the *sovereignty* and *territorial integrity* of other states (7)

**Social Darwinism**: the misapplication of the evolutionary theories of *Charles Darwin*, particularly the idea of the "survival of the fittest," to politics; normally used by *imperialists* and *Nazis* to justify the dominance of one people over another (14)

**Social movement**: a group of individuals and organizations, often only very loosely organized, who share commonalities of view on certain social and political issues (7)

**Social reinforcement mechanism**: in the context of war-fighting, the social pressures that work to sustain loyalty and courage under fire (14)

**Society**: see *Community*

**Soft loans**: development assistance loans offered at concessional rates, usually featuring a nominal rate of interest charged after ten years (16)

**Sovereign state**: a political formation deemed to consist of a territory, people, and a government, endowed with the legal attributes of *sovereignty* (9)

**Sovereignists**: in Québec, those who want to achieve independent statehood, or *sovereignty*, for the province (8)

**Sovereignty**: the idea that an individual, institution, or political formation is the highest source of political authority and is subject to no other authority (9)

**Special Drawing Rights**: the unit of account used by the IMF, based on the weighted average value of five major currencies; today worth approximately US$1.45 (16)

**Special economic zones**: in China, areas, primarily on the coast, that were created to attract foreign investment and industry as part of the *Open Door policy* (16)

**Spheres of influence**: those countries, usually bordering a great power, where that power is deemed to have an appropriate and legitimate interest (15)

**Spin-doctoring**: efforts made by governments and other actors to put the best face, or "spin," on an event in a way that benefits them and their image (5)

**Stakeholder politics**: the willingness of some liberal democratic governments to accord certain groups—particularly those who are able to claim that they have a "stake" in the outcome—a privileged position in the making of policy (7)

**Stalin, Joseph** (1879–1953): leader of the USSR and secretary general of the Communist Party of the Soviet Union from 1922 until his death

**State of nature**: hypothetical construct used by liberal philosophers to imagine what life was like in a presocial stage, i.e., when humans were assumed to be solitary individuals without society (3)

**State-centric model**: a conception of world politics that puts the state (or government of a community) at the centre of analysis (7)

**Stateless communities**: societies, usually preindustrial (sometimes called "primitive"), that exist without formal institutions of governance (3)

**Stateless person**: an individual who has been stripped of his or her citizenship by one state, but not granted citizenship by another state (9)

**Statute of Westminster**: act of the British parliament in 1931 that gave all the self-governing dominions in the British Empire sovereignty in both internal and external affairs (13)

**Stock market crash**: a sudden loss of confidence in the stock market marked by a selling spree that drives down the price of stocks; see also *herd instinct, meltdown* (14)

**Straight baseline**: the line that states are allowed to draw across the mouths of bays (and sometimes around archipelagos) to turn what otherwise would be *high seas* into *internal waters* (10)

**Strategic Defense Initiative**: a plan outlined by the United States Department of Defense in the early 1980s to create a space-based weapons system to destroy nuclear weapons in their various phases of flight (4)

**Strategic Impediments Initiative**: a series of bilateral negotiations between the United States and Japanese

governments in the early 1990s focusing on the elimination of barriers to the Japanese market (10)

**Structural Adjustment Programs**: a program of economic policies, usually involving budgetary restraints, that a state is required to adopt as a condition of receiving financial assistance from the International Monetary Fund (10)

**Structural realism**: a kind of realism (often called "neorealism" because it sought to reassert the continued relevance of realism) that focuses on how the anarchical structure of the international system shapes politics at this level (2)

**Subsequent boundaries**: political borders that are drawn after patterns of human settlement have been established (9)

**Successor states**: the name given to the regimes that emerged from the changes of the post–Cold War period, particularly the sovereign states that were created from the USSR (15)

**Suez crisis**: the conflict that developed over the nationalization of the Suez Canal in 1956 by Egypt and the subsequent invasion of the Sinai and seizure of the Canal by Israel, France, and Britain (15)

**Summit meeting**: any meeting involving the political leadership of two or more governments (7)

**Super 301**: the colloquial name given to the provision of the United States Omnibus Trade and Competitiveness Act of 1988 that permits agencies of the United States government to by-pass multilateral organizations in finding a country's trading practices "unfair" (10)

**Supergun**: a class of artillery weapon that is marked by hugeness of size, calibre, and range, such as the *Pariskanone* of the First World War, so-called because it was capable of bombarding Paris from 120 km (75 miles) away (7)

**Superimposed boundaries**: political borders that are drawn after political communities and borders have already been established, such as the borders superimposed on Europe after the Second World War (9)

**Supranational politics**: a sphere of politics and political institutions that exists "above" the nation-state, but usually "below" the global level (3, 17)

**Surgical strike**: a limited air attack, usually designed to hit a highly specific target—i.e., "with surgical precision" (15)

**Sustainable development**: the idea that economic growth should only be undertaken in a way that does not threaten long-term environmental damage or deplete resources at a nonrenewable rate (16)

*Terra nullius*: (Latin) literally, no one's land; the legal doctrine that a sovereign could lay claim to land deemed to be claimed by no other sovereign or people (9)

**Territorial integrity**: the idea that a particular geographic space belongs to a sovereign state, and that no one else can occupy, use, exploit, or even be in that space without the approval of that state (9)

**Territorial waters**: that part of the ocean adjacent to a state, normally extending to 12 nautical miles from shore, but not including *internal waters*. States exert sovereign jurisdiction over these waters, though foreign vessels have certain rights of passage. (10)

**Terror or terrorism**: a technique of power that uses the fear that humans have of pain and death to bend them to one's will. A terrorist is any actor who uses terror as a political tool. (5, 7)

**Têt offensive**: an wide offensive launched by the Vietnamese communists against cities of South Vietnam beginning on 31 January 1968, providing a turning point in the Vietnam War (7)

**Thatcher, Margaret** (1925– ): British prime minister, 1979–1990, won three consecutive elections; elected to Parliament 1959, served in Edward Heath's cabinet; leader of the Conservative party, 1975–1990; introduced neo-conservative economic and social policies that reduced the role of the state

**Think tank**: an institution, usually but not always a not-for-profit nongovernmental organization, that exists primarily to engage in research and thinking about policy questions (7)

**Third World**: after *Tiers-État*, the group (or "estate") in the Estates-General of prerevolutionary France which represented the majority of the people; the poorer countries of the world, also called "underdeveloped," "developing," or "less developed" countries (16)

**Thirty Years' War**: the name given to the series of European wars fought between the *defenestration of Prague* in 1618 and the *Peace of Westphalia* in 1648 (9)

**Three-mile limit**: from the 18th century to the 1950s, there was general agreement that the *territorial waters* of a state extended three nautical miles from shore—approximately the range of a land-based cannon in the 1700s (10)

**Thucydides** (circa 460–400 BC): Athenian general and historian who wrote *History of the Peloponnesian War*

**Tiananmen massacre**: the name given to the events of the night of 3–4 June 1989, when troops were ordered to clear Tiananmen Square in Beijing of protestors; thousands died when troops opened fire (16)

**Tied aid**: development assistance that is offered on condition that it be spent on goods and services in the donor country (16)

**Tojo Hideki** (1884–1948): Japanese leader during the Second World War; army chief of staff, 1937; minister of war, 1940; prime minister, September 1941; executed by the Allies

**Tools of statecraft**: the term given to the instruments of influence and power used by governments (5)

**Total war**: the name given to the wars of the twentieth century when all the resources of a society were devoted to war-fighting (14)

**Track-two diplomacy**: a form of international dialogue, in which governments (operating on "track one") encourage nongovernmental actors to meet on a separate "track" to engage in talks or relations that might be considered too sensitive or politically difficult for governments (7)

**Trade gap**: the gap between the revenues generated by Southern countries through commodity exports and the expenditures on imports from the industrialized world. In the 1960s, this gap was widely believed to be the major obstacle to Southern development. (16)

**Trade liberalization**: the efforts to remove all barriers to international trade, both tariffs and *nontariff barriers* (17)

**Tragedy of the commons**: a tragedy-like dynamic identified by Garrett Hardin by which it is rational for all members of a community to use a common resource without limitation, on the assumption that the collectivity will absorb the costs (4)

**Transfer pricing**: the propensity of MNCs to set the prices of products traded between their different subsidiaries at rates designed to minimize their tax or duty exposure in different jurisdictions (7)

**Transgovernmental actors**: an official of a government, not sufficiently senior to speak on behalf of that government, whose behaviour crosses a border; for example, the desk officer in the U.S. Department of State and the minister-counsellor in the South African embassy in Washington who have a phone conversation are examples of such actors (7)

**Transnational actors**: any actor in international politics other than a government of a state, whose behaviour crosses a border (7)

**Transnational corporation**: according to Paul Hirst and Grahame Thompson, an MNC has a national home while a TNC has no national home, but is organized and willing to locate anywhere in the world; they argue that there are virtually no examples of true "stateless" corporations (7)

**Transnational security corporations**: international businesses which offer to provide offshore clients, usually governments, intergovernmental organizations, or other MNCs, with a range of security services, including training, counter-subversion, and the use of force in a variety of forms (7)

**Treaty of Rome**: the treaty signed on 25 March 1957 between Belgium, France, West Germany, Italy, Luxembourg, and Netherlands (*the Six*) that created the European Economic Community, a common market that was the forerunner of the European Union (17)

**Treaty of Versailles**: the peace agreement, signed on 28 June 1919, that brought the First World War to an end and created the League of Nations, but also contained the seeds of future conflict (14)

**Trench warfare**: a kind of immobile warfare arising from the digging and construction of trenches for protection against enemy fire; marked by high casualty rates from attempts to breach the line of trenches (14)

**Trigger clause**: a clause in an agreement that invokes a promised response, such as *Article 5* in the North Atlantic Treaty (15)

**Trudeau, Pierre Elliott** (1919– ): prime minister of Canada, 1968–1979, 1980–1984; Liberal Party

**Truman Doctrine**: doctrine proclaimed by Harry S Truman, president of the United States on 12 March 1947, that the United States would support "free peoples" everywhere against totalitarian regimes (15)

**Truman, Harry S** (1884–1972): president of the United States 1945–1953; Democratic Party; under his presidency the U.S. embraced *containment* and encircled the USSR with a series of defensive alliances

**Tung Chee-hwa** (1938– ): shipping magnate and first chief executive of the Hong Kong Special Administrative Region, 1997–

**Ultranationalism**: extreme nationalism, usually marked by an intense intolerance of other peoples or other nations (14)

**Unequal Treaties**: the name given by Chinese to the series of treaties that the Chinese emperor was forced to sign in the 19th century as a result of military defeats by Europeans (12)

**Unilateral declaration of independence (UDI)**: a declaration by one part of a political community that it is independent, without the consent of the other part or parts (11)

**Union flag**: sometimes known as the Union Jack; the flag of Great Britain and Northern Ireland that combines the flags of England, Scotland, and Ireland (but not Wales) into its design (12)

**Universal IGO**: an intergovernmental organization, open to membership of all states in the international system; see *exclusive IGO* (7)

**Universalism**: the assumption, particularly prevalent among *behaviouralists* and *rational choice* enthusiasts, that the patterns of world politics can be universalized—applying to all people at all times in all places—rather than being highly culturally and socially determined (2)

**"Unofficial" missions**: diplomatic missions that technically have no official or *de jure* standing or existence but nonetheless are established to conduct relations between countries that do not have formal diplomatic relations (11)

*Untermenschen*: (German) literally, subhuman; the name given by *Nazis* to those races deemed "undesirable" (14)

**"Vagabond mercenaries"**: highly individualistic and adventuristic soldiers who sell their military skills to whomever will pay (7)

**Vandenberg Resolution**: resolution passed by the United States Senate on 11 June 1948 approving the formation of a defensive alliance linking the U.S. and Western European countries; named after its sponsor, Senator Arthur Vandenberg, Republican of Michigan, chair of the Senate Foreign Relations Committee (15)

**Velvet Divorce**: name given to the separation of Czechoslovakia into the Czech Republic and Slovakia in January 1993, so called because it was smooth and bloodless, unlike the Yugoslav "divorce" occurring at the same time (14)

**Versailles, Treaty of**: see *Treaty of Versailles*

**"Video game war"**: common, if inappropriate, tag used to describe the Persian Gulf war of 1991 (7)

**Voluntary export restraints**: a unilateral imposition of limits on exports to a foreign market; the word "voluntary" ironically added to mask the fact that VERs are invariably imposed under threat of retaliation (10)

**Voluntary restraint agreements**: agreements signed between two trading partners under which one agrees to impose restraints on trade, often under threat from the other partner (10)

**War dead**: those who have died in a particular war and whose deaths become an important political symbol that helps sustain the willingness to fight (14)

**"War on drugs"**: the periodic efforts made by a succession of American presidents to eradicate the domestic drug problem in the United States by trying to stop supply overseas rather than demand domestically (16)

**War**: a condition in which groups—individuals, organizations, or communities—are in conflict with one another, and each uses violence, often highly organized, against the other (5)

**War-guilt clause**: article 231 of the 1919 Versailles Treaty by which Germany was forced to accept responsibility for all the losses of the First World War because of its "aggression" in 1914 (14)

**War-weariness**: the lack of willingness to continue fighting a war that tends to grip a community at a certain point, leading them to end the war (14)

**Warfare state**: a reference to the capacity of the bureaucratic state to organize and galvanize the resources of the nation-state for fighting *total war* (14)

**Warlord period**: in contemporary Chinese politics, the 1920s, 1930s, and 1940s; years which were marked by an absence of central authority and the existence of numerous local chiefs or warlords (13)

**Wars of religion**: the wars fought by Protestants and Catholics in the countries of Western Europe in the 125 years between the Peasant Wars of the 1520s and the *Thirty Years' War* that ended in 1648; these wars were primarily fought *within* countries in the 16th century and *between* countries in the 17th century (9)

**Warsaw uprising**: the revolt against Nazi occupiers staged by the Polish underground Home Army beginning on 31 July 1944 as Soviet troops approached Warsaw. However, Stalin ordered his troops to halt, and refused to allow the United States to overfly Soviet airspace to help the Polish rebels, who surrendered on 2 October. (15)

**Weber, Max** (1864–1920): German political sociologist who worked on the nature of bureaucracy and the modern state

**Welfare state**: the idea, dominant for much of the twentieth century, that welfare for the citizens of a political community should be produced by the state (4)

**Welfare**: the desire to create well-being of all kinds, particularly economic well-being (4)

**Westphalia, Peace of**: See *Peace of Westphalia*

**"White slavery"**: historically, the supposed practice of abducting young European women and forcibly selling them into slavery; today, the name generally given to the transnational trade in prostitutes, usually involving both coercion and manipulation (7)

**Wilson, Woodrow** (1856–1924): president of the United States, 1913–1921; Democratic Party; noted for his contribution to the creation of the League of Nations and national self-determination; see also *Fourteen Points*

**Wojtyla, Karol**: see *John Paul II*

**World economy theory**: an approach to IR that stresses the importance of changing modes of production and different international divisions of labour to explain world politics at any given era in history (2)

**World war**: a war that spans the entire globe and involves most of the countries of the world in war-fighting (14)

**Yalta**: conference held at Yalta in Crimea, 4–11 February 1945, between Stalin, Churchill, and Roosevelt at which the postwar treatment of Germany and Eastern Europe was agreed (15)

**Yeltsin, Boris N.** (1931– ): president of Russia, June 1991–present; foiled *coup d'état* against Mikhail Gorbachev in August 1991; maintained Gorbachev's cooperative stance toward the West

**Yom Kippur war**: the war that resulted from the surprise attack by Egypt and Syria on Israel that began on the sacred holiday of Yom Kippur in 1973 (16)

**Zedillo Ponce de Léon, Ernesto** (1951– ): president of Mexico, 1994–present; Institutional Revolutionary Party (PRI); former minister of budget and planning, minister of education

**Zhou Enlai** (1898–1976): also rendered Chou En-lai, pronounced *joe en lie*; first premier of the People's Republic of China, 1949–76; foreign minister, 1949–1958

**Zimmerman telegram**: telegram sent in 1917 from Alfred Zimmerman, German foreign minister, to the German embassy in Mexico offering to help Mexico regain land seized by the United States in the 1840s (14)

# Index

## A

Abbasid Caliphate, 63, 190, 195

"Able Archer 83," 412, 412fn

Aboriginals, 68, 190
   rights of, 78

**Absolute gains**, 447fn

Abu Musa, 229

Abu Nidal [Sabry Khalil al-Banna], 123

**Acheson, Dean**, 391

**Acid rain**, 95, 163, 163fn

Adams, John Quincy, 376

Aeta, 52

Afghanistan, 68, 430
   Soviet invasion of, 74, 91, 95, 243, 407, 410

Aflatoxin, 252

Africa Watch, 143

Africa, economic condition, 431-32
   effects of war on, 431

African Americans
   in US civil war, 349

**"African Eve,"** 286

Afrikaaners, 299

Agalev (Live Differently Party), 150

Agca, Mehmet Ali, 146-47

**Age of Enlightenment**, 17-18

**Age of exploration**, 209-210

Age of majority, 110fn

Age-ist analysis, 110

Agnelli, Susanna, 108

Ahmadiyya movement, 147

Aidid, Mohamed Farah, 237, 238

*Air Force One*, 111

Alaska
   and fisheries dispute, 163

Albigenses, 195

Albright, Madeleine, 3, 109, 161

Alexander the Great, 134, 183

Alexander VI, Pope, 210

Algeria, 68, 103, 217, 318
   war of independence, 5fn, 339
   civil war in, 154

Allende Gossens, Salvador, 153

**Allophones**, 347

Alpha Five, 135

Alsace-Lorraine
   loss of, 319, 352

Álvarez de Toledo, Fernando, 205

Ambrose, Stephen E., 122

Amchitka nuclear tests, 143

American Colonization Society, 319

American Federation of Labor-Congress of Industrial Organizations, 141

American Friends of the Czech Republic, 142

American Institute in Taiwan, 273

American Revolution, 213, 293

Ames, Aldrich, 159

Amin Dada, Idi, 242

Amin, Hafizullah, 407

Amnesty International, 75, 124, 143, 171

Amritsar massacres, 333

**Anarchical society**, 57

**Anarchism**, 50-51

**Anarchy**, 44-45
   in prisons, 53-54

Anderson, Benedict, 295

Andorra, 229

**Androcentrism**, 17, 42

Andropov, Yuri, 412, 413fn

Angola
   and USSR, 407-408
   mercenaries in, 134, 135
   war of independence, 339

Annan, Kofi, 170

*Anschluss*, 367

Antarctica, 218

Anthrax, 252

Anti-Bolshevism, 386-87

Anti-Comintern Pact, 262

Anti-Corn Law League, 309

Antigua and Barbuda, 222

Anzacs, 332

ANZCERTA, 456

ANZUS treaty, 169, 396

Apartheid, 23, 74-75, 235-36

APEC. *see* Asia Pacific Economic Cooperation

Apollo 11 moon landing, 137

**Appeasement**, 368

Aquino, Corazon, 108

Arab Maghreb Union, 469

Arab states
   boycott against Israel, 267-68
   union of, 468-69

'Arafat, Yasir, 171, 172, 276

Arctic Cooperation Agreement, 248

Arctic Waters Pollution Prevention Act, 245

Argentina, 82, 235, 243, 428
   claim to Falkland Islands, 302
   Dirty War, 143
   seizure of Falklands, 96

Arias Sánchez, Oscar, 172

Aristide, Jean-Bertrand, 428

Aristotle, "rediscovery" of, 203

Arlen, Michael, 139

**Armed forces**, 158

Armenians, Turkish slaughter of, 48

Arms embargo, Bosnia, 351

**Arms race**, 351-52

Article 2.7, 234
   and apartheid, 235
   and capital punishment, 239
   UN Charter, 230

**Article 5**, North Atlantic Treaty, 393

Aryan Nations, 106, 186

Asia Pacific Economic Cooperation forum, 3fn, 28-30, 168, 252, 458
   and ROC participation, 273

Asia Watch, 143

Asian Development Bank, 259

"Asian meltdown," 231

Asoka, 146

Assad, Hafez, 153

Assassination, 60, 159

Association of Southeast Asian Nations (ASEAN), 168, 274
   ASEAN Regional Forum, 150

Assyrians, 189

Aswan High Dam, 398

Athenians, 65-66, 76-77

Atlas Foundation, 151

Augsburg, Peace of, 206

Aum Shinrikyo, 154

Aung San Suu Kyi, Daw, 171, 172

Australia, 29, 46fn, 68, 222
   Australia-New Zealand Closer Economic Relationship Trade Agreement, 230-31
   aboriginals, 190
   ANZUS treaty, 396
   CGDK, 275
   **Cairns Group**, 444
   dispute with Portugal, 243
   First Fleet, 212
   First World War, 332
   French nuclear testing issue, 95, 124
   Jewish immigration, 221
   media and nuclear testing, 137
   New Protectionism, 312
   opposition to globalization, 459
   state governments and nuclear testing, 163
   steel industry, 232
   Suez crisis, 398

Entries in **bold** are defined in the Glossary, pp. 493-512

Dǝ⁺